Marketing Scales Handbook

A Compilation of Multi-Item Measures for Consumer Behavior & Advertising

Volume IV

Gordon C. Bruner II · Paul J. Hensel · Karen E. James

American Marketing Association
Chicago, Illinois USA

Australia · Canada · Mexico · Singapore · Spain · United Kingdom · United States

**Marketing Scales Handbook Volume IV: A Compilation of Multi-Item Measures
for Consumer Behavior & Advertising**
Gordon C. Bruner II, Paul J. Hensel, and Karen E. James

Composed by: Cadmus Professional Communications

Printed in the United States of America by Quebecor World Taunton

2 3 4 5 08 07 06

This book is printed on acid-free paper.

ISBN: 1-58799-205-1

This publication is designed to provide accurate and authoritative information in regard to the subject matter covered. It is sold with the understanding that the publisher is not engaged in rendering legal, accounting, or other professional services. If expert assistance is required, the services of a competent professional person should be sought.

Cover photo: © Arthur S. Aubry/ Getty Images

Library of Congress Cataloging-in-Publication Data

Bruner, Gordon C., 1954–
    Marketing scales handbook: a compilation of multi-item measures/Gordon C. Bruner, Karen E. James, Paul J. Hensel.
        p.   cm
    Includes index.
    1. Marketing research—Statistical methods—Handbooks, manuals, etc. 2. Scaling (Social sciences)—Handbook, manuals, etc.
    I. James, Karen E. II. Hensel, Paul J. III. Title.
    HF5415.3.B785   2001
    658.8′3028—dc20   92-18858
                            CIP

For more information about our products, contact us at:

Thomson Learning Academic
Resource Center
1-800-423-0563

Thomson Higher Education
5191 Natorp Boulevard
Mason, Ohio 45040
USA

Table of Contents

....

Table of Contents

Table of Contents

Part II: Advertising-Related Scales

Acknowledgements

A book of this nature is the result of the efforts of many parties. First, we thank the hundreds of researchers who have developed, used, and/or reported the measures contained herein. We also want to express our appreciation to those researchers who personally provided us with information beyond what was available in print. Many authors were contacted when more information was needed about a scale. Not all of them answered our requests and that may have caused descriptions of some scales to be less complete or, in the worst cases, to be left out of the book for lack of information. But, the following researchers responded to our requests and enabled us to provide more complete information than otherwise would have been possible. Our gratitude is extended to:

Jennifer Aaker
Dana Alden
Craig Andrews
Osei Appiah
Leopoldo Arias-Bolzmann
Sharon Beatty
Ruth Bolton
Paul Bottomley
Amanda Bower
Mike Brady
Sheri Bridges
Scot Burton
Les Carlson
Ben Carr
Goutam Chakraborty
Pierre Chandon
Chang-Hoan Cho
Keith Coulter
Dwane Dean
Pam Ellen
Bob Ferris
Robert Fisher
Mary Gilly
Ron Goldsmith
Kent Grayson
Dwayne Gremler
Kevin Gwinner
Jay Handelman
Thomas Hult
Lynn Kahle
Barbara Kahn
Jikyeong Kang
Richard Klink

Pradeep Korgaonkar
Vickie Lane
Carolyn Lin
Mary Luce
David Luna
Susan Mantel
Craig Martin
Charla Mathwick
Anna Mattila
Page Moreau
Ashesh Mukherjee
Gaby Odekerken-Schroder
Connie Pechmann
Michel Pham
Barbara Phillips
Priya Raghubir
Akshay Rao
Tom Reichert
Michelle Roehm
Greg Rose
Julie Ruth
Sankar Sen
Kim Sheehan
Avi Shoham
L.J. Shrum
Amy Smith
Alina Sorescu
Geoffrey N. Soutar
Deborah Spake
Janet Wagner
Kirk Wakefield
Alisa White

At SIU, we are grateful to Raj Murthy who helped with the **Office of Scale Research.** We also want to express our appreciation to the AMA for its ongoing interest in making this information available. We particularly thank Francesca Van Gorp Cooley, our editor for the first three volumes. With this volume the publication is being managed by Thomson/SW in a co-publishing agreement with AMA. The interest of the new publisher in our past, present, and future work encourages us to continue the series and, in fact, makes it likely that we will develop other publications of benefit to scales users. *Stay tuned!*

Finally, our thanks go out to our respective spouses and families. *May your measures always be valid!*

Gordon C. Bruner II
Southern Illinois University–Carbondale

Paul J. Hensel
University of New Orleans

Karen E. James
Louisiana State University–Shreveport

June 2005

Introduction

Volumes I, II, and III of this series covered the years 1980–1989, 1990–1993, and 1994–1997, respectively. This fourth volume covers the scales that were reported in articles published from 1998 to 2001. As with the earlier books, this one should **not** be viewed simply as a revision of the previously published material as scales from the first three volumes were not automatically included in this fourth book. In fact, the contents of this volume are predominately new. Only scales reported in the first three volumes that were used again during the 1998 to 2001 period were included in V. IV. Thus, the first three volumes have hundreds of scales not contained here. Given that, V. IV should be viewed as *complementing* the preceding volumes rather than superseding them.

A key difference in this volume and the previous ones is that the two largest sections (Consumer Behavior and Organizational Behavior) are being published separately. There are two reasons for this. First, those two sections tend to appeal to different researchers; some researchers only study consumers while others focus on people within organizational contexts, e.g., sales people, retail managers, marketing directors, etc. Second, due to the amount of material to be reviewed and the division of labor among the authors, the CB section was finished well before the OB section. The decision was made to proceed with publication of the CB material and follow later with a book concentrating on the OB scales. The section with advertising-related scales is small enough that it is included with both volumes.

In addition to the time period covered and the type of scales included (CB vs. OB), a few other differences between V. IV and the previous volumes should be noted. It became clear rather quickly when working on this new volume that many more scales were being published in our field than could be reviewed in the time available. One way to facilitate the review work and reduce the number of pages that must be bound was to condense the number of sections in each review. More details about the sections of the reviews are provided in the Table.

We are also more sensitive in this volume to distinguishing between reflective scales and formative ones. The intention of the series has been to focus on the former though some of the latter have been included at times. Only in recent years has our field begun to appreciate the difference between the two. Our rule in this volume was to be a bit more vigilant; if a measure was described as a formative scale it was not reviewed. If it was treated by the authors as a reflective measure with evidence attesting to its reliability (an important characteristic of a reflective measure) then we probably included it except when it was obvious to us that the scale was formative.

As has been true throughout the series, only multi-item scales were reviewed. The first volume in this series reviewed scales with just two items but since then scales have only been reviewed if they had three items or more. Further, a minimum amount of information was required for a scale to be included, with particular emphasis on scale items and information about reliability. Beginning in this volume, any scale which otherwise met the requirements but had a reliability of less than .60 was not included. Such low reliability implies that the scale is of such tenuous quality that it should not be used again without substantial improvement. Even with the scales that are included here with reliabilities greater than .60, we have commented for many of them that more developmental work is called for to improve their psychometric quality.

Along those lines, readers are urged to take care in the selection of scales. Those without a basic understanding of psychometrics are encouraged to improve their ability to evaluate alternative measures and make a selection. A suggested reading list is provided at the end of the book from which a rich explanation of psychometric issues can be found.

Our rule since the beginning has been to attempt to describe multiple uses of a scale in the same review. The problem has always been deciding when two scales that are not exactly the same should be included in the same review. The simple answer is that they were reviewed together when they appeared to be measuring the same construct and had about half or more items in common. This means that there are many cases where substantially different scales for the same or similar constructs exist (e.g., #335–#339). This rule was very hard to apply with respect to some scales, most notably the semantic differential versions of Attitude-Toward-the-Product/Brand (#59) and Attitude-Toward-the-Ad (#562). Although these two have been the most popular constructs to measure in scholarly marketing research using multi-item scales there has been little agreement on how to measure them, i.e., they both have been measured dozens of ways with dozens of items. Several years of working with the hodgepodge of Attitude-Toward-the-Ad scales led to an initial grouping. A full explanation of the logic and analysis that led to the grouping has been published. (See full cite for Bruner 1998 in Readings section.) Unfortunately, similar efforts to unravel the jumble of scales for measuring Attitude-Toward-the-Product/Brand have not been as successful. Given that, many measures have been written up together because, at least on the surface, they appear to be measuring the same construct in roughly the same way (multiple semantic differentials) with authors cherry picking from an identifiable pool of items. For those reviews as well as others, the set of items used in each study is identified so readers can determine which is the most appropriate for their purpose.

Finally, the structure of our scale descriptions was slightly different compared to the previous volumes. In general, the difference is that some of the sections have been dropped (as mentioned above) as either their information was considered less important or because the information could be included in other sections. The change was made in order to speed up the review process by concentrating only on the most important information and it also allowed more scales to be covered in fewer pages. Details of the remaining sections are described in the table below which is a template for the typical scale review in this volume.

TABLE

Description of Scale Review Format

SCALE NAME: A short, descriptive title for the scale is assigned. The name may or may not be the one used by the author. Our goals were to use a name that was as consistent with the content of scale and with other measures of the construct without being overly long and/or cumbersome.

SCALE DESCRIPTION: One or two sentences are used to describe the physical structure of the measure and the psychological construct apparently being assessed. The number of items, the number of points on the scale, and the response format (e.g., Likert, semantic differential) are typically specified. If significantly different names were used by authors for the measure then they are usually noted here.

SCALE ORIGIN: Limited information is given about the creation of the scale, if known. Many, if not most of the scales were developed for use in one study and are not known to have been used again in the review domain.

RELIABILITY: For the most part, reliability is described in terms of internal consistency, most typically with Cronbach's alpha. In rare cases other issues related to reliability are mentioned such as scale stability (test-retest correlations). For those scales which have had lots of uses (e.g., #59, #562), their reliabilities are summarized in general terms in this section and the reliabilities for each of the many individual uses are provided in the Scale Items section, as explained further below.

VALIDITY: Most studies did not report much if any helpful information regarding the various aspects of a scale's validity. Some simply referred to the results of exploratory factor analyses even though that only provides limited evidence of dimensionality. In rare cases, scale authors provided so much information that it is only summarized here and readers are urged to see the article for more details. In some instances the nomological or face validity of scales could be commented upon even if scale authors did not discuss evidence of scale validity.

COMMENTS: This section is not always used but occasionally something significant was observed in writing-up a scale which we felt should be pointed out to readers. For example, if something about the scale was judged to be seriously deficient then improvement is urged before further use of the scale is made. Also, when other studies were considered to be potentially relevant to the scale's usage but were not fully described in the review for some reason then they were cited here as "see also."

REFERENCES: Every source cited in the review is referenced here using the ***Journal of Marketing*** style. Titles of the seven primary journals which were reviewed and from which scales were taken (the review domain) are abbreviated as follows:

Journal of the Academy of Marketing Science = JAMS
Journal of Advertising = JA
Journal of Advertising Research = JAR
Journal of Consumer Research = JCR
Journal of Marketing = JM
Journal of Marketing Research = JMR
Journal of Retailing = JR

Titles of other journals, books, proceedings, and other sources are written out in full. As stated in the Acknowledgements, in many cases the scale authors or users themselves were contacted and provided information that helped with the description. Depending upon the extent of their assistance, they may have been cited as well.

SCALE ITEMS: The statements, adjectives, or questions composing a scale are listed in this section. Also, an indication of the response format is provided unless it is has been adequately specified in the Scale Description section. Where an item is followed by an (r) it means that the numerical response should be reverse coded when calculating scale scores. Other idiosyncrasies may be noted as well. For example, when slightly different versions of the same scale are discussed in the same write-up then an indication is given as to which items were used in particular studies. Finally, for those few scales that have been used many, many times (e.g., #59, #562) then the reliability of the scale is indicated at the end of a line which also states who the authors were and which items were used from a larger set. If a study had more than two reliabilities for a scale due to more studies, more products, pre/post measures, then just the range is reported. However, if a scale has been described more than once in an article with slightly different sets of items then the reliability for each usage is reported separately.

Part I

Consumer-Related Scales

SCALE NAME: Acceptability of Choice Alternatives

SCALE DESCRIPTION: Four seven-point Likert-type statements are used to measure the degree to which a customer believes there are acceptable alternative sources of a product. Although the scale was developed for use with a service provider it would appear to be amenable for use with sellers of physical goods as well. The measure was called *attractiveness of alternatives* by Jones, Mothersbaugh, and Beatty (2000).

SCALE ORIGIN: Although Jones, Mothersbaugh, and Beatty (2000, p. 265) stated that their scale was an "adaptation of scales" previously developed by others (Ping 1993; Rusbult 1980), it is probably more accurate to view the scale as original to Jones, Mothersbaugh, and Beatty (2000) but inspired by the scales used in the previous studies.

RELIABILITY: An alpha of .83 was reported for the scale.

VALIDITY: Based on the CFA and other tests that were conducted on this and other scales, Jones, Mothersbaugh, and Beatty (2000) concluded that their version of the scale was unidimensional and showed evidence of discriminant validity. In addition, the scale was reported to have a variance extracted of .58.

REFERENCES:
Jones, Michael A., David L. Mothersbaugh, and Sharon E. Beatty (2000), "Switching Barriers and Repurchase Intentions in Services," *JR*, 79 (2), 259–274.
Ping, Robert A., Jr. (1993), "The Effects of Satisfaction and Structural Constraints on Retailer Exiting, Voice, Loyalty, Opportunism, and Neglect," *JR*, 69 (Fall), 320–352.
Rusbult, Caryl E. (1980), "Commitment and Satisfaction in Romantic Associations: A Test of the Investment Model," *Journal of Experimental Social Psychology*, 16 (2), 172–186.

SCALE ITEMS: [1]

1. If I needed to change _____, there are other good _____ to choose from.

2. I would probably be happy with the products and services of another_____.

3. Compared to this _____, there are other _____ with which I would probably be equally or more satisfied.

4. Compared to this _____, there are not very many other _____with whom I could be satisfied. (r)

---

[1] A generic descriptor of the provider should go in the blanks, e.g., banks.

SCALE NAME: Affective Response (General)

SCALE DESCRIPTION: The scale is composed of three semantic differential items measuring one's affective response to some stimulus.

SCALE ORIGIN: The scale used by Kim, Allen, and Kardes (1996) as well as Kim, Lim, and Bhargava (1998) was borrowed from Stuart, Shimp, and Engle (1987). It appears the scale was original to the latter.

RELIABILITY: An alpha of .95 (n = 90) was reported by Kim, Allen, and Kardes (1996). Alphas of .95 (n = 36) and .94 (n = 84) were reported by Kim, Lim, and Bhargava (1998) for use of the scale in study 1 and 2, respectively.

VALIDITY: No examination of the scale's validity was reported by either Kim, Allen, and Kardes (1996) or Kim, Lim, and Bhargava (1998).

REFERENCES:
Kim, John, Chris T. Allen, and Frank R. Kardes (1996), "An Investigation of the Mediational Mechanisms Underlying Attitudinal Conditioning," *JMR*, 33 (August), 318–328.
Kim, John, Jeen-Su Lim, and Mukesh Bhargava (1998), "The Role of Affect in Attitude Formation: A Classical Conditioning Approach," *JAMS*, 26 (2), 143–152.
Stuart, Elnora W., Terence A. Shimp, and Randall W. Engle (1987), "Classical Conditioning of Consumer Attitudes: Four Experiments in an Advertising Context," *JCR*, 14 (December), 334–349.

SCALE ITEMS: [1]

1. unpleasant/pleasant

2. dislike very much/like very much

3. left me with a bad feeling/left me with a good feeling

---

[1] The number of points on the response scales used by Kim, Allen, and Kardes (1996) were not specified. Kim, Lim, and Bhargava (1998) used a seven point response format.

SCALE NAME: Affective Response (Negative)

SCALE DESCRIPTION: The scale attempts to measure the degree to which a person who has just been exposed to some stimulus describes his/her emotional response in negative terms such as sadness and anger. The stimulus used in the study conducted by Price, Arnould, and Tierney (1995) was a river rafting trip. In the study by Coulter (1998) the stimulus was a TV program.

SCALE ORIGIN: The scale appears to have been used first as a set of items by Price, Arnould, and Tierney (1995). Three of the items were part of a larger scale used by Edell and Burke (1987) to measure affective reactions to ads. (See #525). Coulter (1998) cited Edell and Burke (1987) as well as Plutchik (1980) for the items in his version of the scale.

RELIABILITY: Alphas of .86 and .87 were reported by Coulter (1998) and Price, Arnould, and Tierney (1995), respectively.

VALIDITY: No specific examination of the scale's validity was reported by Coulter (1998) or Price, Arnould, and Tierney (1995).

REFERENCES:
Coulter, Keith S. (1998), "The Effects of Affective Responses to Media Context on Advertising Evaluations," *JA*, 27 (4), 41–51.
Edell, Julie E. and Marian C. Burke (1987), "The Power of Feelings in Understanding Advertising Effects," *JCR*, 14 (December), 421–433.
Plutchik, Robert (1980), *Emotion: A Psychoevolutionary Synthesis*, New York: Harper and Row Publishers, Inc.
Price, Linda L., Eric J. Arnould, and Patrick Tierney (1995), "Going to Extremes: Managing Service Encounters and Assessing Provider Performance," *JM*, 59 (April), 83 – 97.

SCALE ITEMS: [1]

1. sad

2. sorry

3. regretful

4. angry

5. upset/disturbed

---

[1] Coulter (1998) used items 1, 3, 4, and 5 as well as a 5-point Likert-type response format. Price, Arnould, and Tierney (1995) used items 1-4 with an unknown response format.

SCALE NAME: Affective Response (Negative)

SCALE DESCRIPTION: Various versions of the scale have been used to measure the degree of negative affect one has toward some specified stimulus. Some of the scales differ in their temporal instructions while others vary in the items used. Therefore, the items can be used to measure one's mood state at a particular point in time or, at the other extreme, could be used as something more like a trait measure of affect. Richins' (1997) version in particular is somewhat different in that it focuses just on the fear emotion rather than a broader negative affect. Similarly, Beatty and Ferrell (1998) were interested in the level of negative affect felt during a particular shopping trip and used a three item, seven-point version of the scale.

SCALE ORIGIN: The scale used in several of the studies (Dubé and Morgan 1996; Lord, Lee, and Sauer 1994; Mano and Oliver 1993; Mano 1999) was developed by Watson, Clark, and Tellegen (1988). The ten negative items along with ten positive items comprise the Positive and Negative Affect Schedule (PANAS). Sharing the same items, seven versions of the scale were tested varying in whether the time period of interest was "right now" or "during the last year." Alphas ranged from .84 to .87 using data from college students. Stability of each of these versions was tested using 101 students and with eight week intervals. The resulting test-retest correlations ranged from .39 to .71. A factor analysis of the ten positive and ten negative items indicated that the positive items all had high loadings (> .50) on the same factor. Evidence of the scale's validity was also provided. By design, the scales were supposed to be independent (uncorrelated) and the evidence bore this out.

Although Luce (1998; 2001) drew heavily upon the PANAS items she also added some descriptors of her own. She thought they would be especially relevant to the type of decision-making she was studying.

Richins (1997) drew terms from previous measures as well as her own series of studies to develop and refine several emotion-related scales into the CES (Consumption Emotion Set).

RELIABILITY: The internal consistency of the scale based upon the studies in which it has been reported has been acceptable to very good ranging from .74 (Richins 1997, study 5) to .92 (Dubé and Morgan 1996).

VALIDITY: Although all of the details were not provided in the study by Beatty and Ferrell (1998), the implication was that this scale was unidimensional and showed sufficient evidence of convergent and discriminant validity.

The two-dimensional structure of the positive and negative PANAS items was generally supported in the analysis by Dubé and Morgan (1996).

Caution was urged by Mano (1999) in use of the scale due to the lack of evidence he found in support of a one-dimensional model.

Results of the study by Mano and Oliver (1993) showed how this scale correlates with many other emotion and satisfaction scales that could be used to support the discriminant and convergent validity of the scale. On the other hand, their data also showed that when 43 emotion-related items were factor analyzed, the ten Negative PANAS items did not load together. However, eight of the items loaded together when the analysis was constrained to a two-factor solution.

Richins (1997) expended a great deal of effort in a creative use of MDS (multi-dimensional scaling) to note whether items composing each scale she was creating clustered together.

REFERENCES:

Beatty, Sharon E. and M. Elizabeth Ferrell (1998), "Impulse Buying: Modeling Its Precursors," *JR*, 74 (2), 169–191.

Dubé, Laurette and Michael S. Morgan (1996), "Trend Effects and Gender Differences in Retrospective Judgments of Consumption Emotions," *JCR*, 23 (September), 156–162.

Lord, Kenneth R., Myung-Soo Lee, and Paul L. Sauer (1994), "Program Context Antecedents of Attitude toward Radio Commercials," *JAMS*, 22 (1), 3–15.

Luce, Mary Frances (2001), Personal Correspondence.

Luce, Mary Frances (1998), "Choosing to Avoid: Coping With Negatively Emotion-Laden Consumer Decisions," *JCR*, 24 (March), 409–433.

Mano, Haim (1999), "The Influence of Pre-Existing Negative Affect on Store Purchase Intentions," *JR*, 75 (2), 149–172.

Mano, Haim and Richard L. Oliver (1993), "Assessing the Dimensionality and Structure of the Consumption Experience: Evaluation, Feeling, and Satisfaction," *JCR*, 20 (December), 451–466.

Richins, Marsha L. (1997), "Measuring Emotions in the Consumption Experience," *JCR*, 24 (September), 127–146.

Watson, David, Lee Anna Clark, and Auke Tellegen (1988), "Development and Validation of Brief Measures of Positive and Negative Affect: The PANAS Scales," *Journal of Personality and Social Psychology*, 54 (6), 1063–1070.

SCALE ITEMS: [1]

1. scared

2. afraid

3. upset

4. distressed

5. jittery

6. nervous

7. ashamed

8. guilty

9. irritable

10. hostile

11. panicky

12. troubled

13. sad

14. worried

15. regretful

16. remorseful

17. angry

18. edgy

19. depressed

20. uncomfortable

21. uneasy

22. tense

Beatty and Ferrell (1998): 3, 4, 9 7-point [.76]
Richins (1997): 1, 2, 11 4-point [.74, .82]
Dubé and Morgan (1996): 1-10 7-point [.92]
Lord, Lee, and Sauer (1994): 1-10 [.89]
Luce (1998): 1-10, 12-22 5-point [.91]
Mano (1999): 1-10 5-point [.86, .87]
Mano and Oliver (1993): 1-10 5-point [.87]

[1] The anchors for the scale used by Dubé and Morgan (1996) as well as Mano and Oliver (1993) were *not at all/very much*. Similarly, Richins (1997) used *not at all/strongly*. In contrast, Beatty and Ferrell (1998) used *disagree/agree* and Luce (1998) used *not well at all/extremely well*.

SCALE NAME: Affective Response (Positive)

SCALE DESCRIPTION: The scale is composed of multiple, five-point descriptors measuring one's overall positive emotional reaction to some stimulus. The stimuli examined in the studies by Coulter (1998) as well as Murry and Dacin (1996) were TV programs whereas in the study by Oliver, Rust, and Varki (1997) it was a recreational wildlife theme park.

SCALE ORIGIN: Coulter (1998) cited Edell and Burke (1987) as well as Plutchik (1980) for the items in his version of the scale.

While Murry and Dacin (1996) appear to have selected items from the pool of adjectives offered by Plutchik (1980, p. 170), the scale itself is original to their study. Based on some undescribed pretests, they narrowed the set of items down to twenty-five that would assess positive and negative emotions.

Oliver, Rust, and Varki (1997) described a different origin for their two arousal scales, drawing most directly from the pool of items proposed by Larsen and Diener (1992, p. 31) who had in turn drawn upon the work of others. The six items Oliver, Rust, and Varki (1997) used in their first study ended up being relatively similar to the set used by Murry and Dacin (1996) and are, thus, reported together here. [See #12, V. III for the version of the scale used by Oliver, Rust, and Varki (1997) in their second study.]

RELIABILITY: The version used by Coulter (1998) had an alpha of .91. Murry and Dacin (1996) reported a reliability of .97 for a linear combination of the items. An alpha of .895 was reported for the version of the scale used by Oliver, Rust, and Varki (1997) in their first study.

VALIDITY: No explicit examination of the scale's validity was mentioned by Coulter (1998) or Murry and Dacin (1996). However, a confirmatory factor analysis was conducted by the latter on the set of twenty-five emotion-related terms. Two subscales were expected to relate to a positive emotional dimension and three were expected to relate to a negative emotional dimension. Indeed, a second-order positive emotion factor was found to underlie the happiness (1-6) and contented (7-10) subscales.

Similarly, Oliver, Rust, and Varki (1997) conducted two rounds of factor analysis. The first analysis involved 24 emotion items taken from the sources noted above. Those items loading highest on the first factor (high positive affect) were subsequently examined further in a second factor analysis. Common to both of their studies, two dimensions were identified: affect and arousal. However, loadings on the affect factor varied between the two studies and led to the use of rather different sets of items.

REFERENCES:
Coulter, Keith S. (1998), "The Effects of Affective Responses to Media Context on Advertising Evaluations," *JA*, 27 (4), 41−51.

Edell, Julie E. and Marian C. Burke (1987), "The Power of Feelings in Understanding Advertising Effects," *JCR*, 14 (December), 421–33.

Larsen, Randy J. and Edward Diener (1992), "Promises and Problems with the Circumplex Model of Emotion," *Emotion*, Margaret S. Clark, ed. Newbury Park, CA: Sage Publications, 25–59.

Murry, John P., Jr. and Peter A. Dacin (1996), in "Cognitive Moderators of Negative-Emotion Effects: Implications for Understanding Media Context," *JCR*, 22 (March), 439−447.

Oliver, Richard L., Roland T. Rust, and Sajeev Varki (1997), "Customer Delight: Foundations, Findings, and Managerial Insight," *JR*, 73 (3), 311−336.

Plutchik, Robert (1980), *Emotion: A Psychoevolutionary Synthesis*, New York: Harper and Row Publishers, Inc.

#5 *Affective Response (Positive)*

SCALE ITEMS: [1]

1. delighted

2. happy

3. cheerful

4. pleased

5. friendly

6. eager

7. cooperative

8. tolerant

9. attentive

10. patient

11. contented

12. excited

13. enthused

14. interested

15. amused

---

[1] Coulter (1998) used items 2, 4, 14, and 15 with a 5-point Likert-type response format. Items 1-10 were used by Murry and Dacin (1996) with the following endpoints on the 5-point response scales: *did not feel at all* and *felt very strongly*. Items 2-4 and 11-13 were used by Oliver, Rust, and Varki (1997) and the scale anchors were *never* and *always*.

SCALE NAME: Affective Response (Positive)

SCALE DESCRIPTION: The full version of the scale is composed of ten five-point items and measures the degree of positive affect one has toward some specified stimulus. As noted below, several versions of the scale were created and tested which vary in their temporal instructions. Therefore, the items can be used to measure one's mood state at a particular point in time or, at the other extreme, could be used as something more like a trait measure of affect. Depending upon the set of items used it may be more accurate to describe a scale as measuring arousal rather than affect *per se.*

A four item variation of the scale was used by Babin, Boles, and Darden (1995) and was referred to as *interest*. The three item subset used by Hung (2001) was referred to as *arousal*. Richins' (1997) version of the scale was composed of three, four-point items and was intended to capture the level of excitement a person felt during a consumption experience. Similarly, Beatty and Ferrell (1998) were interested in the level of positive affect felt during a particular shopping trip and used a four item, seven-point version of the scale.

SCALE ORIGIN: The scale was developed by Watson, Clark, and Tellegen (1988). The ten positive items along with ten negative items comprise the Positive and Negative Affect Schedule (PANAS). Sharing the same items, seven versions of the scale were tested varying in whether the time period of interest was "right now" or "during the last year." Alphas ranged from .86 to .90 using data from college students. Stability of each of these versions was tested using 101 students and with eight week intervals. The resulting test-retest correlations ranged from .47 to .68. A factor analysis of the ten positive and ten negative items indicated that the positive items all had high loadings (>.50) on the same factor. Evidence of the scale's validity was also provided. By design, the scales were supposed to be independent (uncorrelated) and the evidence bore this out.

Babin, Boles, and Darden (1995) modified a scale developed by Holbrook and Batra (1988). The latter developed a three item scale to measure *activation,* but the former added the item *interested* and viewed the scale as measuring "the extent to which one's system is energized with respect to allocating attention capacity" to some stimulus (p. 103).

Richins (1997) drew upon terms in previous measures as well as her own series of studies to develop and refine several emotion-related scales into the CES (Consumption Emotion Set).

RELIABILITY: Alphas of .77 (Babin, Boles, and Darden 1995), .88 (Dubé and Morgan 1996), .92 (Hung 2001), .78 (Lord, Lee, and Sauer 1994), and .90 (Mano and Oliver 1993) have been reported for the various versions of the scale. As noted above, reliability was reported by Richins (1997) for only studies four (α = .88) and five (α = .89). The version of the scale used by Beatty and Ferrell (1998) was reported to have a composite reliability of .82. Alphas of .86 and .88 were reported for the version of the scale used by Mano (1999) in pre-task and post-task assessments, respectively.

VALIDITY: The validity of the scale was not specifically addressed in any of the studies conducted by Babin, Boles, and Darden (1995), Lord, Lee, and Sauer (1994), or Mano and Oliver (1993). Dubé and Morgan (1996) stated that a factor analysis was conducted on this scale's items along with those for another scale (V. III, #5) and revealed a two-factor structure. One item (*excited*) loaded on the other factor and was, presumably, dropped from the final version of the scale. Likewise, the analyses conducted by Hung (2001) on twelve items showed three items loaded together in a factor analysis and having an average variance extracted of .79.

Richins (1997) did not directly examine the validity of her scale either. A great deal of effort was expended, however, in a creative use of MDS (multi-dimensional scaling) to note whether items composing each scale clustered together.

Although all of the details were not provided in the study by Beatty and Ferrell (1998), the implication was that this scale was unidimensional and showed sufficient evidence of convergent and discriminant validity.

COMMENTS: See also Kelley and Hoffman (1997).

REFERENCES:

Babin, Barry J., James S. Boles, and William R. Darden (1995), "Salesperson Stereotypes, Consumer Emotions, and Their Impact on Information Processing," *JAMS*, 23 (Spring), 94–105.

Beatty, Sharon E. and M. Elizabeth Ferrell (1998), "Impulse Buying: Modeling Its Precursors," *JR*, 74 (2), 169–191.

Dubé, Laurette and Michael S. Morgan (1996), "Trend Effects and Gender Differences in Retrospective Judgments of Consumption Emotions," *JCR*, 23 (September), 156–162.

Holbrook, Morris B. and Rajeev Batra (1988), "Toward a Standardized Emotional Profile (SEP) Useful in Measuring Responses to the Nonverbal Components of Advertising," *Nonverbal Communication in Advertising*, Sidney Hecker, David W. Stewart, eds. Lexington, MA: D.C. Heath, 95–109.

Hung, Kineta (2001), "Framing Meaning Perceptions with Music: The Case of Teaser Ads," *JA*, 30 (3), 39–49.

Kelley, Scott W. and K. Douglas Hoffman (1997), "An Investigation of Positive Affect, Prosocial Behaviors and Service Quality," *JR*, 73 (3), 407–427.

Lord, Kenneth R., Myung-Soo Lee, and Paul L. Sauer (1994), "Program Context Antecedents of Attitude toward Radio Commercials," *JAMS*, 22 (1), 3–15.

Mano, Haim (1999), "The Influence of Pre-Existing Negative Affect on Store Purchase Intentions," *JR*, 75 (2), 149–172.

Mano, Haim and Richard L. Oliver (1993), "Assessing the Dimensionality and Structure of the Consumption Experience: Evaluation, Feeling, and Satisfaction," *JCR*, 20 (December), 451–466.

Richins, Marsha L. (1997), "Measuring Emotions in the Consumption Experience," *JCR*, 24 (September), 127–146.

Watson, David, Lee Anna Clark, and Auke Tellegen (1988), "Development and Validation of Brief Measures of Positive and Negative Affect: The PANAS Scales," *Journal of Personality and Social Psychology*, 54 (6), 1063–1070.

SCALE ITEMS:

1. enthusiastic

2. interested

3. determined

4. excited

5. inspired

6. alert

7. active

8. strong

9. proud

10. attentive

11. aroused

12. thrilled

Babin, Boles, and Darden (1995): 2, 4, 7, 11 7-point
Beatty and Ferrell (1998): 1, 4, 5, 9 7-point
Dubé and Morgan (1996): 1-10 7-point
Hung (2001): 4, 7, 11 7-point
Lord, Lee, and Sauer (1994): 1-10 5-point
Mano (1999): 1-10 5-point
Mano and Oliver (1993): 1-10 5-point
Richins (1997): 1, 4, 12 4-point

SCALE NAME: Affective Response to Brand

SCALE DESCRIPTION: The scale is composed of three, seven-point Likert-type statements measuring the degree of positive affect a consumer has toward a brand.

SCALE ORIGIN: No information regarding the scale's origin was provided by Chaudhuri and Holbrook (2001). It seems to have been developed for use in their study.

RELIABILITY: An alpha of .96 was reported for the scale Chaudhuri and Holbrook (2001).

VALIDITY: The only information bearing on the scale's validity reported by Chaudhuri and Holbrook (2001) was that there was evidence of its discriminant validity given that its average variance extracted was much higher than its squared correlation with the three other constructs with which it was compared.

REFERENCES:
Chaudhuri, Arjun and Morris B. Holbrook (2001), "The Chain of Effects from Brand Trust and Brand Affect to Brand Performance: The Role of Brand Loyalty," *JM*, 65 (April), 81 – 93.

SCALE ITEMS:

1. I feel good when I use this brand.

2. This brand makes me happy.

3. This brand gives me pleasure.

SCALE NAME: Agreement Response Tendency

SCALE DESCRIPTION: The scale is intended to measure the tendency to agree (or disagree) with items regardless of their content due to an underlying personality trait. This could be considered a measure of *yea-saying*.

SCALE ORIGIN: The scale was developed by Couch and Keniston (1960). An original instrument had 681 items, the majority of which were drawn from previous tests. That was pared down to 360 items and referred to as the over-all agreement score (OAS). Most of the psychometric analysis in their article related to the OAS rather than the short version presented here. Scores on the OAS were then correlated with each of the original 681 items. The fifteen items with the highest correlation were identified by the authors as "the best short scale measure of the agreeing response tendency" (p. 159).

RELIABILITY: An alpha of .77 was reported for the scale by Lastovicka et al. (1999).

VALIDITY: No examination of the scale's validity was reported by Lastovicka et al. (1999) although it was used in the process of validating another scale (#177). In the process of doing that this scale was correlated with another measure of response bias (#462). The correlation was significant but moderately low and negative ($-.33$), thus, raising doubt about what either or both of the scales are measuring.

COMMENTS: Although an impressive amount of testing was done on the OAS, little is known about the psychometric quality of the short version. Caution is urged in using this scale until further testing is conducted.

REFERENCES:
Couch, Arthur and Kenneth Keniston (1960), "Yeasayers and Naysayers: Agreeing Response Set as a Personality Variable," *Journal of Abnormal and Social Psychology*, 60 (2), 151–174.
Lastovicka, John L., Lance A. Bettencourt, Renee Shaw Hughner, and Ronald J. Kuntze (1999), "Lifestyle of the Tight and Frugal: Theory and Measurement," *JCR*, 26 (June), 85–98.

SCALE ITEMS: [1]

1. Novelty has a great appeal to me.

2. I crave excitement.

3. It's a wonderful feeling to sit surrounded by your possessions.

4. There are few things more satisfying than to splurge on something—books, clothes, furniture, etc.

5. Only the desire to achieve great things will bring a man's mind into full activity.

6. Nothing is worse than an offensive odor.

7. In most conversations, I tend to bounce from topic to topic.

8. I really envy the man who can walk up to anybody and tell him off to his face.

9. I could really shock people if I said all of the dirty things I think.

10. There are few more miserable experiences than going to bed night after night knowing you are so upset that worry will not let you sleep.

11. I tend to make decisions on the spur of the moment.

12. Little things upset me.

13. Drop reminders of yourself whenever you go and your life's trail will be well remembered.

14. I like nothing better than having breakfast in bed.

15. My mood is easily influenced by the people around me.

[1] Couch and Keniston (1960) used a seven-point Likert-type response format with *strongly disagree* (1) and *strongly agree* (7) as anchors.

SCALE NAME: Animosity (Economic)

SCALE DESCRIPTION: The scale is composed of five, seven-point Likert-type statements that measure a person's negative feelings towards a specified country because of its economic power over one's own country.

SCALE ORIGIN: The scale was developed by Klein, Ettenson, and Morris (1998). Although the scale was drafted in English, the authors took several steps to ensure the appropriateness of the measure when read in Mandarin Chinese by the respondents.

RELIABILITY: Klein, Ettenson, and Morris (1998) reported the construct reliability of the scale to be .74 (n = 244).

VALIDITY: Results of a single-construct structural equation model showed that the five scale items had significant paths to the construct, the residuals were low, and the fit statistics were strong (Klein, Ettenson, and Morris 1998). Further testing indicated that the scale was distinct from another measure of animosity (#10) as well as ethnocentrism (#163). However, the variance extracted was rather low (.38).

REFERENCES:

Klein, Jill Gabrielle, Richard Ettenson, and Marlene D. Morris (1998), "The Animosity Model of Foreign Product Purchase: An Empirical Test in the People's Republic of China," *JM*, 62 (January), 89 – 100.

SCALE ITEMS: [1]

1. _____ is not a reliable trading partner.

2. _____ wants to gain economic power over _____.

3. _____ is taking advantage of _____ .

4. _____ has too much economic influence in _____ .

5. The _____ are doing business unfairly with _____.

[1] The name of the country of interest should be placed in the first blanks of each item. The name of a country of the respondents should go in the second blanks of 2 to 5. A seven-point, Likert-type response format was used by Klein, Ettenson, and Morris (1998) with anchors ranging from *strongly disagree* (1) to *strongly agree* (7).

#10 *Animosity (War)*

SCALE NAME: Animosity (War)

SCALE DESCRIPTION: The scale is composed of three, seven-point Likert-type statements that measure a person's negative feelings towards a specified country because of something it was responsible for during a war.

SCALE ORIGIN: The scale was developed by Klein, Ettenson, and Morris (1998). Although the scale was drafted in English the authors took several steps to ensure the appropriateness of the measure when read in Mandarin Chinese by the respondents.

RELIABILITY: Klein, Ettenson, and Morris (1998) reported the construct reliability of the scale to be .76 (n = 244).

VALIDITY: Results of a single-construct structural equation model showed that the three scale items had significant paths to the construct (Klein, Ettenson, and Morris 1998). Further testing indicated that the scale was distinct from another measure of animosity (#9) as well as ethnocentrism (#163).

COMMENTS: Klein, Ettenson, and Morris (1998) used the items with a Chinese sample and they responded with reference to Japan and its invasion of China during World War II. Some adjustment in the items will no doubt be necessary if/when the scale is to be used with other countries.

REFERENCES:
Klein, Jill Gabrielle, Richard Ettenson, and Marlene D. Morris (1998), "The Animosity Model of Foreign Product Purchase: An Empirical Test in the People's Republic of China," *JM*, 62 (January), 89 – 100.

SCALE ITEMS: [1]

1. I feel angry toward the _____.

2. I will never forgive _____ for the _____ massacre.

3. _____ should pay for what it did to _____ during the occupation.

---

[1] The name of the country of interest should be placed in the blank of item 1 as well as the first blanks of 2 and 3. The name of a place where a war-time atrocity occurred should go in the second blanks of 2 and 3. A seven-point, Likert-type response format was used by Klein, Ettenson, and Morris (1998) with anchors ranging from *strongly disagree* (1) to *strongly agree* (7).

SCALE NAME: Anxiety (With Computers)

SCALE DESCRIPTION: The eight, seven-point Likert-type statements are used to measure a person's dislike of computers as well as their discomfort using them.

SCALE ORIGIN: The items used by Coyle and Thorson (2001) were taken from a scale by Charlton and Birkett (1995). That scale had 18 items and was itself a subscale of a larger scale. In terms of reliability, this subscale was reported to have an alpha of .93 and a stability (one month) of .92. The authors provided evidence in support of the subscale's known-group validity, e.g., those students judged to have anxiety with computers did in fact score significantly lower on the scale.

It is not clear why Coyle and Thorson (2001) borrowed the particular subset of items that they did, especially since those had the lowest loadings of all the items in Charlton and Birkett's (1995) longer version of the scale.

RELIABILITY: An alpha of .68 (n = 68) was reported for the scale (Coyle and Thorson 2001).

VALIDITY: No examination of the scale's validity was reported by Coyle and Thorson (2001).

COMMENTS: The low reliability of the scale and lack of information about the scale's validity indicate that caution should be exercised in its usage. It would appear from reading the items themselves that the items are tapping into more than one factor.

REFERENCES:
Charlton, John P. and Paul E. Birkett (1995), "The Development and Validation of the Computer Apathy and Anxiety Scale," *Journal of Educational Computing Research*, 13 (1), 41 – 59.
Coyle, James R. and Esther Thorson (2001), "The Effects of Progressive Levels of Interactivity and Vividness in Web Marketing Sites," *JA*, 30 (Fall), 65 – 77.

SCALE ITEMS:

1. I do not have problems in understanding computers. (r)

2. I often get irritated with computers.

3. I dislike the inflexibility of computers.

4. Computers make my life easier. (r)

5. I can't understand why people like computers.

6. I like the challenge that learning to use computers presents. (r)

7. It would not matter to me if I never used a computer again.

8. I think that people attach too much importance to computers these days.

SCALE NAME: Approach-Avoidance (Retail Environment)

SCALE DESCRIPTION: The eight-item, seven-point Likert-type scale measures a consumer's opposing motivations with respect to a particular retail facility, to simultaneously want to be in the environment but also leave it.

SCALE ORIGIN: Mattila and Wirtz (2001) took the items used by Donovan and Rossiter (1982) and phrased them as sentences rather than as questions. The latter said that they, in turn, had taken the general approach-avoidance questions from Mehrabian and Russell (1974) and adapted them for the retail environment.

RELIABILITY: Donovan and Rossiter (1982) reported alphas for several subscales: .88 (all items except #8), .90 (#1–#3), .67 (#4 and #5). (Item #8 was used in the analyses by itself.) Mattila and Wirtz (2001) reported an alpha of .78 for the scale as a whole.

VALIDITY: Although neither study directly evaluated the validity of the scale, Donovan and Rossiter (1982) provided information bearing on it. Specifically, their factor analysis of the eight items showed there were three factors although only one had an eigenvalue greater than one. Ultimately, the authors used subscales (rather than the scale as a whole) in their analyses.

REFERENCES:

Donovan, Robert J. and John R. Rossiter (1982), "Store Atmospherics: An Environmental Psychology Approach," *JR*, 58 (1), 34–57.
Mattila, Anna S. (2004), Personal Correspondence.
Mattila, Anna S. and Jochen Wirtz (2001), "Congruency of Scent and Music as a Driver of In-store Evaluations and Behaviour," *JR*, 77 (2), 273–289.
Mehrabian, Albert and James A. Russell (1974), *An Approach to Environmental Psychology*, Cambridge, MA: The MIT Press.

SCALE ITEMS: [1]

1. I enjoy shopping in this store.

2. I like this store environment.

3. I would avoid having to return to this store. (r)

4. This is a place in which I feel friendly and talkative to a stranger who happens to be next to me.

5. This is a place where I try to avoid people and avoid talking to them. (r)

6. I like to spend time browsing in this store.

7. I want to avoid looking around or exploring the store. (r)

8. This is a sort of place where I end up spending more money than I originally set out to spend.

[1] This is the Likert-type version of the scale used by Mattila and Wirtz (2001). The items used by Donovan and Rossiter (1982) were similar except that they were stated as questions.

SCALE NAME: Arousal

SCALE DESCRIPTION: The scale is typically composed of six, seven-point semantic differentials that are intended to measure one's arousal-related emotional reaction to some environmental stimulus.

SCALE ORIGIN: This scale is taken from the work of Mehrabian and Russell (1974). Given previous work by others as well as their own research, they proposed that there are three factors that compose all emotional reactions to environmental stimuli. They referred to the three factors as pleasure, arousal, and dominance. A series of studies were used to develop measures of each factor. A study of the "final" set of items used 214 University of California undergraduates, each of whom used the scales to evaluate a different subset of six situations. (The analysis was based, therefore, on 1284 observations.) A principal components factor analysis with oblique rotation was used and the expected three factors emerged. Pleasure, arousal, and dominance explained 27%, 23%, and 14% of the available evidence, respectively. Scores on the pleasure scale had correlations of −0.07 and 0.03 with arousal and dominance, respectively. Dominance had a correlation of 0.18 with arousal.

RELIABILITY: The following estimates of reliability (e.g., alpha) have been reported in the various studies: .77 (Donovan et al. 1994); .89 (Holbrook et al. 1984); .81 (Kempf and Smith 1998); .83 (Mattila and Wirtz 2001); .82 (Neelamegham and Jain 1999); .97 (Olney, Holbrook, and Batra 1991); .96 (Simpson, Horton, and Brown 1996); and .87 and .86 (Wirtz, Matilla and Tan 2000).

VALIDITY: No explicit examination of the scale's validity was reported in most of the articles. Some evidence of the scale's unidimensionality came from a principal components factor analysis performed by Donovan et al. (1994) where all six of the arousal-related items loaded highest on the same dimension and lowest on one related to pleasure. Wirtz, Matilla and Tan (2000) performed a confirmatory factor analysis on this scale and a couple of others with the results providing some evidence of each scale's convergent and discriminant validity. Further evidence of the arousal scale's discriminant validity came from noting that its average variance extracted (.82) was higher than it was for the squared correlation between it and any of the other two constructs (Fornell and Larcker 1981). Some evidence of nomological validity came from noting, as expected from previous research, arousal was not related to satisfaction.

COMMENTS: As noted previously, this scale was developed along with two other scales, dominance and pleasure. Although scored separately, they are typically used together in a study.

See also Havlena and Holbrook (1986), and Menon and Kahn (1995), and Mitchell, Kahn, and Knasko (1995).

REFERENCES:

Donovan, Robert J., John R. Rossiter, Gilian Marcoolyn, and Andrew Nesdale (1994), "Store Atmosphere and Purchasing Behavior," *JR*, 70 (3), 283–294.

Fornell, Claes and David F. Larcker (1981), "Evaluating Structural Equation Models with Unobservable Variables and Measurement Error," *JMR*, 18 (February), 39–50.

Havlena, William J. and Morris B. Holbrook (1986), "The Varieties of Consumption Experience: Comparing Two Typologies of Emotion in Consumer Behavior," *JCR*, 13 (December), 394–404.

Holbrook, Morris B., Robert W. Chestnut, Terence A. Oliva, and Eric A. Greenleaf (1984), "Play as a Consumption Experience: The Roles of Emotions, Performance, and Personality in the Enjoyment of Games," *JCR*, 11 (September), 728–739.

Kempf, Deanna S. and Robert E. Smith (1998), "Consumer Processing of Product Trial and the Influence of Prior Advertising: A Structural Modeling Approach," *JMR*, 35 (August), 325–338.

Mattila, Anna S. and Jochen Wirtz (2001), "Congruency of Scent and Music as a Driver of In-store Evaluations and Behaviour," *JR*, 77 (2), 273 – 289.

Mehrabian, Albert and James A. Russell (1974), *An Approach to Environmental Psychology,* Cambridge, MA: The MIT Press.

Menon, Satya and Barbara E. Kahn (1995), "The Impact of Context on Variety Seeking in Product Choices," *JCR*, 22 (December), 285 – 295.

Mitchell, Deborah, Barbara E. Kahn, and Susan C. Knasko (1995), "There's Something in the Air: Effects of Congruent or Incongruent Ambient Odor on Consumer Decision Making," *JCR*, 22 (September), 229 – 238.

Neelamegham, Ramya and Dipak Jain (1999), "Consumer Choice Process for Experience Goods: An Econometric Model and Analysis," *JMR*, 36 (August), 373 – 386.

Olney, Thomas J., Morris B. Holbrook, and Rajeev Batra (1991), "Consumer Responses to Advertising: The Effects of Ad Content, Emotions, and Attitude toward the Ad on Viewing Time," *JCR*, 17 (March), 440 – 453.

Simpson, Penny M., Steve Horton, and Gene Brown (1996), "Male Nudity in Advertisements: A Modified Replication and Extension of Gender and Product Effects," *JAMS*, 24 (Summer), 257–262.

Wirtz, Jochen, Anna S. Matilla, and Rachel L.P. Tan (2000), "The Moderating Role of Target-Arousal on the Impact of Affect on Satisfaction—An Examination in the Context of Service Experience," *JR*, 76 (3), 347–365.

SCALE ITEMS: [1]

Directions: Rate your emotions according to the way the _____ made you feel.

1. stimulated / relaxed

2. excited / calm

3. frenzied / sluggish

4. jittery / dull

5. wide-awake / sleepy

6. aroused / unaroused

[1] All of the reported studies appear to have used the full set of items except for Kempf and Smith (1998) who just used items 1, 2, and 6 and Neelamegham and Jain (1999) who used items 1-3 and 6.

SCALE NAME: Arousal Avoidance

SCALE DESCRIPTION: The scale is composed of 14 sets of items intended to measure the extent to which a person seeks situations in which arousal levels are expected to be low and avoids situations that might generate high arousal.

SCALE ORIGIN: This scale is one of three dimensions of an instrument constructed by Murgatroyd et al. (1978) intended to measure telic dominance, a state of mind in which a person views him- or herself as pursuing some essential goal. Further, this telic state is characterized by attempts to lower arousal. The opposite state was called paratelic. Although this might also be referred to as a personality trait, technically it denotes the probability of an individual being in a given state rather than its opposite. A person is viewed as being able to change to the opposite state under certain conditions.

The subscale used by Shoham, Rose, and Kahle (1998) was arousal avoidance. Murgatroyd et al. (1978) reported an alpha of .734 (n = 119) for the subscale with its stability ranging from .872 (6 hours, n = 32) to .698 (12 months, n = 15). A variety of evidence was reported in support of the scale's construct validity.

RELIABILITY: Shoham, Rose, and Kahle (1998) reported an alpha of .67 (n = 155) for the subscale.

VALIDITY: Although Shoham, Rose, and Kahle (1998) did not report examining the validity of the scale, their results indicated the measure performed as expected in their model and, thus, provided some evidence of the subscale's nomological validity.

COMMENTS: Shoham, Rose, and Kahle (1998) translated the scale into Hebrew before use with a sample of people in Israel.

REFERENCES:

Murgatroyd, Stephen, Cyril Rushton, Michael Apter, and Colette Ray (1978), "The Development of the Telic Dominance Scale," *Journal of Personality Assessment*, 42 (5), 519 – 528.

Shoham, Aviv (2000), Personal Correspondence.

Shoham, Aviv, Gregory M. Rose, and Lynn R. Kahle (1998), "Marketing of Risky Sports: From Intention to Action," *JAMS*, 26 (4), 307–321.

SCALE ITEMS: [1]

Directions: Given a free choice, which of the following statements would you choose or which fits you best? If you are uncertain of which alternative you prefer select the *not sure* option.[1]

1. Leisure activities which are just exciting.
   Leisure activities which have a purpose.*

2. Spending one's life in many different places.
   Spending most of one's life in one place.*

3. Having your tasks set for you.*
   Choosing your own activities.

4. Staying in one job.*
   Having many changes of job.

5. Seldom doing things "for kicks."*
   Often doing things "for kicks."

6. Taking holidays in many different places.
   Taking holidays always in the same place.*

7. Frequently trying strange foods.
   Always eating familiar foods.*

8. Recounting an incident accurately.*
   Exaggerating for effect.

9. Having continuity in the place where you live.*
   Having frequent moves of house.

10. Taking risks.
    Going through life safely.*

11. Wining a game easily.*
    Playing a game with scores very close.

12. Steady routine in life.*
    Continual unexpectedness of surprise.

13. Working in the garden.*
    Picking wild fruit.

14. Traveling a great deal in one's job.
    Working in one office or workshop.

---

[1] The instructions are based upon information from Shoham (2000) and the article by Murgatroyd et al. (1978). A *not sure* option was available for selection with every set of alternative responses. Telic choices (designated above with asterisks) were scored as 1, paratelic choices were not scored, and *not sure* responses were scored as .5. Murgatroyd et al. (1978) summed the item scores whereas Shoham, Rose, and Kahle (1998) appear to have calculated averages.

SCALE NAME: Attitude Toward a Theater's Facilities

SCALE DESCRIPTION: Three items are used to measure a theater attendee's attitude about the physical facilities of a specified theater.

SCALE ORIGIN: Garbarino and Johnson (1999) indicated that they drew upon a variety of sources to develop the items.

RELIABILITY: Garbarino and Johnson (1999) reported the following alphas for the scales as used with three different subsets of theatergoers: .69 (individual ticket buyers), .63 (occasional subscribers), and .67 (consistent subscribers).

VALIDITY: Based on the variety of indicators they examined, Garbarino and Johnson (1999) made a general claim of good fit for their measurement model as well as evidence of good convergent validity. This scale performed adequately on a common test of discriminant validity, but not as well on a more conservative test. The authors admitted that it was "one of the less well captured constructs" (p. 83).

REFERENCES:
Garbarino, Ellen and Mark S. Johnson (1999), "The Different Roles of Satisfaction, Trust, and Commitment in Customer Relationships," *JM*, 63 (April), 70 – 87.

SCALE ITEMS: [1]

1. How would you rate your overall satisfaction with the current theater facilities?

2. I like the intimacy of the theater.

3. How would you rate the theater compared with other off-Broadway companies on the quality of the facilities?

---

[1] Response scale anchors were: *very dissatisfied/very satisfied* (#1), *strongly disagree/strongly agree* (#2), and *much worse/much better* (#3).

SCALE NAME: Attitude Toward Activities (Adventurous)

SCALE DESCRIPTION: The scale is composed of three, seven point items intended to measure a person's general liking of activities that are different from their daily routine.

SCALE ORIGIN: The scale is original to Shoham, Rose, and Kahle (1998). The authors stated that the items were developed after a review of the literature and pretested on a convenience sample of students.

RELIABILITY: An alpha of .60 (n = 155) was reported for the scale by Shoham, Rose, and Kahle (1998).

VALIDITY: The only evidence relating to the scale's validity reported by Shoham, Rose, and Kahle (1998) was that it had moderate, positive correlations with two other scales they developed to measure related attitudes about activities.

COMMENTS: The alpha for the scale is low. Caution should be exercised in use of the scale until its psychometric quality can be improved.

REFERENCES:
Shoham, Aviv, Gregory M. Rose, and Lynn R. Kahle (1998), "Marketing of Risky Sports: From Intention to Action," *JAMS*, 26 (4), 307–321.

SCALE ITEMS: [1]

1. adventures

2. daily and routine activities (r)

3. breaking out of the daily routine

---

[1] These items were responded to using a seven-point scale ranging from *dislike very much* (1) to *like very much* (7).

SCALE NAME: Attitude Toward Activities (Social Status)

SCALE DESCRIPTION: The scale is composed of three, seven-point items intended to measure a person's general liking of activities that could enhance one's social status.

SCALE ORIGIN: The scale is original to Shoham, Rose, and Kahle (1998). The authors stated that the items were developed after a review of the literature and pretested on a convenience sample of students.

RELIABILITY: An alpha of .67 (n = 155) was reported for the scale by Shoham, Rose, and Kahle (1998).

VALIDITY: Very limited evidence relating to the scale's validity was reported by Shoham, Rose, and Kahle (1998). They said it had a moderate, positive correlation with a measure of the value of being well respected (Kahle 1983).

REFERENCES:
Kahle, Lynn R. (1983), *Social Values and Social Change: Adaptation to Life in America* New York: Praeger.
Shoham, Aviv, Gregory M. Rose, and Lynn R. Kahle (1998), "Marketing of Risky Sports: From Intention to Action," *JAMS*, 26 (4), 307–321.

SCALE ITEMS: [1]

1. activities that may harm your social standing (r)

2. activities, the participation in which causes your friends to appreciate you

3. activities that cause an increase in your social status

[1] These items were responded to using a seven-point scale ranging from *dislike very much* (1) to *like very much* (7).

SCALE NAME: Attitude Toward Charitable Organizations

SCALE DESCRIPTION: Five items are used to measure a person's general attitude about charities including how they use money and the role they play in society. The scale is not specific to any particular charity nor does it directly assess the respondent's level of support.

SCALE ORIGIN: The scale is original to Webb, Green, and Brashear (2000). Seventy-eight items were generated based on previous scales and a literature review for the measurement of this construct and a related one (#23). Two rounds of content validation with different sets of judges left 14 items. Further testing eliminated a few more items as discussed below.

RELIABILITY: Alphas of .81 (Study 1) and .82 (Study 2) were reported for the scale by Webb, Green, and Brashear (2000). Variance extracted was .49 (Study 1) and .53 (Study 2).

VALIDITY: Several rounds of EFA and CFA were employed by Webb, Green, and Brashear (2000) in both studies and led to the elimination of some items from the two scales being developed. Ultimately, a two-factor model was found to have a significantly better fit than a one-factor model. This along with other evidence provided support for the discriminant validity of the two scales.

REFERENCES:

Webb, Deborah J., Corliss L. Green, and Thomas G. Brashear (2000), "Development and Validation of Scales to Measure Attitudes Influencing Monetary Donations to Charitable Organizations," *JAMS*, 28 (2), 299 – 309.

SCALE ITEMS:

1. The money given to charities goes for good causes.

2. Much of the money donated to charity is wasted. (r)

3. My image of charitable organizations is positive.

4. Charitable organizations have been quite successful in helping the needy.

5. Charity organizations perform a useful function for society.

SCALE NAME: Attitude Toward Children's TV Programming

SCALE DESCRIPTION: The scale is composed of three, five-point Likert-type items intended to measure the extent to which a person (adult) believes that the television programs aimed at kids are of high quality.

SCALE ORIGIN: The scale appears to be original to Walsh, Laczniak, and Carlson (1998).

RELIABILITY: An alpha of .81 (n = 151) was reported by Walsh, Laczniak, and Carlson (1998).

VALIDITY: No examination of the scale's validity was reported by Walsh, Laczniak, and Carlson (1998).

REFERENCES:
Walsh, Ann D., Russell N. Laczniak, and Les Carlson (1998), "Mothers' Preferences for Regulating Children's Television," *JA*, 27 (3), 23–36.

SCALE ITEMS:

1. The quality of children's TV programs is excellent.

2. Children's TV programs are "tasteful."

3. The educational level of children's TV programs is excellent.

SCALE NAME: Attitude Toward Complaining (Personal Norms)

SCALE DESCRIPTION: The scale is composed of several Likert-type items measuring the extent to which a person agrees that it is appropriate for consumers to complain when they experience a dissatisfying transaction. Richins (1983) used a four item, five-point scale whereas Singh (1990) used a five item, six-point scale. Moorman (1998) used four items and a seven-point scale.

SCALE ORIGIN: The origin of the scale used by Richins (1983) is provided in Richins (1982), which shares the same database. Thirty-one items were generated based upon depth interviews and then tested. A final group of 15 items was factor analyzed, which resulted in three complaint-related factors, one of which is the scale discussed here.

Singh (1990) modified the scale: three items were added and two were dropped. Two of the three items added by Singh were slight modifications of items used in a ten-item measure described by Day (1984).

Moorman (1998) used a six item scale from Richins and Verhage (1985) but two of the items were dropped due to low item-total correlations.

RELIABILITY: Alphas of .71, .62 and .67 were reported by Moorman (1998), Richins (1983), and Singh (1990), respectively.

VALIDITY: Information regarding the unidimensionality of the scale used by Richins (1983) is provided in Richins (1982). Singh (1990) factor analyzed eight items: five from his version of this scale and three items from the Societal Benefits version of the scale (V. II, #18). A two factor structure with negligible cross-loadings resulted.

No information was provided by Moorman (1998) about the validity of the four items she used. Some light can be shed on it, however, by referring to the original study by Richins (1982). She envisioned these items to be part of three different dimensions of complaining. Her data and analysis indicated that three of the items loaded highest on the same factor while the fourth (#4 below) loaded on another factor. Not only does this raise some doubt about the unidimensionality of the four item set used by Moorman (1998) but it also brings into question its validity.

REFERENCES:

Day, Ralph L. (1984), "Modeling Choices Among Alternative Responses to Dissatisfaction," in *Advances in Consumer Research*, V. 11, Tom Kinnear, ed. Ann Arbor, MI: Association for Consumer Research, 496–499.

Moorman, Christine (1998), "Market-Level Effects of Information: Competitive Responses and Consumer Dynamics," *JMR*, 35 (February), 82–98.

Richins, Marsha L (1982), "An Investigation of Consumers' Attitudes Toward Complaining," *Advances in Consumer Research*, V. 9, Andrew Mitchell, ed. Ann Arbor, MI: Association for Consumer Research, 502–506.

Richins, Marsha L. (1983), "An Analysis of Consumer Interaction Styles in the Marketplace," *JCR*, 10 (June), 73–82.

Richins, Marsha L. and Bronislaw J. Verhage (1985), "Seeking Redress for Consumer Dissatisfaction: The Role of Attitudes and Situational-Factors," *Journal of Consumer Policy*, 8 (March), 29–43.

Singh, Jagdip (1990), "A Typology of Consumer Dissatisfaction Response Styles," *JR*, 66 (Spring), 57–97.

SCALE ITEMS: [1]

1. Most people don't make enough complaints to businesses about unsatisfactory products.

2. I feel a sense of accomplishment when I have managed to get a complaint [to a store] taken care of satisfactorily.

3. People are bound to end up with unsatisfactory products once in a while so they shouldn't complain [about them]. (r)

4. It bothers me quite a bit if I don't complain about an unsatisfactory product [when I know I should].

5. It sometimes feels good to get my dissatisfaction and frustration with the product off my chest by complaining.

6. I often complain when I'm dissatisfied with business or products because I feel it is my duty to do so.

7. I don't like people who complain to stores because usually their complaints are unreasonable. (r)

8. People have a responsibility to society to tell stores or manufacturers when products are unsatisfactory.

[1] Richins (1982, 1983) used items 1 and the long versions of 2, 3, and 4. Singh (1990) used a six point scale along with items 5, 6, 7, and the short versions of #3 and #4. Moorman (1998) used items 1, the short version of 2, the long version of 4, and 8. Each author used a Likert-type (agree/disagree) response format.

SCALE NAME: Attitude Toward Coupons

SCALE DESCRIPTION: Five, ten-point semantic differentials composed the scale used by Huff and Alden (1998). The scale was used to measure a consumer's attitude toward coupons in general.

SCALE ORIGIN: Although not explicitly stated by the authors, the scale appears to be original to Huff and Alden (1998). However, four of these items have been used many times in measuring brand attitudes (see #59).

RELIABILITY: Alphas of .96 (n = 250), .90 (n = 200), and .90 (n = 473) were reported for the scale as used in Thailand, Taiwan, and Malaysia, respectively (Huff and Alden 1998).

VALIDITY: No examination of the scale's validity was reported by Huff and Alden (1998).

REFERENCES:
Huff, Lenard C. and Dana L. Alden (1998), "An Investigation of Consumer Response to Sales Promotions In Developing Markets: A Three-Country Analysis," *JAR*, 38 (May/June), 47–56.

SCALE ITEMS: [1]

1. favorable / not favorable

2. good / bad

3. positive / negative

4. valuable / worthless

5. an incentive to buy / a disincentive to buy

[1] A ten-point response scale was used by Huff and Alden (1998) for these items.

SCALE NAME: Attitude Toward Elicitation Method

SCALE DESCRIPTION: The six item, seven-point semantic differential scale attempts to measure a person's opinion of a measure task he or she has just engaged in. The scale assesses several facets of the task such as how easy it was and how well the measure allowed the respondent to express his or her attitude.

SCALE ORIGIN: Bottomley, Doyle, and Green (2000) cited both Leon (1997) and Steenkamp and Van Trijp (1997) as previous users of these items. An examination of those sources indicate that about three items were borrowed from each and used to create a new scale.

RELIABILITY: An alpha of .776 was reported for the scale by Bottomley, Doyle, and Green (2000).

VALIDITY: No discussion of this scale's validity was provided in any of the studies.

REFERENCES:
Bottomley, Paul A., John R. Doyle, and Rodney H. Green (2000), "Testing the Reliability of Elicitation Methods: Direct Rating Versus Point Allocation," *JMR*, 37 (4), 508–513.
Leon, Orfelio G. (1997), "On the Death of SMART and the Birth of GRAPA," *Organizational Behavior and Human Decision Processes*, 71 (3), 249–262.
Steenkamp, Jan-Benedict E.M. and Hans M. Van Trijp (1997), "Attribute Elicitation in Marketing Research: A Comparison of Three Procedures," *Marketing Letters*, 8 (2), 153–165.

SCALE ITEMS:

Directions: We would like to determine your reactions to the measurement task. Was it:

1. easy / difficult

2. reliable / unreliable

3. easy to express my opinion / difficult to express my opinion

4. simple / challenging

5. nice / awful

6. helpful in clearly thinking about the problem / unhelpful in thinking clearly about the problem

SCALE NAME: Attitude Toward Helping Others

SCALE DESCRIPTION: The scale is composed of four statements intended to measure a person's general attitude about how people in society should feel and act towards those in need. It is not specific to any particular charity or type of needy persons. Further, the scale does not directly assess what the respondent is actually doing to help but rather what he or she thinks people in general should do.

SCALE ORIGIN: The scale is original to Webb, Green, and Brashear (2000). Seventy-eight items were generated based on previous scales and a literature review for the measurement of this construct and a related one (#18). Two rounds of content validation with different sets of judges left 14 items. Further testing eliminated a few more items as discussed below.

RELIABILITY: Alphas of .79 (Study One) and .80 (Study Two) were reported for the scale by Webb, Green, and Brashear (2000). Variance extracted was .46 (Study One) and .52 (Study Two).

VALIDITY: Several rounds of EFA and CFA were employed by Webb, Green, and Brashear (2000) in both studies and led to the elimination of some items from the two scales being developed. Ultimately, a two-factor model was found to have a significantly better fit than a one-factor model. This, along with other evidence, provided support for the discriminant validity of the two scales.

REFERENCES:

Webb, Deborah J., Corliss L. Green, and Thomas G. Brashear (2000), "Development and Validation of Scales to Measure Attitudes Influencing Monetary Donations to Charitable Organizations," *JAMS*, 28 (2), 299–309.

SCALE ITEMS:

1. People should be willing to help others who are less fortunate.

2. Helping troubled people with their problems is very important to me.

3. People should be more charitable towards others in society.

4. People in need should receive support from others.

SCALE NAME: Attitude Toward Homosexuality

SCALE DESCRIPTION: The scale is composed of nine, seven-point Likert-type items measuring a person's attitude toward male homosexuality, with the emphasis on the morality of that lifestyle.

SCALE ORIGIN: Bhat, Leigh, and Wardlow (1998) indicated that the nine items they used were taken from the 64-item instrument created by Herek (1984). These particular items were selected due to their high factor loadings (> .70) in the latter's research.

RELIABILITY: An alpha of .935 was reported for the scale by Bhat, Leigh, and Wardlow (1998).

VALIDITY: No examination of the scale's validity was reported by Bhat, Leigh, and Wardlow (1998).

REFERENCES:
Bhat, Subodh, Thomas W. Leigh, and Daniel L. Wardlow (1998), "The Effect of Consumer Prejudices on Ad Processing: Heterosexual Consumers' Responses to Homosexual Imagery in Ads," *JA*, 27 (4), 9 – 28.
Herek, Gregory M. (1984), "Attitudes Toward Lesbians and Gay Men: A Factor-Analytic Study," *Journal of Homosexuality*, 10 (1), 39 – 51.

SCALE ITEMS:

1. The growing number of male homosexuals indicates a decline in American morals.

2. Homosexual behavior between two men is just plain wrong.

3. Male homosexuality is merely a different kind of lifestyle that should *not* be condemned. (r)

4. Male homosexuality is a sin.

5. I think male homosexuals are disgusting.

6. If a man has homosexual feelings, he should do everything he can to overcome them.

7. Male homosexuality is not a problem, but what society makes of it can be a problem. (r)

8. Male homosexuality is a perversion.

9. The idea of male homosexual marriages seems ridiculous to me.

SCALE NAME: Attitude Toward NUTRITION FACTS Label

SCALE DESCRIPTION: The scale is composed of three, seven-point semantic differential items measuring a person's general attitude about the provision of information in the Nutrition Facts labels. (These labels are required on all foods sold in the United States.) The scale was called *Nutrition Facts Attitude* by Burton, Garretson, and Velliquette (1999).

SCALE ORIGIN: Although not explicitly stated, the scale appears to be original to Burton, Garretson, and Velliquette (1999).

RELIABILITY: An alpha of .90 was reported for the scale by Burton, Garretson, and Velliquette (1999).

VALIDITY: No explicit analysis was described bearing on the scale's validity.

REFERENCES:
Burton, Scot, Judith A. Garretson, and Anne M. Velliquette (1999), "Implications of Accurate Usage of Nutrition Facts Panel Information for Food Product Evaluations and Purchase Intentions," *JAMS*, 27 (4), 470–480.

SCALE ITEMS:

For me, providing information about nutrition through the Nutrition Facts label on the back or side panel of food packages is:

1. good / bad

2. valuable / worthless

3. important / unimportant

SCALE NAME: Attitude Toward Private Label Brands

SCALE DESCRIPTION: The scale is composed of six, seven-point Likert-type statements that measure a consumer's attitude about private distributor brands. Not only does the scale capture a consumer's opinion of the general quality level of private brands but it also provides a sense of the consumer's tendency to buy them or not.

SCALE ORIGIN: The scale is original to the study of Burton et al. (1998). They used the following definition of the construct when developing the scale, "a predisposition to respond in a favorable or unfavorable manner due to product evaluations, purchase evaluations, and/or self-evaluations associated with private label grocery products" (p. 298). Twelve items were generated based on this definition and were assessed in a pretest with 140 nonstudent respondents. After several rounds of factor analysis six items remained once weak items or, at the other extreme, redundant items were deleted. This set of items was then subjected to confirmatory factor analysis where it was confirmed to fit a one factor model. The alpha for the scale was .89.

RELIABILITY: An alpha of .873 (n = 333) was reported for the scale by Burton et al. (1998).

VALIDITY: The purpose of the study by Burton et al. (1998) was to develop and test a scale of private label attitude. Given this, much information was provided in the article that supported the scale's validity, only a portion of which is mentioned here. Confirmatory factor analysis not only supported the unidimensionality of the items but provided evidence of their convergent validity as well. Three separate tests provided support for the scale's discriminate validity. By examining the relationship between the scale and measures of several other constructs with which it was hypothesized to be related, support was found for claims of the scale's nomological and predictive validity.

COMMENTS: Based on data gathered in the main study, the mean score on the scale was 25.7 with a median of 26 and standard deviation of 7.5. Scores ranged between 6 and 42 with quartile splits at 21, 26, and 31.

Although the items do not explicitly refer to grocery products, they make the most sense in that context. Further, it was in that context that the items were tested. Further testing would be necessary to determine the appropriateness of the scale for use in a non-grocery product situation.

REFERENCES:
Burton, Scot, Donald R. Lichtenstein, Richard G. Netemeyer, and Judith A. Garretson (1998), "A Scale for Measuring Attitude Toward Private Label Products and an Examination of Its Psychological and Behavioral Correlates," *JAR*, 26 (4), 293–306.

SCALE ITEMS:

1. Buying private label brands makes me feel good.

2. I love it when private label brands are available for the product categories I purchase.

3. For most product categories, the best buy is usually the private label brand.

4. In general, private label brands are poor-quality products. (r)

5. Considering the value for the money, I prefer private label brands to national brands.

6. When I buy a private label brand, I always feel that I am getting a good deal.

SCALE NAME: Attitude Toward Product Price

SCALE DESCRIPTION: The scale is composed of three, seven-point semantic differentials measuring a customer's attitude about the pricing of a particular product offering in a store. Although Manning, Sprott, and Miyazaki (1998) used it with reference to "two bottles of ketchup" the scale appears to be quite amenable for use with a wide range of price perceptions from individual brands to store-level assessments.

SCALE ORIGIN: The scale seems to have been developed by Manning, Sprott, and Miyazaki (1998) for use in their study. However, the items themselves have been routinely used in many attitude scales (e.g., #59).

RELIABILITY: An alpha of .93 was reported for the scale by Manning, Sprott, and Miyazaki (1998).

VALIDITY: No examination of the scale's validity was reported by Manning, Sprott, and Miyazaki (1998).

REFERENCES:
Manning, Kenneth C., David E. Sprott, and Anthony D. Miyazaki (1998), "Consumer Response to Quantity Surcharges: Implications for Retail Price Setters," *JR*, 74 (3), 373 – 399.

SCALE ITEMS:

The pricing of the _____ is:

1. bad / good

2. unfavorable / favorable

3. negative / positive

SCALE NAME: Attitude Toward Sweepstakes

SCALE DESCRIPTION: Five, ten-point semantic differentials composed the scale used by Huff and Alden (1998). The scale was used to measure a consumer's attitude toward sweepstakes in general.

SCALE ORIGIN: Although not explicitly stated by the authors, the scale appears to be original to Huff and Alden (1998).

RELIABILITY: Alphas of .96 (n = 250), .91 (n = 200), and .78 (n = 473) were reported for the scale as used in Thailand, Taiwan, and Malaysia, respectively (Alden 2001; Huff and Alden 1998).

VALIDITY: No examination of the scale's validity was reported by Huff and Alden (1998).

REFERENCES:
Alden, Dana L. (2001), Personal Correspondence.
Huff, Lenard C. and Dana L. Alden (1998), "An Investigation of Consumer Response to Sales Promotions In Developing Markets: A Three-Country Analysis," *JAR*, 38 (May/June), 47–56.

SCALE ITEMS: [1]

1. favorable / not favorable

2. good / bad

3. positive / negative

4. valuable / worthless

5. an incentive to buy / a disincentive to buy

---

[1] A ten-point response scale was used by Huff and Alden (1998) for these items.

SCALE NAME: Attitude Toward The Act

SCALE DESCRIPTION: The scale is characterized by several bi-polar adjectives presumed to measure the subject's overall evaluation of engaging in an activity. In most cases the "activity" is a hypothetical purchase or product usage situation the subject is asked to consider. Theoretically, the construct is viewed as lying between *attitude-toward-the-object* and one's *behavioral intention* with respect to the object. The various versions of the scale discussed here have between three and five items. They are similar in that they have at least two or more items in common with several other versions in the set. Although most users did not describe the number of points on their scales, it appears that the majority employed seven point scales.

SCALE ORIGIN: Oliver and Bearden (1985) cite Ajzen and Fishbein (1980) as the source of their scale. Although none of the other studies were as explicit in describing the origins of their measures, the overlap between their sets of items and those offered in Ajzen and Fishbein (1980, pp. 261, 262, and 267) is too similar to be coincidental. Two of the items below (1 and 4) are also among the set of items recommended by Osgood, Suci, and Tannenbaum (1957) for measuring the evaluative dimension of semantic judgment.

RELIABILITY: Although estimates of internal consistency have ranged from .72 (Allen, Machleit, Kleine 1992) to .97 (Gardner, Mitchell, and Russo 1985) it appears that most configurations of the scale have had reliabilities between .85 and .95. Estimates related to each usage are provided under **Scale Items** (below).

VALIDITY: Bagozzi (1981, 1982) provided some evidence of convergent validity for his six item version of the scale. Bagozzi, Baumgartner, and Yi (1992) did make a general observation that all of their measures had an average variance extracted of over .50, with the mean being .74. Allen, Machleit, Kleine (1992) used LIS-REL to confirm their scale's unidimensionality. The scale was used by Shimp and Sharma (1987) to provide evidence of their CETSCALE's nomological validity.

Discriminant validity was assessed by Childers et al. (2001) using two different tests (the latent variable confidence interval tests and the χ^2 difference test). For both studies the evidence indicated that each scale they used, including *attitude*, was measuring a distinctive construct.

COMMENTS: See also Haugtvedt and Wegener (1994) for a variation on the scale as used to measure attitude toward implementation of a new graduation testing procedure and attitude toward building more nuclear power plants.

REFERENCES:

Ajzen, Icek and Martin Fishbein (1980), *Understanding Attitudes and Predicting Social Behavior*, Englewood Cliffs, NJ: Prentice-Hall, Inc.

Allen, Chris T., Karen A. Machleit, and Susan Schultz Kleine (1992), "A Comparison of Attitudes and Emotions as Predictors of Behavior at Diverse Levels of Behavioral Experience," *JCR*, 18 (March), 493 – 504.

Bagozzi, Richard P. (1981), "Attitudes, Intentions, and Behavior: A Test of Some Key Hypotheses," *Journal of Personality and Social Psychology*, 41 (4), 607 – 627.

Bagozzi, Richard P. (1982), "A Field Investigation of Causal Relations Among Cognitions, Affect, Intentions, and Behavior," *JMR*, 19 (November), 562 – 584.

Bagozzi, Richard P. (1994), Personal Correspondence.

Bagozzi, Richard P., Hans Baumgartner, and Youjae Yi (1992), "State versus Action Orientation and the Theory of Reasoned Action: An Application to Coupon Usage," *JCR*, 18 (March), 505 – 518.

Childers, Terry L., Christopher L. Carr, Joann Peck, and Stephen Carson (2001), "Hedonic and Utilitarian Motivations for Online Retail Shopping Behavior," *JR*, 77 (Winter), 511–535.

Gardner, Meryl Paula, Andrew A. Mitchell, and J. Edward Russo (1985), "Low Involvement Strategies for Processing Advertisements," *JA*, 14 (2), 44–56.

Grossbart, Sanford, Darrel D. Muehling, and Norman Kangun (1986), "Verbal and Visual References to Competition in Comparative Advertising," *JA*, 15 (1), 10–23.

Hastak, Manoj (1990), "Does Retrospective Thought Measurement Influence Subsequent Measures of Cognitive Structure in an Advertising Context?," *JA*, 19 (3), 3–13.

Haugtvedt, Curtis P. and Duane T. Wegener (1994), "Message Order Effects in Persuasion: An Attitude Strength Perspective," *JCR*, 21 (June), 205–218.

Mitchell, Andrew A. (1986), "The Effect of Verbal and Visual Components of Advertisements on Brand Attitudes and Attitude Toward the Advertisement," *JCR*, 13 (June), 12–24.

Mitchell, Andrew A. and Jerry C. Olson (1981), "Are Product Attribute Beliefs the Only Mediator of Advertising Effects on Brand Attitude?," *JMR*, 18 (August), 318–32.

Muehling, Darrel D. (1987), "Comparative Advertising: The Influence of Attitude-Toward-The-Ad on Brand Evaluation," *JA*, 16 (4), 43–49.

Netemeyer, Richard G. and William O. Bearden (1992), "A Comparative Analysis of Two Models of Behavioral Intention," *JAMS*, 20 (Winter), 49–59.

Oliver, Richard L. and William O. Bearden (1985), "Crossover Effects in the Theory of Reasoned Action: A Moderating Influence Attempt," *JCR*, 12 (December), 324–340.

Osgood, Charles E., George J. Suci, and Percy H. Tannenbaum (1957), *The Measurement of Meaning*, Urbana, Illinois: University of Illinois Press.

Raju, P. S. and Manoj Hastak (1983), "Pre-Trial Cognitive Effects of Cents-Off Coupons," *JA*, 12 (2), 24–33.

Sawyer, Alan G. and Daniel J. Howard (1991), "Effects of Omitting Conclusions in Advertisements to Involved and Uninvolved Audiences," *JMR*, 28 (November), 467–474.

Shimp, Terence A. and Subhash Sharma (1987), "Consumer Ethnocentrism: Construction and Validation of The CETSCALE," *JMR*, 24 (August), 280–289.

SCALE ITEMS: [1]

1. bad / good

2. foolish / wise

3. harmful / beneficial

4. unpleasant / pleasant

5. unsafe / safe

6. punishing / rewarding

7. unsatisfactory / satisfactory

8. unfavorable / favorable

9. negative / positive

10. inferior / superior

11. poor /excellent

[1] The items used in particular studies are indicated below with reference to the numbered bi-polar adjectives listed above. Scale reliabilities are shown in brackets.
Allen, Machleit, Kleine (1992): 1, 2, 4, 5, 6 [.72]
Bagozzi (1982): 1, 2, 4, 5, 6 [.95]
Bagozzi, Baumgartner, and Yi (1992; Bagozzi 1994): 1, 4, 8 [.86]
Childers et al. (2001): 1, 4, 10, 11 7-point [.89 & .93]
Gardner, Mitchell, and Russo (1985): 1, 2, 3 [.97]
Grossbart, Muehling, and Kangun (1986): 1, 2, 3 [.95]
Hastak (1990): 1, 2, 3, 4 [> .90]
Mitchell (1986): 1, 2, 3 [.85 and .88]
Mitchell and Olson (1981): 1, 2, 3 [.85]
Muehling (1987): 1, 2, 3 [.90 and .95]
Netemeyer and Bearden (1992): 1, 2, 3 [.90 and .89]
Oliver and Bearden (1985): 1, 2, 4 [.86]
Raju and Hastak (1983): 1, 2, 3, 4 [.87]
Sawyer and Howard (1991): 1, 7, 8, 9 [.96]
Shimp and Sharma (1987): 1, 2, 3 [.92 and .90]

SCALE NAME: Attitude Toward the Act (Consuming a Food Item)

SCALE DESCRIPTION: The multi-item, seven-point semantic-differential is intended to assess a person's attitude about eating a food. The scale was used in the experiments by Shiv and Fedorikhin (1999) as well as Fitzsimons and Shiv (2001) with two snacks (chocolate cake and fruit salad) as a measure of the cognitive aspect of one's desire for the snack. The scale was referred to as *cognitions about consuming a snack* by Shiv and Fedorikhin (1999) and *consumption beliefs* by Fitzsimons and Shiv (2001).

SCALE ORIGIN: Three of the items used by Shiv and Fedorikhin (1999) and Fitzsimons and Shiv (2001) came from a seven item measure of the cognitive part of an attitude reported by Crites, Fabrigar, and Petty (1994). It is described here as something different than mere cognitions regarding an object because it appears that it was used to measure attitude toward an activity, that is, consuming a particular food. Given that, it is more akin to the construct referred to in marketing science as *attitude-toward-the-act* (Aact).

RELIABILITY: Alphas of .88 and .84 were reported for the scale as used with cake and fruit salad, respectively (Shiv and Fedorikhin 1999). Likewise, Fitzsimons and Shiv (2001) reported alphas of .86 and .81 for use of the scale with cake and fruit salad, respectively.

VALIDITY: No examination of the scale's validity was reported in either study. However, Shiv and Fedorikhin (1999) stated that the items in this scale as well as those from two other scales, loaded on unique dimensions in the factor analysis.

REFERENCES:
Crites, Stephen L. Jr., Leandre R. Fabrigar, and Richard E. Petty (1994), "Measuring the Affective and Cognitive Properties of Attitudes: Conceptual and Methodological Issues," *Personality and Social Psychology Bulletin*, 20 (December), 619 – 634.
Fitzsimons, Gavan J. and Baba Shiv (2001), "Nonconscious and Contaminative Effects of Hypothetical Questions on Subsequent Decision Making," *JCR*, 28 (September), 224 – 238.
Shiv, Baba and Alexander Fedorikhin (1999), "Heart and Mind in Conflict: The Interplay of Affect and Cognition in Consumer Decision Making," *JCR*, 26 (December), 278 – 292.

SCALE ITEMS: [1]

1. harmful / beneficial

2. not good for health / good for health

3. a foolish choice / a wise choice

4. useless / useful

5. bad / good

[1] Items 1-4 were used by Shiv and Fedorikhin (1999). Fitzsimons and Shiv (2001) used Items 1-5.

SCALE NAME: Attitude Toward the Brand

SCALE DESCRIPTION: The scale is composed of three, five-point Likert-type statements meant to assess a person's general, overall attitude about a particular brand he or she has been exposed to.

SCALE ORIGIN: Cho, Lee, and Tharp (2001) did not specify the source of the scale but it would appear to have been developed by them for their study.

RELIABILITY: The alpha for the scale was calculated to be .92 (Cho 2001).

VALIDITY: No examination of the scale's validity was reported by Cho, Lee, and Tharp (2001).

REFERENCES:
Cho, Chang-Hoan (2001), Personal Correspondence.
Cho, Chang-Hoan, Jung-Gyo Lee, and Marye Tharp (2001), "Different Forced-Exposure Levels to Banner Advertisements," *JAR*, 41 (July-August), 45–56.

SCALE ITEMS: [1]

1. I like _____.

2. _____ is satisfactory.

3. _____ is desirable.

[1] The name of the brand being evaluated should be placed in the blanks.

SCALE NAME: Attitude Toward the Brand & Product Category

SCALE DESCRIPTION: The scale is composed of six statements attempting to assess a consumer's attitude toward a brand and the category of products it represents.

SCALE ORIGIN: Martin and Stewart (2001) stated that their scale was based on measures used by Park, Milberg, and Lawson (1991) as well as Shavitt (1989).

RELIABILITY: The scale was used twice by Martin and Stewart (2001), once with regard to the core brand and once with regard to a brand extension. The alphas were .83 (core brand) and .86 (extension).

VALIDITY: The typical aspects of scale validity were not provided by Martin and Stewart (2001) although the items in the scale were said to have loaded on one factor (Martin 2004).

COMMENTS: On the face of it, the items in this scale refer to two different though related things (a brand and its product category). It is quite possible for consumers to be favorable towards a product category yet not like a particular brand. Thus, it is difficult to see how the scale could be unidimensional. Care should be taken in using the scale until its psychometric quality can be confirmed.

REFERENCES:

Martin, Ingrid M. (2004), Personal Correspondence.

Martin, Ingrid M. and David W. Stewart (2001), "The Differential Impact of Goal Congruency on Attitudes, Intentions, and the Transfer of Brand Equity," *JMR*, 38 (November), 471–484.

Park, C. Whan, Sandra Milberg, and Robert Lawson (1991), "Evaluation of Brand Extensions: The Role of Product Feature Similarity and Brand Concept Consistency," *JCR*, 18 (2), 185–193.

Shavitt, Sharon (1989), "Operationalizing Functional Theories of Attitudes," in *Attitude Structure and Functions*, Anthony R. Pratkanis, Steven J. Breckler, Anthony G. Greenwald, eds. Hillsdale, NJ: Lawrence Erlbaum Associates, 311–337.

SCALE ITEMS: [1]

1. How favorable are _____?
   not at all favorable / very favorable

2. How likable are _____?
   not at all likable / very likable

3. How pleasing are _____?
   not at all pleasing / very pleasing

4. How favorable is the category of _____?
   not at all favorable / very favorable

5. How likable is the category of _____?
   not at all likable / very likable

6. How pleasing is the category of _____?
   not at all pleasing / very pleasing

---

[1] When measuring attitudes toward the core brand, Martin and Stewart (2001) placed the name/description of the brand in the first three items and placed the name of the product category in the blanks of the last three items.

SCALE NAME: Attitude Toward the Brand (Beer)

SCALE DESCRIPTION: The scale is a six item, seven-point measure of one's attitude toward a specific brand of beer.

SCALE ORIGIN: Although not stated by Aaker and Williams (1998), the items composing this scale have been drawn from two types of scales used in previous studies. The first three items have been used many times to measure brand attitude (see #59). The last two items are similar to statements that have been used to measure purchase intention (e.g., #335).

RELIABILITY: Aaker and Williams (1998) reported an alpha of .86 for the scale.

VALIDITY: No evidence of the scale's validity was presented in the article by Aaker and Williams (1998).

COMMENTS: Because the items composing this scale have come from two scales used to measure different though related constructs, the unidimensionality of this set of items is in doubt.

REFERENCES:
Aaker, Jennifer L. and Patti Williams (1998), "Empathy versus Pride: The Influence of Emotional Appeals Across Cultures," *JCR*, 25 (December), 241–261.

SCALE ITEMS: [1]

1. good / bad

2. likable / not at all likeable

3. favorable / unfavorable

4. How much do you like the brand of beer?

5. Would you try this brand of beer?

6. Would you buy this brand of beer the next time you see it in a store?

[1] The first three items are seven-point semantic differentials. The last three items were recreated here based on the descriptions in the article. Item 3 was responded to using a scale anchored by *extremely dislike* (1) and *extremely like* (7). The response scales for the last two items were anchored by *definitely no* (1) and *definitely yes* (7).

SCALE NAME: Attitude Toward the Brand (Child's Hedonic)

SCALE DESCRIPTION: The scale is composed of four, four-point items that are intended to capture a child's tendency to respond to a brand in a consistently positive (or negative) way with the emphasis on the likeability of the brand.

SCALE ORIGIN: The scale was created in French by Pecheux and Derbaix (1999). (English translations are provided below.) Very similar Likert-type and semantic differential versions were developed and tested. An admirable multi-step process with four different data collections was used to develop and purify the scale.

RELIABILITY: The Likert-type and semantic differential versions of the scale had alphas of .855 and .883, respectively (Pecheux and Derbaix 1999). The stabilities (two week test-retest) were reported to be .594 and .721 for the Likert-type and semantic differential versions, respectively.

VALIDITY: Several aspects of validity were tested by Pecheux and Derbaix (1999). Content validity was dealt with via qualitative studies involving children, mothers, and teachers. Dimensionality was examined multiple times with unidimensionality of the final version being supported by confirmatory factor analysis. Claims for convergent and discriminant validity were made based upon a multitrait-multimethod matrix that was constructed.

REFERENCES:
Pecheux, Claude and Christian Derbaix (1999), "Children and Attitude toward the Brand: A New Measurement Scale," *JAR*, 39 (July/August), 19 – 27.

SCALE ITEMS: [1]

1. I like it very much.

2. I like it.

3. It is great.

4. It is fun.

---

[1] The four-point response format for the Likert-type version of the scale ranged from *Definitely Disagree* to *Definitely Agree*. The semantic differential version of the scale was of the type where one set of anchors was as shown above and the other anchors expressed the negative, e.g., *It is not fun.*

SCALE NAME: Attitude Toward the Brand (Child's Utilitarian)

SCALE DESCRIPTION: The scale is composed of three, four-point items that are intended to capture a child's tendency to respond to a brand in a consistently positive (or negative) way with the emphasis on the utility of the brand.

SCALE ORIGIN: The scale was created in French by Pecheux and Derbaix (1999). (English translations are provided below.) Very similar Likert-type and semantic differential versions were developed and tested. An admirable multi-step process with four different data collections was used to develop and purify the scale.

RELIABILITY: The Likert-type and semantic differential versions of the scale had alphas of .765 and .811, respectively (Pecheux and Derbaix 1999). The stabilities (two week test-retest) were reported to be .612 and .678 for the Likert-type and semantic differential versions, respectively.

VALIDITY: Several aspects of validity were tested by Pecheux and Derbaix (1999). Content validity was dealt with via qualitative studies involving children, mothers, and teachers. Dimensionality was examined multiple times with unidimensionality of the final version bring supported by confirmatory factor analysis. Claims for convergent and discriminant validity were made based upon a mutlitrait-multimethod matrix that was constructed.

REFERENCES:
Pecheux, Claude and Christian Derbaix (1999), "Children and Attitude toward the Brand: A New Measurement Scale," *JAR*, 39 (July/August), 19 – 27.

SCALE ITEMS: [1]

1. It is useful.

2. It is practical / handy.

3. It is useless. (r)

---

[1] The four-point response format for the Likert-type version of the scale ranged from *Definitely Disagree* to *Definitely Agree*. The semantic differential version of the scale was of the type where one set of anchors was as shown above and the other anchors expressed the negative, e.g., *It is not useful.*

SCALE NAME: Attitude Toward the Brand (Usage Benefits)

SCALE DESCRIPTION: The scale is composed of four, five-point Likert-type statements attempting to assess a person's attitude towards a product with the emphasis being on rather specific benefits related to the product's usage. Given the phrasing of the items, the scale may only be useful with a limited set of products. In the study by Bolton, Kannan, and Bramlett (2000), the product was a particular brand of credit card but the scale would seem to be amenable for use with insurance products as well.

SCALE ORIGIN: The scale is apparently original to the study reported by Bolton, Kannan, and Bramlett (2000).

RELIABILITY: Alphas of .76 (focal company) and .75 (competitor) were reported for the scale (Bolton, Kannan, and Bramlett 2000).

VALIDITY: No examination of the scale's validity was reported by Bolton, Kannan, and Bramlett (2000).

REFERENCES:
Bolton, Ruth N., P.K. Kannan, and Matthew D. Bramlett (2000), "Implications of Loyalty Program Membership and Service Experiences for Customer Retention and Value," *JAMS*, 28 (1), 95 – 108.

SCALE ITEMS: [1]

1. _____ is a product you can depend upon in times of emergency.

2. _____ is good for travelers.

3. _____ is best for business people.

4. _____ is a prestigious product.

[1] The response scale used with these items ranged from *strongly agree* to *strongly disagree*. The name of the product should be placed in the blanks.

SCALE NAME: Attitude Toward the Brand Name

SCALE DESCRIPTION: The seven-point semantic differential scale measuring the degree to which a person views a brand name as being acceptable.

SCALE ORIGIN: No information about the source of the scale was provided by Schmitt, Pan, and Tavassoli (1994), but it would appear to be original to their study. A modified version of the scale was used in Chinese by Zhang and Schmitt (2001).

RELIABILITY: An alpha of .97 was reported for the scale by Schmitt, Pan, and Tavassoli (1994). In the studies by Zhang and Schmitt (2001), alphas of .90 (pretest) and .87 (Experiment One) were reported.

VALIDITY: No examination of scale validity was reported by either set of authors.

REFERENCES:
Schmitt, Bernd H., Yigang Pan, and Nader T. Tavassoli (1994), "Language and Consumer Memory: The Impact of Linguistic Differences Between Chinese and English," *JCR*, 21 (December), 419–431.
Zhang, Shi and Bernd H. Schmitt (2001), "Creating Local Brands in Multilingual International Markets," *JMR*, 38 (August), 313 – 325.

SCALE ITEMS: [1]

How acceptable do you think this word is as a brand name?

1. dislike / like

2. negative / positive

3. bad / good

4. disagreeable / agreeable

5. unpleasant / pleasant

6. not at all acceptable / very acceptable

7. not at all satisfactory / very satisfactory

---

[1] The first six items were used by Schmitt, Pan, and Tavassoli (1994) whereas Zhang and Schmitt (2001) used items 1, 3, and 7.

SCALE NAME: Attitude Toward the Brand Name

SCALE DESCRIPTION: Four, seven-point statements are used to assess a person's opinion of the likelihood that a particular name for a brand would be successful in the market place.

SCALE ORIGIN: No information about the source of the scale was provided by Zhang and Schmitt (2001), but it would appear to be original to their study. Note that the scale was presented to the respondents in Chinese.

RELIABILITY: An alpha of .95 was reported for the scale by Zhang and Schmitt (2001).

VALIDITY: No examination of scale validity was reported by Zhang and Schmitt (2001).

REFERENCES:
Zhang, Shi and Bernd H. Schmitt (2001), "Creating Local Brands in Multilingual International Markets," *JMR*, 38 (August), 313–325.

SCALE ITEMS:

1. To what extent do you think this brand name will facilitate the success of the product in the marketplace?
   not at all / large extent

2. How likely do you think you would be to select this brand name in order for the product to be successful in the marketplace?
   not at all likely / very likely

3. How likely is it that the brand name will be judged favorably in the marketplace?
   not at all likely / very likely

4. How much do you think consumers will be satisfied with this brand name?
   not at all / very much

SCALE NAME: Attitude Toward the Company

SCALE DESCRIPTION: Three, seven-point semantic differentials are used to assess a person's general opinion of a company.

SCALE ORIGIN: No source for the scale was specified by Goldsmith, Lafferty and Newell (2001). However, it is simply an extension of the attitude-toward-the-object type measurements which have been popularly applied in scholarly marketing research with such scales as Attitude-Toward-the-Brand (#59) and Attitude-Toward-the-Ad (#562). In fact, in the article by Goldsmith, Lafferty and Newell (2001) the scale is actually referred to as Attitude-Toward-the-Brand.

RELIABILITY: An alpha of .94 was reported for the scale (Goldsmith, Lafferty and Newell 2001).

VALIDITY: Although no rigorous evaluation of the scale's validity was discussed in the article, it was stated that the scale's items along with those measuring the other constructs were examined via principle axis factor analysis with oblique rotation. All of the items were described as loading as expected. This provides some rudimentary evidence of the scale's convergent and discriminant validity.

REFERENCES:
Goldsmith, Ronald E. (2003), Personal Correspondence.
Goldsmith, Ronald E., Barbara A. Lafferty, and Stephen J. Newell (2001), "The Impact of Corporate Credibility and Celebrity Credibility on Consumer Reaction to Advertisements and Brands," *JA*, 29 (3), 30 – 54.

SCALE ITEMS: [1]

Directions: Please rate the following statements on *each* of the seven-point scales below and circle the number that best represents your answer.

My overall impression of the _____ company is:

1. good / bad

2. favorable / unfavorable

3. satisfactory / unsatisfactory

[1] The name of the company being studied should be placed in the blank. This information was supplied by Goldsmith (2003).

SCALE NAME: Attitude Toward the Company

SCALE DESCRIPTION: The five-item, seven-point scale measures a person's attitude toward a company with an emphasis on the favorability of beliefs the person has about the company with regard to a range of business abilities. The scale was called *company evaluation* by Sen and Bhattacharya (2001).

SCALE ORIGIN: Although containing items that are similar to those used in previous measures employed in organizational research (e.g., VIII, #814), the scale used by Sen and Bhattacharya (2001) is probably original to their own research.

RELIABILITY: Sen and Bhattacharya (2001) stated that the scale had an alpha of .87.

VALIDITY: No information regarding the scale's validity was provided by Sen and Bhattacharya (2001).

REFERENCES:

Sen, Sankar and C.B. Bhattacharya (2001), "Does Doing Good Always Lead to Doing Better? Consumer Reactions to Corporate Social Responsibility," *JMR*, 38 (May), 225–243.

SCALE ITEMS: [1]

What is your opinion regarding Company X on each of the following dimensions?

1. manufacturing ability

2. technological innovativeness

3. product quality

4. customer service

5. range of products

---

[1] The anchors for the response scale used by Sen and Bhattacharya (2001) were *very unfavorable* (1) and *very favorable* (7).

SCALE NAME: Attitude Toward the Company (Social Responsibility)

SCALE DESCRIPTION: The scale is composed of six, seven-point items attempting to assess the favorability of beliefs a person has about a company's involvement with and/or position on a range of social issues. The scale was called *CSR (Corporate Social Responsibility) Dimensions* by Sen and Bhattacharya (2001).

SCALE ORIGIN: Although the source of the scale was not explicitly stated by Sen and Bhattacharya (2001), it is probably original to their research.

RELIABILITY: Sen and Bhattacharya (2001) stated that the scale had an alpha of .98.

VALIDITY: No information regarding the scale's validity was provided by Sen and Bhattacharya (2001).

REFERENCES:
Sen, Sankar and C.B. Bhattacharya (2001), "Does Doing Good Always Lead to Doing Better? Consumer Reactions to Corporate Social Responsibility," *JMR*, 38 (May), 225–243.

SCALE ITEMS: [1]

What is your opinion regarding Company X on each of the following dimensions?

1. corporate giving

2. community involvement

3. position on women's issues

4. position on ethnic minority issues

5. position on gay and lesbian issues

6. position on disabled minority issues

[1] The anchors for the response scale used by Sen and Bhattacharya (2001) were *very unfavorable* (1) and *very favorable* (7).

SCALE NAME: Attitude Toward the Innovation

SCALE DESCRIPTION: This eleven item, seven-point scale measures the attitude a consumer has toward a specific new product. The scale is broad enough to tap not only into what a person thinks about a specified product, but also how it is thought others might respond to it. The scale was referred to as *attractiveness of innovation*.

SCALE ORIGIN: The scale was constructed by Boyd and Mason (1999). A set of potential items were developed based on Rogers' (1962) list of innovation characteristics as well as feedback from a focus group. Several judges examined the items for face validity and the scale was tested on a convenience sample (n = 55 college students).

RELIABILITY: An alpha of .91 was reported for the scale (Boyd and Mason 1999).

VALIDITY: No examination of the scale's validity was reported by Boyd and Mason (1999). However, they did state that an exploratory factor analysis showed the items to be unidimensional.

REFERENCES:
Boyd, Thomas C. and Charlotte H. Mason (1999), "The Link Between Attractiveness of 'Extrabrand' Attributes and the Adoption of Innovations," *JAMS*, 27 (3), 306–319.
Rogers, Everett M. (1962), *Diffusion of Innovation*, New York: Free Press.

SCALE ITEMS: [1]

1. _____ is a great idea.

2. _____ would be fun to own.

3. This is the best way to improve the quality of _____.

4. Many people will buy _____.

5. _____ is here to stay.

6. _____ fills a real need for me.

7. _____ is a big improvement over existing _____.

8. _____ can give me real value.

9. _____ is just another gimmick. (r)

10. _____ fills a need for many people.

11. Many people will believe _____ is worth the cost.

[1] The actual product name should be placed in the blanks. The name of the product category should be in the blank of #4 and the second blank in #7. Response scale anchors ranged from *do not agree at all* (1) to *completely agree* (7).

SCALE NAME: Attitude Toward the Mall (Ambience)

SCALE DESCRIPTION: The scale is composed of four, five-point Likert-type statements measuring a shopper's reaction to the music, lighting, and temperature environmental factors at a particular mall he or she is familiar with.

SCALE ORIGIN: The scale is original to Wakefield and Baker (1998).

RELIABILITY: An alpha of .733 (n = 438) was reported for the scale by Wakefield and Baker (1998).

VALIDITY: The items in this scale were found to be unidimensional in an exploratory factor analysis that also included the items for four other scales (Wakefield and Baker 1998). However, confirmatory factor analysis indicated that this scale and two others (#44 and #46) measuring environmental dimensions were highly inter-correlated suggesting that shoppers probably perceive the physical environment in a holistic manner.

REFERENCES:
Wakefield, Kirk L. and Julie Baker (1998), "Excitement at the Mall: Determinants and Effects on Shopping Response," *JR*, 74 (4), 515 – 539.

SCALE ITEMS:

1. The mall plays music that I like.

2. Mall music is played at an appropriate volume.

3. The mall lighting is appropriate.

4. The mall temperature is comfortable.

SCALE NAME: Attitude Toward the Mall (Design)

SCALE DESCRIPTION: The scale is composed of four, five-point Likert-type statements measuring a shopper's reaction to the design and décor of a particular mall with an emphasis on the attractiveness of its interior.

SCALE ORIGIN: The scale is original to Wakefield and Baker (1998).

RELIABILITY: An alpha of .931 (n = 438) was reported for the scale by Wakefield and Baker (1998).

VALIDITY: The items in this scale were found to be unidimensional in an exploratory factor analysis that included the items for five scales (Wakefield and Baker 1998). However, confirmatory factor analysis indicated that this scale and two others (#43 and #47) measuring environmental dimensions were highly intercorrelated suggesting that shoppers probably perceive the physical environment in a holistic manner.

REFERENCES:
Wakefield, Kirk L. and Julie Baker (1998), "Excitement at the Mall: Determinants and Effects on Shopping Response," *JR*, 74 (4), 515 – 539.

SCALE ITEMS:

1. The mall's architecture gives it an attractive character.

2. This mall is decorated in an attractive fashion.

3. The interior wall and floor color schemes are attractive.

4. The overall design of this mall is interesting.

SCALE NAME: Attitude Toward the Mall (Exciting)

SCALE DESCRIPTION: The scale is composed of five, seven-point Likert-type statements measuring the degree to which a shopper believes that a mall is appealing and stimulating.

SCALE ORIGIN: The scale appears to be original to Wakefield and Baker (1998) although ideas for the items came from scales used by Russell and Pratt (1980) as well as Mano and Oliver (1993).

RELIABILITY: An alpha of .975 (n = 438) was reported for the scale by Wakefield and Baker (1998).

VALIDITY: The items in this scale were found to be unidimensional in a confirmatory factor analysis that also included several other scales from the study (Wakefield and Baker 1998).

REFERENCES:
Mano, Haim and Richard L. Oliver (1993), "Assessing the Dimensionality and Structure of the Consumption Experience: Evaluation, Feeling and Satisfaction," *JCR*, 20 (Dec), 451–466.
Russell, James A. and Geraldine Pratt (1980), "A Description of the Affective Quality Attributed to Environments," *Journal of Personality and Social Psychology*, 38 (2), 311–322.
Wakefield, Kirk L. and Julie Baker (1998), "Excitement at the Mall: Determinants and Effects on Shopping Response," *JR*, 74 (4), 515–539.

SCALE ITEMS:

This mall is:

1. unexciting / exciting

2. dull / interesting

3. boring / stimulating

4. unappealing / appealing

5. monotonous / sensational

SCALE NAME: Attitude Toward the Mall (Layout)

SCALE DESCRIPTION: The scale is composed of four, five-point Likert-type statements measuring the degree to which a shopper believes that the layout of a mall is conducive to getting around and accessing stores, food areas, and restrooms.

SCALE ORIGIN: The scale is original to Wakefield and Baker (1998).

RELIABILITY: An alpha of .9043 (n = 438) was reported for the scale by Wakefield and Baker (1998).

VALIDITY: The items in this scale were found to be unidimensional in an exploratory factor analysis that included the items for five scales (Wakefield and Baker 1998). However, confirmatory factor analysis indicated that this scale and two others (#43 and #44) measuring environmental dimensions were highly intercorrelated suggesting that shoppers probably perceive the physical environment in a holistic manner.

REFERENCES:
Wakefield, Kirk L. and Julie Baker (1998), "Excitement at the Mall: Determinants and Effects on Shopping Response," *JR*, 74 (4), 515 – 539.

SCALE ITEMS:

1. The layout makes it easy to get to the stores you want.

2. The layout makes it easy to get to the food areas.

3. The layout makes it easy to get to the restrooms.

4. Overall, the layout makes it easy to get around.

SCALE NAME: Attitude Toward the Mall (Variety)

SCALE DESCRIPTION: The scale is composed of three, five-point Likert-type statements measuring a shopper's evaluation of the excellence of a particular mall in terms of its diversity of stores, entertainment, and food offerings.

SCALE ORIGIN: The scale is original to Wakefield and Baker (1998).

RELIABILITY: An alpha of .86 (n = 438) was reported for the scale by Wakefield and Baker (1998).

VALIDITY: The items in this scale were found to be unidimensional in both exploratory as well as confirmatory factor analyses (Wakefield and Baker 1998).

REFERENCES:
Wakefield, Kirk L. and Julie Baker (1998), "Excitement at the Mall: Determinants and Effects on Shopping Response," *JR*, 74 (4), 515–539.

SCALE ITEMS:

1. The variety of food offered at the mall is excellent.

2. The mall has an excellent variety of stores.

3. This mall has excellent entertainment alternatives.

SCALE NAME: Attitude Toward the Movie (Action)

SCALE DESCRIPTION: Seven, nine-point items are used to measure the degree to which a movie is considered to be exciting and entertaining.

SCALE ORIGIN: As a scale, the origin appears to be Pechmann and Shih (1999), although the items themselves may have been used in the industry for pretesting films.

RELIABILITY: The scale was found to have an alpha of .90 (Pechmann and Shih 1999).

VALIDITY: No examination of the scale's validity was reported by Pechmann and Shih (1999). However, these items along with nine others were factor analyzed in order to determine scale content.

REFERENCES:
Pechmann, Cornelia and Chuan-Fong Shih (1999), "Smoking Scenes in Movies and Antismoking Advertisements Before Movies: Effects on Youth," *JM*, 63 (July), 1–13.

SCALE ITEMS: [1]

1. entertaining

2. funny

3. action-packed

4. exciting

5. happy

6. positive

7. my kind of movie

[1] Pechmann and Shih (1999) gathered responses using a nine-point scale anchored by *unfavorable* (1) and *favorable* (9).

SCALE NAME: Attitude Toward the Movie (Extrinsic Cues)

SCALE DESCRIPTION: The scale is composed of four items and uses a seven-point response format to measure a person's thoughts about a movie's quality. The emphasis is on peripheral aspects of the movie such as sets and special effects.

SCALE ORIGIN: The scale appears to be original to Neelamegham and Jain (1999) but inspiration came from work by Linton and Petrovich (1989).

RELIABILITY: The composite reliabilities were .87 (pre-exposure expectation) and .88 (post-exposure evaluation) (Neelamegham and Jain 1999).

VALIDITY: All items loaded on the same factor when analyzed with items intended to measure two other constructs. Analyses of data from the pre- and post-exposure stages provided mixed support for the scale's discriminant validity and the overall fit of the measurement models that included other scales (Neelamegham and Jain 1999).

REFERENCES:

Linton, James M. and Joseph A. Petrovich (1989), "The Application of the Consumer Information Acquisition Approach to Movie Selection: An Exploratory Study," in *Current Research in Film Audiences, Economics and Law, Vol. 4*, Bruce A. Austin, ed., Norwood, NJ: Ablex Publishing Co., 24–44.

Neelamegham, Ramya and Dipak Jain (1999), "Consumer Choice Process for Experience Goods: An Econometric Model and Analysis," *JMR*, 36 (August), 373–386.

SCALE ITEMS: [1]

1. sets

2. costumes

3. music

4. special effects

---

[1] The scale stem used by Neelamegham and Jain (1999) in the pre-exposure stage of the study apparently asked respondents how well they expected a certain movie to be on these characteristics. In the post-exposure stage the stem probably asked them to rate the movie they saw. The verbal anchors on the response scale in both cases were *very poor* and *excellent*.

SCALE NAME: Attitude Toward the Movie (Intrinsic Cues)

SCALE DESCRIPTION: The scale is composed of three items and uses a seven-point response format to measure a person's thoughts about a movie's quality. The emphasis is on the movie's core attributes such as the story.

SCALE ORIGIN: The scale appears to be original to Neelamegham and Jain (1999) but inspiration came from work by Linton and Petrovich (1989).

RELIABILITY: The composite reliabilities were .90 (pre-exposure expectation) and .89 (post-exposure evaluation) (Neelamegham and Jain 1999).

VALIDITY: All items loaded on the same factor when analyzed with items intended to measure two other constructs. Analyses of data from the pre- and post-exposure stages provided mixed support for the scale's discriminant validity and the overall fit of the measurement models that included other scales (Neelamegham and Jain 1999).

REFERENCES:

Linton, James M. and Joseph A. Petrovich (1989), "The Application of the Consumer Information Acquisition Approach to Movie Selection: An Exploratory Study," in *Current Research in Film Audiences, Economics and Law, Vol. 4*, Bruce A. Austin, ed. Norwood, NJ: Ablex Publishing Co., 24–44.

Neelamegham, Ramya and Dipak Jain (1999), "Consumer Choice Process for Experience Goods: An Econometric Model and Analysis," *JMR*, 36 (August), 373–386.

SCALE ITEMS: [1]

1. plot / story

2. acting

3. supporting cast

[1] The scale stem used by Neelamegham and Jain (1999) in the pre-exposure stage of the study apparently asked respondents how well they expected a certain movie to perform on these characteristics. In the post-exposure stage the stem probably asked them to rate the movie they saw. The verbal anchors on the response scale in both cases were *very poor* and *excellent*.

SCALE NAME: Attitude Toward the Movie (Story)

SCALE DESCRIPTION: The scale is composed of nine, nine-point items measuring the extent to which a movie is considered to have delivered a good story.

SCALE ORIGIN: As a scale, the source appears to be Pechmann and Shih (1999) although the items themselves may have been used in industry for pretesting films.

RELIABILITY: The scale was found to have an alpha of .94 (Pechmann and Shih 1999).

VALIDITY: No examination of the scale's validity was reported by Pechmann and Shih (1999). However, these items along with seven others were factor analyzed in order to determine dimensionality.

REFERENCES:
Pechmann, Cornelia and Chuan-Fong Shih (1999), "Smoking Scenes in Movies and Antismoking Advertisements Before Movies: Effects on Youth," *JM*, 63 (July), 1–13.

SCALE ITEMS: [1]

1. good characters

2. well-acted

3. good story

4. good taste

5. imaginative

6. not confusing

7. not offensive

8. not corny

9. not stupid

---

[1] Pechmann and Shih (1999) gathered responses using a nine point scale anchored by *unfavorable* (1) and *favorable* (9).

SCALE NAME: Attitude Toward the Object (Interesting)

SCALE DESCRIPTION: The scale is composed of five, seven-point semantic differentials attempting to measure a person's thoughts about some specified object with an emphasis on how fun and exciting it is. Neelamegham and Jain (1999) used it specifically as a measure of consumer expectations regarding a movie.

SCALE ORIGIN: The scale appears to be original to Neelamegham and Jain (1999) but the items are typical from measures of involvement, brand attitude, and arousal.

RELIABILITY: The composite reliability was reported to be .94 (Neelamegham and Jain 1999).

VALIDITY: All items loaded on the same factor when analyzed with items intended to measure two other constructs. Although some support was provided of the scale's discriminant validity with respect to the other two scales, the overall fit of the model did not reach a level typically considered as acceptable (Neelamegham and Jain 1999).

REFERENCES:
Neelamegham, Ramya and Dipak Jain (1999), "Consumer Choice Process for Experience Goods: An Econometric Model and Analysis," *JMR*, 36 (August), 373–386.

SCALE ITEMS: [1]

1. fun / not fun

2. appealing / not appealing

3. interesting / boring

4. exciting / unexciting

5. fascinating / dull

[1] The scale stem used by Neelamegham and Jain (1999) apparently asked respondents to what extent they expected the movie to have the listed characteristics.

SCALE NAME: Attitude Toward the Object (Likeability)

SCALE DESCRIPTION: The scale is composed of four single word descriptors and a ten-point response format. It attempts to assess a person's opinion of an object with an emphasis on attributes that make it desirable and attractive. Although these attributes would tend to be most relevant when describing people, Moon (2000) used them with respect to a computer and referred to the scale as *attraction*.

SCALE ORIGIN: Although not explicitly stated as such, the scale would appear to be original to Moon (2000).

RELIABILITY: Alphas of .87 (Experiment One) and .78 (Experiment Two) were reported by Moon (2000).

VALIDITY: No information about the scale's validity was reported by Moon (2000).

REFERENCES:
Moon, Youngme (2000), "Intimate Exchanges: Using Computers to Elicit Self-Disclosure from Consumers," *JCR*, 26 (March), 323–339.

SCALE ITEMS: [1]

1. likable

2. friendly

3. kind

4. helpful

---

[1] The anchors for the ten-point response scale used by Moon (2000) were not stated but were probably of the *agree/disagree* type.

SCALE NAME: Attitude Toward the Offer

SCALE DESCRIPTION: Five, seven-point semantic differentials are used to measure a consumer's evaluation of an offer that has been presented to him/her. Given the phrasing of one of the items, the scale is most suited for an offer that has to do with an event or cause which a consumer has been asked to support in some way and has the potential to "make a difference" to someone or something the consumer cares about.

SCALE ORIGIN: The source of the scale was not identified by Ellen, Mohr, and Webb (2000) and it is likely to be original to their study. Most of the items have been used previously in scales such as attitude-toward-the-brand (#59).

RELIABILITY: An alpha of .87 was reported for the scale (Ellen, Mohr, and Webb 2000).

VALIDITY: No examination of the scale's validity was reported by Ellen, Mohr, and Webb (2000).

COMMENTS: If item #5 (below) is deleted or replaced then it seems quite possible that the scale would be amenable for use with a variety of marketing-related offers presented to consumers.

REFERENCES:
Ellen, Pam Scholder (2003), Personal Correspondence.
Ellen, Pam Scholder, Lois A. Mohr, and Deborah J. Webb (2000), "Charitable Programs and the Retailer: Do They Mix?" *JR*, 76 (3), 393–406.

SCALE ITEMS: [1]

The typical consumer would think the offer:

1. is positive / is negative

2. is good / is bad

3. is beneficial / is harmful

4. is foolish / is wise

5. will make a difference / won't make a difference

[1] The scale stem and items were provided by Ellen (2003).

SCALE NAME: Attitude Toward the Product (Beauty Enhancement)

SCALE DESCRIPTION: Four items are used to assess the degree to which a consumer believes a certain product would be able to improve his/her beauty.

SCALE ORIGIN: Although not explicitly stated by Bower (2001), the scale would appear to be original.

RELIABILITY: An alpha of .85 was reported for the scale (Bower 2001).

VALIDITY: Bower (2001) used confirmatory factor analysis with items composing five scales, one of which was this scale. The evidence suggested a good fit. The scale's average variance extracted was .63. In addition, this was higher that the scale's squared correlation with the other scales. In total, this provides some evidence of the scale's convergent and discriminant validity.

REFERENCES:
Bower, Amanda B. (2001), "Highly Attractive Models in Advertising and the Women Who Loathe Them: The Implementations of Negative Affect for Spokesperson Effectiveness," *JA*, 30 (3), 51–63.

SCALE ITEMS:

To what extent do you think there would be an improvement in your beauty if you used the product?

1. Insignificant / significant

2. Unachievable / achievable

3. Unnoticeable / Noticeable

4. If used properly, this product could be responsible for a significant improvement in the user's beauty. (disagree / agree)

SCALE NAME: Attitude Toward the Product (Digital Camera)

SCALE DESCRIPTION: The twelve item scale is intended to measure a person's attitude toward a digital camera he/she has been exposed to with an emphasis on behavioral aspects of the attitude, i.e., the extent to which the camera would be used. The measure was called *product preference*.

SCALE ORIGIN: Although not stated explicitly, the scale seems to be original to the study by Moreau, Markman, and Lehmann (2001).

RELIABILITY: The alpha reported for the scale by Moreau, Markman, and Lehmann (2001) was .76.

VALIDITY: No information regarding the scale's validity was reported by Moreau, Markman, and Lehmann (2001).

COMMENTS: Because the scale has five items answered on a seven-point response format and seven items with a two-point response format it is inappropriate to simply add up the numerical scores for each item. As done by Moreau, Markman, and Lehmann (2001), scores on each of the twelve items were standardized first and then summed to determine the overall scale score.

REFERENCES:
Moreau, Page C. (2004), Personal Correspondence.
Moreau, Page C., Arthur B. Markman, and Donald R. Lehmann (2001), "What Is It? Categorization Flexibility and Consumers' Responses to Really New Products," *JCR*, 4 (27), 489–498.

SCALE ITEMS: [1]

1. As an overall evaluation of this particular digital camera, I think I would: *dislike it very much / like it very much*

2. I think the features offered as part of this particular digital camera are good.
   strongly disagree / strongly agree

3. I think that this digital camera is an excellent product.
   strongly disagree / strongly agree

4. I would like to use this digital camera on a regular basis.
   strongly disagree / strongly agree

5. Would you recommend this digital camera to your friends?
   definitely would NOT recommend / definitely would recommend

Now, please indicate whether or not (yes/no) you would use the digital camera in each of the following situations:

6. A friend's wedding

7. A family vacation

8. For insurance purposes

9. On a fall trip to Vermont

10. A child's sporting event

11. A reunion

12. A photography class

[1] As clarified by Moreau (2004), the first five items were sentences that were responded to using seven-point scales whereas the last seven items employed a simple *yes/no* response.

SCALE NAME: Attitude Toward the Product (Food)

SCALE DESCRIPTION: The scale was used in a couple of slightly different forms. One was composed of ten, seven-point semantic differentials measuring a consumer's evaluation of a brand. Another had seven items and a nine-point scale to measure attitudes towards a product category. In both cases the set of items appear to be most suited for evaluating a food or beverage presented within the context of an advertisement. Arias-Bolzmann, Chakraborty, and Mowen (2000) used it with respect to a print ad created for a fictitious wine cooler.

SCALE ORIGIN: These items were apparently used first as a set by Arias-Bolzmann, Chakraborty, and Mowen (2000), however, many of the items have been used previously in measuring brand attitude (#59).

RELIABILITY: Alphas of .94 (brand) and .96 (product category) were reported for the scale by Arias-Bolzmann, Chakraborty, and Mowen (2000).

VALIDITY: No information regarding the scales' validity was reported by Arias-Bolzmann, Chakraborty, and Mowen (2000).

REFERENCES:
Arias-Bolzmann, Leopoldo (2002), Personal Correspondence.
Arias-Bolzmann, Leopoldo, Goutam Chakraborty, and John C. Mowen (2000), "Effects of Absurdity in Advertising: The Moderating Role of Product Category Attitude and the Mediating Role of Cognitive Responses," *JA*, 29 (1), 35–48.

SCALE ITEMS: [1]

1. pleasant / unpleasant

2. agreeable / disagreeable

3. satisfactory / unsatisfactory

4. positive / negative

5. tastes good / tastes bad

6. exciting / dull

7. romantic / unromantic

8. powerful / weak

9. social / not social

10. expensive / inexpensive

11. good / bad

[1] The brand version of the scale used items 1 to 10; the product category version used items 1 to 3, 5 to 7, and 11 (Arias-Bolzmann 2002).

SCALE NAME: Attitude Toward the Product (High Tech)

SCALE DESCRIPTION: The multi-item semantic differential scale is used to measure a person's general evaluation of a high tech good or service.

SCALE ORIGIN: Although many of the items have been used previously, particularly to measure attitude-toward-the-brand (#59), this version by Roehm and Sternthal (2001) appears to be unique. Not only are there several bi-polar adjectives that as a set have not had previous usage but the scale as a whole was meant to be used with high tech products rather than any goods or services.

RELIABILITY: Three versions of the scale were used by Roehm and Sternthal (2001) in the four experiments they conducted. Two slightly different ten-item versions were used that had alphas of .93 (study one) and .90 (study three). The alphas for the eight- and 13-item versions were .90 (study four) and .93 (study two), respectively.

VALIDITY: No examination of the scale's validity was reported by Roehm and Sternthal (2001). However, they did state that factor analysis indicated the various versions of the scale were unidimensional.

REFERENCES:
Roehm, Michelle L. and Brian Sternthal (2001), "The Moderating Effect of Knowledge and Resources on the Persuasive Impact of Analogies," *JCR*, 28 (September), 257–272.

SCALE ITEMS: [1]

1. like / dislike

2. useful / not useful

3. high-tech / not high-tech

4. good / bad

5. high quality / low quality

6. practical / impractical

7. worth owning / not worth owning

8. impressive / not impressive

9. valuable / not valuable

10. advanced / not advanced

11. dependable / not dependable

12. simple / complex

13. convenient / inconvenient

---

[1] The eight-item version of the scale was composed of 1, 2, 4, 6–10. The ten-item version was composed of items 1–10 and the 13-item version used all of the listed items (Roehm and Sternthal 2001). A seven-point response format appears to have been used.

SCALE NAME: Attitude Toward the Product/Brand (Semantic Differential)

SCALE DESCRIPTION: The scales consist of various bi-polar adjectives presumed to measure the subject's overall evaluation of the product or brand. The various versions of the scale are similar in that they are not specific to any particular product or brand under investigation although certain adjectives may not be appropriate in some cases. Note that some scale users have referred to their measures as *product evaluation*, e.g., Muthukrishnan and Ramaswami (1999). In Lane (2000), a version was used as a brand extension evaluation. Stafford and Day (1995) made slightly different use of the scale than most of the others by measuring attitudes toward a *service* rather than a *good*. Given the directions used by Gürhan-Canli and Maheswaran (2000), their scale had the sense of a country-of-origin evaluation of a class of products.

SCALE ORIGIN: There is no common origin for these scales and many of them are unique in that the sets of items of which they are composed have been used as a set in just one or two studies. Some items have been used much more than others but *good/bad* is by far the most commonly used bi-polar adjective. Many of the scales have used *favorable/unfavorable* and/or *pleasant/unpleasant*. At the other extreme, there are several items (e.g., #22 to #25) that appear to have been used just once.

Versions of the scale in languages other than English have been reported such as Korean (Taylor, Miracle, and Wilson 1997) and Chinese (Zhang and Schmitt 2001).

RELIABILITY: Reported internal consistencies have ranged from below .70 (Iyer 1988) to .98 (Holbrook and Batra 1987). However, the reliabilities have tended to be on the high side with most of them being greater than .80 if not .90. See last section for specific reliabilities.

VALIDITY: Little if any evidence of scale validity was provided in the majority of the studies. A few studies conducted some testing, however, of unidimensionality (e.g., Anand and Sternthal 1990; MacInnis and Park).

Batra and Stayman (1990) performed confirmatory factor analysis on their ten-item scale and indicated that there were two factors, one more hedonic and the other more utilitarian. However, since use of the two scales separately led to findings not significantly different from those of the combined items, the latter was not discussed any further in the article.

A factor analysis was performed by Bezjian-Avery, Calder, and Iacobucci (1998) on items composing their attitude toward the brand and attitude toward the ad scales (#562). Each set of items appeared to be unidimensional with no cross-loadings greater than .34.

Darley and Smith (1993) conducted several tests to determine if the three multi-item measures they used (brand attitude, ad attitude, and ad credibility) were sufficiently representative of their respective latent constructs. Among the findings was that a three factor model fit the data better than a one factor model. This provides some evidence of the scale's discriminant validity.

Miller and Marks (1992) performed a factor analysis of nine items expected to measure either attitude-toward-the-ad or attitude-toward-the-brand. All of the items had loadings of .65 or higher on the expected factors and was used to support a claim of each scale's discriminant validity.

COMMENTS: See also Debevec and Iyer (1986), Health, McCarthy, and Mothersbaugh (1994), Holmes and Crocker (1987), Kamins and Marks (1987), Maheswaran (1994), Nyer (1997), Pham et al. (2001), Prakash (1992), Sheffet (1983), Smith and Swinyard (1983), Tripp, Jensen, and Carlson (1994), and Unnava, Burnkrant, and Erevelles (1994). Some variations on the scale can also be found in Batra and Stayman (1990), Grossman and Till (1998), as well as Stayman and Batra (1991).

As is obvious from the material presented here, a wide-variety of bi-polar adjectives have been used over the years to measure brand attitude. No one set of items has been declared the optimal scale. Definitive studies of the psychometric quality of alternative versions of the measure are certainly needed. In the meantime, it is clear that some items are much more widely used than others and one should strongly consider using a set that has been used before rather than generating yet another unique set with unknown comparability to previous studies of the construct. Further, some items listed below (13, 37, 41) are probably less suited for measuring Aad and more appropriate for measuring different, though related constructs, e.g., attitude toward the act, behavioral intention.

REFERENCES:
Aaker, Jennifer L. (2000b), "Accessibility or Diagnosticity? Disentangling the Influence of Culture on Persuasion Processes and Attitudes," *JCR*, 26 (March), 340–357.

Aaker, Jennifer L. and Durairaj Maheswaran (1997), "The Effect of Cultural Orientation on Persuasion," *JCR*, 24 (December), 315–328.

Adaval, Rashmi (2001), "Sometimes It Just Feels Right: The Differential Weighting of Affected-Consistent and Affected-Inconsistent Product Information," *JCR*, 28 (June), 1–17.

Ahluwalia, Rohini (2000), "Examination of Psychological Processes Underlying Resistance to Persuasion," *JCR*, 27 (2), 217–232.

Ahluwalia, Rohini, Robert E. Burnkrant, and H. Rao Unnava (2000), "Consumer Response to Negative Publicity: The Moderating Role of Commitment," *JMR*, 37 (May), 203–214.

Ahluwalia, Rohini and Zeynep Gurhan-Canli (2000), "The Effects of Extensions on the Family Brand Name: An Accessibility-Diagnosticity Perspective," *JCR*, 27 (3), 371–381.

Ahluwalia, Rohini, H. Rao Unnava, and Robert E. Burnkrant (2001), "The Moderating Role of Commitment on the Spillover Effect of Marketing Communications," *JMR*, 38 (November), 458–470.

Alpert, Frank H. and Michael A. Kamins (1995), "An Empirical Investigation of Consumer Memory, Attitude, and Perceptions Toward Pioneer and Follower Brands," *JM*, 59 (October), 34–45.

Anand, Punam and Brian Sternthal (1990), "Ease of Message Processing as a Moderator of Repetition Effects in Advertising," *JMR*, 27 (August), 345–353.

Andrews, J. Craig (2001), Personal Correspondence.

Andrews, J. Craig, Scot Burton, and Richard G. Netemeyer (2001), "Are Some Comparative Nutrition Claims Misleading? The Role of Nutrition Knowledge, Ad Claim Type and Disclosure Conditions," *JA*, 29 (3), 29–42.

Andrews, J. Craig, Richard G. Netemeyer, and Scot Burton (1998), "Consumer Generalization of Nutrient Content Claims in Advertising," *JM*, 62 (October), 62–75.

Aylesworth, Andrew B., Ronald C. Goodstein, and Ajay Kalra (1999), "Effect of Archetypal Embeds on Feelings: An Indirect Route to Affecting Attitudes?" *JA*, 28 (3), 73–81.

Babin, Laurie and Alvin C. Burns (1997), "Effects of Print Ad Pictures and Copy Containing Instructions to Imagine on Mental Imagery That Mediates Attitudes," *JA*, 26 (Fall), 33–44.

Baker, William E. (1999), "When Can Affective Conditioning and Mere Exposure Directly Influence Brand Choice?" *JA*, 28 (4), 31–46.

Barone, Michael J., Paul W. Miniard, and Jean B. Romeo (2000), "The Influence of Positive Mood on Brand Extension Evaluations," *JCR*, 26 (March), 386–400.

Batra, Rajeev and Michael L. Ray (1986), "Affective Responses Mediating Acceptance of Advertising," *JCR*, 13 (September), 234–249.

Batra, Rajeev and Stayman (1990), "The Role of Mood in Advertising Effectiveness," *JCR*, 17 (September), 203–214.

Bello, Daniel C., Robert E. Pitts, and Michael J. Etzel (1983), "The Communication Effects of Controversial Sexual Content in Television Programs and Commercials," *JA*, 12 (3), 32–42.

Berger, Ida E. and Andrew A. Mitchell (1989), "The Effect of Advertising on Attitude Accessibility, Attitude Confidence, and the Attitude Behavior Relationship," *JCR*, 16 (December), 269–279.

Bezjian-Avery, Alexa, Bobby Calder, and Dawn Iacobucci (1998), "New Media Interactive Advertising vs. Traditional Advertising," *JAR*, 38 (July/August), 23–32.

Bhat, Subodh, Thomas W. Leigh, and Daniel L. Wardlow (1998), "The Effect of Consumer Prejudices on Ad Processing: Heterosexual Consumers' Responses to Homosexual Imagery in Ads," *JA*, 27 (4), 9–28.

Bone, Paula Fitzgerald and Pam Scholder Ellen (1992), "The Generation and Consequences of Communication Evoked Imagery," *JCR*, 19 (June), 93–104.

Bower, Amanda B. and Stacy Landreth (2001), "Is Beauty Best? Highly Versus Normally Attractive Models in Advertising," *JA*, 30 (1), 1–12.

Bruner, Gordon C. and Anand Kumar (2000), "Web Commercials and Advertising Hierarchy-of-Effects," *JAR*, 40 (Jan-Apr), 35–42.

Burnkrant, Robert E. and H. Rao Unnava (1995), "Effects of Self-Referencing on Persuasion," *JCR*, 22 (June), 17–26.

Campbell, Margaret C. and Ronald C. Goodstein (2001), "The Moderating Effect of Perceived Risk on Consumers' Evaluations of Product Incongruity: Preference for the Norm," *JCR*, 28 (December), 439–449.

Chattopadhyay, Amitava and Kunal Basu (1990), "Humor in Advertising: The Moderating Role of Prior Brand Evaluation," *JMR*, 27 (November), 466–476.

Chattopadhyay, Amitava and Prakash Nedungadi (1992), "Does Attitude Toward the Ad Endure? The Moderating Effects of Attention and Delay," *JCR*, 19 (June), 26–33.

Chao, Paul (2001), "The Moderating Effects of Country of Assembly, Country of Parts, and Country of Design on Hybrid Product Evaluations," *JA*, 30 (Winter), 67–81.

Chao, Paul (2003), Personal Correspondence.

Cox, Dena Saliagas and Anthony D. Cox (1988), "What Does Familiarity Breed? Complexity as a Moderator of Repetition Effects in Advertisement Evaluations," *JCR*, 15 (June), 111–116.

Cox, Dena Saliagas and William B. Locander (1987), "Product Novelty: Does It Moderate the Relationship Between Ad Attitudes and Brand Attitudes," *JA*, 16 (3), 39–44.

Darley, William K. and Robert E. Smith (1993), "Advertising Claim Objectivity: Antecedents and Effects," *JM*, 57 (October), 100–113.

Darley, William K. and Robert E. Smith (1995), "Gender Differences in Information Processing Strategies: An Empirical Test of the Selectivity Model in Advertising Response," *JA*, 24 (Spring), 41–56.

Debevec, Kathleen and Easwar Iyer (1986), "The Influence of Spokespersons in Altering a Product's Gender Image: Implications for Advertising Effectiveness," *JA*, 15 (4), 12–20.

Despande, Rohit and Douglas Stayman (1994), "A Tale of Two Cities: Distinctiveness Theory and Advertising Effectiveness," *JMR*, 31 (February), 57–64.

Droge, Cornelia (1989), "Shaping the Route to Attitude Change: Central Versus Peripheral Processing Through Comparative Versus Noncomparative Advertising," *JMR*, 26 (May), 193–204.

Edell, Julie and Kevin Lane Keller (1989), "The Information Processing of Coordinated Media Campaigns," *JMR*, 26 (May), 149–63.

Ellen, Pam Scholder and Paula Fitzgerald Bone (1998), "Does It Matter If It Smells? Olfactory Stimuli As Advertising Executional Cues," *JA*, 27 (4), 29–39.

Fennis, Bob M. (2003), Personal Correspondence.

Fennis, Bob M. and Arnold B. Bakker (2001), "Stay Tuned-We Will Be Back Right After These Messages: Need to Evaluate Moderates the Transfer of Irritation in Advertising," *JA*, 30 (3), 15–25.

Gardner, Meryl Paula, Andrew A. Mitchell, and J. Edward Russo (1985), "Low Involvement Strategies for Processing Advertisements," *JA*, 14 (2), 4–12, 56.

Gelb, Betsy G. and George M. Zinkhan (1986), "Humor and Advertising Effectiveness After Repeated Exposures to a Radio Commercial," *JA*, 15 (2), 15–20.

Gill, James D., Sanford Grossbart, and Russel N. Laczniak (1988), "Influence of Involvement, Commitment, and Familiarity on Brand Beliefs and Attitudes of Viewers Exposed to Alternative Advertising Claim Strategies," *JA*, 17 (2), 33–43.

Goodstein, Ronald C. (1993), "Category based Applications and Extensions in Advertising: Motivating More Extensive Ad Processing," *JCR*, 20 (June), 87–99.

Gotlieb, Jerry B. and John E. Swan (1990), "An Application of the Elaboration Likelihood Model," *JAMS*, 18 (Summer), 221–228.

Grier, Sonya A. and Rohit Despandé (2001), "Social Dimensions of Consumer Distinctiveness: The Influence of Social Status on Group Identity and Advertising Persuasion," *JMR*, 38 (May), 216–224.

Grossbart, Sanford, Darrel D. Muehling, and Norman Kangun (1986), "Verbal and Visual References to Competition in Comparative Advertising," *JA*, 15 (1), 10–23.

Grossman, Randi Priluck and Brian D. Till (1998), "The Persistence of Classically Conditioned Brand Attitudes," *JA*, 27 (Spring), 23–31.

Gürhan-Canli, Zeynep and Durairaj Maheswaran (1998), "The Effects of Extensions on Brand Name Dilution and Enhancement," *JMR*, 35 (November), 464–473.

Gürhan-Canli, Zeynep and Durairaj Maheswaran (2000a), "Determinants of Country-of-Origin Evaluations," *JCR*, 27 (1), 96–108.

Gürhan-Canli, Zeynep and Durairaj Maheswaran (2000b), "Cultural Variations in Country of Origin Effects," *JMR*, 37 (3), 309–317.

Hastak, Manoj (1990), "Does Retrospective Thought Measurement Influence Subsequent Measures of Cognitive Structure in an Advertising Context?" *JA*, 19 (3), 3–13.

Hastak, Manoj and Jerry C. Olson (1989), "Assessing the Role of Brand Related Cognitive Responses as Mediators of Communication Effects," *JCR*, 15 (March), 444–56.

Health, Timothy B., Michael S. McCarthy, and David L. Mothersbaugh (1994), "Spokesperson Fame and Vividness Effects in the Context of Issue-Relevant Thinking: The Moderating Role of Competitive Setting," *JCR*, 20 (March), 520–534.

Herr, Paul M., Frank R. Kardes, and John Kim (1991), "Effects of Word of Mouth and Product Attribute Information on Persuasion: An Accessibility Diagnosticity Perspective," *JCR*, 17 (March), 454–462.

Holbrook, Morris B. and Rajeev Batra (1987), "Assessing the Role of Emotions as Mediators of Consumer Responses to Advertising," *JCR*, 14 (December), 404–420.

Holmes, John H. and Kenneth E. Crocker (1987), "Predispositions and the Comparative Effectiveness of Rational, Emotional, and Discrepant Appeals for Both High Involvement and Low Involvement Products," *JAMS*, 15 (Spring), 27–35.

Homer, Pamela M. (1990), "The Mediating Role of Attitude Toward the Ad: Some Additional Evidence," *JMR*, 27 (February), 78–86.

Homer, Pamela M. and Lynn R. Kahle (1990), "Source Expertise, Time of Source Identification, and Involvement in Persuasion: An Elaborative Processing Perspective," *JA*, 19 (1), 30–39.

Howard, Daniel J. and Charles Gengler (2001), "Emotional Contagion Effects on Product Attitudes," *JCR*, 28 (September), 189–201.

Iyer, Easwar S. (1988), "The Influence of Verbal Content and Relative Newness on the Effectiveness of Comparative Advertising," *JA*, 17 (3), 15–21.

Kalra, Ajay and Ronald C. Goodstein (1998), "The Impact of Advertising Positioning Strategies on Consumer Price Sensitivity," *JMR*, 35 (May), 210–224.

Kamins, Micheal A. and Lawrance J. Marks (1987), "Advertising Puffery: The Impact of Using Two Sided Claims on Product Attitude and Purchase Intention," *JA*, 16 (4), 6–15.

Kardes, Frank R. and Gurumurthy Kalyanaram (1992), "Order of Entry Effects on Consumer Memory and Judgment: An Information Integration Perspective," *JMR*, 29 (August), 343–357.

Keller, Kevin Lane (1991a), "Cue Compatibility and Framing in Advertising," *JMR*, 28 (February), 42–57.

Keller, Kevin Lane (1991b), "Memory and Evaluation Effects in Competitive Advertising Environments," *JCR*, 17 (March), 463–476.

Kelleris, James J., Anthony D. Cox, and Dena Cox (1993), "The Effect of Background Music on Ad Processing: A Contingency Explanation," *JM*, 57 (October), 114–125.

Kempf, DeAnna S. and Russell N. Laczniak (2001), "Advertising's Influence on Subsequent Product Trial Processing," *JA*, 30 (3), 27–38.

Kempf, DeAnna S. and Robert E. Smith (1998), "Consumer Processing of Product Trial and the Influence of Prior Advertising: A Structural Modeling Approach," *JMR*, 35 (August), 325–338.

Kim, Allen and Frank R. Kardes (1996), "An Investigation of the Mediational Mechanisms Underlying Attitudinal Conditioning," *JMR*, 33 (August), 318–328.

Kim, John, Jeen-Su Lim, and Mukesh Bhargava (1998), "The Role of Affect in Attitude Formation: A Classical Conditioning Approach," *JAMS*, 26 (2), 143–152.

Krishnamurthy, Parthasarathy and Mita Sujan (1999), "Retrospection Versus Anticipation: The Role of the Ad under Retrospective and Anticipatory Self-Referencing," *JCR*, 26 (June), 55–69.

Laczniak, Russell N. and Darrel D. Muehling (1993), "The Relationship Between Experimental Manipulations and Tests of Theory in an Advertising Message Involvement Context," *JA*, 22 (September), 59–74.

Lane, Vicki R. (2003), Personal Correspondence.

Lane, Vicki R. (2000), "The Impact of Ad Repetition and Ad Content on Consumer Perceptions of Incongruent Extensions," *JM*, 64 (2), 80–91.

Leclerc, France (1998), Personal Correspondence.

Leclerc, France and John D. C. Little (1997), "Can Advertising Copy Make FSI Coupons More Effective?" *JMR*, 34 (November), 473–484.

Lim, Jeen-Su, William K. Darley, and John O. Summers (1994), "An Assessment of Country of Origin Effects Under Alternative Presentation Formats," *JAMS*, 22 (3), 272–282.

Loken, Barbara and James Ward (1990), "Alternative Approaches to Understanding the Determinants of Typicality," *JCR*, 17 (September), 111–126.

Lord, Kenneth R., Myung-Soo Lee, and Paul L. Sauer (1994), "Program Context Antecedents of Attitude toward Radio Commercials," *JAMS*, 22 (1), 3–15.

Lord, Kenneth R., Myung-Soo Lee, and Paul L. Sauer (1995), "The Combined Influence Hypothesis Central and Peripheral Antecedents of Attitude Toward the Ad," *JA*, 24 (Spring), 73–85.

Machleit, Karen A., Chris T. Allen, and Thomas J. Madden (1993), "The Mature Brand and Brand Interest: An Alternative Consequence of Ad Evoked Affect," *JM*, 57 (October), 72–82.

MacInnis, Deborah J. and C. Whan Park (1991), "The Differential Role of Characteristics of Music on High and Low Involvement Consumers' Processing of Ads," *JCR*, 18 (September), 161–173.

MacKenzie, Scott B. and Richard J. Lutz (1989), "An Empirical Examination of the Structural Antecedents of Attitude Toward the Ad in an Advertising Pretesting Context," *JM*, 53 (April), 48–65.

MacKenzie, Scott B., Richard J. Lutz, and George E. Belch (1986), "The Role of Attitude Toward the Ad as a Mediator of Advertising Effectiveness: A Test of Competing Explanations," *JMR*, 23 (May), 130–143.

MacKenzie, Scott B. and Richard A. Spreng (1992), "How Does Motivation Moderate the Impact of Central and Peripheral Processing on Brand Attitudes and Intentions," *JCR*, 18 (March), 519–529.

Macklin, M. Carole, Norman T. Bruvold, and Carole Lynn Shea (1985), "Is It Always as Simple as 'Keep It Simple'?" *JA*, 14 (4), 28–35.

Maheswaran, Durairaj (1994), "Country of Origin as a Stereotype: Effects of Consumer Expertise and Attribute Strength on Product Evaluations," *JCR*, 21 (September), 354–365.

McQuarrie, Edward F. and David Glen Mick (1992), "On Resonance: A Critical Pluralistic Inquiry into Advertising Rhetoric," *JCR*, 19 (September), 180–197.

Mick, David Glen (1992), "Levels of Subjective Comprehension in Advertising Processing and Their Relations to Ad Perceptions, Attitudes, and Memory," *JCR*, 18 (March), 411–424.

Miller, Darryl W. and Lawrence J. Marks (1992), "Mental Imagery and Sound Effects in Radio Commercials," *JA*, 21 (4), 83–93.

Miniard, Paul W., Sunil Bhatla, and Randall L. Rose (1990), "On the Formation and Relationship of Ad and Brand Attitudes: An Experimental and Causal Analysis," *JMR*, 27 (August), 290–303.

Miniard, Paul W., Sunil Bhatla, Kenneth R. Lord, Peter R. Dickson, and H. Rao Unnava (1991), "Picture based Persuasion Processes and the Moderating Role of Involvement," *JCR*, 18 (June), 92–107.

Miniard, Paul W., Deepak Sirdeshmukh, and Daniel E. Innis (1992), "Peripheral Persuasion and Brand Choice," *JCR*, 19 (September), 226–239.

Mitchell, Andrew A. (1986), "The Effect of Verbal and Visual Components of Advertisements on Brand Attitudes and Attitude Toward the Advertisement," *JCR*, 13 (June), 12–24.

Mitchell, Andrew A. and Jerry C. Olson (1981), "Are Product Attribute Beliefs the Only Mediator of Advertising Effects on Brand Attitude?" *JMR*, 18 (August), 318–332.

Mittal, Banwari (1990), "The Relative Roles of Brand Beliefs and Attitude Toward the Ad as Mediators of Brand Attitude: A Second Look," *JMR*, 27 (May), 209–219.

Moore, David J., John C. Mowen, and Richard Reardon (1994), "Multiple Sources in Advertising Appeals: When Product Endorsers Are Paid by the Advertising Sponsor," *JAMS*, 22 (Summer), 234–243.

Muehling, Darrel D., Russell N. Laczniak, and Jeffrey J. Stoltman (1991), "The Moderating Effects of Ad Message Involvement: A Reassessment," *JA*, 20 (June), 29–38.

Mukherjee, Ashesh and Wayne D. Hoyer (2001), "The Effect of Novel Attributes on Product Evaluation," *JCR*, 28 (December), 462–472.

Munch, James M. and John L. Swasy (1988), "Rhetorical Question, Summarization Frequency, and Argument Strength Effects on Recall," *JCR*, 15 (June), 69–76.

Murry, John P. Jr., John L. Lastovicka, and Surendra N. Singh (1992), "Feeling and Liking Responses to Television Programs: An Examination of Two Explanations for Media-Context Effects," *JCR*, 18 (March), 441–451.

Muthukrishnan, A. V. and S. Ramaswami (1999), "Contextual Effects on the Revision of Evaluative Judgments: An Extension of the Omission-Detection Framework," *JCR*, 26 (June), 70–84.

Nyer, Prashanth U. (1997), "A Study of the Relationships Between Cognitive Appraisals and Consumption Emotions," *JAMS*, 25 (Fall), 296–304.

Peterson, Robert A., William R. Wilson, and Steven P. Brown (1992), "Effects of Advertised Customer Satisfaction Claims on Consumer Attitudes and Purchase Intentions," *JAR*, 32 (March/April), 34–40.

Pham, Michel Tuan (1996), "Cue Representation and Selection Effects of Arousal on Persuasion," *JCR*, 22 (March), 373–387.

Pham, Michel Tuan, Joel B. Cohen, Johan W. Pracejus, and G. David Hughes (2001), "Affect Monitoring and the Primacy of Feelings in Judgment," *JCR*, 28 (September), 167–188.

Prakash, Ved (1992), "Sex Roles and Advertising Preferences," *JAR*, 32 (May/June), 43–52.

Raju, P.S. and Manoj Hastak (1983), "Pre-Trial Cognitive Effects of Cents-Off Coupons," *JA*, 12 (2), 24–33.

Rosenberg, Edward, Rik Pieters, and Michel Wedel (1997), "Visual Attention to Advertising: A Segment-Level Analysis," *JCR*, 24 (December), 305–314.

Rossiter, John R. and Larry Percy (1980), "Attitude Change Through Visual Imagery in Advertising," *JA*, 9 (2), 10–16.

Samu, Sridhar, H. Shanker Krishnan, and Robert E. Smith (1999), "Using Advertising Alliances for New Product Introduction: Interactions Between Product Complementarity and Promotional Strategies," *JM*, 63 (January), 57–74.

Sanbonmatsu, David and Frank R. Kardes (1988), "The Effects of Physiological Arousal on Information Processing and Persuasion," *JCR*, 15 (December), 379–385.

Sengupta, Jaideep and Gavan J. Fitzsimons (2000), "The Effects of Analyzing Reasons for Brand Preferences: Disruption or Reinforcement?" *JMR*, 37 (3), 318–330.

Sheffet, Mary Jane (1983), "An Experimental Investigation of the Documentation of Advertising Claims," *JA*, 12 (2), 19–29.

Shiv, Baba, Julie A. Edell, and John W. Payne (1997), "Factors Affecting the Impact of Negatively and Positively Framed Ad Messages," *JCR*, 24 (December), 285–294.

Simonin, Bernard L. and Julie A. Ruth (1998), "Is a Company Known by the Company It Keeps? Assessing the Spillover Effects of Brand Alliances on Consumer Brand Attitudes," *JMR*, 35 (February), 30–42.

Simpson, Penny M., Steve Horton, and Gene Brown (1996), "Male Nudity in Advertisements: A Modified Replication and Extension of Gender and Product Effects," *JAMS*, 24 (Summer), 257–262.

Sirgy, M. Joseph, Dhruv Grewal, Tamara F. Mangleburg, Jae-ok Park, Kye-Sung Chon, C. B. Claiborne Johar, and Harold Berkman (1997), "Assessing the Predictive Validity of Two Methods of Measuring Self-Image Conguence," *JAMS*, 25 (Summer), 229–241.

Singh, Mandeep, Siva K. Balasubramanian, and Goutam Chakraborty (2000), "A Comparative Analysis of Three Communication Formats: Advertising, Infomercial, and Direct Experience," *JA*, 29 (Winter), 59–75.

Singh, Surendra N. and Catherine Cole (1993), "The Effects of Length, Content, and Repetition on Television Commercial Effectiveness," *JMR*, 30 (February), 91–104.

Singh, Surendra, V. Parker Lessig, Dongwook Kim, Reetika Gupta, and Mary Ann Hocutt (2000), "Does Your Ad Have Too Many Pictures?" *JAR*, 40 (Jan-Apr), 11–27.

Smith, Robert E. (1993), "Integrating Information From Advertising and Trial: Processes and Effects on Consumer Response to Product Information," *JMR*, 30 (May), 204–219.

Smith, Robert E. and William R. Swinyard (1983), "Attitude Behavior Consistency: The Impact of Product Trial Versus Advertising," *JMR*, 20 (August), 257–267.

Sorescu, Alina B. and Betsy D. Gelb (2000), "Negative Competitive Advertising: Evidence Favoring Fine-Tuning," *JA*, 29 (Winter), 25–40.

Stafford, Marla Royne and Ellen Day (1995), "Retail Services Advertising: The Effects of Appeal, Medium, and Service," *JA*, 24 (Spring), 57–71.

Stevenson, Julie, Gordon C. Bruner II, and Anand Kumar (2000), "Webpage Background and Viewer Attitudes," *JAR*, 40 (January/April), 29–34.

Stayman, Douglas M. and Rajeev Batra (1991), "Encoding and Retrieval of Ad Affect in Memory," *JMR*, 28 (May), 232–239.

Stout, Patricia and Benedicta L. Burda (1989), "Zipped Commercials: Are They Effective?" *JA*, 18 (Number 4), 23–32.

Stuart, Shimp and Engle (1987), "Classical Conditioning of Consumer Attitudes: Four Experiments in an Advertising Context," *JCR*, 14 (December), 334–349.

Sujan, Mita and James R. Bettman (1989), "The Effects of Brand Positioning Strategies on Consumers' Brand and Category Perceptions: Some Insights from Schema Research," *JMR*, 26 (November), 454–467.

Sujan, Mita, James R. Bettman, and Hans Baumgartner (1993), "Influencing Consumer Judgments Using Autobiographical Memories: A Self Referencing Perspective," *JMR*, 30 (November), 422–436.

Szymanski, David M. (2001), "Modality and Offering Effects in Sales Presentations for a Good Versus a Service," *JAMS*, 29 (2), 179–189.

Taylor, Charles R., Gordon E. Miracle, and R. Dale Wilson (1997), "The Impact of Information Level on the Effectiveness of U.S. and Korean Television Commercials," *JA*, 26 (Spring), 1–18.

Till, Brian D. and Michael Busler (2001), "The Match-Up Hypothesis: Physical Attractiveness, Expertise, and the Role of Fit on Brand Attitude, Purchase Intent and Brand Beliefs," *JA*, 29 (3), 1–14.

Till, Brian D. and Terence A. Shimp (1998), "Endorsers In Advertising: The Case of Negative Celebrity Information," *JA*, 27 (Spring), 67–82.

Toncar, Mark and James Munch (2001), "Consumer Responses to Tropes in Print Advertising," *JA*, 30 (1), 55–65.

Tripp, Carolyn, Thomas D. Jensen, and Les Carlson (1994), "The Effects of Multiple Product Endorsements by Celebrities on Consumers' Attitudes and Intentions," *JCR*, 20 (March), 535–547.

Unnava, H. Rao, Robert E. Burnkrant, and Sunil Erevelles (1994), "Effects of Presentation Order and Communication Modality on Recall and Attitude," *JCR*, 21 (September), 481–490.

Viswanathan, Madhubalan and Terry L. Childers (1999), "Understanding How Product Attributes Influence Product Categorization: Development and Validation of Fuzzy Set-Based Measures of Gradedness in Product Categories," *JMR*, 36 (February), 75–94.

Wansink, Brian and Michael L. Ray (1992), "Estimating an Advertisement's Impact on One's Consumption of a Brand," *JAR*, 32 (May/June), 9–16.

Ward, James C., Mary Jo Bitner, and John Barnes (1992), "Measuring the Prototypicality and Meaning of Retail Environments," *JR*, 68 (Summer), 194–220.

Whittler, Tommy E. (1991), "The Effects of Actors' Race in Commercial Advertising: Review and Extension," *JA*, 20 (1), 54–60.

Whittler, Tommy E. and Joan DiMeo (1991), "Viewers' Reactions to Racial Cues in Advertising Stimuli," *JAR*, 31 (December), 37–46.

Yi, Youjae (1990a), "Cognitive and Affective Priming Effects of the Context for Print Advertisements," *JA*, 19 (2), 40–48.

Yi, Youjae (1990b), "The Effects of Contextual Priming in Print Advertisements," *JCR*, 17 (September), 215–222.

Zhang, Shi and Bernd H. Schmitt (2001), "Creating Local Brands in Multilingual International Markets," *JMR*, 38 (August), 313–325.

Zhang, Yong (1996), "Responses to Humorous Advertising: The Moderating Effect of Need for Cognition," *JA*, 25 (Spring), 15–32.

Zhang, Yong and Richard Buda (1999), "Moderating Effects of Need for Cognition on Responses to Positively versus Negatively Framed Advertising Messages," *JA*, 28 (2), 1–15.

Zhang, Yong and Betsy D. Gelb (1996), "Matching Advertising Appeals to Culture: The Influence of Products' Use Conditions," *JA*, 25 (Fall), 29–46.

Zinkhan, George M., William B. Locander, and James H. Leigh (1986), "Dimensional Relationships of Aided Recall and Recognition," *JA*, 15 (1), 38–46.

SCALE ITEMS: [1]

1. good / bad

2. like / dislike

3. pleasant / unpleasant

4. high quality / poor quality

5. agreeable / disagreeable

6. satisfactory / dissatisfactory

7. wise / foolish

8. beneficial / harmful

9. favorable / unfavorable

10. distinctive / common

11. likable / dislikable

12. positive / negative

13. buy / would not buy

14. attractive / unattractive

15. enjoyable / unenjoyable

16. useful / useless

17. desirable / undesirable

18. nice / awful

19. important / unimportant

20. harmless / harmful

21. valuable / worthless

22. appetizing / unappetizing

23. unique / not unique

24. expensive / inexpensive

25. needed / not needed

26. fond of / not fond of

27. superior / inferior

28. interesting / boring

29. tasteful / tasteless

30. appealing / unappealing

31. for me / not for me

32. appropriate / inappropriate

33. reasonable / unreasonable

34. value for money / no value for money

35. fast / slow

36. healthy / unhealthy

37. would definitely consider buying it / would definitely not consider buying it

38. effective / ineffective

39. strong / weak

40. responsible / irresponsible

41. would like to try / would not like to try

Aaker (2000b): 1, 9, 11* 7-point [.82–.93]
Aaker and Maheswaran (1997): 1*, 9*, 13*, 16* 9-point [.89]
Adaval (2001): 1*, 14*, 17* 11-point [>.91]
Ahluwalia (2000): 1, 8, 17 9-point [.96]
Ahluwalia, Burnkrant, and Unnava (2000; Ahluwalia, Unnava, and Burnkrant (2001): 1, 8, 17, 18 9-point [.97]
Ahluwalia, and Gurhan-Canli (2000): 1*, 9*, 12* 7-point [.95]
Alpert and Kamins (1995): 2*, 9*, 12* 7-point [.81 & .77]
Anand and Sternthal (1990): 1, 2, 3, 13, 15 7-point [.91]
Andrews, Burton and Netemeyer (2001): 1, 9, 12 7-point [.96]

Andrews, Netemeyer, and Burton (1998; Andrews 2001): 1, 9, 12 7-point [.96]
Aylesworth, Goodstein, and Kalra (1999): 1, 9, 11 7-point [.90]
Babin and Burns (1997): 1, 14, 17, 28*, 30, 31, 32, 33 7-point [.91]
Baker (1999): 1, 4*, 8, 16 7-point [.84 & .85]
Barone, Miniard, and Romeo (2000): 4*, 9, 17 7-point [.82-.89+]
Batra and Ray (1986): 1, 3, 16, 18, 19 7-point [.80]
Batra and Ray (1986): 3, 16, 18, 19 [.93]
Batra and Stayman (1990): 1, 2, 3, 4*, 5, 8*, 9, 12, 16, 21 [.94]
Bello, Pitts, and Etzel (1983): 1*, 4*, 7*, 8*, 10*, 16*, 17* 7-point [.86]
Berger and Mitchell (1989): 1, 2* 7-point. [.94]
Bezjian-Avery, Calder, and Iacobucci (1998): 1, 2*, 4*, 12, 18, 27, 28, 36 7-point [.88]
Bhat, Leigh, and Wardlow (1998): 2, 9, 12 7-point [.84]
Bone and Ellen (1992): 1, 7, 9, 16 [.86 & .82]
Bower and Landreth (2001): 1, 2, 4*, 9, 12, 38, 39 7-point [.92]
Bruner and Kumar (2000): 1, 9, 12 7-point [.94]
Burnkrant and Unnava (1995): 1, 3, 8, 17, 18, 27 7-point [.91]
Campbell and Goodstein (2001): 1, 9, 17, 30 7-point [.92-.95]
Chao (2001; Chao 2003): 1, 6*, 9 7-point [.97]
Chattopadhyay and Basu (1990): 1, 2, 18* 9-point [.93]
Chattopadhyay and Nedungadi (1992): 1, 2, 18* 9-point [.87]
Cox and Cox (1988): 1, 3, 11 9-point [.94]
Cox and Locander (1987): 1, 3, 11 9-point [.90]
Darley and Smith (1993): 1, 4, 11* [.83]
Darley and Smith (1995): 1, 3, 4, 11* [.85]
Deshpande and Stayman (1994): 1, 3, 4*, 12, 16, 21 7-point [.94]
Droge (1989): 1, 3, 5, 6*, 7, 8 7-point [.942 & .941]
Edell and Keller (1989): 1*, 2* 7-point [.97]
Ellen and Bone (1998): 1, 7, 8, 9, 7-point [.91]
Fennis and Bakker (2001; Fennis 2003): 1, 2*, 3, 7, 12, 14, 16*, 18*, 19, 20, 40, 41 [.89]
Gardner, Mitchell, and Russo (1985): 1, 2*, 4 [.94]
Gelb and Zinkhan (1986): 1, 6*, 9 [.91]
Gill, Grossbart, and Laczniak (1988): 1*, 2*, 9*, 21* 7-point [.95]
Goodstein (1993): 1, 9, 11 7-point [.97 & .98]
Gotlieb and Swan (1990): 1, 6*, 9 [.93]
Grier and Despandé (2001): 1, 3, 4*, 9 7-point [.915]
Grossbart, Muehling, and Kangun (1986): 1, 9, 12 7-point [.96 & .97]
Gurhan-Canli and Maheswaran (1998): 1, 9*, 12 7-point [.98]
Gürhan-Canli and Maheswaran (2000a): 1, 9*, 12 7-point [.91]
Gürhan-Canli and Maheswaran (2000b): 1, 9*, 12, 37 7-point [.97]
Hastak and Olson (1989; Hastak 1990): 1, 2, 4 7- point [.90+]
Health, McCarthy, and Mothersbaugh (1994): 1, 6*, 9 9-point [.88 - .96]
Herr, Kardes, and Kim (1991): 1, 9, 17 11-point [.95]
Holbrook and Batra (1987): 1*, 2*, 9*, 12* 7-point [.98]
Homer (1990): 1, 2, 9 9-point [.85 & .91]
Homer and Kahle (1990): 1, 6*, 17 [.86]
Howard and Gengler (2001): 1, 3, 17 7-point [.94 & .87]

Iyer (1988): 1, 8, 16 7-point [.698]
Kalra and Goodstein (1998): 1*, 2*, 9* 7-point [.92]
Kardes and Kalyanaram (1992): 1*, 6, 9* 11-point [.92+ & .94+]
Keller (1991a): 1, 3, 4, 5, 8, 11, 16, 18, 19 7-point [.94]
Keller (1991b): 1, 3, 4, 11 7-point [.90]
Kelleris, Cox, and Cox (1993): 1, 2, 11*, 28*, 29 7-point [.91]
Kempf and Laczniak (2001): 1, 2, 9 7-point [.97]
Kempf and Smith (1998): 1, 3, 9 [.91]
Kim, Allen, and Kardes (1996): 1, 2*, 3, 4, 14, 27, 28 7-point [.79]
Kim, Lim, and Bhargava (1998): 1, 2*, 3, 4, 14, 27, 28 [.92]
Krishnamurthy and Sujan (1999): 1, 9, 12 9-point [.97]
Laczniak and Muehling (1993): 1*, 2*, 4, 9*, 21 7-point [.94]
Lane (2000, 2003): 4*, 6*, 30 7-point [.83-.90]
Leclerc and Little (1997): 1, 6*, 9 9-point [.95 & .92]
Lim, Darley, and Summers (1994): 1, 9, 11* 7-point [.92 - .94]
Loken and Ward (1990): 1, 4, 6* 11-point [.979]
Lord, Lee, and Sauer (1994, 1995): 1, 3, 9 7-point [.85]
Machleit, Allen, and Madden (1993): 1, 7*, 17 7-point [.86 - .96]
MacInnis and Park (1991): 1*, 9, 11*, 30 7-point [.95]
MacKenzie and Lutz (1989): 1, 3, 9 7-point [.86]
MacKenzie, Lutz, and Belch (1986): 1, 7, 9 7-point [.92]
MacKenzie and Spreng (1992): 1, 3, 9 7-point [.85]
Macklin, Bruvold, and Shea (1985): 1, 3, 18, 21, 27, 28 7-point [.83]
Maheswaran (1994): 1, 9, 16* 9-point [.80 - .92]
McQuarrie and Mick (1992): 1*, 4*, 21 7-point [.88 & .92]
Mick (1992): 1, 3, 21 9-point [.87]
Miller and Marks (1992): 1, 2*, 3, 4, 25 7-point [.84]
Miniard, Bhatla, and Rose (1990): 2, 9, 12 7-point [.97]
Miniard et al. (1991): 2*, 9, 12 7-point [.95]
Miniard, Sirdeshmukh, and Innis (1992) {initial measure}: 9, 12, 30 11-point [.91 - .97]
Miniard, Sirdeshmukh, and Innis (1992) {final measure}: 1, 14, 17 7-point [.91 - .97]
Mitchell (1986): 1, 2, 3 7-point [.89 - .92]
Mitchell and Olson (1981): 1, 2*, 3, 4 5-point [.88]
Mittal (1990): 1, 2, 17 7-point [.81 & .90]
Moore, Mowen, and Reardon (1994): 1, 8, 9 7-point [.90]
Muehling, Laczniak, and Stoltman (1991): 1, 9, 12 7-point [.93]
Mukherjee and Hoyer (2001): 1, 2, 4*, 9, 16*, 17 9-point [.92]
Munch and Swasy (1988): 1, 3, 12 7-point [.89]
Murry, Lastovicka, Singh (1992): 1, 3, 7, 8, 9, 11* 5-point [.91]
Muthukrishnan and Ramaswami (1999): 1, 2, 9 9-point [.89]
Peterson, Wilson, and Brown (1992): 4, 16*, 17*, 23, 24 [.80]
Pham (1996): {experiment 1} 1, 6*, 9 7-point [.98]
Pham (1996): {experiments 2 & 3} 1, 2, 6*, 9 [.86 & .96]
Raju and Hastak (1983): 1, 2*, 4 7-point [.90]
Rosenberg, Pieters, and Wedel (1997): 1, 4*, 34 5-point [.85]
Rossiter and Percy (1980): 1, 3, 27, 28 7-point [.86]

Samu, Krishnan, and Smith (1999): 1, 3, 9 7-point [.94]
Sanbonmatsu and Kardes (1988): 1, 6, 9 9-point [.98]
Sengupta and Fitzsimons (2000): 1*, 2*, 9*, 29* [.94]
Shiv, Edell, and Payne (1997): 1, 3, 4*, 11*, 30 7-point [.91 & .90]
Simonin and Ruth (1998): 1, 9, 12 7-point [.957 - .982]
Simpson, Horton, and Brown (1996): 1, 2, 3, 4, 5, 8*, 9, 12, 16, 21 9-point [.978]
Singh, Balasubramanian, and Chakraborty (2000): 1, 3, 4 7-point [.93]
Singh, Balasubramanian, and Chakraborty (2000): 1, 3, 5 7-point [.94]
Singh and Cole (1993): 2*, 8*, 15, 16, 19, 21, 26 7-point [.95]
Singh et al. (2000): 2*, 15, 16, 19, 20, 21, 26 7-point [.94]
Sirgy et al. (1997): 1*, 6*, 9* 5-point [.77]
Smith (1993): 1, 3, 9 [.97]
Sorescu and Gelb (2000): 1, 9, 12 7-point [.84-.95]
Stafford and Day (1995): 1, 9, 12 7-point [.97]
Stevenson, Bruner, and Kumar (2000): 1, 9, 12 7-point [.89]
Stout and Burda (1989): 2, 9 7-point [.75]
Stuart, Shimp, and Engle (1987): 1, 2*, 3, 4, 14, 27, 28 7-point [.96]
Sujan and Bettman (1989): 1, 9, 12 7-point [.94]
Sujan, Bettman, and Baumgartner (1993): 1, 3, 9, 12 9-point [.97 & .98]
Szymanski (2001): 2, 9, 12 7-point [.78]
Taylor, Miracle, and Wilson (1997): 3, 8, 9, 12 7-point [.96]
Till and Busler (2000): 2*, 9, 12 9-point [.92 & .96]
Till and Shimp (1998): 1, 2, 4, 9, 12, 27, 35 9-point [.93]
Toncar, Mark and James Munch (2001): 1, 3, 12 7-point [.89]
Tripp, Jensen, and Carlson (1994): 1, 2*, 3, 4* 7-point[.88]
Unnava, Burnkrant, and Erevelles (1994): 1*, 14, 17*, 18* 7-point [.78 & .92]
Viswanathan and Childers (1999): 1, 4*, 6* 10-point [.91]
Wansink and Ray (1992): 1*, 4*, 11, 22 7-point [.936]
Ward, Bitner, and Barnes (1992): 1, 4, 6* 11-point [.95]
Whittler and DiMeo (1991): 1, 4*, 6* 15-point [.88]
Whittler (1991): 1, 4*, 6* 15-point [.91 & .88]
Yi (1990a): 1, 2, 3 7-point [.92]
Yi (1990b): 1, 2, 9 7-point [.90]
Zhang (1996): 1, 11*, 18* 9-point [.95]
Zhang and Budda (1999): 1, 11*, 18* 7-point [.86]
Zhang and Gelb (1996): 1, 11*, 18* 9-point [.88]
Zhang and Schmitt (2001): 1, 2, 6* 7-point [.91]
Zinkhan, Locander, and Leigh (1986): 1, 3, 21 8-point [.93]

---

[1] For ease of reporting, the positive anchors (when clear) are listed on the left. Scale items used in specific studies are listed below with an indication of the number of response alternatives, if known. Some authors have used scale anchors that have essentially the same meaning but with minor semantic differences, such as *like very much/dislike very much* instead of *like/dislike*. For purposes of parsimony, one version is reported and slight variations are noted with an asterisk (*). For each study, the reliability of a particular set of items is shown in brackets. In several cases more than one reliability or a range is given because the article reported on multiple samples, experiments, et cetera.

SCALE NAME: Attitude Toward the Brand

SCALE DESCRIPTION: The scale is composed of various semantic differentials used to measure a consumer's evaluation of a product. Depending upon the mix of items used, the scale has some similarity to measures of purchase intention as well as product quality.

SCALE ORIGIN: Although not specifically stated in the article, the scale appears to be original to Peracchio and Meyers-Levy (1994). Some modifications were made in later uses of the scale by Meyers-Levy and Peracchio (1995), Peracchio and Meyers-Levy (1997), and Luna and Peracchio (2001).

RELIABILITY: Alphas of .71 (experiment one, bicycle), .91 (experiment two, bicycle), and .92 (experiment two, clothing) were reported for the scale by Meyers-Levy and Peracchio (1995). An alpha of .89 was reported for scale for both jeans and beer by Peracchio and Meyers-Levy (1994). Peracchio and Meyers-Levy (1997) reported alphas of .85 and .92 for evaluations of beer and ski products, respectively. (No alphas for the scale as used in their second experiment were reported.) Luna and Peracchio (2001) reported an alpha of .85 for the version of the scale they used.

VALIDITY: No specific evidence of the scale's validity was provided in any of the studies. However, in a couple of the studies the authors stated that the items loaded on a single factor (Luna and Peracchio 2001; Peracchio and Meyers-Levy 1994).

COMMENTS: Despite the limited evidence that suggests the scale is internally consistent and unidimensional, more rigorous testing may show that it is tapping into two or more factors. It is not clear except in some general sense what high scores on this scale mean: it could mean that consumers are willing to purchase the item; it could mean that they believe the product is of high quality; or, it could mean they think it represents a good value for the money. These have been considered separate constructs in past research and strong consideration should be given to measuring them with different scales so it is clearer to researchers what a score on the scale means.

REFERENCES:

Luna, David and Laura A. Peracchio (2001), "Moderators of Language Effects in Advertising to Bilinguals: A Psycholinguistic Approach," *JCR*, 28 (September), 284–295.

Meyers-Levy, Joan and Laura A. Peracchio (1995), "Understanding the Effects of Color: How the Correspondence between Available and Required Resources Affects Attitudes," *JCR*, 22 (September), 121–138.

Peracchio, Laura A. and Joan Meyers-Levy (1994), "How Ambiguous Cropped Objects in Ad Photos Can Affect Product Evaluations," *JCR*, 21 (June), 190–204.

Peracchio, Laura A. and Joan Meyers-Levy (1997), "Evaluating Persuasion-Enhancing Techniques from a Resource-Matching Perspective," *JCR*, 24 (September), 178–191.

SCALE ITEMS: [1]

1. I would not purchase this product / I would purchase this product

2. mediocre product / exceptional product

3. not at all high quality / extremely high quality

4. poor value / excellent value

5. poorly made / well made

6. boring / exciting

7. not a worthwhile product / a worthwhile product

8. unappealing product / appealing product

9. common / unique

[1] Peracchio and Meyers-Levy (1994) used items 1 to 5. Meyers-Levy and Peracchio (1995) used items 4, 5, 6, 7, and one similar to 1. Peracchio and Meyers-Levy (1997) used items the same as or similar to 3, 4, 5, and 7 as well as an additional one (8).Variations were made in item 5 in each of those studies depending upon the product being evaluated (e.g., crafted, designed). See articles for specific terms. Luna and Peracchio (2001) used items the same as or similar to 3, 4, and 6 as well as another one (9).

SCALE NAME: Attitude Toward the Product/Brand

SCALE DESCRIPTION: A seven-item, seven-point scale is used to assess a person's attitude toward some specific product or brand. Unlike the more popular approach that depends simply on bi-polar adjectives, this scale is composed of sets of brief, opposing, complete sentences.

SCALE ORIGIN: Shamdasani, Stanaland, and Tan (2001) stated that they drew upon scales used in some previous studies (e.g., Leclerc, Schmitt, and Dube-Rioux 1994; Pan and Schmitt 1996). The core bi-polar adjectives upon which the statements are based have been commonly used in the measurement of the construct. (See #59.)

RELIABILITY: An alpha of .95 was reported for the scale by Shamdasani, Stanaland, and Tan (2001).

VALIDITY: The validity of the scale was not addressed in the study by Shamdasani, Stanaland, and Tan (2001).

REFERENCES:

Leclerc, France, Bernd H. Schmitt, and Laurette Dubé (1994), "Foreign Branding and Its Effects on Product Perceptions and Attitudes," *JMR*, 31 (May), 263–270.

Pan, Yigang and Bernd Schmitt (1996), "Language and Brand Attitudes: Impact of Script and Sound Matching in Chinese and English," *Journal of Consumer Psychology*, 5 (3), 263–277.

Shamdasani, Prem N., Andrea J. S. Stanaland, and Juliana Tan (2001), "Location, Location, Location: Insights for Advertising Placement on the Web," *JAR*, 41 (July-August), 7–21.

SCALE ITEMS:

1. This is a bad product / This is a good product.

2. I dislike the product / I like the product.

3. I feel negative toward the product / I feel positive toward the product.

4. The product is awful / The product is nice.

5. The product is unpleasant / The product is pleasant.

6. The product is unattractive / The product is attractive.

7. I approve of the product / I disapprove of the product.

SCALE NAME: Attitude Toward the Sales Promotion (Convenience)

SCALE DESCRIPTION: The scale has three Likert-type statements that measure a consumer's attitude about a specific sales promotion device, the emphasis being on the belief that the promotion reduces search and decision costs.

SCALE ORIGIN: The source of the scale was not specifically stated by Chandon, Wansink and Laurent (2000) but it seems to be original to them. Note that the scale was developed and tested in French; the English phrasings provided below are translations the authors provided in the published version of the article.

RELIABILITY: The scale has an alpha of .603 (Chandon, Wansink and Laurent 2000; Chandon 2003).

VALIDITY: The scale was one of six used to examine the benefits of sales promotions. The items in this scale along with those for the other five scales were analyzed in a first-order CFA. Although the details were not provided, the implication was that all the scales showed evidence of convergent and discriminant validity. A second-order CFA supported a two dimensional structure (hedonic and utilitarian) with the construct measured by this scale (convenience) loading higher on the utilitarian factor.

COMMENTS: The very low alpha suggests that the scale has a barely acceptable level of internal consistency. Caution is urged in use of the scale until its reliability can be substantially improved.

REFERENCES:
Chandon, Pierre (2003), Personal Correspondence.
Chandon, Pierre, Brian Wansink, and Gilles Laurent (2000), "A Benefit Congruency Framework of Sales Promotion Effectiveness," *JM*, 64 (4), 65–81.

SCALE ITEMS: [1]

With this type of promotion:

1. These promotions remind me that I need the product.

2. These promotions make my life easy.

3. I can remember what I need.

---

[1] Although the details of the response format were not provided by Chandon, Wansink and Laurent (2000), the typical Likert-type *agree/disagree* format appears to have been used.

SCALE NAME: Attitude Toward the Sales Promotion (Entertainment)

SCALE DESCRIPTION: The scale is composed of three Likert-type statements intended to measure a consumer's attitude about a specific sales promotion tactic, the emphasis being on the fun and enjoyment that can come from it.

SCALE ORIGIN: The source of the scale was not specifically stated by Chandon, Wansink and Laurent (2000) but it seems to be original to them. Note that the scale was developed and tested in French; the English phrasings provided below are translations the authors provided in the published version of the article.

RELIABILITY: The scale has an alpha of .831 (Chandon, Wansink and Laurent 2000; Chandon 2003).

VALIDITY: The scale was one of six used to examine the benefits of sales promotions. The items in this scale along with those for the other five scales were analyzed in a first-order CFA. Although the details were not provided, the implication was that all the scales showed evidence of convergent and discriminant validity. A second-order CFA supported a two dimensional structure (hedonic and utilitarian) with the construct measured by this scale (entertainment) loading highest on the hedonic factor.

REFERENCES:
Chandon, Pierre (2003), Personal Correspondence.
Chandon, Pierre, Brian Wansink, and Gilles Laurent (2000), "A Benefit Congruency Framework of Sales Promotion Effectiveness," *JM*, 64 (4), 65–81.

SCALE ITEMS: [1]

With this type of promotion:

1. these promotions are fun.

2. these promotions are entertaining.

3. these promotions are enjoyable.

---

[1] Although the details of the response format were not provided by Chandon, Wansink and Laurent (2000), the typical Likert-type *agree/disagree* format appears to have been used.

SCALE NAME: Attitude Toward the Sales Promotion (Exploration)

SCALE DESCRIPTION: Three Likert-type statements are used to measure a consumer's attitude about a specific sales promotion technique, the emphasis being on the role played by the promotion device in helping to satisfy the desire to try new products and brands.

SCALE ORIGIN: The source of the scale was not specifically stated by Chandon, Wansink and Laurent (2000) but it seems to be original to them. Note that the scale was developed and tested in French; the English phrasings provided below are translations the authors provided in the published version of the article.

RELIABILITY: The scale has an alpha of .778 (Chandon, Wansink and Laurent 2000; Chandon 2003).

VALIDITY: The scale was one of six used to examine the benefits of sales promotions. The items in this scale along with those for the other five scales were analyzed in a first-order CFA. Although the details were not provided, the implication was that all the scales showed evidence of convergent and discriminant validity. A second-order CFA supported a two dimensional structure (hedonic and utilitarian) with the construct measured by this scale (exploration) loading highest on the hedonic factor.

REFERENCES:
Chandon, Pierre (2003), Personal Correspondence.
Chandon, Pierre, Brian Wansink, and Gilles Laurent (2000), "A Benefit Congruency Framework of Sales Promotion Effectiveness," *JM*, 64 (4), 65–81.

SCALE ITEMS: [1]

With this type of promotion:

1. I feel like trying new brands.

2. I can avoid always buying the same brands.

3. I can get new ideas of things to buy.

---

[1] Although the details of the response format were not provided by Chandon, Wansink and Laurent (2000), the typical Likert-type *agree/disagree* format appears to have been used.

SCALE NAME: Attitude Toward the Sales Promotion (Overall)

SCALE DESCRIPTION: Three statements are used to measure a consumer's general attitude about a specific sales promotion device he/she is familiar with. The scale was referred to as *overall evaluation of the promotion* by Chandon, Wansink and Laurent (2000).

SCALE ORIGIN: The source of the scale was not specifically stated by Chandon, Wansink and Laurent (2000) but it seems to be original to them. Note that the scale was developed and tested in French; the English phrasings provided below are translations the authors provided in the published version of the article.

RELIABILITY: An alpha of .83 was reported for the scale (Chandon, Wansink and Laurent 2000).

VALIDITY: No examination of the scale's validity was reported by Chandon, Wansink and Laurent (2000).

REFERENCES:
Chandon, Pierre, Brian Wansink, and Gilles Laurent (2000), "A Benefit Congruency Framework of Sales Promotion Effectiveness," *JM*, 64 (4), 65–81.

SCALE ITEMS: [1]

1. I like this type of promotion a lot.

2. I wish there were more promotions like this.

3. With this type of promotion, I feel like buying the product.

---

[1] No information about the response format was provided by Chandon, Wansink and Laurent (2000). However, the typical Likert-type *agree/disagree* format appears to be appropriate for use with it.

SCALE NAME: Attitude Toward the Sales Promotion (Pride)

SCALE DESCRIPTION: The scale uses three Likert-type statements to measure a consumer's attitude about a specific sales promotion technique, the emphasis being on the belief that taking advantage of the promotion would make one feel good and responsible. The scale was called the *value expression benefit* by Chandon, Wansink and Laurent (2000).

SCALE ORIGIN: The source of the scale was not specifically stated by Chandon, Wansink and Laurent (2000) but it seems to be original to them. Note that the scale was developed and tested in French; the English phrasings provided below are translations the authors provided in the published version of the article.

RELIABILITY: The scale has an alpha of .826 (Chandon, Wansink and Laurent 2000; Chandon 2003).

VALIDITY: The scale was one of six used to examine the benefits of sales promotions. The items in this scale along with those for the other five scales were analyzed in a first-order CFA. Although the details were not provided, the implication was that all the scales showed evidence of convergent and discriminant validity. A second-order CFA supported a two dimensional structure (hedonic and utilitarian) with the construct measured by this scale (pride) split loading but being somewhat more aligned with the hedonic factor.

REFERENCES:

Chandon, Pierre (2003), Personal Correspondence.

Chandon, Pierre, Brian Wansink, and Gilles Laurent (2000), "A Benefit Congruency Framework of Sales Promotion Effectiveness," *JM*, 64 (4), 65–81.

SCALE ITEMS: [1]

With this type of promotion:

1. I feel good about myself.

2. I can be proud of my purchase.

3. I feel like I am a smart shopper.

---

[1] Although the details of the response format were not provided by Chandon, Wansink and Laurent (2000), the typical Likert-type *agree/disagree* format appears to have been used.

SCALE NAME: Attitude Toward the Sales Promotion (Quality)

SCALE DESCRIPTION: The scale is composed of three Likert-type statements intended to measure a consumer's attitude about a specific sales promotion device, the emphasis being on the belief that the deal facilitates the purchase of a better quality product than normal.

SCALE ORIGIN: The source of the scale was not specifically stated by Chandon, Wansink and Laurent (2000) but it seems to be original to them. Note that the scale was developed and tested in French. The English phrasings provided below are translations the authors provided in the published version of the article.

RELIABILITY: The scale has an alpha of .714 (Chandon, Wansink and Laurent 2000; Chandon 2003).

VALIDITY: The scale was one of six used to examine the benefits of sales promotions. The items in this scale along with those for the other five scales were analyzed in a first-order CFA. Although the details were not provided, the implication was that all the scales showed evidence of convergent and discriminant validity. A second-order CFA supported a two dimensional structure (hedonic and utilitarian) with the construct measured by this scale (quality) loading much higher on the utilitarian factor.

REFERENCES:
Chandon, Pierre (2003), Personal Correspondence.
Chandon, Pierre, Brian Wansink, and Gilles Laurent (2000), "A Benefit Congruency Framework of Sales Promotion Effectiveness," *JM*, 64 (4), 65–81.

SCALE ITEMS: [1]

With this type of promotion:

1. I can have a higher-quality product at the same price.

2. I can afford a better-than-usual product.

3. I can upgrade to a better brand.

---

[1] Although the details of the response format were not provided by Chandon, Wansink and Laurent (2000), the typical Likert-type *agree/disagree* format appears to have been used.

SCALE NAME: Attitude Toward the Sales Promotion (Savings)

SCALE DESCRIPTION: Three statements with a Likert-type response format are used to measure a consumer's attitude about a specific sales promotion device, the emphasis being on the belief that the deal results in a monetary savings.

SCALE ORIGIN: The source of the scale was not specifically stated by Chandon, Wansink and Laurent (2000) but it seems to be original to them although the items are similar to other measures of sales promotion used in the past. Note that the scale was developed and tested in French. The English phrasings provided below are translations the authors provided in the published version of the article.

RELIABILITY: The scale has an alpha of .875 (Chandon, Wansink and Laurent 2000; Chandon 2003).

VALIDITY: The scale was one of six used to examine the benefits of sales promotions. The items in this scale along with those for the other five scales were analyzed in a first-order CFA. Although the details were not provided, the implication was that all the scales showed evidence of convergent and discriminant validity. A second-order CFA supported a two dimensional structure (hedonic and utilitarian) with the construct measured by this scale (savings) loading highest on the utilitarian factor.

REFERENCES:
Chandon, Pierre (2003), Personal Correspondence.
Chandon, Pierre, Brian Wansink, and Gilles Laurent (2000), "A Benefit Congruency Framework of Sales Promotion Effectiveness," *JM*, 64 (4), 65–81.

SCALE ITEMS: [1]

With this type of promotion:

1. I really save money.

2. I feel that I am getting a good deal.

3. I really spend less.

---

[1] Although the details of the response format were not provided by Chandon, Wansink and Laurent (2000), the typical Likert-type *agree/disagree* format appears to have been used.

SCALE NAME: Attitude Toward the Service Provider

SCALE DESCRIPTION: The scale is composed of three, seven-point bi-polar adjectives used to measure one's attitude toward a person or organization that renders a service. As used by Hui, Thakor, and Gill (1998), another item was also part of the scale. Further, their scale measured one's evaluation of the *service* rather than the service provider per se.

SCALE ORIGIN: Stafford (1996; 1998; Day and Stafford 1997) cites previous studies as being the source of the items but the scale as a whole appears to be original to her. Specifically, the scale is a typical attitude-toward-the-brand measure modified with the scale stem(s) to focus the respondent's attention on the provider of some service rather than on a product.

Hui, Thakor, and Gill (1998) did not specify the source of their scale.

RELIABILITY: Alphas of .97 and .96 have been reported for the scale as used in experiments by Stafford (1996) and (1998), respectively. The alpha for the scale in the study by Day and Stafford (1997, Day 1999) was .94. For their four item version of the scale, Hui, Thakor, and Gill (1998) reported an alpha of .95.

VALIDITY: No examination of the scale's validity has been reported in any of the studies.

REFERENCES:
Day, Ellen and Marla Royne Stafford (1997), "Age-Related Cues in Retail Services Advertising: Their Effects on Younger Consumers," *JR*, 73 (2), 211–233.
Hui, Michael K., Mrugank V. Thakor, and Ravi Gill (1998), "The Effect of Delay Type and Service Stage on Consumers' Reactions to Waiting," *JCR*, 24 (March), 469–479.
Stafford, Marla Royne (1996), "Tangibility in Services Advertising: An Investigation of Verbal versus Visual Cues," *JA*, 25 (Fall), 13–28.
Stafford, Marla Royne (1998), "Advertising Sex-Typed Services: The Effects of Sex, Service Type, and Employee Type on Consumer Attitudes," *JA*, 27 (2), 65–82.
Stafford, Marla Royne (1999), Personal Correspondence.

SCALE ITEMS: [1]

1. My feelings toward <u>service provider</u> are:
   bad / good
2. I feel <u>favorable/unfavorable</u> toward <u>service provider</u>.
3. I have <u>negative/positive</u> feelings toward <u>service provider</u>.
4. How much do you like the service?
   not at all / extremely so

[1] The stems show here for the first three items were those used in Stafford (1998). It is not known if in the other studies these same stems were used or if just one overall stem was used at the beginning. The fourth item is one used Hui, Thakor, and Gill (1998), reconstructed based upon information provided in their article. An eight-point response format was used with the item.

SCALE NAME: Attitude Toward the Service Provider

SCALE DESCRIPTION: The seven-point semantic differential scale is used to measure evaluations of a service provider a person knows about or has interacted with. The scale may make most sense to use with professionals such as dentists as was done by Raghubir and Corfman (1999) in one of their studies.

SCALE ORIGIN: Although not explicitly stated by Raghubir and Corfman (1999), the scale appears to have been developed for use in their study. A nine-item version of the scale was used in study one while one of the items was dropped when the scale was used in their second study.

RELIABILITY: An alpha of .91 was reported for both the nine- and eight- item versions of the scale (Raghubir and Corfman 1999).

VALIDITY: No examination of the scale's validity was reported by Raghubir and Corfman (1999). However, they did indicate that the items from this scale and those measuring beliefs about the service provider (#181) loaded on two different factors.

REFERENCES:
Raghubir, Priya and Kim Corfman (1999), "When Do Price Promotions Affect Pretrial Brand Evaluations?" *JMR*, 36 (May), 211–222.

SCALE ITEMS: [1]

1. not at all good / very good

2. not at all better / much better

3. not at all professional / very professional

4. not at all qualified / very qualified

5. not at all competent / very competent

6. not at all reliable / very reliable

7. not at all busy / very busy

8. not at all quality conscious / very quality conscious

9. not at all well-known / very well-known

[1] Item 2 was not used in the eight-item version of the scale.

SCALE NAME: Attitude Toward the Sponsor

SCALE DESCRIPTION: The scale is composed of three, seven-point Likert type statements measuring a person's attitude about the effect of a company's support for a particular event on one's attitude toward that company. The emphasis is on the degree to which sponsorship could improve one's opinion of the sponsor. The events examined by Speed and Thompson (2000) were related to sports.

SCALE ORIGIN: Although not explicitly stated by the authors, the scale appears to be original to the study by Speed and Thompson (2000). Some qualitative work by the authors led to generation of items for several scales used to create the independent variables in the model. This was followed by a pretest which aided in identifying items for deletion or modification. It was not clear whether or not the items used to create this scale and the other dependent measures were part of this process.

RELIABILITY: An alpha of .95 was reported for the scale by Speed and Thompson (2000).

VALIDITY: Based on data from the main study, a CFA was performed on items from this scale and two others (the dependent variables). The results provided evidence of this scale's convergent and discriminant validity.

REFERENCES:
Speed, Richard and Peter Thompson (2000), "Determinants of Sports Sponsorship Response," *JAMS*, 28 (2), 226–238.

SCALE ITEMS:

1. This sponsorship makes me feel more favorable toward the sponsor.

2. This sponsorship would improve my perception of the sponsor.

3. This sponsor would make me like the sponsor more.

SCALE NAME: Attitude Toward the Sport (Adventurous)

SCALE DESCRIPTION: The scale is composed of three, seven-point Likert-type items intended to measure a person's general attitude about some specified sporting activity with an emphasis on how adventurous it is.

SCALE ORIGIN: The scale is original to Shoham, Rose, and Kahle (1998).

RELIABILITY: An alpha of .88 (n = 155) was reported for the scale by Shoham, Rose, and Kahle (1998).

VALIDITY: The only evidence relating to the scale's validity reported by Shoham, Rose, and Kahle (1998) was that it had moderate, positive correlations with two other scales they developed to measure related attitudes about a sport. (See #73 and #75.)

REFERENCES:
Shoham, Aviv (2000), Personal Correspondence.
Shoham, Aviv, Gregory M. Rose, and Lynn R. Kahle (1998), "Marketing of Risky Sports: From Intention to Action," *JAMS*, 26 (4), 307–321.

SCALE ITEMS: [1]

1. People who take part in this sport are adventurous.

2. This sport is an adventure I think I'll enjoy.

3. I like the adventures that practitioners in this sport have.

---

[1] These items were responded to using a response scale ranging from *definitely disagree* (1) to *definitely agree* (7) (Shoham 2000).

SCALE NAME: Attitude Toward the Sport (Curiosity-Arousing)

SCALE DESCRIPTION: The scale is composed of three, seven-point Likert-type items intended to measure a person's general interest in some specified sporting activity.

SCALE ORIGIN: The scale is original to Shoham, Rose, and Kahle (1998).

RELIABILITY: An alpha of .93 (n = 155) was reported for the scale by Shoham, Rose, and Kahle (1998).

VALIDITY: The only evidence relating to the scale's validity reported by Shoham, Rose, and Kahle (1998) was that it had moderate, positive correlations with two other scales they developed to measure related attitudes about a sport. (See #72 and #75.)

REFERENCES:
Shoham, Aviv (2000), Personal Correspondence.
Shoham, Aviv, Gregory M. Rose, and Lynn R. Kahle (1998), "Marketing of Risky Sports: From Intention to Action," *JAMS*, 26 (4), 307–321.

SCALE ITEMS: [1]

1. I think I'd want to experience this sport to know more about it.

2. It would be interesting to find out how I would feel if I participated in this sport.

3. I am interested in this sport.

---

[1] These items were responded to using a response scale ranging from *definitely disagree* (1) to *definitely agree* (7) (Shoham 2000).

SCALE NAME: Attitude Toward the Sport (Social Status)

SCALE DESCRIPTION: The scale is composed of three, seven-point Likert-type items intended to measure a person's general attitude about some specified sporting activity with an emphasis on how it enhances participants' social status.

SCALE ORIGIN: The scale is original to Shoham, Rose, and Kahle (1998).

RELIABILITY: An alpha of .89 (n = 155) was reported for the scale by Shoham, Rose, and Kahle (1998).

VALIDITY: The only evidence relating to the scale's validity reported by Shoham, Rose, and Kahle (1998) was that it had a moderate, positive correlation with a measure of the value of being well respected (Kahle 1983).

REFERENCES:

Kahle, Lynn R. (1983), *Social Values and Social Change: Adaptation to Life in America*, New York: Praeger.

Shoham, Aviv (2000), Personal Correspondence.

Shoham, Aviv, Gregory M. Rose, and Lynn R. Kahle (1998), "Marketing of Risky Sports: From Intention to Action," *JAMS*, 26 (4), 307–321.

SCALE ITEMS: [1]

1. In society today, people who participate in this sport are appreciated.

2. My friends would think highly of me if I participated in this sport.

3. My social status will be enhanced if I participate in this sport.

---

[1] These items were responded to using a response scale ranging from *definitely disagree* (1) to *definitely agree* (7) (Shoham 2000).

SCALE NAME: Attitude Toward the Sport (Thrilling)

SCALE DESCRIPTION: The scale is composed of three, seven-point Likert-type items intended to measure a person's general attitude about some specified sporting activity with an emphasis on how thrilling it is.

SCALE ORIGIN: The scale is original to Shoham, Rose, and Kahle (1998).

RELIABILITY: An alpha of .88 (n = 155) was reported for the scale by Shoham, Rose, and Kahle (1998).

VALIDITY: The only evidence relating to the scale's validity reported by Shoham, Rose, and Kahle (1998) was that it had moderate, positive correlations with two other scales they developed to measure related attitudes about a sport. (See #72 and #73).

REFERENCES:
Shoham, Aviv (2000), Personal Correspondence.
Shoham, Aviv, Gregory M. Rose, and Lynn R. Kahle (1998), "Marketing of Risky Sports: From Intention to Action," *JAMS*, 26 (4), 307–321.

SCALE ITEMS: [1]

1. This sport is so thrilling.

2. This sport gives people a thrill.

3. People who participate in this sport do not get thrills. (r)

[1] These items were responded to using a response scale ranging from *definitely disagree* (1) to *definitely agree* (7) (Shoham 2000).

SCALE NAME: Attitude Toward the Task

SCALE DESCRIPTION: The scale is composed of three, seven-point semantic differentials that are used to assess a person's thoughts and feelings with regard to a task he/she has recently engaged in. The measure was referred to as *task enjoyment* by Park, Jun, and MacInnis (2000).

SCALE ORIGIN: Although some similar ideas can be found in previous research with regard to subjects' reactions to an experimental task as well as general attitude measures, this set of items appears to be original to Park, Jun, and MacInnis (2000).

RELIABILITY: An alpha of .87 was reported for the scale (Park, Jun, and MacInnis 2000).

VALIDITY: No examination of the scale's validity was reported by Park, Jun, and MacInnis (2000).

COMMENTS: As used by Park, Jun, and MacInnis (2000) the scale relates to a task being investigated in a study. However, by changing the instructions the scale appears to be amenable for use with a variety of other activities, objects, or ideas.

REFERENCES:
Park, C. Whan, Sung Youl Jun, and Deborah J. MacInnis (2000), "Choosing What I Want Versus Rejecting What I Don't Want: An Application of Decision Framing to Product Option Choice Decisions," *JMR*, 37 (May), 187–202.

SCALE ITEMS: [1]

1. Not enjoyable at all / very enjoyable

2. Not interesting at all / very interesting

3. Not pleasant at all / very pleasant

[1] The scale stem was not provided in the article by Park, Jun, and MacInnis (2000) but was likely to have been something like "*using the following items, please indicate your opinions about the task you just engaged in.*"

SCALE NAME: Attitude Toward the Website (Affect)

SCALE DESCRIPTION: The scale is composed of three items measuring a person's attitude towards a website with an emphasis on his/her affective reaction to the site.

SCALE ORIGIN: Although not explicitly stated by Lynch, Kent, and Srinivasan (2001), the scale appears to be original to their study.

RELIABILITY: Alphas of .827 (CD player) and .896 (t-shirt) were reported by Lynch, Kent, and Srinivasan (2001).

VALIDITY: No information bearing on the scale's validity was reported by Lynch, Kent, and Srinivasan (2001). However, they did indicate for both product categories they studied that the items loaded high on the same dimension in factor analyses.

REFERENCES:
Lynch, Patrick D., Robert J. Kent, and Srini S. Srinivasan (2001), "The Global Internet Shopper: Evidence from Shopping Tasks in Twelve Countries," *JAR*, 41 (3), 15–23.

SCALE ITEMS:

1. The site has a good reputation.

2. This website is trustworthy.

3. This website will keep its promises and commitments.

SCALE NAME: Attitude Toward the Website (Economic Value)

SCALE DESCRIPTION: The scale is composed of three, seven-point Likert-type statements and appears to measure the extent to which a consumer views the prices charged by a specific website for the products it carries to be reasonable.

SCALE ORIGIN: Several steps were followed by Mathwick, Malhotra, and Rigdon (2001) in developing this scale as well as the others used in their study. First, they drew upon previous scales of similar constructs along with qualitative research by the Catalog Coalition (1993) to generate items. Then, various types of pretesting followed which helped reduced the set of items and provide a sense of content validity. Ultimately, the study produced an instrument that the authors referred to as the *experiential value scale* which has seven dimensions and 19 items.

RELIABILITY: An alpha of .78 was reported for the scale by Mathwick, Malhotra, and Rigdon (2001). The composite reliability was also .83.

VALIDITY: Confirmation factor analysis was used to provide evidence of the scale's unidimensionality as well as its convergent validity (Mathwick, Malhotra, and Rigdon 2001). Discriminant validity was difficult to test due to the multidimensional, hierarchically organized constructs that were hypothesized to compose the model. However, some limited evidence of discriminant validity was provided.

COMMENTS: Although developed as part of the *experiential value scale*, this subscale appears to be useful by itself if a researcher so desires to use it apart from the rest of the subscales.

REFERENCES:

A commercial research project sponsored by a consortium of catalog retailers led by Sears Shop At Home Services (1993), *Catalog Coalition Research Project*, Hoffman Estates, IL: Sears Shop At Home Services.

Mathwick, Charla, Naresh Malhotra, and Edward Rigdon (2001), "Experiential Value: Conceptualization, Measurement and Application in the Catalog and Internet Shopping Environment," *JR*, 77 (Spring), 39–56.

SCALE ITEMS: [1]

1. _____ products are a good economic value.

2. Overall, I am happy with _____'s prices.

3. The prices of the product(s) I purchased from _____'s Internet site are too high, given the quality of the merchandise. (r)

[1] The name of the company should be placed in the blanks.

SCALE NAME: Attitude Toward the Website (Entertaining)

SCALE DESCRIPTION: The unipolar scale is intended to measure the extent to which a person considers a website to be fun and exciting. It is composed of six terms and utilizes a five-point response format.

SCALE ORIGIN: The scale is original to the study by Chen and Wells (1999). Beginning with 141 adjectives used by judges to rate 120 websites, various means were used to trim the list down to 65 items. Those items were factor analyzed and high loading items on the first three factors formed the basis for three scales, each emphasizing a different dimension of attitude toward a website: entertainment, informativeness, and organization.

RELIABILITY: Chen and Wells (1999) reported an alpha of .92.

VALIDITY: Besides noting that the items loaded together in a factor analysis, Chen and Wells (1999) did not report examining the scale's validity.

REFERENCES:
Chen, Qimei and William D. Wells (1999), "Attitude toward the Site," *JAR*, 39 (September/October), 27–37.

SCALE ITEMS: [1]

1. Fun

2. Exciting

3. Cool

4. Imaginative

5. Entertaining

6. Flashy

[1] The anchors for the five-point response scale used with the items were *not at all applies* and *very much applies*.

SCALE NAME: Attitude Toward the Website (Entertaining)

SCALE DESCRIPTION: The three-item, seven-point Likert-type scale is intended to measure how entertaining a person believes a website to be.

SCALE ORIGIN: Several steps were followed by Mathwick, Malhotra, and Rigdon (2001) in developing this scale as well as the others used in their study. First, they drew upon previous scales of similar constructs along with qualitative research by the Catalog Coalition (1993) to generate items. Then, various types of pretesting followed which helped reduced the set of items and provide a sense of content validity. Ultimately, the study produced an instrument that the authors referred to as the *experiential value scale* which has seven dimensions and 19 items.

RELIABILITY: An alpha of .88 was reported for the scale by Mathwick, Malhotra, and Rigdon (2001). The composite reliability was .91.

VALIDITY: Confirmation factor analysis was used to provide evidence of the scale's unidimensionality as well as its convergent validity (Mathwick, Malhotra, and Rigdon 2001). Discriminant validity was difficult to test due to the multidimensional, hierarchically organized constructs that were hypothesized to compose the model. However, some limited evidence of discriminant validity was provided.

COMMENTS: Although developed as part of the *experiential value scale*, this subscale appears to be useful by itself if a researcher so desires to use it apart from the rest of the subscales.

REFERENCES:
A commercial research project sponsored by a consortium of catalog retailers led by Sears Shop At Home Services (1993), *Catalog Coalition Research Project*, Hoffman Estates, IL: Sears Shop At Home Services.
Mathwick, Charla, Naresh Malhotra, and Edward Rigdon (2001), "Experiential Value: Conceptualization, Measurement and Application in the Catalog and Internet Shopping Environment," *JR*, 77 (Spring), 39–56.

SCALE ITEMS: [1]

1. I think _____'s Internet site is very entertaining.

2. The enthusiasm of _____'s Internet site is catching; it picks me up.

3. _____ doesn't sell products – it entertains me.

[1] The name of the company should be placed in the blanks.

SCALE NAME: Attitude Toward the Website (Escapism)

SCALE DESCRIPTION: The scale is composed of three, seven-point Likert-type statements and appears to measure the extent to which a person views shopping at a specific website as helping provide the sense of leaving his/her normal world for a while.

SCALE ORIGIN: Several steps were followed by Mathwick, Malhotra, and Rigdon (2001) in developing this scale as well as the others used in their study. First, they drew upon previous scales of similar constructs along with qualitative research by the Catalog coalition (1993) to generate items. Then, various types of pretesting followed which helped reduced the set of items and provide a sense of content validity. Ultimately, the study produced an instrument that the authors referred to as the *experiential value scale* which has seven dimensions and 19 items.

RELIABILITY: An alpha of .79 was reported for the scale by Mathwick, Malhotra, and Rigdon (2001). The composite reliability was also .79.

VALIDITY: Confirmation factor analysis was used to provide evidence of the scale's unidimensionality as well as its convergent validity (Mathwick, Malhotra, and Rigdon 2001). Discriminant validity was difficult to test due to the multidimensional, hierarchically organized constructs that were hypothesized to compose the model. However, some limited evidence of discriminant validity was provided.

COMMENTS: Although developed as part of the *experiential value scale*, this subscale appears to be useful by itself if a researcher so desires to use it apart from the rest of the subscales.

REFERENCES:
A commercial research project sponsored by a consortium of catalog retailers led by Sears Shop At Home Services (1993), *Catalog Coalition Research Project*, Hoffman Estates, IL: Sears Shop At Home Services.
Mathwick, Charla, Naresh Malhotra, and Edward Rigdon (2001), "Experiential Value: Conceptualization, Measurement and Application in the Catalog and Internet Shopping Environment," *JR*, 77 (Spring), 39–56.

SCALE ITEMS: [1]

1. Shopping from _____'s Internet site "gets me away from it all."

2. Shopping from _____ makes me feel like I am in another world.

3. I get so involved when I shop from _____ that I forget everything else.

[1] The name of the company should be placed in the blanks.

SCALE NAME: Attitude Toward the Website (General)

SCALE DESCRIPTION: The scale is composed of six items intended to measure a person's general evaluation of a website. The scale was called *attitude toward the site* by Chen and Wells (1999).

SCALE ORIGIN: The scale is original to the study by Chen and Wells (1999). They asked a sample of people experienced with the web to describe "good" and "bad" websites. Based on that feedback, the scale items were developed.

RELIABILITY: Alphas of .92 and .81 have been reported for the scale by Chen and Wells (1999) and Shamdasani, Stanaland, and Tan (2001), respectively.

VALIDITY: Besides noting that a factor analysis indicated the scale items were unidimensional, Chen and Wells (1999) did not report examining the scale's validity. No examination of the scale's validity was reported by Shamdasani, Stanaland, and Tan (2001).

REFERENCES:
Chen, Qimei and William D. Wells (1999), "Attitude toward the Site," *JAR*, 39 (September/October), 27–37.
Shamdasani, Prem N., Andrea J. S. Stanaland, and Juliana Tan (2001), "Location, Location, Location: Insights for Advertising Placement on the Web," *JAR*, 41 (July-August), 7–21.

SCALE ITEMS: [1]

Directions: The following items assess your general favorability toward the website you just visited. Circle the number that best indicates your agreement or disagreement with each statement.

1. This website makes it easy for me to build a relationship with this company.

2. I would like to visit this website again in the future.

3. I'm satisfied with the service provided by this website.

4. I feel comfortable in surfing the website.

5. I feel surfing this website is a good way for me to spend my time.

6. Compared with other websites, I would rate this one as . . .

---

[1] As used by Chen and Well (1999), the first five items were answered with a five-point response scale anchored by *definitely disagree/definitely agree* whereas the anchors for the sixth item was *one of the worst/ one of the best*. The response format used by Shamdasani, Stanaland, and Tan (2001) was similar except that they used seven-point scales.

SCALE NAME: Attitude Toward the Website (General)

SCALE DESCRIPTION: The scale is composed of three, seven-point Likert-type statements used to measure a person's overall evaluation of a website. The scale was symbolized as Aws by the first users (Stevenson, Bruner, and Kumar 2000).

SCALE ORIGIN: The scale is original to the study by Stevenson, Bruner, and Kumar (2000). However, they indicated that the items were adapted from a measure of attitude toward the brand by Chattopadhyay and Basu (1990).

RELIABILITY: Alphas of .97 and .93 was reported for the scale by Bruner and Kumar (2000) and Stevenson, Bruner, and Kumar (2000), respectively.

VALIDITY: No examination of the scale's validity was reported in these studies. However, another study was conducted by these authors with that as one of its purposes (Bruner and Kumar 2002). Using a procedure called *similarity analysis*, the evidence indicated that the scale showed greater evidence of validity than two other competing measures of the same construct.

REFERENCES:
Bruner II, Gordon C. and Anand Kumar (2000), "Web Commercials and Advertising Hierarchy-of-Effects," *JAR*, 40 (Jan-Apr), 35– 42.
Bruner II, Gordon C. and Anand Kumar (2002), "Similarity Analysis Of Three Attitude-Toward-The-Website Scales," *Quarterly Journal of Electronic Commerce*, 3 (2), 163–172.
Stevenson, Julie, Gordon C. Bruner II, and Anand Kumar (2000), "Webpage Background and Viewer Attitudes," *JAR*, 40 (January/April), 29–34.

SCALE ITEMS:

1. I like the website I saw.

2. I think it is a good website.

3. I think it is a nice website.

SCALE NAME: Attitude Toward the Website (General)

SCALE DESCRIPTION: The three, seven-point semantic differentials are used to measure a person's general attitude toward some specified website.

SCALE ORIGIN: Coyle and Thorson (2001) did not cite any previous study as the source of the scale, thus, it is likely to be original to their study. However, it is very similar to at least one other Aws scale (Burns 2000) and it uses items that have been commonly used over the years to measure attitude-toward-the-brand and attitude-toward-the-ad.

RELIABILITY: An alpha of .84 (n = 68) was reported for the scale (Coyle and Thorson 2001).

VALIDITY: No examination of the scale's validity was reported by Coyle and Thorson (2001).

REFERENCES:
Burns, Kellie S. (2000), "Branding in Cyberspace: Using the Congruity of Consumer and Website Personality to Unravel Online User Satisfaction," in *Proceedings of the American Academy of Advertising*, Mary Alice Shaver, ed., 9–18.
Coyle, James R. and Esther Thorson (2001), "The Effects of Progressive Levels of Interactivity and Vividness in Web Marketing Sites," *JA*, 30 (Fall), 65–77.

SCALE ITEMS:

1. bad / good

2. unfavorable / favorable

3. dislike / like

SCALE NAME: Attitude Toward the Website (Informative)

SCALE DESCRIPTION: The uni-polar scale is intended to measure the extent to which a person considers a website to be useful and intelligent. It is composed of six terms and utilizes a five-point response format.

SCALE ORIGIN: The scale is original to the study by Chen and Wells (1999). Beginning with 141 adjectives used by judges to rate 120 websites, various means were used to trim the list down to 65 items. Those items were factor analyzed and high loading items on the first three factors formed the basis for three scales, each emphasizing a different dimension of attitude toward a website: entertainment, informativeness, and organization.

RELIABILITY: Chen and Wells (1999) reported an alpha of .94.

VALIDITY: Besides noting that the items loaded together in a factor analysis, Chen and Wells (1999) did not report examining the scale's validity.

REFERENCES:
Chen, Qimei and William D. Wells (1999), "Attitude Toward the Site," *JAR*, 39 (September/October), 27–37.

SCALE ITEMS: [1]

1. Informative

2. Intelligent

3. Knowledgeable

4. Resourceful

5. Useful

6. Helpful

[1] The anchors for the five-point response scale used with the items were *not at all applies* and *very much applies*.

SCALE NAME: Attitude Toward the Website (Organized)

SCALE DESCRIPTION: The uni-polar scale is intended to measure the extent to which a person considers a website to lack clear structure and ease of use. It is composed of four terms and utilizes a five-point response format.

SCALE ORIGIN: The scale is original to the study by Chen and Wells (1999). Beginning with 141 adjectives used by judges to rate 120 websites, various means were used to trim the list down to 65 items. Those items were factor analyzed and high loading items on the first three factors formed the basis for three scales, each emphasizing a different dimension of attitude toward a website: entertainment, informativeness, and organization.

RELIABILITY: Chen and Wells (1999) reported an alpha of .84.

VALIDITY: Besides noting that the items loaded together in a factor analysis, Chen and Wells (1999) did not report examining the scale's validity.

REFERENCES:
Chen, Qimei and William D. Wells (1999), "Attitude Toward the Site," *JAR*, 39 (September/October), 27–37.

SCALE ITEMS: [1]

1. Messy

2. Cumbersome

3. Confusing

4. Irritating

---

[1] The anchors for the five-point response scale used with the items were *not at all applies* and *very much applies*.

SCALE NAME: Attitude Toward the Website (Quality)

SCALE DESCRIPTION: The scale is composed of four items that are intended to measure a person's attitude towards a website with an emphasis on the helpfulness of the site and its ease of use.

SCALE ORIGIN: Although not explicitly stated by Lynch, Kent, and Srinivasan (2001), the scale appears to be original to their study.

RELIABILITY: Alphas of .783 (CD player) and .848 (t-shirt) were reported by Lynch, Kent, and Srinivasan (2001).

VALIDITY: No information bearing on the scale's validity was reported by Lynch, Kent, and Srinivasan (2001). However, they did indicate for both product categories they studied that the items loaded high on the same dimension in factor analyses.

REFERENCES:
Lynch, Patrick D., Robert J. Kent, and Srini S. Srinivasan (2001), "The Global Internet Shopper: Evidence from Shopping Tasks in Twelve Countries," *JAR*, 41 (3), 15–23.

SCALE ITEMS: [1]

1. Was this site easy to use?

2. How would you rate the quality of this site's search engine?

3. Did the site have helpful pictures and graphics?

4. How complete was the information at this website?

[1] The response format was not described by Lynch, Kent, and Srinivasan (2001). However, the anchors for these items might have been something like *very/not very*.

SCALE NAME: Attitude Toward the Website (Shopping Efficiency)

SCALE DESCRIPTION: The three-item, seven-point Likert-type scale is intended to measure the extent to which a consumer believes that shopping at a particular website is an efficient use of his/her time.

SCALE ORIGIN: Several steps were followed by Mathwick, Malhotra, and Rigdon (2001) in developing this scale as well as the others used in their study. First, they drew upon previous scales of similar constructs along with qualitative research by the Catalog Coalition (1993) to generate items. Then, various types of pretesting followed which helped reduced the set of items and provide a sense of content validity. Ultimately, the study produced an instrument that the authors referred to as the *experiential value scale* which has seven dimensions and 19 items.

RELIABILITY: An alpha of .74 was reported for the scale by Mathwick, Malhotra, and Rigdon (2001). The composite reliability was .75.

VALIDITY: Confirmation factor analysis was used to provide evidence of the scale's unidimensionality as well as its convergent validity (Mathwick, Malhotra, and Rigdon 2001). Discriminant validity was difficult to test due to the multidimensional, hierarchically organized constructs that were hypothesized to compose the model. However, some limited evidence of discriminant validity was provided.

COMMENTS: Although developed as part of the *experiential value scale*, this subscale appears to be useful by itself if a researcher so desires to use it apart from the rest of the subscales.

REFERENCES:
A commercial research project sponsored by a consortium of catalog retailers led by Sears Shop At Home Services (1993), *Catalog Coalition Research Project*, Hoffman Estates, IL: Sears Shop At Home Services.
Mathwick, Charla, Naresh Malhotra, and Edward Rigdon (2001), "Experiential Value: Conceptualization, Measurement and Application in the Catalog and Internet Shopping Environment," *JR*, 77 (Spring), 39–56.

SCALE ITEMS: [1]

1. Shopping from _____ is an efficient way to manage my time.

2. Shopping from _____'s Internet site is makes my life easier.

3. Shopping from _____'s Internet site fits with my schedule.

---

[1] The name of the company should be placed in the blanks.

SCALE NAME: Attitude Toward the Website (Trust)

SCALE DESCRIPTION: Three Likert-type items are used to measure a person's attitude towards a website with an emphasis on the integrity and veracity of the site.

SCALE ORIGIN: Although not explicitly stated by Lynch, Kent, and Srinivasan (2001), the scale appears to be original to their study.

RELIABILITY: Alphas of .839 (CD player) and .863 (t-shirt) were reported by Lynch, Kent, and Srinivasan (2001).

VALIDITY: No information bearing on the scale's validity was reported by Lynch, Kent, and Srinivasan (2001). However, they did indicate for both product categories they studied that the items loaded high on the same dimension in factor analyses.

REFERENCES:
Lynch, Patrick D., Robert J. Kent, and Srini S. Srinivasan (2001), "The Global Internet Shopper: Evidence from Shopping Tasks in Twelve Countries," *JAR*, 41 (3), 15–23.

SCALE ITEMS: [1]

1. The site has a good reputation.

2. This website is trustworthy.

3. This website will keep its promises and commitments.

[1] The response format was not described by Lynch, Kent, and Srinivasan (2001). However, the anchors for these items were probably *agree/disagree*.

SCALE NAME: Attitude Toward the Website (Visual Appeal)

SCALE DESCRIPTION: The three-item, seven-point Likert-type scale is intended to measure how visually attractive a person believes a website to be.

SCALE ORIGIN: Several steps were followed by Mathwick, Malhotra, and Rigdon (2001) in developing this scale as well as the others used in their study. First, they drew upon previous scales of similar constructs along with qualitative research by the Catalog Coalition (1993) to generate items. Then, various types of pretesting followed which helped reduced the set of items and provide a sense of content validity. Ultimately, the study produced an instrument that the authors referred to as the *experiential value scale* which has seven dimensions and 19 items.

RELIABILITY: An alpha of .92 was reported for the scale by Mathwick, Malhotra, and Rigdon (2001). The composite reliability was .93.

VALIDITY: Confirmation factor analysis was used to provide evidence of the scale's unidimensionality as well as its convergent validity (Mathwick, Malhotra, and Rigdon 2001). Discriminant validity was difficult to test due to the multidimensional, hierarchically organized constructs that were hypothesized to compose the model. However, some limited evidence of discriminant validity was provided.

COMMENTS: Although developed as part of the *experiential value scale*, this subscale appears to be useful by itself if a researcher so desires to use it apart from the rest of the subscales.

REFERENCES:

A commercial research project sponsored by a consortium of catalog retailers led by Sears Shop At Home Services (1993), *Catalog Coalition Research Project*, Hoffman Estates, IL: Sears Shop At Home Services.

Mathwick, Charla, Naresh Malhotra, and Edward Rigdon (2001), "Experiential Value: Conceptualization, Measurement and Application in the Catalog and Internet Shopping Environment," *JR*, 77 (Spring), 39–56.

SCALE ITEMS: [1]

1. The way _____ displays its products is attractive.

2. _____'s Internet site is aesthetically appealing.

3. I like the way _____'s Internet site looks.

---

[1] The name of the company should be placed in the blanks.

SCALE NAME: Balanced Inventory of Desirable Responding

SCALE DESCRIPTION: The scale is intended to measure both the tendency to give self-reports that are honest but positively biased (*self-deceptive positivity*) as well as deliberate self-presentation to others (*impression management*). Scores are based upon the extent to which respondents consider forty statements about their behavior to be true.

SCALE ORIGIN: This version of the BIDR scale was developed by Paulhus (1984) but is based upon a earlier instrument by Sackeim and Gur (1978). Alphas have been reported to range from .75 to .86 for the impression management component, .68 to .80 for the self-deceptive positivity component, and .83 for the scale as a whole (Paulhus 1988). The stability (5-week test-retest) was reported to be .65 for impression management and .69 for self-deceptive positivity (Paulhus 1988). A variety of data have been presented in support of the scale's validity among which is a correlation of .71 between the complete BIDR and the Marlowe-Crowne #462, scale (Paulhus 1988). (See Robinson, Shaver, and Wrightsman 1991 for more details.)

RELIABILITY: An alpha of .75 was reported for the scale by Lastovicka et al. (1999). Just the impression management portion of the scale was used in the studies by Bearden, Hardesty, and Rose (2001) and Tian, Bearden, and Hunter (2001) with alphas of .81 and .77 being reported for it, respectively.

VALIDITY: No examination of BIDR's validity was reported by Lastovicka et al. (1999), Bearden, Hardesty, and Rose (2001), or Tian, Bearden, and Hunter (2001) although it was used in each case in the process of validating other scales.

COMMENTS: With the 40 items of the BIDR intentionally tapping into two constructs, it is highly unlikely that the BIDR is unidimensional, a characteristic that is now viewed as essential for proper measurement of any construct (Gerbing and Anderson 1988). If the sets of items composing the two components are shown to be unidimensional and those two factors are shown to load appropriately on a higher order factor (desirable responding) then a composite score of all 40 items might be acceptable.

See also Mick (1996).

REFERENCES:

Bearden, William O., David M. Hardesty, and Randall L. Rose (2001), "Consumer Self Confidence: Refinements in Conceptualization and Measurement," *JCR*, 28 (June), 121–134.

Gerbing, David W. and James C. Anderson (1988), "An Updated Paradigm for Scale Development Incorporating Unidimensionality and Its Assessment," *JMR*, 25 (May), 186–192.

Lastovicka, John L., Lance A. Bettencourt, Renee Shaw Hughner, and Ronald J. Kuntze (1999), "Lifestyle of the Tight and Frugal: Theory and Measurement," *JCR*, 26 (June), 85–98.

Mick, David Glen (1996), "Are Studies of Dark Side Variables Confounded by Socially Desirable Responding? The Case of Materialism," *JCR*, 23 (September), 106–119.

Paulhus, Delroy L. (1984), "Two-Component Models of Socially Desirable Responding," *Journal of Personality and Social Psychology*, 46 (3), 598–609.

Paulhus, Delroy L. (1988), "Assessing Self-Deception and Impression Management in Self-Reports: the Balanced Inventory of Desirable Responding," doctoral dissertation, University of British Columbia.

Robinson, John P., Phillip R. Shaver, and Lawrence S. Wrightsman (1991), *Measures of Personality and Social Psychological Attitudes*, San Diego: Academic Press.

Sackeim, H. A. and R. C. Gur (1978), "Self-deception, Self-confrontation and Consciousness," in *Consciousness and Self-Regulation: Advances in Research, V. 2*, G. E. Schwartz and D. Shapiro, eds., New York: Plenum 139–197.

Tian, Kelly T., William O. Bearden, and Gary L. Hunter (2001), "Consumers' Need for Uniqueness: Scale Development and Validation," *JCR*, 28 (June), 50–66.

SCALE ITEMS: [1]

1. My first impressions of people usually turn out to be right. (r)

2. It would be hard for me to break any of my bad habits.

3. I don't care to know what other people really think of me.

4. I have not always been honest with myself. (r)

5. I always know why I like things.

6. When my emotions are aroused, it biases my thinking. (r)

7. Once I've made up my mind, other people can seldom change my opinion.

8. I am not a safe driver when I exceed the speed limit. (r)

9. I am fully in control of my own fate.

10. It's hard for me to shut off a disturbing thought. (r)

11. I never regret my decisions.

12. I sometimes lose out on things because I can't make up my mind soon enough. (r)

13. The reason I vote is because my vote can make a difference.

14. My parents were not always fair when they punished me. (r)

15. I am a completely rational person.

16. I rarely appreciate criticism. (r)

17. I am very confident of my judgments.

18. I have sometimes doubted my ability as a lover. (r)

19. It's all right with me if some people happen to dislike me.

20. I don't always know the reasons why I do the things I do. (r)

21. I sometimes tell lies if I have to. (r)

22. I never cover up my mistakes.

23. There have been occasions when I have taken advantage of someone. (r)

24. I never swear.

25. I sometimes try to get even rather than forgive and forget. (r)

26. I always obey laws, even if I'm unlikely to get caught.

27. I have said something bad about a friend behind his or her back. (r)

28. When I hear people talking privately, I avoid listening.

29. I have received too much change from a salesperson without telling him or her. (r)

30. I always declare everything at customs.

31. When I was young I sometimes stole things. (r)

32. I have never dropped litter on the street.

33. I sometimes drive faster than the speed limit. (r)

34. I never read sexy books or magazines.

35. I have done things that I don't tell other people about. (r)

36. I never take things that don't belong to me.

37. I have taken sick-leave from work or school even though I wasn't really sick. (r)

38. I have never damaged a library book or store merchandise without reporting it.

39. I have some pretty awful habits. (r)

40. I don't gossip about other's people's business.

[1] The first 20 items are intended to measure self-deceptive positivity and the last 20 items measure impression management. The response format used by Paulhus (1984, 1988) ranged from 1 (not true) to 7 (very true). A dichotomous scoring procedure was used such that only items receiving a 6 or 7 were counted and added one point a piece. Bearden, Hardesty, and Rose (2001) as well as Tian, Bearden, and Hunter (2001) only used the 20 items composing the impression management subscale.

SCALE NAME: Behavioral Intention

SCALE DESCRIPTION: The semantic differential scale measures the stated inclination of a person to engage in a specified behavior. In most of the studies described below the behavior was a purchase but the items are general enough to refer to non-purchase behaviors as well (e.g., likelihood of shopping at a store, paying attention to an ad, using a coupon). One version of the scale used by Machleit, Allen, and Madden (1993) (referred to as *contact intention*) measured the motivation to try the brand if in the market for the product. Some have used the scale to measure *patronage intention* (Day and Stafford 1997; Stafford 1996; Wakefield and Baker 1998) while Urbany et al. (1997) adjusted it to measure *willingness to rent an apartment*. The various versions of the scale differ in the number and set of items employed as well as the scale stem. However, the uses are similar in that they have multiple items in common.

SCALE ORIGIN: Little information was provided in most of the studies about the origin of the particular sets of items they used. Since it is unlikely that they would have independently arrived at such similar sets of items, they must have, instead, built upon some unspecified source and from each other. The books by Fishbein (Fishbein and Ajzen 1975; Ajzen and Fishbein 1980) are possible sources although only item #1 (below) figures prominently in those books as a way to measure behavioral intention.

Taylor, Miracle, and Wilson (1997) developed a Korean version of the scale using the back-translation method.

RELIABILITY: Reported internal consistencies have tended to be very good and have ranged from .80 (Zhang and Buda 1999) to .99 (Jones, Mothersbaugh, and Beatty 2000).

VALIDITY: In none of the studies was the scale's validity fully addressed. Although not specifically examining the validity of behavioral intention, Machleit, Allen, and Madden (1993) used confirmatory factor analysis to provide evidence that another measure (brand interest) and two measures of behavioral intention (purchase and contact) were not measures of the same construct (discriminant validity). Similarly, a couple of tests generally described by Urbany et al. (1997) provided support for a claim of discriminant validity for the scale but the details relative to this particular scale were not given.

A correlation matrix was provided by MacKenzie and Spreng (1992) between the items in the behavioral intention scale as well as several others that sheds some limited light on the issue of validity. For example, the inter-correlations of the intention scale items ranged between .47 and .88 which provides some evidence that the items are measuring the same thing. In contrast, the correlations between the intention items and items measuring related but theoretically distinct constructs were much lower.

Based on the CFA and other tests that were conducted on this and other scales, both Jones, Mothersbaugh, and Beatty (2000) as well as Madrigal (2000) concluded that their versions of the scale were unidimensional and showed evidence of discriminant validity.

COMMENTS: See also Dabholkar (1994), Dabholkar, Thorpe, and Rentz (1996), Lim, Darley, and Summers (1994), Prakash (1992), Schuhwerk & Lefkoff-Hagius (1995), and Tripp, Jensen, and Carlson (1994).

REFERENCES:

Ajzen, Icek and Martin Fishbein (1980), *Understanding Attitudes and Predicting Social Behavior*, Englewood Cliffs, NJ: Prentice-Hall Inc.

Bruner II, Gordon C. and Anand Kumar (2000), "Web Commercials and Advertising Hierarchy-of-Effects," *JAR*, 40 (Jan-Apr), 35–42.

Chattopadhyay, Amitava and Kunal Basu (1990), "Humor in Advertising: The Moderating Role of Prior Brand Evaluation," *JMR*, 27 (November), 466–476.

Dabholkar, Pratibha (1994), "Incorporating Choice into an Attitudinal Framework: Analyzing Models of Mental Comparison Processes," *JCR*, 21 (June), 100–118.

Dabholkar, Pratibha, Dayle I. Thorpe, and Joseph O. Rentz (1996), "A Measure of Service Quality for Retail Stores: Scale Development and Validation," *JAMS*, 24 (Winter), 3–16.

Day, Ellen and Marla Royne Stafford (1997), "Age-Related Cues in Retail Services Advertising: Their Effects on Younger Consumers," *JR*, 73 (2), 211–233.

Fishbein, Martin and Icek Ajzen (1975), *Belief, Attitude, Intention, and Behavior: An Introduction to Theory and Research*, Reading, Mass.: Addison-Wesley.

Gill, James D., Sanford Grossbart, and Russell N. Laczniak (1988), "Influence of Involvement, Commitment and Familiarity on Brand Beliefs and Attitudes of Viewers Exposed to Alternative Claim Strategies," *JA*, 17 (2), 33–43.

Goldsmith, Ronald E., Barbara A. Lafferty, and Stephen J. Newell (2001), "The Impact of Corporate Credibility and Celebrity Credibility on Consumer Reaction to Advertisements and Brands," *JA*, 29 (3), 30–54.

Gotlieb, Jerry B. and Dan Sarel (1991), "Comparative Advertising Effectiveness: The Role of Involvement and Source Credibility," *JA*, 20 (1), 38–45.

Gotlieb, Jerry B. and Dan Sarel (1992), "The Influence of Type of Advertisement, Price, and Source Credibility on Percieved Quality," *JAMS*, 20 (Summer), 253–260.

Grossbart, Sanford, Darrel D. Muehling, and Norman Kangun (1986), "Verbal and Visual References to Competition in Comparative Advertising," *JA*, 15 (1), 10–23.

Homer, Pamela M. (1995), "Ad Size as an Indicator of Perceived Advertising Costs and Effort: The Effects on Memory and Perceptions," *JA*, 24 (Winter), 1–12.

Jones, Michael A., David L. Mothersbaugh, and Sharon E. Beatty (2000), "Switching Barriers and Repurchase Intentions in Services," *JR*, 79 (2), 259–274.

Lacher, Kathleen T. and Richard Mizerski (1994), "An Exploratory Study of the Responses and Relationships Involved in the Evaluation of, and in the Intention to Purchase New Rock Music," *JCR*, 21 (September), 366–380.

Lim, Jeen-Su, William K. Darley, and John O. Summers (1994), "An Assessment of Country of Origin Effects Under Alternative Presentation Formats," *JAMS*, 22 (3), 272–282.

Machleit, Karen A., Chris T. Allen, and Thomas J. Madden (1993), "The Mature Brand and Brand Interest: An Alternative Consequence of Ad-Evoked Affect," *JM*, 57 (October), 72–82.

MacKenzie, Scott B., Richard J. Lutz, and George E. Belch (1986), "The Role of Attitude Toward the Ad as a Mediator of Advertising Effectiveness: A Test of Competing Explanations," *JMR*, 23 (May), 130–143.

MacKenzie, Scott B. and Richard A. Spreng (1992), "How Does Motivation Moderate the Impact of Central and Peripheral Processing on Brand Attitudes and Intentions," *JCR*, 18 (March), 519–529.

Madrigal, Robert (2000), "The Influence of Social Alliances with Sports Teams on Intentions to Purchase Corporate Sponsors' Products," *JA*, 29 (Winter), 13–24.

Netemeyer, Richard G. and William O. Bearden (1992), "A Comparative Analysis of Two Models of Behavioral Intention," *JAMS*, 20 (Winter), 49–59.

Oliver, Richard L. and William O. Bearden (1985), "Crossover Effects in the Theory of Reasoned Action: A Moderating Influence Attempt," *JCR*, 12 (December), 324–340.

Prakash, Ved (1992), "Sex Roles and Advertising Preferences," *JAR*, 32 (May/June), 43–52.

Schuhwerk, Melody E. and Roxanne Lefkoff-Hagius (1995), "Green or Non-Green? Does Type of Appeal Matter When Advertising a Green Product?" *JA*, 24 (Summer), 45–54.

Shimp, Terence A. and Subhash Sharma (1987), "Consumer Ethnocentrism: Construction and Validation of The CETSCALE," *JMR*, 24 (August), 280–289.

Simpson, Penny M., Steve Horton, and Gene Brown (1996), "Male Nudity in Advertisements: A Modified Replication and Extension of Gender and Product Effects," *JAMS*, 24 (Summer), 257–262.

Singh, Mandeep, Siva K. Balasubramanian, and Goutam Chakraborty (2000), "A Comparative Analysis of Three Communication Formats: Advertising, Infomercial, and Direct Experience," *JA*, 29 (Winter), 59–75.

Singh, Surendra N. and Catherine Cole (1993), "The Effects of Length, Content, and Repetition on Television Commercial Effectiveness," *JMR*, 30 (February), 91–104.

Singh, Surendra N., V. Parker Lessig, Dongwook Kim, Reetika Gupta, and Mary Ann Hocutt (2000), "Does Your Ad Have Too Many Pictures?" *JAR*, 40 (Jan-Apr), 11–27.

Stafford, Marla Royne (1996), "Tangibility in Services Advertising: An Investigation of Verbal versus Visual Cues," *JA*, 25 (Fall), 13–28.

Stafford, Marla Royne and Ellen Day (1995), "Retail Services Advertising: The Effects of Appeal, Medium, and Service," *JA*, 24 (Spring), 57–71.

Stevenson, Julie, Gordon C. Bruner II, and Anand Kumar (2000), "Webpage Background and Viewer Attitudes," *JAR*, 40 (January/April), 29–34.

Szymanski, David M (2001), "Modality and Offering Effects in Sales Presentations for a Good Versus a Service," *JAMS*, 29 (2), 179–189.

Taylor, Charles R., Gordon E. Miracle, and R. Dale Wilson (1997), "The Impact of Information Level on the Effectiveness of U.S. and Korean Television Commercials," *JA*, 26 (Spring), 1–18.

Till, Brian D. and Michael Busler (2001), "The Match-Up Hypothesis: Physical Attractiveness, Expertise, and the Role of Fit on Brand Attitude, Purchase Intent and Brand Beliefs," *JA*, 29 (3), 1–14.

Tripp, Carolyn, Thomas D. Jensen, and Les Carlson (1994), "The Effects of Multiple Product Endorsements by Celebrities on Consumers' Attitudes and Intentions," *JCR*, 20 (March), 535–547.

Urbany, Joel E., William O. Bearden, Ajit Kaicker, and Melinda Smith-de Borrero (1997), "Transaction Utility Effects When Quality is Uncertain," *JAMS*, 25 (Winter), 45–55.

Wakefield, Kirk L. and Julie Baker (1998), "Excitement at the Mall: Determinants and Effects on Shopping Response," *JR*, 74 (4), 515–539.

Yi, Youjae (1990a), "Cognitive and Affective Priming Effects of the Context for Print Advertisements," *JA*, 19 (2), 40–48.

Yi, Youjae (1990b), "The Effects of Contextual Priming in Print Advertisements," *JCR*, 17 (September), 215–222.

Zhang, Yong (1996), "Responses to Humorous Advertising: The Moderating Effect of Need for Cognition," *JA*, 25 (Spring), 15–32.

Zhang, Yong and Richard Buda (1999), "Moderating Effects of Need for Cognition on Responses to Positively versus Negatively Framed Advertising Messages," *JA*, 28 (2), 1–15.

SCALE ITEMS: [1]

1. unlikely / likely

2. non-existent / existent

3. improbable / probable

4. impossible / possible

5. uncertain / certain

6. definitely would not use / definitely would use

7. not at all / very frequent

8. no chance / certain chance

9. probably not / probably

Bruner and Kumar (2000): 1, 3, 4 7-point [.91]
Chattopadhyay and Basu (1990): 1, 3, 4 [.93]
Dabholkar (1994): 1, 4, 6 mixed points [.87 & .90]
Day and Stafford (1997): 1, 3, 4 7-point [.93 & .95]
Gill, Grossbart, and Laczniak (1988) 1, 2, 3, 4 [.861]
Goldsmith, Lafferty and Newell (2001): 1*, 3, 4 7-point [.92]
Gotlieb and Sarel (1991, 1992): 1, 3, 4 [.89 & .93]
Grossbart, Muehling, and Kangun (1986): 1, 3, 5 [.92]
Homer (1995): 1*, 3*, 4* 9-point [.97]
Jones, Mothersbaugh, and Beatty (2000): 1, 3*, 4, 8 10-point [.99]
Lacher and Mizerski (1994): 1, 3, 4 6-point [.92 & .94]
Lim, Darley, and Summers (1994): 1, 3, 4 [.90-.94]
Machleit, Allen, and Madden (1993): 1, 3, 4 [>.95]
MacKenzie, Lutz, and Belch (1986): 1, 3, 4 [.88 & .90]
MacKensie and Spreng (1992): 1, 3, 4 [.88]
Madrigal (2000): 1, 3, 8 7-point [.81]
Netemeyer and Bearden (1992): 1, 3, 4 [.91& .90]
Oliver and Bearden (1985): 1, 3, 4, 5 [.87]
Shimp and Sharma (1987): 1, 3, 5 [.84]
Simpson, Horton, and Brown (1996): 1, 3, 4 9-point [.96]
Singh, Balasubramanian, and Chakraborty (2000): 1, 3, 4 7-point [.95 & .93]
Singh and Cole (1993): 1, 3, 4 [.93]
Singh et al. (2000): 1, 3, 4 7-point [.95]
Stafford (1996): 1, 3, 4 7-point [.94]
Stafford and Day (1995): 1, 3, 4 7-point [.94]
Stevenson, Bruner, and Kumar (2000): 1, 3, 4 7-point [.95]
Szymanski (2001): 1*, 6*, 9 7-point [.94]
Taylor, Miracle, and Wilson (1997): 1, 3, 4 7-point [.98 & .97]
Till and Busler (2000): 1, 3, 6* 9-point [.95 & .96]
Tripp, Jensen, and Carlson (1994): 1, 2, 3, 4 7-point [.93]
Urbany et al. (1997): 1, 3, 5, 6* mixed points [.91]
Wakefield and Baker (1998): 1, 3, 4, 7 7-point [.96]
Yi (1990a, 1990b): 1, 3, 4 [.89 & .92]
Zhang (1996): 1, 3, 4 9-point [.80]
Zhang and Buda (1999): 1, 3, 4 7-point [.80]

[1] An asterisk (*) indicates that the actual item used in the indicated study varied somewhat from that shown in the list. Scale stems have varied depending upon the object of the intention.

SCALE NAME: Behavioral Intention

SCALE DESCRIPTION: The three-item, nine-point scale measures the likelihood that a person will use some object again. The statements appear to be amenable for use with a variety of objects such as goods, services, facilities, and even people.

SCALE ORIGIN: The scale was developed by Cronin, Brady, and Hult (2000) based on similar statements used previously in services research.

RELIABILITY: Cronin, Brady, and Hult (2000) reported a construct reliability of .87 for the scale.

VALIDITY: Confirmatory factor analysis was conducted by Cronin, Brady, and Hult (2000) on this scale and several others. Some evidence of the scale's discriminant validity came from noting that the average variance extracted (68%) was greater than the shared variances with the other constructs (Fornell and Larcker 1981).

COMMENTS: Based on the combined sample from six different service industries (n = 1,944), the scale had a mean of 7.08 and a standard deviation of 1.79.

REFERENCES:

Cronin, Jr., J. Joseph, Michael K. Brady, and G. Tomas M. Hult (2000), "Assessing the Effects of Quality, Value, and Customer Satisfaction on Consumer Behavioral Intentions in Service Environments," *JR*, 79 (2), 193–218.

Fornell, Claes and David F. Larcker (1981), "Evaluating Structural Equation Models with Unobservable Variables and Measurement Error," *JMR*, 18 (February), 39–50.

SCALE ITEMS: [1]

1. The probability that I will use this _____ again is:

2. The likelihood that I would recommend this _____ to a friend is:

3. If I had to do it over again, I would make the same choice.

---

[1] A nine-point response scale was used by Cronin, Brady, and Hult (2000) with anchors of *very low* and *very high*. The blanks should be filled with the name of the object of interest. The object of interest to Cronin, Brady, and Hult (2000) was "facility's services."

#94 *Bored*

SCALE NAME: Bored

SCALE DESCRIPTION: The scale measures the degree to which one reports a low degree of arousal, specifically feeling sluggish and drowsy. It appears like the scale can be used to measure the emotional response to a stimulus (e.g., Mano and Oliver 1993) or more as a mood that one has felt prior to being exposed to a stimulus (e.g., Mano 1999).

SCALE ORIGIN: Although not expressly indicated by Mano and Oliver (1993), the items appear to have been used first as a summated scale by Mano (1991). In his study with 224 college students the scale was reported to have an alpha of .87. Cluster and factor analyses grouped these three items together by themselves.

Mano (1999) expressly identified his earlier work (1991) as the source of the scale although items #4 and #5 were not part of it.

RELIABILITY: An alpha of .80 was reported for the version of the scale used by Mano and Oliver (1993). Alphas of .84 and .86 were reported for the version of the scale used by Mano (1999) in pre-task and post-task assessments, respectively.

VALIDITY: The validity of the scale was not specifically addressed in either study. Mano (1999) did indicate, however, that factor analysis supported a one factor solution.

REFERENCES:
Mano, Haim (1991), "The Structure and Intensity of Emotional Experiences: Method and Context Convergence," *Multivariate Behavioral Research*, 26 (3), 149–172.
Mano, Haim (1999), "The Influence of Pre-Existing Negative Affect on Store Purchase Intentions," *JR*, 75 (2), 149–172.
Mano, Haim and Richard L. Oliver (1993), "Assessing the Dimensionality and Structure of the Consumption Experience: Evaluation, Feeling, and Satisfaction," *JCR*, 20 (December), 451–466.

SCALE ITEMS: [1]

1. sleepy

2. sluggish

3. drowsy

4. bored

5. tired

---

[1] Both studies used a five-point response format. Mano and Oliver (1993) used items #1 to #3 and indicated that the anchors were *not at all* and *very much*. Mano (1999) used all five items but did not specify the anchors on the response scale.

SCALE NAME: Boycott Issue Importance

SCALE DESCRIPTION: Four statements and a seven-point response scale are used to assess a person's concern about activities a company is engaged in that are the basis for a boycott it is experiencing.

SCALE ORIGIN: The source of the scale was not specified but it appears to be original to Sen, Gurhan-Canli, and Morwitz (2001).

RELIABILITY: An alpha of .91 (n = 166) was reported for the scale by Sen, Gurhan-Canli, and Morwitz (2001).

VALIDITY: No examination of the scale's validity was described in the article by Sen, Gurhan-Canli, and Morwitz (2001).

REFERENCES:
Sen, Sankar, Zeynep Gurhan-Canli, and Vicki Morwitz (2001), "Withholding Consumption: A Social Dilemma Perspective on Consumer Boycotts," *JCR*, 28 (December), 399–417.

SCALE ITEMS: [1]

1. How much or how little do you care about the issue over which _____ is being boycotted?
   Do not care at all / care a great deal

2. To what extent are you concerned about _____?
   Not at all concerned / extremely concerned

3. How bothered are you by the reported _____?
   Not at all bothered / extremely bothered

4. How important or unimportant is it to you that firms such as _____ avoid _____?
   not at all important / extremely important

[1] The name of the company should be placed in the blank of #1 and the first blank of #4. The other blanks of #2-#4 are for a phrase describing a boycott issue, e.g., animal testing practices.

SCALE NAME: Boycott Likelihood

SCALE DESCRIPTION: The seven-point semantic differential scale is intended to measure a person's attitude toward a boycott of a specified marketer and propensity to engage in it personally.

SCALE ORIGIN: The source of the scale was not specified but it appears to be original to Sen, Gurhan-Canli, and Morwitz (2001). A five-item version was used in their first study while a seven-item version was used in the second study.

RELIABILITY: Alphas of .92 (n = 147) and .96 (n = 166) were reported for the five- and seven-item versions, respectively (Sen, Gurhan-Canli, and Morwitz 2001).

VALIDITY: No examination of the scale's validity was described in the article by Sen, Gurhan-Canli, and Morwitz (2001).

COMMENTS: Given that the seven-item version of the scale has three items measuring intention and four measuring attitude it seems possible that the scale is not unidimensional. This issue should be clarified in future research.

REFERENCES:
Sen, Sankar (2003), Personal Correspondence.
Sen, Sankar, Zeynep Gurhan-Canli, and Vicki Morwitz (2001), "Withholding Consumption: A Social Dilemma Perspective on Consumer Boycotts," *JCR*, 28 (December), 399–417.

SCALE ITEMS: [1]

Based on the information you just read, how likely or unlikely would you be
to participate in this boycott?

1. Definitely not boycott / definitely boycott

2. Extremely unlikely / extremely likely

3. Not at all probable / highly probable

Based on what you just read, how do you feel about boycotting _____?

4. Very negative / very positive

5. Not at all favorable / very favorable

6. Very bad idea / very good idea

7. Not at all useful / very useful

[1] The scale instructions were provided by Sen (2003). Items 1, 4-7 were used in study 1 and study 2 used all of the items. The object of the boycott should be placed in the blank shown before item 4, e.g., *the movie theaters, P&G*.

SCALE NAME: Brand Belief

SCALE DESCRIPTION: Three, seven-point semantic differentials are used to measure one's belief that a specified product attribute is possessed by a product or set of products sharing the same brand name (family). The attributes studied by Loken and John (1993) were *gentleness* and *quality*. John, Loken, and Joiner (1998) examined *gentleness* and *hygienicness*. Ahluwalia, and Gurhan-Canli (2000) focused on *reliability*.

SCALE ORIGIN: The origin of the scale was not specified by Loken and John (1993) but appears to have been developed by them for their study. Ahluwalia and Gurhan-Canli (2000) did not specify the source of their scale but it does not seem likely that its similarity to the scales used by John, Loken, and Joiner (1998) and Loken and John (1993) was merely a coincidence.

RELIABILITY: An alpha of .95 was reported by Ahluwalia and Gurhan-Canli (2000). John, Loken, and Joiner (1998) reported alphas of .887 (study one, average over seven products), .95 (study one, family), .976 (study three, average over six products), and .929 (study three, family) with reference to the *gentleness* attribute. Likewise, John, Loken, and Joiner (1998) reported alphas of .97 (study two, average over five products), .94 (study two, family), .974 (study three, average over six products), and .92 (study three, family) with reference to how *hygienic* the products were perceived to be. Alphas of .92 and .97 were reported by Loken and John (1993) for the scale when measuring *gentleness* and *quality* attributes shared by a family of products, respectively.

VALIDITY: No evidence regarding the validity of the scale was reported in any of the studies.

REFERENCES:
Ahluwalia, Rohini and Zeynep Gurhan-Canli (2000), "The Effects of Extensions on the Family Brand Name: An Accessibility-Diagnosticity Perspective," *JCR*, 27 (3), 371–381.
John, Deborah Roedder, Barbara Loken, and Christopher Joiner (1998), "The Negative Impact of Extensions: Can Flagship Products Be Diluted?" *JM*, 62 (January), 19–32.
Loken, Barbara and Deborah Roedder John (1993), "Diluting Brand Beliefs: When Do Brand Extensions Have a Negative Impact," *JM*, 57 (July), 71–84.

SCALE ITEMS: [1]

Brand X is (Family X are) _____.

1. strongly disagree / strongly agree

2. extremely unlikely / extremely likely

3. not at all probable / very probable

---

[1] The specific product brand name (or family name) as well as the focal attribute should be specified in this phrase.

SCALE NAME: Brand Consciousness

SCALE DESCRIPTION: It is a three-item, five point Likert-type summated ratings scale measuring the degree to which a person expresses a desire to buy "brand name products." The implication is that the consumer prefers nationally known brands rather than private distributor brands or generic goods.

SCALE ORIGIN: The source of the scale was not stated by Donthu and Gilliland (1996) but it is likely to be original to their study.

RELIABILITY: An alpha of .80 was reported for the scale by both Donthu and Gilliland (1996) as well as Donthu and Garcia (1999).

VALIDITY: No specific examination of the scale's validity was reported by Donthu and Gilliland (1996).

REFERENCES:
Donthu, Naveen and Adriana Garcia (1999), "The Internet Shopper," *JAR*, 39 (May/June), 52–58.
Donthu, Naveen and David Gilliland (1996), "The Infomercial Shopper," *JAR*, 36 (March/April), 69–76.

SCALE ITEMS:

1. I usually purchase brand name products.

2. Store brands are of poor quality. (r)

3. All brands are about the same. (r)

SCALE NAME: Brand Distinctiveness

SCALE DESCRIPTION: The scale is composed of six, five-point Likert-type statements measuring brand associations with an emphasis on the consumer's awareness of the brand and the extent to which it stands out in his/her own mind.

SCALE ORIGIN: Although Yoo, Donthu, and Lee (2000) may have drawn inspiration from previous measures, ultimately their scale appears to be original to them.

RELIABILITY: Yoo, Donthu, and Lee (2000) reported the scale to have a composite reliability of .94.

VALIDITY: Factor analyses (EFA and CFA) were used to check the dimensionality of this scale along with eight others used in the study. Based on the results, the authors concluded that all items loaded on their respective factors as expected providing some sense of the scales' convergent and discriminant validities. The average variance extracted for this scale was .72.

REFERENCES:
Yoo, Boonghee, Naveen Donthu, and Sungho Lee (2000), "An Examination of Selected Marketing Mix Elements and Brand Equity," *JAMS*, 28 (2), 195–211.

SCALE ITEMS: [1]

1. I know what _____ looks like.

2. I can recognize _____ among competing brands.

3. I am aware of _____.

4. Some characteristics of _____ come to mind quickly.

5. I can quickly recall the symbol or logo of _____.

6. I have difficulty in imagining _____ in my mind. (r)

[1] The brand name of a product was placed in the blanks by Yoo, Donthu, and Lee (2000).

SCALE NAME: Brand Equity

SCALE DESCRIPTION: The scale is composed of four, five-point Likert-type statements measuring the relative value of a specified brand to a consumer compared to similar competing brands due to its name (above and beyond its features and quality).

SCALE ORIGIN: Yoo, Donthu, and Lee (2000) generated 18 items based upon their definition of the construct. They attempted to emphasize in the items that all product characteristics except the name were the same. Ultimately, 14 of the items were not retained for the final version of the scale since they did not significantly contribute to the scale's reliability.

RELIABILITY: Yoo, Donthu, and Lee (2000) reported the scale to have a composite reliability of .93.

VALIDITY: Factor analyses (EFA and CFA) were used to check the dimensionality of this scale along with eight others used in the study. Based on the results, the authors concluded that all items loaded on their respective factors as expected providing some sense of the scales' convergent and discriminant validities. The average variance extracted for this scale was .77.

REFERENCES:
Yoo, Boonghee, Naveen Donthu, and Sungho Lee (2000), "An Examination of Selected Marketing Mix Elements and Brand Equity," *JAMS*, 28 (2), 195–211.

SCALE ITEMS: [1]

1. It makes sense to buy _____ instead of any other brand, even if they are the same.

2. Even if another brand has the same features as _____, I would prefer to buy _____.

3. If there is another brand as good as _____, I prefer to buy _____.

4. If another brand is not different from _____ in any way, it seems smarter to purchase _____.

[1] The brand name of a product was placed in the blanks by Yoo, Donthu, and Lee (2000).

SCALE NAME: Brand Extension Fit

SCALE DESCRIPTION: Four, seven-point semantic differentials are used to measure one's opinion of the degree to which a new brand by a company is consistent with the image of other products by the company with the same name. The scale was called a *discrepancy index* by Ahluwalia and Gurhan-Canli (2000).

SCALE ORIGIN: Although not stated explicitly, the scale appears to be original to the study by John, Loken, and Joiner (1998). Similarly, the source was not specified by Ahluwalia and Gurhan-Canli (2000). However, given that the items were basically the same in both studies it is unlikely that they originated from different sources.

RELIABILITY: An alpha of .90 (n = 39) was reported by Ahluwalia and Gurhan-Canli (2000). John, Loken, and Joiner (1998) reported alphas of .974, .963, .977 for the scale as used in studies one (n = 101), two (n = 118), and three (n = 116), respectively.

VALIDITY: No evidence regarding the validity of the scale was reported by Ahluwalia and Gurhan-Canli (2000) or John, Loken, and Joiner (1998).

REFERENCES:
Ahluwalia, Rohini and Zeynep Gurhan-Canli (2000), "The Effects of Extensions on the Family Brand Name: An Accessibility-Diagnosticity Perspective," *JCR*, 27 (3), 371–381.
John, Deborah Roedder, Barbara Loken, and Christopher Joiner (1998), "The Negative Impact of Extensions: Can Flagship Products Be Diluted?" *JM*, 62 (January), 19–32.

SCALE ITEMS: [1]

Using the phrases below, please indicate how you think _____ compares to the image of _____.

1. consistent / inconsistent

2. similar / different

3. representative / unrepresentative

4. typical / atypical

[1] The scale stem was not provided by Ahluwalia and Gurhan-Canli (2000) nor John, Loken, and Joiner (1998) but could have been something like this. The first blank should have the name of the brand extension whereas the last blank has the name of the company or the family brand name.

SCALE NAME: Brand Extension Fit

SCALE DESCRIPTION: The scale is composed of five, seven-point statements that assess the appropriateness of a new product being introduced by a company to carry the same brand name as a previous product by the company.

SCALE ORIGIN: The scale is apparently original to Bridges, Keller, and Sood (2000).

RELIABILITY: An alpha of .95 was reported for the scale (Bridges, Keller, and Sood 2000).

VALIDITY: No explicit examination of the scale's validity was provided by Bridges, Keller, and Sood (2000).

REFERENCES:
Bridges, Sheri (2003), Personal Correspondence.
Bridges, Sheri, Kevin Lane Keller, and Sanjay Sood (2000), "Communication Strategies for Brand Extensions: Enhancing Perceived Fit by Establishing Explanatory Links," *JA*, 29 (Winter), 1–11.

SCALE ITEMS: [1]

1. How appropriate do you think a *product 2* is for the company that makes *brand-product 1*?
   Not at all appropriate / very appropriate for company

2. To what extent do you think it makes sense for *brand-product 1* and *product 2* to have the same brand name?
   Makes no sense at all / makes a lot of sense

3. What do you think about the fit between the *brand-product 2* and the company that makes it?
   Bad fit between company and product / good fit between company and product

4. How well do you think you understand the relationship or connection between *brand-product 1* and *brand-product 2*?
   Don't understand at all / understand very well

5. How confident are you that you can explain why the makers of *brand-product 1* are planning to introduce a *product 2* under the same brand name?
   Not at all confident / extremely confident

---

[1] The items were provided by Bridges (2003). The italicized words in each statement should be replaced with either the brand name and/or the generic product name as shown. Sometimes both are used and sometimes just one.

SCALE NAME: Brand Extension Fit

SCALE DESCRIPTION: The seven-item, seven-point scale measures the extent to which a person views a proposed new product with the same name as a familiar product as being similar in numerous ways.

SCALE ORIGIN: Although bearing some conceptual similarity to measures that had been developed previously by Smith (Smith and Andrews 1995; Smith and Park 1992), this scale appears to be original to the study by Klink and Smith (2001). (See V. III, #660 and #901.)

RELIABILITY: Alphas of .91 (study one) and .93 (study two) were reported for the scale in Klink and Smith (2001).

VALIDITY: The only information bearing on the scale's validity reported by Klink and Smith (2001) was that the scale had a strong correlation (r = .74) with a measure of the general similarity between a brand extension and its parent (Loken and Ward 1987).

REFERENCES:

Klink, Richard R (2004), Personal Correspondence.

Klink, Richard R. and Daniel C. Smith (2001), "Threats to the External Validity of Brand Extension Research," *JMR*, 38 (August), 326–335.

Loken, Barbara and James Ward (1987), "Measures of Attribute Structure Underlying Product Typicality," in *Advances in Consumer Research, V. 14*, M. Wallendorf and P.F. Anderson, eds., Provo, UT: Association for Consumer Research, 22–28.

Smith, Daniel C. and C. Whan Park (1992), "The Effects of Brand Extensions on Market Share and Advertising Efficiency," *JMR*, 29 (August), 296–313.

Smith, Daniel C. and Jonlee Andrews (1995), "Rethinking the Effect of Perceived Fit on Customers' Evaluations of New Products," *JAMS*, 23 (1), 4–14.

SCALE ITEMS: [1]

Please indicate how similar you believe _____ are to _____'s existing products in terms of the following characteristics:

1. Component parts

2. Product features

3. Product functions

4. Needs they satisfy

5. Usage situations

6. Manufacturing processes

7. Servicing

[1] The scale stem was provided by Klink (2004). The generic name of the new product is placed in the first blank (e.g., smoke detectors) and the name of the company (or familiar brand, e.g., Maytag) is placed in the second blank. Anchors on the seven-point response scale were *not very similar* and *very similar*.

#104 *Brand Extension Fit (Usage-Based)*

SCALE NAME: Brand Extension Fit (Usage-Based)

SCALE DESCRIPTION: The scale is composed of three statements attempting to assess a consumer's perception of the similarity of two products based on when/how they are used, such as a well-known core brand and a proposed extension.

SCALE ORIGIN: Martin and Stewart (2001) stated that their scale was based on measures used by Chakravarti, MacInnis, and Nakamoto (1989) as well as Ratneshwar and Shocker (1991). Those previous studies used one item measures of product similarity thus, this multi-item scale appears to be original to Martin and Stewart (2001).

RELIABILITY: The alpha for the scale was .82 (Martin and Stewart 2001).

VALIDITY: The typical aspects of scale validity were not provided by Martin and Stewart (2001) although some information bearing on the scale's nomological validity was discussed.

REFERENCES:

Chakravarti, Dipankar, Deborah J. MacInnis, and Kent Nakamoto (1989), "Product Category Perceptions, Elaborative Processing and Brand Name Extension Strategies," in *Advances in Consumer Research, V. 17*, Thomas Srull, ed., Provo, UT: Association for Consumer Research, 910–916.

Martin, Ingrid M. and David W. Stewart (2001), "The Differential Impact of Goal Congruency on Attitudes, Intentions, and the Transfer of Brand Equity," *JMR*, 38 (November), 471–484.

Ratneshwar, Srinivsan and Allan D. Shocker (1991), "Substitution in Use and the Role of Usage Context in Product Category Structures," *JMR*, 28 (August), 281–95.

SCALE ITEMS: [1]

1. How similar are _____ and _____ in terms of how/when they are used?
   not at all similar / very similar

2. How likely are you to use _____ and _____ together?
   Not at all likely / very likely

3. How appropriate is it to use _____ to _____?
   not at all appropriate / very appropriate

---

[1] The blanks in the first two items are filled with the names for (or descriptions of) the core brand and the extension. As used by Martin and Stewart (2001), the first blank in item 3 refers to the brand while the second blank refers to a usage context, e.g., *how appropriate is it to use Reebok athletic wear to exercise?*

SCALE NAME: Brand Parity

SCALE DESCRIPTION: Four, seven-point Likert-type statements are used to assess a consumer's opinion regarding the extent to which all brands in a specified product category are of similar quality and there are no meaningful differences. The scale was referred to by Batra and Sinha (2000) as *degree of quality variation in category*.

SCALE ORIGIN: The source of the scale was not identified by Batra and Sinha (2000) but it would appear to be original to their study.

RELIABILITY: An alpha of .88 was reported for the scale by Batra and Sinha (2000).

VALIDITY: Some typical tests of convergent and discriminant validity were conducted by Batra and Sinha (2000) using confirmatory factor analysis. Although two of the four scales they used had some problems, this one did not. Evidence was provided of its convergent and discriminant validities and its average variance extracted was .65.

REFERENCES:
Batra, Rajeev and Indrajit Sinha (2000), "Consumer-Level Factors Moderating the Success of Private Label Brands," *JR*, 79 (2), 175–191.

SCALE ITEMS: [1]

1. All brands of _____ are basically the same in quality.

2. I don't think that there are any significant differences among different brands of _____ in terms of quality.

3. _____ brands do not vary a lot in terms of quality.

4. There are only minor variations among brands of _____ in terms of quality.

[1] Within each item the blank should be filled with the name of the product category of interest.

SCALE NAME: Brand Personality (Competence)

SCALE DESCRIPTION: The scale is composed of nine-items and a five-point response format indicating the degree to which a consumer views a brand as having personality-like characteristics typified by the following facets: reliable, intelligent, and successful.

SCALE ORIGIN: The scale was constructed by Aaker (1997) as part of a larger set of 42 items which were proposed for the measurement of five brand-personality dimensions. She viewed these measures as being distinct from those of product-related attributes which are more utilitarian in function. In contrast, brand personality is supposed to serve a symbolic or self-expressive function. Before conducting the two initial studies, two pretests were used to reduce an initial list of items (309) to something more manageable (114).

RELIABILITY: An alpha of .93 was reported for the scale by Aaker (1997) based upon data from the first study. With data from a subsample of the first study's respondents (n = 81), the scale's stability (two month test-retest reliability) was estimated to be .76. Aaker (1999) reported an alpha level between .92 and .98 (Study 2).

VALIDITY: Aaker (1997) indicated that a variety of steps and analyses were taken with data from both Study 1 and 2 that provided support for the stability of the five-factor structure represented in the full set of 42 items.

COMMENTS: Using the combined results of Studies 1 and 2, Aaker (1997) reported the mean and standard deviation for this scale to be 3.17 and 1.02, respectively.

REFERENCES:
Aaker, Jennifer L. (1997), "Dimensions of Brand Personality," *JMR*, 34 (August), 347–356.
Aaker, Jennifer L. (1999), "The Malleable Self: The Role of Self-Expression in Persuasion," *JMR*, 36 (February), 45–57.

SCALE ITEMS: [1]

1. reliable

2. hard-working

3. secure

4. intelligent

5. technical

6. corporate

7. successful

8. leader

9. confident

[1] A five-point response format was used with *not at all descriptive* and *extremely descriptive* as the verbal anchors.

SCALE NAME: Brand Personality (Excitement)

SCALE DESCRIPTION: The scale is composed of eleven items and a five-point response format indicating the degree to which a consumer views a brand as having personality-like characteristics typified by the following facets: daring, spirited, imaginative, and up-to-date.

SCALE ORIGIN: The scale was constructed by Aaker (1997) as part of a larger set of 42 items which were proposed for the measurement of five brand-personality dimensions. She viewed these measures as being distinct from those of product-related attributes which are more utilitarian in function. In contrast, brand personality is supposed to serve a symbolic or self-expressive function. Before conducting the two initial studies, two pretests were used to reduce an initial list of items (309) to something more manageable (114).

RELIABILITY: An alpha of .95 was reported for the scale by Aaker (1997) based upon data from the first study. With data from a subsample of the first study's respondents (n = 81), the scale's stability (two month test-retest reliability) was estimated to be .74. In a later set of studies, .90 (Study 1) and something between .92 and .98 (Study 2) were the levels of alpha reported (Aaker 1999).

VALIDITY: Aaker (1997) indicated that a variety of steps and analyses were taken with data from both Study 1 and 2 that provided support for the stability of the five-factor structure represented in the full set of 42 items.

COMMENTS: Using the combined results of Studies 1 and 2, Aaker (1997) reported the mean and standard deviation for this scale to be 2.79 and 1.05, respectively.

REFERENCES:
Aaker, Jennifer L. (1997), "Dimensions of Brand Personality," *JMR*, 34 (August), 347–356.
Aaker, Jennifer L. (1999), "The Malleable Self: The Role of Self-Expression in Persuasion," *JMR*, 36 (February), 45–57.

SCALE ITEMS: [1]

1. daring

2. trendy

3. exciting

4. spirited

5. cool

6. young

7. imaginative

8. unique

9. up-to-date

10. independent

11. contemporary

---

[1] A five-point response format was used with *not at all descriptive* and *extremely descriptive* as the verbal anchors.

SCALE NAME: Brand Personality (Ruggedness)

SCALE DESCRIPTION: The scale is composed of five items and a five-point response format indicating the degree to which a consumer views a brand as having personality-like characteristics typified by toughness and masculinity.

SCALE ORIGIN: The scale was constructed by Aaker (1997) as part of a larger set of 42 items which were proposed for the measurement of five brand-personality dimensions. She viewed these measures as being distinct from those of product-related attributes which are more utilitarian in function. In contrast, brand personality is supposed to serve a symbolic or self-expressive function. Before conducting the two initial studies, two pretests were used to reduce an initial list of items (309) to something more manageable (114).

RELIABILITY: An alpha of **.90** was reported for the scale by Aaker (1997) based upon data from the first study. With data from a subsample of the first study's respondents (n = 81), the scale's stability (two month test-retest reliability) was estimated to be .77. In a later set of studies, .96 (Study 1) and something between .92 and .98 (Study 2) were the levels of alpha reported (Aaker 1999).

VALIDITY: Aaker (1997) indicated that a variety of steps and analyses were taken with data from both Study 1 and 2 that provided support for the stability of the five-factor structure represented in the full set of 42 items.

COMMENTS: Using the combined results of Studies 1 and 2, the mean and standard deviation for this scale was reported to be 2.49 and 1.08, respectively (Aaker 1997).

REFERENCES:
Aaker, Jennifer L. (1997), "Dimensions of Brand Personality," *JMR*, 34 (August), 347–356.
Aaker, Jennifer L. (1999), "The Malleable Self: The Role of Self-Expression in Persuasion," *JMR*, 36 (February), 45–57.

SCALE ITEMS: [1]

1. outdoorsy

2. masculine

3. Western

4. tough

5. rugged

[1] A five-point response format was used with *not at all descriptive* and *extremely descriptive* as the verbal anchors.

SCALE NAME: Brand Personality (Sincerity)

SCALE DESCRIPTION: The scale is composed of eleven items and a five-point response format indicating the degree to which a consumer views a brand as having personality-like characteristics typified by the following facets: down-to-earth, honest, wholesome, and cheerful.

SCALE ORIGIN: The scale was constructed by Aaker (1997) as part of a larger set of 42 items which were proposed for the measurement of five brand-personality dimensions. She viewed these measures as being distinct from those of product-related attributes which are more utilitarian in function. In contrast, brand personality is supposed to serve a symbolic or self-expressive function. Before conducting the two initial studies, two pretests were used to reduce an initial list of items (309) to something more manageable (114).

RELIABILITY: An alpha of .93 was reported for the scale by Aaker (1997) based upon data from the first study. With data from a subsample of the first study's respondents (n = 81), the scale's stability (two month test-retest reliability) was estimated to be .75. Aaker (1999) reported an alpha level between .92 and .98 (Study 2).

VALIDITY: Aaker (1997) reported a variety of steps and analyses were taken with data from both Study 1 and 2 that provided support for the stability of the five-factor structure represented in the full set of 42 items.

COMMENTS: Using the combined results of Studies 1 and 2, Aaker (1997) indicated that the mean and standard deviation for this scale were 2.72 and .99, respectively.

REFERENCES:
Aaker, Jennifer L. (1997), "Dimensions of Brand Personality," *JMR*, 34 (August), 347–356.
Aaker, Jennifer L. (1999), "The Malleable Self: The Role of Self-Expression in Persuasion," *JMR*, 36 (February), 45–57.

SCALE ITEMS: [1]

1. down-to-earth
2. family-oriented
3. small-town
4. honest
5. sincere
6. real
7. wholesome
8. original
9. cheerful
10. sentimental
11. friendly

[1] A five-point response format was used with *not at all descriptive* and *extremely descriptive* as the verbal anchors.

SCALE NAME: Brand Personality (Sophistication)

SCALE DESCRIPTION: The scale is composed of six items and a five-point response format indicating the degree to which a consumer views a brand as having personality-like characteristics typified by good looks and charm.

SCALE ORIGIN: The scale was constructed by Aaker (1997) as part of a larger set of 42 items which were proposed for the measurement of five brand-personality dimensions. She viewed these measures as being distinct from those of product-related attributes which are more utilitarian in function. In contrast, brand personality is supposed to serve a symbolic or self-expressive function. Before conducting the two initial studies, two pretests were used to reduce an initial list of items (309) to something more manageable (114).

RELIABILITY: An alpha of .91 was reported for the scale by Aaker (1997) based upon data from the first study. With data from a subsample of the first study's respondents (n = 81), the scale's stability (two month test-retest reliability) was estimated to be .75. Aaker (1999) reported an alpha level between .92 and .98 (Study 2).

VALIDITY: Aaker (1997) indicated that a variety of steps and analyses were taken with data from both Study 1 and 2 that provided support for the stability of the five-factor structure represented in the full set of 42 items.

COMMENTS: Using the combined results of Studies 1 and 2, Aaker (1997) reported the mean and standard deviation for this scale to be 2.66 and 1.02, respectively.

REFERENCES:
Aaker, Jennifer L. (1997), "Dimensions of Brand Personality," *JMR*, 34 (August), 347–356.
Aaker, Jennifer L. (1999), "The Malleable Self: The Role of Self-Expression in Persuasion," *JMR*, 36 (February), 45–57.

SCALE ITEMS: [1]

1. upper class

2. glamorous

3. good looking

4. charming

5. feminine

6. smooth

---

[1] A five-point response format was used with *not at all descriptive* and *extremely descriptive* as the verbal anchors.

SCALE NAME: Brand Superiority

SCALE DESCRIPTION: Three semantic differentials are used to measure the degree to which a person believes that the information to which he/she has been exposed describes a product and its features in a positive manner and indicates it is better than the competition. The scale was referred to as an *information valence index* by Ahluwalia and Gürhan-Canli (2000) and *description index* by Gürhan-Canli and Maheswaran (2000b).

SCALE ORIGIN: The scale appears to be original to Maheswaran (1994). Aaker and Maheswaran (1997) used it with few if any changes. Ahluwalia and Gurhan-Canli (2000) as well as Gürhan-Canli and Maheswaran (2000b) did not specify the source of their scales but it does not seem likely that their similarity to the Maheswaran (1994) and Aaker and Maheswaran (1997) scales would be a coincidence.

RELIABILITY: Alphas for the scale as used in Experiments 1 and 2 by Aaker and Maheswaran (1997) were .84 and .83, respectively. Alphas of .87 (PCs) and .81 (stereo systems) were reported for the scale by Maheswaran (1994) in Studies 1 and 2, respectively. Alphas of .88 and .94 were reported by Ahluwalia and Gurhan-Canli (2000) and Gürhan-Canli and Maheswaran (2000b), respectively.

VALIDITY: No information regarding the scale's validity was reported in any of the articles. However, some sense of the scale's validity comes from its successful use as a manipulation check in each case.

COMMENTS: The information medium used by Maheswaran (1994) as well as Gürhan-Canli and Maheswaran (2000b) was a booklet that subjects read. In the study by Ahluwalia and Gurhan-Canli (2000), the product information was provided to subjects in the form of a *Consumer Reports* type article. Despite its use in these cases with print media, it appears that the scale is amenable for use with a variety of media to which the subjects could be exposed (e.g., TV, radio, Internet), commercial (advertising) or otherwise (publicity).

REFERENCES:

Aaker, Jennifer L. (1998), Personal Correspondence.

Aaker, Jennifer L. and Durairaj Maheswaran (1997), "The Effect of Cultural Orientation on Persuasion," *JCR*, 24 (December), 315–328.

Ahluwalia, Rohini and Zeynep Gürhan-Canli (2000), "The Effects of Extensions on the Family Brand Name: An Accessibility-Diagnosticity Perspective," *JCR*, 27 (3), 371–381.

Gürhan-Canli, Zeynep and Durairaj Maheswaran (2000b), "Cultural Variations in Country of Origin Effects," *JMR*, 37 (3), 309–317.

Maheswaran, Durairaj (1994), "Country of Origin as a Stereotype: Effects of Consumer Expertise and Attribute Strength on Product Evaluations," *JCR*, 21 (September), 354–365.

SCALE ITEMS: [1]

Directions: The product description of the <u>*brand name/model*</u> indicated it as:

1. having few positive features / having many positive features

2. having many negative features / having few negative features

3. inferior to competing brands / superior to competing brands

---

[1] These are the items and scale stem used by Aaker and Maheswaran (1997; Aaker 1998). Numerical anchors on the nine-point scale ranged from -4 to +4. The items used by Maheswaran (1994) appear to be the same or very similar except that they used 1 and 9 as the numerical anchors. The items used by Ahluwalia and Gurhan-Canli (2000) as well as Gürhan-Canli and Maheswaran (2000b) were apparently the same as those shown above except that in the first two items the term *attributes* was used instead of *features*. They both used response scales with seven points.

SCALE NAME: Browsing

SCALE DESCRIPTION: Three, seven-point Likert-type statements are used to measure the level to which a consumer was "window shopping" and simply "looking around" during some specific shopping trip. This is opposed to the type of search that occurs when shopping time is focused on looking for items towards which purchase intentions have already been developed.

SCALE ORIGIN: The scale was developed by Beatty and Ferrell (1998) after examining related research by Jeon (1990) as well as Bloch et al. (1986, 1989).

RELIABILITY: Beatty and Ferrell (1998) reported a composite reliability of .72 for the scale.

VALIDITY: Although the details related to this scale were not provided, the implication was that it was unidimensional and showed sufficient evidence of convergent and discriminant validity (Beatty and Ferrell 1998).

REFERENCES:
Beatty, Sharon E. and Elizabeth Ferrell (1998), "Impulse Buying: Modeling Its Precursors," *JR*, 74 (2), 169–191.
Bloch, Peter H., Daniel L. Sherrell, and Nancy M. Ridgway (1986), "Consumer Search: An Extended Framework," *JCR*, 13 (June), 119–126.
Bloch, Peter H., Nancy M. Ridgway, and Daniel L. Sherrell (1989), "Extending the Concept of Shopping: An Investigation of Browsing Activity," *JAMS*, 17 (1), 13–21.
Jeon, Jung-Ok (1990), "An Empirical Investigation of the Relationship Between Affective States, In-store Browsing, and Impulse Buying," doctoral dissertation, The University of Alabama.

SCALE ITEMS:

1. The percent of time I spent just looking around on the trip was fairly high.

2. I would say that I was primarily "just looking around" on this trip.

3. I devoted most of my attention to the items I planned to buy on this trip. (r)

SCALE NAME: Calmness

SCALE DESCRIPTION: The scale measures the degree to which one reports a low degree of arousal, specifically feeling calm and relaxed. It appears like the scale can be used to measure the emotional response to a stimulus (e.g., Mano and Oliver 1993) or more as a mood that one has felt prior to exposure to a stimulus (e.g., Mano 1999).

SCALE ORIGIN: Although not expressly indicated, the items used by Mano and Oliver (1993) appear to have been used first as a summated scale by Mano (1991). With 224 college students the scale was reported to have an alpha of .80. A cluster analysis grouped these three items together by themselves but in a factor analysis the items loaded along with three more related to *quietness*.

Mano (1999) identified his earlier work (1991) as the source of the scale although item #4 (below) was not part of it.

RELIABILITY: An alpha of .77 (n = 118) was reported for the scale by Mano and Oliver (1993). Alphas of .81 (n = 151) and .83 were reported for the version of the scale used by Mano (1999) in pre-task and post-task assessments, respectively.

VALIDITY: The validity of the scale was not specifically addressed in either study. Mano (1999) did indicate, however, that factor analysis supported a one factor solution.

REFERENCES:
Mano, Haim (1991), "The Structure and Intensity of Emotional Experiences: Method and Context Convergence," *Multivariate Behavioral Research*, 26 (3), 389–411.
Mano, Haim (1999), "The Influence of Pre-Existing Negative Affect on Store Purchase Intentions," *JR*, 75 (2), 149–172.
Mano, Haim and Richard L. Oliver (1993), "Assessing the Dimensionality and Structure of the Consumption Experience: Evaluation, Feeling, and Satisfaction," *JCR*, 20 (December), 451–466.

SCALE ITEMS: [1]

1. calm

2. at rest

3. relaxed

4. serene

---

[1] Both studies used a five-point response format. Mano and Oliver (1993) used items 1 to 3 and indicated that the anchors were *not at all* and *very much*. Mano (1999) used all four items but did not specify the anchors on the response scale.

SCALE NAME: Cause Marketing (Commitment by Business)

SCALE DESCRIPTION: The scale is composed of four, seven-point semantic differentials used to evaluate a potential donor's opinion of the commitment by a business to a particular charity or cause.

SCALE ORIGIN: The source of the scale was not identified by Ellen, Mohr, and Webb (2000) and it is likely to be original to their study.

RELIABILITY: An alpha of .91 was reported for the scale (Ellen, Mohr, and Webb 2000).

VALIDITY: No examination of the scale's validity was reported by Ellen, Mohr, and Webb (2000).

COMMENTS: Ellen, Mohr, and Webb (2000) examined the collection of cash and goods by retailers for donation to some cause. Adjustment of the scale instructions could easily tailor the scale for other types of cause marketing or charitable activities.

REFERENCES:
Ellen, Pam Scholder (2003), Personal Correspondence.
Ellen, Pam Scholder, Lois A. Mohr, and Deborah J. Webb (2000), "Charitable Programs and the Retailer: Do They Mix?" *JR*, 76 (3), 393–406.

SCALE ITEMS: [1]

If a business collects customers' donations, matches them and then delivers them to the charity, do you think the business...?

1. is *not* committed to the charity / is committed to the charity

2. has little invested in the charity / has a lot invested in the charity

3. is *not* interested in the charity / is very interested in the charity

4. is giving a little to the charity / is giving a lot to the charity

---

[1] The scale stem and items were provided by Ellen (2003).

SCALE NAME: Cause Marketing (Congruency With Business)

SCALE DESCRIPTION: Three, seven-point, semantic differentials items are used to measure a person's evaluation of the extent to which there is a reasonable relationship between a certain type of business and its involvement in a certain cause or charitable activity.

SCALE ORIGIN: The source of the scale was not identified by Ellen, Mohr, and Webb (2000) and it is likely to be original to their study.

RELIABILITY: An alpha of .87 was reported for the scale (Ellen, Mohr, and Webb 2000).

VALIDITY: No examination of the scale's validity was reported by Ellen, Mohr, and Webb (2000).

COMMENTS: Ellen, Mohr, and Webb (2000) examined the collection of cash and goods by retailers for donation to some cause. Adjustment of the scale instructions could easily tailor the scale for other types of cause marketing.

REFERENCES:
Ellen, Pam Scholder (2003), Personal Correspondence.
Ellen, Pam Scholder, Lois A. Mohr, and Deborah J. Webb (2000), "Charitable Programs and the Retailer: Do They Mix?" *JR*, 76 (3), 393–406.

SCALE ITEMS: [1]

What do you think about a *type of retailer* collecting *types of products?*

1. does *not* make sense given their business / makes sense given their business

2. is *not* consistent with their business / is consistent with their business

3. is *not* related to what they sell / is related to what they sell

[1] The scale stem and items were provided by Ellen (2003).

SCALE NAME: Cause Marketing (Resources Expended by Business)

SCALE DESCRIPTION: The scale is composed of four, seven-point semantic differentials used to evaluate a potential donor's opinion of the time and energy spent by a business in conducting some particular charitable or cause-related activity.

SCALE ORIGIN: The source of the scale was not identified by Ellen, Mohr, and Webb (2000) and it is likely to be original to their study.

RELIABILITY: An alpha of .91 was reported for the scale (Ellen, Mohr, and Webb 2000).

VALIDITY: No examination of the scale's validity was reported by Ellen, Mohr, and Webb (2000).

COMMENTS: Ellen, Mohr, and Webb (2000) examined the collection of cash and goods by retailers for donation to some cause. Adjustment of the scale instructions could easily tailor the scale for other types of cause marketing.

REFERENCES:
Ellen, Pam Scholder (2003), Personal Correspondence.
Ellen, Pam Scholder, Lois A. Mohr, and Deborah J. Webb (2000), "Charitable Programs and the Retailer: Do They Mix?" *JR*, 76 (3), 393–406.

SCALE ITEMS: [1]

If a company decides to *collect products*, do you think this would. . . ?

1. take little energy / take a lot of energy

2. take little time / take a lot of time

3. take little effort / take a lot of effort

4. require few resources / require a lot of resources

[1] The scale stem and items were provided by Ellen (2003).

SCALE NAME: Change Seeking

SCALE DESCRIPTION: The scale is composed of seven statements measuring the degree to which a person expresses a desire for variation or stimulation in his/her life. The scale is viewed as a measure of *optimum stimulation level*.

SCALE ORIGIN: The scale came from Steenkamp and Baumgartner (1995). It was developed to be a short form of the CSI (Change Seeker Index), the 95-item instrument created by Garlington and Shimota (1964). (See V. II, #52.) Six of the items in this short form are also a subset of the well-known 40-item arousal seeking scale by Mehrabian and Russell (1974). (See V. II, #14.) The studies conducted by Steenkamp and Baumgartner (1995) first reduced the scale from 95 items to seven and then cross-validated those seven in three countries and with two types of subjects.

RELIABILITY: Baumgartner and Steenkamp (2001) reported an overall alpha of .75 in their pan-European survey with alphas for individual countries ranging from .60 to .81. As used in study two by Campbell and Goodstein (2001), the alpha of the scale was .82.

VALIDITY: The purpose of the study by Baumgartner and Steenkamp (2001) was to examine response styles as a source of contamination in questionnaire measures and the effect that might have on the validity of conclusions drawn from such data. Although most of the results were reported at an overall level one finding pertinent to this scale was that the mean level of contamination in scale scores was estimated to be 2% (ranging from 1%-4% for eleven European countries), among the lowest average amounts of contamination found for the 14 scales that were examined.

No examination of the scale's validity was reported by Campbell and Goodstein (2001).

REFERENCES:
Baumgartner, Hans and Jan-Benedict E.M. Steenkamp (2001), "Response Styles in Marketing Research: A Cross-National Investigation," *JMR*, 38 (May), 143–156.
Campbell, Margaret C. and Ronald C. Goodstein (2001), "The Moderating Effect of Perceived Risk on Consumers' Evaluations of Product Incongruity: Preference for the Norm," *JCR*, 28 (December), 439–449.
Garlington, Warren K. and Helen E. Shimota (1964), "The Change Seeker Index: A Measure of the Need for Variable Stimulus Input," *Psychological Reports*, 14, 919–924.
Mehrabian, Albert and James A. Russell (1974), *An Approach to Environmental Psychology*, Cambridge, MA: The MIT Press.
Steenkamp, Jan-Benedict E.M. and Hans Baumgartner (1995), "Development and Cross-Cultural Validation of a Short form of CSI as a Measure of Optimum Stimulation Level," *International Journal of Research in Marketing*, 12 (2), 97–104.

SCALE ITEMS: [1]

1. I like to continue doing the same old things rather than trying new and different things. (r)

2. I like to experience novelty and change in my daily routine.

---

[1] The response format used by Campbell and Goodstein (2001) was not described. Steenkamp and Baumgartner (1995) used a five-point scale ranging from *completely false* to *completely true*.

#117 *Change Seeking*

3. I like a job that offers change, variety, and travel, even if it involves some danger.

4. I am continually seeking new ideas and experiences.

5. I like continually changing activities.

6. When things get boring, I like to find some new and unfamiliar experience.

7. I prefer a routine way of life to an unpredictable one full of change. (r)

SCALE NAME: Commercial Friendship Perception

SCALE DESCRIPTION: The eleven-item, seven-point scale is used to measure the extent to which one person in a professional relationship considers the other party to be a friend. One party is the service provider and the other is the service receiver (client, patient, customer). Very slight changes in the scale can be made to measure either the client's perspective or the service provider's. The scale touches on three key facets of the construct: instrumentality, sociability, and reciprocity. The type of service provider studied by Price and Arnould (1999) was a hairstylist.

SCALE ORIGIN: The scale is original to Price and Arnould (1999). Five studies (three quantitative studies, two qualitative) were described in the article, each with some bearing on the construct. Items appear to have been generated after review of existing literature on friendship and service provider/customer relationships. The emphasis of the studies appears to have been on the client version of the scale; the service provider version was only examined in Study 3.

RELIABILITY: Alphas of .94 (Study 1, n = 193), .96 (Study 3, n = 65), and .98 (Study 4, n = 171) were reported for the client version of the scale (Price and Arnould 1999). An alpha of .92 (Study 3, n = 62) was reported for service provider version of the scale.

VALIDITY: Although a lot of descriptive information was gathered in the studies that help to understand the construct, Price and Arnould (1999) did not appear to be explicitly validating the scale nor did they make claims about the scale's validity. They did, however, indicate that the items on the client version of the scale loaded on a single factor in each of the three quantitative studies. Likewise, based upon the data from Study 3, the service provider version was reported to be unidimensional as well.

REFERENCES:
Price, Linda L. and Eric J. Arnould (1999), "Commercial Friendships: Service Provider-Client Relationships in Context," *JM*, 63 (October), 38–56.

SCALE ITEMS: [1]

1. I think of _____ as a friend.

2. It feels like a meeting with one of my friends.

3. I feel like I know this _____ well.

4. I am able to share my true thoughts and feelings with this _____.

5. I feel close to this _____ during the service interaction.

6. _____ seems to care about me.

7. I want to give something back to this _____.

8. I like doing little things to please this _____.

9. If something out of the ordinary occurs, _____ generally responds to it as a special situation and accommodates my needs.

10. _____ provides me with extras.

11. _____ goes out of his or her way for me.

---

[1] A personal name should be placed in the blanks of items 1, 4, 6, and 9–11; for all others (except 2) the term for the <u>category</u> of service provider or service receiver should be used, e.g., hairstylist or client. Price and Arnould (1999) did not specify the verbal anchors used with their seven-point response scale but they were probably Likert-type (*strongly agree / strongly disagree*).

SCALE NAME: Commercial Friendship Perception

SCALE DESCRIPTION: The scale is composed of three, seven-point Likert-type statements attempting to assess the extent to which a customer in a professional relationship considers the sales person to be a friend and someone to have a relationship with beyond the current sales event.

SCALE ORIGIN: Evans et al. (2000) indicated that they had tried to adopt items for their study from past research. No specific origin was cited for this scale and it appears to be unique enough that it may be safest to consider it to be original to their study. They said that all of their measures were modified based on pretesting.

RELIABILITY: An alpha of .74 was reported for the scale (Evans et al. 2000).

VALIDITY: No explicit evidence of the scale's validity was provided by Evans et al. (2000).

REFERENCES:
Evans, Kenneth R., Robert E. Kleine III, Timothy D. Landry, and Lawrence A. Crosby (2000), "How First Impressions of a Customer Impact Effectiveness in an Initial Sales Encounter," *JAMS*, 28 (4), 512–526.

SCALE ITEMS:

1. The agent is someone I could get along with as a friend.

2. The agent did use the first meeting to get acquainted.

3. The agent is someone with whom I can have a lasting, business-like relationship.

#120 *Commitment (Brand)*

SCALE NAME: Commitment (Brand)

SCALE DESCRIPTION: The purpose of the scale is to assess the degree to which a consumer expresses devotion to a specified brand versus a willingness to accept alterative brands even if they are cheaper or more convenient. The scale is composed of three, nine-point Likert-type statements. The scale was called *commitment to the target brand* by Ahluwalia (2000; Ahluwalia, Burnkrant, and Unnava 2000; Ahluwalia, Unnava, and Burnkrant 2001).

SCALE ORIGIN: The scale used by Ahluwalia (2000; Ahluwalia, Burnkrant, and Unnava 2000; Ahluwalia, Unnava, and Burnkrant 2001) is original to Beatty, Kahle, and Homer (1988). They called it *brand commitment* rather than *brand loyalty* since the latter suggests a behavioral dimension which the former does not. Their work provided evidence that commitment is distinct from purchase involvement and ego involvement but is influenced by them. The construct reliability was .75 and variance extracted as .51.

RELIABILITY: The alpha for the scale used by Ahluwalia (2000) was .62 (Ahluwalia 2002). (The "lab study" in Ahluwalia [2000] seems to be the same as what is referred to as Experiment One in Ahluwalia, Burnkrant, and Unnava [2000] and Experiment Two in Ahluwalia, Unnava, and Burnkrant [2001].)

VALIDITY: No examination of the scale's validity was reported by Ahluwalia (2000; Ahluwalia, Burnkrant, and Unnava 2000; Ahluwalia, Unnava, and Burnkrant 2001).

REFERENCES:

Ahluwalia, Rohini (2000), "Examination of Psychological Processes Underlying Resistance to Persuasion," *JCR*, 27 (2), 217–232.

Ahluwalia, Rohini, Robert E. Burnkrant, and H. Rao Unnava (2000), "Consumer Response to Negative Publicity: The Moderating Role of Commitment," *JMR*, 37 (May), 203–214.

Ahluwalia, Rohini, H. Rao Unnava, and Robert E. Burnkrant (2001), "The Moderating Role of Commitment on the Spillover Effect of Marketing Communications," *JMR*, 38 (Nov.), 458–470.

Beatty, Sharon E., Lynn R. Kahle, and Pamela Homer (1988), "The Involvement-Commitment Model: Theory and Implications," *Journal of Business Research*, 16 (2), 149–167.

SCALE ITEMS: [1]

1. If _____ was not available at the store, it would make little difference to me if I had to choose another brand. (r)

2. I consider myself to be highly loyal to _____.

3. When another brand is on sale, I will generally purchase it rather than _____. (r)

---

[1] Responses to these items were measured by Ahluwalia (2000; Ahluwalia, Burnkrant, and Unnava 2000; Ahluwalia, Unnava, and Burnkrant 2001) on a nine-point Likert-type scale with *disagree/agree* anchors.

SCALE NAME: Commitment (Brand)

SCALE DESCRIPTION: The scale is composed of three, five-point Likert-type statements attempting to capture a consumer's general loyalty to a specified brand.

SCALE ORIGIN: Although Yoo, Donthu, and Lee (2000) may have drawn inspiration from previous measures, especially Beatty and Kahle (1988), ultimately their scale appears to be original to them.

RELIABILITY: Yoo, Donthu, and Lee (2000) reported the scale to have a composite reliability of .90.

VALIDITY: Factor analyses (EFA and CFA) were used to check the dimensionality of this scale along with eight others used in the study. Based on the results, the authors concluded that all items loaded on their respective factors as expected providing some sense of the scales' convergent and discriminant validities. The average variance extracted for this scale was .75.

REFERENCES:

Beatty, Sharon E. and Lynn R. Kahle (1988), "Alternative Hierarchies of the Attitude-Behavior Relationship: The Impact of Brand Commitment and Habit," *JAMS*, 16 (2), 1–10.

Yoo, Boonghee, Naveen Donthu, and Sungho Lee (2000), "An Examination of Selected Marketing Mix Elements and Brand Equity," *JAMS*, 28 (2), 195–211.

SCALE ITEMS: [1]

1. I consider myself to be loyal to _____ .

2. _____ would be my first choice.

3. I would not buy other brands if _____ is available at the store.

---

[1] The brand name of a product was placed in the blanks by Yoo, Donthu, and Lee (2000).

SCALE NAME: Commitment (Information Complexity)

SCALE DESCRIPTION: The scale is composed of three, seven-point Likert-type statements that are intended to measure the strength of a consumer's commitment to an object (e.g., company or brand) with an emphasis on the apparent complexity of the consumer's cognitive structures with respect to the object.

SCALE ORIGIN: Pritchard, Havitz, and Howard (1999) constructed the scale using an admirable and rigorous process. Briefly, the items for this scale were generated along with many others thought to tap into a hypothesized multidimensional view of commitment. An initial pool of 65 items was reduced to 51 by examining the content validity of the items using a panel of judges. Testing of the 51 items was conducted in two separate studies followed by further psychometric assessment using the combined samples. Ultimately, 13 items remained that provided a "simple structure" solution of four commitment factors: resistance to change (#124), volitional choice (#125), information complexity, and position involvement (#123).

RELIABILITY: Pritchard, Havitz, and Howard (1999) reported the construct reliability for the scale to be .83.

VALIDITY: A variety of tests reported by Pritchard, Havitz, and Howard (1999) provided evidence of the scale's discriminant and convergent validity. Variance extracted for the scale was .62.

REFERENCES:

Pritchard, Mark P., Mark E. Havitz, and Dennis R. Howard (1999), "Analyzing the Commitment-Loyalty Link in Service Contexts," *JAMS*, 27 (3), 333–348.

SCALE ITEMS: [1]

1. I don't really know that much about _____. (r)

2. I consider myself to be an educated consumer regarding _____.

3. I am knowledgeable about _____.

[1] Response scale anchors ranged from *strongly disagree* (1) to *strongly agree* (7). The name of the company/ brand should be placed in the blanks.

SCALE NAME: Commitment (Position Involvement)

SCALE DESCRIPTION: The scale is composed of three, seven-point Likert-type statements that are intended to measure the strength of a consumer's commitment to a company/brand with an emphasis on the extent of his/her psychological identification with the company/brand. As currently phrased, the items relate to airlines.

SCALE ORIGIN: Pritchard, Havitz, and Howard (1999) constructed the scale using an admirable and rigorous process. Briefly, the items for this scale were generated along with many others thought to tap into a hypothesized multidimensional view of commitment. An initial pool of 65 items was reduced to 51 by examining the content validity of the items using a panel of judges. Testing of the 51 items was conducted in two separate studies followed by further psychometric assessment using the combined samples. Ultimately, 13 items remained that provided a "simple structure" solution of four commitment factors: resistance to change (#124), volitional choice (#125), information complexity (#122), and position involvement.

RELIABILITY: Pritchard, Havitz, and Howard (1999) reported the construct reliability for the scale to be .84.

VALIDITY: A variety of tests reported by Pritchard, Havitz, and Howard (1999) provided evidence of the scale's discriminant and convergent validity. Variance extracted for the scale was .63.

COMMENTS: Although the items are written with airlines in mind, they appear to amenable for adaptation for other product categories.

REFERENCES:
Pritchard, Mark P., Mark E. Havitz, and Dennis R. Howard (1999), "Analyzing the Commitment-Loyalty Link in Service Contexts," *JAMS*, 27 (3), 333–348.

SCALE ITEMS: [1]

1. I prefer to fly with _____ because their image comes closest to reflecting my lifestyle.

2. When I fly with _____ it reflects the kind of person I am.

3. I prefer to fly with _____ because their service makes me feel important.

---

[1] Response scale anchors ranged from *strongly disagree* (1) to *strongly agree* (7). The name of the company/brand should be placed in the blanks.

SCALE NAME: Commitment (Resistance to Change)

SCALE DESCRIPTION: The scale is composed of four, seven-point Likert-type statements that are intended to measure the strength of a consumer's commitment to a company/brand with an emphasis on his/her stated opposition to changing preferences. As currently phrased, the items relate to airlines.

SCALE ORIGIN: Pritchard, Havitz, and Howard (1999) constructed the scale using an admirable and rigorous process. Briefly, the items for this scale were generated along with many others thought to tap into a hypothesized multidimensional view of commitment. An initial pool of 65 items was reduced to 51 by examining the content validity of the items using a panel of judges. Testing of the 51 items was conducted in two separate studies followed by further psychometric assessment using the combined samples. Ultimately, 13 items remained that provided a "simple structure" solution of four commitment factors: resistance to change, volitional choice (#125), information complexity (#122), and position involvement (#123).

RELIABILITY: Pritchard, Havitz, and Howard (1999) reported the construct reliability for the scale to be .81.

VALIDITY: A variety of tests reported by Pritchard, Havitz, and Howard (1999) provided evidence of the scale's discriminant and convergent validity. Variance extracted for the scale was .53.

COMMENTS: Although the items are written with airlines in mind, they appear to amenable for adaptation for other product categories.

REFERENCES:
Pritchard, Mark P., Mark E. Havitz, and Dennis R. Howard (1999), "Analyzing the Commitment-Loyalty Link in Service Contexts," *JAMS*, 27 (3), 333–348.

SCALE ITEMS: [1]

1. My preference to fly with _____ would not willingly change.

2. It would be difficult to change my beliefs about _____.

3. Even if close friends recommended another airline, I would not change my preference for _____.

4. To change my preference from _____ would require major rethinking.

[1] Response scale anchors ranged from *strongly disagree* (1) to *strongly agree* (7). The name of the company/brand should be placed in the blanks.

SCALE NAME: Commitment (Volitional Choice)

SCALE DESCRIPTION: The scale is composed of three, seven-point Likert-type statements that are intended to measure the strength of a consumer's commitment to a company/brand with an emphasis on his/her stated freedom in making the choice. As currently phrased, the items relate to airlines.

SCALE ORIGIN: Pritchard, Havitz, and Howard (1999) constructed the scale using an admirable and rigorous process. Briefly, the items for this scale were generated along with many others thought to tap into a hypothesized multidimensional view of commitment. An initial pool of 65 items was reduced to 51 by examining the content validity of the items using a panel of judges. Testing of the 51 items was conducted in two separate studies followed by further psychometric assessment using the combined samples. Ultimately, 13 items remained that provided a "simple structure" solution of four commitment factors: resistance to change (#124), volitional choice, information complexity (#122), and position involvement (#123).

RELIABILITY: Pritchard, Havitz, and Howard (1999) reported the construct reliability for the scale to be .80.

VALIDITY: A variety of tests reported by Pritchard, Havitz, and Howard (1999) provided evidence of the scale's discriminant and convergent validity. Variance extracted for the scale was .57.

COMMENTS: Although the items are written with airlines in mind, they appear to amenable for adaptation for other product categories.

REFERENCES:
Pritchard, Mark P., Mark E. Havitz, and Dennis R. Howard (1999), "Analyzing the Commitment-Loyalty Link in Service Contexts," *JAMS*, 27 (3), 333–348.

SCALE ITEMS: [1]

1. My decision to fly with _____ was freely chosen from several alternatives.

2. I did not control the decision on whether to fly with _____. (r)

3. I am fully responsible for the decision to fly with _____.

[1] Response scale anchors ranged from *strongly disagree* (1) to *strongly agree* (7). The name of the company/brand should be placed in the blanks.

#126 *Commitment to a Theater*

SCALE NAME: Commitment to a Theater

SCALE DESCRIPTION: The scale is composed of four, five-point Likert-type items used to measure a theater attendee's identification with, loyalty to, and concern for a specified theater.

SCALE ORIGIN: Garbarino and Johnson (1999) indicated that they drew upon a variety of sources to develop the items.

RELIABILITY: Garbarino and Johnson (1999) reported the following alphas for the scales as used with three different subsets of theatergoers: .87 (individual ticket buyers), .87 (occasional subscribers), and .82 (consistent subscribers).

VALIDITY: Based on the variety of indicators they examined, Garbarino and Johnson (1999) made a general claim of good fit for their measurement model as well as evidence of good convergent validity. This scale performed adequately on a couple of tests of discriminant validity.

REFERENCES:
Garbarino, Ellen and Mark S. Johnson (1999), "The Different Roles of Satisfaction, Trust, and Commitment in Customer Relationships," *JM*, 63 (April), 70–87.

SCALE ITEMS:

1. I am proud to belong to this theater.

2. I feel a sense of belonging to this theater.

3. I care about the long-term success of this theater.

4. I am a loyal patron of this theater.

SCALE NAME: Commitment to Retailer

SCALE DESCRIPTION: The scale is composed of three, seven-point Likert-type statements that measure a customer's enduring desire to continue a relationship with a retailer as well as the willingness to sustain the relationship over time.

SCALE ORIGIN: The source of the scale was not explicitly described by De Wulf, Odekerken-Schröder, and Iacobucci (2001) but it would appear to be original to their studies. The items appear to be among those that were developed using the back-translation method for versions in American English and Dutch and then pretested in the U.S., Netherlands, and Belgium (Flemish-speaking area).

RELIABILITY: Composite reliabilities were calculated by for two types of stores for each of three countries (De Wulf, Odekerken-Schröder, and Iacobucci 2001). The reliabilities for food stores were .84, .75, and .75 for the U.S., Netherlands, and Belgium, respectively (Odekerken-Schröder 2004). For apparel stores, the reliabilities were .86, .73, and .72 for the U.S., Netherlands, and Belgium, respectively.

VALIDITY: Along with two other scales (relationship satisfaction [#401] and trustworthiness [#481]), De Wulf, Odekerken-Schröder, and Iacobucci (2001) used scale averages as indicators of a second-order factor (relationship quality). Evidence was provided in support of the scale's unidimensionality as well as its convergent validity. Partial metric invariance across countries was supported too.

REFERENCES:
De Wulf, Kristof, Gaby Odekerken-Schröder, and Dawn Iacobucci (2001), "Investments in Consumer Relationships: A Cross-Country and Cross-Industry Exploration," *JM*, 65 (October), 33–50.
Odekerken-Schröder, Gaby (2004), Personal Correspondence.

SCALE ITEMS: [1]

1. I am willing "to go the extra mile" to remain a customer of this _____.

2. I feel loyal towards this _____.

3. Even if this _____ would be more difficult to reach, I would still keep buying there.

---

[1] An appropriate descriptor of the business entity should be placed in the blanks. De Wulf, Odekerken-Schröder, and Iacobucci (2001) used the term "store" but other terms such as "retailer" may be possible as well.

SCALE NAME: Commitment to Service Provider

SCALE DESCRIPTION: Four, five-point Likert-type items compose the scale. The scale is used to measure the degree to which a customer expresses intent to continue doing business with a particular service organization. The context in which the respondents were given this scale was after being told to remember a recent service experience that led to their lodging a complaint.

SCALE ORIGIN: Although Tax, Brown, and Chandrashekaran (1998) may have drawn inspiration from previous measures, this scale appears to be original to their study.

RELIABILITY: An alpha of .92 (n = 257) was reported for the scale by Tax, Brown, and Chandrashekaran (1998).

VALIDITY: It is not clear what support if any was found for the validity of the scale in the study by Tax, Brown, and Chandrashekaran (1998).

REFERENCES:
Tax, Stephen S., Stephen W. Brown, and Murali Chandrashekaran (1998), "Customer Evaluations of Service Complaint Experiences: Implications for Relationship Marketing," *JM*, 62 (April), 60–76.

SCALE ITEMS:

1. If I needed to use this type of service again, I would have changed service providers for a small cost savings. (r)

2. I wanted to continue dealing with this organization.

3. If this organization sold other products I needed, I would have bought them from this organization.

4. If other options were available, I would have preferred switching service providers. (r)

SCALE NAME: Commitment to Service Provider

SCALE DESCRIPTION: The scale is used to measure the extent to which one person (a client) expresses intentions to continue a relationship with another person/party (professional service provider). The type of service provider studied by Price and Arnould (1999) was a hairstylist.

SCALE ORIGIN: The scale appears to be original to Price and Arnould (1999).

RELIABILITY: Alphas of .79 (Study 1, n = 197), .93 (Study 3, n = 45), and .95 (Study 4, n = 187) were reported for the scale by Price and Arnould (1999).

VALIDITY: No information about the scale's validity was provided by Price and Arnould (1999).

REFERENCES:
Price, Linda L. and Eric J. Arnould (1999), "Commercial Friendships: Service Provider-Client Relationships in Context," *JM*, 63 (October), 38–56.

SCALE ITEMS: [1]

1. I feel a commitment to continuing a relationship with this _____.

2. I would expend extra effort to continue seeing this _____.

3. I feel loyal to this _____.

4. I intend to make an appointment with this _____ again.

5. I would continue to do business with this _____ even if his/her prices increase somewhat.

[1] In studies 1 and 3 only items 1 and 2 were used whereas study four used all five (Price and Arnould 1999). Study 1 used a five-point response format whereas a seven-point scale was used in Studies 3 and 4. The term for the <u>category</u> of service provider should be placed in the blanks, e.g., hairstylist.

SCALE NAME: Commitment to Service Provider

SCALE DESCRIPTION: Three, five-point Likert-type statements are used to measure the extent to which a customer views a relationship with a particular service provider as being important to his/her self-concept.

SCALE ORIGIN: Ganesh, Arnold, and Reynolds (2000) drew upon a scale developed by Morgan and Hunt (1994) to develop their scale. The latter's scale had seven items and measured the relationship commitment between a company and one of its major suppliers.

RELIABILITY: An alpha of .82 was reported for the scale (Ganesh, Arnold, and Reynolds 2000).

VALIDITY: While Ganesh, Arnold, and Reynolds (2000) did not examine the scale's validity they did include its items in an EFA along with items intended to measure two other constructs. All items loaded strongly on the expected dimensions with no significant cross-loadings.

REFERENCES:

Ganesh, Jaishanker, Mark J. Arnold, and Kristy E. Reynolds (2000), "Understanding the Customer Base of Service Providers: An Examination of the Differences Between Switchers and Stayers," *JM*, 64 (3), 65–87.

Morgan, Robert M. and Shelby D. Hunt (1994), "The Commitment-Trust Theory of Relationship Marketing," *JM*, 58 (July), 20–38.

SCALE ITEMS: [1]

1. The relationship I share with my _____ is something that the _____ and I are very committed to.

2. The relationship I share with my _____ is something that is very important to me.

3. The relationship I share with my _____ is something that deserves my maximum effort to maintain.

[1] The generic term for the service provider should be placed in the blanks, e.g., bank.

SCALE NAME: Communication Avoidance (Parent/Child)

SCALE DESCRIPTION: The scale is composed of three, five point Likert-type items measuring the degree to which a person (a parent) believes that it is best to leave children alone and not discuss their worries with them.

SCALE ORIGIN: The items seem to originate from Schaefer and Bell (1958) but may have been used even earlier. They discuss a considerable amount of testing of the items as part of a larger multi-scaled instrument. While the three-item version reported here was not tested in their studies, five- and eight-item versions were. The findings indicated that they had somewhat low internal consistency and test-retest stability.

RELIABILITY: Alphas of .66 and .77 were reported for the scale by Carlson and Grossbart (1988) and Carlson, Laczniak, and Walsh (2001), respectively.

VALIDITY: No examination of scale validity was reported by Carlson and Grossbart (1988).

COMMENTS: See also Walsh, Laczniak, and Carlson (1998).

REFERENCES:
Carlson, Les and Sanford Grossbart (1988), "Parental Style and Consumer Socialization of Children," *JCR*, 15 (June), 77–94.
Carlson, Les, Russell N. Laczniak, and Ann Walsh (2001), "Socializing Children about Television: An Intergenerational Study," *JAMS*, 29 (3), 276–288.
Schaefer, Earl S. and Richard Q. Bell (1958), "Development of a Parental Attitude Research Instrument," *Child Development*, 29 (September), 339–361.
Walsh, Ann D., Russell N. Laczniak, and Les Carlson (1998), "Mothers' Preferences for Regulating Children's Television," *JA*, 27 (3), 23–36.

SCALE ITEMS:

Directions: Please indicate your opinion by checking one response (strongly disagree, disagree, neither disagree or agree, agree, strongly agree) for each statement. Check one for each statement.

1. If you let children talk about their troubles they end up complaining even more.

2. Parents who start a child talking about his/her worries don't realize that sometimes it's better to leave well enough alone.

3. If a child has upset feelings it is best to leave him/her alone and not make it look serious.

SCALE NAME: Communication Effectiveness with Service Provider

SCALE DESCRIPTION: Three, five-point statements are used to measure the extent to which one person (a client) believes that another person/party has listened and understood his/her requests and performs the service with them in mind. The type of service provider studied by Price and Arnould (1999) was a hairstylist.

SCALE ORIGIN: The scale appears to be original to Price and Arnould (1999).

RELIABILITY: An alpha of .78 was reported for the scale by Price and Arnould (1999).

VALIDITY: No information about the scale's validity was provided by Price and Arnould (1999).

REFERENCES:
Price, Linda L. and Eric J. Arnould (1999), "Commercial Friendships: Service Provider-Client Relationships in Context," *JM*, 63 (October), 38–56.

SCALE ITEMS: [1]

1. I am not able to communicate my needs effectively to this _____. (r)

2. _____ listens carefully to my requests.

3. _____ tries to perform the service close to my specification.

[1] The name of the service provider should go in the blanks of items 2 and 3; for 1, the term for the <u>category</u> of service provider should be used, e.g., hairstylist.

SCALE NAME: Communication Encouragement (Parent/Child)

SCALE DESCRIPTION: The scale is composed of four, five-point Likert-type statements measuring the degree to which a person (a parent) believes that children should be free to candidly express their own views and disagreements with parents when they feel like it. This scale was called *encouraging verbalization* by Schaefer and Bell (1958).

SCALE ORIGIN: The items seem to originate from Schaefer and Bell (1958) but may have been used even earlier. They discuss a considerable amount of testing of the items as part of a larger multi-scaled instrument. While the four-item version reported here was not tested in their studies, five- and eight-item versions were. The findings indicated that they had rather low internal consistency and test-retest stability.

RELIABILITY: Carlson and Grossbart (1988) reported an alpha of .69 for the scale. An alpha of .71 was reported by Carlson, Laczniak, and Walsh (2001). Alphas of .69 (U.S.) and .61 (Japan) were reported for the scale by Rose (1999).

VALIDITY: No examination of scale validity was reported by Carlson and Grossbart (1988) or Carlson, Laczniak, and Walsh (2001). Rose (1999) stated that a CFA indicated the set of scales they used "formed the expected dimensions" (p. 111). In particular, this scale and one measuring nurturance (#289) produced a warmth dimension in a second order factor model.

COMMENTS: See also Walsh, Laczniak, and Carlson (1998).

REFERENCES:
Carlson, Les and Sanford Grossbart (1988), "Parental Style and Consumer Socialization of Children," *JCR*, 15 (June), 77–94.
Carlson, Les, Russell N. Laczniak, and Ann Walsh (2001), "Socializing Children about Television: An Intergenerational Study," *JAMS*, 29 (3), 276–288.
Rose, Gregory M. (2002), Personal Correspondence.
Rose, Gregory M. (1999), "Consumer Socialization, Parental Style, and Development Timetables in the United States and Japan," *JM*, 63 (July), 105–119.
Schaefer, Earl S. and Richard Q. Bell (1958), "Development of a Parental Attitude Research Instrument," *Child Development*, 29 (September), 339–361.
Walsh, Ann D., Russell N. Laczniak, and Les Carlson (1998), "Mothers' Preferences for Regulating Children's Television," *JA*, 27 (3), 23–36.

SCALE ITEMS:

Directions: Please indicate your opinion by checking one response (strongly disagree, disagree, neither disagree or agree, agree, strongly agree) for each statement. Check one for each statement.

1. Children should be allowed to disagree with their parents if they feel their own ideas are better.

2. Children should be encouraged to tell their parents about it whenever they feel family rules are unreasonable.

3. A child has a right to his/her own point of view and ought to be allowed to express it.

4. A child's ideas should be seriously considered before making family decisions.

SCALE NAME: Competence of Service Provider

SCALE DESCRIPTION: The four-item, seven-point scale measures the extent to which one person (a client) believes that another person/party is able to perform a certain service. The type of service provider studied by Price and Arnould (1999) was a hairstylist.

SCALE ORIGIN: The scale appears to be original to Price and Arnould (1999).

RELIABILITY: Alphas of .73 (n = 45) and .92 (n = 187) were reported for the scale by Price and Arnould (1999).

VALIDITY: No information about the scale's validity was provided by Price and Arnould (1999).

REFERENCES:
Price, Linda L. and Eric J. Arnould (1999), "Commercial Friendships: Service Provider-Client Relationships in Context," *JM*, 63 (October), 38–56.

SCALE ITEMS:

1. incapable / capable

2. inefficient / efficient

3. disorganized / organized

4. hasty / thorough

SCALE NAME: Compulsive Buying

SCALE DESCRIPTION: The scale provides a measure of the degree to which a consumer makes an excessive amount of purchases given his/her disposable income as a means of dealing with undesirable mood states. Compulsive buyers are thought to engage in purchasing behavior to alleviate negative feelings. Some improvement in mood may follow buying episodes but are temporary and the behavior "becomes very difficult to stop and ultimately results in harmful consequences" (O'Guinn and Faber 1989, p. 155).

SCALE ORIGIN: The scale was constructed and tested by Faber and O'Guinn (1992). The scale built upon earlier work buy the authors (Faber, O'Guinn, and Krych 1987; Faber and O'Guinn 1989; O'Guinn and Faber 1989). The version used by Babin, Darden, and Griffin (1994) was based upon that earlier work rather than the "final" version of the scale and because of that is a little different.

RELIABILITY: An alpha of .76 was reported for the five-item version of the scale used by Babin, Darden, and Griffin (1994). The full seven-item version of the scale was reported by Faber and O'Guinn (1992) as having an alpha of .95. Although not explicitly stated, Lastovicka et al. (1999) appear to have used the seven-item version of the scale and reported an alpha of .75 for it.

VALIDITY: Faber and O'Guinn (1992) provided data in support of the scale's face, criterion, and external validities. In addition, their factor analysis indicated that the items were unidimensional.

Lastovicka et al. (1999) used this scale in the process of validating another scale (#177). Based upon that, their data indicated that scores on the compulsive buying scale had low but significant negative correlations with frugality and a measure of response bias (#91). The former supports, as might be expected, that those who are compulsive buyers are not very frugal. The latter is more confusing; it appears to suggest that as compulsive buying tendencies increase the tendency to give exaggeratedly desirable responses decrease. The implication of this finding as it relates to the scale's validity is worthy of further investigation.

COMMENTS: As constructed and used by Faber and O'Guinn (1992) the scale items are weighted to produce the scale score. Those scoring two standard deviations from the mean were labeled as compulsive buyers. Faber (2000) has indicated that the sale has been used successfully by others without weighting (e.g., Babin, Darden, and Griffin 1994).

See also Faber et al. (1995).

REFERENCES:

Babin, Barry J., William R. Darden, and Mitch Griffin (1994), "Work and/or Fun: Measuring Hedonic and Utilitarian Shopping Value," *JCR*, 20 (March), 644–656.

Faber, Ronald J. (2000), Personal Correspondence.

Faber, Ronald J., Gary A. Christenson, Martine De Zwaan, and James Mitchell (1995), "Two forms of Compulsive Consumption: Comorbidity of Compulsive Buying and Binge Eating," *JCR*, 22 (December), 296–304.

Faber, Ronald J. and Thomas C. O'Guinn (1989), "Classifying Compulsive Consumers: Advances in the Development of a Diagnostic Tool," in *Advances in Consumer Research, V. 16*, Thomas K. Srull, ed., Provo: UT: Association for Consumer Research 738–44.

Faber, Ronald J. and Thomas C. O'Guinn (1992), "A Clinical Screener for Compulsive Buying," *JCR*, 19 (December), 459–469.

Faber, Ronald J., Thomas C. O'Guinn, and Raymond Krych (1987), "Compulsive Consumption," in *Advances in Consumer Research, V. 14*, Melanie Wallendorf and Paul Anderson, eds., Provo: UT: Association for Consumer Research, 132–35.

Lastovicka, John L., Lance A. Bettencourt, Renee Shaw Hughner, and Ronald J. Kuntze (1999), "Lifestyle of the Tight and Frugal: Theory and Measurement," *JCR*, 26 (June), 85–98.

O'Guinn, Thomas C. and Ronald J. Faber (1989), "Compulsive Buying: A Phenomenological Exploration," *JCR*, 16 (2), 147–157.

SCALE ITEMS: [1]

Please indicate how often you have done each of the following things.

1. Felt others would be horrified if they knew of my spending habits.

2. Bought things even though I couldn't afford them.

3. Wrote a check when I knew I didn't have enough money in the bank to cover it.

4. Bought myself something in order to make myself feel better.

5. Felt anxious or nervous on days I didn't go shopping.

6. Made only the minimum payments on my credit cards.

7. If I have any money left at the end of the pay period, I just have to spend it.

8. Having more money would solve my problems.

9. I have bought something, got home, and didn't know why I had bought it.

[1] The version used by Faber and O'Guinn (1992) used the first six items with a five-point frequency response scale (*very often* to *never*) while a five-point Likert-type scale was used with item 7. Babin, Darden, and Griffin (1994) used a Likert-type response format and versions of items similar to 1, 5, 6 and added items 8 and 9. Lastovicka et al. (1999) did not report the exact items or response format they used.
© 1992 R. Faber and T. O'Guinn

SCALE NAME: Conformity Motivation (ATCSI)

SCALE DESCRIPTION: The scale is composed of thirteen, six-point statements measuring the degree to which a person looks to others to determine how to behave and desires to act in accordance with group norms. This measure was called Attention to Social Comparison Information (ATSCI) by Lennox and Wolfe (1984). A three-item variation of the scale was created by Ailawadi, Neslin, and Gedenk (2001).

SCALE ORIGIN: The scale was constructed by Lennox and Wolfe (1984) in the process of refining an index of self-monitoring measures presented earlier by Snyder (1974). The scale was developed in several stages with the final version being tested on 224 college students who were required to participate as part of a course. Testing occurred in small groups. The scale had an alpha of .83 and item-total correlations between .34 and .60. It was concluded that this should not be considered a component of the self-monitoring construct though it does seem to measure tendency to conform.

RELIABILITY: An alpha of .82 was reported for the scale by Bearden et al. (1989). Alphas of .85, .83, .88, and .89 were reported by Bearden and Rose (1990) for the scale in studies one to four, respectively. Gulas and McKeage (2000) reported an alpha of .85 for the scale. The composite reliability for the version used by Ailawadi, Neslin, and Gedenk (2001) was .824.

VALIDITY: This scale was used by Bearden et al. (1989) to help validate two other scales constructed in the study. In contrast, one of the purposes of the studies conducted by Bearden and Rose (1990) was to evaluate the validity of the scale. These studies provided evidence of the scale's convergent and discriminant validity.

The items in the version used by Ailawadi, Neslin, and Gedenk (2001) were examined along with those belonging to 14 other scales in a confirmatory factor analysis. The fit of the measurement model was acceptable and general evidence was cited in support of the scale's discriminant validity.

REFERENCES:
Ailawadi, Kusum L., Scott A. Neslin, and Karen Gedenk (2001), "Pursuing the Value-Conscious Consumer: Store Brands Versus National Brand Promotions," *JM*, 65 (1), 71–89.

Bearden, William O., Richard G. Netemeyer, and Jesse E. Teel (1989), "Measurement of Consumer Susceptibility to Interpersonal Influence," *JCR*, 15 (March), 473–481.

Bearden, William O. and Randall L. Rose (1990), "Attention to Social Comparison Information: An Individual Difference Factor Affecting Consumer Conformity," *JCR*, 16 (March), 461–471.

Gulas, Charles A. and Kim McKeage (2000), "Extending Social Comparison: An Examination of the Unintended Consequences of Idealized Advertising Imagery," *JA*, 29 (2), 17–28.

Lennox, Richard D. and Raymond N. Wolfe (1984), "Revision of the Self-Monitoring Scale," *Journal of Personality and Social Psychology*, 46 (6), 1349–1364.

Snyder, Mark (1974), "The Self-Monitoring of Expressive Behavior," *Journal of Personality and Social Psychology*, 30 (October), 526–537.

#136 *Conformity Motivation (ATCSI)*

SCALE ITEMS: [1]

1. It is my feeling that if everyone else in a group is behaving in a certain manner, this must be the way to behave.

2. I actively avoid wearing clothes that are not in style.

3. At parties I usually try to behave in a manner that makes me fit in.

4. When I am uncertain how to act in a social situation, I look to the behavior of others for cues.

5. I try to pay attention to the reaction of others to my behavior in order to avoid being out of place.

6. I find that I tend to pick up slang expressions from others and use them as part of my own vocabulary.

7. I tend to pay attention to what others are wearing.

8. The slightest look of disapproval in the eyes of a person with whom I am interacting is enough to make me change my approach.

9. It's important to me to fit in with the group I'm with.

10. My behavior often depends on how I feel others wish me to behave.

11. If I am the least bit uncertain as to how to act in a social situation, I look to the behavior of others for cues.

12. I usually keep up with clothing style changes by watching what others wear.

13. When in a social situation, I tend not to follow the crowd, but instead behave in a manner that suits my particular mood at the time. (r)

14. It bothers me if other people disapprove of my choices.

---

[1] Bearden et al. (1989, 1990) used a response format with anchors of *Generally False* (0) and *Certainly, Always True* (5). The response format used by Gulas and McKeage (2000) was not reported. A five-point Likert-type scale (*strongly disagree/strongly agree*) was used by Ailawadi, Neslin, and Gedenk (2001) and the items were 10, 14, and a condensed version of 9.

SCALE NAME: Conformity Motivation (Consumption)

SCALE DESCRIPTION: It is a seven-item, seven-point Likert-type scale purported to measure the degree to which a consumer is concerned about adhering to group norms with special regard for what products/brands to buy. The scale was referred to by Kahle (1995b; Shoham, Rose, and Kahle 1998) as *role-relaxed consumer*.

SCALE ORIGIN: Although the construct was discussed in Kahle (1995a), it was in a follow-up article (1995b) where the scale was apparently presented for the first time.

RELIABILITY: Alphas of .76 and .67 were reported for the scale by Kahle (1995b) and Shoham, Rose, and Kahle (1998), respectively.

VALIDITY: Although some sense of the scale's nomological validity can be construed from the performance of the scale with other variables with which it was expected to be related, no rigorous examination of the scale's discriminant or convergent validities was reported by Kahle (1995b) or Shoham, Rose, and Kahle (1998).

COMMENTS: Kahle (1995) reported a mean score of 21.96 for the scale along with a standard deviation of 7.5.

REFERENCES:
Kahle, Lynn R. (1995a), "Observations: Role-Relaxed Consumers: A Trend of the Nineties," *JAR*, 35 (2), 37–47.
Kahle, Lynn R. (1995b), "Observations: Role-Relaxed Consumers: Empirical Evidence," *JAR*, 35 (May/June), 59–62.
Shoham, Aviv, Gregory M. Rose, and Lynn R. Kahle (1998), "Marketing of Risky Sports: From Intention to Action," *JAMS*, 26 (4), 307–321.

SCALE ITEMS:

Directions: People have differing opinions when it comes to shopping for and buying products. We'd like your opinion about the statements listed below. If you *agree* strongly with a statement, you may mark a one (1) or two (2). If you *disagree* strongly, you may mark a six (6) or a seven (7). You can mark any number from one to seven to tell us how you feel.

1. How elegant and attractive a product is, is as important as how well it works.

2. It is important that others think well of how I dress and look.

3. When I am uncertain how to act in a social situation, I try to do what others are doing.

4. My friends and I tend to buy the same brands.

5. If I were to buy something expensive, I would worry about what others would think of me.

6. I buy brands that will make me look good in front of my friends.

7. When I buy the same things my friends buy, I feel closer to them.

SCALE NAME: Congruency (Beliefs/Information)

SCALE DESCRIPTION: The scale is composed of three items intended to measure the similarity (or lack thereof) between a person's prior beliefs about a brand and some new information he/she has been exposed to.

SCALE ORIGIN: The scale is apparently original to Gurhan-Canli and Maheswaran (1998).

RELIABILITY: An alpha of .95 was reported for the scale by Gurhan-Canli and Maheswaran (1998).

VALIDITY: No information regarding the scale's validity was reported by Gurhan-Canli and Maheswaran (1998).

REFERENCES:
Gurhan-Canli, Zeynep and Durairaj Maheswaran (1998), "The Effects of Extensions on Brand Name Dilution and Enhancement," *JMR*, 35 (November), 464–473.

SCALE ITEMS: [1]

1. How different was the information from what you expected?
   not at all / very different

2. Indicate the extent to which the information was:
   totally expected / unexpected

3. Indicate the extent to which the information was:
   not at all surprising / very surprising

[1] Gurhan-Canli and Maheswaran (1998) did not provide the exact phrasing of the scale stems. Also, it is not clear how many points were used on their response scales although it appears to have been seven.

SCALE NAME: Consumer Activism

SCALE DESCRIPTION: The scale is composed of seven, five-point statements designed to measure the degree to which a person is involved in activities that are typically considered to be wise or proper for consumers to engage in. Two of the items, #6 and #7, tap into conservation motivations or even environmentalism. As used by Palan (1998), the scale was completed by adolescents about their own behavior as well as by their parents who described the perceived degree of their child's activism.

SCALE ORIGIN: The scale used by Palan (1998) was apparently developed by Moschis and Churchill (1978). The latter reported an alpha of .64 for the scale.

RELIABILITY: Palan (1998) reported alphas of .84, .81, and .71 for use of the scale with mothers, fathers, and adolescents, respectively.

VALIDITY: Factor analyses were separately run by Palan (1998) on the responses from mothers, fathers, and children. In each case the items loaded on one factor providing some evidence of the scale's unidimensionality. Using the Multi-trait, Multi-Informant method, evidence was provided in support of the scale's convergent and discriminant validities.

REFERENCES:

Moschis, George P. and Gilbert A. Churchill, Jr. (1978), "Consumer Socialization: A Theoretical and Empirical Analysis," *JMR*, 15 (November), 599–609.

Palan, Kay M. (1998), "Relationships Between Family Communication and Consumer Activities of Adolescents: An Exploratory Study," *JAMS*, 26 (4), 338–349.

SCALE ITEMS: [1]

1. I (My child) carefully read(s) most of the things they write on packages or labels.

2. I (My child) plan(s) how to spend my (his or her) money.

3. I (My child) compare(s) prices and brands before buying something that costs a lot of money.

4. I (My child) keep(s) track of the money I (he or she) spend(s) and save(s).

5. I (My child) shop(s) around before buying something that costs a lot of money.

6. I (My child) try (tries) to buy recyclable containers instead of disposable ones.

7. I (My child) makes sure that the lights and TV set at home are off when they are not being used.

---

[1] As noted by the parentheses in the statements, the phrasing of the items varies slightly depending upon who fills out the scale. Responses to the items were made on five-point scales with anchors ranging from *never* (1) to *very often* (5).

SCALE NAME: Consumer Skills Development (Child's)

SCALE DESCRIPTION: The scale is composed of five, eleven-point statements measuring at what age a parent believes that a typical child is able to engage in certain activities that indicate the beginning of the "consumer" role. Although children "consume" products from the day they are born, the skills referred to in this scale are those that develop later when children become more active and independent such as when they begin to purchase products themselves.

SCALE ORIGIN: The items are original to Rose (1999). This scale and a companion one were envisioned as capturing a "developmental timetable" dimension. This has to do with a parent's beliefs about typical ages when certain emotional and cognitive developments occur in children. The scale was developed following empirical testing of a larger pool of items.

RELIABILITY: Alphas of .77 (U.S.) and .68 (Japan) were reported for the scale by Rose (1999).

VALIDITY: The validity of the scale was not addressed by Rose (1999). However, results of a factor analysis of the items in this scale and those of another related scale (#590) were presented. It showed that the items proposed for the two scales loaded appropriately for both the U.S. and the Japanese samples.

REFERENCES:
Rose, Gregory M. (2002), Personal Correspondence.
Rose, Gregory M. (1999), "Consumer Socialization, Parental Style, and Development Timetables in the United States and Japan," *JM*, 63 (July), 105–119.

SCALE ITEMS: [1]

Directions: Now we would like to find out at what age you believe a typical child can do each of the following things:

1. spend money carefully

2. receive an allowance

3. purchase groceries by himself or herself

4. purchase things with his or her own money

5. prepare his or her own lunch

---

[1] The response format for these items was anchored by 2 to 12+ with the numbers referring to a child's age (Rose 2002).

SCALE NAME: Convenience of Technology Assisted Shopping

SCALE DESCRIPTION: The scale is composed of three, seven-point Likert-type items used to measure the degree to which a person views shopping that utilizes a technological device or system as being a less time consuming way to shop.

SCALE ORIGIN: The scale appears to be original to the studies reported by Childers et al. (2001).

RELIABILITY: Using LISREL, the reliability of the scale was calculated to be .921 (hedonic motivations) and .862 (utilitarian motivations) in the studies reported by Childers et al. (2001).

VALIDITY: Discriminant validity was assessed using two different tests (the latent variable confidence interval tests and the χ^2 difference test). For both studies the evidence indicated that each scale, including convenience, was measuring a distinctive construct.

COMMENTS: The phrase "technology assisted shopping" in each item (below) appears like it could be replaced with more specific names when wanting to adapt the scale for particular devices such as wireless PDAs.

REFERENCES:
Childers, Terry L., Christopher L. Carr, Joann Peck, and Stephen Carson (2001), "Hedonic and Utilitarian Motivations for Online Retail Shopping Behavior," *JR*, 77 (Winter), 511–535.

SCALE ITEMS:

1. Technology assisted shopping would allow me to save time when shopping.

2. Using technology assisted shopping would make my shopping less time consuming.

3. Using technology assisted shopping would be a convenient way to shop.

SCALE NAME: Corporate Social Responsibility (Company Ability)

SCALE DESCRIPTION: The nine-item, seven-point Likert-type scale attempts to assess a person's beliefs about the ability of companies (in general) to produce and deliver quality goods and services while also being socially responsible.

SCALE ORIGIN: The source of the scale was not described by Sen and Bhattacharya (2001) but it appears to have been developed by them for this or a related study.

RELIABILITY: Sen and Bhattacharya (2001) stated that the scale had an alpha of .87.

VALIDITY: No information regarding the scale's validity was provided by Sen and Bhattacharya (2001).

REFERENCES:
Sen, Sankar and C.B. Bhattacharya (2001), "Does Doing Good Always Lead to Doing Better? Consumer Reactions to Corporate Social Responsibility," *JMR*, 38 (May), 225–243.

SCALE ITEMS: [1]

1. Socially responsible behavior detracts from companies' ability to provide the best possible products. (r)

2. Socially responsible behavior is a drain on a company's resources. (r)

3. Socially responsible behavior by firms is often a cover-up for inferior product offerings. (r)

4. Socially responsible firms produce worse products than do firms that do not worry about social responsibility. (r)

5. All else equal, a socially responsible firm is likely to have lower technological expertise than a firm that is not socially responsible. (r)

6. Firms that devote resources towards socially responsible actions have fewer resources available for increasing employee effectiveness. (r)

7. A company can be both socially responsible and manufacture products of high value.

8. Firms engage in socially responsible behaviors to compensate for inferior product offerings. (r)

9. Resources devoted to social responsibility come at the expense of improved product offerings. (r)

[1] The anchors for the response scale used by Sen and Bhattacharya (2001) were *strongly disagree* (1) and *strongly agree* (7).

SCALE NAME: Corporate Social Responsibility (Personal Support)

SCALE DESCRIPTION: The ten-item, seven-point scale attempts to measure the extent to which a person supports a range of social issues that companies might be involved with.

SCALE ORIGIN: The source of the scale was not described by Sen and Bhattacharya (2001) but it appears to have been developed by them for this or a related study.

RELIABILITY: Sen and Bhattacharya (2001) stated that the scale had an alpha of .89.

VALIDITY: No information regarding the scale's validity was provided by Sen and Bhattacharya (2001).

REFERENCES:
Sen, Sankar and C.B. Bhattacharya (2001), "Does Doing Good Always Lead to Doing Better? Consumer Reactions to Corporate Social Responsibility," *JMR*, 38 (May), 225–243.

SCALE ITEMS: [1]

What is your position on each of the following issues?

1. equal opportunity employment practices

2. special employment support for women

3. special employment support for gays and lesbians

4. special employment support for ethnic minorities

5. special employment support for disabled people

6. special educational opportunities for women

7. special educational opportunities for ethnic minorities

8. special educational opportunities for disabled people

9. abortion rights (right to choose)

10. affirmative action

[1] The anchors for the response scale used by Sen and Bhattacharya (2001) were *do not support at all* (1) and *strongly support* (7).

SCALE NAME: Country-of-Origin Product Image (General)

SCALE DESCRIPTION: The scale is composed of six, seven-point Likert-type statements that measure a person's quality-related attitude about products produced in a specified country.

SCALE ORIGIN: Five of the six items used by Klein, Ettenson, and Morris (1998) come from a set of items developed by Darling and Arnold (1988). A set of thirteen items were used by the latter but they were not summated into a scale.

RELIABILITY: Klein, Ettenson, and Morris (1998) reported the construct reliability of the scale to be .73 (n = 244).

VALIDITY: Results of a single-construct structural equation model showed that the six scale items had significant paths to the construct and the residuals were low (Klein, Ettenson, and Morris 1998). Most indicators (e.g., AGFI) indicated a good level of model fit. However, the variance extracted was very low (.32).

REFERENCES:

Darling, John R. and Danny R. Arnold (1988), "The Competitive Position Abroad of Products and Marketing Practices of the United States, Japan, and Selected European Countries," *Journal of Consumer Marketing*, 5 (Fall), 61–68.

Klein, Jill Gabrielle, Richard Ettenson, and Marlene D. Morris (1998), "The Animosity Model of Foreign Product Purchase: An Empirical Test in the People's Republic of China," *JM*, 62 (January), 89–100.

SCALE ITEMS: [1]

1. Products made in _____ are carefully produced and have fine workmanship.

2. Products made in _____ are generally of a lower quality than similar products available from other countries. (r)

3. Products made in _____ show a very high degree of technological advancement.

4. Products made in _____ usually show a clever use of color and design.

5. Products made in _____ are usually quite reliable and seem to last the desired length of time.

6. Products made in _____ are usually a good value for the money.

[1] The name of the country of interest should be placed in the blanks. A seven-point, Likert-type response format was used by Klein, Ettenson, and Morris (1998) with anchors ranging from *strongly disagree* (1) to *strongly agree* (7).

SCALE NAME: Country-of-Origin Product Purchase Intention

SCALE DESCRIPTION: The scale is composed of six, seven-point Likert-type statements that measure a person's willingness to buy products made in another particular country. Technically, because of the lack of specificity in the measure (time frame, product), this scale may lean more towards being a measure of attitude-toward-the-act than purchase intention. The scale was called *willingness to buy* by Klein, Ettenson, and Morris (1998).

SCALE ORIGIN: The scale may be original to Klein, Ettenson, and Morris (1998) although it has one item used in a scale by Darling and Wood (1990).

RELIABILITY: Klein, Ettenson, and Morris (1998) reported the construct reliability of the scale to be .79 (n = 244).

VALIDITY: Results of a single-construct structural equation model showed that the six scale items had significant paths to the construct and the residuals were low (Klein, Ettenson, and Morris 1998). Most indicators (e.g., AGFI) indicated a good level of model fit. However, the variance extracted was very low (.39).

REFERENCES:

Klein, Jill Gabrielle, Richard Ettenson, and Marlene D. Morris (1998), "The Animosity Model of Foreign Product Purchase: An Empirical Test in the People's Republic of China," *JM*, 62 (January), 89–100.
Darling, John R. and Van R. Wood (1990), "A Longitudinal Study Comparing Perceptions of U.S. and Japanese Consumer Products in a Third/Neutral Country: Finland 1975 to 1985," *Journal of International Business Studies*, 21 (3), 427–450.

SCALE ITEMS: [1]

1. I would feel guilty if I bought a _____ product. (r)

2. I would never buy a _____ car. (r)

3. Whenever possible, I avoid buying _____ products. (r)

4. Whenever available, I would prefer to buy products made in _____.

5. I do not like the idea of owning _____ products. (r)

6. If two products were equal in quality, but one was from _____ and one was from _____, I would pay 10% more for the product from _____. (r)

[1] The name of the country of interest should be placed in the blanks of items 1–5 as well as the first blank of 6. The name of another country should go in the second and third blanks of 6. A seven-point, Likert-type response format was used by Klein, Ettenson, and Morris (1998) with anchors ranging from *strongly disagree* (1) to *strongly agree* (7).

SCALE NAME: Coviewing TV (Parent/Child)

SCALE DESCRIPTION: The scale measures what time during the week a parent reports typically watching TV with his/her children. The version by Carlson and Grossbart (1988) had an extra dimension intended to capture the importance of coviewing.

SCALE ORIGIN: The scale is indicated as being original to Carlson and Grossbart (1988; Grossbart, Carlson, and Walsh 1991).

RELIABILITY: Carlson and Grossbart (1988; Grossbart, Carlson, and Walsh 1991) reported an alpha of .90 and a beta of .85 for the scale. Alphas of .80 and .85 were estimated by Rose (2000; Rose, Bush, and Kahle 1998) for the scale in the U.S. and Japan, respectively. Rose and Grossbart (1999) reported alphas of .90 and .80 for the scale in the U.S. and the Japanese samples, respectively.

VALIDITY: No examination of scale validity was reported by Carlson and Grossbart (1988; Grossbart, Carlson, and Walsh 1991) or Rose (Rose, Bush, and Kahle 1998; Rose and Grossbart 1999).

REFERENCES:

Carlson, Les and Sanford Grossbart (1988), "Parental Style and Consumer Socialization of Children," *JCR*, 15 (June), 77–94.

Grossbart, Sanford, Les Carlson, and Ann Walsh (1991), "Consumer Socialization and Frequency of Shopping with Children," *JAMS*, 19 (Summer), 155–163.

Rose, Gregory M. and Sanford Grossbart (1999), "Consumer Socialization, Parental Style, and Development Timetables in the United States and Japan," *JM*, 63 (July), 105–119.

Rose, Gregory M. (2000), Personal Correspondence.

Rose, Gregory M. (2002), Personal Correspondence.

Rose, Gregory M., Victoria D. Bush, and Lynn Kahle (1998), "The Influence of Family Communication Patterns on Parental Reactions toward Advertising: A Cross-National Examination," *JA*, 27 (4), 71–85.

SCALE ITEMS: [1]

I watch TV with my children on:

1. . . . weekdays.

2. . . . Saturdays.

3. . . . Sundays.

4. It is important for my child and I to watch TV together so I know what kind of programs he/she is watching.

---

[1] The anchors for the five-point response scale used with the first three items were *very seldom* to *very often*. A five-point Likert-type response scale was used with item 4. Carlson and Grossbart (1988) used items 1–4 whereas Rose (Rose, Bush, and Kahle 1998; Rose and Grossbart 1999; 2002) only used the first three items.

SCALE NAME: Crime Estimates

SCALE DESCRIPTION: The scale is composed of 18 questions that are purported to measure a person's sense of the incidence of crime in the country with particular emphasis on New York City.

SCALE ORIGIN: Although not explicitly stated in the article, the scale appears to be based on work by Shapiro (1987). The impetus for the scale appears to be the expectation that television viewing influences consumers' perceptions of social reality, among them the exaggerated sense of the prevalence of crime in the country.

RELIABILITY: Alphas of .81 (n = 71) and .80 (n = 162) were reported for the scale as it was used in study one and two, respectively (Shrum, Wyer, and O'Guinn 1998).

VALIDITY: No information regarding the scale's validity was reported by Shrum, Wyer, and O'Guinn (1998).

COMMENTS: The scale items appear to tap into multiple constructs thus bringing into doubt the unidimensionality of the scale. If the scale is a reflective measure then unidimensionality is a problem but it might not be if the scale is argued to be a set of formative indicators. See Diamantopoulous and Winklhofer (2001) for more details.

REFERENCES:

Diamantopoulous, Adamantios and Heidi M. Winklhofer (2001), "Index Construction with Formative Indicators: An Alternative to Scale Development," *JMR*, 38 (May), 269–277.

Shapiro, Michael A. (1987), "The Influence of Communication-Source Coded Memory Traces on World View," doctoral dissertation, University of Wisconsin-Madison.

Shrum, L.J., Robert S. Wyer, Jr., and Thomas C. O'Guinn (1998), "The Effects of Television Consumption on Social Perceptions: The Use of Priming Procedures to Investigate Psychological Processes," *JCR*, 24 (March), 447–458.

SCALE ITEMS: [1]

Directions: Express your answers to the following questions as a <u>percentage</u>. If you think the event listed is very unlikely to happen, then you will write in a very small percentage. If you think the event listed is very likely, then you should give a large percentage. Please guess or estimate the answer as well as you can. Please write the answer as a percentage in the space given. Once you have given an answer, please do not go back and change that answer. Unless otherwise indicated, all questions refer to the United States.

1. During any given week, about how many people out of one hundred are involved in some kind of violence? _____

2. What percent of all crimes are violent crimes–like murder, rape, robbery, and aggravated assault? _____

3. What proportion of murders are committed by strangers? _____

4. What do you think the chances are that if you were to walk home alone at night on residential streets in New York City each night for a month, you would be the victim of a serious crime? _____

5. If a child were to play alone in a park for an hour during daylight each day for a month, what do you think the chances are that he would be the victim of a violent crime? _____

6. If you were to walk by yourself for an hour every night in a park in New York City for a month, what do you think the chances are that you would be the victim of a serious crime? _____

7. What do you think the chances are that an unaccompanied woman would be the victim of a violent crime late at night in a New York City subway? _____

8. What do you think the chances are that you, a member of your family, or one of your close friends might be the victim of an assault during the next year? _____

9. What percentage of the time do you think that policemen who shoot at running persons actually hit them? _____

10. How likely do you think it is that your house or the house of one of your close friends would be broken into during the next year? _____

11. If you were seriously harmed by someone, what are the chances that person would be a stranger? _____

12. What proportion of all murders do you think are committed by people who could be classified as mentally ill? _____

13. Of mentally ill people, what proportion would you say are violent? _____

14. What are the odds that you personally will be attacked or robbed within the next year? _____

15. When police arrive at the scene of violence, what percentage of the time must they use force and violence? _____

Directions: Express your answer to the following questions with a specific number. Please guess or estimate the answer as well as you can. Please write the answer in the space given.

16. How many times per month does the average policeman have to draw a gun? _____

17. How many murders do you think take place in Los Angeles every year? _____

18. During the last year, how many people do you think were murdered in the New York City subways? _____

---

[1] These are the directions used by Shapiro (1987). Presumably, the directions used by Shrum, Wyer, and O'Guinn (1998) were similar. Because items had different response formats, z-scores were calculated before item scores were averaged.

SCALE NAME: Cultural Orientation (Horizontal Collectivism)

SCALE DESCRIPTION: The scale is composed of eight items measuring the degree to which one's self is viewed in terms of its interdependence on the group, where similarity and equality of members is stressed.

SCALE ORIGIN: The scale was constructed by Singelis et al. (1995). A considerable amount of research was conducted to develop an instrument that would reflect the distinctions between two dimensions of cultural orientation: horizontal/vertical and collectivism/individualism. Given this, four scales were developed and tested. Confirmatory factor analysis showed that the four-factor model provided better fit than the two- and one-factor models. The reliability (alpha) for the horizontal individualism scale was .74.

RELIABILITY: An alpha of .70 was reported for the scale by Gürhan-Canli and Maheswaran (2000b).

VALIDITY: No examination of the scale's validity was reported by Gürhan-Canli and Maheswaran (2000b).

REFERENCES:
Gürhan-Canli, Zeynep and Durairaj Maheswaran (2000b), "Cultural Variations in Country of Origin Effects," *JMR*, 37 (3), 309–317.
Singelis, Theodore M., Harry C. Triandis, Dharm P.S. Bhawuk, and Michele J. Gelfand (1995), "Horizontal and Vertical Dimensions of Individualism and Collectivism: A Theoretical and Measurement Refinement," *Cross-Cultural Research*, 29 (August), 341–375.

SCALE ITEMS: [1]

1. The well-being of my coworkers is important to me.

2. If a coworker gets a prize, I would feel proud.

3. If a relative were in financial difficulty, I would help within my means.

4. It is important to maintain harmony within my group.

5. I like sharing little things with my neighbors.

6. I feel good when I cooperate with others.

7. My happiness depends very much on the happiness of those around me.

8. To me, pleasure is spending time with others.

---

[1] Gürhan-Canli and Maheswaran (2000b) used a seven-point response format but did not describe the exact nature of the verbal anchors. The original format by Singelis et al. (1995) appears to have been a nine-point scale with anchors ranging from *never or definitely no* to always or *definitely yes*.

SCALE NAME: Cultural Orientation (Horizontal Individualism)

SCALE DESCRIPTION: The purpose of the eight-item scale is to measure the degree to which a person expresses a tendency towards self-reliance. One's self is viewed in terms of its autonomy from the group though not in terms of relative status.

SCALE ORIGIN: The scale was constructed by Singelis et al. (1995). A considerable amount of research was conducted to develop an instrument that would reflect the distinctions between two dimensions of cultural orientation: horizontal/vertical and collectivism/individualism. Given this, four scales were developed and tested. Confirmatory factor analysis showed that the four-factor model provided better fit than the two- and one-factor models. The reliability (alpha) for the horizontal individualism scale was .67.

RELIABILITY: An alpha of .74 was reported for the scale by Gürhan-Canli and Maheswaran (2000b).

VALIDITY: No examination of the scale's validity was reported by Gürhan-Canli and Maheswaran (2000b).

REFERENCES:

Gürhan-Canli, Zeynep and Durairaj Maheswaran (2000b), "Cultural Variations in Country of Origin Effects," *JMR*, 37 (3), 309–317.

Singelis, Theodore M., Harry C. Triandis, Dharm P.S. Bhawuk, and Michele J. Gelfand (1995), "Horizontal and Vertical Dimensions of Individualism and Collectivism: A Theoretical and Measurement Refinement," *Cross-Cultural Research*, 29 (August), 341–375.

SCALE ITEMS: [1]

1. I often do "my own thing."

2. One should live one's life independently of others.

3. I like my privacy.

4. I prefer to be direct and forthright when discussing with people.

5. I am a unique individual.

6. What happens to me is my own doing.

7. When I succeed, it is usually because of my abilities.

8. I enjoy being unique and different from others in many ways.

---

[1] Gürhan-Canli and Maheswaran (2000b) used a seven-point response format but did not describe the exact nature of the verbal anchors. The original format by Singelis et al. (1995) appears to have been a nine-point scale with anchors ranging from *never or definitely no* to always or *definitely yes*.

SCALE NAME: Cultural Orientation (Vertical Collectivism)

SCALE DESCRIPTION: The scale is composed of eight items that attempt to assess the extent to which a person sees one's self as a member of a group but with members having different amounts of status. Although interdependence is accepted, so is inequality though service and sacrifice are stressed.

SCALE ORIGIN: The scale was constructed by Singelis et al. (1995). A considerable amount of research was conducted to develop an instrument that would reflect the distinctions between two dimensions of cultural orientation: horizontal/vertical and collectivism/individualism. Given this, four scales were developed and tested. Confirmatory factor analysis showed that the four-factor model provided better fit than the two- and one-factor models. The reliability (alpha) for the horizontal individualism scale was .68.

RELIABILITY: An alpha of .76 was reported for the scale by Gürhan-Canli and Maheswaran (2000b).

VALIDITY: No examination of the scale's validity was reported by Gürhan-Canli and Maheswaran (2000b).

REFERENCES:

Gürhan-Canli, Zeynep and Durairaj Maheswaran (2000b), "Cultural Variations in Country of Origin Effects," *JMR*, 37 (3), 309–317.

Singelis, Theodore M., Harry C. Triandis, Dharm P.S. Bhawuk, and Michele J. Gelfand (1995), "Horizontal and Vertical Dimensions of Individualism and Collectivism: A Theoretical and Measurement Refinement," *Cross-Cultural Research*, 29 (August), 341–375.

SCALE ITEMS: [1]

1. I would sacrifice an activity that I enjoy very much if my family did not approve of it.

2. I would do what would please my family even if I detested that activity.

3. Before taking a major trip, I consult with most members of my family and many friends.

4. I usually sacrifice my self-interest for the benefit of my group.

5. Children should be taught to place duty before pleasure.

6. I hate to disagree with others in my group.

7. We should keep our aging parents with us at home.

8. Children should feel honored if their parents receive a distinguished award.

---

[1] Gürhan-Canli and Maheswaran (2000b) used a seven-point response format but did not describe the exact nature of the verbal anchors. The original format by Singelis et al. (1995) appears to have been a nine-point scale with anchors ranging from *never or definitely no* to always or *definitely yes*.

SCALE NAME: Cultural Orientation (Vertical Individualism)

SCALE DESCRIPTION: The eight-item scale measures the degree to which a person expresses a tendency to relate to others such that social hierarchy and achievement of status through competition is important.

SCALE ORIGIN: The scale was constructed by Singelis et al. (1995). A considerable amount of research was conducted to develop an instrument that would reflect the distinctions between two dimensions of cultural orientation: horizontal/vertical and collectivism/individualism. Given this, four scales were developed and tested. Confirmatory factor analysis showed that the four-factor model provided better fit than the two- and one-factor models. The reliability (alpha) for the vertical individualism scale was .74.

RELIABILITY: An alpha of .72 was reported for the scale by Gürhan-Canli and Maheswaran (2000b).

VALIDITY: No examination of the scale's validity was reported by Gürhan-Canli and Maheswaran (2000b).

REFERENCES:

Gürhan-Canli, Zeynep and Durairaj Maheswaran (2000b), "Cultural Variations in Country of Origin Effects," *JMR*, 37 (3), 309–317.

Singelis, Theodore M., Harry C. Triandis, Dharm P.S. Bhawuk, and Michele J. Gelfand (1995), "Horizontal and Vertical Dimensions of Individualism and Collectivism: A Theoretical and Measurement Refinement," *Cross-Cultural Research*, 29 (August), 341–375.

SCALE ITEMS: [1]

1. It annoys me when other people perform better than I do.

2. Competition is the law of nature.

3. When another person does better than I do, I get tense and aroused.

4. Without competition, it is not possible to have a good society.

5. Winning is everything.

6. It is important that I do my job better than others.

7. I enjoy working in situations involving competition with others.

8. Some people emphasize winning: I'm not one of them. (r)

---

[1] Gürhan-Canli and Maheswaran (2000b) used a seven-point response format but did not describe the exact nature of the verbal anchors. The original format by Singelis et al. (1995) appears to have been a nine-point scale with anchors ranging from *never or definitely no* to always or *definitely yes*.

SCALE NAME: Decision Basis (Head Vs. Heart)

SCALE DESCRIPTION: The five-item, seven-point scale is intended to assess the basis on which a person thinks a decision was made. Essentially, the scale attempts to measure the relative roles played by affect and cognition in a particular decision a person has made. The scale was used by Shiv and Fedorikhin (1999) with regard to a selection of a snack but appears to be amenable for us with a variety of decisions.

SCALE ORIGIN: Although the authors have drawn some of the items from work by others, the scale as a whole appears to be original to Shiv and Fedorikhin (1999).

RELIABILITY: An alpha of .91 was reported for the scale (Shiv and Fedorikhin 1999).

VALIDITY: No examination of the scale's validity was reported by Shiv and Fedorikhin (1999). However, they did report that the items in this scale as well as those from two other scales loaded on unique dimensions in a factor analysis.

REFERENCES:
Shiv, Baba and Alexander Fedorikhin (1999), "Heart and Mind in Conflict: The Interplay of Affect and Cognition in Consumer Decision Making," *JCR*, 26 (December), 278–292.

SCALE ITEMS: [1]

My final decision _____ was driven by:

1. My thoughts / my feelings

2. My willpower / my desire

3. My prudent self / my impulsive self

4. The rational side of me / the emotional side of me

5. My head / my heart

---

[1] The nature of the decision can be specified in the blank. The phrase used by Shiv and Fedorikhin (1999) was *about which snack to choose.*

SCALE NAME: Decision-Making Style

SCALE DESCRIPTION: Six, six-point Likert-type statements are used to measure a person's tendency to use either an analytical or intuitive mental strategy for processing brand-related information and making a decision.

SCALE ORIGIN: The scale is original to Mantel and Kardes (1999).

RELIABILITY: The alpha for the scale was reported to be .75 (Mantel and Kardes 1999).

VALIDITY: Use of confirmatory factor analysis by Mantel and Kardes (1999) on the set of items provided support for the scale's unidimensionality. Beyond that, several tests of discriminant validity were conducted that confirmed the scale was measuring something distinct from something potentially similar such as need for cognition, (#283).

REFERENCES:
Mantel, Susan Powell and Frank R. Kardes (1999), "The Role of Direction of Comparison, Attribute-Based Processing, and Attitude-Based Processing in Consumer Preference," *JCR*, 25 (March), 335–352.

SCALE ITEMS:

1. The answer just came to me. (r)

2. In making my decision, I focused more on my personal impressions and feelings rather than on complex tradeoffs between attributes. (r)

3. I tried to use as much attribute information as possible.

4. I carefully compared the two brands on several different attributes.

5. My decision was based on facts rather than on general impressions and feelings.

6. My decision was based on careful thinking and reasoning.

SCALE NAME: Desire for Friendship with Service Provider

SCALE DESCRIPTION: The scale is used to measure the extent to which one person (a client) does not want to have a personal relationship with another person/party (professional service provider). The type of service provider studied by Price and Arnould (1999) was a hairstylist.

SCALE ORIGIN: The scale appears to be original to Price and Arnould (1999).

RELIABILITY: Alphas of .54 (Study 1, n = 197) and .89 (Study 4, n = 187) were reported for the scale by Price and Arnould (1999).

VALIDITY: No information about the scale's validity was provided by Price and Arnould (1999).

REFERENCES:
Price, Linda L. and Eric J. Arnould (1999), "Commercial Friendships: Service Provider-Client Relationships in Context," *JM*, 63 (October), 38–56.

SCALE ITEMS: [1]

1. I don't want to share feelings with this _____ because of our professional relationship.

2. My professional relationship with this _____ limits our personal relationship.

3. I don't want to be friends with my _____ because of our professional relationship.

---

[1] In Study 1 a five-point response format was used whereas a seven-point scale was used in Study 4 (Price and Arnould 1999). The term for the <u>category</u> of service provider should be placed in the blanks, e.g., hairstylist.

SCALE NAME: Disconfirmation Sensitivity

SCALE DESCRIPTION: The scale attempts to measure a consumer's tendency to experience greater satisfaction (dissatisfaction) than the average consumer when products perform better (worse) than expected.

SCALE ORIGIN: The scale is apparently original to the studies by Kopalle and Lehmann (2001).

RELIABILITY: Alphas of .53 (Study 1) and .64 (Study 2) were reported for the scale (Kopalle and Lehmann 2001).

VALIDITY: While an in-depth analysis of the scale's validity was not provided by Kopalle and Lehmann (2001), they did indicate that factor analyses of items from several scales showed the items in this scale to be unidimensional in both studies.

COMMENTS: A four-item version was used in Study 1 but it had such a poor reliability that for Study 2 the authors made slight wording changes to the items and added two more items. That improved alpha somewhat but it was still lower than desired. The authors suggested the low internal consistency was due to the scale capturing two aspects of the construct. Indeed, further work is called for to improve and establish the scale's psychometric quality.

REFERENCES:
Kopalle, Praveen K. and Donald R. Lehmann (2001), "Strategic Management of Expectations: The Role of Disconfirmation Sensitivity and Perfectionism," *JMR*, 38 (August), 386–394.

SCALE ITEMS: [1]

1. I notice when product performance does not match the quality I expect from the product.

2. Customers should be delighted when products perform better than expected.

3. I am not at all satisfied when products perform worse than I expect.

4. I am very satisfied when products perform better than I expect.

5. Customers are legitimately irritated when products perform worse than expected.

6. I typically compare a product's performance to my expectations for that product.

[1] A six-point response format was used by Kopalle and Lehmann (2001) in Study 1 while a seven-point scale was used in the second study.

SCALE NAME: Distribution Intensity

SCALE DESCRIPTION: The scale is composed of three, five-point Likert-type statements attempting to capture a consumer's sense of the relative amount of retail stores that carry a specified brand.

SCALE ORIGIN: Although Yoo, Donthu, and Lee (2000) drew inspiration from work by Smith (1992), the scale they used appears to be original to them.

RELIABILITY: Yoo, Donthu, and Lee (2000) reported the scale to have a composite reliability of .87.

VALIDITY: Factor analyses (EFA and CFA) were used to check the dimensionality of this scale along with eight others used in the study. Based on the results, the authors concluded that all items loaded on their respective factors as expected providing some sense of the scales' convergent and discriminant validities. The average variance extracted for this scale was .70.

REFERENCES:
Smith, Daniel C. (1992), "Brand Extensions and Advertising Efficiency: What Can and Cannot Be Expected," *JAR*, 32 (Nov-Dec), 11–20.
Yoo, Boonghee, Naveen Donthu, and Sungho Lee (2000), "An Examination of Selected Marketing Mix Elements and Brand Equity," *JAMS*, 28 (2), 195–211.

SCALE ITEMS: [1]

1. More stores sell _____ as compared to its competing brands.

2. The number of stores that deal with _____ is more than that of its competing brands.

3. _____ is distributed through as many stores as possible.

[1] The brand name of a product was placed in the blanks by Yoo, Donthu, and Lee (2000).

SCALE NAME: Ease of Use

SCALE DESCRIPTION: The scale is composed of four semantic differentials used to assess a person's opinion about a product's complexity, with emphasis on the amount of knowledge needed by the user to effectively use the product.

SCALE ORIGIN: The scale was developed by Mukherjee and Hoyer (2001).

RELIABILITY: An alpha of .74 was reported for the scale (Mukherjee and Hoyer 2001).

VALIDITY: No examination of the scale's validity was reported by Mukherjee and Hoyer (2001).

COMMENTS: Although the scale was developed for use with high tech products, it appears to be amenable for use with low tech products too if the object is to determine its ease of use.

REFERENCES:
Mukherjee, Ashesh and Wayne D. Hoyer (2001), "The Effect of Novel Attributes on Product Evaluation," *JCR*, 28 (December), 462– 472.

SCALE ITEMS:

1. Difficult to use / easy to use

2. High complexity / low complexity

3. A lot of knowledge required for effective use / little knowledge required for effective use

4. Many new procedures need to be mastered for effective use / few new procedures need to be mastered for effective use

SCALE NAME: Ease of Use (Technology Assisted Shopping)

SCALE DESCRIPTION: Three, seven-point Likert-type items are used to measure the degree to which the process involved in using a technological device or system is viewed by a person as understandable and easy.

SCALE ORIGIN: The construct and original scale were part of the Technology Acceptance Model (TAM) developed and tested by Davis (1986). The model became very popular and adjustments were made by other users over time and for varying contexts. Childers et al. (2001) drew upon Davis' (1989) ease of use scale and adapted it for their study, particularly so it would pertain to shopping.

RELIABILITY: Using LISREL, the reliability of the scale was calculated to be .791 (hedonic motivations) and .989 (utilitarian motivations) in the studies reported by Childers et al. (2001).

VALIDITY: Discriminant validity was assessed using two different tests (the latent variable confidence interval tests and the χ^2 difference test). For both studies the evidence indicated that each scale, including ease of use, was measuring a distinctive construct.

COMMENTS: The phrase "technology assisted shopping" in each item (below) appears like it could be replaced with more specific names when wanting to adapt the scale for particular devices such as wireless PDAs.

REFERENCES:
Childers, Terry L., Christopher L. Carr, Joann Peck, and Stephen Carson (2001), "Hedonic and Utilitarian Motivations for Online Retail Shopping Behavior," *JR*, 77 (Winter), 511–535.
Davis, Fred D. (1986), "Technology Acceptance Model for Empirically Testing New End-User Information Systems: Theory and Results," doctoral dissertation, MIT Sloan School of Management.
Davis, Fred D. (1989), "Perceived Usefulness, Perceived Ease of Use, and User Acceptance of Information Technology," *MIS Quarterly*, 19 (September), 319–340.

SCALE ITEMS:

1. Technology assisted shopping would be clear and understandable.

2. Technology assisted shopping would not require a lot of mental effort.

3. Technology assisted shopping would be easy to use.

#159 *Embarrassment*

SCALE NAME: Embarrassment

SCALE DESCRIPTION: Multiple semantic differentials are used to assess a person's negative, affective reaction to some stimulus that increases the perceived possibility of unwanted social evaluation.

SCALE ORIGIN: The scale was apparently developed by Dahl, Manchanda, and Argo (2001) drawing upon previous research (Modigliani 1968; Parrott and Smith 1991).

RELIABILITY: An alpha of .88 was reported for the scale used in both studies by Dahl, Manchanda, and Argo (2001) even though there was a difference in the number of items used in the two administrations (see below).

VALIDITY: No examination of the scale's validity was reported by Dahl, Manchanda, and Argo (2001). It was stated, however, that the three item version used in the first study was unidimensional.

REFERENCES:

Dahl, Darren W., Rajesh V. Manchanda, and Jennifer J. Argo (2001), "Embarrassment in Consumer Purchase: The Roles of Social Presence and Purchase Familiarity," *JCR*, 28 (December), 473–481.

Modigliani, Andre (1968), "Embarrassment and Embarrassability," *Sociometry*, 31 (3), 313–326.

Parrott, W. Gerrod and Stephanie F. Smith (1991), "Embarrassment: Actual vs. Typical Cases, Classical vs. Prototypical Representations," *Cognition and Emotion*, 5 (September-November), 467–488.

SCALE ITEMS: [1]

1. not embarrassed at all / very embarrassed

2. not uncomfortable at all / very uncomfortable

3. not awkward at all / very awkward

4. not self-conscious at all / very self-conscious

[1] In their first study, Dahl, Manchanda, and Argo (2001) used items 1-3 whereas in their second study they used all four items. A seven-point scale was employed in both cases.

SCALE NAME: Environmentalism

SCALE DESCRIPTION: Sixteen, five-point Likert-type statements are used to measure a person's attitude about a wide range of ecological issues with an emphasis on conservation and pollution. The developers of the scale referred to it as *Environmental Concern* (Weigel and Weigel 1978).

SCALE ORIGIN: The scale was developed by Weigel and Weigel (1978) although the items were selected from a pool that had performed well in previous study (Tognacci et al. 1972). Weigel and Weigel (1978) reported on the results of using the scale in several studies. Among the findings was that the scale's internal consistency was above .80 and it had a stability (6 week test-retest) of .83. Evidence was also provided that attested to the scale's known-groups validity.

RELIABILITY: An alpha of .68 (n = 57) was reported for the scale by Lastovicka et al. (1999).

VALIDITY: Lastovicka et al. (1999) used this scale in the process of validating another scale (#177). Based upon that, their data indicated that scores on this environmentalism scale were not significantly related to scores on the frugality scale or two measures of response bias (#462 and #91). It was significantly related (r = .54) to another measure of environmentalism (#161). This pattern of correlations provides a limited sense of the scale's discriminant and convergent validities.

REFERENCES:
Lastovicka, John L., Lance A. Bettencourt, Renee Shaw Hughner, and Ronald J. Kuntze (1999), "Lifestyle of the Tight and Frugal: Theory and Measurement," *JCR*, 26 (June), 85–98.
Tognacci, Louis N., Russell H. Weigel, Marvin F. Wideen, and David T. A. Vernon (1972), "Environmental Quality: How Universal is Public Concern?" *Environment and Behavior*, 4 (March), 73–86.
Weigel, Russell and Joan Weigel (1978), "Environmental Concern: The Development of a Measure," *Environment and Behavior*, 10 (March), 3–15.

SCALE ITEMS:

1. The federal government will have to introduce harsh measures to halt pollution since few people will regulate themselves.

2. We should not worry about killing too many game animals because in the long run things will balance out. (r)

3. I'd be willing to make personal sacrifices for the sake of slowing down pollution even though the immediate results may not seem significant.

4. Pollution is *not* personally affecting my life. (r)

5. The benefits of modern consumer products are more important than the pollution that results from their production and use. (r)

6. We must prevent any type of animal from becoming extinct, even if it means sacrificing some things for ourselves.

7. Course focusing on the conservation of natural resources should be taught in the public schools.

8. Although there is continual contamination of our lakes, streams, and air, nature's purifying processes soon return them to normal. (r)

9. Because government has such good inspection and control agencies, it's very unlikely that pollution due to energy production will become excessive. (r)

10. The government should provide each citizen with a list of agencies and organizations to which citizens could report grievances concerning pollution.

11. Predators such as hawks, crows, skunks, and coyotes which prey on farmers' grain crops and poultry should be eliminated. (r)

12. The currently active anti-pollution organizations are really more interested in disrupting society than they are in fighting pollution. (r)

13. Even if public transportation was more efficient than it is, I would prefer to drive my car to work. (r)

14. Industry is trying its best to develop effective anti-pollution technology. (r)

15. If asked, I would contribute time, money, or both to an organization like the Sierra Club that works to improve the quality of the environment.

16. I would be willing to accept an increase in my family's expenses of $100 next year to promote the wise use of natural resources.

SCALE NAME: Environmentalism

SCALE DESCRIPTION: The scale is composed of twelve Likert-type items and is purported to measure one's world view as it pertains to the environment and man's relationship to it. Response to most of the items appears to hinge on whether humans should adapt to the environment or rather that it is appropriate to use the environment as mankind desires. The scale was referred to the *New Environmental Paradigm* by its creators (Dunlap and Van Liere 1978) because this view was seen as contrasting with the more dominant paradigm of the time that was not particularly pro-environment. It might also be referred to as *ecological concern, eco-centrism,* or *green orientation.*

SCALE ORIGIN: The scale was constructed by Dunlap and Van Liere (1978). Alphas of .81 (general public) and .76 (environmentalists) were reported. The scale was unidimensional and showed modest evidence of validity.

RELIABILITY: Schuhwerk and Lefkoff-Hagius (1995) reported an alpha of .83 (n = 71) for the scale. An alpha of .78 (n = 57) was reported by Lastovicka et al. (1999).

VALIDITY: Lastovicka et al. (1999) used this scale in the process of validating another scale (#177). Based upon that, their data indicated that scores on the environmental paradigm scale were not significantly related to scores on the frugality scale or two measures of response bias (#462 and #91). It was significantly related (r = .54) to another measure of environmentalism (#160). This pattern of correlations provides some sense of the scale's discriminant and convergent validities.

Similarly, Schuhwerk and Lefkoff-Hagius (1995) did not report explicit validation effort but they did compare scores on this scale with one they created measuring a related construct. (See V. III, #202). The correlation of the two scales was .65, giving some hint of the scale's convergent validity.

REFERENCES:
Dunlap, Riley E. and Kent D. Van Liere (1978), "The New Environmental Paradigm," *The Journal of Environmental Education*, 9 (Summer), 10–19.
Lastovicka, John L., Lance A. Bettencourt, Renee Shaw Hughner, and Ronald J. Kuntze (1999), "Lifestyle of the Tight and Frugal: Theory and Measurement," *JCR*, 26 (June), 85–98.
Schuhwerk, Melody E. and Roxanne Lefkoff-Hagius (1995), "Green or Non-Green? Does Type of Appeal Matter When Advertising a Green Product?" *JA*, 24 (Summer), 45–54.

SCALE ITEMS: [1]

1. We are approaching the limit of the number of people the earth can support.

2. The balance of nature is very delicate and easily upset.

3. Humans have the right to modify the natural environment to suit their needs. (r)

4. Mankind was created to rule over the rest of nature. (r)

5. When humans interfere with nature it often produces disastrous consequences.

6. Plants and animals exist primarily to be used by humans. (r)

7. To maintain a healthy economy we will have to develop a "steady state" economy where industrial growth is controlled.

8. Humans must live in harmony with nature in order to survive.

9. The earth is like a spaceship with only limited room and resources.

10. Humans need not adapt to the natural environment because they can remake it to suit their needs. (r)

11. There are limits to growth beyond which our industrialized society cannot expand.

12. Mankind is severely abusing the environment.

[1] The response format used by Lastovicka et al. (1999) as well as Schuhwerk and Lefkoff-Hagius (1995) was not described. A four-point format was used by Dunlap and Van Liere (1978).

SCALE NAME: Ethnic Identification (Affirmation and Belonging)

SCALE DESCRIPTION: Five, seven-point Likert-type statements are used to measure the degree to which a person expresses a sense of attachment to an ethnic group and have positive affect towards it. The items were developed so that they are not specific to any one group but could be used with people who might be members of a variety of ethnic minorities.

SCALE ORIGIN: The scale used by Appiah (2001) is one component of the Multigroup Ethnic Identity Measure by Phinney (1992). The full instrument has 14 items that the author described as tapping into three dimensions of ethnic identity, one of which is the scale shown here (affirmation and belongingness). Alphas for this subscale were reported by Phinney (1992) to be .75 for high school students and .86 for college students.

RELIABILITY: An alpha of .87 was reported for the scale by Appiah (2001).

VALIDITY: No examination of the scale's validity was reported by Appiah (2001).

REFERENCES:

Appiah, Osei (2001), "Ethnic Identification on Adolescents' Evaluations of Advertisements," *JAR*, 41 (5), 7–22.

Phinney, Jean S. (1992), "The Multigroup Ethnic Identity Measure: A New Measure for Use with Diverse Groups," *Journal of Adolescent Research*, 7 (April), 156–176.

SCALE ITEMS:

1. I am happy that I am a member of the ethnic group I belong to.

2. I have a strong sense of belonging to my own ethnic group.

3. I have a lot of pride in my ethnic group and its accomplishments.

4. I feel a strong attachment to my ethnic group.

5. I feel good about my cultural or ethnic background.

SCALE NAME: Ethnocentrism (CETSCALE)

SCALE DESCRIPTION: It is a seventeen-item, seven-point Likert-type summated ratings scale measuring a respondent's attitude toward the appropriateness of purchasing American-made products versus those manufactured in other countries. The scale was called CETSCALE (consumers' ethnocentric tendencies) by its originators (Shimp and Sharma 1987). The scale has been used in a variety of languages and countries. A ten-item version of the scale has been used in some studies and a revised version of the scale was used by Herche (1992).

SCALE ORIGIN: The scale is original to the studies reported by Shimp and Sharma (1987). Development of the scale passed through several stages and employed numerous different samples. The information provided below is primarily based upon the final seventeen-item version of the scale rather than larger preliminary sets.

Four separate samples were used to assess the psychometric properties of the CETSCALE. One sample used names and addresses obtained from a list broker. One thousand questionnaires were mailed to each of three deliberately chosen cities: Detroit, Denver, and Los Angeles. The response rate was just less than a third for each area. At the same time, 950 questionnaires were sent to former panel members in the Carolinas. The response rate was nearly 60%. The total sample size in this "four-areas study" was 1535. The "Carolinas study" was composed of a group of 417 people who were a part of the "four-areas study." Data for the former study was collected two years prior to the latter. A smaller, ten-item version of the scale was tested in national consumer good study. A total of more than 2000 completed responses were received. A fourth study examined data from 145 college students. Although having varying proportions, each of the samples except for the student group had respondents representing most age and income groups.

RELIABILITY: The alpha for the ten-item version used by Gürhan-Canli and Maheswaran (2000b) was .70 (n = 168). The revised version of the scale used by Herche (1992) was reported to have an alpha of .93 (n = 520). Klein, Ettenson, and Morris (1998) reported a construct reliability of .83 (n = 244) for a six-item version of the scale modified for use in China. Netemeyer, Durvasula, and Lichtenstein (1991) reported alphas of .91, .92, .94, and .95 for the Japanese (n = 76), French (n = 70), German (n = 73), and American (n = 71) samples, respectively.

Alphas of between .94 and .96 were found for the scale in the four samples used by Shimp and Sharma (1987). Test-retest reliability was estimated with the student sample only. With a five-week interval between administrations, a correlation of .77 was reported.

Sharma, Shimp, and Shin (1995) reported a reliability coefficient of .91 for the CETSCALE based upon a holdout sample (n = 333).

Composite reliabilities of .939 (n = 990), .952 (n = 1,153), and .937 (n = 974) were reported for the short version of the scale used by Steenkamp and Baumgartner (1998) for Belgium, Great Britain, and Greece, respectively.

VALIDITY: Although bearing somewhat on the scale's predictive validity, the study by Herche (1992) did not directly assess the scale's construct validity. However, the revised version of the scale he used was discussed in an earlier paper (Herche 1990) as being a superior measure to the original CETSCALE. In that earlier paper Herche argued that the absence of negatively stated items in the scale made it vulnerable to response bias. He developed a version of the scale with seven of the original items stated in the opposite direction which were reverse coded during summation. The evidence indicated that the revised version of the scale explained substantially more variance than the original and had a better factor structure. He later recanted his recommendations (Herche and Engelland 1994, 1996) by providing evidence that there may be a significant threat to a scale's unidimensionality when both reversed- and standard-polarity items are included.

Klein, Ettenson, and Morris (1998) began with the ten- item version of the scale modified for the Chinese sample. However, fit statistics from a measurement model indicated that some adjustment was justified. The statistics improved when the scale was trimmed to six items. Further, some evidence of the scale's discriminant validity came from finding it was distinct from two types of animosity measures: #9 and #10. However, the variance extracted for the six-item scale was less than the minimum of .50 recommended by Fornell and Larcker (1981).

Using the original version of the scale and confirmatory factor analysis Netemeyer, Durvasula, and Lichtenstein (1991) found evidence that it was unidimensional and had adequate discriminant validity. Moderate support was also found for the scale's nomological validity. Convergent, discriminant, and nomological validity were addressed by Shimp and Sharma (1987) who provided evidence of the scale's quality.

Sharma, Shimp, and Shin (1995) made a general claim of discriminant and convergent validity for all of their scales based upon results of a CFA.

Steenkamp and Baumgartner (1998) examined the invariance of the scale in a cross-national study. Evidence was provided in support of partial metric and scalar invariance.

COMMENTS: See also Steenkamp, Hofstede, and Wedel (1999) as well as Baumgartner and Steenkamp (2001).

REFERENCES:

Baumgartner, Hans and Jan-Benedict E.M. Steenkamp (2001), "Response Styles in Marketing Research: A Cross-National Investigation," *JMR*, 38 (May), 143–156.

Fornell, Claes and David F. Larcker (1981), "Evaluating Structural Equation Models with Unobservable Variables and Measurement Error," *JMR*, 18 (February), 39–50.

Gürhan-Canli, Zeynep and Durairaj Maheswaran (2000b), "Cultural Variations in Country of Origin Effects," *JMR*, 37 (3), 309–317.

Herche, Joel (1990), "The Measurement of Consumer Ethnocentrism: Revisiting the CETSCALE," in *Proceedings of the Thirteenth Annual Conference of the Academy of Marketing Science*, B. J. Dunlap, ed., Western Carolina University, 371–375.

Herche, Joel (1992), "A Note on the Predictive Validity of the CETSCALE," *JAMS*, 20 (Summer), 261–264.

Herche, Joel and Brian Engelland (1994), "Reversed-Polarity Items, Attribution Effects and Scale Dimensionality," Office of Scale Research Technical Report #9401, Marketing Department, Southern Illinois University, Carbondale, Illinois, 62901-4629. .

Herche, Joel and Brian Engelland (1996), "Reversed-Polarity Items and Scale Unidimensionality," *JAMS*, 24 (Fall), 366–374.

Herche, Joel, Jill Gabrielle Klein, Richard Ettenson, and Marlene D. Morris (1998), "The Animosity Model of Foreign Product Purchase: An Empirical Test in the People's Republic of China," *JM*, 62 (January), 89–100.

Klein, Jill Gabrielle, Richard Ettenson, and Marlene D. Morris (1998), "The Animosity Model of Foreign Product Purchase: An Empirical Test in the People's Republic of China," *JM*, 62 (January), 89–100.

Netemeyer, Richard G., Srinvas Durvasula, and Donald R. Lichtenstein (1991), "A Cross-National Assessment of the Reliability and Validity of the CETSCALE," *JMR*, 28 (August), 320–327.

Sharma, Subhash, Terence A. Shimp, and Jeongshin Shin (1995), "Consumer Ethnocentrism: A Test of Antecedents and Moderators," *JAMS*, 23 (Winter), 26–37.

Shimp, Terence A. and Subhash Sharma (1987), "Consumer Ethnocentrism: Construction and Validation of the CETSCALE," *JMR*, 24 (August), 280–289.

Steenkamp, Jan-Benedict E.M. and Hans Baumgartner (1998), "Assessing Measurement Invariance in Cross-National Consumer Research," *JCR*, 25 (June), 78–90.

Steenkamp, Jan-Benedict E. M., Frenkel ter Hofstede, and Michel Wedel (1999), "A Cross-National Investigation into the Individual and National Cultural Antecedents of Consumer Innovativeness," *JM*, 63 (April), 55–69.

SCALE ITEMS: [1]

1. American people should always buy American-made products instead of imports.

2. Only those products that are unavailable in the U.S. should be imported.

3. Buy American-made products. Keep America working.

4. American products first, last, and foremost.

5. Purchasing foreign-made products is un-American.

6. It is not right to purchase foreign products, because it puts Americans out of jobs.

7. A real American should always buy American-made products.

8. We should purchase products manufactured in America instead of letting other countries get rich off us.

9. It is always best to purchase American products.

10. There should be very little trading or purchasing of goods from other countries unless out of necessity.

11. Americans should not buy foreign products, because this hurts American business and causes unemployment.

12. Curbs should be put on all imports.

13. It may cost me in the long-run but I prefer to support American products.

14. Foreigners should not be allowed to put their products on our markets.

15. Foreign products should be taxed heavily to reduce their entry into the U.S.

16. We should buy from foreign countries only those products that we cannot obtain within our own country.

17. American consumers who purchase products made in other countries are responsible for putting their fellow Americans out of work.

[1] The seven items altered by Herche (1990, 1992) were 1, 5, 7, 9, 12, 14, and 17. The alterations in each case essentially amounted to the addition of the word "not" in the sentence. The ten items used in the national consumer good study by Shimp and Sharma (1987) were 2, 4 to 8, 11, 13, 16, and 17. Gürhan-Canli and Maheswaran (2000b) as well as Steenkamp and Baumgartner (1998) apparently used that same ten-item version of the scale. The items composing the final version of the scale used by Klein, Ettenson, and Morris (1998) were 4-6, 8, 16, and 17. Presumably, the items are modified to reflect the county of interest.

SCALE NAME: Event/Product Congruence (Functional)

SCALE DESCRIPTION: This three-item, seven-point Likert-type scale attempts to assess a person's sense of the extent to which a specified product is probably used by the participant's in a specific event.

SCALE ORIGIN: Gwinner and Eaton (1999) developed the scale based upon previous conceptual work by Gwinner (1997). The scale was used to help test various "match-up" hypotheses. The items were constructed with sports events in mind but appear to be amenable for use in other types of events as well.

RELIABILITY: An alpha of .89 was reported for the scale (Gwinner and Eaton 1999).

VALIDITY: No examination of the scale's validity was reported by Gwinner and Eaton (1999).

REFERENCES:
Gwinner, Kevin P (1997), "A Model of Image Creation and Image Transfer in Event Sponsorship," *International Marketing Review*, 14 (3), 145–158.
Gwinner, Kevin P. and John Eaton (1999), "Building Brand Image Through Event Sponsorship: The Role of Image Transfer," *JA*, 28 (4), 47–57.

SCALE ITEMS: [1]

1. It is likely that *participants* in the *event* use *brand*.

2. When I watch the *event*, I often see *brand* being *used*.

3. *Brand* is not a product that *participants* in the *event* would consider *using*. (r)

---

[1] The italicized words in the scale items are meant to be replaced with those terms appropriate in the context of the study in which they are used. *Participants* could be such things as *driver*, *rider*, or *player*.

SCALE NAME: Event/Product Congruence (Image)

SCALE DESCRIPTION: The scale is composed of three, seven-point Likert-type sentences that attempt to assess a person's sense of the similarity between the images of an event and a specified product that could be associated with it in some way, e.g., sponsorship.

SCALE ORIGIN: Gwinner and Eaton (1999) developed the scale based upon previous conceptual work by Gwinner (1997). The scale was used to help test various "match-up" hypotheses. The items were constructed with sports events in mind but appear to be amenable for use in other types of events as well.

RELIABILITY: An alpha of .90 was reported for the scale (Gwinner and Eaton 1999).

VALIDITY: No examination of the scale's validity was reported by Gwinner and Eaton (1999).

REFERENCES:
Gwinner, Kevin P. (1997), "A Model of Image Creation and Image Transfer in Event Sponsorship," *International Marketing Review*, 14 (3), 145–158.
Gwinner, Kevin P. and John Eaton (1999), "Building Brand Image Through Event Sponsorship: The Role of Image Transfer," *JA*, 28 (4), 47–57.

SCALE ITEMS: [1]

1. The *event* and *brand* have a similar image.

2. The ideas I associate with *brand* are related to the ideas I associate with the *event*.

3. My image of the *event* is very different from the image I have of *brand*. (r)

---

[1] The italicized words in the scale items are meant to be replaced the particular brand and event names being studied.

SCALE NAME: Event/Sponsor Congruence

SCALE DESCRIPTION: The scale is composed of five, seven-point Likert type statements measuring a person's sense of fit between an event and the company that is sponsoring it. The events examined by Speed and Thompson (2000) were related to sports.

SCALE ORIGIN: The scale is original to the study by Speed and Thompson (2000). Some qualitative work by the authors led to generation of items for this scale as well as several others. This was followed by a pretest which aided in identifying items for deletion or modification.

RELIABILITY: An alpha of .95 was reported for the scale by Speed and Thompson (2000).

VALIDITY: The initial qualitative work conducted by the authors provides some evidence of its content validity. Based on data from the main study, a CFA was performed on items from several scales. The results provided evidence of this scale's convergent and discriminant validity.

REFERENCES:
Speed, Richard and Peter Thompson (2000), "Determinants of Sports Sponsorship Response," *JAMS*, 28 (2), 226–238.

SCALE ITEMS:

1. There is a logical connection between the event and the sponsor.

2. The image of the event and the image of the sponsor are similar.

3. The sponsor and the event fit together well.

4. The company and the event stand for similar things.

5. It makes sense to me that this company sponsors this event.

SCALE NAME: Exploratory Consumer Tendencies

SCALE DESCRIPTION: The scale is composed of multiple Likert-type items measuring the degree to which a person expresses preference for situations calling for greater exploratory consumer behavior and that produce stimulation from one's environment. The scale was referred to as *optimum stimulation level* (OSL) by Menon and Kahn (1995) although it would appear that OSL is a more general personality trait that is one determinant of (rather than being equivalent to) the consumer behaviors referred to in this scale. Following Baumgartner and Steenkamp (1996), Van Trijp, Hoyer, and Inman (1996) referred to their measure as *exploratory acquisition of products* and viewed it as measuring the consumer's need for variety. The eight-item subset used by Keaveney and Parthasarathy (2001) was referred to as *propensity for risk-taking behavior*. A three-item subset used by Ganesh, Arnold, and Reynolds (2000) was called *risk aversion*.

SCALE ORIGIN: The scale used by Menon and Kahn (1995) is a 30-item subset of 39 items developed by Raju (1980). An initial pool of ninety items related to exploratory behavior and lifestyle were compiled and then tested for low social desirability bias and high item-total correlations. Thirty-nine items were found to meet the criteria and were tested with two separate samples. Menon and Kahn (1995) used those items which Raju's (1980) findings indicated had the highest correlations with arousal-seeking tendency (Mehrabian and Russell 1974, pp. 218, 219) and were not specific to any product category (Kahn 1997).

Van Trijp, Hoyer, and Inman (1996) used a six-item version of a scale validated by Baumgartner and Steenkamp (1996) that in turn was mostly composed of items taken from Raju (1980). Van Trijp, Hoyer, and Inman (1996) indicated that using Baumgartner and Steenkamp's (1996) own data the six-item scale had a extremely high correlation (r=.96) with the 10-item version.

Ganesh, Arnold, and Reynolds (2000) as well as Keaveney and Parthasarathy (2001) stated that they borrowed the items from Raju (1980).

RELIABILITY: Alphas of .88 and .79 were reported by Menon and Kahn (1995) and Van Trijp, Hoyer, and Inman (1996), respectively, for their different versions of the scale. Keaveney and Parthasarathy (2001) reported alphas of .91 and .93 for the version of the scale they used in their studies one and two, respectively. An alpha of .74 was reported for the version of the scale used by Ganesh, Arnold, and Reynolds (2000).

VALIDITY: No examination of the scale's validity was reported in any of the studies. While Ganesh, Arnold, and Reynolds (2000) did not examine the scale's validity they did include its items in an EFA along with items intended to measure two other constructs. All items loaded strongly on the expected dimension with no significant cross-loadings.

COMMENTS: Although the full scale has high internal consistency it almost certainly does not have unidimensionality. This conclusion is based upon comments by Raju (1980) that his judgment and the results of a factor analysis led to the breaking up of the large set of items into seven different scales. Testing is called for to determine the dimensionality of this set of thirty items (a subset of Raju's 39 items). If it is not unidimensional then it would be inappropriate to use as a summated rating scale (Gerbing and Anderson 1988).

The range of scores on the six-item version of the scale (Van Trijp, Hoyer, and Inman 1996) was from 6 to 29 with a mean of 17.7 and a standard deviation of 3.9.

See also Steenkamp, Hofstede, and Wedel (1999) as well as Baumgartner and Steenkamp (2001).

REFERENCES:

Baumgartner, Hans and Jan-Benedict E. M. Steenkamp (1996), "Exploratory Consumer Buying Behavior: Conceptualization and Measurement," *International Journal of Research in Marketing*, 13 (2), 121–137.

Baumgartner, Hans and Jan-Benedict E. M. Steenkamp (2001), "Response Styles in Marketing Research: A Cross-National Investigation," *JMR*, 38 (May), 143–156.

Ganesh, Jaishanker, Mark J. Arnold, and Kristy E. Reynolds (2000), "Understanding the Customer Base of Service Providers: An Examination of the Differences Between Switchers and Stayers," *JM*, 64 (3), 65–87.

Gerbing, David W. and James C. Anderson (1988), "An Updated Paradigm for Scale Development Incorporating Uni-dimensionality and Its Assessment," *JMR*, 25 (May), 186–192.

Kahn, Barbara E. (1997), Personal Correspondence.

Keaveney, Susan M. and Madhavan Parthasarathy (2001), "Customer Switching Behavior in Online Services: An Exploratory Study of the Role of Selected Attitudinal, Behavioral, and Demographic Factors," *JAMS*, 29 (Fall), 374–390.

Mehrabian, Albert and James A. Russell (1974), *An Approach to Environmental Psychology*, Cambridge, MA: The MIT Press.

Menon, Satya and Barbara E. Kahn (1995), "The Impact of Context on Variety Seeking in Product Choices," *JCR*, 22 (December), 285–295.

Raju, P. S. (1980), "Optimum Stimulation Level: Its Relationship to Personality, Demographics, and Exploratory Behavior," *JCR*, 7 (December), 272–282.

Steenkamp, Jan-Benedict E.M., Frenkel ter Hofstede, and Michel Wedel (1999), "A Cross-National Investigation into the Individual and National Cultural Antecedents of Consumer Innovativeness," *JM*, 63 (April), 55–69.

Van Trijp, Has C. M., Wayne D. Hoyer, and J. Jeffrey Inman (1996), "Why Switch? Product Category-Level Explanations for True Variety-Seeking Behavior," *JMR*, 33 (August), 281–292.

SCALE ITEMS:

1. Even though certain food products are available in a number of different flavors, I always tend to buy the same flavor. (r)

2. When I eat out, I like to try the most unusual items the restaurant serves, even if I am not sure I would like them.

3. I like to shop around and look at displays.

4. I like to browse through mail order catalogs even when I don't plan to buy anything.

5. When I see a new or different brand on the shelf, I pick it up just to see what it is like.

6. I often read the information on the packages of products just out of curiosity.

7. I am the kind of person who would try any new product once.

8. A new store or restaurant is not something I would be eager to find out about. (r)

9. When I go to a restaurant, I feel it is safer to order dishes I am familiar with. (r)

10. I am very cautious in trying new/different products.

11. Even for an important date or dinner, I wouldn't be wary of trying a new or unfamiliar restaurant.

12. I generally read even my junk mail just to know what it is about.

13. I enjoy sampling different brands of commonplace products for the sake of comparison.

14. I would rather stick with a brand I usually buy than try something I am not very sure of. (r)

15. I usually throw away mail advertisements without reading them. (r)

16. If I like a brand, I rarely switch from it just to try something different. (r)

17. I often read advertisements just out of curiosity.

18. I would prefer to keep using old appliances and gadgets even if it means having to get them fixed, rather than buy new ones every few years. (r)

19. I would rather wait for others to try a new store or restaurant than try it myself. (r)

20. I get bored with buying the same brands even if they are good.

21. When I see a new brand somewhat different from the usual, I investigate it.

22. I never buy something I don't know about at the risk of making a mistake. (r)

23. I would get tired of flying the same airline every time.

24. If I buy appliances, I will buy only well established brands. (r)

25. Investigating new brands of grocery and other similar products is generally a waste of time. (r)

26. I rarely read advertisements that just seem to contain a lot of information. (r)

27. A lot of times I feel the urge to buy something really different from the brands I usually buy.

28. I enjoy taking chances in buying unfamiliar brands just to get some variety in my purchases.

29. If I did a lot of flying, I would probably like to try all the different airlines, instead of flying just one most of the time.

30. I enjoy exploring several different alternatives or brands while shopping.

Ganesh, Arnold, and Reynolds (2000): 10, 14, 28 5-point
Keaveney and Parthasarathy (2001): 2, 7, 9, 10, 11, 14, 22 7-point
Menon and Kahn (1995): 1-30 9-point
Van Trijp, Hoyer, and Inman (1996): 1, 9, 10, 14, 16, 28 5-point

SCALE NAME: Familiarity (Brand)

SCALE DESCRIPTION: The scale is composed of three, seven-point semantic differentials intended to measure a person's familiarity with a specified brand name.

SCALE ORIGIN: Although similar in concept to previous measures of familiarity (e.g., V. I, #101 and #102), this set of items appears to be original to the study by Simonin and Ruth (1998).

RELIABILITY: Alphas of .80 and .94 were reported for the scale as used with a car brands and microprocessor brands, respectively (Simonin and Ruth 1998).

VALIDITY: In general terms, Simonin and Ruth (1998) reported evidence of the scale's convergent and discriminant validity from analysis of their measurement model.

REFERENCES:
Simonin, Bernard L. and Julie A. Ruth (1998), "Is a Company Known by the Company It Keeps? Assessing the Spillover Effects of Brand Alliances on Consumer Brand Attitudes," *JMR*, 35 (February), 30–42.
Ruth, Julie A. (2001), Personal Correspondence.

SCALE ITEMS: [1]

Please indicate how familiar you are with the _____ brand name.

1. not at all familiar / extremely familiar

2. definitely do not recognize / definitely recognize

3. definitely have not heard of it before / definitely have heard of it before

[1] The directions and items were provided by Ruth (2001). Responses to the items were made on a seven-point scale and the name of the brand was put in the blank of the directions.

#169 *Familiarity (Object)*

SCALE NAME: Familiarity (Object)

SCALE DESCRIPTION: Three, seven-point semantic differentials are used to measure a person's aware-ness and recognition of some specific object. In the study by Roehm (2001), the focal object was a portion of a song used as background music in a mock radio advertisement.

SCALE ORIGIN: Although bearing similarity to some previous measures of familiarity, this scale appears to be original to the study by Roehm (2001).

RELIABILITY: Alphas of .96 (48 MBA students) and .86 (44 community members) were reported for the scale (Roehm 2001).

VALIDITY: No information regarding the scale's validity was reported by Roehm (2001).

REFERENCES:
Roehm, Michelle L. (2001), "Instrumental Vs. Vocal Versions of Popular Music in Advertising," *JAR*, 41 (3), 49–58.

SCALE ITEMS:

1. Not at all familiar / highly familiar

2. Don't know it well at all / know it very well

3. Don't recognize it right away / recognize it right away

SCALE NAME: Familiarity (Product Category & Brand)

SCALE DESCRIPTION: The scale is composed of seven statements attempting to assess a consumer's familiarity and experience with a brand and several other things related to the brand such as the products carrying the brand name, the advertising for the brand, the stores carrying the products, and the product category.

SCALE ORIGIN: Although not stated explicitly, the scale appears to have been created by Martin and Stewart (2001). The scale was developed for use in studying brand extensions.

RELIABILITY: An alpha of .91 was reported for the scale (Martin and Stewart 2001).

VALIDITY: The validity of the scale was not discussed by Martin and Stewart (2001).

COMMENTS: On the face of it, the items in this scale refer to several different though possibly related things. Despite its high internal consistency it is difficult to see how the scale could be unidimensional. Care should be taken in using the scale until its psychometric quality can be confirmed.

REFERENCES:
Martin, Ingrid M. and David W. Stewart (2001), "The Differential Impact of Goal Congruency on Attitudes, Intentions, and the Transfer of Brand Equity," *JMR*, 38 (Nov), 471–484.

SCALE ITEMS: [1]

1. How familiar are you with _____?

2. How familiar are you with _____ _____?

3. How familiar are you with the types of retail stores that carry _____ products?

4. How familiar are you with the type of advertising that _____ currently uses?

5. How familiar are you with _____ in general?

6. How familiar are you with _____ in general?

7. How much experience do you have with _____ products?

[1] With items 1, 3, 4, and 7 the name of the brand should be placed in the blanks. With item 2, the name of the brand goes in the first blank and the name or description of the products the brand is currently known for should go in the second blank. In item 5, the blank should be filled with a name or description of the product category that the brand has been known for whereas in 6 the extension category is named. As for the scale anchors, items 1-6 used *not at all familiar* to *very familiar* whereas #7 used *no experience at all* to *much experience*.

SCALE NAME: Family Communication (Concept-Oriented, Child's View)

SCALE DESCRIPTION: The scale is composed of six, five-point Likert-type statements that measure the extent to which a child indicates that his/her mother takes an active interest in his/her use of money and the purchase of products. The tone of the items is positive such that the child's role is respected rather than his/her opinion being ignored and/or his/her purchases being dictated.

SCALE ORIGIN: Mangleburg and Bristol (1998) stated that they drew their items from the scales by Moschis, Moore, and Smith (1984). The version of this scale stated from the point of view of the parent can be found in V. I (#178) as well as V. II (#181) of this series.

RELIABILITY: A composite reliability of .74 was reported for the scale by Mangleburg and Bristol (1998).

VALIDITY: Although confirmatory factor analysis was conducted by Mangleburg and Bristol (1998), the exact details bearing on the validity of this scale were not reported.

REFERENCES:

Mangleburg, Tamara F. and Terry Bristol (1998), "Socialization and Adolescents' Skepticism Toward Advertising," *JA*, 27 (3), 11–21.

Moschis, George P., Roy. L. Moore , and Ruth B. Smith (1984), "The Impact of Family Communication on Adolescent Consumer Socialization," in *Advances in Consumer Research, V. 11*, Thomas C. Kinnear, ed., Provo, UT: Association for Consumer Research, 314–319.

SCALE ITEMS:

1. My (step)mother asks me to help in buying things for the family.

2. My (step)mother asks me what I think about the things I buy for myself.

3. My (step)mother says I should decide about things I should or should not buy.

4. My (step)mother says that buying things I like is important even if others do not like them.

5. My (step)mother lets me decide how to spend my own money.

6. My (step)mother asks me for advice about buying things.

SCALE NAME: Family Communication (Concept-Oriented, Parent's View)

SCALE DESCRIPTION: The scale is composed of statements using a five-point response format that measure how often a parent encourages his/her children to form their own consumption preferences. The tone suggested in the items is of positive communication where the child's role, assistance, and opinion is respected rather than their purchases being dictated to them.

SCALE ORIGIN: Rose, Bush, and Kahle (1998) stated that their scale was composed of five items taken from a scale by Moschis, Moore, and Smith (1984) and three items from the work of Ward, Wackman, and Wartella (1977). Carlson and Grossbart (1988; Grossbart, Carlson, and Walsh 1991) either drew from that same study or other work by Moschis. Rose (1999) used subsets of these items to compose two scales, one to measure a family's *concept-orientation* and the other to measure the *extent of family communication*.

RELIABILITY: Carlson and Grossbart (1988; Grossbart, Carlson, and Walsh 1991) reported an alpha of .71 for the version of the scale they used. Alphas of .77 and .76 were reported by Rose, Bush, and Kahle (1998) for the scales they used in the U.S. and Japan, respectively. For the *concept-oriented* scale Rose (1999) reported alphas of .70 (U.S.) and .68 (Japan); for *extent of family communication* an alpha of .71 was reported for both U.S. and Japanese samples.

VALIDITY: No examination of the scale's validity was reported in any of the studies. The unidimensionality of the full set of items is in doubt and should be carefully checked before treating the set as a summated measure.

REFERENCES:

Carlson, Les and Sanford Grossbart (1988), "Parental Style and Consumer Socialization of Children," *JCR*, 15 (June), 77–94.

Grossbart, Sanford, Les Carlson, and Ann Walsh (1991), "Consumer Socialization and Frequency of Shopping with Children," *JAMS*, 19 (Summer), 155–163.

Moschis, George P., Roy. L. Moore, and Ruth B. Smith (1984), "The Impact of Family Communication on Adolescent Consumer Socialization," in *Advances in Consumer Research, V. 11*, Thomas C. Kinnear, ed., Provo, UT: Association for Consumer Research, 314–319.

Rose, Gregory M. (1999), "Consumer Socialization, Parental Style, and Development Timetables in the United States and Japan," *JM*, 63 (July), 105–119.

Rose, Gregory M. (2000), Personal Correspondence.

Rose, Gregory M. (2002), Personal Correspondence.

Rose, Gregory M., Victoria D. Bush, and Lynn Kahle (1998), "The Influence of Family Communication Patterns on Parental Reactions toward Advertising: A Cross-National Examination," *JA*, 27 (4), 71–85.

Ward, Scott, Daniel B. Wackman, and Ellen Wartella (1977), *How Children Learn to Buy: The Development of Consumer Information Processing Skills*, Beverly Hills: Sage Publications.

#172 *Family Communication (Concept-Oriented, Parent's View)*

SCALE ITEMS: [1]

1. I ask my child to help me buy things for the family.

2. I tell my child that buying things that he/she likes is important even if others don't like them.

3. I ask my child for advice about buying things.

4. I ask my child about things that I buy for myself.

5. I let my child decide which things he/she should or shouldn't buy.

6. I let my child decide how to spend his/her money.

7. I ask my child what he/she thinks about things that he/she buys for him/herself.

8. My children and I talk about buying things.

9. I ask my child his/her preference when I buy something for him/her.

10. I talk to him/her about where different products can be bought.

11. To teach my child to become a consumer I allow my child to learn from his/her own experience.

[1] Each study used the same five-point response scale where 1 = *very seldom*, 2 = *seldom*, 3 = *sometimes*, 4 = *often*, and 5 = *very often* (Rose 2000, 2002). Rose, Bush, and Kahle (1998) used all of the items except for #2 and #6. Rose (1999, 2002) used #1–7 to measure *concept-orientation* and #8–#10 to measure *extent of family communication*. Carlson and Grossbart (1988; Grossbart, Carlson, and Walsh 1991) used items the same or similar to #1–#3, #5–#7, and #11.

SCALE NAME: Family Communication (Socio-Oriented, Child's View)

SCALE DESCRIPTION: The scale is composed of six, five-point Likert-type statements that measure the extent to which a child indicates that his/her mother tells him/her what to buy or not buy. The tone of the items is that the child believes the parent is concerned about how the child's money is used and wants to have a lot of control over the decisions.

SCALE ORIGIN: Mangleburg and Bristol (1998) stated that they drew their items from the scales by Moschis, Moore, and Smith (1984). A version of this scale stated from the point-of-view of the parent can be found in V. I (#181) of this series.

RELIABILITY: A composite reliability of .80 was reported for the scale by Mangleburg and Bristol (1998).

VALIDITY: Although confirmatory factor analysis was conducted by Mangleburg and Bristol (1998), the exact details bearing on the validity of this scale were not reported.

REFERENCES:
Mangleburg, Tamara F. and Terry Bristol (1998), "Socialization and Adolescents' Skepticism Toward Advertising," *JA*, 27 (3), 11–21.
Moschis, George P., Roy. L. Moore, and Ruth B. Smith (1984), "The Impact of Family Communication on Adolescent Consumer Socialization," in *Advances in Consumer Research, V. 11*, Thomas C. Kinnear, ed., Provo, UT: Association for Consumer Research, 314–319.

SCALE ITEMS:

1. My (step)mother tells me what types of things I can buy.

2. My (step)mother wants to know what I do with my money.

3. My (step)mother complains when I buy something that she does not like.

4. My (step)mother says that I should not ask questions about things that teenagers do not usually buy.

5. My (step)mother tells me that I can't buy certain things.

6. My (step)mother says that she knows what is best for me and that I should not question her.

SCALE NAME: Family Communication (Socio-Oriented, Parent's View)

SCALE DESCRIPTION: The scale attempts to measure the degree to which a parent reports telling a child what to buy or not buy. This is in contrast to taking an interest in what the child wants to purchase and being lenient in allowing it.

SCALE ORIGIN: Ideas for some of the items used by Carlson and Grossbart (1988) came from the research of Moschis (1978, p. 45) as well as Ward, Wackman, and Wartella (1977).

Rose, Bush, and Kahle (1998) cited Moschis, Moore, and Smith (1984) as the source of the scale. Indeed, four of the five items used by the former are the same or similar to statements in the six-item scale used by the latter.

RELIABILITY: Carlson and Grossbart (1988) reported an alpha of .56 and a beta of .51 for their scale. Alphas of .70 and .68 were reported by Rose, Bush, and Kahle (1998) for their versions of the scale in the U.S. and Japan, respectively. Rose (1999) reported alphas of .68 and .70 for the scale in the U.S. and the Japanese samples, respectively.

VALIDITY: No examination of the scale's validity was reported by Carlson and Grossbart (1988) or Rose, Bush, and Kahle (1998).

COMMENTS: The low alphas may indicate a lack of unidimensionality. This may be due to respondent behavior not being consistent across product categories.

REFERENCES:

Carlson, Les and Sanford Grossbart (1988), "Parental Style and Consumer Socialization of Children," *JCR*, 15 (June), 77–94.

Moschis, George P. (1978), *Acquisition of the Consumer Role By Adolescents, Research Monograph No. 82*, Atlanta, Georgia: Publishing Services Division, College of Business Administration, Georgia State University.

Moschis, George P., Roy L. Moore, and Ruth B. Smith (1984), "The Impact of Family Communication on Adolescent Consumer Socialization," in *Advances in Consumer Research, V. 11*, Thomas C. Kinnear, ed., Provo, UT: Association for Consumer Research, 314–319.

Rose, Gregory M. (1999), "Consumer Socialization, Parental Style, and Development Timetables in the United States and Japan," *JM*, 63 (July), 105–119.

Rose, Gregory M. (2000), Personal Correspondence.

Rose, Gregory M. (2002), Personal Correspondence.

Rose, Gregory M., Victoria D. Bush, and Lynn Kahle (1998), "The Influence of Family Communication Patterns on Parental Reactions toward Advertising: A Cross-National Examination," *JA*, 27 (4), 71–85.

Ward, Scott, Daniel B. Wackman, and Ellen Wartella (1977), *How Children Learn to Buy: The Development of Consumer Information Processing Skills*, Beverly Hills: Sage Publications.

SCALE ITEMS: [1]

1. I tell my child he/she shouldn't ask questions about things children do not usually buy.

2. I tell my child he/she is not allowed to buy certain things.

3. I tell my child what things he/she should or shouldn't buy.

4. I want to know what my child does with his/her money.

5. I complain when I do not like something my child bought for him/herself.

6. To teach my child to become a consumer I stop him/her from doing certain things.

7. I tell my child not to buy certain things.

---

[1] Carlson and Grossbart (1988) used items 1-6 in a five-point Likert-type format. Rose (Rose, Bush, and Kahle 1998; 1999; 2002) used item 7 and other items similar to 2, 3, 4, and 5. The anchors for the scale were 1 = *very seldom*, 2 = *seldom*, 3 = *sometimes*, 4 = *often*, and 5 = *very often* (Rose 2000, 2002).

#175 *Financial Pressure (Specific Shopping Trip)*

SCALE NAME: Financial Pressure (Specific Shopping Trip)

SCALE DESCRIPTION: Three, seven-point Likert-type statements are used to measure the degree to which a shopper perceives having sufficient money to cover what is intended to be purchased as well as a few unplanned items during a particular shopping episode. The scale was called *money available* by Beatty and Ferrell (1998).

SCALE ORIGIN: The scale was developed by Beatty and Ferrell (1998) by modifying a previous measure geared for teenagers (Beatty and Talpade 1994).

RELIABILITY: Beatty and Ferrell (1998) reported a composite reliability of .72 for the scale.

VALIDITY: Although the details related to this scale were not provided, the implication was that it was unidimensional and showed sufficient evidence of convergent and discriminant validity (Beatty and Ferrell 1998).

REFERENCES:
Beatty, Sharon E. and M. Elizabeth Ferrell (1998), "Impulse Buying: Modeling Its Precursors," *JR*, 74 (2), 169–191.
Beatty, Sharon E. and Salil Talpade (1994), "Adolescent Influence in Family Decision Making: A Replication with Extension," *JCR*, 21 (September), 332–341.

SCALE ITEMS:

1. I do not feel I can afford to make any unplanned purchases on this trip. (r)

2. I am on a tight budget while on this shopping trip.

3. I feel that I have enough money on this shopping trip so that I can splurge a little if I find something I really like. (r)

SCALE NAME: Friendliness

SCALE DESCRIPTION: The six-item, five-point scale measures the extent to which a person considers another person to be likeable and pleasant to be around. Due to the phrasing of the last two items, the focus of the scale is on the perceived friendliness of a service provider by a client. The service provider studied by Price and Arnould (1999) was a hairstylist.

SCALE ORIGIN: The scale appears to be original to Price and Arnould (1999).

RELIABILITY: An alpha of .85 was reported for the scale by Price and Arnould (1999).

VALIDITY: No information about the scale's validity was provided by Price and Arnould (1999).

COMMENTS: With some rephrasing of items #5 and #6 (below) the scale appears to be usable in a non-commercial context.

REFERENCES:
Price, Linda L. and Eric J. Arnould (1999), "Commercial Friendships: Service Provider-Client Relationships in Context," *JM*, 63 (October), 38–56.

SCALE ITEMS: [1]

1. _____ likes to talk with people.

2. _____ is friendly.

3. _____ tries to establish a personal relationship.

4. _____ is very pleasant.

5. _____ treats me like just a customer rather than as a person with specific needs and desires. (r)

6. I like this _____ as a person.

[1] The name of the service provider should go in the blanks of all of the items except for #6 which should have the term for the <u>category</u> of service provider, e.g., hairstylist.

SCALE NAME: Frugality

SCALE DESCRIPTION: The scale is composed of eight, six-point Likert-type items that are intended to measure a consumer lifestyle trait characterized by the extent that a person is both restrained in acquiring products as well as being resourceful in using them.

SCALE ORIGIN: The scale was developed by Lastovicka et al. (1999). A model multi-study process was used to generate items, examine reliability and validity, as well as establish norms. Although some details are mentioned in this review, much more information is available in the article and is worth consulting.

RELIABILITY: The following alphas were reported for the scale by Lastovicka et al. (1999): .85 (106 college students, Study 1A), .87 (107 college students, Study 1B), .88 (57 university staff, Study 2), .73 (convenience sample of 90 airline passengers, Study 3), and .80 (164 randomly selected adults, Study 6).

VALIDITY: The six studies conducted by Lastovicka et al. (1999) broadly and deeply addressed the validity of the scale. Briefly, study 1 involved item generation and scale purification. Studies 2 and 3 examined the scale's discriminant validity. In the fourth study a multitrait-multimethod analysis was conducted. Nomological validity was examined in Study 5. A known-groups evaluation was made in Study 6. In general, across the various methods used and forms of validity assessed, the scale was found to be valid and free from response-set tendencies, e.g., social desirability bias.

COMMENTS: One of the goals of Study 6 was to get a sense of scale norms with a general adult sample. Scores were found to be normally distributed with a mean of 40 and standard deviation of 4.

REFERENCES:
Lastovicka, John L., Lance A. Bettencourt, Renee Shaw Hughner, and Ronald J. Kuntze (1999), "Lifestyle of the Tight and Frugal: Theory and Measurement," *JCR*, 26 (June), 85–98.

SCALE ITEMS:

1. If you take good care of your possessions, you will definitely save money in the long run.

2. There are many things that are normally thrown away that are still quite useful.

3. Making better use of my resources makes me feel good.

4. If you can re-use an item you already have, there's no sense in buying something new.

5. I believe in being careful in how I spend my money.

6. I discipline myself to get the most from my money.

7. I am willing to wait on a purchase I want so that I can save money.

8. There are things I resist buying today so I can save for tomorrow.

SCALE NAME: Goal Similarity (Brand/Ideals)

SCALE DESCRIPTION: The scale is composed of three statements attempting to assess a consumer's belief of how well a brand can achieve a certain goal. The scale was called *goodness-of-fit* by Martin and Stewart (2001).

SCALE ORIGIN: Martin and Stewart (2001) stated that their scale was based on the goals-based approach to measuring product similarity and their scale was apparently inspired by the work of Barsalou (e.g., 1985). As used by Martin and Stewart (2001), the scale was applied to the study of brand extensions.

RELIABILITY: The alpha for the scale was .69 (Martin and Stewart 2001).

VALIDITY: The typical aspects of scale validity were not provided by Martin and Stewart (2001) although some information bearing on the scale's nomological validity was discussed.

REFERENCES:

Barsalou, Lawrence W. (1985), "Ideals, Central Tendency, and Frequency of Instantiation as Determinants of Graded Structure in Categories," *Journal of Experimental Psychology: Learning, Memory, and Cognition*, 11 (4), 629–654.

Martin, Ingrid M., and David W. Stewart (2001), "The Differential Impact of Goal Congruency on Attitudes, Intentions, and the Transfer of Brand Equity," *JMR*, 38 (Nov), 471–484.

SCALE ITEMS: [1]

1. How well do _____ _____ fit with the goal of wanting high quality, colorful clothing?
   not at all well / very well

2. How consistent are _____ _____ with the goal of wanting high quality, colorful clothing?
   not at all consistent / very consistent

3. How well do _____ _____ exemplify the goal of wanting high quality, colorful clothing?
   extremely poor example / extremely good example

[1] The first blank in each item should have the brand name (e.g., *Benetton's*) while the second blank is the product category name (e.g., *dress leather shoes*). To adapt the items for other product categories the ending phrases of each item can be rephrased so as to apply to other goals.

SCALE NAME: Goal Similarity (Product Category/Ideals)

SCALE DESCRIPTION: Three items are used to measure a consumer's belief of how well a product category is thought to achieve certain goals. The scale was called *ideals at the category level* by Martin and Stewart (2001).

SCALE ORIGIN: Martin and Stewart (2001) stated that their scale was based on the goals-based approach to measuring product similarity and their scale was apparently inspired by the work of Barsalou (e.g., 1985). As used by Martin and Stewart (2001), the scale was applied to the study of brand extensions.

RELIABILITY: The alpha for the scale was .81 (Martin and Stewart 2001).

VALIDITY: The typical aspects of scale validity were not provided by Martin and Stewart (2001) although some information bearing on the scale's nomological validity was discussed.

REFERENCES:
Barsalou, Lawrence W. (1985), "Ideals, Central Tendency, and Frequency of Instantiation as Determinants of Graded Structure in Categories," *Journal of Experimental Psychology: Learning, Memory, and Cognition*, 11 (4), 629–654.
Martin, Ingrid M., and David W. Stewart (2001), "The Differential Impact of Goal Congruency on Attitudes, Intentions, and the Transfer of Brand Equity," *JMR*, 38 (Nov), 471–484.

SCALE ITEMS: [1]

1. How likely is it that _____ would be made of high quality, soft, pliable leather?

2. How likely is it that _____ would come in bright, stylish colors to complete that fashionable, yet casual image?

3. How likely is it that _____ would come in many bright colors to mix and match with your wardrobe?

[1] The blank in each item should have the product category name or description (e.g., *dress leather shoes*). To adapt the items for other product categories the ending phrases of each item can be rephrased so as to apply to other ideals. The anchors of the response scale were *not at all likely* to *very likely*; the number of points on the scale were not stated.

SCALE NAME: Health Behaviors (Preventive)

SCALE DESCRIPTION: The scale is composed of seventeen, three-point items measuring the extent to which a person engages in numerous activities related to maintaining good health.

SCALE ORIGIN: Items from several measures developed by Moorman and Matulich (1993) were used for this scale. (See #85, #120, and #164 in V. II of this series.) Jayanti and Burns (1998) pretested and modified those multiple measures scales to produce one scale.

RELIABILITY: An alpha of .81 (n = 175) was reported for the scale by Jayanti and Burns (1998).

VALIDITY: Although rigorous examination of the scale's validity was not reported by Jayanti and Burns (1998), some general evidence related to the convergent and discriminant validities of all of their scales was mentioned.

COMMENTS: Jayanti and Burns (1998) used one scale to measure what Moorman and Matulich (1993) used multiple scales to measure. This raises the question of whether or not this scale is truly unidimensional.

REFERENCES:
Jayanti, Rama K. and Alvin C. Burns (1998), "The Antecedents of Preventive Health Care Behavior: An Empirical Study," *JAMS*, 26 (Winter), 6–15.
Moorman, Christine and Erika Matulich (1993), "A Model of Consumers' Preventive Health Motivation and Health Ability," *JCR*, 20 (September), 208–228.

SCALE ITEMS: [1]

How often do you undertake the following activities?

1. Eat a well-balanced diet.

2. See your dentist for regular check-ups.

3. Eat fresh fruit and vegetables.

4. Reduce amount of salt in your diet.

5. Watch for salt content in diet.

6. Exercise regularly.

7. Watch the amount of fat you consume.

8. Take precautions against sexually transmitted diseases.

---

[1] The response scale was anchored by *never* (1), *sometimes* (2), and *always* (3).

9. Pay attention to your sugar intake.

10. Pay attention to the amount of red meat you eat.

11. Cut back on snacks and treats.

12. Avoid foods with additives and preservatives.

13. Get enough rest and sleep.

14. Reduce stress and anxiety.

15. Maintain a balance between "work" and "play."

16. Pay attention to the amount of alcohol you drink.

17. Try to avoid smoking.

SCALE NAME: Health Club Beliefs

SCALE DESCRIPTION: The six-item, seven-point scale is used to measure beliefs regarding an exercise and fitness service (health club) a person has used or is at least aware of.

SCALE ORIGIN: Although not explicitly stated by Raghubir and Corfman (1999), the scale appears to have been developed for use in their study.

RELIABILITY: An alpha of .91 was reported for the scale (Raghubir and Corfman 1999).

VALIDITY: No examination of the scale's validity was reported by Raghubir and Corfman (1999). However, they did indicate that the items for this scale and those measuring attitude toward the health club (#70) loaded on two different factors.

REFERENCES:
Raghubir, Priya and Kim Corfman (1999), "When Do Price Promotions Affect Pretrial Brand Evaluations?" *JMR*, 36 (May), 211–222.

SCALE ITEMS: [1]

1. The health club uses the latest equipment.

2. The health club offers a full range of services.

3. The health club is well maintained.

4. The club's facilities are hygienic.

5. The health club uses the latest technology.

6. The club is targeting a high-income clientele.

---

[1] The response format used by Raghubir and Corfman (1999) had *not at all likely* (1) and *very likely* (7) as anchors.

SCALE NAME: Health Consciousness

SCALE DESCRIPTION: The scale is composed of six, five-point Likert-type items intended to measure the degree to which being concerned and sensitive about health issues is part of a person's daily life.

SCALE ORIGIN: Jayanti and Burns (1998) stated that they adapted their scale from one used by Kraft and Goodell (1993).

RELIABILITY: An alpha of .75 (n = 175) was reported for the scale by Jayanti and Burns (1998).

VALIDITY: Although rigorous examination of the scale's validity was not reported by Jayanti and Burns (1998), some general evidence related to the convergent and discriminant validities of all of their scales was mentioned.

REFERENCES:
Jayanti, Rama K. and Alvin C. Burns (1998), "The Antecedents of Preventive Health Care Behavior: An Empirical Study," *JAMS*, 26 (Winter), 6–15.
Kraft, Frederick and Phillips W. Goodell (1993), "Identifying the Health Conscious Consumer," *Journal of Health Care Marketing*, 13 (Fall), 18–25.

SCALE ITEMS:

1. I worry that there are harmful chemicals in my food.

2. I am concerned about my drinking water quality.

3. I usually read the ingredients on food labels.

4. I read more health-related articles than I did 3 years ago.

5. I am interested in information about my health.

6. I am concerned about my health all the time.

SCALE NAME: Health Knowledge

SCALE DESCRIPTION: The scale is composed of five, five-point Likert-type items intended to measure the level of familiarity a person states as having about preventive health care behaviors.

SCALE ORIGIN: The scale developed by Jayanti and Burns (1998) was loosely based upon a measure used by Brucks (1985) and modified for the health care context.

RELIABILITY: An alpha of .86 (n = 175) was reported for the scale by Jayanti and Burns (1998).

VALIDITY: Although rigorous examination of the scale's validity was not reported by Jayanti and Burns (1998), some general evidence related to the convergent and discriminant validities of all of their scales was mentioned.

REFERENCES:
Brucks, Merrie (1985), "The Effect of Product Class Knowledge on Information Search Behavior," *JCR*, 12 (June), 1–16.
Jayanti, Rama K. and Alvin C. Burns (1998), "The Antecedents of Preventive Health Care Behavior: An Empirical Study," *JAMS*, 26 (Winter), 6–15.

SCALE ITEMS:

1. I am very knowledgeable about taking care of my general health compared to an average person.

2. I am familiar with preventing minor and temporary problems such as colds and viruses.

3. I am familiar with preventing minor and chronic problems such as allergies and dry skin.

4. I am familiar with preventing major and temporary problems such as flu and measles.

5. I am familiar with preventing major and chronic problems such as hypertension and diabetes.

SCALE NAME: Health Motivation

SCALE DESCRIPTION: The Likert-like scale is intended to measure the degree to which people say they are concerned about health hazards and try to take actions to protect themselves before the problems occur. As noted below, several versions of the scale have been used, each with a slightly different emphasis. Moorman (1990) used a subset of the scale that emphasized actions taken to protect one's self before health problems occur. In the same study she also had a six-item scale that focused on the motivation to not take action to protect one's health unless a problem has occurred. Moorman and Matulich (1993) as well as Jayanti and Burns (1998) used different combinations of items from those two previous scales.

SCALE ORIGIN: The scale was developed by Moorman (1993). The work reported in Moorman (1990) led to the use of two scales but further examination led to a combination of those items in the subsequent study (Moorman 1994). Measures were pretested on 67 undergraduate students. Then, in the main study the scales were purified further using alpha, item-total correlations, and LISREL.

RELIABILITY: Alphas of .76 and .80 (n = 180) were reported by Moorman (1990) for the three- and six-item versions of the scale, respectively. Alphas of .82 (n = 404) and .78 (n = 175) were reported for the eight- and six-item versions used by Moorman and Matulich (1993) and Jayanti and Burns (1998), respectively.

VALIDITY: Limited analysis by Moorman (1990) led her to treat the set of items as two scales. Although specific details were not provided in the article, Moorman and Matulich (1993) engaged in more rigorous purification activities in both the pretest and the main study which led them to view the items as unidimensional and internally consistent.

Although rigorous examination of the scale's validity was not reported by Jayanti and Burns (1998), some general evidence related to the convergent and discriminant validities of all of their scales was mentioned.

COMMENTS: The mean score of the sample on the scale was reported by Moorman and Matulich (1993) to be 4.01 with a standard deviation of 1.11. It is worth noting that Moorman (1994) prefers that the health motivation measure be viewed as one scale rather than two.

REFERENCES:

Jayanti, Rama K. and Alvin C. Burns (1998), "The Antecedents of Preventive Health Care Behavior: An Empirical Study," *JAMS*, 26 (Winter), 6–15.

Moorman, Christine (1990), "The Effects of Stimulus and Consumer Characteristics on the Utilization of Nutrition Information," *JCR*, 17 (December), 362–374.

Moorman, Christine (1993), Personal Correspondence.

Moorman, Christine (1994), Personal Correspondence.

Moorman, Christine and Erika Matulich (1993), "A Model of Consumers' Preventive Health Motivation and Health Ability," *JCR*, 20 (September), 208–228.

SCALE ITEMS: [1]

1. I try to prevent health problems before I feel any symptoms.

2. I am concerned about health hazards and try to take action to prevent them.

3. I try to protect myself against health hazards I hear about.

4. I don't worry about health hazards until they become a problem for me or someone close to me. (r)

5. There are so many things that can hurt you these days. I'm not going to worry about them. (r)

6. I often worry about the health hazards I hear about, but don't do anything about them. (r)

7. I don't take any action against health hazards I hear about until I know I have a problem. (r)

8. I'd rather enjoy life than try to make sure I'm not exposing myself to a health hazard. (r)

9. I don't think health hazards I hear about will happen to me.

[1] Items #1 to #3 were used by Moorman (1990) to measure a *preventative health orientation* and items #4 to #9 were used to measure a *curative health orientation*. Moorman and Matulich (1993) used items #1 to #8 and a seven-point scale. Items similar to or the same as #1, #2, #4, #5, #7, #8 were used with a five-point response format by Jayanti and Burns (1998).

#185 *Health Value*

SCALE NAME: Health Value

SCALE DESCRIPTION: The scale is composed of five, five-point items intended to measure a person's attitude toward the costs/benefits of engaging in preventive health care behavior.

SCALE ORIGIN: Jayanti and Burns (1998) stated that they developed the scale for their study.

RELIABILITY: An alpha of .91 (n = 175) was reported for the scale by Jayanti and Burns (1998).

VALIDITY: Although rigorous examination of the scale's validity was not reported by Jayanti and Burns (1998), some general evidence related to the convergent and discriminant validities of all of their scales was mentioned.

REFERENCES:
Jayanti, Rama K. and Alvin C. Burns (1998), "The Antecedents of Preventive Health Care Behavior: An Empirical Study," *JAMS*, 26 (Winter), 6–15.

SCALE ITEMS: [1]

1. avoid tension

2. stay healthy longer

3. enjoy life more

4. stay fit longer

5. look younger

---

[1] The response scale was anchored by *not worth the benefit at all* (1) and *very much worth the benefit* (5).

SCALE NAME: Homophily

SCALE DESCRIPTION: The scale is composed of five, seven-point statements intended to measure the extent to which a person thinks he/she is similar to someone else in terms of such things as values, likes, experiences, and tastes in products.

SCALE ORIGIN: The scale was developed by Wolfinbarger and Gilly (1993). Alphas of .89 and .95 were reported when the scale was used with gift givers and gift receivers, respectively.

RELIABILITY: Alphas of .86 and .84 were reported by Gilly et al. (1998) when the scale was used with information seekers and their sources, respectively.

VALIDITY: No information about the scale's validity was reported by Gilly et al. (1998).

REFERENCES:
Gilly, Mary C., John L. Graham, Mary Finley Wolfinbarger, and Laura J. Yale (1998), "A Dyadic Study of Interpersonal Information Search," *JAMS*, 26 (2), 83–100.
Wolfinbarger, Mary Finley and Mary C. Gilly (1993), "The Encoding and Decoding of Gift Symbolism," working paper, University of California at Irvine.

SCALE ITEMS: [1]

1. Considering your outlook on life, how similar are you and this person?

2. Considering your likes and dislikes, how similar are you and this person?

3. Considering your values and experiences, how similar are you and this person?

4. How similar are this person's tastes in products compared to yours?

5. How similar are this person's tastes in gifts compared to yours?

---

[1] The response scale was anchored by *more dissimilar than anyone else I know* (1) and *more similar than anyone else I know* (7).

SCALE NAME: Impulse Buying (Product Specific)

SCALE DESCRIPTION: The scale is composed of five, seven-point Likert-type statements measuring the extent to which a consumer indicates experiencing a strong urge to spontaneously make a particular purchase without much hesitation or consideration of the consequences. The scale was called *impulsivity* by Beatty and Ferrell (1998).

SCALE ORIGIN: The scale was developed in dissertation research conducted by Jeon (1990).

RELIABILITY: Beatty and Ferrell (1998) reported an alpha for the scale of .70.

VALIDITY: Although the details related to this scale were not provided, the implication was that it was unidimensional and showed sufficient evidence of convergent and discriminant validity (Beatty and Ferrell 1998).

REFERENCES:

Beatty, Sharon E. and M. Elizabeth Ferrell (1998), "Impulse Buying: Modeling Its Precursors," *JR*, 74 (2), 169–191.

Jeon, Jung-Ok (1990), "An Empirical Investigation of the Relationship Between Affective States, In-store Browsing, and Impulse Buying," doctoral dissertation, University of Alabama.

SCALE ITEMS:

1. When I bought _____, I felt a spontaneous urge to buy it.

2. When I bought _____, I felt I wouldn't be able to get it off my mind until I bought it.

3. When I bought _____, I really did not consider the consequences of the purchase.

4. When I bought _____, I did it without much hesitation.

5. When I saw _____, I couldn't resist it.

SCALE NAME: Impulse Buying (Trip Specific)

SCALE DESCRIPTION: The scale is composed of four, seven-point Likert-type statements measuring the extent to which a consumer indicates that during a specific shopping trip one or more sudden urges to purchase were experienced. One distinction between this and some other impulse buying scales is that this one does not explicitly measure whether anything was actually bought but just that the motivation to buy spontaneously was felt. The scale was called *urge to purchase* by Beatty and Ferrell (1998).

SCALE ORIGIN: Beatty and Ferrell (1998) stated that items for the scale were drawn from several sources.

RELIABILITY: A composite reliability of .80 was reported for the scale (Beatty and Ferrell 1998).

VALIDITY: Although all of the details were not provided, the implication was that this scale was unidimensional and showed sufficient evidence of convergent and discriminant validity (Beatty and Ferrell 1998).

REFERENCES:
Beatty, Sharon E. and M. Elizabeth Ferrell (1998), "Impulse Buying: Modeling Its Precursors," *JR*, 74 (2), 169–191.

SCALE ITEMS:

1. I experienced a number of sudden urges to buy things I had not planned to purchase on this trip.

2. On this trip I saw a number of things I wanted to buy even though they were not on my shopping list.

3. I experienced no strong urges to make unplanned purchases on this trip. (r)

4. On this trip, I felt a sudden urge to buy something.

SCALE NAME: Impulse Buying Tendency

SCALE DESCRIPTION: The scale is intended to measure the extent to which a consumer is likely to make unplanned, immediate, and unreflective purchases. The version used by Burton et al. (1998) added a grocery store context to the scale.

SCALE ORIGIN: The scale used by Mick (1996) was developed by Martin, Weun, and Beatty (1993). Several rounds of testing whittled a group of 65 potential items down to an eight-item, two factor structure with an alpha of .86. Several tests of this version of the scale provided support for a claim of convergent validity.

However, the scale's lack of unidimensionality led to some redevelopment effort such that Weun, Jones, and Beatty subsequently (1997, 1998) presented a five-item version. Evidence was provided in support of the scale's unidimensionality as well as its discriminant and convergent validities. The alphas for this version of the scale were reported to range between .80 to .85. Beatty and Ferrell (1998) used three of the five items as their scale.

The version of the scale used by Burton et al. (1998) used five items from Martin, Weun, and Beatty's (1993) scale and added four more items that were assessed in a pretest.

RELIABILITY: Beatty and Ferrell (1998) reported a composite reliability of .81 for the three-item version of the scale they used. Alphas of .83 and .82 were reported for versions of the scale used by Burton et al. (1998) and Mick (1996), respectively.

VALIDITY: In the study by Beatty and Ferrell (1998) items from the original scale were deleted in order to improve the fit of the measurement model. Although all of the details were not provided, the implication was that the three-item scale was unidimensional and showed sufficient evidence of convergent and discriminant validity. No examination of the scale's validity was described by either Burton et al. (1998) or Mick (1996).

REFERENCES:

Beatty, Sharon E. and M. Elizabeth Ferrell (1998), "Impulse Buying: Modeling Its Precursors," *JR*, 74 (2), 169–191.

Burton, Scot, Donald R. Lichtenstein, Richard G. Netemeyer, and Judith A. Garretson (1998), "A Scale for Measuring Attitude Toward Private Label Products and an Examination of Its Psychological and Behavioral Correlates," *JAMS*, 26 (4), 293–306.

Martin, Wendy K., Seungoog Weun, and Sharon Beatty (1993), "Validation of an Impulse Tendency Scale," paper presented at the Association of Consumer Research conference, Nashville, Tennessee.

Mick, David Glen (1996), "Are Studies of Dark Side Variables Confounded by Socially Desirable Responding? The Case of Materialism," *JCR*, 23 (September), 106–119.

Weun, Seungoog, Michael A. Jones, and Sharon E. Beatty (1997), "A Parsimonious Scale to Measure Impulse Buying Tendency," in *Proceedings of the American Marketing Association Educators' Summer Conference*, American Marketing Association Educators, 306–307.

Weun, Seungoog, Michael A. Jones, and Sharon E. Beatty (1998), "Development and Validation of the Impulse Buying Tendency Scale," *Psychological Reports*, 82, 1123–1133.

SCALE ITEMS: [1]

Directions: Please indicate the degree to which the following statements describe your behavior when you are shopping at a mall. Think about the last few times you have been shopping in a mall. Please respond to each question by circling the number from 1 to 7 that most closely corresponds to your position.

1. Even when I see something I really like, I do not buy it unless it is a planned purchase. (r)

2. When I go shopping, I buy things I had not intended to purchase.

3. I avoid buying things that are not on my shopping list. (r)

4. It is fun to buy spontaneously.

5. I do not buy until I can make sure I am getting a real bargain. (r)

6. When I see something new that really interests me, I buy it right away just to see what it is like.

7. I buy some things without hesitation if I like them when I first see them.

8. When I see something new I really want, I purchase it immediately, even if I had not planned to buy it.

9. I am a person who makes unplanned purchases.

10. When I see something that really interests me, I buy it without considering the consequences.

11. For me, buying grocery items is a spontaneous occurrence.

12. For me, buying grocery items can come from "out of the blue."

13. Generally speaking, I would consider myself to be an impulsive shopper.

14. When it comes to making grocery purchases, I usually purchase on impulse.

Beatty and Ferrell (1998): 2, 4, 9
Burton et al. (1998): 1–5, 11–14
Martin, Weun, and Beatty (1993): 1–8
Mick (1996): 1–8
Weun, Jones, and Beatty (1997): 2, 4, 5, 9, 10
Weun, Jones, and Beatty (1998): 2, 3, 4, 9, 10

[1] These directions were provided in one of the stages of testing conducted by Martin, Weun, and Beatty (1993) and would need to be adjusted for different conditions. Several of the users have employed a seven-point Likert-type response format.

SCALE NAME: Impulse Buying Tendency

SCALE DESCRIPTION: It is a four-item, five-point Likert-type summated ratings scale measuring the degree to which a person not only indicates that he/she engages in unplanned consumer choice but likes to purchase that way.

SCALE ORIGIN: The source of the scale was not stated by Donthu and Gilliland (1996) but it is likely to be original to their study.

RELIABILITY: An alpha of .87 was reported for the scale by both Donthu and Gilliland (1996) and Donthu and Garcia (1999).

VALIDITY: No specific examination of the scale's validity was reported by Donthu and Gilliland (1996).

REFERENCES:
Donthu, Naveen and Adriana Garcia (1999), "The Internet Shopper," *JAR*, 39 (May/June), 52–58.
Donthu, Naveen and David Gilliland (1996), "The Infomercial Shopper," *JAR*, 36 (March/April), 69–76.

SCALE ITEMS:

1. I often make unplanned purchases.

2. I like to purchase things on a whim.

3. I think twice before committing myself. (r)

4. I always stick to my shopping list. (r)

SCALE NAME: Impulsivity

SCALE DESCRIPTION: The three-item, seven-point scale is intended to assess the degree to which a person describes him/herself as impulsive with a sense that the person realizes this tendency is not a positive attribute.

SCALE ORIGIN: Shiv and Fedorikhin (1999) drew items from the *Consumer Impulsiveness Scale* by Puri (1996). That scale had 12 items that represented two factors: hedonic and prudent. The three items used by Shiv and Fedorikhin (1999) came from the hedonic dimension.

RELIABILITY: An alpha of .77 was reported for the scale (Shiv and Fedorikhin 1999). The stability of the scale (four week test-retest) was reported to be .79.

VALIDITY: No examination of the scale's validity was reported by Shiv and Fedorikhin (1999).

REFERENCES:
Puri, Radhika (1996), "Measuring and Modifying Consumer Impulsiveness: A Cost-Benefit Accessibility Framework," *Journal of Consumer Psychology*, 5 (2), 87–114.
Shiv, Baba and Alexander Fedorikhin (1999), "Heart and Mind in Conflict: The Interplay of Affect and Cognition in Consumer Decision Making," *JCR*, 26 (December), 278–292.

SCALE ITEMS: [1]

1. impulsive

2. careless

3. easily tempted

---

[1] The verbal anchors used by Shiv and Fedorikhin (1999) were: *seldom would describe me* (1), *sometimes would describe me* (4), and *usually would describe me* (7).

SCALE NAME: Independence (Child from Parent)

SCALE DESCRIPTION: The scale is composed of six, five-point statements measuring how often a parent believes that a particular child of his/hers tries to do things on their own without assistance from the parent.

SCALE ORIGIN: Rose (1999, 2002) cited Schaefer and Finkelstein (1975) as the source of the scale.

RELIABILITY: Alphas of .76 (U.S.) and .74 (Japan) were reported for the scale by Rose (1999).

VALIDITY: Rose (1999) stated that a CFA indicated the set of scales they used "formed the expected dimensions" (p. 111). In particular, this scale and two others (protective parental style [#303] and excluding outside influences [#301]) measured an anxious-emotional involvement dimension in a second order factor model.

REFERENCES:

Rose, Gregory M. (2002), Personal Correspondence.

Rose, Gregory M. (1999), "Consumer Socialization, Parental Style, and Development Timetables in the United States and Japan," *JM*, 63 (July), 105–119.

Schaefer, Earl S. and N. W. Finkelstein (1975), "Child Behavior Toward Parent: An Inventory and Factor Analysis," Paper presented at the *American Psychological Association Annual Meeting*, Chicago (August 31).

SCALE ITEMS: [1]

1. Tries to do things for him/herself.

2. Does his/her chores without my help.

3. Keeps busy for long periods of time without my attention.

4. Will take help from me only after trying to do something him/herself.

5. Thinks of things to do him/herself.

6. Decides by him/herself how to do things.

---

[1] The response format for these items was anchored by *very seldom* (1) to *very often* (5) (Rose 2002).

SCALE NAME: Independence/Interdependence

SCALE DESCRIPTION: The scale measures the degree to which a person expresses preference for individualism and separation from others (independence) or connectedness and relations with others (interdependence).

SCALE ORIGIN: The original 24-item version of the scale was constructed by Singelis (1994). He proposed that there are two images of self: one reflects independence of others while the other emphasizes interdependence on others. Further, these two self images can coexist in a person. Singelis developed and tested two 12-item subscales, one for each dimension. Results from several studies provided evidence in support of the two factor model as well as for the reliability and validity of each subscale. Alphas for the interdependence subscale were reported as .73 (n = 360) and .74 (n = 160); likewise, alphas for the independence subscale were .69 (n = 360) and .70 (n = 160).

Aaker (2000b; and Williams 1998) reported using a 31-item version of the scale. This is based upon a 30-item unpublished version by Singelis (Aaker 2000b). The 31st item was being tested for the Japanese version of the scale but Aaker does not recommend its use (2000a).

RELIABILITY: Aaker and Williams (1998) reported that the scale had an alpha of .90 (n = 151). Aaker (2000b) reported alphas of .90 (experiment 1), .87 (experiment 2), and .91 (experiment 3) for her use of the scale. As used by Aaker and Lee (2001), the independent subscale had an alpha of .77 while the interdependent subscale had an alpha of .74.

VALIDITY: No evidence of the scale's validity was presented in any of the articles. Aaker and Williams (1998) did, however, indicate that a factor analysis was conducted which yielded just one factor. They speculated that their sample size or insufficient situational variability in the items may have been the reason for not finding the expected two dimensional structure.

COMMENTS: Given that the set of items were developed and tested by Singelis (1984) as a pair of subscales the implications of treating them as one scale are not clear. However, it is probably safest to separately calculate scores for the two subscales. Aaker concurs (2000a).

Further, several items in the scale were deliberately written by Singelis (1994) to be suitable for students. If the scale is to be used with a non-student sample, adjustment in those items will be necessary which in turn will call for retesting the scale's dimensionality and validity.

REFERENCES:
Aaker, Jennifer L. (2000a), Personal Correspondence.

Aaker, Jennifer L. (2000b), "Accessibility or Diagnosticity? Disentangling the Influence of Culture on Persuasion Processes and Attitudes," *JCR*, 26 (March), 340–357.

Aaker, Jennifer L. and Angela Y. Lee (2001), "I Seek Pleasures and We Avoid Pains: The Role of Self-Regulatory Goals in Information Processing and Persuasion," *JCR*, 28 (June), 33–49.

Aaker, Jennifer L. and Patti Williams (1998), "Empathy versus Pride: The Influence of Emotional Appeals Across Cultures," *JCR*, 25 (December), 241–261.

Singelis, Theodore M. (1994), "The Measurement of Independent and Interdependent Self-Construals," *Personality and Social Psychology Bulletin*, 20 (October), 580–591.

SCALE ITEMS: [1]

1. I have respect for the authority figures with whom I interact.

2. It is important for me to maintain harmony within my group.

3. My happiness depends on the happiness of those around me.

4. I would offer my seat in a bus to my professor (boss).

5. I respect people who are modest about themselves.

6. I will sacrifice my self-interest for the benefit of the group I am in.

7. I often have the feeling that my relationships with others are more important than my own accomplishments.

8. I should take into consideration my parents' advice when making education (career) plans.

9. It is important to me to respect decisions made by the group.

10. I will stay in a group if they need me, even when I'm not happy with the group.

11. If my brother or sister fails, I feel responsible.

12. Even when I strongly disagree with group members, I avoid an argument.

13. I feel my fate is intertwined with the fate of those around me.

14. I feel good when I cooperate with others.

15. I usually go along with what others do, even when I would rather do something different.

16. I'd rather say "No" directly, than risk being misunderstood.

17. Speaking up during a class (or a meeting) is not a problem for me.

18. Having a lively imagination is important to me.

19. I am comfortable with being singled out for praise or rewards.

20. I am the same person at home that I am at school.

21. Being able to take care of myself is a primary concern for me.

22. I act the same way no matter whom I am with.

23. I feel comfortable using someone's first name soon after I meet them, even when they are much older than I am.

24. I prefer to be direct and forthright when dealing with people I've just met.

25. I enjoy being unique and different from others in many respects.

26. My personal identity independent of others is very important to me.

27. I value being in good health above everything.

28. I do my own thing, regardless of what others think.

29. I feel it is important for me to act as an independent person.

30. I try to do what is best for me, regardless of how that might affect others.

[1] The first fifteen items represent the interdependence subscale whereas the final fifteen are the independence subscale. A seven-point, Likert-type response format was used by Singelis (1994).

SCALE NAME: Indexicality (Corporal)

SCALE DESCRIPTION: The scale is made up of three, seven-point items used to measure the degree to which an object is important or distinctive to a person due to its association with someone from the person's past who had been in physical contact with the object.

SCALE ORIGIN: The scale appears to be original to Grayson and Shulman (2000). Their goal was to use the concept of semiotics to better understand how meanings become associated with special possessions.

RELIABILITY: An alpha of .84 was reported for the scale (Grayson and Shulman 2000).

VALIDITY: No examination of the scale's validity was reported by Grayson and Shulman (2000). They did, however, present the results of an exploratory factor analysis of the items in this scale and three others. The results showed that the items on this scale loaded highest on the same factor.

REFERENCES:
Grayson, Kent (2002), Personal Correspondence.
Grayson, Kent and David Shulman (2000), "Indexicality and the Verification Function of Irreplaceable Possessions: A Semiotic Analysis," *JCR*, 27 (1), 17–30.

SCALE ITEMS: [1]

Directions: Please read the following statements about the possession you selected and mark how well each statement describes the possession.

1. It is special because a special person (or people) was once physically in contact with it.

2. It is special because a special person (or people) actually touched it.

3. If I lost it, I would lose a connection with someone.

[1] The response scale was anchored by *does not describe this possession at all* and *describes this possession very well* (Grayson 2002).

SCALE NAME: Indexicality (Temporal)

SCALE DESCRIPTION: Five, seven-point statements are used to measure the extent to which an object is important or distinctive to a person due to its association with a time or event in the person's past.

SCALE ORIGIN: The scale appears to be original to Grayson and Shulman (2000). Their goal was to use the concept of semiotics to better understand how meanings become associated with special possessions.

RELIABILITY: An alpha of .85 was reported for the scale (Grayson and Shulman 2000).

VALIDITY: No examination of the scale's validity was reported by Grayson and Shulman (2000). They did, however, present the results of an exploratory factor analysis of the items in this scale and three others. The results showed that the items on this scale loaded highest on the same factor.

REFERENCES:
Grayson, Kent (2002), Personal Correspondence.
Grayson, Kent and David Shulman (2002), "Indexicality and the Verification Function of Irreplaceable Possessions: A Semiotic Analysis," *JCR*, 27 (1), 17–30.

SCALE ITEMS: [1]

Directions: Please read the following statements about the possession you selected and mark how well each statement describes the possession.

1. When I look at it or touch it, I am transported back in time.

2. It is proof of something from my past.

3. When I look at it, I think about who I was when I got it.

4. It is evidence that something happened.

5. If I lost it, I would lose an important part of my history.

---

[1] The response scale was anchored by *does not describe this possession at all* and *describes this possession very well* (Grayson 2002).

SCALE NAME: Innovativeness (General)

SCALE DESCRIPTION: It is a three-item, five-point Likert-type summated ratings scale measuring the degree to which a person expresses a desire to take chances and try new things.

SCALE ORIGIN: The source of the scale was not stated by Donthu and Gilliland (1996) but it is likely to be original to their study.

RELIABILITY: Alphas of .70 (Donthu and Gilliland 1996) and .74 (Donthu and Garcia 1999) have been reported for the scale.

VALIDITY: No specific examination of the scale's validity was reported by Donthu and Gilliland (1996).

REFERENCES:

Donthu, Naveen and Adriana Garcia (1999), "The Internet Shopper," *JAR*, 39 (May/June), 52–58.
Donthu, Naveen and David Gilliland (1996), "The Infomercial Shopper," *JAR*, 36 (March/April), 69–76.

SCALE ITEMS:

1. I like to take chances.

2. I like to experiment with new ways of doing things.

3. New products are usually gimmicks. (r)

SCALE NAME: Innovativeness (Product Purchase)

SCALE DESCRIPTION: The scale is composed of three, five-point Likert-type statements and attempts to assess the degree to which a consumer engages in exploratory behaviors, particularly when it comes to trying out new and different products.

SCALE ORIGIN: Darden and Perreault (1976) were cited by Ailawadi, Neslin, and Gedenk (2001) as the source of the scale they used, however, the former had taken items from the work of Wells and Tigert (1971). (See V. I, #125.) A close examination reveals that only one item from Wells and Tigert (1971) is among the three shown below. Given all of this, it is probably safest to describe this scale as being original though inspired by previous work.

RELIABILITY: A composite reliability of .81 was reported for the scale (Ailawadi, Neslin, and Gedenk 2001).

VALIDITY: The items in this scale along with those belonging to 14 other scales were included in a confirmatory factor analysis. The fit of the measurement model was acceptable and general evidence was cited in support of the scale's discriminant validity.

REFERENCES:
Ailawadi, Kusum L., Scott A. Neslin, and Karen Gedenk (2001), "Pursuing the Value-Conscious Consumer: Store Brands Versus National Brand Promotions," *JM*, 65 (1), 71–89.
Darden, William R. and William D. Perreault, Jr. (1976), "Identifying Interurban Shoppers: Multiproduct Purchase Patterns and Segmentation Profiles," *JMR*, 13 (Feb.), 51–60.
Wells, William D. and Douglas Tigert (1971), "Activities, Interests, and Opinions," *JAR*, 11 (Aug.), 27–35.

SCALE ITEMS:

1. When I see a product somewhat different from the usual, I check it out.

2. I am often among the first people to try a new product.

3. I like to try new and different things.

SCALE NAME: Innovativeness (Product Specific)

SCALE DESCRIPTION: The four-item, seven-point Likert-type scale measures the extent to which a person expresses a tendency to buy the newest products within a specific product category and not wait for feedback from others before doing so.

SCALE ORIGIN: Although drawing inspiration from a scale by Goldsmith and Hofacker (1991; V. III, #188), this scale is distinct and should be considered original to Klink and Smith (2001).

RELIABILITY: An alpha of .84 was reported for the scale by Klink and Smith (2001).

VALIDITY: The only information bearing on the scale's validity reported by Klink and Smith (2001) was that the scale had a strong correlation (r = .81) with a two-item measure of general innovativeness.

REFERENCES:
Goldsmith, Ronald E. and Charles F. Hofacker (1991), "Measuring Consumer Innovativeness," *JAMS*, 19 (Summer), 209–221.
Klink, Richard R. (2001), Personal Correspondence.
Klink, Richard R. and Daniel C. Smith (2001), "Threats to the External Validity of Brand Extension Research," *JMR*, 38 (August), 326–335.

SCALE ITEMS: [1]

1. Overall, I like buying the latest _____.

2. If I needed to purchase a _____, I would buy the latest one available.

3. In general, if a new _____ was introduced, I would not wait to see how others liked the product before I would buy it.

4. When I see a new brand of _____ in the store, I often buy it because it is new.

---

[1] The generic name of the product should be placed in the blanks (e.g., home safety products). Anchors on the seven-point response scale were *agree/disagree*. The scale items were provided by Klink (2004).

SCALE NAME: Intention to Support a Theater

SCALE DESCRIPTION: The scale is composed of three, five-point Likert-type items used to measure a theater attendee's plans for future behavioral involvement with a specified theater from attending productions to volunteering time.

SCALE ORIGIN: Garbarino and Johnson (1999) indicated that they drew upon a variety of sources to develop the items.

RELIABILITY: Garbarino and Johnson (1999) reported the following alphas for the scales as used with three different subsets of theatergoers: .75 (individual ticket buyers), .71 (occasional subscribers), and .58 (consistent subscribers).

VALIDITY: Based on the variety of indicators they examined, Garbarino and Johnson (1999) made a general claim of good fit for their measurement model as well as evidence of good convergent validity. This scale performed adequately on a couple of tests of discriminant validity.

REFERENCES:
Garbarino, Ellen and Mark S. Johnson (1999), "The Different Roles of Satisfaction, Trust, and Commitment in Customer Relationships," *JM*, 63 (April), 70–87.

SCALE ITEMS:

1. I plan to attend future performances at this theater.

2. I plan to subscribe to this theater in the future.

3. I would consider donating my time or money to this theater.

SCALE NAME: Intergenerational Communication (Preferences)

SCALE DESCRIPTION: The scale is composed of four, seven-point statements measuring preferences at the brand, store, and company levels that have been communicated in some way from a parent to a child. Two versions of the scale are presented (below). One has to do with the *frequency* with which these preferences have been communicated by the parents. The other focuses on the *degree of influence* the parent's opinions have had on the child.

SCALE ORIGIN: The scale is original to Viswanathan, Childers, and Moore (2000). It is part of a larger instrument they developed called IGEN, referring to intergenerational communication and influence. The instrument as a whole covers three dimensions (skills, preferences, and attitudes) and has two versions of scales for those three dimensions (*frequency* and *degree of influence*). Initially, 37 items were generated. After a thorough pretest which involved examination of dimensionality, reliability, and validity the set was reduced to 12 items with each dimension represented by four items.

RELIABILITY: Viswanathan, Childers, and Moore (2000) reported the following alphas for the *frequency* version of the scale: .80 (U.S.), .80 (Thailand), .78 (young adults), .70 (parents). For the *degree of influence* version the alphas were .77 (U.S.), .81 (Thailand), .76 (college students), .76 (students' parents).

VALIDITY: The pretest and three follow-up studies thoroughly examined the scales' psychometric quality (Viswanathan, Childers, and Moore 2000). The evidence appeared to favor a three factor model and a variety of evidence was found in support of each scales' convergent, discriminant, and nomological validities.

COMMENTS: Data for Studies 1 and 2 were collected along with the data referred to in Childers and Rao (1992).

REFERENCES:

Childers, Terry L. and Akshay R. Rao (1992), "The Influence of Familial and Peer-based Reference Groups on Consumer Decisions," *JCR*, 19 (Sept), 198–211.

Viswanathan, Madhubalan, Terry L. Childers, and Elizabeth S. Moore (2000), "The Measurement of Intergenerational Communication and Influence on Consumption: Development, Validation, and Cross-Cultural Comparison of the IGEN Scale," *JAMS*, 28 (3), 406–424.

SCALE ITEMS: [1]

Directions: The following set of questions deals with the communication and influence that your family may have on your purchasing behavior. Two questions follow each statement. The first pertains to whether your parents/family have communicated in some way the basic idea behind the statement to you. The second question deals with how much you were influenced by your parents/family and their opinions.

1. Why they buy the brands or products they purchase.

2. Their preferences for shopping at different types of stores.

3. Their preferences for different styles of products.

4. Their preferences for different companies and the products/brands made by these different companies.

[1] (The frequency version of the scale would have the following question after each item):
Have your parents communicated this to you?
Very often / never
(The degree of influence version would have the following question after each item):
How much were you influenced by their opinions on this issue?
A large extent / not at all

SCALE NAME: Intergenerational Communication (Skills)

SCALE DESCRIPTION: The four-item, seven-point scale is used to measure cognitions regarding various aspects of "proper" consumer behavior (paying bills, decision-making, purchasing) that have been communicated in some way from a parent to a child. Two versions of the scale are presented (below). One has to do with the *frequency* with which these skills have been communicated by the parents. The other focuses on the *degree of influence* parent's opinions have had on the child.

SCALE ORIGIN: The scale is original to Viswanathan, Childers, and Moore (2000). It is part of a larger instrument they developed called IGEN, referring to intergenerational communication and influence. The instrument as a whole covers three dimensions (skills, preferences, and attitudes) and has two versions of scales for those three dimensions (*frequency* and *degree of influence*). Initially, 37 items were generated. After a thorough pretest which involved examination of dimensionality, reliability, and validity the set was reduced to 12 items with each dimension represented by four items.

RELIABILITY: Viswanathan, Childers, and Moore (2000) reported the following alphas for the *frequency* version of the scale: .72 (U.S.), .78 (Thailand), .70 (young adults), .80 (parents). For the *degree of influence* version the alphas were .70 (U.S.), .77 (Thailand), .69 (college students), .75 (students' parents).

VALIDITY: The pretest and three follow-up studies thoroughly examined the scales' psychometric quality (Viswanathan, Childers, and Moore 2000). The evidence appeared to favor a three factor model and a variety of evidence was found in support of each scales' convergent, discriminant, and nomological validities.

COMMENTS: Data for studies one and two were collected along with the data referred to in Childers and Rao (1992).

REFERENCES:
Childers, Terry L. and Akshay R. Rao (1992), "The Influence of Familial and Peer-based Reference Groups on Consumer Decisions," *JCR*, 19 (Sept), 198–211.
Viswanathan, Madhubalan, Terry L. Childers, and Elizabeth S. Moore (2000), "The Measurement of Intergenerational Communication and Influence on Consumption: Development, Validation, and Cross-Cultural Comparison of the IGEN Scale," *JAMS*, 28 (3), 406–424.

SCALE ITEMS: [1]

Directions: The following set of questions deals with the communication and influence that your family may have on your purchasing behavior. Two questions follow each statement. The first pertains to whether your parents/family have communicated in some way the basic idea behind the statement to you. The second question deals with how much you were influenced by your parents/family and their opinions.

1. It is advantageous to be good at money saving, planning future finances, budgeting regularly, paying bills on time, and keeping periodic track of accounts.

2. Their views on "how to choose between products and brands" while shopping.

3. Their views on "how to evaluate information related to a product, its price, its advertisements, and the stores where it is sold."

4. The best way to shop is to compare two or more brands carefully on several features such as price, quality, and expected life and buy the one which gives the best overall value.

[1] (The frequency version of the scale would have the following question after each item):
Have your parents communicated this to you?
Very often / never
(The degree of influence version would have the following question after each item):
How much were you influenced by their opinions on this issue?
A large extent / not at all

SCALE NAME: Internet Services Adoption (Financial & Information)

SCALE DESCRIPTION: The scale is composed of seven, five-point items that measure the likelihood that a person might use the web in the future to access a wide range of services that either involve financial services (banking), communication (e-mail), or in-depth information (encyclopedias).

SCALE ORIGIN: The scale is original to Lin (1999). Twenty-three items were generated that had to do with a broad range of customer-related online services. Using exploratory factor analysis, the items were concluded to represent three dimensions with the set composing this scale to be one of them. Three items of the original 23 were dropped due to low loadings.

RELIABILITY: The scale was reported to have an alpha of .89 (Lin 1999).

VALIDITY: Although no examination of the scale's validity was reported by Lin (1999) an exploratory factor analysis was conducted. This provided some evidence of the scale's unidimensionality. Despite this, the items appear to tap into more than one dimension. More rigorous examination appears to be called for to test the scale's dimensionality as well as the discriminant validity between it and a companion scale that also tapped into an information-related dimension (#203).

REFERENCES:
Lin, Carolyn A. (1999), "Online-Service Adoption Likelihood," *JAR*, 39 (March/April), 79–89.
Lin, Carolyn A. (2001), Personal Correspondence.

SCALE ITEMS: [1]

When you surf the Internet, you are also able to do shopping, banking and order a lot of services directly from your computer. Please indicate how likely it is that you might use the following services:

1. Electronic mail services for sending and receiving messages to and from others

2. Electronic yellow-page services for finding telephone numbers

3. Accounting services for doing your taxes

4. Banking services for paying your bills, making money transfers, and balancing bank accounts

5. Financial services for getting updated trading information on stocks and bonds

6. Library service for checking references from different libraries

7. Encyclopedia services with moving video and sound

---

[1] Responses to these statements were measured using the following scale: *never* (1), *rarely* (2), *sometimes* (3), *often* (4), and *very often* (5) (Lin 2001).

SCALE NAME: Internet Services Adoption (Infotainment)

SCALE DESCRIPTION: The eight-item, five-point scale measures the likelihood that a person might use the web in the future to access a wide range of information and light entertainment-type services such as reading news, sports, movie reviews, and weather.

SCALE ORIGIN: The scale is original to Lin (1999). Twenty-three items were generated that had to do with a broad range of customer-related online services. Using exploratory factor analysis, the items were concluded to represent three dimensions with the set composing this scale to be one of them. Three items of the original 23 were dropped due to low loadings.

RELIABILITY: The scale was reported to have an alpha of .89 (Lin 1999).

VALIDITY: Although no examination of the scale's validity was reported by Lin (1999) an exploratory factor analysis was conducted. This provided some evidence of the scale's unidimensionality. More rigorous examination appears to be called for to determine the discriminant validity between this scale and a companion scale that also tapped into an information-related dimension (#202).

REFERENCES:
Lin, Carolyn A. (1999), "Online-Service Adoption Likelihood," *JAR*, 39 (March/April), 79–89.
Lin, Carolyn A. (2001), Personal Correspondence.

SCALE ITEMS: [1]

When you surf the Internet, you are also able to do shopping, banking and order a lot of services directly from your computer. Please indicate how likely it is that you might use the following services:

1. Newspaper services for reading a regular newspaper on screen

2. Magazine services for reading a regular magazine on screen

3. TV news services for reading the stories of TV network news programs

4. Sports services for getting sports statistics and updated sports news

5. TV program services for getting the plots of TV series or soap operas

6. Movie services for getting reviews of movie releases

7. Weather services for checking the weather conditions around the country or the world

8. Local advertising service for checking retail store ads

---

[1] Responses to these statements were measured using the following scale: *never* (1), *rarely* (2), *sometimes* (3), *often* (4), and *very often* (5) (Lin 2001).

SCALE NAME: Internet Services Adoption (Ordering)

SCALE DESCRIPTION: The five-item, five-point scale measures the likelihood that a person might use the web in the future to make reservations and/or purchase a wide range of products such as food, tickets, and clothes.

SCALE ORIGIN: The scale is original to Lin (1999). Twenty-three items were generated that had to do with a broad range of customer-related online services. Using exploratory factor analysis, the items were concluded to represent three dimensions with the set composing this scale to be one of them. Three items of the original 23 were dropped due to low loadings.

RELIABILITY: The scale was reported to have an alpha of .86 (Lin 1999).

VALIDITY: Although no examination of the scale's validity was reported by Lin (1999) an exploratory factor analysis was conducted. This provided some evidence of the scale's unidimensionality.

REFERENCES:
Lin, Carolyn A. (1999), "Online-Service Adoption Likelihood," *JAR*, 39 (March/April), 79–89.
Lin, Carolyn A. (2001), Personal Correspondence.

SCALE ITEMS: [1]

When you surf the Internet, you are also able to do shopping, banking and order a lot of services directly from your computer. Please indicate how likely it is that you might use the following services:

1. Merchandising services for shopping for clothes, shoes, and other necessities

2. Grocery services for directly ordering grocery items for pickup or delivery

3. Restaurant services for ordering food delivery or making dinner reservations

4. Travel services for booking tickets or rental cars

5. Ticketmaster services for booking movie, concert, or sports game tickets

[1] Responses to these statements were measured using the following scale: *never* (1), *rarely* (2), *sometimes* (3), *often* (4), and *very often* (5) (Lin 2001).

SCALE NAME: Internet Shopping (Convenience)

SCALE DESCRIPTION: The three-item, seven-point scale measures the extent to which a person thinks that Internet stores are easier to shop at and save more time compared to shopping at traditional retail stores. The scale is attempting to tap into a very general attitude, not specific to any particular website or store.

SCALE ORIGIN: The scale is original to Szymanski and Hise (2000). They said that the items for the scale were inspired by statements made by focus group members during the qualitative phase of their research.

RELIABILITY: An alpha of .69 was reported for the scale (Szymanski and Hise 2000).

VALIDITY: Apart from evidence that the scale is unidimensional, no examination of the scale's validity was reported by Szymanski and Hise (2000).

COMMENTS: If the phrase *store fronts* in the scale stem is viewed as awkward or confusing then a term such as *websites* could be used instead without having to make any other changes to the scale.

REFERENCES:
Szymanski, David M. and Richard T. Hise (2000), "e-Satisfaction: An Initial Examination," *JR*, 76 (3), 309–322.

SCALE ITEMS: [1]

Evaluate Internet store fronts relative to traditional retail stores on each of the following dimensions:

1. Total shopping time

2. Convenience

3. Ease of browsing

---

[1] The anchors used by Szymanski and Hise (2000) for the response scale were *much worse than traditional stores* (1) and *much better than traditional stores* (7).

SCALE NAME: Internet Shopping (Site Design)

SCALE DESCRIPTION: Three, seven-point items are used to assess the degree to which a person thinks websites of retailers are doing a good job of helping customers to navigate easily and find desired information quickly. The scale is attempting to tap into a very general attitude, not specific to any particular vendor's website.

SCALE ORIGIN: The scale is original to Szymanski and Hise (2000). They said that the items for the scale were inspired by statements made by focus group members during the qualitative phase of their research.

RELIABILITY: An alpha of .72 was reported for the scale (Szymanski and Hise 2000).

VALIDITY: Apart from evidence that the scale is unidimensional, no examination of the scale's validity was reported by Szymanski and Hise (2000).

COMMENTS: If the phrase *store fronts* in the scale stem is viewed as awkward or confusing then a term such as *websites* could be used instead without having to make any other changes to the scale.

REFERENCES:
Szymanski, David M. and Richard T. Hise (2000), "e-Satisfaction: An Initial Examination," *JR*, 76 (3), 309–322.

SCALE ITEMS: [1]

In general, how good of a job are Internet store fronts doing on the following dimensions:

1. presenting uncluttered screens

2. providing easy-to-follow search paths

3. presenting information fast

[1] The anchors used by Szymanski and Hise (2000) for the response scale were *poor job* (1) and *excellent job* (7).

SCALE NAME: Internet Shopping Experience

SCALE DESCRIPTION: The three-item, seven-point scale is intended to measure the extent to which a person has made purchases via the Internet in the past year. Although the scale is based upon a respondent's answers with respect to three specific goods, in total they are intended to be representative of all *search goods* (as opposed to *experience goods*). See below for more detail.

SCALE ORIGIN: The scale is original to Shim et al. (2001). The authors desired a scale that measured online shopping experience with *search goods* rather than *experience goods*, that is, goods that mainly involved the gathering of factual information versus those that were chosen based on experience using the senses. Five goods were tested and the ones that scored highest on factual information and lowest on sensory experience were computer software, books, and videos.

RELIABILITY: Shim et al. (2001) reported the construct reliability of the scale to be .71.

VALIDITY: Little information regarding the scale's validity was reported by Shim et al. (2001). It was stated, however, that the variance extracted was only 45%. This means that the variance explained by the construct is smaller than the variance due to measurement error bringing the validity of the measure into question (Fornell and Larcker 1981).

REFERENCES:

Fornell, Claes and David F. Larcker (1981), "Evaluating Structural Equation Models with Unobservable Variables and Measurement Error," *JMR*, 18 (February), 39–50.

Shim, Soyeon (2002), Personal Correspondence.

Shim, Soyeon, Mary Ann Eastlick, Sherry L. Lotz, and Patricia Warrington (2001), "An Online Prepurchase Intentions Model: The Role of Intention to Search," *JR*, 77 (3), 397–416.

SCALE ITEMS: [1]

In the past twelve months, how many purchases have you made through the Internet for the following products?

1. computer software

2. books

3. videos

---

[1] The following seven-point response scale was used with these items by Shim et al. (2001; 2002):
(0 times)–(1–2)–(3–4)–(5–6)–(7–8)–(9–10)–(11+ times)

SCALE NAME: Internet Usage (Economic Motivation)

SCALE DESCRIPTION: Four, five-point Likert-type items are used to assess the degree to which a person uses the web because of its potential for making business transactions (prepurchase information gathering and purchasing) more convenient and cheap.

SCALE ORIGIN: The scale is original to the work of Korgaonkar and Wolin (1999). After reviewing previous research and the results of six focus groups the authors generated 41 items thought to relate to the reasons why people use the web as well as their concerns about using it. Eight factors were originally expected but their analysis (exploratory factor analysis) ultimately led to the development of seven scales.

RELIABILITY: An alpha of .65 was reported for the scale (Korgaonkar and Wolin 1999).

VALIDITY: No explicit examination of the scale's validity was reported by Korgaonkar and Wolin (1999). However, the items composing this scale loaded together and highest on this dimension in the seven factor solution based upon principal components factor analysis with varimax rotation.

REFERENCES:
Korgaonkar, Pradeep K. and Lori D. Wolin (1999), "A Multivariate Analysis of Web Usage," *JAR*, 39 (March/April), 53–68.

SCALE ITEMS: [1]

1. I enjoy the convenience of shopping on the web.

2. When I want to buy a big-ticket item, I use the web to search for bargain prices.

3. I use the web to research a company, industry, or stock.

4. I use the web because it saves money.

---

[1] The response format used by Korgaonkar and Wolin (1999) with these items was anchored by *strongly disagree* (1) and *strongly agree* (5).

SCALE NAME: Internet Usage (Entertainment Motivation)

SCALE DESCRIPTION: The three-item, five-point scale measures the frequency with which a person uses the web as a form of entertainment in hopes of finding fun and excitement.

SCALE ORIGIN: The scale is original to Lin (1999) although she drew inspiration from previous studies of other media.

RELIABILITY: The scale was reported to have an alpha of .88 (Lin 1999).

VALIDITY: Although no examination of the scale's validity was reported by Lin (1999) an exploratory factor analysis was conducted. This provided some evidence of the scale's unidimensionality.

REFERENCES:
Lin, Carolyn A. (1999), "Online-Service Adoption Likelihood," *JAR*, 39 (March/April), 79–89.
Lin, Carolyn A. (2001), Personal Correspondence.

SCALE ITEMS: [1]

These days you can surf the Internet to get news, information and entertainment materials or exchange messages with other people who are also online. Please indicate how likely it is for you to surf the Internet for the following reasons:

1. To have fun.

2. To find excitement.

3. To entertain yourself.

[1] Responses to these statements were measured using the following scale: *never* (1), *rarely* (2), *sometimes* (3), *often* (4), and *very often* (5) (Lin 2001).

SCALE NAME: Internet Usage (Escape Motivation)

SCALE DESCRIPTION: The scale is composed of eleven, five-point Likert-type items that appear to capture the degree to which a person considers using the web to be exciting, allows one to escape from reality, and helps deal with loneliness.

SCALE ORIGIN: The scale is original to the work of Korgaonkar and Wolin (1999). After reviewing previous research and the results of six focus groups the authors generated 41 items thought to relate to the reasons why people use the web as well as their concerns about using it. Eight factors were originally expected but their analysis (exploratory factor analysis) ultimately led to the development of seven scales.

RELIABILITY: An alpha of .91 was reported for the scale (Korgaonkar and Wolin 1999).

VALIDITY: No explicit examination of the scale's validity was reported by Korgaonkar and Wolin (1999). Items in this scale were expected to represent two factors: entertainment and overcoming loneliness. However, the seven-factor solution based upon principal components factor analysis with varimax rotation led to the items merging into one scale.

REFERENCES:
Korgaonkar, Pradeep K. (2001), Personal Correspondence.
Korgaonkar, Pradeep K. and Lori D. Wolin (1999), "A Multivariate Analysis of Web Usage," *JAR*, 39 (March/April), 53–68.

SCALE ITEMS: [1]

I use the web:

1. So I can escape from reality.

2. Because it stirs me up.

3. Because it arouses my emotions and feelings.

4. Because it makes me feel less lonely.

5. So I can get away from what I am doing.

6. So I can forget about work.

7. Because it shows me how to get along with others.

8. Because it helps me unwind.

9. So I won't be alone.

10. I do not like to use the web alone.

11. Because it takes me into another world.

[1] The response format used by Korgaonkar and Wolin (1999) with these items was anchored by *strongly disagree* (1) and *strongly agree* (5). The scale stem was supplied by Korgaonkar (2001).

SCALE NAME: Internet Usage (Escape Motivation)

SCALE DESCRIPTION: The eight-item, five point scale measures the frequency with which a person uses the web as a way of mentally escaping discomforts of life such as boredom, loneliness, and other problems.

SCALE ORIGIN: The scale is original to Lin (1999) although she drew inspiration from previous studies of other media.

RELIABILITY: The scale was reported to have an alpha of .91 (Lin 1999).

VALIDITY: Although no examination of the scale's validity was reported by Lin (1999) an exploratory factor analysis was conducted. This provided some evidence of the scale's unidimensionality. Despite this, it appears that the items are tapping into more than one dimension. More rigorous examination of the scale's dimensionality is called for in future research.

REFERENCES:
Lin, Carolyn A. (1999), "Online-Service Adoption Likelihood," *JAR*, 39 (March/April), 79–89.
Lin, Carolyn A. (2001), Personal Correspondence.

SCALE ITEMS: [1]

These days you can surf the Internet to get news, information and entertainment materials or exchange messages with other people who are also online. Please indicate how likely it is for you to surf the Internet for the following reasons:

1. To keep yourself company.

2. To keep yourself from being bored.

3. To get advice to help to help solve your daily problems.

4. To forget about your problems.

5. To tune out what's going on around you.

6. To relax yourself.

7. To chat with people who share the same interest on the network.

8. To make friends with people who share the same interests on the network.

---

[1] Responses to these statements were measured using the following scale: *never* (1), *rarely* (2), *sometimes* (3), *often* (4), and *very often* (5) (Lin 2001).

SCALE NAME: Internet Usage (Financial Security Concerns)

SCALE DESCRIPTION: The scale is composed of seven, five-point Likert-type items that measure the extent to which a person expresses concern about using the web due to security and personal privacy reasons especially as they relate to financial transactions such as using a credit card and banking.

SCALE ORIGIN: The scale is original to the work of Korgaonkar and Wolin (1999). After reviewing previous research and the results of six focus groups the authors generated 41 items thought to relate to the reasons why people use the web as well as their concerns about using it. Eight factors were originally expected but their analysis (exploratory factor analysis) ultimately led to the development of seven scales.

RELIABILITY: An alpha of .80 was reported for the scale (Korgaonkar and Wolin 1999).

VALIDITY: No explicit examination of the scale's validity was reported by Korgaonkar and Wolin (1999). However, the items composing this scale loaded together and highest on this dimension in the seven-factor solution based upon principal components factor analysis with varimax rotation.

REFERENCES:
Korgaonkar, Pradeep K. and Lori D. Wolin (1999), "A Multivariate Analysis of Web Usage," *JAR*, 39 (March/April), 53–68.

SCALE ITEMS: [1]

1. I am worried about the security of financial transactions on the web.

2. I am concerned that my personal financial information may be shared with businesses without my consent.

3. I am uncomfortable giving my credit card number on the web.

4. I am concerned over the security of personal information on the web.

5. When I send a message over the Web, I feel concerned that it may be read by some other person or company without my knowledge.

6. I am uncomfortable conducting personal banking transactions via the web.

7. To me, the use of the web will be more appealing if proper safeguards were in place.

---

[1] The response format used by Korgaonkar and Wolin (1999) with these items was anchored by *strongly disagree* (1) and *strongly agree* (5).

SCALE NAME: Internet Usage (Information Motivation)

SCALE DESCRIPTION: The scale is composed of five, five-point Likert-type items that appear to capture the extent to which a person uses the web due to its ability to help locate information quickly and cheaply.

SCALE ORIGIN: The scale is original to the work of Korgaonkar and Wolin (1999). After reviewing previous research and the results of six focus groups the authors generated 41 items thought to relate to the reasons why people use the web as well as their concerns about using it. Eight factors were originally expected but their analysis (exploratory factor analysis) ultimately led to the development of seven scales.

RELIABILITY: An alpha of .77 was reported for the scale (Korgaonkar and Wolin 1999).

VALIDITY: No explicit examination of the scale's validity was reported by Korgaonkar and Wolin (1999). However, the items composing this scale loaded together and highest on this dimension in the seven-factor solution based upon principal components factor analysis with varimax rotation.

REFERENCES:
Korgaonkar, Pradeep K. and Lori D. Wolin (1999), "A Multivariate Analysis of Web Usage," *JAR*, 39 (March/April), 53–68.

SCALE ITEMS: [1]

1. I use the web because it gives quick and easy access to large volumes of information.

2. Overall, I learn a lot from using the Web.

3. I use the web so I can learn about things happening in the world.

4. Overall, information obtained from the Web is useful.

5. I use the web because it makes acquiring information inexpensive.

[1] The response format used by Korgaonkar and Wolin (1999) with these items was anchored by *strongly disagree* (1) and *strongly agree* (5).

SCALE NAME: Internet Usage (Information Motivation)

SCALE DESCRIPTION: The scale is composed of three, five-point items that measure the frequency with which a person uses the web in order to keep up with local, national, and international news.

SCALE ORIGIN: The scale is original to Lin (1999) although she drew inspiration from previous studies of other media.

RELIABILITY: The scale was reported to have an alpha of .88 (Lin 1999).

VALIDITY: Although no examination of the scale's validity was reported by Lin (1999) an exploratory factor analysis was conducted. This provided some evidence of the scale's unidimensionality.

REFERENCES:
Lin, Carolyn A. (1999), "Online-Service Adoption Likelihood," *JAR*, 39 (March/April), 79–89.
Lin, Carolyn A. (2001), Personal Correspondence.

SCALE ITEMS: [1]

These days you can surf the Internet to get news, information and entertainment materials or exchange messages with other people who are also online. Please indicate how likely it is for you to surf the Internet for the following reasons:

1. To get news to keep up with what's going on in your community.

2. To get news to keep up with what's going on in the country.

3. To get news to keep up with what's going on around the world.

[1] Responses to these statements were measured using the following scale: *never* (1), *rarely* (2), *sometimes* (3), *often* (4), and *very often* (5) (Lin 2001).

SCALE NAME: Internet Usage (Interactive Control Motivation)

SCALE DESCRIPTION: Six, five-point Likert-type items are used to measure the degree to which a person uses the web because it provides an experience that is both exciting and manageable.

SCALE ORIGIN: The scale is original to the work of Korgaonkar and Wolin (1999). After reviewing previous research and the results of six focus groups the authors generated 41 items thought to relate to the reasons why people use the web as well as their concerns about using it. Eight factors were originally expected but their analysis (exploratory factor analysis) ultimately led to the development of seven scales.

RELIABILITY: An alpha of .83 was reported for the scale (Korgaonkar and Wolin 1999).

VALIDITY: No explicit examination of the scale's validity was reported by Korgaonkar and Wolin (1999). However, the items composing this scale loaded together and highest on this dimension in the seven-factor solution based upon principal components factor analysis with Varimax rotation.

REFERENCES:
Korgaonkar, Pradeep K. (2001), Personal Correspondence.
Korgaonkar, Pradeep K. and Lori D. Wolin (1999), "A Multivariate Analysis of Web Usage," *JAR*, 39 (March/April), 53–68.

SCALE ITEMS: [1]

I use the web:

1. Because I decide if I want to continue scrolling through the sites or not.

2. Because it gives me the control over what and when I want to use it.

3. Because it is interactive.

4. Because I enjoy it.

5. Because it is thrilling.

6. Because I find it exciting.

[1] The response format used by Korgaonkar and Wolin (1999) with these items was anchored by *strongly disagree* (1) and *strongly agree* (5). The scale stem was supplied by Korgaonkar (2001).

SCALE NAME: Internet Usage (Privacy Concerns)

SCALE DESCRIPTION: The scale is composed of three, five-point Likert-type statements that measure the degree to which a person is troubled about use of the web because of personal privacy concerns as well as "spam" (unwanted solicitations).

SCALE ORIGIN: The scale is original to the work of Korgaonkar and Wolin (1999). After reviewing previous research and the results of six focus groups the authors generated 41 items thought to relate to the reasons why people use the web as well as their concerns about using it. Eight factors were originally expected but their analysis (exploratory factor analysis) ultimately led to the development of seven scales.

RELIABILITY: An alpha of .76 was reported for the scale (Korgaonkar and Wolin 1999).

VALIDITY: No explicit examination of the scale's validity was reported by Korgaonkar and Wolin (1999). However, the items composing this scale loaded together and highest on this dimension in the seven-factor solution based upon principal components factor analysis with varimax rotation.

REFERENCES:
Korgaonkar, Pradeep K. and Lori D. Wolin (1999), "A Multivariate Analysis of Web Usage," *JAR*, 39 (March/April), 53–68.

SCALE ITEMS: [1]

1. I detest the fact that the web is becoming a haven for electronic junk mail.

2. I wish I had more control over unwanted messages sent by businesses on the web.

3. I dislike the fact that marketers are able to find out personal information of on-line shoppers.

---

[1] The response format used by Korgaonkar and Wolin (1999) with these items was anchored by *strongly disagree* (1) and *strongly agree* (5).

SCALE NAME: Internet Usage (Privacy Concerns)

SCALE DESCRIPTION: The scale is composed of fifteen, seven-point statements measuring the level of concern a person has about privacy on the Internet with an emphasis on e-mail activities.

SCALE ORIGIN: Sheehan and Hoy (1999) stated that they adapted their scale from previous measures of privacy. The scale was constructed with the expectation that five of the fifteen practices would evoke low concern, five would evoke moderate concern, and the remaining five would generate high concern.

RELIABILITY: An alpha of .92 was reported for the scale (Sheehan and Hoy 1999).

VALIDITY: No examination of the scale's validity was reported by Sheehan and Hoy (1999).

REFERENCES:
Sheehan, Kim Bartel and Mariea Grubbs Hoy (1999), "Flaming, Complaining, Abstaining: How Online Users Respond to Privacy Concerns," *JA*, 28 (3), 37–51.

SCALE ITEMS: [1]

Please indicate your level of concern about your own privacy for each situation.

1. You receive e-mail from a company you have sent e-mail to in the past.

2. You receive e-mail from a company whose webpage you recently visited.

3. You receive an e-mail and have no idea how the company got your address.

4. A company requests your e-mail address only to send information of interest.

5. A notice on a webpage states that information collected is used by other divisions of that company.

6. A notice on a webpage states that information collected on that webpage may be sold to other companies.

7. You are asked to provide your name to access homepage.

8. You are asked to provide names of newsgroups read to access a homepage.

9. You are asked to provide your Social Security Number to access a homepage.

10. You receive e-mail about a new product from a company you currently do business with.

11. You receive e-mail about a new product from a known company you don't do business with.

12. You receive e-mail about a new product from a company you've never heard of.

13. A webpage requires your e-mail address to access the page. Upon registration, you will receive a mouse pad.

14. A webpage requires your e-mail address to access the page. Upon registration, you will receive a 24% discount on future purchases.

15. A webpage requires your e-mail address to access the page. Upon registration, you will be entered in a contest to win a computer (value: $1000).

[1] The response scale used by Sheehan and Hoy (1999) had *not at all concerned* (1) and *extremely concerned* (7) as anchors.

SCALE NAME: Internet Usage (Socialization Motivation)

SCALE DESCRIPTION: Five, five-point Likert-type items are used to measure the extent to which a person uses the web because it facilitates interpersonal communication and activities.

SCALE ORIGIN: The scale is original to the work of Korgaonkar and Wolin (1999). After reviewing previous research and the results of six focus groups the authors generated 41 items thought to relate to the reasons why people use the web as well as their concerns about using it. Eight factors were originally expected but their analysis (exploratory factor analysis) ultimately led to the development of seven scales.

RELIABILITY: An alpha of .80 was reported for the scale (Korgaonkar and Wolin 1999).

VALIDITY: No explicit examination of the scale's validity was reported by Korgaonkar and Wolin (1999). However, the items composing this scale loaded together and highest on this dimension in the seven-factor solution based upon principal components factor analysis with varimax rotation.

COMMENTS: Items #4 and #5 (below) had loadings below .50 in the factor solution reported by Korgaonkar and Wolin (1999). In addition, the items appear on the surface to hold less content in common with the other items. Given this, they should be used cautiously if not dropped or modified.

REFERENCES:

Korgaonkar, Pradeep K. and Lori D. Wolin (1999), "A Multivariate Analysis of Web Usage," *JAR*, 39 (March/April), 53–68.

SCALE ITEMS: [1]

1. When I visit my friends we often use the web.

2. I use the web with my friends.

3. Often, I talk to my friends about sites on the web.

4. I enjoy telling people about the web sites I like.

5. I use the web because it is a part of my usual routine.

---

[1] The response format used by Korgaonkar and Wolin (1999) with these items was anchored by *strongly disagree* (1) and *strongly agree* (5).

SCALE NAME: Internet Usage Intention (Information)

SCALE DESCRIPTION: The three-item, seven-point scale is used to measure the extent to which a person intends to use the Internet versus a store to gather prepurchase information. Although the scale is based upon a respondent's answers with respect to three specific goods, in total they are intended to be representative of all *search goods* (as opposed to *experience goods*). See below for more detail.

SCALE ORIGIN: The scale is original to Shim et al. (2001). The authors desired a scale that measured online shopping as it pertained to *search goods* rather than *experience goods*, that is, goods that mainly involved the gathering of factual information versus those that were chosen based on experience using the senses. Five goods were tested and the ones that scored highest on factual information and lowest on sensory experience were computer software, books, and videos.

RELIABILITY: Shim et al. (2001) reported the construct reliability of the scale to be .79.

VALIDITY: Except for the saying that the variance extracted for the scale was 56.1%, little information regarding the scale's validity was reported by Shim et al. (2001).

REFERENCES:
Shim, Soyeon (2002), Personal Correspondence.
Shim, Soyeon, Mary Ann Eastlick, Sherry L. Lotz, and Patricia Warrington (2001), "An Online Prepurchase Intentions Model: The Role of Intention to Search," *JR*, 77 (3), 397–416.

SCALE ITEMS: [1]

Directions: Say that you are planning to buy the following products during the next three months. Regardless of where you eventually but these products, indicate how likely you would seek product information through the Internet or stores?

1. computer software

2. books

3. videos

---

[1] A seven-point response scale was used with these items by Shim et al. (2001; 2002) that was anchored by *definitely store search* (1) and *definitely Internet search* (7).

SCALE NAME: Internet Usage Intention (Purchase)

SCALE DESCRIPTION: The scale is composed of three, seven-point items that are used to measure the degree to which a person expresses the intention to use the Internet versus a store to buy products. Although the scale is based upon a respondent's answers with respect to three specific goods, in total they are intended to be representative of all *search goods* (as opposed to *experience goods*). See below for more detail.

SCALE ORIGIN: The scale is original to Shim et al. (2001). The authors desired a scale that measured online shopping as it pertained to *search goods* rather than *experience goods*, that is, goods that mainly involved the gathering of factual information versus those that were chosen based on experience using the senses. Five goods were tested and the ones that scored highest on factual information and lowest on sensory experience were computer software, books, and videos.

RELIABILITY: Shim et al. (2001) reported the construct reliability of the scale to be .90.

VALIDITY: Except for the saying that the variance extracted for the scale was 75.8%, little information regarding the scale's validity was reported by Shim et al. (2001).

REFERENCES:
Shim, Soyeon, Mary Ann Eastlick, Sherry L. Lotz, and Patricia Warrington (2001), "An Online Prepurchase Intentions Model: The Role of Intention to Search," *JR*, 77 (3), 397–416.
Shim, Soyeon (2002), Personal Correspondence.

SCALE ITEMS: [1]

After the product information search, how likely would you choose a store or Internet for shopping for the following products?

1. computer software

2. books

3. videos

---

[1] A seven-point response scale was used with these items by Shim et al. (2001; 2002) that was anchored by *definitely store buying* (1) and *definitely Internet buying* (7).

SCALE NAME: Involvement (Brand)

SCALE DESCRIPTION: The scale is composed of three, seven-point items that measure how much a person expresses that a product with a particular brand name is important to him/her.

SCALE ORIGIN: Although not stated explicitly, the scale is apparently original to Kirmani, Sood, and Bridges (1999).

RELIABILITY: An alpha of .88 was reported for the scale (Kirmani, Sood, and Bridges 1999).

VALIDITY: No examination of the scale's validity was reported by Kirmani, Sood, and Bridges (1999).

REFERENCES:
Kirmani, Amna, Sanjay Sood, and Sheri Bridges (1999), "The Ownership Effect in Consumer Responses to Brand Line Stretches," *JM*, 63 (January), 88–101.

SCALE ITEMS: [1]

1. uninvolving / involving

2. I relate to _____ _____.

3. _____ _____ are important to me.

---

[1] The verbal anchors used by Kirmani, Sood, and Bridges (1999) with #2 and #3 were not specified, however, the typical Likert-type approach (*agree/disagree*) would appear to be appropriate. Also, in those same items, the first blank should contain the brand name and the second one has the generic product name, e.g., *Gap* jeans.

SCALE NAME: Involvement (Cents-Off Offers)

SCALE DESCRIPTION: It is a seven-item, seven-point Likert-type scale measuring a consumer's propensity to buy brands that have price-off offers despite the amount of money involved. This measures a general tendency rather than the likelihood that the behavior occurs for any particular product category. The authors of the scale called it *cents-off proneness* (Burton et al. 1998; Lichtenstein, Netemeyer, and Burton 1995; Lichtenstein, Burton, and Netemeyer 1997).

SCALE ORIGIN: The scale is original to the studies by Lichtenstein, Netemeyer, and Burton (1995) though some of the items are similar to ones developed previously by the same authors for other measures (e.g., Lichtenstein, Netemeyer, and Burton 1990). In an effort to develop several deal proneness measures, 91 items were generated and tested with 341 nonstudent adults. Using factor analysis and other tests, seven items were deleted leaving 84 to be used in the two studies reported in Lichtenstein, Netemeyer, and Burton (1995). Lichtenstein, Burton, and Netemeyer (1997) presented 49 of the items for the measurement of eight different deal proneness types.

RELIABILITY: An alpha of .90 was reported for the scale by Lichtenstein, Netemeyer, and Burton (1995; Lichtenstein, Burton, and Netemeyer 1997) for both studies as well as by Burton et al. (1998).

VALIDITY: Confirmatory factor analyses were used in both studies by Lichtenstein, Netemeyer, and Burton (1995; Lichtenstein, Burton, and Netemeyer 1997). A variety of data were produced in support of the scale's unidimensionality and discriminant validity. No examination of the scale's validity was reported by Burton et al. (1998).

COMMENTS: Lichtenstein, Netemeyer, and Burton (1995) reported means on the scale of 25.08 and 25.18 for Study 1 and 2, respectively.

REFERENCES:

Burton, Scot, Donald R. Lichtenstein, Richard G. Netemeyer, and Judith A. Garretson (1998), "A Scale for Measuring Attitude Toward Private Label Products and an Examination of Its Psychological and Behavioral Correlates," *JAMS*, 26 (4), 293–306.

Lichtenstein, Donald R., Scot Burton, and Richard G. Netemeyer (1997), "An Examination of Deal Proneness Across Sales Promotion Types: A Consumer Segmentation Perspective," *JR*, 73 (2), 283–297.

Lichtenstein, Donald R., Richard D. Netemeyer, and Scot Burton (1990), "Distinguishing Coupon Proneness From Value Consciousness: An Acquisition-Transaction Utility Theory Perspective," *JM*, 54 (July), 54–67.

Lichtenstein, Donald R., Richard D. Netemeyer, and Scot Burton (1995), "Assessing the Domain Specificity of Deal Proneness: A Field Study," *JCR*, 22 (December), 314–326.

SCALE ITEMS:

1. Buying products with cents-off deals makes me feel good.

2. I am more likely to buy a brand if it has a cents-off deal on the label.

3. I enjoy buying products with cents-off deals, regardless of the amount I save by doing so.

4. Compared to most people, I would say I have a positive attitude toward cents-off deals.

5. Beyond the money I save, buying products with cents-off deals gives me a sense of joy.

6. Cents-off deals can save a shopper a lot of money.

7. Compared to most people, I am more likely to buy products with cents-off deals.

SCALE NAME: Involvement (Coupons)

SCALE DESCRIPTION: It is an multi-item, seven-point Likert-type scale measuring the degree to which a consumer reports using coupons and enjoying it. A five-item version was used by Lichtenstein, Ridgway, and Netemeyer (1993), Lichtenstein, Netemeyer, and Burton (1995), Lichtenstein, Burton, and Netemeyer (1997), and Burton et al. (1998, 1999). In these studies the scale was referred to as *coupon proneness*.

SCALE ORIGIN: The scale is original to Lichtenstein, Netemeyer, and Burton (1990). Five marketing academicians judged the appropriateness of 33 items generated to represent the construct. Twenty-five items remained after this procedure. Based upon a second round of five additional judges assessing the face validity of the items, all items were retained. The items were then interspersed throughout a questionnaire given to 263 undergraduate and graduate business students. The eight items composing the final version of the scale were those that had corrected item-total correlations equal to or greater than .40. Confirmatory factor analysis provided evidence that the items were unidimensional and had discriminant validity. The construct reliability was calculated to be .88.

RELIABILITY: An alpha of .84 was calculated for the scale as used by Biwa, Srinivasan, and Srivastava (1997; Biwa 1998). Burton et al. (1998) reported an alpha of .86. In Study 1 by Burton, Lichtenstein, and Netemeyer (1999) an alpha of .88 was reported; in Study 2 it was merely reported to be greater than .85. Lastovicka et al. (1999) reported an alpha of .88.

The internal consistency of the scale was calculated by Lichtenstein, Netemeyer, and Burton (1990) to be .88 and item-total correlations were above .40. Alphas of .88 and .86 were reported for the scale by Lichtenstein, Netemeyer, and Burton (1995) for Study 1 (Lichtenstein, Burton, and Netemeyer 1997) and 2, respectively.

VALIDITY: In the process of validating another scale (#26), Burton et al. (1998) conducted multiple tests of the scale's discriminant validity. The evidence provided support for a claim of discriminant validity for the Involvement (Coupons) scale as well.

Lastovicka et al. (1999) used this scale in the process of validating another scale (#177). Based upon that, their data indicated that scores on the coupon involvement scale were not significantly related to either frugality or a measure of response bias (#91).

Confirmatory factor analyses were used in each of the studies by Lichtenstein et al. (1990, 1993, 1995, 1997) and the evidence indicated that the scale was unidimensional and showed evidence of discriminant validity. Lichtenstein, Ridgway, and Netemeyer (1993) stated that after using CFA, items with low standardized factor loadings were dropped. This is likely to be the reason that fewer items composed the scale in the later studies compared to the first.

COMMENTS: Lichtenstein, Netemeyer, and Burton (1995) reported means on the scale of 19.26 and 19.18 for Study 1 and 2, respectively.

REFERENCES:

Biwa, Kapil (1998), Personal Correspondence.

Biwa, Kapil, Srini S. Srinivasan, and Rajendra K. Srivastava (1997), "Coupon Attractiveness and Coupon Proneness: A Framework for Modeling Coupon Redemption," *JMR*, 34 (November), 517–525.

Burton, Scot (2000), Personal Correspondence.

Burton, Scot, Donald R. Lichtenstein, and Richard G. Netemeyer (1999), "Exposure to Sales Flyers and Increased Purchases in Retail Supermarkets," *JAR*, 39 (September/October), 7–14.

Burton, Scot, Donald R. Lichtenstein, Richard G. Netemeyer, and Judith A. Garretson (1998), "A Scale for Measuring Attitude Toward Private Label Products and an Examination of Its Psychological and Behavioral Correlates," *JAMS*, 26 (4), 293–306.

Lastovicka, John L., Lance A. Bettencourt, Renee Shaw Hughner, and Ronald J. Kuntze (1999), "Lifestyle of the Tight and Frugal: Theory and Measurement," *JCR*, 26 (June), 85–98.

Lichtenstein, Donald R., Scot Burton, and Richard G. Netemeyer (1997), "An Examination of Deal Proneness Across Sales Promotion Types: A Consumer Segmentation Perspective," *JR*, 73 (2), 283–297.

Lichtenstein, Donald R., Richard D. Netemeyer, and Scot Burton (1990), "Distinguishing Coupon Proneness From Value Consciousness: An Acquisition-Transaction Utility Theory Perspective," *JM*, 54 (July), 54–67.

Lichtenstein, Donald R., Richard D. Netemeyer, and Scot Burton (1995), "Assessing the Domain Specificity of Deal Proneness: A Field Study," *JCR*, 22 (December), 314–326.

Lichtenstein, Donald R., Nancy M. Ridgway, and Richard G. Netemeyer (1993), "Price Perceptions and Consumer Shopping Behavior: A Field Study," *JMR*, 30 (May), 234–245.

SCALE ITEMS: [1]

1. Redeeming coupons makes me feel good.

2. I enjoy clipping coupons out of the newspapers.

3. When I use coupons, I feel that I am getting a good deal.

4. I enjoy using coupons, regardless of the amount I save by doing so.

5. I have favorite brands, but most of the time I buy the brand I have a coupon for.

6. I am more likely to buy brands for which I have a coupon.

7. Coupons have caused me to buy products I normally would not buy.

8. Beyond the money I save, redeeming coupons gives me a sense of joy.

[1] All of the above items were used by Lichtenstein, Netemeyer, and Burton (1990) but only items 1 to 4, and 8 were used by Burton et al. (1998, 1999, 2000), Lichtenstein, Burton, and Netemeyer (1997), Lichtenstein, Ridgway, and Netemeyer (1993) as well as Lichtenstein, Netemeyer, and Burton (1995). Biwa, Srinivasan, and Srivastava (1997) as well as Lastovicka et al. (1999) were not explicit about which items they used but it would appear they used the original version of the scale.

SCALE NAME: Involvement (Ego with Service Provider)

SCALE DESCRIPTION: Three, five-point Likert-type statements are used to measure the extent to which a customer views a service provider he/she uses and the image that the provider has as being important to his/her self-concept.

SCALE ORIGIN: Ganesh, Arnold, and Reynolds (2000) cited several previous studies on which they drew in the development of their scale.

RELIABILITY: An alpha of .71 was reported for the scale (Ganesh, Arnold, and Reynolds 2000).

VALIDITY: No examination of the scale's validity was reported by Ganesh, Arnold, and Reynolds (2000). They did, however, factor analyze the items in this scale along with those of a related scale (#235). The items for this scale loaded highest on the same dimension with no substantial loadings on the other dimension.

REFERENCES:
Ganesh, Jaishanker, Mark J. Arnold, and Kristy E. Reynolds (2000), "Understanding the Customer Base of Service Providers: An Examination of the Differences Between Switchers and Stayers," *JM*, 64 (3), 65–87.

SCALE ITEMS: [1]

1. The brand image of the _____ played a major role in my decision to become a customer of the _____.

2. The _____ I use says a lot about who I am.

3. It is important for me to choose a _____ that "feels" right.

[1] The generic term for the service provider should be placed in the blanks, e.g., bank.

SCALE NAME: Involvement (End-of-Aisle Displays)

SCALE DESCRIPTION: It is a seven-item, seven-point Likert-type scale measuring a consumer's attitude toward end-of-aisle displays and stated tendency to buy products displayed on them. This measures a general tendency rather than the likelihood that the behavior occurs for any particular product category. Lichtenstein, Burton, and Netemeyer (1997) and Lichtenstein, Netemeyer, and Burton (1995) referred the scale as *end-of-aisle-display proneness* whereas Burton et al. (1998) called it *display proneness*.

SCALE ORIGIN: The scale is original to the studies by Lichtenstein, Netemeyer, and Burton (1995) though some of the items are similar to ones developed previously by the same authors for other measures (e.g., Lichtenstein, Netemeyer, and Burton 1990). In an effort to develop several deal proneness measures 91 items were generated and tested with 341 nonstudent adults. Using factor analysis and other tests, seven items were deleted leaving 84 to be used in the two studies reported in Lichtenstein, Netemeyer, and Burton (1995). Lichtenstein, Burton, and Netemeyer (1997) presented 49 of the items for the measurement of eight different deal proneness types.

RELIABILITY: Alphas of .89 and .90 were reported for the scale by Lichtenstein, Netemeyer, and Burton (1995) for Study 1 (Lichtenstein, Burton, and Netemeyer 1997) and 2, respectively. Burton et al. (1998) also reported an alpha of .90.

VALIDITY: Confirmatory factor analyses were used in both studies by Lichtenstein, Netemeyer, and Burton (1995; Lichtenstein, Burton, and Netemeyer 1997) and it was concluded that the scale was unidimensional and showed evidence of discriminant validity. No examination of the scale's validity was reported by Burton et al. (1998).

COMMENTS: Lichtenstein, Netemeyer, and Burton (1995) reported means on the scale of 18.93 and 18.55 for Study 1 and 2, respectively.

REFERENCES:
Burton, Scot, Donald R. Lichtenstein, Richard G. Netemeyer, and Judith A. Garretson (1998), "A Scale for Measuring Attitude Toward Private Label Products and an Examination of Its Psychological and Behavioral Correlates," *JAMS*, 26 (4), 293–306.
Lichtenstein, Donald R., Scot Burton, and Richard G. Netemeyer (1997), "An Examination of Deal Proneness Across Sales Promotion Types: A Consumer Segmentation Perspective," *JMR*, 73 (2), 283–297.
Lichtenstein, Donald R., Richard D. Netemeyer, and Scot Burton (1990), "Distinguishing Coupon Proneness From Value Consciousness: An Acquisition-Transaction Utility Theory Perspective," *JM*, 54 (July), 54–67.
Lichtenstein, Donald R., Richard D. Netemeyer, and Scot Burton (1995), "Assessing the Domain Specificity of Deal Proneness: A Field Study," *JCR*, 22 (December), 314–326.

SCALE ITEMS:

1. You usually save money when you buy a product from an end-of-aisle display.

2. I am more likely to buy brands that are displayed at the end of the aisle.

3. End-of-aisle displays have influenced me to buy brands I normally would not buy.

4. Beyond the money I save, buying from end-of-aisle displays gives me a sense of joy.

5. I believe that one can save a lot of money buying from end-of-aisle displays.

6. The prices of products displayed at the ends of aisles are usually good.

7. Compared to most people, I am more likely to buy brands on end-of-aisle displays.

SCALE NAME: Involvement (Enduring)

SCALE DESCRIPTION: It is a twenty-item, seven-point semantic differential scale measuring the enduring and intrinsic (rather than situational) relevance of an object to a person. The scale is easily customized to measure involvement with a product category, a particular brand, an ad for a particular brand, or a particular purchase decision. The scale was referred to as Personal Involvement Inventory (PII) by the originator (Zaichkowsky 1985).

Abbreviated versions of the scale have been used in several studies. Even Zaichkowsky (1994) herself introduced a version with just ten items.

For a greatly modified version of the scale see Steenkamp and Wedel (1991) where store involvement was measured in Holland. Also see McQuarrie and Munson (1987) for another modified version of the scale (RPII). Finally, Neese and Taylor (1994) used only positive anchors to make two Likert-type scales for the study of luxury sedans.

SCALE ORIGIN: While previous research was reviewed and may have provided ideas for scale items, the scale as a unit was generated and tested first by Zaichkowsky (1985). Construction of the scale used four data sets of 286 undergraduate psychology students; two data sets with 49 MBA students; and two data sets with 57 clerical and administrative staff members. The stability of the measure was checked over two subject groups for four products producing test-retest correlations from .88 to .93. Internal consistency was calculated with the same data and ranged from .95 to .97 (Cronbach's alpha). Content validity was demonstrated by the scale through use of expert judges at two points: first, by reducing the list of word pairs to those most appropriate for measuring the construct; second, by successful classification of open- ended statements from subjects. Criterion validity was examined by demonstrating the similarity between subjects' average involvement levels with four products and the expected degree of involvement based upon previous studies. Construct validity was checked for three products by noting the association between subjects' scale scores and their statements of behavior expected to reflect involvement. For each of the three products there was a positive relationship between scale scores and responses to statements.

The scale used by Maheswaran and Meyers-Levy (1990) may not have been directly derived from the Zaichkowsky measure and is very short but is similar enough to be viewed here as measuring the same thing.

RELIABILITY: Reported internal consistencies have ranged from .80 (Lord, Lee, and Sauer 1994) to .98 (Houston and Walker 1996). Zaichkowsky (1994) reported that the abbreviated version of the scale she tested had stability scores (3 week test-retest) ranging between .73 and .84 depending upon the ad.

VALIDITY: No test of validity was reported by most of the studies. A factor analysis of the twenty-item scale performed by Mick (1992) produced a two-factor solution. Only the sixteen items loading strongly on the first factor were retained for calculating scale scores.

Houston and Walker (1996) were concerned about the dimensionality of the scale and tested it further using CFA. While evidence was found for two factors, the test for discriminant validity they applied was not met which led them to treat the two dimensions as one for purposes of the scale.

Similarly, Zaichkowsky (1994) found evidence that the abbreviated scale was not unidimensional but in fact contained both a five-item cognitive involvement subscale and a five-item affective involvement subscale.

COMMENTS: Zaichkowsky (1985) admitted that a smaller number of items composing the scale might be almost as reliable as the twenty-item version but warned against haphazardly reducing the number of items.

She also pointed out that while the scale could be used for various purposes, her work had mainly focused on demonstrating its quality regarding product involvement. More research was called for to verify its quality for other objects such as ads and purchase decisions. She provided such testing and a shorter version in her 1994 article.

See also Dean (1999), Celsi and Olson (1998), Gotlieb and Sarel (1991), Gotlieb and Swan (1990), Haugtvedt and Wegener (1994), Machleit, Allen, and Madden (1993), Mano and Oliver (1993), Mishra, Umesh, and Stem (1993), Mittal (1990), Murry, Lastovicka, and Singh (1992), Samu, Krishnan, and Smith (1999), Singh and Cole (1993), and Spreng, MacKenzie, and Olshavsky (1996) for other uses of the scale.

REFERENCES:

Bower, Amanda B. and Stacy Landreth (2001), "Is Beauty Best? Highly Versus Normally Attractive Models in Advertising," *JA*, 30 (1), 1–12.

Celsi, Richard L. and Jerry C. Olson (1988), "The Role of Involvement in Attention and Comprehension Processes," *JCR*, 15 (September), 210–224.

Coyle, James R. and Esther Thorson (2001), "The Effects of Progressive Levels of Interactivity and Vividness in Web Marketing Sites," *JA*, 30 (Fall), 65–77.

Dean, Dwane Hal (1999), "Brand Endorsement, Popularity, and Event Sponsorship as Advertising Cues Affecting Consumer Pre-Purchase Attitudes," *JA*, 28 (3), 1–12.

Gotlieb, Jerry B. and John E. Swan (1990), "An Application of the Elaboration Likelihood Model," *JAMS*, 18 (Summer), 221–228.

Gotlieb, Jerry B. and Dan Sarel (1991), "Comparative Advertising Effectiveness: The Role of Involvement and Source Credibility," *JA*, 20 (1), 38–45.

Haugtvedt, Curtis P. and Duane T. Wegener (1994), "Message Order Effects in Persuasion: An Attitude Strength Perspective," *JCR*, 21 (June), 205–218.

Houston, Mark B. and Beth A. Walker (1996), "Self-Relevance and Purchase Goals: Mapping a Consumer Decision," *JAMS*, 24 (Summer), 232–245.

Laczniak, Russell N. and Darrel D. Muehling (1993), "The Relationship Between Experimental Manipulations and Tests of Theory in an Advertising Message Involvement Context," *JA*, 22 (September), 59–74.

Lichtenstein, Donald R., Peter H. Bloch, and William C. Black (1988), "Correlates of Price Acceptability," *JCR*, 15 (Sept.), 243–252.

Lichtenstein, Donald R., Richard D. Netemeyer, and Scot Burton (1990), "Distinguishing Coupon Proneness From Value Consciousness: An Acquisition-Transaction Utility Theory Perspective," *JM*, 54 (July), 54–67.

Lord, Kenneth R., Myung-Soo Lee, and Paul L. Sauer (1994), "Program Context Antecedents of Attitude toward Radio Commercials," *JAMS*, 22 (1), 3–15.

Maheswaran, Durairja and Joan Meyers-Levy (1990), "The Influence of Message Framing and Issue Involvement," *JMR*, 27 (August), 361–367.

Machleit, Karen A., Chris T. Allen, and Thomas J. Madden (1993), "The Mature Brand and Brand Interest: An Alternative Consequence of Ad-Evoked Affect," *JM*, 57 (October), 72–82.

Mano, Haim and Richard L. Oliver (1993), "Assessing the Dimensionality and Structure of the Consumption Experience: Evaluation, Feeling, and Satisfaction," *JCR*, 20 (December), 451–466.

Marks, Lawrence J. (1994), Personal Correspondence.

McQuarrie, Edward F. and J. Michael Munson (1987), "The Zaichkowsky Personal Inventory: Modification and Extension," *Advances in Consumer Research*, 14 (?), 36–40.

Mick, David Glen (1992), "Levels of Subjective Comprehension in Advertising Processing and Their Relations to Ad Perceptions, Attitudes, and Memory," *JCR*, 18 (March), 411–424.

Miller, Darryl W. and Lawrence J. Marks (1992), "Mental Imagery and Sound Effects in Radio Commercials," *JA*, 21 (4), 83–93.

Mishra, Sanjay, U. N. Umesh, and Donald E. Stem, Jr. (1993), "Antecedents of the Attraction Effect: An Information-Processing Approach," *JMR*, 30 (August), 331–349.

Mittal, Banwari (1990), "The Relative Roles of Brand Beliefs and Attitude Toward the Ad as Mediators of Brand Attitude: A Second Look," *JMR*, 27 (May), 209–219.

Muehling, Darrel D. (1994), Personal Correspondence.

Murry, John P. Jr., John L. Lastovicka, and Surendra N. Singh (1992), "Feeling and Liking Responses to Television Programs: An Examination of Two Explanations for Media-Context Effects," *JCR*, 18 (March), 441–451.

Neese, William T. and Ronald D. Taylor (1994), "Verbal Strategies for Indirect Comparative Advertising," *JAR*, 34 (March/April), 56–69.

Samu, Sridhar, H. Shanker Krishnan, and Robert E. Smith (1999), "Using Advertising Alliances for New Product Introduction: Interactions Between Product Complementarity and Promotional Strategies," *JM*, 63 (January), 57–74.

Singh, Surendra N. and Catherine Cole (1993), "The Effects of Length, Content, and Repetition on Television Commercial Effectiveness," *JMR*, 30 (February), 91–104.

Spreng, Richard A., Scott B. MacKenzie, and Richard W. Olshavsky (1996), "A Reexamination of the Determinants of Consumer Satisfaction," *JM*, 60 (July), 15–32.

Stafford, Marla Royne (1996), "Tangibility in Services Advertising: An Investigation of Verbal versus Visual Cues," *JA*, 25 (Fall), 13–28.

Stafford, Marla Royne (1998), "Advertising Sex-Typed Services: The Effects of Sex, Service Type, and Employee Type on Consumer Attitudes," *JA*, 27 (2), 65–82.

Steenkamp, Jan-Benedict E. M. and Michel Wedel (1991), "Segmenting Retail Markets on Store Image Using a Consumer-Based Methodology," *JR*, 67 (Fall), 300–320.

Wakefield, Kirk L. and Julie Baker (1998), "Excitement at the Mall: Determinants and Effects on Shopping Response," *JR*, 74 (4), 515–539.

Zaichkowsky, Judith L. (1985), "Measuring the Involvement Construct," *JCR*, 12 (December), 341–352.

Zaichkowsky, Judith L. (1994), "The Personal Involvement Inventory: Reduction, Revision, and Application to Advertising," *JA*, 23 (December), 59–70.

SCALE ITEMS: [1]

1. unimportant / important

2. of no concern / of concern to me

3. irrelevant / relevant

4. means nothing to me / means a lot to me

5. useless / useful

6. worthless / valuable

7. trivial / fundamental

8. not beneficial / beneficial

9. doesn't matter / matters to me

10. uninterested / interested

11. insignificant / significant

12. superfluous / vital

13. boring / interesting

14. unexciting / exciting

15. unappealing / appealing

16. mundane / fascinating

17. nonessential / essential

18. undesirable / desirable

19. unwanted / wanted

20. not needed / needed

21. not involved / highly involved

22. uninvolving / involving

Bower and Landreth (2001): 1, 2, 3, 9 [.90]
Coyle and Thorson (2001): 13, 14, 15, 22 [.82, .92]
Houston and Walker (1996): 1–20 [.98]
Laczniak and Muehling (1993; Muehling 1994)
Lichtenstein et al. (1988): 1 to 6, 8, 17, 20 [.93]
Lichtenstein et al. (1990): 1 to 4, 6, 8, 9, 13 to 15, 17 [.90]
Lord, Lee, and Sauer (1994): 1 to 3, 8, 12 [.80]
Maheswaran and Joan Meyers-Levy (1990): short phrases based on 3, 10, 21 [.89]
Mick (1992): 1–6, 8–11, 13–16, 18, 19 [.96]
Miller and Marks (1992; Marks 1994): 1–20 [.94]
Stafford (1996): 1–20 [.97]
Stafford (1998): 1, 3, 4, 6, 13–16, 20, 22 [.92]
Wakefield and Baker (1998): 1, 4, 9, 13–15 [.96]
Zaichkowsky (1985): 1–20 [.95–.97]
Zaichkowsky (1994): 1, 3, 4, 6, 13–16, 20, 22 [.91–.95]

[1] Seven-point response formats have been typically used. Where known, the items used by particular authors are listed along with their respective reliabilities.

SCALE NAME: Involvement (Event)

SCALE DESCRIPTION: The scale is composed of four, seven-point Likert type statements measuring a person's interest in some specific event and its importance to him/her. The events examined by Speed and Thompson (2000) were related to sports.

SCALE ORIGIN: The scale is original to the study by Speed and Thompson (2000). Some qualitative work by the authors led to generation of items for this scale as well as several others. This was followed by a pretest which aided in identifying items for deletion or modification.

RELIABILITY: An alpha of .96 was reported for the scale by Speed and Thompson (2000).

VALIDITY: The initial qualitative work conducted by the authors provides some evidence of its content validity. Based on data from the main study, a CFA was performed on items from several scales. The results provided evidence of this scale's convergent and discriminant validity.

REFERENCES:
Speed, Richard and Peter Thompson (2000), "Determinants of Sports Sponsorship Response," *JAMS*, 28 (2), 226–238.

SCALE ITEMS:

1. I am a strong supporter of this event.

2. I would want to attend this event.

3. I enjoy following coverage of this event.

4. This event is important to me.

#228 *Involvement (Movie Watching)*

SCALE NAME: Involvement (Movie Watching)

SCALE DESCRIPTION: The four-item scale measures a person's interest in movies, with an emphasis on watching them more, going to a theater to see them, and seeing them before others do.

SCALE ORIGIN: Inspiration for some of the items developed by Neelamegham and Jain (1999) came from the innovativeness scale by Goldsmith and Hofacker (1991).

RELIABILITY: The composite reliability was reported to be .82 (Neelamegham and Jain 1999).

VALIDITY: All items loaded on a single factor and model fit was acceptable (Neelamegham and Jain 1999).

REFERENCES:
Goldsmith, Ronald E. and Charles F. Hofacker (1991), "Measuring Consumer Innovativeness," *JAMS*, 19 (Summer), 209–221.
Neelamegham, Ramya and Dipak Jain (1999), "Consumer Choice Process for Experience Goods: An Econometric Model and Analysis," *JMR*, 36 (August), 373–386.

SCALE ITEMS: [1]

1. I watch a lot more movies than others.

2. I am interested in watching new movies.

3. I do not like watching movies before others. (r)

4. How often do you go to the movies in a theater?

[1] The first three items were responded to using a Likert-type format (*totally agree/totally disagree*). The potential responses for item 4 were: *once a week/once every two weeks/once a month/once every six months/ not more than once a year/don't go.*

SCALE NAME: Involvement (Online Services)

SCALE DESCRIPTION: The scale is composed of seven, seven-point Likert-type items that gauge the level of interest, experience, and expertise a person expresses having with regard to Internet-related services.

SCALE ORIGIN: The scale was developed by Keaveney and Parthasarathy (2001) based upon a scale used by Zinkhan and Locander (1988). (See V. I, #140.)

RELIABILITY: An alpha of .80 was reported for the scale by Keaveney and Parthasarathy (2001).

VALIDITY: No examination of the scale's validity was reported by Keaveney and Parthasarathy (2001).

COMMENTS: A casual examination of the items indicates that they touch on several issues such as interest in online services, Internet expertise, and experience in purchasing online. Given this, it is possible that the scale is not unidimensional. Further, testing appears to be called for.

REFERENCES:

Keaveney, Susan M. and Madhavan Parthasarathy (2001), "Customer Switching Behavior in Online Services: An Exploratory Study of the Role of Selected Attitudinal, Behavioral, and Demographic Factors," *JAMS*, 29 (Fall), 374–390.

Zinkhan George M. and William B. Locander (1988), "ESSCA: A Multidimensional Analysis Tool for Marketing Research," *JAMS*, 16 (Spring), 36–46.

SCALE ITEMS:

1. I am very interested in online services.

2. My level of involvement with online services is high.

3. I am particularly engaged in the online service environment.

4. I consider myself an expert on the online electronic environment.

5. I consider myself an Internet expert.

6. I purchase products from online vendors regularly.

7. My level of expertise regarding personal computers is high.

SCALE NAME: Involvement (Premiums)

SCALE DESCRIPTION: It is a six-item, seven-point Likert-type scale measuring a consumer's fondness for purchasing products that have another item with them for free. This measures a general tendency rather than the likelihood that the behavior occurs for any particular product category. Lichtenstein, Burton, and Netemeyer (1997) and Lichtenstein, Netemeyer, and Burton (1995) referred to the scale as *free-gift-with-purchase proneness* and Burton et al. (1998) called it *free gift proneness*.

SCALE ORIGIN: The scale is original to the studies by Lichtenstein, Netemeyer, and Burton (1995) though some of the items are similar to ones developed previously by the same authors for other measures (e.g., Lichtenstein, Netemeyer, and Burton 1990). In an effort to develop several deal proneness measures 91 items were generated and tested with 341 nonstudent adults. Using factor analysis and other tests, 7 items were deleted leaving 84 to be used in the 2 studies described below. Lichtenstein, Burton, and Netemeyer (1997) presented 49 of the items for the measurement of 8 different deal proneness types.

RELIABILITY: An alpha of .91 was reported for the scale by Lichtenstein, Netemeyer, and Burton (1995; Lichtenstein, Burton, and Netemeyer 1997) for both Study 1 and 2. Burton et al. (1998) also reported an alpha of .91.

VALIDITY: Confirmatory factor analyses were used in the studies by Lichtenstein, Netemeyer, and Burton (1995; Lichtenstein, Burton, and Netemeyer 1997) and it was concluded that the scale was unidimensional and showed evidence of discriminant validity. No examination of the scale's validity was reported by Burton et al. (1998).

COMMENTS: Lichtenstein, Netemeyer, and Burton (1995) reported means on the scale of 17.74 and 15.93 for Study 1 and 2, respectively.

REFERENCES:

Burton, Scot, Donald R. Lichtenstein, Richard G. Netemeyer, and Judith A. Garretson (1998), "A Scale for Measuring Attitude Toward Private Label Products and an Examination of Its Psychological and Behavioral Correlates," *JAMS*, 26 (4), 293–306.

Lichtenstein, Donald R., Scot Burton, and Richard G. Netemeyer (1997), "An Examination of Deal Proneness Across Sales Promotion Types: A Consumer Segmentation Perspective," *JR*, 73 (2), 283–297.

Lichtenstein, Donald R., Richard D. Netemeyer, and Scot Burton (1990), "Distinguishing Coupon Proneness From Value Consciousness: An Acquisition-Transaction Utility Theory Perspective," *JM*, 54 (July), 54–67.

Lichtenstein, Donald R., Richard D. Netemeyer, and Scot Burton (1995), "Assessing the Domain Specificity of Deal Proneness: A Field Study," *JCR*, 22 (December), 314–326.

SCALE ITEMS:

1. I enjoy buying products that come with a free gift.

2. I enjoy buying a brand that comes with a free gift, regardless of the value of the free gift.

3. I have favorite brands, but when I encounter a free gift offer, I am more likely to buy the brand that comes with the free gift.

4. Seeing a brand that comes with a free gift has influenced me to buy brands I normally would not buy.

5. Beyond the money I save, buying a brand that comes with a free gift gives me a sense of joy.

6. Compared to most people, I am more likely to buy brands that come with free gifts.

SCALE NAME: Involvement (Product Class)

SCALE DESCRIPTION: The scale is composed of Likert-type statements measuring a person's interest in some specified category of products. The scale was apparently used twice by Beatty and Talpade (1994): once for the sample (teens) to evaluate relative contributions in a decision regarding a durable product for *teenager* use and another time related to a durable product for *family* use. A three-item version of the scale was used by Flynn, Goldsmith, and Eastman (1996). Another variation on the scale was used by Kopalle and Lehmann (2001).

SCALE ORIGIN: The four-item scale is original to Beatty and Talpade (1994) though three of the items were adapted from a scale reported by Mittal and Lee (1988, 1989) and another item was adapted from a scale by Bloch (1981). The three-item scale used by Flynn, Goldsmith, and Eastman (1996) was apparently based upon the version reported by Mittal and Lee (1989). The source of the version used by Kopalle and Lehmann (2001) was not stated but two of its items are similar enough to those in this scale that it was assumed here that they have a common origin.

RELIABILITY: Alphas of .74 and .80 were reported by Beatty and Talpade (1994) for the family and teenager applications of the scale, respectively. An alpha of .93 was estimated for the scale in Study 3 (fashion) by Flynn, Goldsmith, and Eastman (1996; Goldsmith 1997). Kopalle and Lehmann (2001) reported an alpha of .89 for their version of the scale.

VALIDITY: The validity of the scale was not directly assessed by Beatty and Talpade (1994) nor Flynn, Goldsmith, and Eastman (1996). However, since it was part of an effort in the latter study to examine the nomological validity of two other scales, some sense of its own nomological validity can be gained. For example, high positive correlations were found between involvement and opinion leadership, innovativeness, and product knowledge. No relationship was found between involvement and opinion seeking.

COMMENTS: See also Baumgartner and Steenkamp (2001).

REFERENCES:
Baumgartner, Hans and Jan-Benedict E.M. Steenkamp (2001), "Response Styles in Marketing Research: A Cross-National Investigation," *JMR*, 38 (May), 143–156.
Beatty, Sharon E. and Salil Talpade (1994), "Adolescent Influence in Family Decision Making: A Replication with Extension," *JCR*, 21 (September), 332–341.
Bloch, Peter E. (1981), "An Exploration into the Scaling of Consumers' Involvement with a Product Class," in *Advances in Consumer Research, V. 8*, Kent B. Monroe, ed. Ann Arbor, MI: Association for Consumer Research, 61–65.
Flynn, Leisa R., Ronald E. Goldsmith, and Jacqueline K. Eastman (1996), "Opinion Leaders and Opinion Seekers: Two New Measurement Scales," *JAMS*, 24 (Spring), 137–147.
Goldsmith, Ronald E. (1997), Personal Correspondence.
Kopalle, Praveen K. and Donald R. Lehmann (2001), "Strategic Management of Expectations: The Role of Disconfirmation Sensitivity and Perfectionism," *JMR*, 38 (August), 386–394.
Mittal, Banwari and Myung-Soo Lee (1988), "Separating Brand-Choice Involvement from Product Involvement via Consumer Involvement Profiles," in *Advances in Consumer Research, V. 15*, Michael J. Houston, ed. Provo, UT: Association for Consumer Research, 43–46.
Mittal, Banwari and Myung-Soo Lee (1989), "A Causal Model of Consumer Involvement," *Journal of Economic Psychology*, 10 (3), 363–389.

SCALE ITEMS: [1]

1. In general I have a strong interest in this product category.

2. This product category is very important to me.

3. This product category matters a lot to me.

4. I get bored when other people talk to me about this product category. (r)

5. The product category is very relevant to me.

---

[1] The version of the scale by Beatty and Talpade (1994) was composed of the first four items and used a five-point response format. Flynn, Goldsmith, and Eastman (1996) used items #1 to #3 with some slight differences in wording. In their Study 1, Kopalle and Lehmann (2001) used items similar to #2, #3, and #5 with a six-point response format. In their second study they used #2 and #5 with a seven-item scale.

SCALE NAME: Involvement (Product Class)

SCALE DESCRIPTION: Three Likert-type statements with a seven-point response format are used to assess a consumer's enduring interest in a related group of products.

SCALE ORIGIN: The source of the scale was not explicitly described by De Wulf, Odekerken-Schröder, and Iacobucci (2001) but it would appear to be original to their studies. The items seem to be among those that were developed using the back-translation method for versions in American English and Dutch and then pretested in the U.S., Netherlands, and Belgium (Flemish-speaking area).

RELIABILITY: Composite reliabilities were calculated for two types of stores for each of three countries (De Wulf, Odekerken-Schröder, and Iacobucci 2001). The reliabilities for food stores were .79, .91, and .86 for the U.S., Netherlands, and Belgium, respectively (Odekerken-Schröder 2004). For apparel stores, the reliabilities were .86, .91, and .86 for the U.S., Netherlands, and Belgium, respectively.

VALIDITY: Although De Wulf, Odekerken-Schröder, and Iacobucci (2001) provided a lot of information about most of the measures they used, evidence of this scale's validity was not specifically given.

REFERENCES:
De Wulf, Kristof, Gaby Odekerken-Schröder, and Dawn Iacobucci (2001), "Investments in Consumer Relationships: A Cross-Country and Cross-Industry Exploration," *JM*, 65 (October), 33–50.
Odekerken-Schröder, Gaby (2004), Personal Correspondence.

SCALE ITEMS: [1]

1. Generally, I am someone who finds it important what _____ he or she buys.

2. Generally, I am someone who is interested in the kind of _____ he or she buys.

3. Generally, I am someone for whom it means a lot what _____ he or she buys.

---

[1] An appropriate descriptor of the product category should be placed in the blanks.

SCALE NAME: Involvement (Product)

SCALE DESCRIPTION: The scale is composed of five, five-point Likert-type statements meant to assess a person's general involvement with a particular product category.

SCALE ORIGIN: Cho, Lee, and Tharp (2001) did not specify the source of the scale. Although it could be assumed that the scale as a whole is original to these authors, the key descriptors in each item have been routinely used in previous research, e.g., #226.

RELIABILITY: Although not explicitly stated in the article, the scale was used with respect to several product categories. The alphas for the scale ranged from .81 to .85 (Cho 2001).

VALIDITY: No examination of the scale's validity was reported by Cho, Lee, and Tharp (2001).

COMMENTS: The dimensionality of the scale is dubious because the last item is an indictor of purchase intention.

REFERENCES:
Cho, Chang-Hoan (2001), Personal Correspondence.
Cho, Chang-Hoan, Jung-Gyo Lee, and Marye Tharp (2001), "Different Forced-Exposure Levels to Banner Advertisements," *JAR*, 41 (July-August), 45–56.

SCALE ITEMS: [1]

1. I am interested in _____ in general.

2. _____ are important to me.

3. I get involved with what _____ I use.

4. _____ are relevant to my life.

5. I am going to purchase _____ in the next six months.

[1] Names of product categories are to be place in the blanks, e.g., computer products.

SCALE NAME: Involvement (Promotional Games)

SCALE DESCRIPTION: It is a six-item, seven-point Likert-type scale measuring a consumer's enjoyment of contests/sweepstakes and tendency to buy products associated with such games. This measures a general tendency rather than the likelihood that the behavior occurs for any particular product category. Lichtenstein, Netemeyer, and Burton (1995; Lichtenstein, Burton, and Netemeyer 1997) referred to the scale as *contest/sweepstakes proneness* and Burton et al. (1998) called it *contest proneness*.

SCALE ORIGIN: The scale is original to the studies by Lichtenstein, Netemeyer, and Burton (1995) though some of the items are similar to ones developed previously by the same authors for other measures (e.g., Lichtenstein, Netemeyer, and Burton 1990). In an effort to develop several deal proneness measures 91 items were generated and tested with 341 nonstudent adults. Using factor analysis and other tests, seven items were deleted leaving 84 to be used in the two studies reported in Lichtenstein, Netemeyer, and Burton (1995). Lichtenstein, Burton, and Netemeyer (1997) presented 49 of the items for the measurement of eight different deal proneness types.

RELIABILITY: Alphas of .90 and .91 were reported for the scale by Lichtenstein, Netemeyer, and Burton (1995) for Study 1 (Lichtenstein, Burton, and Netemeyer 1997) and 2, respectively. Burton et al. (1998) also reported an alpha of .91.

VALIDITY: Confirmatory factor analyses were used in both studies by Lichtenstein, Netemeyer, and Burton (1995; Lichtenstein, Burton, and Netemeyer 1997) and it was concluded that the scale was unidimensional and showed evidence of discriminant validity. No examination of the scale's validity was reported by Burton et al. (1998).

COMMENTS: Lichtenstein, Netemeyer, and Burton (1995) reported means on the scale of 12.94 and 10.73 for Study 1 and 2, respectively.

REFERENCES:

Burton, Scot, Donald R. Lichtenstein, Richard G. Netemeyer, and Judith A. Garretson (1998), "A Scale for Measuring Attitude Toward Private Label Products and an Examination of Its Psychological and Behavioral Correlates," *JAMS*, 26 (4), 293–306.

Lichtenstein, Donald R., Scot Burton, and Richard G. Netemeyer (1997), "An Examination of Deal Proneness Across Sales Promotion Types: A Consumer Segmentation Perspective," *JR*, 73 (2), 283–297.

Lichtenstein, Donald R., Richard G. Netemeyer, and Scot Burton (1990), "Distinguishing Coupon Proneness From Value Consciousness: An Acquisition-Transaction Utility Theory Perspective," *JM*, 54 (July), 54–67.

Lichtenstein, Donald R., Richard D. Netemeyer, and Scot Burton (1995), "Assessing the Domain Specificity of Deal Proneness: A Field Study," *JCR*, 22 (December), 314–326.

SCALE ITEMS:

1. I enjoy entering manufacturers' contests.

2. When I buy a brand that is connected to a contest or sweepstake, I feel that it is a good deal.

3. I have favorite brands, but if possible, I buy the brand that is connected with a contest or sweepstakes.

4. I feel compelled to respond to contest or sweepstakes offers.

5. Manufacturers' contests and sweepstakes are fun to enter, even if I know I'll never win.

6. If I am indifferent between two brands, I would purchase the one that has a contest or sweepstakes associated with it.

#235 *Involvement (Purchase of Bank Services)*

SCALE NAME: Involvement (Purchase of Bank Services)

SCALE DESCRIPTION: Six, five-point Likert-type statements are used to measure the time and effort expended by a consumer in selecting a bank in which to open an account.

SCALE ORIGIN: Ganesh, Arnold, and Reynolds (2000) cited several previous studies on which they drew in the development of their scale.

RELIABILITY: An alpha of .84 was reported for the scale (Ganesh, Arnold, and Reynolds 2000).

VALIDITY: No examination of the scale's validity was reported by Ganesh, Arnold, and Reynolds (2000). They did, however, factor analyze the items in this scale along with those of a related scale (#224). The items for this scale loaded highest on the same dimension with no substantial loadings on the other dimension.

REFERENCES:
Ganesh, Jaishanker, Mark J. Arnold, and Kristy E. Reynolds (2000), "Understanding the Customer Base of Service Providers: An Examination of the Differences Between Switchers and Stayers," *JM*, 64 (3), 65–87.

SCALE ITEMS:

1. I constantly compare the prices and rates offered by various banks in my area.

2. I visited multiple banks in the area before I opened an account with the current bank.

3. I compared the prices and rates of several banks in my area before I selected my current bank.

4. After deciding on my current bank, I have discussed my choice with family and friends.

5. After deciding on my current bank, I have compared my bank with other banks in the area.

6. After deciding on my current bank, I have weighed the pros and cons of my choice.

SCALE NAME: Involvement (Rebates)

SCALE DESCRIPTION: It is a six-item, seven-point Likert-type scale measuring a consumer's enjoyment of cash refund offers and tendency to buy products associated with such offers. This measures a general tendency rather than the likelihood that the behavior occurs for any particular product category. Lichtenstein, Netemeyer, and Burton (1995; Lichtenstein, Burton, and Netemeyer 1997) referred the scale as *rebate/refund proneness*. Burton et al. (1998) called it *rebate proneness*.

SCALE ORIGIN: The scale is original to the studies by Lichtenstein, Netemeyer, and Burton (1995) though some of the items are similar to ones developed previously by the same authors for other measures (e.g., Lichtenstein, Netemeyer, and Burton 1990). In an effort to develop several deal proneness measures 91 items were generated and tested with 341 nonstudent adults. Using factor analysis and other tests, seven items were deleted leaving 84 to be used in the two studies reported in Lichtenstein, Netemeyer, and Burton (1995). Lichtenstein, Burton, and Netemeyer (1997) presented 49 of the items for the measurement of eight different deal proneness types.

RELIABILITY: Alphas of .86 and .83 were reported for the scale by Lichtenstein, Netemeyer, and Burton (1995) for Study 1 (Lichtenstein, Burton, and Netemeyer 1997) and 2 respectively. Burton et al. (1998) reported an alpha of .83.

VALIDITY: Confirmatory factor analyses were used in both studies by Lichtenstein, Netemeyer, and Burton (1995; Lichtenstein, Burton, and Netemeyer 1997) and it was concluded that the scale was unidimensional and showed evidence of discriminant validity. No examination of the scale's validity was reported by Burton et al. (1998).

COMMENTS: Lichtenstein, Netemeyer, and Burton (1995) reported means on the scale of 16.15 and 16.10 for Study 1 and 2, respectively.

REFERENCES:

Burton, Scot, Donald R. Lichtenstein, Richard G. Netemeyer, and Judith A. Garretson (1998), "A Scale for Measuring Attitude Toward Private Label Products and an Examination of Its Psychological and Behavioral Correlates," *JAMS*, 26 (4), 293–306.

Lichtenstein, Donald R., Scot Burton, and Richard G. Netemeyer (1997), "An Examination of Deal Proneness Across Sales Promotion Types: A Consumer Segmentation Perspective," *JR*, 73 (2), 283–297.

Lichtenstein, Donald R., Richard G. Netemeyer, and Scot Burton (1990), "Distinguishing Coupon Proneness From Value Consciousness: An Acquisition-Transaction Utility Theory Perspective," *JM*, 54 (July), 54–67.

Lichtenstein, Donald R., Richard D. Netemeyer, and Scot Burton (1995), "Assessing the Domain Specificity of Deal Proneness: A Field Study," *JCR*, 22 (December), 314–326.

SCALE ITEMS:

1. Receiving cash rebates makes me feel good.

2. I enjoy buying brands that offer cash rebates, regardless of the amount of money I save by doing so.

3. By the time you pay postage, mail-in cash rebates are *not* worth the hassle. (r)

4. I have favorite brands, but if possible, I buy the brand that offers a cash rebate.

5. Beyond the money I save, buying products that offer a rebate gives me a sense of joy.

6. I'm usually *not* motivated to respond to rebate offers. (r)

SCALE NAME: Involvement (Sales Promotion Deals)

SCALE DESCRIPTION: It is a eight-item, seven-point Likert-type scale measuring a consumer's enjoyment of sales promotion deals and tendency to buy products associated with such offers. This measures a general tendency rather than the likelihood that the behavior occurs for any particular product category. Burton et al. (1998) and Lichtenstein, Netemeyer, and Burton (1995) referred the scale as *general deal proneness*.

SCALE ORIGIN: The scale is original to the studies by Lichtenstein, Netemeyer, and Burton (1995) though some of the items are similar to ones developed previously by the same authors for other measures (e.g., Lichtenstein, Netemeyer, and Burton 1990). In an effort to develop a deal proneness measure not specific to any particular type of deal 43 items were generated and purified to a final set of eight using a pretest sample.

RELIABILITY: An alpha of .90 was reported for the scale by Burton et al. (1998). Alphas of .90 and .91 were reported for the scale by Lichtenstein, Netemeyer, and Burton (1995) for a pretest and Study 2, respectively.

VALIDITY: Confirmatory factor analysis was used by Lichtenstein, Netemeyer, and Burton (1995) to conclude that the scale was unidimensional and showed evidence of discriminant validity. Some evidence of the scale's predictive validity was also indicated since the scale had significant positive associations with most of the marketplace behaviors examined in the study. No information relating to the scale's validity was reported by Burton et al. (1998).

COMMENTS: Lichtenstein, Netemeyer, and Burton (1995) reported means on the scale of 32.66 and 36.06 for the pretest and Study 2, respectively. See also Baumgartner and Steenkamp (2001).

REFERENCES:

Baumgartner, Hans and Jan-Benedict E.M. Steenkamp (2001), "Response Styles in Marketing Research: A Cross-National Investigation," *JMR*, 38 (May), 143–156.

Burton, Scot, Donald R. Lichtenstein, Richard G. Netemeyer, and Judith A. Garretson (1998), "A Scale for Measuring Attitude Toward Private Label Products and an Examination of Its Psychological and Behavioral Correlates," *JAMS*, 26 (4), 293–306.

Lichtenstein, Donald R., Richard D. Netemeyer, and Scot Burton (1990), "Distinguishing Coupon Proneness From Value Consciousness: An Acquisition-Transaction Utility Theory Perspective," *JM*, 54 (July), 54–67.

Lichtenstein, Donald R., Richard D. Netemeyer, and Scot Burton (1995), "Assessing the Domain Specificity of Deal Proneness: A Field Study," *JCR*, 22 (December), 314–326.

SCALE ITEMS:

1. I enjoy buying a brand that is "on deal."

2. Beyond the money I save, buying brands on deal makes me happy.

3. Compared to other people, I am very likely to purchase brands that come with promotional offers.

4. Receiving a promotional deal with a product purchase makes me feel like I am a good shopper.

5. I'm usually *not* motivated to respond to promotional deals on products. (r)

6. When I purchase a brand that is offering a special promotion, I feel that it is a good buy.

7. I feel like a successful shopper when I purchase products that offer special promotions.

8. I love special promotional offer for products.

SCALE NAME: Involvement (Sales)

SCALE DESCRIPTION: It is a six-item, seven-point Likert-type scale measuring a consumer's tendency to buy the brands that are on sale. This measures a general tendency rather than the likelihood that the behavior occurs for any particular product category. Given this, Lichtenstein and colleagues (1993, 1995, 1997; Burton et al. 1998, 1999) referred to the scale as *sale proneness*.

SCALE ORIGIN: The scale is original to Lichtenstein, Ridgway, and Netemeyer (1993). Eight items in Lichtenstein, Netemeyer, and Burton's (1990) coupon proneness scale were modified and more were generated specifically for this study. A total of 18 items were tested along with many others in a pretest. The sample was composed of 341 nonstudent adult consumers who had the grocery- shopping responsibility for their households. Factor analysis and coefficient alpha were used to eliminate weaker items. The sixteen items remaining for this scale were reported to have an alpha of .90. These items were used in the main study although the next round of analysis eliminated ten of them. Of the remaining six items in the final version of the scale, three were very similar to items used by Lichtenstein, Netemeyer, and Burton (1990).

RELIABILITY: The main study by Lichtenstein, Ridgway, and Netemeyer (1993; Lichtenstein, Burton, and Netemeyer 1997; and Study 1 by Lichtenstein, Netemeyer, and Burton 1995) showed an alpha for the scale of .88. An alpha of .86 was reported for the scale by Lichtenstein, Netemeyer, and Burton (1995) in their Study 2. Burton et al. (1998) also reported an alpha of .86 for the scale. In Study 1 by Burton, Lichtenstein, and Netemeyer (1999) an alpha of .88 was reported; in Study 2 it was merely reported to be greater than .85.

VALIDITY: Confirmatory factor analyses were used in the studies by Lichtenstein et al. (1993, 1995, 1997) and it was concluded that the scale was unidimensional and showed evidence of discriminant validity.

COMMENTS: Lichtenstein, Netemeyer, and Burton (1995) reported means on the scale of 23.56 and 24.54 for Study 1 and 2, respectively.

REFERENCES:

Burton, Scot, Donald R. Lichtenstein, and Richard G. Netemeyer (1999), "Exposure to Sales Flyers and Increased Purchases in Retail Supermarkets," *JAR*, 39 (September/October), 7–14.

Burton, Scot, Donald R. Lichtenstein, Richard G. Netemeyer, and Judith A. Garretson (1998), "A Scale for Measuring Attitude Toward Private Label Products and an Examination of Its Psychological and Behavioral Correlates," *JAMS*, 26 (4), 293–306.

Lichtenstein, Donald R., Scot Burton, and Richard G. Netemeyer (1997), "An Examination of Deal Proneness Across Sales Promotion Types: A Consumer Segmentation Perspective," *JR*, 73 (2), 283–297.

Lichtenstein, Donald R., Richard D. Netemeyer, and Scot Burton (1990), "Distinguishing Coupon Proneness From Value Consciousness: An Acquisition-Transaction Utility Theory Perspective," *JM*, 54 (July), 54–67.

Lichtenstein, Donald R., Richard D. Netemeyer, and Scot Burton (1995), "Assessing the Domain Specificity of Deal Proneness: A Field Study," *JCR*, 22 (December), 314–326.

Lichtenstein, Donald R., Nancy M. Ridgway, and Richard G. Netemeyer (1993), "Price Perceptions and Consumer Shopping Behavior: A Field Study," *JMR*, 30 (May), 234–245.

#238 *Involvement (Sales)*

SCALE ITEMS:

1. If a product is on sale, that can be a reason for me to buy it.

2. When I buy a brand that's on sale, I feel that I am getting a good deal.

3. I have favorite brands, but most of the time I buy the brand that's on sale.

4. One should try to buy the brand that's on sale.

5. I am more likely to buy brands that are on sale.

6. Compared to most people, I am more likely to buy brands that are on special.

SCALE NAME: Involvement (Situational)

SCALE DESCRIPTION: It is a multi-item, seven-point semantic differential scale measuring the temporary (rather than enduring and/or intrinsic) relevance of an object to a person. Whereas enduring involvement is ongoing and probably related to a product class, situational involvement is a passing motivation given that it is related to a certain product-related situation. The scale is easily customized to measure involvement with a product category, a particular brand, an ad for a particular brand, or a particular purchase decision.

SCALE ORIGIN: The items for the scale come from the Personal Involvement Inventory (PII) by Zaich-kowsky (1985). However, that scale was constructed to assess enduring involvement. In contrast, the studies listed here used a subset of the PII items and specifically modified instructions to measure a distinct though related construct: situational involvement.

RELIABILITY: An alpha of .99 was reported for the scale by Houston and Walker (1996). Lichtenstein, Nete-meyer, and Burton (1990) reported the reliability (LISREL estimate) of their version of the scale to be .96. Alphas of .89 and .93 were reported for the version of the scale used by Mantel and Kardes (1999) for low- and high-involvement manipulation checks, respectively.

VALIDITY: Houston and Walker (1996) examined the discriminant validity of the scale with the larger version of the scale (#226). They concluded that the two were related but distinct constructs. They also stated that the items composing the situational involvement scale loaded on a single factor in principle components analysis.

Although the scale may have been used to help validate another scale or two developed in the study, no explicit test of the situational involvement scale's validity was reported by Lichtenstein, Netemeyer, and Burton (1990).

Similarly, the validity of the scale was not specifically tested by Mantel and Kardes (1999) but, as a manipulation check, some sense of the scale's concurrent validity comes from confirmation that the manipulation of subjects occurred as expected.

REFERENCES:
Houston, Mark B. and Beth A. Walker (1996), "Self-Relevance and Purchase Goals: Mapping a Consumer Decision," *JAMS*, 24 (Summer), 232–245.

Lichtenstein, Donald R., Richard D. Netemeyer, and Scot Burton (1990), "Distinguishing Coupon Proneness From Value Consciousness: An Acquisition-Transaction Utility Theory Perspective," *JM*, 54 (July), 54–67.

Mantel, Susan Powell and Frank R. Kardes (1999), "The Role of Direction of Comparison, Attribute-Based Processing, and Attitude-Based Processing in Consumer Preference," *JCR*, 25 (March), 335–352.

Zaichkowsky, Judith L. (1985), "Measuring the Involvement Construct," *JCR*, 12 (December), 341–352.

SCALE ITEMS: [1]

1. unimportant / important

2. of no concern / of concern to me

3. irrelevant / relevant

 4. means nothing to me / means a lot to me

 5. worthless / valuable

 6. not beneficial / beneficial

 7. doesn't matter / matters to me

 8. boring / interesting

 9. unexciting / exciting

10. unappealing / appealing

11. nonessential / essential

12. insignificant / significant to me

13. undesirable / desirable

[1] Directions should be provided for respondents that focus attention on the object/action towards which situational involvement is being measured. Houston and Walker (1996) used items 1-4, 7, and 12 whereas by Lichtenstein, Netemeyer, and Burton (1990) used items 1-11. Items 1, 3, 4, 5, 7, and 13 were used by Mantel and Kardes (1999).

SCALE NAME: Involvement (Special Possession)

SCALE DESCRIPTION : The scale uses three, seven-point statements to measure the degree to which a person pays relatively more attention to a particular possession than to other possessions. The investment of time and thought in the object "layers' more meaning on it and makes it even more important to the owner. The scale was called *psychic energy* by Grayson and Shulman (2000).

SCALE ORIGIN: The scale appears to be original to Grayson and Shulman (2000). Their goal was to use the concept of semiotics to better understand how meanings become associated with special possessions.

RELIABILITY: An alpha of .62 was reported for the scale by Grayson and Shulman (2000).

VALIDITY: No examination of the scale's validity was reported by Grayson and Shulman (2000). They did, however, present the results of an exploratory factor analysis of the items in this scale and three others. The results showed that the items on this scale loaded highest on the same factor.

COMMENTS: The low alpha indicates that the scale is barely reliable. The scale should be used cautiously until its psychometric quality is improved.

REFERENCES:
Grayson, Kent (2002), Personal Correspondence.
Grayson, Kent and David Shulman (2000), "Indexicality and the Verification Function of Irreplaceable Possessions: A Semiotic Analysis," *JCR*, 27 (1), 17–30.

SCALE ITEMS: [1]

Directions: Please read the following statements about the possession you selected and mark how well each statement describes the possession.

1. I think about it a lot.

2. I have invested a lot of energy in it.

3. Over time, more and more meaning gets layered into it.

[1] The response scale was anchored by *does not describe this possession at all* and *describes this possession very well* (Grayson 2002).

SCALE NAME: Involvement (Study)

SCALE DESCRIPTION: The four-item scale measures a subject's interest in a study he/she has just participated in. In addition, one item taps into the subject's motivation to process information related to the focal stimulus of the study.

SCALE ORIGIN: The scale is apparently original to Li, Miniard, and Barone (2000). They wanted to manipulate knowledge but not motivation and this scale was used to determine the extent to which that might have inadvertently occurred. Thus, the scale was used as a sort of manipulation check although, in this case, they wanted to confirm that subjects' involvement did not vary significantly across experimental treatments.

RELIABILITY: An alpha of .86 was reported for the scale (Li, Miniard, and Barone 2000).

VALIDITY: No examination of the scale's validity was reported by Li, Miniard, and Barone (2000).

REFERENCES:
Li, Faun, Pual M. Miniard, and Michael J. Barone (2000), "The Facilitating Influence of Consumer Knowledge on the Effectiveness of Daily Value Reference Information," *JAMS*, 28 (3), 425–436.

SCALE ITEMS: [1]

1. To what extent is the study of concern to you?
   no concern / great concern to me

2. How important is the study to you?
   not important at all / very important

3. I was highly involved in this research project.

4. It was important to me to carefully evaluate the _____.

---

[1] The exact phrasing of items 1 and 2 was not provided in the article by Li, Miniard, and Barone (2000). They are reconstructed here based on the description provided. Items 3 and 4 used a Likert-type response scale format. The focal stimulus should be described in #4. In the study by Li, Miniard, and Barone (2000) the object was a nutritional label.

SCALE NAME: Involvement (Two-For-One Deals)

SCALE DESCRIPTION: It is a six-item, seven-point Likert-type scale measuring a consumer's inclination to buy brands that have "two-for-one" offers despite the amount of money being saved. This measures a general tendency rather than the likelihood that the behavior occurs for any particular product category. Lichtenstein, Netemeyer, and Burton (1995; Lichtenstein, Burton, and Netemeyer 1997) referred to the scale as *buy one - get one free proneness* while Burton et al. (1998) called theirs *one-free proneness*.

SCALE ORIGIN: The scale is original to the studies by Lichtenstein, Netemeyer, and Burton (1995) though some of the items are similar to ones developed previously by the same authors for other measures (e.g., Lichtenstein, Netemeyer, and Burton 1990). In an effort to develop several deal proneness measures 91 items were generated and tested with 341 nonstudent adults. Using factor analysis and other tests, seven items were deleted leaving 84 to be used in the two studies reported in Lichtenstein, Netemeyer, and Burton (1995). Lichtenstein, Burton, and Netemeyer (1997) presented 49 of the items for the measurement of eight different deal proneness types.

RELIABILITY: Alphas of .86 and .84 were reported for the scale by Lichtenstein, Netemeyer, and Burton (1995) for Study 1 (Lichtenstein, Burton, and Netemeyer 1997) and 2, respectively. Burton et al. (1998) also reported an alpha of .84.

VALIDITY: Confirmatory factor analyses were used in both studies by Lichtenstein, Netemeyer, and Burton (1995; Lichtenstein, Burton, and Netemeyer 1997). A variety of data were produced in support of the scale's unidimensionality and discriminant validity. No examination of the scale's validity was reported by Burton et al. (1998).

COMMENTS: Lichtenstein, Netemeyer, and Burton (1995) reported means on the scale of 28.96 and 30.05 for Study 1 and 2, respectively.

REFERENCES:

Burton, Scot, Donald R. Lichtenstein, Richard G. Netemeyer, and Judith A. Garretson (1998), "A Scale for Measuring Attitude Toward Private Label Products and an Examination of Its Psychological and Behavioral Correlates," *JAMS*, 26 (4), 293–306.

Lichtenstein, Donald R., Scot Burton, and Richard G. Netemeyer (1997), "An Examination of Deal Proneness Across Sales Promotion Types: A Consumer Segmentation Perspective," *JR*, 73 (2), 283–297.

Lichtenstein, Donald R., Richard D. Netemeyer, and Scot Burton (1990), "Distinguishing Coupon Proneness From Value Consciousness: An Acquisition-Transaction Utility Theory Perspective," *JM*, 54 (July), 54–67.

Lichtenstein, Donald R., Richard D. Netemeyer, and Scot Burton (1995), "Assessing the Domain Specificity of Deal Proneness: A Field Study," *JCR*, 22 (December), 314–326.

SCALE ITEMS:

1. I enjoy buying a brand that offers a "buy-one-get-one-free" deal.

2. When I buy a product on a "buy-one-get-one-free" offer, I feel that I am getting a good deal.

3. I enjoy buying a product that offers a "2 for 1" deal, regardless of the amount I save by doing so.

4. I have favorite brands, but if I see a "2 for 1" offer, I am more likely to buy that brand.

5. When I take advantage of a "buy-one-get-one-free" offer, I feel good.

6. I don't believe that "2 for 1" deals save you much money. (r)

SCALE NAME: Justice (Accessibility)

SCALE DESCRIPTION: The scale is composed of four, five-point Likert-type items. The items are intended to measure the degree to which a customer was able to easily lodge a complaint with the other party in a transaction. The context in which the respondents were given this scale was after being told to remember a recent service experience that led to their lodging a complaint.

SCALE ORIGIN: Although Tax, Brown, and Chandrashekaran (1998) may have drawn inspiration from previous measures, this scale appears to be original to their study.

RELIABILITY: An alpha of .86 (n = 257) was reported for the scale by Tax, Brown, and Chandrashekaran (1998).

VALIDITY: Although specific details of the validation were not presented by Tax, Brown, and Chandrashekaran (1998), they did state that evidence was found "for discriminant validity among all the variables in the study" (p. 67). Likewise, all of the subdimensions such as this one were described as being unidimensional.

COMMENTS: In the study by Tax, Brown, and Chandrashekaran (1998) this scale was used to measure one subdimension of *procedural justice*. That overall scale was composed of five subscales and was reported to have an alpha of .86.

REFERENCES:
Tax, Stephen S., Stephen W. Brown, and Murali Chandrashekaran (1998), "Customer Evaluations of Service Complaint Experiences: Implications for Relationship Marketing," *JM*, 62 (April), 60–76.

SCALE ITEMS:

1. It was hard to figure who to complain to in this organization. (r)

2. The complaint process was easy to access.

3. It was difficult to determine where to lodge my complaint. (r)

4. They made it easy for me to voice my complaint.

SCALE NAME: Justice (Decision Control)

SCALE DESCRIPTION: The four, five-point Likert-type items measure the degree that a person indicates having influence over the outcome of a complaint compared to the other party in a transaction. The context in which the respondents were given this scale was after being told to remember a recent service experience that led to their lodging a complaint.

SCALE ORIGIN: Although Tax, Brown, and Chandrashekaran (1998) may have drawn inspiration from previous measures, this scale appears to be original to their study.

RELIABILITY: An alpha of .83 (n = 257) was reported for the scale by Tax, Brown, and Chandrashekaran (1998).

VALIDITY: Although specific details of the validation were not presented by Tax, Brown, and Chandrashekaran (1998), they did state that evidence was found "for discriminant validity among all the variables in the study" (p. 67). Likewise, all of the subdimensions such as this one were described as being unidimensional.

COMMENTS: In the study by Tax, Brown, and Chandrashekaran (1998) this scale was used to measure one subdimension of *procedural justice*. That overall scale was composed of five subscales and was reported to have an alpha of .86.

REFERENCES:
Tax, Stephen S., Stephen W. Brown, and Murali Chandrashekaran (1998), "Customer Evaluations of Service Complaint Experiences: Implications for Relationship Marketing," *JM*, 62 (April), 60–76.

SCALE ITEMS:

1. I had some control over the result I received from the complaint.

2. The organization solely determined the outcome I received. (r)

3. The final decision was jointly shared by me and the firm.

4. I had no say in the outcome of the complaint. (r)

SCALE NAME: Justice (Distributive)

SCALE DESCRIPTION: The scale is used to measure the degree to which a customer who lodged a complaint thinks that the resolution of the problem was appropriate. In the study by Tax, Brown, and Chandrashekaran (1998) the respondents were given this scale after being told to remember a recent service experience that led to their lodging a complaint. Similarly, in Smith, Bolton, and Wagner (1999) subjects were asked to imagine a visit to a service provider they had been to before and what they would do if a service failure occurred.

SCALE ORIGIN: Tax, Brown, and Chandrashekaran (1998) as well as Smith, Bolton, and Wagner (1999) appear to have drawn upon dissertation work by Tax (1993).

RELIABILITY: An alpha of .97 was reported for the scale by Tax, Brown, and Chandrashekaran (1998). The version of the scale used by Smith, Bolton, and Wagner (1999; Smith 2002) had alphas of .88 and .91 as used with restaurants and hotels, respectively.

VALIDITY: Although specific details of the validation were not presented by Tax, Brown, and Chandrashekaran (1998), they did state that evidence was found "for discriminant validity among all the variables in the study" (p. 67). Smith, Bolton, and Wagner (1999) indicated that there was evidence of their scale's convergent and discriminant validity but it appears to be based upon the pattern of loadings in an exploratory factor analysis.

REFERENCES:

Smith, Amy K. (2002), Personal Correspondence.

Smith, Amy K., Ruth N. Bolton, and Janet Wagner (1999), "A Model of Customer Satisfaction with Service Encounters Involving Failure and Recovery," *JMR*, 36 (August), 356–372.

Tax, Stephen S. (1993), "The Role of Perceived Justice in Complaint Resolutions: Implications for Services and Relationship Marketing," doctoral dissertation, Arizona State University.

Tax, Stephen S., Stephen W. Brown, and Murali Chandrashekaran (1998), "Customer Evaluations of Service Complaint Experiences: Implications for Relationship Marketing," *JM*, 62 (April), 60–76.

SCALE ITEMS: [1]

1. The result of the complaint was not right. (r)

2. In resolving the complaint the firm gave me what I needed.

3. I did not receive what I required. (r)

4. I got what I deserved.

5. My outcome was probably not as good as others who have complained to this firm. (r)

6. The result I received from the complaint was fair.

[1] Tax, Brown, and Chandrashekaran (1998) used a five-point response scale with their items whereas Smith, Bolton, and Wagner (1999) used a seven-point format. Also, the items used by the latter were similar to #1, #2, #4, and #6 and were phrased with respect to a restaurant (Study 1) and a hotel (Study 2).

#246 *Justice (Effort)*

SCALE NAME: Justice (Effort)

SCALE DESCRIPTION: The four, five-point Likert-type items measure the degree that a person reports that the other party in a transaction put a lot of effort into solving a problem. The context in which the respondents were given this scale was after being told to remember a recent service experience that led to their lodging a complaint.

SCALE ORIGIN: Although Tax, Brown, and Chandrashekaran (1998) may have drawn inspiration from previous measures, this scale appears to be original to their study.

RELIABILITY: An alpha of .93 (n = 257) was reported for the scale by Tax, Brown, and Chandrashekaran (1998).

VALIDITY: Although specific details of the validation were not presented by Tax, Brown, and Chandrashekaran (1998), they did state that evidence was found "for discriminant validity among all the variables in the study" (p. 67). Likewise, all of the subdimensions such as this one were described as being unidimensional.

COMMENTS: In the study by Tax, Brown, and Chandrashekaran (1998) this scale was used to measure one subdimension of *interactional justice*. That overall scale was composed of five subscales and was reported to have an alpha of .91.

REFERENCES:
Tax, Stephen S., Stephen W. Brown, and Murali Chandrashekaran (1998), "Customer Evaluations of Service Complaint Experiences: Implications for Relationship Marketing," *JM*, 62 (April), 60–76.

SCALE ITEMS:

1. They tried hard to resolve the problem.

2. They put little effort into resolving the complaint. (r)

3. They put a lot of positive energy into handling my problem.

4. They were not very persistent in trying to solve my problem. (r)

SCALE NAME: Justice (Empathy)

SCALE DESCRIPTION: The scale is composed of four, five-point Likert-type items. The measure is intended to capture the extent to which a person reports that the other party in a transaction seemed concerned about a problem that occurred with a service that was provided. The context in which the respondents were given this scale was after being told to remember a recent service experience that led to their lodging a complaint.

SCALE ORIGIN: Although Tax, Brown, and Chandrashekaran (1998) may have drawn inspiration from previous measures, this scale appears to be original to their study.

RELIABILITY: An alpha of .94 (n = 257) was reported for the scale by Tax, Brown, and Chandrashekaran (1998).

VALIDITY: Although specific details of the validation were not presented by Tax, Brown, and Chandrashekaran (1998), they did state that evidence was found "for discriminant validity among all the variables in the study" (p. 67). Likewise, all of the subdimensions such as this one were described as being unidimensional.

COMMENTS: In the study by Tax, Brown, and Chandrashekaran (1998) this scale was used to measure one subdimension of *interactional justice*. That overall scale was composed of five subscales and was reported to have an alpha of .91.

REFERENCES:
Tax, Stephen S., Stephen W. Brown, and Murali Chandrashekaran (1998), "Customer Evaluations of Service Complaint Experiences: Implications for Relationship Marketing," *JM*, 62 (April), 60–76.

SCALE ITEMS:

1. They seemed very concerned about my problem.

2. They were not very empathetic. (r)

3. The people were sympathetic and caring.

4. They did not seem very understanding about the problems I had experienced. (r)

SCALE NAME: Justice (Explanation)

SCALE DESCRIPTION: Four, five-point Likert-type items compose the scale. The measure is intended to capture the degree to which a person reports that the other party in a transaction gave an explanation for a problem that occurred with a service that was provided. The context in which the respondents were given this scale was after being told to remember a recent service experience that led to their lodging a complaint.

SCALE ORIGIN: Although Tax, Brown, and Chandrashekaran (1998) may have drawn inspiration from previous measures, this scale appears to be original to their study.

RELIABILITY: An alpha of .84 (n = 257) was reported for the scale by Tax, Brown, and Chandrashekaran (1998).

VALIDITY: Although specific details of the validation were not presented by Tax, Brown, and Chandrashekaran (1998), they did state that evidence was found "for discriminant validity among all the variables in the study" (p. 67). Likewise, all of the subdimensions such as this one were described as being unidimensional.

COMMENTS: In the study by Tax, Brown, and Chandrashekaran (1998) this scale was used to measure one subdimension of *interactional justice*. That overall scale was composed of five subscales and was reported to have an alpha of .91.

REFERENCES:
Tax, Stephen S., Stephen W. Brown, and Murali Chandrashekaran (1998), "Customer Evaluations of Service Complaint Experiences: Implications for Relationship Marketing," *JA*, 62 (April), 60–76.

SCALE ITEMS:

1. They did not tell me the cause of the service failure. (r)

2. I was given a reasonable explanation as to why the original problem occurred.

3. No reason was given for the poor service I received. (r)

4. They told me why the service had failed in the first place.

SCALE NAME: Justice (Flexibility)

SCALE DESCRIPTION: Four, five-point Likert-type items compose the scale. The items are intended to measure the degree that a customer who lodged a complaint thinks that the other party in the transaction adjusted procedures in order to resolve the problem. The context in which the respondents were given this scale was after being told to remember a recent service experience that led to their lodging a complaint.

SCALE ORIGIN: Although Tax, Brown, and Chandrashekaran (1998) may have drawn inspiration from previous measures, this scale appears to be original to their study.

RELIABILITY: An alpha of .89 (n = 257) was reported for the scale by Tax, Brown, and Chandrashekaran (1998).

VALIDITY: Although specific details of the validation were not presented by Tax, Brown, and Chandrashekaran (1998), they did state that evidence was found "for discriminant validity among all the variables in the study" (p. 67). Likewise, all of the subdimensions such as this one were described as being unidimensional.

COMMENTS: In the study by Tax, Brown, and Chandrashekaran (1998) this scale was used to measure one subdimension of *procedural justice*. That overall scale was composed of five subscales and was reported to have an alpha of .86.

REFERENCES:
Tax, Stephen S., Stephen W. Brown, and Murali Chandrashekaran (1998), "Customer Evaluations of Service Complaint Experiences: Implications for Relationship Marketing," *JM*, 62 (April), 60–76.

SCALE ITEMS:

1. They adapted their complaint handling procedures to satisfy my needs.

2. They would not adapt their complaint handling procedures to deal with my situation. (r)

3. The people showed flexibility in responding to my complaint.

4. Their complaint process was too rigid. (r)

SCALE NAME: Justice (Honesty)

SCALE DESCRIPTION: Four, five-point Likert-type items compose the scale. The measure is intended to capture the degree to which a person thinks that the other party in a transaction was telling the truth. The context in which the respondents were given this scale was after being told to remember a recent service experience that led to their lodging a complaint.

SCALE ORIGIN: Although Tax, Brown, and Chandrashekaran (1998) may have drawn inspiration from previous measures, this scale appears to be original to their study.

RELIABILITY: An alpha of .91 (n = 257) was reported for the scale by Tax, Brown, and Chandrashekaran (1998).

VALIDITY: Although specific details of the validation were not presented by Tax, Brown, and Chandrashekaran (1998), they did state that evidence was found "for discriminant validity among all the variables in the study" (p. 67). Likewise, all of the subdimensions such as this one were described as being unidimensional.

COMMENTS: In the study by Tax, Brown, and Chandrashekaran (1998) this scale was used to measure one subdimension of *interactional justice*. That overall scale was composed of five subscales and was reported to have an alpha of .91.

REFERENCES:

Tax, Stephen S., Stephen W. Brown, and Murali Chandrashekaran (1998), "Customer Evaluations of Service Complaint Experiences: Implications for Relationship Marketing," *JM*, 62 (April), 60–76.

SCALE ITEMS:

1. They communicated honestly with me.

2. They told me something that was a lie. (r)

3. I believe what they told me.

4. They did not appear to be telling the truth. (r)

SCALE NAME: Justice (Interactional)

SCALE DESCRIPTION: The four-item, seven-point Likert-type scale is intended to measure the degree to which a customer who lodged a complaint with a service provider thinks that the concern and effort put forth by employees to solve the problem was appropriate. In Smith, Bolton, and Wagner (1999) subjects were asked to imagine a visit to a service provider they had been to before and what they would do if a service failure occurred.

SCALE ORIGIN: Smith, Bolton, and Wagner (1999) drew upon dissertation work by Tax (1993).

RELIABILITY: The scale had alphas of .88 and .91 as used with restaurants and hotels, respectively (Smith, Bolton, and Wagner 1999; Smith 2002).

VALIDITY: Smith, Bolton, and Wagner (1999) indicated that there was evidence of their scale's convergent and discriminant validity but it appears to be based upon the pattern of loadings in an exploratory factor analysis.

REFERENCES:

Smith, Amy K. (2002), Personal Correspondence.

Smith, Amy K., Ruth N. Bolton, and Janet Wagner (1999), "A Model of Customer Satisfaction with Service Encounters Involving Failure and Recovery," *JMR*, 36 (August), 356–372.

Tax, Stephen S. (1993), "The Role of Perceived Justice in Complaint Resolutions: Implications for Services and Relationship Marketing," doctoral dissertation, Arizona State University.

SCALE ITEMS:

1. The employees were appropriately concerned about my problem.

2. The employees did not put the proper effort into resolving my problem. (r)

3. The employees' communications with me were appropriate.

4. The employees did not give me the courtesy I was due. (r)

SCALE NAME: Justice (Politeness)

SCALE DESCRIPTION: The scale is composed of four, five-point Likert-type items. The items measure the degree that a person reports that the other party in a transaction was pleasant and acted courteously. The context in which the respondents were given this scale was after being told to remember a recent service experience that led to their lodging a complaint.

SCALE ORIGIN: Although Tax, Brown, and Chandrashekaran (1998) may have drawn inspiration from previous measures, this scale appears to be original to their study.

RELIABILITY: An alpha of .94 (n = 257) was reported for the scale by Tax, Brown, and Chandrashekaran (1998).

VALIDITY: Although specific details of the validation were not presented by Tax, Brown, and Chandrashekaran (1998), they did state that evidence was found "for discriminant validity among all the variables in the study" (p. 67). Likewise, all of the subdimensions such as this one were described as being unidimensional.

COMMENTS: In the study by Tax, Brown, and Chandrashekaran (1998) this scale was used to measure one subdimension of *interactional justice*. That overall scale was composed of five subscales and was reported to have an alpha of .91.

REFERENCES:
Tax, Stephen S., Stephen W. Brown, and Murali Chandrashekaran (1998), "Customer Evaluations of Service Complaint Experiences: Implications for Relationship Marketing," *JM*, 62 (April), 60–76.

SCALE ITEMS:

1. I felt I was treated rudely. (r)

2. The people were courteous to me.

3. The people were not polite to me. (r)

4. They were quite pleasant to deal with.

SCALE NAME: Justice (Process Control)

SCALE DESCRIPTION: Four, five-point Likert-type items compose the scale. The items are used to measure the extent to which a customer who lodged a complaint thinks that he/she was allowed the opportunity to fully describe the problem to the other party in the transaction. The context in which the respondents were given this scale was after being told to remember a recent service experience that led to their lodging a complaint.

SCALE ORIGIN: Although Tax, Brown, and Chandrashekaran (1998) may have drawn inspiration from previous measures, this scale appears to be original to their study.

RELIABILITY: An alpha of .89 (n = 257) was reported for the scale by Tax, Brown, and Chandrashekaran (1998).

VALIDITY: Although specific details of the validation were not presented by Tax, Brown, and Chandrashekaran (1998), they did state that evidence was found "for discriminant validity among all the variables in the study" (p. 67). Likewise, all of the subdimensions such as this one were described as being unidimensional.

COMMENTS: In the study by Tax, Brown, and Chandrashekaran (1998) this scale was used to measure one subdimension of *procedural justice*. That overall scale was composed of five subscales and was reported to have an alpha .86.

REFERENCES:
Tax, Stephen S., Stephen W. Brown, and Murali Chandrashekaran (1998), "Customer Evaluations of Service Complaint Experiences: Implications for Relationship Marketing," *JM*, 62 (April), 60–76.

SCALE ITEMS:

1. They did not let me explain the events which led to my complaint. (r)

2. I got a chance to tell them the details of my problem.

3. I was not given an opportunity to tell my side of the story. (r)

4. They listened to my entire complaint.

SCALE NAME: Justice (Speed)

SCALE DESCRIPTION: Four, five-point Likert-type items compose the scale. The scale is intended to measure the degree to which a customer who has lodged a complaint thinks that it has been dealt with quickly. The context in which the respondents were given this scale was after being told to remember a recent service experience that led to their lodging a complaint.

SCALE ORIGIN: Although Tax, Brown, and Chandrashekaran (1998) may have drawn inspiration from previous measures, this scale appears to be original to their study.

RELIABILITY: An alpha of .91 (n = 257) was reported for the scale by Tax, Brown, and Chandrashekaran (1998).

VALIDITY: Although specific details of the validation were not presented by Tax, Brown, and Chandrashekaran (1998), they did state that evidence was found "for discriminant validity among all the variables in the study" (p. 67). Likewise, all of the subdimensions such as this one were described as being unidimensional.

COMMENTS: In the study by Tax, Brown, and Chandrashekaran (1998) this scale was used to measure one subdimension of *procedural justice*. That overall scale was composed of five subscales and was reported to have an alpha of .86.

REFERENCES:
Tax, Stephen S., Stephen W. Brown, and Murali Chandrashekaran (1998), "Customer Evaluations of Service Complaint Experiences: Implications for Relationship Marketing," *JM*, 62 (April), 60–76.

SCALE ITEMS:

1. They responded quickly to my complaint.

2. The time taken to resolve the problem was longer than necessary, under the circumstances. (r)

3. I was pleased with the length of time it took for them to resolve my complaint.

4. They were very slow in responding to the problem. (r)

SCALE NAME: Knowledge (Cars)

SCALE DESCRIPTION: The seven-point scale is a measure of the relative knowledge a person reports having about cars and their operation compared to the "average" buyer. Srinivasan and Ratchford (1991) and Sambandam and Lord (1995) used a Likert version of the scale whereas Bottomley, Doyle, and Green (2000) used a semantic differential variation.

SCALE ORIGIN: Although not expressly stated in the article, the scale appears to be have been first used in published research by Srinivasan and Ratchford (1991) which was based upon the dissertation of Srinivasan (1987). Some initial assessment of scale reliability and face validity was made in pre-test stage of the study.

Bottomley, Doyle, and Green (2000) did not indicate the source of their scale. It would appear to be a modification of the previous scales given its similarity to them.

RELIABILITY: The short, semantic differential version of the scale by Bottomley, Doyle, and Green (2000) was reported to have an alpha of .89. An alpha of .87 was reported for the scale by Srinivasan and Ratchford (1991). Sambandam and Lord (1995) found their version of the scale to have a construct reliability of .93.

VALIDITY: No discussion of this scale's validity was provided in any of the studies.

REFERENCES:

Bottomley, Paul A., John R. Doyle, and Rodney H. Green (2000), "Testing the Reliability of Elicitation Methods: Direct Rating Versus Point Allocation," *JMR*, 37 (4), 508–513.

Sambandam, Rajan Kenneth R. Lord (1995), "Switching Behavior in Automobile Markets: A Consideration-Sets Model," *JAMS*, 23 (Winter), 57–65.

Srinivasan, Narasimhan (1987), "A Causal Model of External Search For Information For Durables: A Particular Investigation in the Case of New Automobiles," doctoral dissertation, State University of New York at Buffalo.

Srinivasan, Narasimhan and Brian T. Ratchford (1991), "An Empirical Test of a External Search for Automobiles," *JCR*, 18 (September), 233–242.

SCALE ITEMS: [1]

Directions: There are no right or wrong answers to the following statements and a large number of people agree and disagree. Kindly indicate your personal opinion by circling any one number for each statement.

1. Compared to the average person, I know a lot about cars.

2. I like to work on cars myself.

3. I don't understand a lot of my car's workings. **(r)**

4. I know how an internal combustion engine works.

5. My friends consider me an expert on cars.

6. Please rate your knowledge of cars compared to the average buyer by circling one number:
   One of the least knowledgeable / One of the most knowledgeable

7. Please circle one of the numbers below to describe <u>your</u> familiarity with cars:
   Not at all familiar / Extremely familiar

---

[1] Sambandam and Lord (1995) used all of the items except 7. Bottomley, Doyle, and Green (2000) used semantic differential versions of items 5-7: *a novice/an expert, much less knowledgeable / much more knowledgeable,* and *much less familiar / much more familiar.*

SCALE NAME: Knowledge (Cars)

SCALE DESCRIPTION: Ten, seven-point statements are used to assess a consumer's knowledge about and familiarity with automobiles, at least in terms of the information needed to make a purchase decision. The scale was called *product experience* by Mason et al. (2001).

SCALE ORIGIN: Mason et al. (2001) cited Brucks (1985) as well as Park and Lessig (1981) as sources of the original items which were adapted for use in this scale.

RELIABILITY: Mason et al. (2001) reported an alpha of .87 for the scale.

VALIDITY: The analysis conducted by Mason et al. (2001) seems to have provided some information regarding the scale's validity, however, those details were not provided in the article.

COMMENTS: Although some of the statements refer to students, the phrases appear to be easily adaptable for other reference groups to make the scale more widely applicable. See a variation on this scale applied to car tires by Kopalle and Lehmann (2001) and called *expertise*.

REFERENCES:
Brucks, Merrie (1985), "The Effects of Product Class Knowledge on Information Search Behavior," *JCR*, 12 (1), 1–16.
Kopalle, Praveen K. and Donald R. Lehmann (2001), "Strategic Management of Expectations: The Role of Disconfirmation Sensitivity and Perfectionism," *JMR*, 38 (August), 386–394.
Mason, Kevin, Thomas Jensen, Scot Burton, and Dave Roach (2001), "The Accuracy of Brand and Attribute Judgments: The Role of Information Relevancy, Product Experience, and Attribute-Relationship Schemata," *JAMS*, 29 (3), 307–317.
Park, Whan C. and V. Parker Lessig (1981), "Familiarity and Its Impact on Consumer Decision Biases and Heuristics," *JCR*, 8 (2), 223–230.

SCALE ITEMS: [1]

1. Please rate your knowledge of automobiles.

2. Relative to people you know, how would you rate your knowledge of automobiles?

3. Relative to a professional race car driver, how would you rate your knowledge about automobiles?

4. Based on your current knowledge about automobiles, how comfortable would you be in making an automobile purchase today?

5. How much information about automobiles have you been exposed to during your lifetime?

6. Compared to other students, how much time do you spend reading automobile-related magazines?

7. How familiar are you with the features available on new automobiles?

8. Compared to other students, how much time do you spend in an automobile per week?

9. Compared to other students, how many automobiles have you purchased in your life?

10. Compared to other students, how many times have you been the primary decision maker in the purchasing of an automobile?

---

[1] The response scale anchors used for the following items by Mason et al. (2001) were: *very unknowledgeable / very knowledgeable* (#1 - #3), *very uncomfortable / very comfortable* (#4), *very little / very much* (#5, #6, #8), *very unfamiliar / very familiar* (#7), *very few / very many* (#9, #10).

SCALE NAME: Knowledge (Marketplace)

SCALE DESCRIPTION: The scale is composed of three, seven-point Likert-type statements that measure the extent to which a person indicates that he/she is an informed consumer.

SCALE ORIGIN: Mangleburg and Bristol (1998) stated that they developed this scale for use in their study.

RELIABILITY: A composite reliability of .65 was reported for the scale by Mangleburg and Bristol (1998).

VALIDITY: Although confirmatory factor analysis was conducted by Mangleburg and Bristol (1998), the exact details bearing on the validity of this scale were not reported.

COMMENTS: The reliability of the scale is low and caution is urged in the scale's use until its psychometric quality can be substantially improved.

REFERENCES:
Mangleburg, Tamara F. and Terry Bristol (1998), "Socialization and Adolescents' Skepticism Toward Advertising," *JA*, 27 (3), 11–21.

SCALE ITEMS:

1. I am a knowledgeable consumer.

2. I know a lot about different types of stores.

3. I am usually well-informed about what is a reasonable price to pay for something.

SCALE NAME: Knowledge (Product Classes)

SCALE DESCRIPTION: The scale attempts to measure a consumer's opinion of the knowledge he/she has across five representative product categories compared to "the average person."

SCALE ORIGIN: The scale was developed by Bearden, Hardesty, and Rose (2001) based upon inspiration drawn from a scale by Park, Mothersbaugh, and Feick (1994). See V. III, #223.

RELIABILITY: An alpha of .66 was reported for the scale (Bearden, Hardesty, and Rose 2001).

VALIDITY: No examination of the scale's validity was reported by Bearden, Hardesty, and Rose (2001).

COMMENTS: The internal consistency of the scale is lower than desired probably because the construct itself (subjective knowledge) varies from category to category rather than being similar in degree.

REFERENCES:
Bearden, William O., David M. Hardesty, and Randall L. Rose (2001), "Consumer Self Confidence: Refinements in Conceptualization and Measurement," *JCR*, 28 (June), 121–134.

SCALE ITEMS: [1]

Directions: Please rate your knowledge of the following products as compared to the average person:

1. CD players

2. Lawn care products

3. Long distance telephone services

4. Cold remedies

5. Televisions

[1] The scale anchors were *one of the least knowledgeable* (1) to *one of the most knowledgeable* (7).

SCALE NAME: Knowledge (Product Classes)

SCALE DESCRIPTION: The scale is composed of three, seven-point items measuring the degree to which a consumer considers him/herself to be knowledgeable and experienced compared to others as it regards various types of products on the market.

SCALE ORIGIN: Mukherjee and Hoyer (2001) did not specify the source of the scale but it would appear to be original to their work.

RELIABILITY: The scale had an alpha above .80 for four product categories and was .81 pooled across those categories (Mukherjee 2003).

VALIDITY: No examination of the scale's validity was reported by Mukherjee and Hoyer (2001).

COMMENTS: The scale appears to be amenable for use with either one product category or several. If the scale is used with just one product category it seems to measure a person's knowledge of the different subtypes within that category, their features, and possibly the brands and models themselves. In contrast, if the score is summated across several product categories then it appears a broader type of knowledge is being assessed. However, since a person's knowledge can vary greatly from category to category, the unidimensionality of such a scale would be in doubt and brings into question just what it is the scale is measuring.

REFERENCES:
Mukherjee, Ashesh (2003), Personal Correspondence.
Mukherjee, Ashesh and Wayne D. Hoyer (2001), "The Effect of Novel Attributes on Product Evaluation," *JCR*, 28 (December), 462–472.

SCALE ITEMS: [1]

1. Compared to others you know, how knowledgeable are you about the features of different types of _____ in the market?
   not at all knowledgeable / very knowledgeable

2. In general, how knowledgeable are you about different types of _____ in the market?
   not at all knowledgeable / very knowledgeable

3. Compared to your friends, how much experience do you have with different types of _____?
   very little experience / a lot of experience

[1] The product class of interest should be placed in the blank of each question. As used by Mukherjee (2003; and Hoyer 2001), these items were used with four product classes: cameras, washing machines, computers, and refrigerators.

SCALE NAME: Knowledge (Product)

SCALE DESCRIPTION: The scale is composed of five, seven-point items measuring a person's familiarity and experience with a good or service. As used by Roehm and Sternthal (2001), the scale measured knowledge with a particular brand, however, the items seem to be amenable for use with a product class as well.

SCALE ORIGIN: Although the items are similar to some that have been used to measure this construct or a similar one in the past, this particular set of items appears to be original to Roehm and Sternthal (2001).

RELIABILITY: An alpha of .89 was reported for the scale (Roehm and Sternthal 2001).

VALIDITY: No examination of the scale's validity was reported by Roehm and Sternthal (2001). However, they did state that the items were unidimensional per factor analysis.

REFERENCES:
Roehm, Michelle L. (2003), Personal Correspondence.
Roehm, Michelle L. and Brian Sternthal (2001), "The Moderating Effect of Knowledge and Resources on the Persuasive Impact of Analogies," *JCR*, 28 (September), 257–272.

SCALE ITEMS: [1]

1. How often do you use _____?
   Never / Constantly

2. How familiar do you consider yourself with _____?
   Unfamiliar / Very familiar

3. How much of a _____ expert would you call yourself?
   Not at all expert / Extremely expert

4. How well-acquainted with _____ are you?
   Not at all acquainted / Very well acquainted

5. How regularly do you use _____?
   Not very regularly / Very regularly

---

[1] The phrasing of the questions and the response format was provided by Roehm (2003). The name of the product should be placed in the blanks.

SCALE NAME: Language Proficiency

SCALE DESCRIPTION: The five-point, twelve-item scale is meant to assess how well a person can use a certain language in various situations.

SCALE ORIGIN: The scale used by Luna and Peracchio (2001) was developed by them using a mixture of items taken from the work of Clark (1981), Liu, Bates, and Li (1992), MacIntyre, Noels, and Clément (1997).

RELIABILITY: An alpha of .94 was reported by Luna and Peracchio (2001) for the scale as used with regard to both English and Spanish.

VALIDITY: Although Luna and Peracchio (2001) did not report examining the validity of the scale, some sense of its predictive validity comes from the fact that subjects, all bilingual, were significantly more proficient (according to the scale) in their first (dominant) language than in their second language.

REFERENCES:

Clark, John (1981), "Language," in *College Students' Knowledge and Beliefs, A Survey of Global Understanding: The Final Report of the Global Understanding Project*, Thomas Barrows, ed. New Rochelle, NY: Change Magazine Press.

Liu, Hua, Elizabeth Bates, and Ping Li (1992), "Sentence Interpretation in English-Chinese Bilinguals," *Applied Psycholinguistics*, 13 (December), 451–484.

Luna, David (2003), Personal Correspondence.

Luna, David and Laura A. Peracchio (2001), "Moderators of Language Effects in Advertising to Bilinguals: A Psycholinguistic Approach," *JCR*, 28 (September), 284–295.

MacIntyre, Peter D., Kimberly A. Noels, and Richard Clément (1997), "Biases in Self-Ratings of Second Language Proficiency: The Role of Language Anxiety," *Language Learning*, 47 (June), 265–287.

SCALE ITEMS: [1]

How proficient are you currently in each of your languages regarding the following areas?

	Comprehension	Writing	Reading
Spanish	1 2 3 4 5	1 2 3 4 5	1 2 3 4 5
English	1 2 3 4 5	1 2 3 4 5	1 2 3 4 5

#261 *Language Proficiency*

How well do you think you can do these things in English and Spanish?

	English	Spanish
Understand cooking directions, such as those in a recipe.	1 2 3 4 5	1 2 3 4 5
Understand newspaper headlines.	1 2 3 4 5	1 2 3 4 5
Read personal letters or notes written to you.	1 2 3 4 5	1 2 3 4 5
Read popular novels without using a dictionary.	1 2 3 4 5	1 2 3 4 5
Make out a shopping list.	1 2 3 4 5	1 2 3 4 5
Fill out a job application form requiring information about your interests and qualifications.	1 2 3 4 5	1 2 3 4 5
Write a letter to a friend.	1 2 3 4 5	1 2 3 4 5
Leave a note for someone explaining where you will be or when you will come home.	1 2 3 4 5	1 2 3 4 5
Write an advertisement to sell a bicycle.	1 2 3 4 5	1 2 3 4 5

[1] This is the form of the scale as used by Luna and Peracchio (2001; Luna 2003) in their study of Spanish and English usage. In the first section above the anchors they used were *not at all proficient* (1) and *proficient like a native speaker* (5). In the second section, the anchors were *can't do very well at all* (1) and *can do very well* (5).

SCALE NAME: Legitimation

SCALE DESCRIPTION: The eight-item, seven-point Likert-type scale is intended to measure a person's attitude toward an organization with the emphasis on how well it operates within socially acceptable norms. More specifically, the scale taps into two types of legitimacy: pragmatic and social. The former involves actions of the organization that a person perceives as increasing his/her own self-interest. The latter has to do with the consistency of the organization's actions with the welfare of the community and society in which it operates.

SCALE ORIGIN: Handelman and Arnold (1999) generated 16 items intended to measure the construct, half of which were adapted from work by Elsbach (1994).

RELIABILITY: No overall reliability was reported for the scale. However, according to Handelman (2002), the separate components (pragmatic and social) both had alphas of .89.

VALIDITY: Handelman and Arnold (1999) used both EFA and CFA to examine the structure of this scale and another one (#469). They reported that after purifying the scales the items loaded on their respective factors. It should also be noted that even though statements related to either pragmatic or social legitimation were included in the scale the factor analyses did <u>not</u> indicate that there were two clear dimensions. Thus, it appears appropriate to consider the set of items as forming one unidimensional measure of legitimation.

REFERENCES:
Elsbach, Kimberly D. (1994), "Managing Organizational Legitimacy in the California Cattle Industry: The Construction and Effectiveness of Verbal Accounts," *Administrative Science Quarterly*, 39 (March), 57–88.
Handelman, Jay M. (2002), Personal Correspondence.
Handelman, Jay M. and Stephen J. Arnold (1999), "The Role of Marketing Actions with a Social Dimension: Appeals to the Institutional Environment," *JM*, 63 (July), 33–48.

SCALE ITEMS: [1]

1. _____ sets an example for how other retailers should conduct their activities.

2. _____ carries products that satisfy my needs.

3. _____ is committed to meeting the standards that people expect of retailers.

4. _____ is the kind of place that I can get my money's worth.

5. _____ carries the latest trends in products and services that meet my needs.

6. _____ genuinely listens to the demands that people put on it.

7. It requires quite a bit of effort for me to shop at _____. (r)

8. _____ sets an example for how other retailers ought to behave.

[1] The name of the retailer should be placed in the blanks. Also, items 1, 3, 6, and 8 are supposed to tap into social legitimacy whereas the others tap into pragmatic legitimacy (Handelman and Arnold 1999).

SCALE NAME: Loyalty (Active)

SCALE DESCRIPTION: Three, five-point Likert-type statements are used to measure the extent to which a customer intends to engage in certain proactive activities with regard to a service provider such as spreading positive word-of-mouth about it and using more of its services.

SCALE ORIGIN: Ganesh, Arnold, and Reynolds (2000) cited several previous studies on which they drew in the development of their scale.

RELIABILITY: An alpha of .77 was reported for the scale (Ganesh, Arnold, and Reynolds 2000).

VALIDITY: No examination of the scale's validity was reported by Ganesh, Arnold, and Reynolds (2000). They did, however, factor analyze the items in this scale along with those of a related scale (#265). The items for this scale loaded highest on the same dimension with no substantial loadings on the other dimension.

REFERENCES:

Ganesh, Jaishanker, Mark J. Arnold, and Kristy E. Reynolds (2000), "Understanding the Customer Base of Service Providers: An Examination of the Differences Between Switchers and Stayers," *JM*, 64 (3), 65–87.

SCALE ITEMS: [1]

1. I would recommend my _____ to my friends and family.

2. I am likely to make negative comments about my _____ to my friends and family. (r)

3. In the near future, I intend to use more of the services offered by my _____.

---

[1] The generic term for the service provider should be placed in the blanks, e.g., bank.

SCALE NAME: Loyalty (Brand)

SCALE DESCRIPTION: Four statements and a seven-point response scale are used to assess a person's tendency over time to purchase a specified brand within a specified product category.

SCALE ORIGIN: The source of the scale was not specified but it appears to be original to Sen, Gurhan-Canli, and Morwitz (2001).

RELIABILITY: An alpha of .91 (n = 166) was reported for the scale by Sen, Gurhan-Canli, and Morwitz (2001).

VALIDITY: No examination of the scale's validity was described in the article by Sen, Gurhan-Canli, and Morwitz (2001).

REFERENCES:
Sen, Sankar, Zeynep Gurhan-Canli, and Vicki Morwitz (2001), "Withholding Consumption: A Social Dilemma Perspective on Consumer Boycotts," *JCR*, 28 (December), 399–417.

SCALE ITEMS: [1]

1. How much would you say you like or dislike *brand product*?
   Dislike very much / like very much

2. When you buy *product,* to what extent do you buy *brand*?
   Never buy / always buy

3. When you buy *product,* to what extent are you "loyal" to *brand*?
   Never buy / always buy

---

[1] As indicated above, Sen, Gurhan-Canli, and Morwitz (2001) put the name of the product category in some of the blanks, e.g., toothpaste. The brand name was put in the other blanks, e.g., Colgate.

#265 *Loyalty (Passive)*

SCALE NAME: Loyalty (Passive)

SCALE DESCRIPTION: The scale is composed of three, five-point Likert-type statements that measure the extent to which a customer intends to remain a customer of a specific service provider for the foreseeable future despite typical market actions that it or its competitors might take, e.g., change in prices charged.

SCALE ORIGIN: Ganesh, Arnold, and Reynolds (2000) cited several previous studies on which they drew in the development of their scale.

RELIABILITY: An alpha of .72 was reported for the scale (Ganesh, Arnold, and Reynolds 2000).

VALIDITY: No examination of the scale's validity was reported by Ganesh, Arnold, and Reynolds (2000). They did, however, factor analyze the items in this scale along with those of a related scale (#263). The items for this scale loaded highest on the same dimension with no substantial loadings on the other dimension.

REFERENCES:
Ganesh, Jaishanker, Mark J. Arnold, and Kristy E. Reynolds (2000), "Understanding the Customer Base of Service Providers: An Examination of the Differences Between Switchers and Stayers," *JM*, 64 (3), 65–87.

SCALE ITEMS: [1]

1. If my current _____ were to raise the price of *its services*, I would still continue to be a customer of the _____ .

2. If a competing _____ were to offer a better *price* on their services, I would switch. (r)

3. As long as I live in this neighborhood, I do not foresee myself switching to a different _____ .

---

[1] The generic term for the service provider should be placed in the blanks of each item, e.g., bank. For the first two items, the terms in italics are not those used by Ganesh, Arnold, and Reynolds (2000) but have been changed to make the statements more flexible for use with a variety of service providers rather than just banks.

SCALE NAME: Loyalty (Product)

SCALE DESCRIPTION: The scale is composed of three statements that attempt to measure a consumer's tendency to buy the same brand within a specified product category rather than seek variation.

SCALE ORIGIN: Campo, Gijsbrechts, and Nisol (2000) indicated that their scale was based on one by Baumgartner and Steenkamp (1996). Specifically, the former used one item from a scale by the latter that was intended to measure exploratory tendencies.

RELIABILITY: Alphas of .856 (cereals) and .890 (margarine) were reported for the scale by Campo, Gijsbrechts, and Nisol (2000).

VALIDITY: No information about the scale's validity was provided by Campo, Gijsbrechts, and Nisol (2000). They did imply, however, that the scale was unidimensional based on the results of a principal components factor analysis of all scale items in their questionnaire.

REFERENCES:
Baumgartner, Hans and Jan-Benedict E. M. Steenkamp (1996), "Exploratory Consumer Buying Behavior: Conceptualization and Measurement," *International Journal of Research in Marketing*, 132, 121–137.
Campo, Katia, Els Gijsbrechts, and Patricia Nisol (2000), "Towards Understanding Consumer Response to Stock-Outs," *JR*, 79 (2), 219–242.

SCALE ITEMS: [1]

1. I think of myself as a loyal buyer of _____.

2. I would rather stick with a brand I usually buy than try something I am not sure of.

3. I like to switch between different brands of _____. (r)

[1] The response format used by Campo, Gijsbrechts, and Nisol (2000) was not described but could easily have been of a Likert-type. The name of the product category should be placed in the blanks.

SCALE NAME: Loyalty (Store)

SCALE DESCRIPTION: The four, seven-point Likert-type items are used to measure a person's commitment to a specified marketer. Reynolds and Beatty (1999a, 1999b) used two versions of the scale, one with respect to a company that customers had done business with and one with a "sales associate" they had interacted with at the store/business. The phrasing of the two is similar enough that they are discussed together here.

SCALE ORIGIN: Inspiration for the scales came from earlier work by the authors (Beatty et al. 1996) as well as others (Higie, Feick, and Price 1987).

RELIABILITY: Reynolds and Beatty (1999a) reported a composite reliability of .91 for both versions of the scale. In Reynolds and Beatty (1999b), the alphas were .86 (sales associate) and .83 (store).

VALIDITY: A claim of convergent validity was made by Reynolds and Beatty (1999a) based upon the significance of the item loadings in the CFA. Evidence of the discriminant validity of their two loyalty measures (salesperson and company) came from noting that the variance extracted for each was much higher than the correlation between them.

REFERENCES:
Beatty, Sharon E., Morris L. Mayer, James E. Coleman, Kristy Ellis Reynolds, and Jungki Lee (1996), "Customer-Sales Associate Retail Relationships," *JR*, 72 (Fall), 223–247.
Higie, Robin A., Lawrence F. Feick, and Linda L. Price (1987), "Types and Amount of Word-of-Mouth Communication about Retailers," *JR*, 63 (Fall), 260–278.
Reynolds, Kristy E. and Sharon E. Beatty (1999a), "Customer Benefits and Company Consequences of Customer-Salesperson Relationships in Retailing," *JR*, 75 (1), 11–32.
Reynolds, Kristy E. and Sharon E. Beatty (1999b), "A Relationship Customer Typology," *JR*, 75 (4), 509–523.

SCALE ITEMS: [1]

1. I am very loyal to _____.

2. I am very committed to _____.

3. I don't consider myself a loyal _____ customer. (r)

4. I don't plan to shop at _____ in the future. (r)

[1] This is the company version of the scale. The name of the business of interest should be placed in the blanks. Slight adjustments in phrasing are necessary for measuring loyalty to a salesperson working at the store/company.

SCALE NAME: Loyalty (Store)

SCALE DESCRIPTION: The three-item scale attempts to measure a consumer's tendency to concentrate purchases at one store. Although the items refer to supermarkets, that term could be easily changed when wanting to measure loyalty to other types of retailers.

SCALE ORIGIN: Campo, Gijsbrechts, and Nisol (2000) indicated that their scale was based on one by Baumgartner and Steenkamp (1996). It is more accurate to say that the former received inspiration from the latter's measure of exploratory tendencies since the two scales do not share any items in common.

RELIABILITY: Alphas of .676 (cereals) and .714 (margarine) were reported for the scale by Campo, Gijsbrechts, and Nisol (2000).

VALIDITY: No information about the scale's validity was provided by Campo, Gijsbrechts, and Nisol (2000). They did imply, however, that the scale was unidimensional based on the results of a principal components factor analysis of all scale items in their questionnaire.

REFERENCES:
Baumgartner, Hans and Jan-Benedict E. M. Steenkamp (1996), "Exploratory Consumer Buying Behavior: Conceptualization and Measurement," *International Journal of Research in Marketing*, 13 (2), 121–137.
Campo, Katia, Els Gijsbrechts, and Patricia Nisol (2000), "Towards Understanding Consumer Response to Stock-Outs," *JR*, 79 (2), 219–242.

SCALE ITEMS: [1]

1. I think of myself as a loyal customer of my supermarket.

2. I would rather stay with the supermarket I usually frequent than trying a different store I'm not very sure of.

3. I like to switch between different supermarkets. (r)

---

[1] The response format used by Campo, Gijsbrechts, and Nisol (2000) was not described but could easily have been of a Likert-type.

SCALE NAME: Loyalty (Store)

SCALE DESCRIPTION: The scale is composed of three, five-point Likert-type statements and attempts to assess the degree to which a consumer has a favorite grocery store (unspecified) and expresses a willingness to go to the effort to shop there in particular.

SCALE ORIGIN: The source of the scale was not identified by Ailawadi, Neslin, and Gedenk (2001). Although the scale items bear some conceptual similarity to those developed for use in other brand loyalty and loyalty proneness scales, it is probably safest to describe this scale as being original to the work of Ailawadi, Neslin, and Gedenk (2001).

RELIABILITY: A composite reliability of .876 was reported for the scale (Ailawadi, Neslin, and Gedenk 2001).

VALIDITY: The items in this scale along with those belonging to 14 other scales were included in a confirmatory factor analysis. The fit of the measurement model was acceptable and general evidence was cited in support of the scale's discriminant validity.

COMMENTS: Although the scale was developed and used by Ailawadi, Neslin, and Gedenk (2001) with reference to grocery stores, the items appear to be amenable for slight adjustment so they can be used with other types of malls, shops, restaurants, bars, etc.

REFERENCES:
Ailawadi, Kusum L., Scott A. Neslin, and Karen Gedenk (2001), "Pursuing the Value-Conscious Consumer: Store Brands Versus National Brand Promotions," *JM*, 65 (1), 71–89.

SCALE ITEMS:

1. I prefer to always shop at one grocery store.

2. I am willing to make an effort to shop at my favorite grocery store.

3. Usually, I care a lot about which particular grocery store I shop at.

SCALE NAME: Loyalty (Store)

SCALE DESCRIPTION: Three questions are used to assess the degree to which a customer focuses purchases of a certain product category on a specified store. The emphasis of the scale is on behavioral loyalty rather than a more attitudinal aspect such as commitment.

SCALE ORIGIN: The source of the scale was not explicitly described by De Wulf, Odekerken-Schröder, and Iacobucci (2001) but it would appear to be original to their studies. The items seem to be among those that were developed using the back-translation method for versions in American English and Dutch and then pretested in the U.S., Netherlands, and Belgium (Flemish-speaking area).

RELIABILITY: Composite reliabilities were reported by De Wulf, Odekerken-Schröder, and Iacobucci (2001) for two types of stores for each of three countries. The reliabilities for food stores were .92, .86, and .89 for the U.S., Netherlands, and Belgium, respectively. For apparel stores, the reliabilities were .93, .90, and .87 for the U.S., Netherlands, and Belgium, respectively.

VALIDITY: A great deal of information regarding the scale's validity was provided by De Wulf, Odekerken-Schröder, and Iacobucci (2001). In brief, evidence was provided in support of the scale's unidimensionality as well as its convergent and discriminant validities. The average variance extracted for the six uses of the scale ranged from .68 to .81. Full metric invariance across countries was supported too.

REFERENCES:
De Wulf, Kristof, Gaby Odekerken-Schröder, and Dawn Iacobucci (2001), "Investments in Consumer Relationships: A Cross-Country and Cross-Industry Exploration," *JM*, 65 (October), 33–50.
Odekerken-Schröder, Gaby (2004), Personal Correspondence.

SCALE ITEMS: [1]

1. What percentage of your total expenditures for _____ do you spend in this store?

2. Of the ten times you select a store to buy _____, how many times do you select this store?

3. How often do you buy _____ in this store compared to other stores where you buy _____?

[1] The name of the primary product category carried by the store should be placed in the blanks, e.g., clothing, groceries. For item 1 respondents were expected to write down a percentage between 0% and 100%. The extreme anchors for items 2 and 3 were *much less frequently* and *much more frequently* (Odekerken-Schröder 2004).

SCALE NAME: Loyalty Intentions (Supermarket Merchandise)

SCALE DESCRIPTION: The scale is composed of three, five-point items measuring a consumer's stated likelihood of shopping at a specified supermarket as well as recommending it to a friend.

SCALE ORIGIN: Sirohi, McLaughlin, and Wittink (1998) did not specify where their measure came from. It appears that it is original to their study.

RELIABILITY: Construct reliability was reported to be .87 (Sirohi, McLaughlin, and Wittink 1998).

VALIDITY: An average variance extracted of .70 was reported for the scale by Sirohi, McLaughlin, and Wittink (1998).

REFERENCES:
Sirohi, Niren, Edward W. McLaughlin, and Dick R. Wittink (1998), "A Model of Consumer Perceptions and Store Loyalty Intentions for a Supermarket Retailer," *JR*, 74 (2), 223–245.

SCALE ITEMS: [1]

1. Likelihood to continue shopping

2. Likelihood to use the store for more of your grocery needs in the next twelve months

3. Likelihood to recommend the supermarket to a friend

---

[1] The response format for the items was a five-point scale ranging from *extremely likely* to *not at all likely*.

SCALE NAME: Loyalty Proneness (Brand)

SCALE DESCRIPTION: The scale is composed of three, five-point Likert-type statements and attempts to assess the degree to which a consumer expresses having favorite brands in many product categories and the tendency to focus on those brands when shopping. This is in contrast to being brand loyal in only a few select product categories or having little loyalty at all.

SCALE ORIGIN: The source of the scale was not identified by Ailawadi, Neslin, and Gedenk (2001). Although the scale items bear some conceptual similarity to those developed for use in other brand loyalty and loyalty proneness scales, it is probably safest to describe this scale as being original to the work of Ailawadi, Neslin, and Gedenk (2001).

RELIABILITY: A composite reliability of .865 was reported for the scale (Ailawadi, Neslin, and Gedenk 2001).

VALIDITY: The items in this scale along with those belonging to 14 other scales were included in a confirmatory factor analysis. The fit of the measurement model was acceptable and general evidence was cited in support of the scale's discriminant validity.

REFERENCES:
Ailawadi, Kusum L., Scott A. Neslin, and Karen Gedenk (2001), "Pursuing the Value-Conscious Consumer: Store Brands Versus National Brand Promotions," *JM*, 65 (1), 71–89.

SCALE ITEMS:

1. I prefer one brand of most products I buy.

2. I am willing to make an effort to search for my favorite brand.

3. Usually, I care a lot about which particular brand I buy.

SCALE NAME: Loyalty Proneness (Product)

SCALE DESCRIPTION: The scale is a five-item, seven-point Likert-type measure assessing a consumer's general tendency to buy the same brands over time rather than switching around to try other brands. The measure is not as specific as normally considered of "brand loyalty" where the tendency to purchase a particular brand is assessed rather than the propensity to be loyal in all sorts of purchases.

SCALE ORIGIN: The scale used by Burton et al. (1998) as well as Lichtenstein, Netemeyer, and Burton (1990) appears to be original although they drew upon Raju (1980) for two of their items.

RELIABILITY: The alpha reported by Burton et al. (1998) was .92. Lichtenstein, Netemeyer, and Burton (1990) reported the reliability of the scale to be .88.

VALIDITY: No test of validity was reported by either Burton et al. (1998) or Lichtenstein, Netemeyer, and Burton (1990).

REFERENCES:

Burton, Scot, Donald R. Lichtenstein, Richard G. Netemeyer, and Judith A. Garretson (1998), "A Scale for Measuring Attitude Toward Private Label Products and an Examination of Its Psychological and Behavioral Correlates," *JAMS*, 26 (4), 293–306.

Lichtenstein, Donald R., Richard D. Netemeyer, and Scot Burton (1990), "Distinguishing Coupon Proneness From Value Consciousness: An Acquisition Transaction Utility Theory Perspective," *JM*, 54 (July), 54–67.

Raju, P. S. (1980), "Optimum Stimulation Level: Its Relationship to Personality, Demographics, and Exploratory Behavior," *JCR*, 7 (December), 272–282.

SCALE ITEMS:

1. I generally buy the same brands I have always bought.

2. Once I have made a choice on which brand to purchase, I am likely to continue to buy it without considering other brands.

3. Once I get used to a brand, I hate to switch.

4. If I like a brand, I rarely switch from it just to try something different.

5. Even though certain products are available in a number of different brands, I always tend to buy the same brand.

SCALE NAME: Loyalty Proneness (Retail)

SCALE DESCRIPTION: Three Likert-type statements with a seven-point response format are used to assess a consumer's expressed desire to be a regular customer of a retailer within a certain product category. This is in contrast to being a regular customer simply out of routine.

SCALE ORIGIN: The source of the scale was not explicitly described by De Wulf, Odekerken-Schröder, and Iacobucci (2001) but it would appear to be original to their studies. The items seem to be among those that were developed using the back-translation method for versions in American English and Dutch and then pre-tested in the U.S., Netherlands, and Belgium (Flemish-speaking area).

RELIABILITY: Composite reliabilities were calculated for two types of stores for each of three countries (De Wulf, Odekerken-Schröder, and Iacobucci 2001). The reliabilities for food stores were .87, .88, and .87 for the U.S., Netherlands, and Belgium, respectively (Odekerken-Schröder 2004). For apparel stores, the reliabilities were .89, .89, and .85 for the U.S., Netherlands, and Belgium, respectively.

VALIDITY: Although De Wulf, Odekerken-Schröder, and Iacobucci (2001) provided a lot of information about most of the measures they used, evidence of this scale's validity was not specifically given.

REFERENCES:

De Wulf, Kristof, Gaby Odekerken-Schröder, and Dawn Iacobucci (2001), "Investments in Consumer Relationships: A Cross-Country and Cross-Industry Exploration," *JM*, 65 (October), 33–50.
Odekerken-Schröder, Gaby (2004), Personal Correspondence.

SCALE ITEMS: [1]

1. Generally, I am someone who likes to be a regular customer of a _____.

2. Generally, I am someone who wants to be a steady customer of the same _____.

3. Generally, I am someone who is willing to "go the extra mile" to buy at the same _____.

---

[1] An appropriate descriptor of the business entity should be placed in the blanks. De Wulf, Odekerken-Schröder, and Iacobucci (2001) used the terms "apparel store" and "supermarket."

SCALE NAME: Market Maven

SCALE DESCRIPTION: The scale is composed of three, five-point Likert-type statements and attempts to assess the degree to which a consumer views him/herself as an opinion leader with regard to shopping in general. This is in contrast to being an opinion leader for one specific product category.

SCALE ORIGIN: The work by Feick and Price (1987) was cited by Ailawadi, Neslin, and Gedenk (2001) as the source of the scale they used. While there is some conceptual similarity between the scales by the sets of authors there is not enough to consider them to be the same scale. It is best therefore, to describe this scale as being original to Ailawadi, Neslin, and Gedenk (2001) but inspired by the work by Feick and Price (1987).

RELIABILITY: A composite reliability of .876 was reported for the scale (Ailawadi, Neslin, and Gedenk 2001).

VALIDITY: The items in this scale along with those belonging to 14 other scales were included in a confirmatory factor analysis. The fit of the measurement model was acceptable and general evidence was cited in support of the scale's discriminant validity.

REFERENCES:

Ailawadi, Kusum L., Scott A. Neslin, and Karen Gedenk (2001), "Pursuing the Value-Conscious Consumer: Store Brands Versus National Brand Promotions," *JM*, 65 (1), 71–89.

Feick, Lawrence F. and Linda L. Price (1987), "The Market Maven: A Diffuser of Marketplace Information," *JM*, 51 (January), 83–97.

SCALE ITEMS:

1. I am somewhat of an expert when it comes to shopping.

2. People think of me as a good source of shopping information.

3. I enjoy giving people tips on shopping.

SCALE NAME: Marketplace Activism (Direct)

SCALE DESCRIPTION: The scale's three, seven-point items are intended to capture the extent to which a consumer has taken action after being dissatisfied with a product by going to the marketing channel member(s) perceived to have some responsibility for resolving the problem. Actions such as complaining to a marketer and returning products to a store are sometimes referred to as *voice behaviors* (e.g., Moorman 1998, p. 85). The timeframe referred to in the scale is a year and the product category is food; both of these appear to be amenable for change if need be.

SCALE ORIGIN: The use of these items as a set seems to be original to Moorman (1998) although she drew upon concepts and items by Day and Bodur (1978), Grønhaug and Zaltman (1981), and Warland, Herrmann, and Moore (1984).

RELIABILITY: An alpha of .87 was reported for the scale by Moorman (1998).

VALIDITY: No information regarding the scale's validity was reported by Moorman (1998). However, in developing the scale and others like it an exploratory factor analysis was conducted on several marketplace activism items and it provided evidence that the three items in this scale loaded together.

COMMENTS: The scale's mean was reported to be 4.03 with a standard deviation of 1.63 (Moorman 1998).

REFERENCES:
Day, Ralph L. and Muzaffer Bodur (1978), "Consumer Response to Dissatisfaction with Services and Intangibles," in *Advances in Consumer Research, V. 5,* H. Keith Hunt, ed. Ann Arbor, MI: Association for Consumer Research, 263–272.
Grønhaug, Kjell and Gerald Zaltman (1981), "Complainers and Noncomplainers Revisited: Another Look at the Data," in *Advances in Consumer Research, V. 8,* Kent B. Monroe, ed. Ann Arbor, MI: Association for Consumer Research, 83–87.
Moorman, Christine (1998), "Market-Level Effects of Information: Competitive Responses and Consumer Dynamics," *JMR,* 35 (February), 82–98.
Warland, Rex H., Robert O. Herrmann, and Dan E. Moore (1984), "Consumer Complaining and Community Involvement: An Exploration of Their Theoretical and Empirical Linkages," *Journal of Consumer Affairs,* 18 (Summer), 64–78.

SCALE ITEMS: [1]

During the past year when you have felt dissatisfied with the content of a food product, to what degree did you take any of the following actions?

1. Returned the product to the store.

2. Complained to the company who manufactured the product.

3. Complained to the store carrying the product.

[1] Moorman (1998) used a response format ranging from *never when I feel dissatisfied* (1) to *always when I feel dissatisfied* (7).

SCALE NAME: Materialism

SCALE DESCRIPTION: The scale is composed of five-point, Likert-type statements intended to capture the emphasis a person places on material things and the belief that those things bring happiness.

SCALE ORIGIN: The scale used by Sirgy et al. (1998) is original to Richins (1987). Interestingly, her analysis of the items showed that they were not unidimensional. She dropped item #7 (below) and used the other six to compose two scales. Ultimately, she developed stronger measures of three materialism subconstructs (Richins and Dawson 1992). (See scales #169 - #171 in V. II of this series.)

RELIABILITY: Sirgy et al. (1998) used the scale with six different samples in five different countries. Alphas ranged from .303 for the Chinese sample (n = 191) to .686 for the Canadian sample (n = 180).

VALIDITY: Because of the scale's moderate and significant correlations with another measure of materialism, the authors claimed support for the scale's convergent validity. However, the validity of the scale is suspect given that so much of the in-depth work on materialism (Belk 1985; Richins and Dawson 1992) indicates that it is a multifaceted construct, not captured in any one scale.

REFERENCES:

Belk, Russell W. (1985), "Materialism: Trait Aspects of Living in the Material World," *JCR*, 12 (December), 265–280.

Richins, Marsha L. (1987), "Media, Materialism, and Human Happiness," in *Advances in Consumer Research, V. 14*, Melanie Wallendorf, Paul Anderson, eds., Ann Arbor, MI: Association for Consumer Research, 352–356.

Richins, Marsha L. and Scott Dawson (1992), "A Consumer Values Orientation for Materialism and its Measurement: Scale Development and Validation," *JCR*, 19 (December), 303–316.

Sirgy M. Joseph, Dong-Jin Lee, Rustan Kosenko, H. Lee Meadow, Don Rahtz, Murris Cicic, Guang Xi-Jin, Duygun Yarsuvat, David L. Blenkhorn, and Newell Wright (1998), "Does Television Viewership Play a Role in the Perception of Quality of Life?" *Journal of Advertising*, 27 (Spring), 125–142.

SCALE ITEMS: [1]

1. It is important to me to have really nice things.

2. I would like to be rich enough to buy anything I want.

3. I'd be happier if I could afford to buy more things.

4. It sometimes bothers me quite a bit that I can't afford to buy all of the things I would like.

5. People place too much emphasis on material things. (r)

6. It's really true that money can buy happiness.

7. The things I own give me a great deal of pleasure.

[1] Depending upon the country, some items were ultimately dropped from this set when calculating scores.

SCALE NAME: Mood (Global)

SCALE DESCRIPTION: It is a multi-item semantic differential measuring a particular state of feeling that has a transient duration. The scale measures mood at a particular point in time on a simple good/bad continuum rather than attempting to assess various dimensions of mood.

SCALE ORIGIN: Although Swinyard (1993) says that the scale is adapted from a scale developed by Peterson and Sauber (1983) they are enough different to be treated separately here. It does appear that both scales measure the same construct but the items are very different. Pham (1996) as well as Lee and Sternthal (1999) did not describe the origin of their scales but the similarity between them all suggests the source is Swinyard (1993).

RELIABILITY: Barone, Miniard, and Romeo (2000) reported alphas of ranging from .90 to .93 depending upon the study it was used in and whether it was administered at the beginning or the end of an experimental session. Alphas of .94 and .85 were reported for the versions of the scale used by Pham (1996) and Swinyard (1993), respectively. The latter indicated that data were collected for another item but it was not used in the final version of the scale due to its unacceptably low item-total correlation. Lee and Sternthal (1999) used the scale in four studies with alphas being reported for three of the studies: .93 (Study 1) and .90 (Studies 3 and 4).

VALIDITY: No examination of the scale's validity was reported in any of the studies. Pham (1996) did state, however, that a factor analysis of the items in this scale as well as two others (V. III, #23 and #203) yielded a three-factor solution in which the items shown below loaded on one factor.

REFERENCES:

Barone, Michael J., Paul W. Miniard, and Jean B. Romeo (2000), "The Influence of Positive Mood on Brand Extension Evaluations," *JCR*, 26 (March), 386–400.

Lee, Angela Y. and Brian Sternthal (1999), "The Effects of Positive Mood on Memory," *JCR*, 26 (September), 115–127.

Peterson, Robert and Matthew Sauber (1983), "A Mood Scale for Survey Research," in Proceedings of the American Marketing Association's Educators' Conference, Chicago: American Marketing Association, 409–414.

Pham, Michel Tuan (1996), "Cue Representation and Selection Effects of Arousal on Persuasion," *JCR*, 22 (March), 373–387.

Swinyard, William R. (1993), "The Effects of Mood, Involvement, and Quality of Store Experience on Shopping Intentions," *JCR*, 20 (September), 271–280.

SCALE ITEMS: [1]

1. sad / happy

2. bad mood / good mood

3. irritable / pleased

4. depressed / cheerful

#278 *Mood (Global)*

Barone, Miniard, and Romeo (2000): 1–4 7-point
Lee and Sternthal (1999): 1–4 7-point
Pham (1996): 1*, 2, 3* 7-point
Swinyard (1996): 1–4 7-point

[1] The asterisk indicates that one of the anchors of a pair used in a study was different from what is shown here.

SCALE NAME: Mood (Global)

SCALE DESCRIPTION: The eight-item, eleven-point uni-polar scale is meant to assess a person's mood at some point in time. As used by Adaval (2001), the scale assessed what subjects said they were feeling during a mood-inducing activity. Because a diverse set of emotions are mixed together in the scale, the most that a researcher can conclude is that a person experienced a generally positive or negative mood.

SCALE ORIGIN: Although Adaval (2001) reported that the items were borrowed from Penner et al. (1994), only three of the eight came from that source. The other five items have been used in previous measures of mood or affect.

RELIABILITY: An alpha of .97 was reported for the scale (Adaval 2001).

VALIDITY: No examination of the scale's validity was reported.

COMMENTS: Despite the high alpha that was reported, the diversity of items in the scale creates the possibility for the set to be tapping into multiple dimensions rather than just one as would be expected. Confirmation of the scale's unidimensionality is urged before use of scale in the future.

REFERENCES:

Adaval, Rashmi (2001), "Sometimes It Just Feels Right: The Differential Weighting of Affected-Consistent and Affected-Inconsistent Product Information," *JCR*, 28 (June), 1–17.

Penner, Louis A., Saul Shiffman, Jean A. Paty, and Barbara A. Fritzche (1994), "Individual Differences in Intraperson Variability in Mood," *Journal of Personality and Social Psychology*, 66 (4), 712–721.

SCALE ITEMS: [1]

1. Happy

2. Angry (r)

3. Pleasant

4. Sad (r)

5. Delighted

6. Glad

7. Unpleasant (r)

8. Distressed (r)

[1] The response scale used with these items by Adaval (2001) ranged from 0 (*not at all*) to 10 (*extremely*). The directions were not provided but apparently asked subjects to report the degree to which they experienced the emotions in some task they had just engaged in.

SCALE NAME: National Brand Promotion Usage (In-Store)

SCALE DESCRIPTION: The scale is composed of four, five-point statements and attempts to assess the frequency with which a consumer takes advantage of <u>in-store</u> promotions on national brands.

SCALE ORIGIN: Ailawadi, Neslin, and Gedenk (2001) did not indicate any other source for the scale thus it is assumed that it was original to their study.

RELIABILITY: A composite reliability of .767 was reported for the scale (Ailawadi, Neslin, and Gedenk 2001).

VALIDITY: The items in this scale along with those belonging to two other scales were included in a confirmatory factor analysis. The fit of the measurement model was acceptable and general evidence was cited in support of the scale's discriminant validity.

REFERENCES:

Ailawadi, Kusum L., Scott A. Neslin, and Karen Gedenk (2001), "Pursuing the Value-Conscious Consumer: Store Brands Versus National Brand Promotions," *JM*, 65 (1), 71–89.

SCALE ITEMS: [1]

1. I am influenced by special displays of national brands in the store.

2. I use a coupon if I see it on a package or in the store.

3. I pick up and use the store flyer when I am shopping in the store.

4. I take advantage of specials on national brands in the store.

---

[1] The anchors Ailawadi, Neslin, and Gedenk (2001) used with this scale were *never* and *very often*.

SCALE NAME: National Brand Promotion Usage (Out-of-Store)

SCALE DESCRIPTION: Four, five-point statements are used to measure the frequency with which a consumer gathers coupons for national brands as well as information from store flyers about national brands <u>before</u> going shopping.

SCALE ORIGIN: Ailawadi, Neslin, and Gedenk (2001) did not indicate any other source for the scale thus it is assumed that it was original to their study.

RELIABILITY: A composite reliability of .799 was reported for the scale (Ailawadi, Neslin, and Gedenk 2001).

VALIDITY: The items in this scale along with those belonging to two other scales were included in a confirmatory factor analysis. The fit of the measurement model was acceptable and general evidence was cited in support of the scale's discriminant validity.

REFERENCES:
Ailawadi, Kusum L., Scott A. Neslin, and Karen Gedenk (2001), "Pursuing the Value-Conscious Consumer: Store Brands Versus National Brand Promotions," *JM*, 65 (1), 71–89.

SCALE ITEMS: [1]

1. I clip coupons for national brands from newspapers and magazines.

2. I take along coupons for national brands and use them when I go shopping.

3. I scan store flyers for sales on national brands before going shopping.

4. I use store flyers to decide what to buy and where to shop.

---

[1] The anchors Ailawadi, Neslin, and Gedenk (2001) used with this scale were *never* and *very often*.

SCALE NAME: Navigation of Technology Assisted Shopping

SCALE DESCRIPTION: The scale is composed of four, seven-point Likert-type items used to measure the degree to which a person views a technological device or system's navigation function (getting around and moving through some environment) to be flexible in its usability. Due to one of the items (#4) as well as the context in which it was used, the scale relates most to how a technology facilitates the online shopping experience.

SCALE ORIGIN: The scale appears to be original to the studies reported by Childers et al. (2001).

RELIABILITY: Using LISREL, the reliability of the scale was calculated to be .774 (hedonic motivations) and .905 (utilitarian motivations) in the studies reported by Childers et al. (2001).

VALIDITY: Discriminant validity was assessed using two different tests (the latent variable confidence interval tests and the χ^2 difference test). For both studies the evidence indicated that each scale, including navigation, was measuring a distinctive construct.

COMMENTS: The phrase "technology assisted shopping" in each item (below) appears like it could be replaced with more specific names when wanting to adapt the scale for particular devices such as wireless PDAs.

REFERENCES:
Childers, Terry L., Christopher L. Carr, Joann Peck, and Stephen Carson (2001), "Hedonic and Utilitarian Motivations for Online Retail Shopping Behavior," *JR*, 77 (Winter), 511–535.

SCALE ITEMS:

1. Using technology assisted shopping would allow flexibility in tracking down information.

2. Use of technology assisted shopping would offer a very free environment which I could navigate as I saw fit.

3. Use of technology assisted shopping would allow navigation through the environment.

4. Use of technology assisted shopping would allow me to move fluidly through the shopping environment.

SCALE NAME: Need for Cognition

SCALE DESCRIPTION: The scale is composed of eighteen Likert-type items that are supposed to measure a person's tendency to engage in and enjoy effortful information processing. An abbreviated version of the scale was used by Ailawadi, Neslin, and Gedenk (2001).

SCALE ORIGIN: The scale was developed by Cacioppo, Petty, and Kao (1984) which was itself a short form of a thirty-four item version (Cacioppo and Petty 1982). The short version was reported to have a theta coefficient (maximized Cronbach's alpha) of .90 compared to the long version's .91. Also, the two versions of the scale had a correlation of .95. Finally, factor analysis indicated that all items except one had substantial and higher loadings on the first factor than subsequent factors. It is unclear why the weak item was not suggested for elimination in future use and, since factor loadings were not presented in the article, it is unknown which particular item it was.

RELIABILITY: Alphas of .88 (Batra and Stayman 1990), .88 (Darley and Smith 1993, 1995), .86 (Inman, Peter, and Raghubir 1997), .80 (Manning, Sprott, and Miyazaki 1998), .89 (Mantel and Kardes 1999), and .86 (Zhang and Budda 1999) have been reported for the scale. Roehm and Sternthal (2001) used the scale in four experiments with the alphas from two of them being .90 (n = 29) and .87 (n = 39). A composite reliability of .882 was reported for the scale used by Ailawadi, Neslin, and Gedenk (2001).

VALIDITY: No information regarding the full scale's validity was reported in any of the marketing studies. The items in the short version of the scale used by Ailawadi, Neslin, and Gedenk (2001) were examined along with those belonging to 14 other scales in a confirmatory factor analysis. The fit of the measurement model was acceptable and general evidence was cited in support of the scale's discriminant validity.

COMMENTS: Also see Garbarino and Edell (1997), Inman, McAlister, and Hoyer (1990), MacKenzie (1986), Meyers-Levy and Tybout (1989; 1997), O'Guinn and Shrum (1997), Peracchio and Tybout (1996), Samu, Krishnan, and Smith (1999), and Zhang (1996) for other uses of the scale.

REFERENCES:
Ailawadi, Kusum L., Scott A. Neslin, and Karen Gedenk (2001), "Pursuing the Value-Conscious Consumer: Store Brands Versus National Brand Promotions," *JM*, 65 (1), 71–89.
Batra, Rajeev and Batra Stayman (1990), "The Role of Mood in Advertising Effectiveness," *JCR*, 17 (September), 203–214.
Cacioppo, John T. and Richard E. Petty (1982), "The Need for Cognition," *Journal of Personality and Social Psychology*, 42 (1), 116–131.
Cacioppo, John T., Richard E. Petty, and Chuan Feng Kao (1984), "The Efficient Assessment of Need for Cognition," *Journal of Personality Assessment*, 48 (3), 306, 307.
Darley, William K. and Robert E. Smith (1993), "Advertising Claim Objectivity: Antecedents and Effects," *JM*, 57 (October), 100–113.
Darley, William K. and Robert E. Smith (1995), "Gender Differences in Information Processing Strategies: An Empirical Test of the Selectivity Model in Advertising Response," *JA*, 24 (Spring), 41–56.
Garbarino, Ellen C. and Julie A. Edell (1997), "Cognitive Effort, Affect, and Choice," *JCR*, 24 (September), 147–158.
Inman, J. Jeffrey, Leigh McAlister, and Wayne D. Hoyer (1990), "Promotion Signal: Proxy for a Price Cut?" *JCR*, 17 (June), 74–81.

Inman, J. Jeffrey, Anil C. Peter, and Priya Raghubir (1997), "Framing the Deal: The Role of Restrictions in Accentuating Deal Value," *JCR*, 24 (June), 68–79.

MacKenzie, Scott B. (1986), "The Role of Attention in Mediating the Effect of Advertising on Attribute Importance," *JCR*, 13 (September), 174–195.

Manning, Kenneth C., David E. Sprott, and Anthony D. Miyazaki (1998), "Consumer Response to Quantity Surcharges: Implications for Retail Price Setters," *JR*, 74 (3), 373–399.

Mantel, Susan Powell and Frank R. Kardes (1999), "The Role of Direction of Comparison, Attribute-Based Processing, and Attitude-Based Processing in Consumer Preference," *JCR*, 25 (March), 335–352.

Meyers-Levy, Joan and Alice M. Tybout (1989), "Schema Congruity as a Basis for Product Evaluation," *JCR*, 16 (June), 39–54.

Meyers-Levy, Joan and Alice M. Tybout (1997), "Context Effects at Encoding and Judgment in Consumption Settings: The Role of Cognitive Resources," *JCR*, 24 (June), 1–14.

O'Guinn, Thomas C. and L. J. Shrum (1997), "The Role of Television in the Construction of Consumer Reality," *JCR*, 23 (March), 278–294.

Peracchio, Laura A. and Alice M. Tybout (1996), "The Moderating Role of Prior Knowledge in Schema-Based Product Evaluation," *JCR*, 23 (December), 177–192.

Roehm, Michelle L. and Brian Sternthal (2001), "The Moderating Effect of Knowledge and Resources on the Persuasive Impact of Analogies," *JCR*, 28 (September), 257–272.

Samu, Sridhar, H. Shanker Krishnan, and Robert E. Smith (1999), "Using Advertising Alliances for New Product Introduction: Interactions Between Product Complementarity and Promotional Strategies," *JM*, 63 (January), 57–74.

Zhang, Yong (1996), "Responses to Humorous Advertising: The Moderating Effect of Need for Cognition," *JA*, 25 (Spring), 15–32.

Zhang, Yong and Richard Buda (1999), "Moderating Effects of Need for Cognition on Responses to Positively versus Negatively Framed Advertising Messages," *JA*, 28 (2), 1–15.

SCALE ITEMS: [1]

1. I would prefer complex to simple problems.

2. I like to have the responsibility of handling a situation that requires a lot of thinking.

3. Thinking is not my idea of fun. (r)

4. I would rather do something that requires little thought than something that is sure to challenge my thinking abilities. (r)

5. I try to anticipate and avoid situations where there is a likely chance I will have to think in depth about something. (r)

6. I find satisfaction in deliberating hard and for long hours.

7. I only think as hard as I have to. (r)

8. I prefer to think about small, daily projects to long-term ones. (r)

9. I like tasks that require little thought once I have learned them. (r)

10. The idea of relying on thought to make my way to the top appeals to me.

11. I really enjoy a task that involves coming up with new solutions to problems.

12. Learning new ways to think doesn't excite me very much. (r)

13. I prefer my life to be filled with puzzles that I must solve.

14. The notion of thinking abstractly is appealing to me.

15. I would prefer a task that is intellectual, difficult, and important to one that is somewhat important but does not require much thought.

16. I feel relief rather than satisfaction after completing a task that required a lot of mental effort. (r)

17. It's enough for me that something gets the job done: I don't care how or why it works. (r)

18. I usually end up deliberating about issues even when they do not affect me personally.

[1] The response format used in the reported articles is rarely described but a five- or seven-point *agree / disagree* style would be appropriate. The short version of the scale used by Ailawadi, Neslin, and Gedenk (2001) was composed of item 3, 7, and a slightly different phrasing of 9.

SCALE NAME: Need For Evaluation

SCALE DESCRIPTION: The scale is composed of sixteen statements intended to measure the extent to which a person chronically engages in evaluative responding across situations and objects, i.e., people are differentially motivated to engage in evaluation. No biological basis for this "need" is presumed although it is possible. Instead, it is viewed as a "self-attributed motive," a component of the self-concept.

SCALE ORIGIN: The scale is original to an unpublished masters thesis by Jarvis that was ultimately reported in Jarvis and Petty (1996). That article provides information about five studies attesting to the scale's reliability and validity. A collapsed data set of the three samples showed an internal consistency (alpha) of .85. A test of scale stability (10-week test-retest) showed a correlation of .84. As for the scale's dimensionality, the data were mixed about the existence of one or two factors. Surprisingly, the factor loadings for many of the items were consistently much lower than would be acceptable in scholarly marketing research ($< .50$). Finally, the scale did not have a significant correlation with either the Social Desirability Scale (#462, Crowne and Marlowe 1964) or the Balanced Inventory of Desirable Responding (#91, Paulhus 1988).

Fennis and Bakker (2001) used a Dutch translation of the scale.

RELIABILITY: An alpha of .84 was reported for the scale (Fennis and Bakker 2001).

VALIDITY: No examination of the scale's validity was reported by Fennis and Bakker (2001) although they did state a factor analysis of the items showed they were unidimensional.

REFERENCES:
Crowne, Douglas P. and David Marlowe (1960), "A New Scale of Social Desirability Independent of Psychopathology," *Journal of Consulting Psychology*, 24 (August), 349–354.
Fennis, Bob M. and Arnold B. Bakker (2001), "Stay Tuned-We Will Be Back Right After These Messages: Need to Evaluate Moderates the Transfer of Irritation in Advertising," *JA*, 30 (3), 15–25.
Jarvis, W. Blair and Richard E. Petty (1996), "The Need to Evaluate," *Journal of Personality and Social Psychology*, 70 (1), 172–194.
Paulhus, Delroy L. (1988), *Assessing Self-Deception and Impression Management in Self-Reports: the Balanced Inventory of Desirable Responding*, Vancouver, B.C., Canada: Department of Psychology, University of British Columbia.

SCALE ITEMS: [1]

1. I form opinions about everything.

2. I prefer to avoid taking extreme positions. (r)

3. It is very important to me to hold strong opinions.

4. I want to know exactly what is good and bad about everything.

5. I often prefer to remain neutral about complex issues. (r)

6. If something does not affect me, I do not usually determine if it is good or bad. (r)

7. I enjoy strongly liking and disliking new things.

8. There are things for which I do not have a preference. (r)

9. It bothers me to remain neutral.

10. I like to have strong opinions even when I am not personally involved.

11. I have many more opinions than the average person.

12. I would rather have a strong opinion than no opinion at all.

13. I pay a lot of attention to whether things are good or bad.

14. I only form strong opinions when I have to. (r)

15. I like to decide that new things are really good or really bad.

16. I am pretty much indifferent to many important issues. (r)

---

[1] No information about the response format was provided by Fennis and Bakker (2001). However, Jarvis and Petty (1996) used a five-point scale that ranged from *extremely uncharacteristic* (1) to *extremely characteristic* (5).

SCALE NAME: Need for Unique Products

SCALE DESCRIPTION: The scale is composed of eight Likert-type statements measuring the degree to which a person expresses the motivation to have unique consumer products that few others possess. The scale was called *desire for unique consumer products* (DUCP) by Lynn and Harris (1997).

SCALE ORIGIN: The scale used by Tian, Bearden, and Hunter (2001) was developed by Lynn and Harris (1997). The article by the latter provides a variety of evidence from multiple studies attesting to the reliability and validity of the scale. Briefly, multiple estimates of internal consistency were above .78 and its stability (two week test-retest) was .85. The unidimensional factor structure was generalizable across multiple samples. The pattern of correlations with measures of several personality traits was as expected. Evidence of the scale's predictive validity was also provided.

RELIABILITY: An alpha of .85 (n = 121 college students) was reported for the scale as used by Tian, Bearden, and Hunter (2001).

VALIDITY: Although it was not the purpose of Tian, Bearden, and Hunter (2001) to validate the scale, they used it in the process of validating their own scale: consumer's need for uniqueness (#286, CNFU). Among the findings were that CNFU had a moderately strong positive correlation (r = .65) with DUCP.

REFERENCES:

Lynn, Michael and Judy Harris (1997), "The Desire for Unique Consumer Products: A New Individual Differences Scale," *Psychology & Marketing*, 14 (September), 601–616.

Tian, Kelly T., William O. Bearden, and Gary L. Hunter (2001), "Consumers' Need for Uniqueness: Scale Development and Validation," *JCR*, 28 (June), 50–66.

SCALE ITEMS:

1. I am very attracted to rare objects.

2. I tend to be a fashion leader rather than a fashion follower.

3. I am more likely to buy a product if it is scarce.

4. I would prefer to have things custom-made than to have them ready-made.

5. I enjoy having things that others do not.

6. I rarely pass up the opportunity to order custom features on the products I buy.

7. I like to try new goods and services before others do.

8. I enjoy shopping at stores that carry merchandise which is different and unusual.

SCALE NAME: Need for Uniqueness (Consumer's)

SCALE DESCRIPTION: Thirty-one, five-point, Likert-type statements are used to assess a trait having to do with a consumer's motivation to purchase and own products that help provide a sense of distinctiveness from other people. The construct can be viewed as a desire for counterconformity for the purpose of enhancing one's personal and social identity. Visual communication of uniqueness is stressed in the scale rather than verbal. The creators of the scale (Tian, Bearden, and Hunter 2001) referred to it as CNFU (consumer's need for uniqueness).

SCALE ORIGIN: The scale is original to Tian, Bearden, and Hunter (2001). The article provided descriptions of an impressive series of studies having to do with the development and validation of the scale. The construct was hypothesized to have three dimensions: creative choice counterconformity, unpopular choice counterconformity, and avoidance of similarity. As confirmed in the analysis, the scale was expected to reflect the structure of a higher-order factor with three correlated subfactors. Despite this, the authors explained that their primary interest was in the higher-order construct rather than the individual dimensions composing it.

RELIABILITY: Among the many tests of the scale's reliability, alphas of .94 (n = 273) and .95 (n = 621) were reported for the student and mail survey samples, respectively. One and two-year measures of the scale's stability were made. Test-retest correlations of .81 (n = 84) and .73 (n = 346) were found using subsamples of the consumer mail survey sample.

VALIDITY: A variety of studies bearing on the scale's validity were conducted. In total, the tests provided evidence of the scale's known-groups validity, and discriminant validity, and nonomological validity. Further, the scale did not appear to be sensitive to social desirability response bias.

REFERENCES:
Tian, Kelly T., William O. Bearden, and Gary L. Hunter (2001), "Consumers' Need for Uniqueness: Scale Development and Validation," *JCR*, 28 (June), 50–66.

SCALE ITEMS:

1. I collect unusual products as a way of telling people I'm different.

2. I have sometimes purchased unusual products or brands as a way to create a more distinctive personal image.

3. I often look for one-of-a-kind products or brands so that I create a style that is all my own.

4. Often when buying merchandise, an important goal is to find something that communicates my uniqueness.

5. I often combine possessions in such a way that I create a personal image for myself that can't be duplicated.

6. I often try to find a more interesting version of run-of-the-mill products because I enjoy being original.

7. I actively seek to develop my personal uniqueness by buying special products or brands.

8. Having an eye for products that are interesting and unusual assists me in establishing a distinctive image.

9. The products and brands that I like best are the ones that express my individuality.

10. I often think of the things I buy and do in terms of how I can use them to shape a more unusual personal image.

11. I'm often on the lookout for new products or brands that will add to my personal uniqueness.

12. When dressing, I have sometimes dared to be different in ways that others are likely to disapprove.

13. As far as I'm concerned, when it comes to the products I buy and the situations in which I use them, customs and rules are made to be broken.

14. I often dress unconventionally even when it's likely to offend others.

15. I rarely act in agreement with what others think are the right things to buy.

16. Concern for being out of place doesn't prevent me from wearing what I want to wear.

17. When it comes to the products I buy and the situations in which I use them, I have often broken customs and rules.

18. I have often violated the understood rules of my social group regarding what to buy or own.

19. I have often gone against the understood rules of my social group regarding when and how certain products are properly used.

20. I enjoy challenging the prevailing taste of people I know by buying something they wouldn't seem to accept.

21. If someone hinted that I had been dressing inappropriately for a social situation, I would continue dressing in the same manner.

22. When I dress differently, I'm often aware that others think I'm peculiar, but I don't care.

23. When products or brands I like become extremely popular, I lose interest in them.

24. I avoid products or brands that have been accepted and purchased by the average consumer.

25. When a product I own becomes popular among the general population, I begin using it less.

26. I often try to avoid products or brands that I know are bought by the general population.

27. As a rule, I dislike products or brands that are customarily purchased by everyone.

28. I give up wearing fashions I've purchased once they become popular among the general public.

29. The more commonplace a product or brand is among the general population, the less interested I am in buying it.

30. Products don't seem to hold much value when they are purchased regularly by everyone.

31. When a style of clothing I own becomes too commonplace, I usually quit wearing it.

SCALE NAME: Need for Uniqueness (General)

SCALE DESCRIPTION: The scale is composed of 32 Likert-type statements measuring the extent to which a person expresses the motivation to be different from other people. The NFU scale approaches the motivation in a positive way rather than treating it negatively such as with mal-adaption or deviancy.

SCALE ORIGIN: The scale used by Tian, Bearden, and Hunter (2001) was developed by Snyder and Fromkin (1977, 1980). A considerable amount of testing was done to validate the scale. For example, the authors used expert judges to reduce a set of 300 items down to 117. That set was further reduced to the final 32 by noting which ones had a prescribed pattern of correlation (or lack thereof) with other scales. Its internal consistency reliability (KR-20) in multiple administrations ranged from .68 to .82. The scale's stability was estimated to be .91 (two month test-retest) and .68 (four month test-retest). Further, with multiple samples it was determined that the scale was not susceptible to social desirability bias. Factor analysis showed the set of items represented three dimensions.

RELIABILITY: Alphas of .70 (n = 121 college students) and .85 (n = 235 college students) were reported for the scale as used by Tian, Bearden, and Hunter (2001).

VALIDITY: Although it was not the purpose of Tian, Bearden, and Hunter (2001) to validate the scale, they did use it in the process of validating their own scale: consumer's need for uniqueness (CNFU, #286). Among the findings were that CNFU had a moderate positive correlation (r = .44) with NFU. Interestingly, when examined at the subscale level, the CNFU correlated highest (r = .46) with the dimension most related to counterconformity and much less with other two dimensions.

COMMENTS: There is little doubt that the NFU scale is multidimensional. The question is whether or not it is appropriate to use one score to represent responses to the multiple dimensions. Further testing is needed to resolve this issue.

For other uses of the scale see Ariely and Levav (2000) as well as Simonson and Nowlis (2000).

REFERENCES:
Ariely, Dan and Jonathon Levav (2000), "Sequential Choice in Group Settings: Taking the Road Less Traveled and Enjoyed," *JCR*, 27 (3), 279–290.

Simonson, Itamar and Stephen M. Nowlis (2000), "The Role of Explanations and Need for Uniqueness in Consumer Decision Making: Unconventional Choices Based on Reasons," *JCR*, 27 (1), 49–68.

Snyder, C. R. and Howard L. Fromkin (1977), "Abnormality as a Positive Characteristic: The Development and Validation of a Scale Measuring Need for Uniqueness," *Journal of Abnormal Psychology*, 86 (5), 518–527.

Snyder, C. R. (1980), *Uniqueness*, New York: Plenum Press.

Tian, Kelly T., William O. Bearden, and Gary L. Hunter (2001), "Consumers' Need for Uniqueness: Scale Development and Validation," *JCR*, 28 (June), 50–66.

SCALE ITEMS: [1]

Directions: The following statements concern your perceptions about yourself in a variety of situations. Your task is to indicate the strength of your agreement with each statement, utilizing a scale in which 1 denotes strong disagreement, 5 denotes strong agreement, and 2, 3, and 4 represent intermediate judgments. There are no "right" or "wrong" answers, so select the number that most closely reflects you on each statement. Take your time and consider each statement carefully.

1. When I am in a group of strangers, I am not reluctant to express my opinion publicly.

2. I find that criticism affects my self-esteem. (r)

3. I sometimes hesitate to use my own ideas for fear they might be impractical. (r)

4. I think society should let reason lead it to new customs and throw aside old habits or mere traditions.

5. People frequently succeed in changing my mind. (r)

6. I find it sometimes amusing to upset the dignity of teachers, judges, and "cultured" people.

7. I like wearing a uniform because it makes me proud to be a member of the organization it represents. (r)

8. People have sometimes called me "stuck-up."

9. Others' disagreements make me uncomfortable. (r)

10. I do not always need to live by the rules and standards of society.

11. I am unable to express my feelings if they result in undesirable consequences. (r)

12. Being a success in one's career means making a contribution that no one else has made.

13. It bothers me if people think I am being too unconventional. (r)

14. I always try to follow rules. (r)

15. If I disagree with a superior on his or her views, I usually do not keep it to myself.

16. I speak up in meetings in order to oppose those whom I feel are wrong.

17. Feeling "different" in a crowd of people makes me feel uncomfortable. (r)

18. If I must die, let it be an unusual death rather than an ordinary death in bed.

19. I would rather be just like everyone else than be called a "freak." (r)

20. I must admit I find it hard to work under strict rules and regulations.

21. I would rather be known for always trying new ideas than for employing well- trusted methods.

22. It is better always to agree with the opinions of others than to be considered a disagreeable person. (r)

23. I do not like to say unusual things to people. (r)

24. I tend to express my opinions publicly, regardless of what others say.

25. As a rule, I strongly defend my own opinions.

26. I do not like to go my own way. (r)

27. When I am with a group of people, I agree with their ideas so that no arguments will arise. (r)

28. I tend to keep quiet in the presence of persons of higher rank, experience, etc. (r)

29. I have been quite independent and free from family rule.

30. Whenever I take part in group activities, I am somewhat of a nonconformist.

31. In most things in life, I believe in playing it safe rather than taking a gamble. (r)

32. It is better to break rules than always to conform with an impersonal society.

---

[1] These are the directions, response format, and items as described by Snyder and Fromkin (1980, pp. 79, 80). They used a five-point scale.

SCALE NAME: Nostalgia Proneness

SCALE DESCRIPTION: It is an eight-item, nine-point Likert-type scale measuring the degree of preference one has towards objects that were more common in the past. This measure has also been referred to as *attitude toward the past* (ATP) and as the *Nostalgia Index*.

SCALE ORIGIN: A twenty item scale was developed and refined by Holbrook (1993) as detailed below.

RELIABILITY: The construct reliability and alpha for the scale were reported by Holbrook (1993) to be .78 in Study 1 and .73 in Study 2. The larger twenty item version of the scale was reported by Holbrook and Schindler (1994) to have an alpha of .77 while the eight-item subset had a construct reliability of .68. As admitted by the authors, the level of reliability should be higher and deserves further developmental effort.

VALIDITY: In Study 1 a confirmatory factor analysis was performed on the original version of the scale and it did not appear to be unidimensional (Holbrook 1993). After eliminating some items, the eight items shown below were found to fit a one factor model. A confirmatory factor analysis in Study 2 also provided some evidence of the eight items' unidimensionality.

This same process occurred in Holbrook and Schindler (1994). A confirmatory factor analysis supported the single-factor model for the eight item version of the scale but not for the full twenty-item measure.

COMMENTS: See also Steenkamp, Hofstede, and Wedel (1999) as well as Baumgartner and Steenkamp (2001).

REFERENCES:

Baumgartner, Hans and Jan-Benedict E.M. Steenkamp (2001), "Response Styles in Marketing Research: A Cross-National Investigation," *JMR*, 38 (May), 143–156.

Holbrook, Morris B. (1993), "Nostalgia and Consumption Preferences: Some Emerging Patterns of Consumer Tastes," *JCR*, 20 (September), 245–256.

Holbrook, Morris B. and Robert M. Schindler (1994), "Age, Sex, and Attitude Toward the Past as Predictors of Consumers' Aesthetic Tastes for Cultural Products," *JMR*, 31 (August), 412–422.

Steenkamp, Jan-Benedict E.M., Frenkel ter Hofstede, and Michel Wedel (1999), "A Cross-National Investigation into the Individual and National Cultural Antecedents of Consumer Innovativeness," *JM*, 63 (April), 55–69.

SCALE ITEMS:

1. They don't make 'em like they used to.

2. Things used to be better in the good old days.

3. Products are getting shoddier and shoddier.

4. Technological change will insure a brighter future. (r)

5. History involves a steady improvement in human welfare. (r)

6. We are experiencing a decline in the quality of life.

7. Steady growth in GNP has brought increased human happiness. (r)

8. Modern business constantly builds a better tomorrow. (r)

SCALE NAME: Nurturance (Parental)

SCALE DESCRIPTION: The scale is composed of multiple five-point Likert-type items measuring the degree to which a person (a parent) describes the interaction with his/her children as being warm, affectionate, and encouraging.

SCALE ORIGIN: The items in the scale are from the Child Rearing Practices Report (Block 1965) as tested and modified by Rickel and Biasatti (1982). Using three samples representing a broad range of socioeconomic factors, Rickel and Biasatti (1982) offered an eighteen-item scale of nurturance in which all items loaded on the same factor with loadings of .40 or higher. The alphas for this eighteen-item version of the scale were found to be .84, .82, and .73 for the three samples tested.

RELIABILITY: Carlson and Grossbart (1988) reported an alpha of .90 for the scale. An alpha of .87 was reported by Carlson, Laczniak, and Walsh (2001) for the version of the scale they used. Alphas of .82 (U.S.) and .74 (Japan) were reported for the scale by Rose (1999).

VALIDITY: No examination of scale validity was reported by Carlson and Grossbart (1988) or Carlson, Laczniak, and Walsh (2001). Rose (1999) stated that a CFA indicated the set of scales they used "formed the expected dimensions" (p. 111). In particular, this scale and one measuring verbalization encouragement (#133) produced a warmth dimension in a second order factor model.

COMMENTS: See also Walsh, Laczniak, and Carlson (1998).

REFERENCES:

Block, Jeanne H. (1965), *The Child Rearing Practices Report*, Berkeley, CA: University of California, Institute of Human Development.

Carlson, Les and Sanford Grossbart (1988), "Parental Style and Consumer Socialization of Children," *JCR*, 15 (June), 77–94.

Carlson, Les, Russell N. Laczniak, and Ann Walsh (2001), "Socializing Children about Television: An Intergenerational Study," *JAMS*, 29 (3), 276–288.

Rickel, Annette U. and Lawrence L. Biasatti (1982), "Modification of the Child Rearing Practices Report," *Journal of Clinical Psychology*, 38 (January), 129–134.

Rose, Gregory M. (2002), Personal Correspondence.

Rose, Gregory M. (1999), "Consumer Socialization, Parental Style, and Development Timetables in the United States and Japan," *JM*, 63 (July), 105–119.

Walsh, Ann D., Russell N. Laczniak, and Les Carlson (1998), "Mothers' Preferences for Regulating Children's Television," *JA*, 27 (3), 23–36.

SCALE ITEMS:

Directions: Please indicate your opinion by checking one response (*strongly disagree, disagree, neither disagree or agree, agree, strongly agree*) for each statement.

1. My child and I have warm intimate moments together.*

2. I encourage my child to talk about his troubles.*

3. I joke and play with my child.*

4. I make sure my child knows that I appreciate what he tries to accomplish.*

5. I encourage my child to wonder and think about life.*

6. I feel that a child should have time to daydream, think, and even loaf sometimes.

7. I express my affection by hugging, kissing, and holding my child.*

8. I talk it over and reason with my child when he misbehaves.*

9. I find it interesting and educational to be with my child for long periods.

10. I encourage my child to be curious, to explore, and question things.

11. I find some of my greatest satisfactions in my child.

12. When I am angry with my child, I let him know about it.

13. I respect my child's opinion and encourage him to express it.*

14. I feel that a child should be given comfort and understanding when he is scared and upset.*

15. I am easygoing and relaxed with my child.

16. I trust my child to behave as he should, even when I am not with him.

17. I believe in praising a child when he is good and think it gets better results that punishing him when he is bad.

18. I usually take into account my child's preference when making plans for the family.

---

[1] The nine items with the asterisks compose the subset used by Carlson and Grossbart (1988) as well as Rose (1999; 2002) and are listed here in order of factor loading strength as reported by Rickel and Biasatti (1982). The version of the scale used by Carlson, Laczniak, and Walsh (2001) had only seven of these items (unspecified).

SCALE NAME: Nutrition Information Interest

SCALE DESCRIPTION: The scale is composed of five, seven-point Likert-type statements measuring the desire of a person to receive and process nutritional information about food products.

SCALE ORIGIN: The scale used by Moorman (1998) is a modification of one she used previously (Moorman 1990). The earlier one made reference to looking for certain nutrient information for two specific foods whereas the newer scale is more general.

RELIABILITY: An alpha of .91 was reported for the scale (Moorman 1998).

VALIDITY: No information regarding the scale's validity was provided by Moorman (1998).

COMMENTS: The scale's mean was reported to be 5.76 with a standard deviation of 1.33 (Moorman 1998). See also Andrews, Netemeyer, and Burton (1998) as well as Andrews, Burton and Netemeyer (2001).

REFERENCES:

Andrews, J. Craig, Scot Burton, and Richard G. Netemeyer (2001), "Are Some Comparative Nutrition Claims Misleading? The Role of Nutrition Knowledge, Ad Claim Type and Disclosure Conditions," *JA*, 29 (3), 29–42.

Andrews, J. Craig, Richard G. Netemeyer, and Scot Burton (1998), "Consumer Generalization of Nutrient Content Claims in Advertising," *JM*, 62 (October), 62–75.

Moorman, Christine (1990), "The Effects of Stimulus and Consumer Characteristics on the Utilization of Nutrition Information," *JCR*, 17 (December), 362–374.

Moorman, Christine (1998), "Market-Level Effects of Information: Competitive Responses and Consumer Dynamics," *JMR*, 35 (February), 82–98.

SCALE ITEMS: [1]

1. I want to know more about nutrition information.

2. I wish more nutrition information were widely available.

3. I enjoy reading about nutrition information.

4. I am interested in looking for nutrition information on labels.

5. I would like to receive additional nutritional information about food products.

[1] Moorman (1998) used a Likert-type response format ranging from *strongly disagree* (1) to *strongly agree* (7).

SCALE NAME: Nutrition Information Usage

SCALE DESCRIPTION: It is a three-item, seven-point scale measuring the degree to which people say they are interested and do things which indicate concern about nutritional information on food packaging. The scale was referred to as *enduring motivation to process* by Moorman (1990) and *motivation to process nutrition information* by Burton, Garretson, and Velliquette (1999).

SCALE ORIGIN: The scale was developed by Moorman (1990). Burton, Garretson, and Velliquette (1999) made slight changes to it for their usage.

RELIABILITY: Alphas of .94 and .92 have been reported for the scale as used by Moorman (1990) and Burton, Garretson, and Velliquette (1999), respectively.

VALIDITY: No explicit analysis was described in either study of the scale's validity. However, based upon principal components analysis with Varimax rotation, Moorman (1993) concluded that the items were unidimensional.

REFERENCES:

Burton, Scot, Judith A. Garretson, and Anne M. Velliquette (1999), "Implications of Accurate Usage of Nutrition Facts Panel Information for Food Product Evaluations and Purchase Intentions," *JAMS*, 27 (4), 470–480.

Moorman, Christine (1990), "The Effects of Stimulus and Consumer Characteristics on the Utilization of Nutrition Information," *JCR*, 17 (December), 362–374.

Moorman, Christine (1993), Personal Correspondence.

SCALE ITEMS: [1]

1. *In general*, how often do you read nutritional labels / *the NUTRITION FACTS panel that reports nutrient information on food product packages?*
   not often / very often

2. *In general*, how interested are you in reading nutrition and health-related information at the grocery store?
   not interested / very interested

3. *Generally*, how often / *frequently* do you read nutrition labels at the grocery store / *on packaged foods?*
   not frequently at all / very frequently

---

[1] The italicized phrases shown in each item are the variations used by Burton, Garretson, and Velliquette (1999) and the anchors shown after each item were those that they used. The verbal anchors used by Moorman (1990, 1993) ranged from *never* (1) to *very often* (7).

SCALE NAME: Nutrition Information Usage

SCALE DESCRIPTION: The scale is composed of four, seven-point Likert-type statements measuring the extent to which a person spends time and effort reading nutritional information from sources such as food labels, advertisements, books, and magazines.

SCALE ORIGIN: The scale was developed by Moorman (1998).

RELIABILITY: An alpha of .71 was reported for the scale (Moorman 1998).

VALIDITY: No information regarding the scale's validity was provided by Moorman (1998).

COMMENTS: The scale's mean was reported to be 5.45 with a standard deviation of 1.41 (Moorman 1998).

REFERENCES:
Moorman, Christine (1998), "Market-Level Effects of Information: Competitive Responses and Consumer Dynamics," *JMR*, 35 (February), 82–98.

SCALE ITEMS: [1]

1. I usually pay attention to nutrition information when I see it in an ad or elsewhere.

2. I use nutrition information on the label when making most of my food selections.

3. I don't spend much time in the supermarket reading nutrition information. (r)

4. I read about nutrition in magazines and books.

---

[1] Moorman (1998) used a Likert-type response format ranging from *strongly disagree* (1) to *strongly agree* (7).

SCALE NAME: Nutrition Knowledge (Objective)

SCALE DESCRIPTION: The sale is composed of fifteen objective statements intended to measure one's understanding of some basic information about human nutrition. All statements had five possible answers with the fifth always being *Don't Know*. The instrument was called *Nutrition Information Questionnaire* by Andrews, Netemeyer, and Burton (1998).

SCALE ORIGIN: The scale is original to Andrews, Netemeyer, and Burton (1998). They developed 64 items based upon previous nutrition research. Data were collected from a sample of 19 graduate students in nutrition and 40 nonstudent adults. Using discriminant analysis a twelve-item subset was found to significantly separate the experts from the nonexperts. This version of the scale had an alpha of .71. After adding three items specific to their study and retesting it, the final 15-item scale had an alpha of .69.

RELIABILITY: No information about the scale's reliability in the main study was reported by Andrews, Netemeyer, and Burton (1998).

VALIDITY: The evidence collected by Andrews, Netemeyer, and Burton (1998) in their pretest amounts to known-group validity.

COMMENTS: See other uses of this scale by some of the same authors (Andrews, Burton and Netemeyer 2001; Burton, Garretson, and Velliquette 1999). The authors stress that the value of the scale should not be judged merely by its reliability (Andrews 2001). Its purpose was not merely to have all items converge but to be a general measure of a person's understanding of a range of nutrition-related facts and accepted beliefs. Given this, assessment of its value should view internal consistency as just one aspect of its quality. Further, it could be argued that the measure is actually a *formative* scale rather than a *reflective* one and, if so, internal consistency is not particularly relevant (Diamantopoulous and Winklhofer 2001).

REFERENCES:

Andrews, J. Craig (2001), Personal Correspondence.

Andrews, J. Craig, Scot Burton, and Richard G. Netemeyer (2001), "Are Some Comparative Nutrition Claims Misleading? The Role of Nutrition Knowledge, Ad Claim Type and Disclosure Conditions" *JA*, 29 (3), 29–42.

Andrews, J. Craig, Richard G. Netemeyer, and Scot Burton (1998), "Consumer Generalization of Nutrient Content Claims in Advertising," *JM*, 62 (October), 62–75.

Burton, Scot, Judith A. Garretson, and Anne M. Velliquette (1999), "Implications of Accurate Usage of Nutrition Facts Panel Information for Food Product Evaluations and Purchase Intentions," *JAMS*, 27 (4), 470–480.

Diamantopoulous, Adamantios and Heidi M. Winklhofer (2001), "Index Construction with Formative Indicators: An Alternative to Scale Development," *JMR*, 38 (May), 269–277.

SCALE ITEMS: [1]

1. Saturated fats are usually found in:

     a) Vegetables and vegetable oils
     b) Animal products like meat and dairy
     c) Grain products such as bread and cereal
     d) None of the above
     e) Don't Know

2. Which kind of fat is more likely to be a liquid rather than a solid?

     a) Saturated fats
     b) Polyunsaturated fats
     c) They are equally likely to be liquids
     d) None of the above
     e) Don't Know

3. Which kind of fat is more likely to raise people's blood cholesterol level?

     a) Saturated fats
     b) Polyunsaturated fats
     c) Both of them
     d) None of the above
     e) Don't Know

4. Which kind of fat is higher in calories?

     a) Saturated fats
     b) Polyunsaturated fats
     c) They are both the same
     d) None of the above
     e) Don't Know

5. If you eat 2000 calories a day, your daily *saturated fat* intake should be less than how many grams?

     a) 20
     b) 25
     c) 30
     d) 35
     e) Don't Know

6. Nutrition guidelines suggest that no more than _____ percent of the calories consumed in a day should come from *fat*.

    a)   10%
    b)   20%
    c)   30%
    d)   40%
    e)   Don't Know

7. Risk of high blood pressure is most likely to be reduced by eating a diet with:

    a)   Less sugar
    b)   More iron
    c)   More fiber
    d)   Less salt
    e)   Don't Know

8. A gram of fat provides about _____ as many calories as a gram of protein.

    a)   One-half
    b)   Twice
    c)   Four times
    d)   Six times
    e)   Don't Know

9. Vegetables, fruits, and grain products provide:

    a)   Complex carbohydrates
    b)   Dietary fiber
    c)   Both complex carbohydrates and dietary fiber
    d)   Neither complex carbohydrates or dietary fiber
    e)   Don't Know

10. Which food group provides protein, B vitamins, iron, and zinc?

    a)   Meat, poultry, and fish
    b)   Milk and diary products
    c)   Fruits
    d)   Grain products such as bread, cereal, and rice
    e)   Don't Know

11. Nutrition guidelines suggest that no more than _____ percent of the calories consumed in a day should come from *saturated fat*.

    a) 1%
    b) 10%
    c) 20%
    d) 30%
    e) Don't Know

12. Is cholesterol found in:

    a) Vegetables and vegetable oils
    b) Animal products like meat and dairy
    c) All foods containing fat or oil
    d) None of the above
    e) Don't Know

13. If you eat 2000 calories a day, your daily *sodium* intake should be less than how many milligrams?

    a) 500
    b) 2400
    c) 4300
    d) 6000
    e) Don't Know

14. Normal blood pressure in adults is systolic less than _____ and diastolic less than _____.

    a) 140 mmHg, 85 mmHg
    b) 180 mmHg, 95 mmHg
    c) 105 mmHg, 95 mmHg
    d) 200 mmHg, 110 mmHg
    e) Don't Know

15. Based on a 2000 calorie diet, per serving sodium levels are considered *high* when they exceed:

    a) 140 mg
    b) 480 mg
    c) 620 mg
    d) 2400 mg
    e) Don't Know

[1] The correct answers are bolded.

SCALE NAME: Nutrition Knowledge (Subjective)

SCALE DESCRIPTION: The scale is a three-item, seven-point global self-reported measure of one's perceived understanding of nutrition.

SCALE ORIGIN: Although not explicitly stated, the scale is apparently original to Burton, Garretson, and Velliquette (1999).

RELIABILITY: An alpha of .87 was reported for the scale by Burton, Garretson, and Velliquette (1999).

VALIDITY: No explicit analysis was described in the study of the scale's validity.

REFERENCES:
Burton, Scot (2001), Personal Correspondence.
Burton, Scot, Judith A. Garretson, and Anne M. Velliquette (1999), "Implications of Accurate Usage of Nutrition Facts Panel Information for Food Product Evaluations and Purchase Intentions," *JAMS*, 27 (4), 470–480.

SCALE ITEMS: [1]

1. In general, how much do you think you know about the topic of nutrition?
   not at all knowledgeable / extremely knowledgeable

2. I do not really know very much about nutrition in general. (r)
   strongly disagree / strongly agree

3. Compared to most people, I am quite knowledgeable about nutrition.
   strongly disagree / strongly agree

---

[1] The italicized responses after each item are the anchors used by Burton, Garretson, and Velliquette (1999; Burton 2001).

SCALE NAME: Obedience Expectations For Kids at School

SCALE DESCRIPTION: The scale has three, forced choice statements used to measure the degree to which a parent believes a child should obey school teachers and rules. This was referred to in some of the studies as *values conformity*.

SCALE ORIGIN: While this scale bears similarity to a construct described in Baumrind (1971), correspondence with Carlson indicates that the article did not highlight data collected with the scale but via observation. Carlson obtained the scale items in personal correspondence with Baumrind.

RELIABILITY: Carlson and Grossbart (1988) reported an alpha of .69 for the scale. Carlson, Laczniak, and Walsh (2001) reported an alpha of .64. Alphas of .70 (U.S.) and .71 (Japan) were reported for the scale by Rose (1999).

VALIDITY: No examination of scale validity was reported by Carlson and Grossbart (1988) or Carlson, Laczniak, and Walsh (2001). Rose (1999) stated that a CFA indicated a set of scales they used "formed the expected dimensions" (p. 111). In particular, this scale and two others (#172 and #304) produced a restrictiveness dimension in a second order factor model.

COMMENTS: See also Walsh, Laczniak, and Carlson (1998).

REFERENCES:
Baumrind, Diana (1971), "Current Patterns of Parental Authority," *Developmental Psychology Monograph*, 4 (January), 1–103.
Carlson, Les and Sanford Grossbart (1988), "Parental Style and Consumer Socialization of Children," *JCR*, 15 (June), 77–94.
Carlson, Les, Russell N. Laczniak, and Ann Walsh (2001), "Socializing Children about Television: An Intergenerational Study," *JAMS*, 29 (3), 276–288.
Rose, Gregory M. (2002), Personal Correspondence.
Rose, Gregory M. (1999), "Consumer Socialization, Parental Style, and Development Timetables in the United States and Japan," *JM*, 63 (July), 105–119.
Walsh, Ann D., Russell N. Laczniak, and Les Carlson (1998), "Mothers' Preferences for Regulating Children's Television," *JA*, 27 (3), 23–36.

SCALE ITEMS: [1]

Directions: Please indicate your opinion by checking one response (A or B) for each statement. There are no right or wrong answers, so answer according to your opinion. It is important to answer all questions even if you are not completely sure of your answer. Just check the response (A or B) that comes closest to your opinion. Some statements may seem alike but are necessary to show slight differences of opinion. All questions refer to your youngest child who attends this school.

A. A child must learn to conform to all school rules and regulations.
B. A child should not have to conform to all school rules. (r)

A. Some public school rules are so arbitrary or foolish that I would not insist that they be obeyed by my child.

B. I would expect my school-age child to obey all school rules.

A. A child should not have to obey all demands of his/her teachers.

B. A child should be taught to obey all his/her teachers' demands.

---

[1] Selection of answer A of a pair should be scored as a 1 while answer B should be scored as a 2, reverse scoring where indicated. Higher scores on the scale mean that parents expect their children to obey rules and authority figures with particular emphasis on the school context.

SCALE NAME: Occupation Estimates

SCALE DESCRIPTION: The scale is composed of five questions that are purported to measure a person's sense of the extent to which certain professions are part of the workforce. These particular occupations are specified due to being highlighted in prime-time TV shows and could be perceived as a larger proportion of the population than they really are.

SCALE ORIGIN: Although not explicitly stated in the article, the scale appears to be based on work by Shapiro (1987). The impetus for the scale appears to be the expectation that television viewing influences consumers' perceptions of social reality, among them the exaggerated sense of what proportion of the population have jobs similar to those most prevalent on TV shows.

RELIABILITY: Alphas of .84 (n = 71) and .78 (n = 162) were reported for the scale as it was used in Study 1 and 2, respectively (Shrum, Wyer, and O'Guinn 1998).

VALIDITY: No information regarding the scale's validity was reported by Shrum, Wyer, and O'Guinn (1998).

COMMENTS: The scale items appear to be tapping into multiple constructs and due to that bring into doubt the unidimensionality of the scale. If the scale is a reflective measure then that is a problem but it might not be a relevant issue if the scale is argued to be a set of formative indicators. See Diamantopoulous and Winklhofer (2001) for more details.

REFERENCES:

Diamantopoulous, Adamantios and Heidi M. Winklhofer (2001), "Index Construction with Formative Indicators: An Alternative to Scale Development," *JMR*, 38 (May), 269–277.

Shapiro, Michael A. (1987), "The Influence of Communication-Source Coded Memory Traces on World View," doctoral dissertation, University of Wisconsin-Madison.

Shrum, L.J., Robert S. Wyer, Jr., and Thomas C. O'Guinn (1998), "The Effects of Television Consumption on Social Perceptions: The Use of Priming Procedures to Investigate Psychological Processes," *JCR*, 24 (March), 447–458.

SCALE ITEMS: [1]

Directions: Express your answers to the following questions as a <u>percentage</u>. If you think the event listed is very unlikely to happen, then you will write in a very small percentage. If you think the event listed is very likely, then you should give a large percentage. Please guess or estimate the answer as well as you can. Please write the answer as a percentage in the space given. Once you have given an answer, please do not go back and change that answer. Unless otherwise indicated, all questions refer to the United States.

1. About what percentage of all males have jobs work in law enforcement and crime detection – like policemen, sheriffs, and detectives? _____

2. What percentage of the U.S. workforce are professional workers? _____

3. What percentage of the U.S. workforce are doctors? _____

4. What percentage of the U.S. workforce are scientists? _____

5. What percentage of the U.S. workforce are lawyers? _____

---

[1] These are the directions used by Shapiro (1987). Presumably, the directions used by Shrum, Wyer, and O'Guinn (1998) were similar.

SCALE NAME: Opinion Leadership (Domain Specific)

SCALE DESCRIPTION: The scale has been used in various forms to measure a person's tendency to provide information to others. Although it has been referred to as a measure of opinion leadership in all of the studies, an examination of the items suggests that it might be more accurate to think of it in more limited terms, e.g., the degree to which one provides information to others. Even if a person talks about a topic a lot that does not necessarily mean that the information is believed and acted upon (persuasion). These activities are critical indicators that one is, indeed, *leading* the opinions of others yet it is weak or missing from this scale.

SCALE ORIGIN: The scale was developed by Rogers (1961) and discussed by Rogers and Cartano (1962). The six item scale was used in a 1957 study of the diffusion of new farm ideas among Ohio farmers. Personal interviews were completed with a state-wide random area sample of 104 farm operators. A split-half reliability of .703 was calculated for the scale. In that study, a crude version of the sociometric technique of measuring opinion leadership produced scores with a correlation of .225 with the scale scores (Rogers 1961; Rogers and Cartano 1962). The validity of the scale was examined in several studies by correlating scale scores with scores from the key informant method as well as the sociometric technique. While positive correlations were found, they were not high.

A seven-item version of this scale was used by King and Summers (1970). A series of studies using the modified scale reported alphas ranging from .5 to .87.

Childers (1986) reported an alpha of .66 that was raised to a .68 when one of the seven items was removed from the summated scale. He also found low nomological validity for the scale.

The most thorough examination of the scale's psychometric properties was made by Flynn, Goldsmith, and Eastman (1994). They reported on the testing and modification of the scale in four studies. In brief, they found that the original version of the scale was not unidimensional. Problems seem to stem from the inclusion of item 5 (below) and their findings supported its deletion. Despite the scale having acceptable reliability and unidimensionality with the deletion of item 5, the authors raised other questions about the scale and felt it necessarily to construct another one (Flynn, Goldsmith, and Eastman 1996). (See V. III, #243).

RELIABILITY: The final version of the scale used by Childers (1986) had an alpha of .83. Alphas of .82 (Davis and Rubin 1983), .91 (Flynn, Goldsmith, and Eastman 1996), and .76 (Gilly et al. 1998) have been reported.

VALIDITY: Nomological validity was assessed by Childers (1986) who examined the pattern of correlations between the modified opinion leadership scale and scales measuring other constructs with which it should correlate, according to theory. As expected, the scale had significant though low correlations with several related variables: curiosity about product operation, product usage creativity, perceived risk of adopting cable TV, and ownership of technically oriented products. It did not have a significant correlation with risk preferences. Validity was also examined by comparing known groups' scores on the scale for predictable differences. Subscribers to cable TV had significantly higher scores than non-subscribers but no significant difference was found between those who subscribed to premium cable and those who just bought the basic service.

Davis and Rubin (1983) compared scores on their energy-related version of the scale with whether or not a person had purchased a solar energy device in the past. This produced a highly significant Kendalls Tau (.47).

In order to provide a sense of the convergent validity of their own opinion leadership scale Flynn, Goldsmith, and Eastman (1996) correlated scores on that scale with those on this scale. In both administrations of Study 5 the correlations were positive and significant supporting a claim of convergent validity of the new scale. Interestingly, the correlation between this old scale and a measure of perceived knowledge was just as strong which means it is, indeed, primarily emphasizing *information* rather than *persuasion*.

COMMENTS: Although not used in the main study reported by Feick and Price (1987), this scale was used in one of their pilot studies to examine the discriminant validity of a one-item generalized opinion leadership scale and a six-item Market Maven scale.

REFERENCES:
Childers, Terry L. (1986), "Assessment of the Psychometric Properties of an Opinion Leadership Scale," *JMR*, 23 (May), 184–188.

Davis, Duane L. and Ronald S. Rubin (1983), "Identifying the Energy Conscious Consumer: The Case of the Opinion Leader," *JAMS*, 11 (Spring), 169–190.

Feick, Lawrence F. and Linda L. Price (1987), "The Market Maven: A Diffuser of Marketplace Information," *JM*, 51 (January), 83–97.

Flynn, Leisa R., Ronald E. Goldsmith, and Jacqueline K. Eastman (1994), "The King and Summers Opinion Leadership Scale: Revision and Refinement," *Journal of Business Research*, 31 (September), 55–64.

Flynn, Leisa R., Ronald E. Goldsmith, and Jacqueline K. Eastman (1996), "Opinion Leaders and Opinion Seekers: Two New Measurement Scales," *JAMS*, 24 (Spring), 137–147.

Gilly, Mary C., John L. Graham, Mary Finley Wolfinbarger, and Laura J. Yale (1998), "A Dyadic Study of Interpersonal Information Search," *JAMS*, 26 (2), 83–100.

King, Charles W. and John O. Summers (1970), "Overlap of Opinion Leadership Across Consumer Product Categories," *JMR*, 7 (Feb.), 43–50.

Rogers, Everett M. (1961), *Characteristics of Agricultural Innovators and Other Adopter Categories*, Research Bulletin 882, Wooster, Ohio: Ohio Agricultural Experiment Station.

Rogers, Everett M. and David G. Cartano (1962), "Methods of Measuring Opinion Leadership," *Public Opinion Quarterly*, 26 (Fall), 435–441.

SCALE ITEMS: [1]

1. In general, do you talk to your friends and neighbors about _____.
   Very Often / Never

2. When you talk to you friends and neighbors about _____ do you:
   give a great deal of information / give very little information

3. During the past six months, how many people have you told about _____ ?
   told a number of people / told no one

4. Compared with your circle of friends, how likely are you to be asked about _____ ?
   very likely to be asked / not at all likely to be asked

5. If you and your friend were to discuss _____, what part would you be most likely to play? Would you mainly listen to your friends' ideas or would you try to convince them of your ideas?
   convince your friend of your ideas / listen to your friends' ideas

6. In discussions of _____, which of the following happens most often:
   you tell your friends about _____ / your friends tell you about _____

7. *Overall* in all of your discussions with friends and neighbors are you:
   often used as a source of advice / not used as a source of advice

---

[1] The name of the object should go in the blank. The version shown above is basically what was used by Childers (1986) as well as Flynn, Goldsmith, and Eastman (1996) except that neither used item 5. The six-item version of the scale (no item 5) is apparently the form used by Gilly et al. (1998) along with a seven-point response format. The full scale with a dichotomous response format (*yes / no*) was used by King and Summers (1971) as well as Davis and Rubin (1983).

SCALE NAME: Outshopping

SCALE DESCRIPTION: The scale is composed of three open-ended statements measuring the degree to which a person shops for clothing, shoes, and electronics outside of the town in which he/she resides.

SCALE ORIGIN: The scale is original to Wakefield and Baker (1998). The three particular product categories mentioned in the items were specified because of their relevance to products carried by the object of the study (mall tenants).

RELIABILITY: An alpha of .905 (n = 438) was reported for the scale by Wakefield and Baker (1998).

VALIDITY: The items in this scale were found to be unidimensional in a confirmatory factor analysis that also included several other scales from the study (Wakefield and Baker 1998).

REFERENCES:
Wakefield, Kirk L. and Julie Baker (1998), "Excitement at the Mall: Determinants and Effects on Shopping Response," *JR*, 74 (4), 515–539.

SCALE ITEMS: [1]

What percentage of your shopping is outside of _____?

1. I buy ___% of clothing *outside* of _____.

2. I buy ___% of shoes *outside* of _____.

3. I buy ___% of electronics *outside* of _____.

---

[1] The blank in the scale stem as well as the last blank in each item should have the name of the focal town placed in it. The first blank in each item is for respondents to write in their estimation of the portion of their shopping for that product category that takes place outside the specified town.

SCALE NAME: Parent-Adolescent Communication (Openness)

SCALE DESCRIPTION: The scale is designed to measure a person's perception of the openness of the communication between a parent and a child. If the scale is filled out by a child then the communication with a specific parent is described whereas when a parent fills out the scale, communication with a specific child is described. The scale is composed of ten, five-point Likert-type statements.

SCALE ORIGIN: The scale used by Palan (1998) was developed by Barnes and Olson (1982). The latter envisioned parent-child communication to have positive (openness) and negative aspects (problems). The openness aspect represented a free-flow exchange of information and lack of constraint between the parent and child. (See #300 for a description of the problems aspect.) Alphas ranging from .81 to .91 have been reported for this scale (Barnes and Olson 1982; Masselam et al. 1990).

RELIABILITY: Palan (1998) reported alphas of .85, .90, .79. and .81 for use of the scale by adolescents about the mothers, adolescents about their fathers, mothers about their children, and fathers about their children, respectively.

VALIDITY: One of the purposes of the study by Palan (1998) was to examine the validity of the Parent-Adolescent Communication scale. As indicated below, the validation was conducted on a sum of the scores of the items from the openness and the problems scales, with the scores from the latter being reversed. Using the Multi-trait, Multi-Informant method, evidence was provided in support of the combined scale's convergent and discriminant validities.

COMMENTS: Palan (1998) as a well as other users of the scale have summed the scores to this scale along with those from its companion scale, #300. This is because it is their combination that is viewed as representing the construct *communication quality*.

REFERENCES:

Barnes, Howard L. and David H. Olson (1982), "Parent-Adolescent Communication Scale," in *Family Inventories: Inventories Used in a National Survey of Families Across the Family Life Cycle*, David H. Olson , H. I. McCubbin , H. Barnes, A. Larsen., M. Muxen, and M. Wilson, ed. St. Paul: University of Minnesota, Family Social Science, 33–48.

Masselam, Venus S., Robert F. Marcus, and Clayton L. Stunkard (1990), "Parent-Adolescent Communication, Family Functioning, and School Performance," *Adolescence*, 25 (99), 725–737.

Palan, Kay M. (1998), "Relationships Between Family Communication and Consumer Activities of Adolescents: An Exploratory Study," *JAMS*, 26 (4), 338–349.

SCALE ITEMS: [1]

1. I can discuss my beliefs with my mother (father, child) without feeling restrained or embarrassed.

2. My mother (father, child) is always a good listener.

3. My mother (father, child) can tell how I am feeling without asking.

4. I am very satisfied with how my mother (father, child) and I talk together.

5. If I were in trouble, I could tell my mother (father, child).

6. I openly show affection to my mother (father, child).

7. When I ask questions, I get honest answers from my mother (father, child).

8. My mother (father, child) tries to understand my point of view.

9. I find it easy to discuss problems with my mother (father, child).

10. I find it easy to express all my true feelings to my mother (father, child).

[1] As noted by the parentheses in the statements, the phrasing of the items varies slightly depending upon who fills out the scale.

SCALE NAME: Parent-Adolescent Communication (Problems)

SCALE DESCRIPTION: The scale is designed to measure a person's perception of the problems involved in the communication between a parent and a child. If the scale is filled out by a child then the communication with a specific parent is described whereas when a parent fills out the scale, communication with a specific child is described. The scale is composed of ten, five-point Likert-type statements.

SCALE ORIGIN: The scale used by Palan (1998) was developed by Barnes and Olson (1982). The latter envisioned parent-child communication to have positive (openness) and negative aspects (problems). The problems aspect represented such things as hesitancy, selectivity, and caution in the exchange of information between the parent and child. (See #299 for a description of the openness aspect.) Alphas ranging from .74 to .79 have been reported for this scale (Barnes and Olson 1982; Masselam et al. 1990).

RELIABILITY: Palan (1998) reported alphas of .71, .71, .69. and .81 for use of the scale by adolescents about their mothers, adolescents about their fathers, mothers about their children, and fathers about their children, respectively.

VALIDITY: One of the purposes of the study by Palan (1998) was to examine the validity of the Parent-Adolescent Communication scale. As indicated below, the validation was conducted on a sum of the scores of the items from the openness and the problems scales, with the scores from the latter being reversed. Using the Multi-trait, Multi-Informant method, evidence was provided in support of the combined scale's convergent and discriminant validities.

COMMENTS: Palan (1998) as a well as other users of the scale have summed the scores to this scale as well as its companion scale, #299. This is because it is their combination that is viewed as representing communication quality.

REFERENCES:

Barnes, Howard L. and David H. Olson (1982), "Parent-Adolescent Communication Scale," in *Family Inventories: Inventories Used in a National Survey of Families Across the Family Life Cycle*, David H. Olson, H. I. McCubbin , H. Barnes, A. Larsen, M. Muxen, and M. Wilson, eds. St. Paul: University of Minnesota, Family Social Science 33–48.

Masselam, Venus S., Robert F. Marcus, and Clayton L. Stunkard (1990), "Parent-Adolescent Communication, Family Functioning, and School Performance," *Adolescence*, 25 (99), 725–737.

Palan, Kay M. (1998), "Relationships Between Family Communication and Consumer Activities of Adolescents: An Exploratory Study," *JAMS*, 26 (4), 338–349.

SCALE ITEMS: [1]

1. Sometimes I have trouble believing everything my mother (father, child) tells me.

2. I am sometimes afraid to ask my mother (father, child) for what I want.

3. My mother (father, child) has a tendency to say things to me that would be better left unsaid.

4. When we are having a problem, I often give my mother (father, child) the silent treatment.

5. I am careful about what I say to my mother (father, child).

6. When talking to my mother (father, child), I have a tendency to say things that would be better left unsaid.

7. There are topics I avoid discussing with my mother (father, child).

8. My mother (father, child) nags/bothers me.

9. My mother (father, child) insults me when she (he) is angry with me.

10. I don't think I can tell my mother (father, child) how I really feel about some things.

---

[1] As noted by the parentheses in the statements, the phrasing of the items varies slightly depending upon who fills out the scale.

SCALE NAME: Parental Exclusion of Outside Influences

SCALE DESCRIPTION: The scale is composed of three, five point Likert-type statements measuring the degree to which a person believes that a child should not learn to doubt his/her parent's views. It could also be viewed as a measure of parental ethnocentrism.

SCALE ORIGIN: The items seem to originate from Schaefer and Bell (1958) but may have been used even earlier. They discussed a considerable amount of testing of the items as part of a larger multi-scaled instrument. While the versions reported here were not tested in their studies, five- and eight-item versions were. The findings indicated that they had low but acceptable internal consistency and test-retest stability.

RELIABILITY: Carlson and Grossbart (1988) reported an alpha of .74 for the scale. Alphas of .67 (U.S.) and .53 (Japan) were reported for the scale by Rose (1999).

VALIDITY: No examination of scale validity was reported by Carlson and Grossbart (1988). Rose (1999) stated that a CFA indicated the set of scales they used "formed the expected dimensions" (p. 111). In particular, this scale and two others (#192 and #303) measured an anxious-emotional involvement dimension in a second order factor model.

COMMENTS: The reliability of the scale is low enough that some care should be exercised in its use as currently configured. Consideration should be given to improving the scale, possibly by testing longer versions. Additional items could come from those used by Schaefer and Bell (1958).

REFERENCES:

Carlson, Les and Sanford Grossbart (1988), "Parental Style and Consumer Socialization of Children," *JCR*, 15 (June), 77–94.

Rose, Gregory M. (1999), "Consumer Socialization, Parental Style, and Development Timetables in the United States and Japan," *JM*, 63 (July), 105–119.

Schaefer, Earl S. and Richard Q. Bell (1958), "Development of a Parental Attitude Research Instrument," *Child Development*, 29 (September), 339–361.

SCALE ITEMS:

Directions: Please indicate your opinion by checking one response (*strongly disagree, disagree, neither disagree or agree, agree, strongly agree*) for each statement. Check one for each statement.

1. A parent should never be made to look wrong in their children's eyes.

2. It's best for a child if he/she never gets started wondering whether their parent's views are right.

3. Children should never learn things outside the home which make them doubt their parent's ideas.

SCALE NAME: Parental Style (Authoritarian)

SCALE DESCRIPTION: The scale is composed of forced-choice items measuring the degree to which a parent expects unquestioning obedience and respect from his/her children.

SCALE ORIGIN: While this scale bears similarity to a construct described in Baumrind (1971), correspondence with Carlson indicated that the article did not highlight data collected with the scale but via observation. Carlson obtained the scale items in personal correspondence with Baumrind.

RELIABILITY: Carlson and Grossbart (1988) reported an alpha for the scale of .60. An alpha of .53 was reported for the version of the scale used by Carlson, Laczniak, and Walsh (2001).

VALIDITY: No examination of scale validity was reported in the studies reviewed.

COMMENTS: The low alpha indicates that the scale does not have good internal consistency and should be used cautiously until its reliability can be substantially improved.
    See also Walsh, Laczniak, and Carlson (1998).

REFERENCES:

Baumrind, Diana (1971), "Current Patterns of Parental Authority," *Developmental Psychology Monograph*, 4 (January), 1–103.

Carlson, Les and Sanford Grossbart (1988), "Parental Style and Consumer Socialization of Children," *JCR*, 15 (June), 77–94.

Carlson, Les, Russell N. Laczniak, and Ann Walsh (2001), "Socializing Children about Television: An Intergenerational Study," *JAMS*, 29 (3), 276–288.

Walsh, Ann D., Russell N. Laczniak, and Les Carlson (1998), "Mothers' Preferences for Regulating Children's Television," *JA*, 27 (3), 23–36.

SCALE ITEMS: [1]

Directions: Please indicate your opinion by checking one response (A or B) for each statement. There are no right or wrong answers, so answer according to your opinion. It is important to answer all questions even if you are not completely sure of your answer. Just check the response (A or B) that comes closest to your opinion. Some statements may seem alike but are necessary to show slight differences of opinion. All questions refer to your youngest child who attends this school.

    A. A child should be able to question the authority of his/her parents.
    B. A child should honor his/her mother and father and accept their authority.

    A. The preservation of order and tradition should be highly valued.
    B. There is no reason for the younger generation to preserve the order and traditions set by the older generation. (r)

    A. When a child is called, he/she should come immediately.
    B. A child should not have to come immediately when he/she is called. (r)

    A. Not all parents deserve the respect of their children.
    B. A child should respect his/her parents because they are his/her parents.

A. I don't mind it particularly when my child argues with me.
B. I don't particularly like my child to argue with me.

Children would be less likely to get into trouble with the law:

A. if parents taught their children respect for authority.
B. if parents listened more to what their children had to say. (r)

A. Parents should take seriously the opinions of young children.
B. Most young children change their minds so frequently that it is hard to take their opinions seriously.

[1] This is the version of the scale used by Carlson and Grossbart (1988); the version of the scale used by Carlson, Laczniak, and Walsh (2001) had only six of the items (unspecified). Selection of answer A of a pair should be scored as a 1 while answer B should be scored as a 2, reverse scoring where indicated. Higher scores on the scale mean that parents expect their children to respect and obey them with little or no back-talking.

SCALE NAME: Parental Style (Protective)

SCALE DESCRIPTION: The scale is composed of statements measuring the degree to which a person (a parent) believes that a child should be shielded from discouraging and difficult situations. The statements are extreme enough that they might be viewed as reflecting over-protectedness on the part of those who agree with them. This scale was called *fostering dependency* by Schaefer and Bell (1958), Carlson and Grossbart (1988), and Rose (1999).

SCALE ORIGIN: The items seem to originate from Schaefer and Bell (1958) but may have been used even earlier. They discussed a considerable amount of testing of the items as part of a larger multi-scaled instrument. While the versions reported here were not tested in their studies, five- and eight-item versions were. The findings indicated that they had low but acceptable internal consistency and test-retest stability.

RELIABILITY: Carlson and Grossbart (1988) reported an alpha of .60 for the scale. Alphas of .70 (U.S.) and .60 (Japan) were reported for the scale by Rose (1999).

VALIDITY: No examination of scale validity was reported by Carlson and Grossbart (1988). Rose (1999) stated that a CFA indicated the set of scales they used "formed the expected dimensions" (p. 111). In particular, this scale and two others (#192 and #301) measured an anxious-emotional involvement dimension in a second order factor model.

REFERENCES:

Carlson, Les and Sanford Grossbart (1988), "Parental Style and Consumer Socialization of Children," *JCR*, 15 (June), 77–94.

Rose, Gregory M. (1999), "Consumer Socialization, Parental Style, and Development Timetables in the United States and Japan," *JM*, 63 (July), 105–119.

Schaefer, Earl S. and Richard Q. Bell (1958), "Development of a Parental Attitude Research Instrument," *Child Development*, 29 (September), 339–361.

SCALE ITEMS: [1]

Directions: Please indicate your opinion by checking one response (*strongly disagree, disagree, neither disagree or agree, agree, strongly agree*) for each statement. Check one for each statement.

1. A mother should do her best to avoid disappointment for her child.

2. A good mother should shelter her child from life's little difficulties.

3. Children should be kept away from all hard jobs which might be discouraging.

4. Parents should know better than to allow their children to be exposed to difficult situations.

[1] Carlson and Grossbart (1988) used items 3 and 4 whereas Rose (1999) used all four.

SCALE NAME: Parental Style (Strict)

SCALE DESCRIPTION: The scale is composed of five point Likert-type statements measuring the degree to which a parent believes that being strict with children is the appropriate method for raising them.

SCALE ORIGIN: The items seem to originate from Schaefer and Bell (1958) but may have been used even earlier. They discussed a considerable amount of testing of the items as part of a larger multi-scaled instrument. While the three- and four-item versions reported here were not tested in their studies, five- and eight-item versions were. The findings indicated that they had reasonable though not high internal consistency and test-retest stability.

RELIABILITY: Carlson and Grossbart (1988) reported an alpha of .81 for the scale. Carlson, Laczniak, and Walsh (2001) reported an alpha of .85. Alphas of .72 (U.S.) and .69 (Japan) were reported for the scale by Rose (1999).

VALIDITY: No examination of scale validity was reported by Carlson and Grossbart (1988) or Carlson, Laczniak, and Walsh (2001). Rose (1999) stated that a CFA indicated the set of scales they used "formed the expected dimensions" (p. 111). In particular, this scale and two others (#295 and #304) produced a restrictiveness dimension in a second order factor model.

COMMENTS: See also Walsh, Laczniak, and Carlson (1998).

REFERENCES:
Carlson, Les and Sanford Grossbart (1988), "Parental Style and Consumer Socialization of Children," *JCR*, 15 (June), 77–94.
Carlson, Les, Russell N. Laczniak, and Ann Walsh (2001), "Socializing Children about Television: An Intergenerational Study," *JAMS*, 29 (3), 276–288.
Rose, Gregory M. (1999), "Consumer Socialization, Parental Style, and Development Timetables in the United States and Japan," *JM*, 63 (July), 105–119.
Schaefer, Earl S. and Richard Q. Bell (1958), "Development of a Parental Attitude Research Instrument," *Child Development*, 29 (September), 339–361.
Walsh, Ann D., Russell N. Laczniak, and Les Carlson (1998), "Mothers' Preferences for Regulating Children's Television," *JA*, 27 (3), 23–36.

SCALE ITEMS: [1]

Directions: Please indicate your opinion by checking one response (*strongly disagree, disagree, neither disagree or agree, agree, strongly agree*) for each statement. Check one for each statement.

1. A child will be grateful later on for strict training.

2. Strict discipline develops a fine, strong character.

3. Children who are held to strong rules grow up to be the best adults.

4. Most children should have more discipline than they get.

---

[1] The version of the scale used by Carlson, Laczniak, and Walsh (2001) had only three of these items (unspecified).

SCALE NAME: Perfectionism

SCALE DESCRIPTION: The scale is composed of eight, Likert-type statements measuring a person's need for accuracy and the tendency to experience displeasure with self when mistakes are made.

SCALE ORIGIN: Kopalle and Lehmann (2001) stated that they drew upon measures by Frost (1990; 1993) as well as Hewitt and Flett (1991).

RELIABILITY: Alphas of .69 (Study 1) and .88 (Study 2) were reported for the scale (Kopalle and Lehmann 2001).

VALIDITY: While an in-depth analysis of the scale's validity was not provided by Kopalle and Lehmann (2001), they did indicate that factor analyses of items from several scales showed the items in this scale to be unidimensional in both studies.

REFERENCES:

Frost, Randy O., Richard G. Heimberg, Craig S. Holt, and Jill I. Mattia (1993), "A Comparison of Two Measures of Perfectionism," *Personality and Individual Differences*, 14 (1), 119–26.

Frost, Randy O., Patricia Marten, Cathleen Lahart, and Robin Rosenblate (1990), "The Dimensions of Perfectionism," *Cognitive Therapy and Research*, 14 (5), 449–68.

Hewitt, Paul L. and Gordon L. Flett (1991), "A Perfectionism in the Self and Social Contexts: Conceptualization, Assessment, and Association with Psychopathology," *Journal of Personality and Social Psychology*, 60 (3), 456–70.

Kopalle, Praveen K. and Donald R. Lehmann (2001), "Strategic Management of Expectations: The Role of Disconfirmation Sensitivity and Perfectionism," *JMR*, 38 (August), 386–394.

SCALE ITEMS: [1]

1. I hate being less than the best at things.

2. I get mad at myself when I make mistakes.

3. It is very important for me to be right.

4. It makes me uneasy to see an error in my work.

5. One of my goals is to be perfect in everything I do.

6. I should be upset if I make a mistake.

7. Little errors bother me a lot.

8. People will probably think less of me if I make a mistake.

[1] A six-point response format was used by Kopalle and Lehmann (2001) in Study 1 while a seven-point scale was used in the second study.

SCALE NAME: Performance Expectations (Prepurchase)

SCALE DESCRIPTION: Five, seven point items compose the scale. The items are intended to measure some quality-related aspects of a service provider thought to be true by a potential customer prior to actually making the purchase and/or receiving the service. As currently written, the items are most appropriate for a hotel but might be adjustable for other types of service providers. Further, they are stated tentatively since respondents would not have actually visited the service provider at the time they complete the scale.

SCALE ORIGIN: Although drawing upon the work of others (e.g., Parasuraman, Zeithaml, and Berry 1988), the scale was developed for the study conducted by Voss, Parasuraman, and Grewal (1998).

RELIABILITY: Average construct reliability was reported to be .90 (Voss, Parasuraman, and Grewal 1998).

VALIDITY: Voss, Parasuraman, and Grewal (1998) reported an average variance extracted of .75. Evidence was also supplied in support of the scale's convergent and discriminant validities.

REFERENCES:
Parasuraman, A., Valarie A. Zeithaml, and Leonard L. Berry (1988), "SERVQUAL: A Multiple-Item Scale for Measuring Consumer Perceptions of Service Quality," *JR*, 64 (Spring), 12–40.
Voss, Glenn B., A. Parasuraman, and Dhruv Grewal (1998), "The Roles of Price, Performance, and Expectations in Determining Satisfaction in Service Exchanges," *JM*, 62 (October), 46–61.

SCALE ITEMS: [1]

If I were to stay at this hotel:

1. the hotel would offer excellent overall service.

2. the hotel would offer accurate and dependable service.

3. the employees would be courteous at all times.

4. the employees would provide prompt assistance at check-in.

5. the employees would provide personal, individualized attention.

[1] Responses to all items were made using a seven-point scale anchored by *definitely would not* (1) and *definitely would* (7).

SCALE NAME: Performance Perceptions (Postpurchase)

SCALE DESCRIPTION: Five, seven-point items compose the scale. The items are intended to measure a customer's quality-related perceptions of a service provider after making a purchase and/or receiving the service. As currently written, the items are most appropriate for a hotel but might be adjusted for other types of service providers.

SCALE ORIGIN: Although drawing upon the work of others (e.g., Parasuraman, Zeithaml, and Berry 1988), the scale was developed for the study conducted by Voss, Parasuraman, and Grewal (1998).

RELIABILITY: Average construct reliability was reported to be .83 (Voss, Parasuraman, and Grewal 1998).

VALIDITY: Voss, Parasuraman, and Grewal (1998) reported an average variance extracted of .62. Evidence was also supplied in support of the scale's convergent and discriminant validities.

REFERENCES:
Parasuraman, A., Valarie A. Zeithaml, and Leonard L. Berry (1988), "SERVQUAL: A Multiple-Item Scale for Measuring Consumer Perceptions of Service Quality," *JR*, 64 (Spring), 12–40.
Voss, Glenn B., A. Parasuraman, and Dhruv Grewal (1998), "The Roles of Price, Performance, and Expectations in Determining Satisfaction in Service Exchanges," *JM*, 62 (October), 46–61.

SCALE ITEMS: [1]

1. The service provided by this hotel was:
   Very low quality / very high quality

2. The service provided by this hotel was:
   Unreliable / reliable

3. The hotel's employees were:
   Courteous / discourteous (r)

4. The hotel's employees were:
   Helpful / not helpful (r)

5. The hotel's employees were:
   Caring / uncaring (r)

---

[1] Responses to all items were made using a seven-point scale using the anchors shown.

SCALE NAME: Pleasantness

SCALE DESCRIPTION: The scale measures the degree to which one reports experiencing a pleasing feeling. It appears like the scale can be used to measure the emotional response to a stimulus (e.g., Mano and Oliver 1993) or a mood that one feels prior to exposure to a stimulus of interest (e.g., Mano 1999).

SCALE ORIGIN: Dawson, Bloch, and Ridgway (1990) stated that they took items for their scale from Mehrabian (1980).

Although not expressly indicated by Mano and Oliver (1993), the items they used appear to have been used first as a summated scale by Mano (1991). In his study with 224 college students the scale was reported to have an alpha of .82. Cluster and factor analyses grouped these three items together by themselves.

Mano (1999) identified his earlier work (1991) as the source of the scale.

It may also be noted that this scale is very similar to one used to measure essentially the same construct except that this one uses uni-polar adjectives whereas the other one uses bi-polar adjectives. That latter has been used many times and derives from the work of Mehrabian and Russell (1974).

RELIABILITY: Alphas of .72 (n = 278) and .81 (n = 118) were reported for the versions of the scale used by Dawson, Bloch, and Ridgway (1990) and Mano and Oliver (1993), respectively. Alphas of .78 (n = 151) and .76 were reported for the version of the scale used by Mano (1999) in pre-task and post-task assessments, respectively.

VALIDITY: Dawson, Bloch, and Ridgway (1990) performed an exploratory factor analysis on the items composing this scale as well as three other items composing an Arousal scale. Although the items loaded highest on their respective factors it was mentioned that one item (happy) had split loadings.

Mano (1999) indicated that factor analysis supported a one factor solution.

REFERENCES:

Dawson, Scott, Peter H. Bloch, and Nancy M. Ridgway (1990), "Shopping Motives, Emotional States, and Retail Outcomes," *JR*, 66 (Winter), 408–427.

Mano, Haim (1991), "The Structure and Intensity of Emotional Experiences: Method and Context Convergence," *Multivariate Behavioral Research*, 26 (3), 389–411.

Mano, Haim (1999), "The Influence of Pre-Existing Negative Affect on Store Purchase Intentions," *JR*, 75 (2), 149–172.

Mano, Haim and Richard L. Oliver (1993), "Assessing the Dimensionality and Structure of the Consumption Experience: Evaluation, Feeling, and Satisfaction," *JCR*, 20 (December), 451–466.

Mehrabian, Albert (1980), *Basic Dimensions for a General Psychological Theory*, Cambridge: MA: Oelgeschlager, Gunn and Hain.

Mehrabian, Albert and James A. Russell (1974), *An Approach to Environmental Psychology*, Cambridge, MA: The MIT Press.

#308 *Pleasantness*

SCALE ITEMS: [1]

1. in a good mood

2. happy

3. satisfied

4. pleased

5. contented

6. relaxed

---

[1] Each study used a five-point response format. The anchors of the scale used by Dawson, Bloch, and Ridgway (1990) were *does not describe at all* and *describes a great deal*. Mano and Oliver (1993) used items 1 to 4 and indicated that the anchors were *not at all* and *very much*. Mano (1999) used that same set of four items but did not specify the anchors on the response scale.

SCALE NAME: Pleasantness

SCALE DESCRIPTION: The scale is supposed to measure the pleasantness-related dimension of a feeling a person is experiencing at some point in time or immediately after exposure to some stimulus. Three versions were used by Broach, Page, and Wilson (1995): one to measure how subjects felt before the experimental manipulation (*prior pleasantness*), one to measure the effect of the treatment (*program pleasantness*), and one to measure the feeling evoked by an ad (*commercial pleasantness*). The version used by Ellen and Bone (1998) had to do with the smell of an object.

SCALE ORIGIN: Broach, Page, and Wilson (1995) stated that the items for the scale were selected from Averill's (1975) semantic atlas of emotional words. However, use of the terms as a set in a summated format appears to be original to their own study. The scale was pretested with about 25 undergraduate students. The alphas for the version used with four different programs ranged from .85 to .96. Similarly, alphas for the *commercial pleasantness* version of the scale ranged from .90 to .96.

Ellen and Bone (1998) did not specify the source of their scale.

RELIABILITY: Alphas ranging from .86 to .97 (*prior pleasantness*), .84 to .94 (*program pleasantness*), and .85 to .97 (*commercial pleasantness*) were reported for the scale (Broach, Page, and Wilson 1995). Ellen and Bone (1998) reported an alpha of .96 for the version of the scale they used.

VALIDITY: No examination of the scale's validity was reported by Broach, Page, and Wilson (1995) or Ellen and Bone (1998).

REFERENCES:
Averill, James R. (1975), "A Semantic Atlas of Emotional Concepts," *JSAS Catalogue of Selected Documents in Psychology*, 330.
Broach, V. Carter, Jr., Thomas J. Page, Jr., and R. Dale Wilson (1995), "Television Programming and Its Influence on Viewers' Perceptions of Commercials: The Role of Program Arousal and Pleasantness," *JA*, 24 (Winter), 45–54.
Ellen, Pam Scholder and Paula Fitzgerald Bone (1998), "Does It Matter If It Smells? Olfactory Stimuli As Advertising Executional Cues" *JA*, 27 (4), 29–39.

SCALE ITEMS: [1]

1. negative / positive

2. bad / good

3. awful / nice

4. sad / happy

#309 *Pleasantness*

5. unpleasant / pleasant

6. agreeable / disagreeable

---

[1] Ellen and Bone (1998) used items 2, 5, and 6 in a seven-point format. Broach, Page, and Wilson (1995) used items 1-5 in a seven-point format with the following scale stems:

- for version measuring prior pleasantness: "At this time I feel . . ."
- for version measuring program pleasantness: "Did the program as a whole make you feel . . ."
- for version measuring commercial pleasantness: "Did the commercial as a whole make you feel . . ."

SCALE NAME: Pleasure

SCALE DESCRIPTION: The scale is used to assess one's affective reaction to an environmental stimulus with an emphasis on its degree of pleasantness. As used by Raghunathan and Irwin (2001), the scale was considered a measure of mood.

SCALE ORIGIN: Several of the items come from the work of Mehrabian and Russell (1974). Given previous work by others as well as their own research, they proposed that there are three dimensions that underlie all emotional reactions to environmental stimuli. They referred to the three factors as pleasure, arousal, and dominance. A series of studies were used to develop measures of each factor. A study of the "final" set of items used 214 University of California undergraduates, each of whom used the scales to evaluate a different subset of six situations. (The analysis was based, therefore, on 1284 observations.) A principal components factor analysis with oblique rotation was used and the expected three factors emerged. Pleasure, arousal, and dominance explained 27%, 23%, and 14% of the available variance, respectively. Scores on the pleasure scale had correlations of 0.07 and 0.03 with arousal and dominance, respectively.

RELIABILITY: The internal consistency for this scale has tended to be good across studies with a variety of samples, typically having reliabilities well above .80. Specific reliabilities are reported below along with the items used by the various researchers in their respective studies.

VALIDITY: Aylesworth and MacKenzie (1998) collected data on all six items shown below but dropped item #6 in calculating scale scores due to the item's unacceptably low factor loading as well as its low communality estimate compared to the other items.

Some idea of the scale's convergent validity can be taken from correlations between it and another scale used to measure the same construct (Bateson and Hui 1992, p. 278). In three different situations the correlations were .65 or higher providing evidence that the two measures were tapping into the same construct.

A principal components factor analysis performed by Donovan et al. (1994) indicated that all six of the pleasure-related items loaded highest on the same dimension and low on one related to arousal.

Wirtz, Matilla, and Tan (2000) performed a confirmatory factor analysis on this scale and a couple of others with the results providing some evidence of each scale's convergent and discriminant validity. Further evidence of the scale's discriminant validity came from noting that its average variance extracted was higher than it was for the squared correlation between it and any of the other two constructs (Fornell and Larcker 1981). Some evidence of nomological validity came from noting, as expected from previous research, that pleasure had a high correlation with satisfaction.

COMMENTS: As noted above, this scale was originally developed along with two other scales, arousal and dominance. Although scored separately, they are frequently used together in a study.

See also Havlena and Holbrook (1986), Hui and Bateson (1991), Menon and Kahn (1995), Mitchell, Kahn, and Knasko (1995), Nyer (1997), and Olney, Holbrook, and Batra (1991).

REFERENCES:

Aylesworth, Andrew B. and Scott B. MacKenzie (1998), "Context Is Key: The Effect of Program-Induced Mood on Thoughts about the Ad," *JA*, 27 (Summer), 17–31.

Bateson, John E. G. and Michael K. Hui (1992), "The Ecological Validity of Photographic Slides and Video-tapes in Simulating the Service Setting," *JCR*, 19 (September), 271–281.

Donovan, Robert J., John R. Rossiter, Gilian Marcoolyn, and Andrew Nesdale (1994), "Store Atmosphere and Purchasing Behavior," *JR*, 70 (3), 283–294.

Fornell, Claes and David F. Larcker (1981), "Evaluating Structural Equation Models with Unobservable Variables and Measurement Error," *JMR*, 18 (February), 39–50.

Havlena, William J. and Morris B. Holbrook (1986), "The Varieties of Consumption Experience: Comparing Two Typologies of Emotion in Consumer Behavior," *JCR*, 13 (December), 394–404.

Holbrook, Morris B., Robert W. Chestnut, Terence A. Oliva, and Eric A. Greenleaf (1984), "Play as a Consumption Experience: The Roles of Emotions, Performance, and Personality in the Enjoyment of Games," *JCR*, 11 (September), 728–739.

Howard, Daniel J., and Charles Gengler (2001), "Emotional Contagion Effects on Product Attitudes," *JCR*, 28 (September), 189–201.

Hui, Michael K. and John E. G. Bateson (1991), "Perceived Control and the Effects of Crowding and Consumer Choice on the Service Experience," *JCR*, 18 (September), 174–184.

Hui, Michael K. and David K. Tse (1996), "What to Tell Consumers in Waits of Different Lengths: An Integrative Model of Service Evaluation," *JM*, 60 (April), 81–90.

Hui, Michael K., Mrugank V. Thakor, and Ravi Gill (1998), "The Effect of Delay Type and Service Stage on Consumers' Reactions to Waiting," *JCR*, 24 (March), 469–479.

Mattila, Anna S. and Jochen Wirtz (2001), "Congruency of Scent and Music as a Driver of In-store Evaluations and Behaviour," *JR*, 77 (2), 273–289.

Mehrabian, Albert and James A. Russell (1974), *An Approach to Environmental Psychology*, Cambridge, MA: The MIT Press.

Menon, Satya and Barbara E. Kahn (1995), "The Impact of Context on Variety Seeking in Product Choices," *JCR*, 22 (December), 285–295.

Mitchell, Deborah, Barbara E. Kahn, and Susan C. Knasko (1995), "There's Something in the Air: Effects of Congruent or Incongruent Ambient Odor on Consumer Decision Making," *JCR*, 22 (September), 229–238.

Neelamegham, Ramya and Dipak Jain (1999), "Consumer Choice Process for Experience Goods: An Econometric Model and Analysis," *JMR*, 36 (August), 373–386.

Nyer, Prashanth U. (1997), "A Study of the relationships Between Cognitive Appraisals and Consumption Emotions," *JAMS*, 25 (Fall), 296–304.

Olney, Thomas J., Morris B. Holbrook, and Rajeev Batra (1991), "Consumer Responses to Advertising: The Effects of Ad Content, Emotions, and Attitude toward the Ad on Viewing Time," *JCR*, 17 (March), 440–453.

Raghunathan, Rajagopal and Julie Irwin (2001), "Walking the Hedonic Product Treadmill: Default Contrast and Mood-Based Assimilation in Judgments of Predicted Happiness with a Target Product," *JCR*, 28 (December), 355–368.

Simpson, Penny M., Steve Horton, and Gene Brown (1996), "Male Nudity in Advertisements: A Modified Replication and Extension of Gender and Product Effects," *JAMS*, 24 (Summer), 257–262.

Wirtz, Jochen, Anna S. Matilla, and Rachel L.P. Tan (2000), "The Moderating Role of Target-Arousal on the Impact of Affect on Satisfaction-An Examination in the Context of Service Experience," *JR*, 76 (3), 347–365.

SCALE ITEMS: [1]

Rate your emotions according to the way the _____ made you feel.

1. happy / unhappy

2. pleased / annoyed

3. satisfied / unsatisfied

4. contented / melancholic

5. hopeful / despairing

6. relaxed / bored

7. joyful / not joyful

Aylesworth and MacKenzie (1998): 1–5 [.85]
Bateson and Hui (1992): item set unknown [.86]
Donovan et al. (1994): 1–6 [.88]
Holbrook et al. (1984): 1–6 [.89]
Howard and Gengler (2001): 1, 2*, 7 7-point [.80–.92]
Hui and Tse (1996): 1–3, 6 [.87]
Hui, Thakor, and Gill (1998): 1–3 [.89]
Mattila and Wirtz (2001): 1–6 7-point [.89]
Neelamegham and Jain (1999): 2–4, 7-point [.85]
Raghunathan and Irwin (2001): 1–3 11-point [.76, .83]
Simpson, Horton, and Brown (1996): 1–6 [.96]
Wirtz, Matilla and Tan (2000): 1–6 [.92]

[1] This is a possible scale stem that can be used with the items. The asterisk next to some of the items indicates that one item of a pair was different from what is shown in the list.

SCALE NAME: Prestige Importance

SCALE DESCRIPTION: Three, seven-point uni-polar items are used to measure how much a person considers prestige to be an important criterion when shopping for a specified product. The product category examined by Kirmani, Sood, and Bridges (1999) was jeans.

SCALE ORIGIN: Although not stated explicitly, the scale is apparently original to Kirmani, Sood, and Bridges (1999).

RELIABILITY: An alpha of .91 was reported for the scale (Kirmani, Sood, and Bridges 1999).

VALIDITY: No examination of the scale's validity was reported by Kirmani, Sood, and Bridges (1999).

REFERENCES:

Kirmani, Amna, Sanjay Sood, and Sheri Bridges (1999), "The Ownership Effect in Consumer Responses to Brand Line Stretches," *JM*, 63 (January), 88–101.

SCALE ITEMS: [1]

1. prestige

2. exclusivity

3. status

---

[1] The verbal anchors used by Kirmani, Sood, and Bridges (1999) with these items were not specified, however, the typical Likert-type approach (*agree / disagree*) would appear to be appropriate.

SCALE NAME: Prestigiousness

SCALE DESCRIPTION: The scale is composed of three, seven-point uni-polar items that measure how much a person considers some specific object to be high class and exclusive.

SCALE ORIGIN: Although not stated explicitly, the scale is apparently original to Kirmani, Sood, and Bridges (1999).

RELIABILITY: An alpha of .96 was reported for the scale (Kirmani, Sood, and Bridges 1999).

VALIDITY: No examination of the scale's validity was reported by Kirmani, Sood, and Bridges (1999).

REFERENCES:
Kirmani, Amna, Sanjay Sood, and Sheri Bridges (1999), "The Ownership Effect in Consumer Responses to Brand Line Stretches," *JM*, 63 (January), 88–101.

SCALE ITEMS: [1]

1. prestigious

2. exclusive

3. high status

---

[1] The verbal anchors used by Kirmani, Sood, and Bridges (1999) with these items were not specified, however, the typical Likert-type approach (*agree / disagree*) would appear to be appropriate.

SCALE NAME: Price (Internal Reference)

SCALE DESCRIPTION: The scale is composed of three, open-ended items intended to measure the price(s) a consumer mentally links to some specific product. Grewal et al. (1998) referred to the scale as *internal reference price*.

SCALE ORIGIN: Although the authors drew upon items used in past research (Lichtenstein and Bearden 1989; Urbany, Bearden, and Weilbaker 1988), Grewal et al. (1998) used them as a summated rating scale.

RELIABILITY: Composite reliability for the scale was reported to be .91 (Grewal et al. 1998).

VALIDITY: A variety of tests conducted by Grewal et al. (1998) indicated the scale was unidimensional and showed evidence of discriminant validity. The variance extracted was .97.

REFERENCES:

Grewal, Dhruv, R. Krishnan, Julie Baker, and Norm Borin (1998), "The Effect of Store Name, Brand Name and Price Discounts on Consumers' Evaluations and Purchase Intentions," *JR*, 74 (3), 331–352.

Lichtenstein, Donald R. and William O. Bearden (1989), "Contextual Influences on Perceptions of Merchant-Supplied Reference Prices," *JCR*, 16 (1), 55–66.

Urbany, Joel E., William O. Bearden, and Dan C. Weilbaker (1988), "The Effect of Plausible and Exaggerated Reference Prices on Consumer Perceptions and Price Search," *JCR*, 15 (June), 95–100.

SCALE ITEMS: [1]

1. Retailer's normal price.

2. Average market price.

3. Fair price for the _____.

---

[1] The generic name of the product category should be placed in the blank. Responses were open-ended and in a standard monetary unit value (e.g., dollars).

SCALE NAME: Price (Product)

SCALE DESCRIPTION: The scale is composed of three, five-point Likert-type statements attempting to capture a consumer's subjective sense of a product's price with an emphasis on its expensiveness.

SCALE ORIGIN: Although Yoo, Donthu, and Lee (2000) said they drew upon items by Smith and Park (1992), ultimately their scale appears to be original to them.

RELIABILITY: Yoo, Donthu, and Lee (2000) reported the scale to have a composite reliability of .88.

VALIDITY: Factor analyses (EFA and CFA) were used to check the dimensionality of this scale along with eight others used in the study. Based on the results, the authors concluded that all items loaded on their respective factors as expected providing some sense of the scales' convergent and discriminant validities. The average variance extracted for this scale was .72.

REFERENCES:
Smith, Daniel C. and Whan Park (1992), "The Effects of Brand Extensions on Market Share and Advertising Efficiency," *JMR*, 29 (August), 296–313.
Yoo, Boonghee, Naveen Donthu, and Sungho Lee (2000), "An Examination of Selected Marketing Mix Elements and Brand Equity," *JAMS*, 28 (2), 195–211.

SCALE ITEMS: [1]

1. The price of _____ is high.

2. The price of _____ is low. (r)

3. _____ is expensive.

---

[1] The brand name of a product was placed in the blanks by Yoo, Donthu, and Lee (2000).

SCALE NAME: Price Consciousness

SCALE DESCRIPTION: The scale is composed of various, Likert-type items measuring the degree to which a consumer focuses on sales and trying to get the "best price."

SCALE ORIGIN: These items below and/or inspiration for them came from an early classic study of psychographics by Wells and Tigert (1971). One thousand questionnaires were mailed to homemaker members of the Market Facts mail panel. In addition to gathering demographic, product use, and media data, the survey contained 300 statements which have served as the basis for the construction of many lifestyle-related scales ever since. While the four items for this scale are reported in the article, they were not analyzed as a multi-item scale. The purpose of the article was to explain how psychographics could improve upon mere demographic description of target audiences and product users. No psychometric information was reported.

One of the first known uses of the items as a multi-item scale was in Darden and Perreault (1976). Analysis was based on self-administered questionnaires completed by 278 suburban housewives randomly selected in Athens, Georgia. A split-half reliability of .70 was reported for the scale. Price consciousness did <u>not</u> significantly differentiate between the outshopping groups.

RELIABILITY: An alpha of .67 was reported by Dickerson and Gentry (1983). Barak and Stern (1985/1986) say only that the scale's alpha was above .5. The version of the scale used by Donthu (and Garcia 1999; and Gilliland 1996) was reported to have alphas of .72 and .81, respectively. The construct reliability (LISREL) for the version of the scale used by Mittal (1994) was reported to be .69.

An alpha of .65 was reported for the scale used by Tat and Bejou (1994). Alphas of .67 and .66 were reported for blacks and whites, respectively. The internal consistency of the scale is somewhat low and care should be exercised in its use.

VALIDITY: The validity of the scale was not specifically addressed by Mittal (1994) except to say the tests that were conducted provided support for discriminant validity. Tat and Bejou (1994) did not directly test the validity of the scale. However, they did perform a couple of factor analyses on a total set of 24 items to purify the scales they developed. Factor loadings for the overall sample were respectable but the loading of item #5 (below) was rather low for blacks (.40) compared to whites (.74).

COMMENTS: It is noteworthy that this scale in some of its forms displays low reliability. A possible reason for this is that three slightly different subconstructs are being measured such as comparison shopping, inspection of prices on products at the store, and watching ads for sales. Some attention should be given to this issue along with some redevelopmental effort if the scale is to be used again.

See also Arora (1985), Burnett and Bush (1986), Heslop, Moran, and Cousineau (1981), Korgaonkar (1984), and Schnaars and Schiffman (1984) for other uses or variations on the measure.

REFERENCES:

Arora, Raj (1985), "Involvement: Its Measurement for Retail Store Research," *JAMS*, 13 (Spring), 229–241.

Barak, Benny and Barbara Stern (1985/1986), "Women's Age in Advertising: An Examination of Two Consumer Age Profiles," *JAR*, 25 (Dec./Jan.), 38–47.

Burnett, John J. and Alan J. Bush (1986), "Profiling the Yuppies," *JAR*, 26 (April/May), 27–35.

Darden, William R. and William D. Perreault, Jr. (1976), "Identifying Interurban Shoppers: Multiproduct Purchase Patterns and Segmentation Profiles," *JMR*, 13 (Feb.), 51–60.

Dickerson, Mary D. and James W. Gentry (1983), "Characteristics of Adopters and Non-Adopters of Home Computers," *JCR*, 10 (Sept.), 225–235.

Donthu, Naveen and Adriana Garcia (1999), "The Internet Shopper," *JAR*, 39 (May/June), 52–58.

Donthu, Naveen and David Gilliland (1996), "The Infomercial Shopper," *JAR*, 36 (March/April), 69–76.

Heslop, Louise A., Lori Moran, and Amy Cousineau (1981), "Consciousness in Energy Conservation Behavior: An Exploratory Study," *JAMS*, 8 (Dec.), 299–305.

Korgaonkar, Pradeep K. (1984), "Consumer Shopping Orientations, Non-Store Retailers, and Consumers' Patronage Intentions: A Multivariate Investigation," *JAMS*, 12 (Winter), 11–22.

Mittal, Banwari (1994), "An Integrated Framework for Relating Diverse Consumer Characteristics to Supermarket Coupon Redemption," *JMR*, 31 (November), 533–544.

Schhaars, Steven P. and Leon G. Schiffman (1984), "An Application of a Segmetation Design Based on the Hybrid of Canonical Correlation and Simple Cross-Tabulation," *JAMS*, 12 (Fall), 177–189.

Tat, Peter K. and David Bejou (1994), "Examining Black Consumer Motives For Coupon Usage," *JAR*, 34 (March/April), 29–35.

Wells, William D. and Douglas Tigert (1971), "Activities, Interests, and Opinions," *JAR*, 11 (Aug.), 27–35.

SCALE ITEMS: [1]

1. I shop a lot for "specials."

2. I find myself checking the prices in the grocery store even for small items.

3. I usually watch the advertisements for announcements of sales.

4. A person can save a lot of money by shopping around for bargains.

5. I check the prices even for inexpensive items.

6. I pay attention to sales and specials.

7. Clothing, furniture, appliances, . . .whatever I buy, I shop around to get the best prices.

8. I usually purchase the cheapest item.

9. I usually purchase items on sale only.

Barak and Stern (1985/1986): 1, 2, 3, 4 6-point
Dickerson and Gentry (1983): 1, 2, 3, 4 6-point
Donthu and Garcia (1999): 2*, 4, 8, 9 5-point
Donthu and Gilliland (1996): 2*, 4, 8, 9 5-point
Mittal (1994): 1, 2, 7 5-point
Tat and Bejou (1994): 1, 5, 6 5-point

[1] Asterisks indicate that a scale item used in a study was similar to one shown but varied somewhat in phrasing.

SCALE NAME: Price Consciousness

SCALE DESCRIPTION: Three Likert-type statements are used to measure a consumer's stated tendency to make product purchase decisions that are heavily influenced by price.

SCALE ORIGIN: The scale was apparently developed by Lichtenstein, Bloch, and Black (1988). In their usage, the items specifically referred to "running shoes" whereas in the other studies the phrasing seems to have been more general.

RELIABILITY: The reliability of the scale was reported to be .66 in the studies by Lichtenstein, Bloch, and Black (1988) as well as Baumgartner and Steenkamp (2001). The latter's pan-European survey of eleven countries reported alphas ranging from .60 to .75. Alphas of .78, .74, and .69 were reported by Huff and Alden (1998) for the scale as used in Thailand, Taiwan, and Malaysia, respectively.

VALIDITY: The purpose of the study by Baumgartner and Steenkamp (2001) was to examine response styles as a source of contamination in questionnaire measures and the effect that might have on the validity of conclusions drawn from such data. Although most of the results were reported at an overall level one finding pertinent to this scale was that the mean level of contamination in scale scores was estimated to be 4% (ranging from 1%-15% for eleven European countries), lower than the average amount of contamination found for the 14 scales examined.

No examination of the scale's validity was reported in the other studies.

REFERENCES:

Baumgartner, Hans and Jan-Benedict E.M. Steenkamp (2001), "Response Styles in Marketing Research: A Cross-National Investigation," *JMR*, 38 (May), 143–156.

Huff, Lenard C. and Dana L. Alden (1998), "An Investigation of Consumer Response to Sales Promotions In Developing Markets: A Three-Country Analysis," *JAR*, 38 (May/June), 47–56.

Lichtenstein, Donald R., Peter H. Bloch, and William C. Black (1988), "Correlates of Price Acceptability," *JCR*, 15 (Sept.), 243–252.

SCALE ITEMS: [1]

1. I usually buy consumer products when they are on sale.

2. I buy the lowest price brand that will suit my needs.

3. When it comes to choosing most consumer products, I rely heavily on price.

[1] A ten-point response scale ranging from *strongly disagree* (1) to *strongly agree* (10) was used by Huff and Alden (1998) for these items. Five-point scales were used in the other studies.

SCALE NAME: Price Consciousness

SCALE DESCRIPTION: A five-item, seven-point Likert-type scale measuring a consumer's willingness to expend the time and energy necessary to shop around if need be to purchase grocery products at the lowest prices. A four-item version was used by Manning, Sprott, and Miyazaki (1998).

SCALE ORIGIN: The scale is original to Lichtenstein, Ridgway, and Netemeyer (1993). While a few items were found in previous research, many were generated specifically for this study. A total of 18 items were tested along with many others in a pretest. The sample was composed of 341 nonstudent adult consumers who had the grocery-shopping responsibility for their households. Factor analysis and coefficient alpha were used to eliminate weaker items. The thirteen items remaining were reported to have an alpha of .84. These items were used in the main study although the next round of analysis eliminated eight of them leaving the final version of the scale with five items.

RELIABILITY: Burton et al. (1998) reported an alpha of .86. In Study 1 by Burton, Lichtenstein, and Netemeyer (1999) an alpha of .84 was reported; in Study 2 it was merely reported to be greater than .85. The main study by Lichtenstein, Ridgway, and Netemeyer (1993) showed an alpha for the scale of .85. Lastovicka et al. (1999) reported an alpha of .80. Alphas of .84 and .80 were reported for the versions of the scale used by Manning, Sprott, and Miyazaki (1998) and Miyazaki, Sprott, and Manning (2000), respectively.

VALIDITY: Lastovicka et al. (1999) used this scale in the process of validating another scale (#177). Based upon that, their data indicated that scores on the price consciousness scale had a moderate positive correlation with frugality as well as with a measure of response bias (#91). The former supports, as might be expected, that those who are price conscious are also frugal. The latter correlation is more confusing; it appears to suggest that as price consciousness increases the tendency to give exaggeratedly desirable responses increases too. The implication of this finding as it relates to the scale's validity is worthy of further investigation.

Confirmatory factor analysis was used by Lichtenstein, Ridgway, and Netemeyer (1993) to conclude that the scale was unidimensional and showed evidence of discriminant validity. No examination of the scale's validity was reported in the articles by the other users of the scale.

REFERENCES:
Burton, Scot, Donald R. Lichtenstein, and Richard G. Netemeyer (1999), "Exposure to Sales Flyers and Increased Purchases in Retail Supermarkets," *JAR*, 39 (September/October), 7–14.

Burton, Scot, Donald R. Lichtenstein, Richard G. Netemeyer, and Judith A. Garretson (1998), "A Scale for Measuring Attitude Toward Private Label Products and an Examination of Its Psychological and Behavioral Correlates," *JAMS*, 26 (4), 293–306.

Lastovicka, John L., Lance A. Bettencourt, Renee Shaw Hughner, and Ronald J. Kuntze (1999), "Lifestyle of the Tight and Frugal: Theory and Measurement," *JCR*, 26 (June), 85–98.

Lichtenstein, Donald R., Nancy M. Ridgway, and Richard G. Netemeyer (1993), "Price Perceptions and Consumer Shopping Behavior: A Field Study," *JMR*, 30 (May), 234–245.

Manning, Kenneth C. (2001), Personal Correspondence.

Manning, Kenneth C., David E. Sprott, and Anthony D. Miyazaki (1998), "Consumer Response to Quantity Surcharges: Implications for Retail Price Setters," *JR*, 74 (3), 373–399.

Miyazaki, Anthony D., David E. Sprott, and Kenneth C. Manning (2000), "Unit Prices on Retail Shelf Labels: An Assessment of Information Prominence," *JR*, 76 (1), 93–112.

#317 *Price Consciousness*

SCALE ITEMS: [1]

1. I am not willing to go to extra effort to find lower prices. **(r)**

2. I will grocery shop at more than one store to take advantage of low prices.

3. The money saved by finding low prices is usually not worth the time and effort. **(r)**

4. I would never shop at more than one store to find low prices. **(r)**

5. The time it takes to find low prices is usually not worth the effort. **(r)**

[1] The reported studies apparently used all of the items except for Manning, Sprott, and Miyazaki (1998) who did not use item 3 (Manning 2001).

SCALE NAME: Price Consciousness

SCALE DESCRIPTION: The scale is composed of three, five-point Likert-type statements and attempts to assess the degree to which a consumer engages in comparative shopping and is intent on getting the "best price."

SCALE ORIGIN: Darden and Perreault (1976) were cited by Ailawadi, Neslin, and Gedenk (2001) as the source of the scale they used, however, the former had taken items from the work of Wells and Tigert (1971). (See #315.) A close examination reveals that only one item from Wells and Tigert (1971) is among the three shown below. Given all of this, it is probably safest to describe this scale as being original though inspired by previous work.

RELIABILITY: A composite reliability of .826 was reported for the scale (Ailawadi, Neslin, and Gedenk 2001).

VALIDITY: The items in this scale along with those belonging to 14 other scales were included in a confirmatory factor analysis. The fit of the measurement model was acceptable and general evidence was cited in support of the scale's discriminant validity.

REFERENCES:

Ailawadi, Kusum L., Scott A. Neslin, and Karen Gedenk (2001), "Pursuing the Value-Conscious Consumer: Store Brands Versus National Brand Promotions," *JM*, 65 (1), 71–89.

Darden, William R. and William D. Perreault, Jr. (1976), "Identifying Interurban Shoppers: Multiproduct Purchase Patterns and Segmentation Profiles," *JMR*, 13 (Feb.), 51–60.

Wells, William D. and Douglas Tigert (1971), "Activities, Interests, and Opinions," *JAR*, 11 (Aug.), 27–35.

SCALE ITEMS:

1. I compare prices of at least a few brands before I choose one.

2. I find myself checking the prices even for small items.

3. It is important to me to get the best price for the products I buy.

SCALE NAME: Price Dealing Intensity

SCALE DESCRIPTION: The scale is composed of three, five-point Likert-type statements attempting to capture a consumer's relative sense of the amount of price dealing that is conducted for a specified brand compared to its competing brands. The emphasis seems to be on the overuse of deals.

SCALE ORIGIN: Although Yoo, Donthu, and Lee (2000) may have drawn inspiration from previous measures, ultimately their scale appears to be original to them.

RELIABILITY: Yoo, Donthu, and Lee (2000) reported the scale to have a composite reliability of .80.

VALIDITY: Factor analyses (EFA and CFA) were used to check the dimensionality of this scale along with eight others used in the study. Based on the results, the authors concluded that all items loaded on their respective factors as expected providing some sense of the scales' convergent and discriminant validities. The average variance extracted for this scale was .58.

REFERENCES:

Yoo, Boonghee, Naveen Donthu, and Sungho Lee (2000), "An Examination of Selected Marketing Mix Elements and Brand Equity," *JAMS*, 28 (2), 195–211.

SCALE ITEMS: [1]

1. Price deals for _____ are frequently offered.

2. Too many times price deals for _____ are presented.

3. Price deals for _____ are emphasized more than seems reasonable.

---

[1] The brand name of a product was placed in the blanks by Yoo, Donthu, and Lee (2000).

SCALE NAME: Price Perceptions (Postpurchase)

SCALE DESCRIPTION: Three, seven-point items compose the scale. The items are intended to measure the degree to which a customer of a service provider considers a certain price paid for a service to be fair and reasonable. As currently written, the items are most appropriate for a hotel but are amenable for modification and use with other types of services.

SCALE ORIGIN: The scale is original to the study by Voss, Parasuraman, and Grewal (1998).

RELIABILITY: Average construct reliability was reported to be .84 (Voss, Parasuraman, and Grewal 1998).

VALIDITY: Voss, Parasuraman, and Grewal (1998) reported an average variance extracted of .63. Evidence was also supplied in support of the scale's convergent and discriminant validities.

REFERENCES:
Voss, Glenn B., A. Parasuraman, and Dhruv Grewal (1998), "The Roles of Price, Performance, and Expectations in Determining Satisfaction in Service Exchanges," *JM*, 62 (October), 46–61.

SCALE ITEMS: [1]

1. Paying $79 ($129) for this hotel room was a very:
   unreasonable price / reasonable price

2. I was satisfied paying $79 ($129) per night:
   disagree very strongly / agree very strongly

3. $79 ($129) for a room at this hotel was a rip-off:
   disagree very strongly / agree very strongly (r)

[1] Responses to all items were made using a seven-point scale using the anchors shown. Only one price was shown at a time in the items depending upon the experimental treatment.

SCALE NAME: Price Perceptions (Prepurchase)

SCALE DESCRIPTION: Three, seven-point items compose the scale. The items are intended to measure the degree to which a potential customer of a service provider considers a certain price charged for a service to be fair and reasonable. As currently written, the items are most appropriate for a hotel but are amenable for modification for other types of services.

SCALE ORIGIN: The scale is original to the study by Voss, Parasuraman, and Grewal (1998).

RELIABILITY: Average construct reliability was reported to be .78 (Voss, Parasuraman, and Grewal 1998).

VALIDITY: Voss, Parasuraman, and Grewal (1998) reported an average variance extracted of .55. Evidence was also supplied in support of the scale's convergent and discriminant validities.

REFERENCES:
Voss, Glenn B., A. Parasuraman, and Dhruv Grewal (1998), "The Roles of Price, Performance, and Expectations in Determining Satisfaction in Service Exchanges," *JM*, 62 (October), 46–61.

SCALE ITEMS: [1]

1. Paying $79 ($129) for a hotel room is very:
   unreasonable / reasonable

2. $79 ($129) for a hotel room is very:
   inexpensive / expensive (r)

3. I would be pleased to pay $79 ($129) for a hotel room in downtown (city name):
   disagree very strongly / agree very strongly

[1] Responses to all items were made using a seven-point scale using the anchors shown. Only one price was shown at a time in the items depending upon the experimental treatment.

SCALE NAME: Price Prominence

SCALE DESCRIPTION: The scale is composed of nine, seven-point Likert-type items measuring the degree to which a consumer believes that the unit price information provided on a grocer's shelf label to which he/she has been exposed was noticeable and stands out from other information on the label. Respondents are instructed that their answers are relative to shelf labels they are familiar with from grocery stores where they have shopped.

SCALE ORIGIN: Although not explicitly identified as such, the scale seems to be original to Miyazaki, Sprott, and Manning (2000). The scale was used in a pretest (n = 40) as a manipulation check and the psychometric information provided below is based on that small sample.

RELIABILITY: An alpha of .92 was reported for the scale (Miyazaki, Sprott, and Manning 2000).

VALIDITY: No rigorous examination of the scale's validity was reported by Miyazaki, Sprott, and Manning (2000). However, the principal components factor analysis they conducted provided evidence of the scale's unidimensionality. Further, evidence of the scale's content validity comes from noting that the labels that were judged *a priori* by the authors to noticeably differ in the prominence of the price information they provided were indeed found to have significantly different scores on the scale and in the expected directions.

REFERENCES:
Miyazaki, Anthony D., David E. Sprott, and Kenneth C. Manning (2000), "Unit Prices on Retail Shelf Labels: An Assessment of Information Prominence," *JR*, 76 (1), 93–112.

SCALE ITEMS: [1]

Directions: Below are several statements regarding the price labels you saw. Please indicate the extent of your agreement or disagreement with the statements relative to other grocery store shelf labels with which you are familiar.

1. Is clearly distinguishable from other information presented in the label.

2. Is highly noticeable.

3. Would be easy to overlook. (r)

4. Is easy to identify.

5. Is more prominent.

6. Stands out from the other information on the label.

7. Is presented in a large font relative to other information on the label.

8. Is clearly labeled.

9. Is shown in an uncluttered portion of the label.

[1] A seven-point Likert-type response format (*disagree / agree*) was used by Miyazaki, Sprott, and Manning (2000). The directions used with the scale were not provided in the article. Those provided here represent instructions that could possibly be used.

SCALE NAME: Price-Quality Relationship

SCALE DESCRIPTION: Four, seven-point Likert-type items are used to measure a consumer's belief that there is a positive relationship between product price and quality.

SCALE ORIGIN: This multi-item summated scale is original to Lichtenstein, Ridgway, and Netemeyer (1993). Inspiration for the scale came from several previous studies of the topic. In particular, item #1 is very similar to the one item measure used by Peterson and Wilson (1985).

RELIABILITY: The main study by Lichtenstein, Ridgway, and Netemeyer (1993) showed an alpha for the scale of .78. Burton et al. (1998) reported an alpha of .85.

VALIDITY: Confirmatory factor analysis was used by Lichtenstein, Ridgway, and Netemeyer (1993) to conclude that the scale was unidimensional and showed evidence of discriminant validity. No examination of the scale's validity was reported by Burton et al. (1998).

REFERENCES:

Burton, Scot, Donald R. Lichtenstein, Richard G. Netemeyer, and Judith A. Garretson (1998), "A Scale for Measuring Attitude Toward Private Label Products and an Examination of Its Psychological and Behavioral Correlates," *JAMS*, 26 (4), 293–306.

Lichtenstein, Donald R., Nancy M. Ridgway, and Richard G. Netemeyer (1993), "Price Perceptions and Consumer Shopping Behavior: A Field Study," *JMR*, 30 (May), 234–245.

Peterson, Robert A. and William R. Wilson (1985), "Perceived Risk and Price-Reliance Schema as Price-Perceived-Quality Mediators," in *Perceived Quality: How Consumers View Stores and Merchandise*, Jacob Jacoby and Jerry C. Olson , ed. Lexington, MA: D. C. Heath and Company, 247–267.

SCALE ITEMS:

1. Generally speaking, the higher the price of a product, the higher the quality.

2. The old saying "you get what you pay for" is generally true.

3. The price of a product is a good indicator of its quality.

4. You always have to pay a bit more for the best.

#324 *Prices (Store)*

SCALE NAME: Prices (Store)

SCALE DESCRIPTION: The seven-point, three-item scale is meant to measure a consumer's expectation of the relative price level of products for sale at a specified vendor. As used by Jain and Srivastava (2000), respondents had not been to the store and only had the information provided in the experimental scenario. Thus, the scale would appear to be most relevant when a new store or online vendor has opened and the interest is in what consumers think about its price level based on what little they know about it from advertising, friends, et cetera.

SCALE ORIGIN: No information was provided by Jain and Srivastava (2000) about the source of the scale. It would appear to original to their study.

RELIABILITY: The alpha for the scale was .82 (Jain and Srivastava 2000).

VALIDITY: No examination of the scale's validity was reported by Jain and Srivastava (2000).

REFERENCES:
Jain, Sanjay and Joydeep Srivastava (2000), "An Experimental and Theoretical Analysis of Price-Matching Refund Policies," *JMR*, 37 (3), 351–362.

SCALE ITEMS: [1]

1. My overall expectations about the prices at _____ are:
   Not at all expensive / very expensive

2. I expect the prices at _____ to be:
   Low / high

3. Compared to other _____ stores, the prices at _____ are most likely to be:
   Much lower than average / much higher than average

---

[1] The blanks in the first two items as well as the second blank in the last item are supposed to have the name of the vendor in them. The first blank in the last item should have the category name, e.g., electronics.

SCALE NAME: Problem Solving Capacity (Beauty Product)

SCALE DESCRIPTION: Three Likert-type statements are used to measure a person's opinion of the degree to which a particular product has the ability to remedy some unsatisfactory aspect of one's physical appearance.

SCALE ORIGIN: The scale is apparently original to Bower and Landreth (2001).

RELIABILITY: Alphas of .83 (Study 1) and .76 (Study 2) were reported for the scale (Bower and Landreth 2001).

VALIDITY: No explicit examination of the scale's validity was described by Bower and Landreth (2001). However, the scale was used a manipulation check and showed that, as expected, two products previously thought to be problem solvers did score higher than two products thought to be beauty enhancers. This provides some limited evidence of the scale's validity.

REFERENCES:
Bower, Amanda B. (2003), Personal Correspondence.
Bower, Amanda B. and Stacy Landreth (2001), "Is Beauty Best? Highly Versus Normally Attractive Models in Advertising" *JA*, 30 (1), 1–12.

SCALE ITEMS: [1]

1. This is the kind of product I would use to "fix" a beauty problem.

2. This product could be used to hide or change a part of my physical appearance that I didn't like.

3. This product would improve the appearance of an unsatisfactory physical feature.

---

[1] Anchors for the response scale were *strong disagree* (1) and *strongly agree* (7). The items and anchors were provided by Bower (2003).

SCALE NAME: Product Information Relevancy

SCALE DESCRIPTION: Four, five-point Likert-type statements are used to assess the helpfulness of some product-related information in a brand rating task. It is assumed that the information has been provided to a respondent as part of a study and the concern is how relevant the respondent found the information to be in completing the product evaluation task.

SCALE ORIGIN: Although not explicitly stated, the scale appears to have been developed specifically for use in the study by Mason et al. (2001).

RELIABILITY: Mason et al. (2001) reported an alpha of .74 for the scale.

VALIDITY: No information regarding the scale's validity was reported by Mason et al. (2001). However, the scale was used as a manipulation check and since the difference between scale scores for two conditions agreed with expectations then that provides a sense of the scale's *known groups* validity.

REFERENCES:

Mason, Kevin, Thomas Jensen, Scot Burton, and Dave Roach (2001), "The Accuracy of Brand and Attribute Judgments: The Role of Information Relevancy, Product Experience, and Attribute-Relationship Schemata," *JAMS*, 29 (3), 307–317.

SCALE ITEMS: [1]

1. The information provided was relevant to the ratings task.

2. The information provided was helpful in answering other questions.

3. The information that was provided would help me in making a choice of _____ to purchase.

4. The information that was provided aided me in completing the ratings task.

[1] The name of the product category being evaluated should be placed in the blank.

SCALE NAME: Product Innovativeness

SCALE DESCRIPTION: A three-item, seven-point scale is used to measure how new and different a product is compared to current products the consumer is aware of and the perceived impact it would have on the consumer's behavior.

SCALE ORIGIN: Inspiration for the scale by Moreau, Lehmann, and Markman (2001) came from Robertson (1971) and probably even more so from measures (non-summated) used by Olshavsky and Spreng (1996).

RELIABILITY: The internal consistencies (alpha) reported for the scale by Moreau, Lehmann, and Markman (2001) were .87 (Study 1) and .82 (Study 2).

VALIDITY: No information regarding the scale's validity was provided by Moreau, Lehmann, and Markman (2001).

REFERENCES:

Moreau, C. Page, Donald R. Lehmann, and Arthur B. Markman (2001), "Entrenched Knowledge Structures and Consumer Response to New Products," *JMR*, 38 (February), 14–29.
Olshavsky, Richard W. and Richard A. Spreng (1996), "An Exploratory Study of the Innovation Evaluation Process," *Journal of Product Innovation Management*, 13 (6), 512–529.
Robertson, Thomas S. (1971), *Innovative Behavior and Communication*, New York: Holt, Rinehart, and Winston.

SCALE ITEMS: [1]

1. How different is this product from other products you currently know about?

2. How innovative do you think this product is?

3. To what extent would this product change your behavior?

[1] These items have been created based upon descriptions provided in the article by Moreau, Lehmann, and Markman (2001). No information was provided about the anchors used on the response scales. See Olshavsky and Spreng (1996) for possibilities.

SCALE NAME: Program Liking

SCALE DESCRIPTION: The scale is composed of statements measuring one's liking of a television program.

SCALE ORIGIN: The scale used by Murry and Dacin (1996) is exactly the same as the one used earlier by Murry, Lastovicka, and Singh (1992). While not certain, the scale appears to have been developed as part of that earlier study. The version of the scale used by Coulter (1998) borrowed two items from the previous version and added a third.

RELIABILITY: Alphas of .94, .93, and 89 were reported by Coulter (1998), Murry and Dacin (1996), and Murry, Lastovicka, and Singh (1992) for their respective versions of the scale.

VALIDITY: No explicit examination of the scale's validity was reported by Coulter (1998), Murry and Dacin (1996), or Murry, Lastovicka, and Singh (1992). However, Coulter (1998) did use LISREL and mentioned that all indicators loaded on their appropriate latent constructs. Similarly, a confirmatory factor analysis was conducted by Murry and Dacin (1996) on a set of fifteen items thought to deal with three different but related constructs. Indeed, the six items composing the program liking scale loaded high on the same dimension.

REFERENCES:
Coulter, Keith S. (1998), "The Effects of Affective Responses to Media Context on Advertising Evaluations," *JA*, 27 (4), 41–51.
Murry, John P., Jr. and Peter A. Dacin (1996), "Cognitive Moderators of Negative-Emotion Effects: Implications for Understanding Media Context," *JCR*, 22 (March), 439–447.
Murry, John P., John L. Lastovicka, and Surendra N. Singh (1992), "Feeling and Liking Responses to Television Programs: An Examination of Two Explanations for Media-Context Effects," *JCR*, 18 (March), 441–451.

SCALE ITEMS: [1]

1. If I knew this program was going to be on television I would look forward to watching it.

2. I liked watching this program.

3. I would never watch a rerun of this program on television. (r)

4. I am glad I had a chance to see this program.

5. There is something about this program that appeals to me.

6. I disliked watching this program more than I do most other TV programs. (r)

7. I think that this is a program I'd be interested in watching in the future.

[1] Coulter (1998) used items 1, 4, and 7. Murry and Dacin (1996) as well as Murry, Lastovicka, and Singh (1992) used items 1-6. A seven-point Likert-type response format appears to have been used in each case.

SCALE NAME: Purchase Communication (Parent-Adolescent)

SCALE DESCRIPTION: The scale is designed to measure the extent of parent-child interaction with regard to various aspects of shopping and spending money. If the scale is filled out by a child then the communication with parents is described whereas when a parent fills out the scale, communication with a specific child is described. The scale has been variously referred to as *parental communication* (Bush, Smith, and Martin 1999), *family communication* (Moschis and Moore 1984), and *consumption interaction* (Palan 1998).

SCALE ORIGIN: Bush, Smith, and Martin (1999) used items from Moschis and Moore (1984) whose scale was similar to, if not the same as, the scales used by both Ward and Wackman (1971) and Moore and Stephens (1975). While the two earlier studies used the items as a summated scale, neither reports any reliability or validity information. The Moschis and Moore (1984) scale also has some items in common with a measure reported by Moschis (1978, p. 45).

The versions used by Palan (1998) were composed of items adapted from a twelve-item scale used by Moschis (1978).

RELIABILITY: Alphas of .72 and .62 were reported for the versions of the scale used by Bush, Smith, and Martin (1999) and Moschis and Moore (1984), respectively. Palan (1998) reported alphas of .76, .78, and .42 for use of his versions of the scale as used by mothers, fathers, and adolescents, respectively.

VALIDITY: Factor analyses were separately run by Palan (1998) on the responses from mothers, fathers, and children. In each case five-items loaded on one factor while another item loaded by itself on a second factor. This indicates the scale is not unidimensional. Using the Multi-trait, Multi-Informant method, evidence was provided in support of the scale's convergent validity. However, evidence of the scale's discriminant validity was lacking. No evidence of the scale's validity was provided by Bush, Smith, and Martin (1999) or Moschis and Moore (1984).

COMMENTS: The Palan versions of the scales are not unidimensional and the child's version is not reliable. Palan (1998) indicated that removing item 3 (child's version below) increased alpha to .52, but that is still unacceptably low. Refinement of Palan's versions is needed, especially before it is used again with adolescents.

REFERENCES:

Bush, Alan J., Rachel Smith, and Craig Martin (1999), "The Influence of Consumer Socialization Variables on Attitude Toward Advertising: A Comparison of African-Americans and Caucasians," *JA*, 28 (3), 13–24.

Moore, Roy L. and Lowndes F. Stephens (1975), "Some Communication and Demographic Determinants of Adolescent Consumer Learning," *JCR*, 2 (September), 80–92.

Moschis, George P. (1978), *Acquisition of the Consumer Role by Adolescents*, Research Monograph No. 82, Georgia State University: Publishing Services Division.

Moschis, George P. and Roy L. Moore (1984), "Anticipatory Consumer Socialization," *JAMS*, 12 (Fall), 109–23.

Palan, Kay M. (1998), "Relationships Between Family Communication and Consumer Activities of Adolescents: An Exploratory Study," *JAMS*, 26 (4), 338–349.

Ward, Scott and Daniel Wackman (1971), "Family and Media Influences on Adolescent Consumer Learning," *American Behavioral Scientist*, 14 (January-February), 415–27.

#329 *Purchase Communication (Parent-Adolescent)*

SCALE ITEMS: [1]

<u>Child's version</u>

1. My parents and I talk about things we see or hear advertised.

2. I try to get my parents to buy things I see advertised.

3. I get my parents to buy things that are advertised.

4. I ask my parents for advice about buying things.

5. I go shopping with my parents.

6. My parents and I don't agree on what things I should or shouldn't buy.

7. My parents tell me what things I should or should not buy.

8. My parents tell me what they do with their money.

9. My parents tell me why they bought some things for themselves.

<u>Parent's Version</u>

1. I talk with my child about buying things.

2. I go shopping with my child.

3. I tell my child what things he or she should or should not buy.

4. I tell my child what I do with my money.

5. I talk with my child about things we see or hear advertised.

6. I tell my child why I bought some things for myself.

[1] Items 1-6 of the child's version were used by Moschis and Moore (1984). Bush, Smith, and Martin (1999) also used in the child's version with items similar or the same as 1-3 and 5. For the child's version of the scale Palan (1998) used items 7-9 and items similar to 1, 4, and 5. He used all six items of the parent's version. All versions of the scale used five-point scales with anchors ranging from *never* to *very often*.

SCALE NAME: Purchase Communication (Peer)

SCALE DESCRIPTION: Three, Likert-type statements are used to measure a person's interest in talking about products as well as seeking information from friends.

SCALE ORIGIN: These items were part of an early classic study of psychographics by Wells and Tigert (1971). One thousand questionnaires were mailed to homemaker members of the Market Facts mail panel. In addition to gathering demographic, product use, and media data, the survey contained 300 statements which have served as the basis for the construction of many lifestyle-related scales ever since. While the three items for this scale are reported in the article they were not analyzed as a multi-item scale. The purpose of the article was to explain how psychographics could improve upon mere demographic description of target audiences and product users. No psychometric information was reported.

One of the first known uses of the items as a multi-item scale was in Darden and Perreault (1976). Analysis was based on self-administered questionnaires completed by 278 suburban housewives randomly selected in Athens, Georgia. A split-half reliability of .53 was reported for the scale. Although several lifestyle variables differentiated between the groups of outshoppers, *information seeking* was not one of them.

Interestingly, Bush, Smith, and Martin (1999) stated a different origin for their scale. Specifically, they indicated that they used a modified version of a scale by Mochis (1981).

RELIABILITY: Alphas of .82 (n = 208) and .55 (n = 639) were reported by Bush, Smith, and Martin (1999) and Dickerson and Gentry (1983), respectively.

VALIDITY: No examination of the scale's validity has been reported although Dickerson and Gentry (1983) did say that the items loaded together in a factor analysis.

REFERENCES:

Bush, Alan J., Rachel Smith, and Craig Martin (1999), "The Influence of Consumer Socialization Variables on Attitude Toward Advertising: A Comparison of African-Americans and Caucasians," *JA*, 28 (3), 13–24.

Darden, William R. and William D. Perreault, Jr. (1976), "Identifying Interurban Shoppers: Multiproduct Purchase Patterns and Segmentation Profiles," *JMR*, 13 (Feb.), 51–60.

Dickerson, Mary D. and James W. Gentry (1983), "Characteristics of Adopters and Non-Adopters of Home Computers," *JCR*, 10 (Sept.), 225–235.

Martin, Craig A. (2001), Personal Correspondence.

Moschis, George P. (1981), "Patterns of Consumer Learning," *JAMS*, 9 (Spring), 110–26.

Wells, William D. and Douglas Tigert (1971), "Activities, Interests, and Opinions," *JAR*, 11 (Aug.), 27–35.

SCALE ITEMS: [1]

1. I often seek out the advice of my friends regarding which brand to buy.

2. I spend a lot of time talking with my friends about products and brands.

3. My neighbors or friends usually give me good advice on what brands to buy in the grocery store.

[1] Dickerson and Gentry (1983) used a six-point *disagree / agree* response format whereas Bush, Smith, and Martin (1999; Martin 2001) used a five-point scale.

SCALE NAME: Purchase Frequency (Product Specific)

SCALE DESCRIPTION: Three, seven-point scales are used to assess a consumer's experience with purchasing a particular product.

SCALE ORIGIN: Dahl, Manchanda, and Argo (2001) did not state the source of the scale but it would appear to be original to them.

RELIABILITY: An alpha of .80 was reported for the scale (Dahl, Manchanda, and Argo 2001).

VALIDITY: No examination of the scale's validity was reported by Dahl, Manchanda, and Argo (2001). It was stated, however, that the three items were unidimensional per a factor analysis.

REFERENCES:
Dahl, Darren W., Rajesh V. Manchanda, and Jennifer J. Argo (2001), "Embarrassment in Consumer Purchase: The Roles of Social Presence and Purchase Familiarity," *JCR*, 28 (December), 473–481.

SCALE ITEMS: [1]

1. How often do you purchase _____?
   very rarely / very often

2. When was the last time you purchased _____?
   never have purchased / purchased within the last month

3. How familiar are you with purchasing _____?
   not familiar / very familiar

[1] The questions are recreated here based upon paraphrasing provided in the article by Dahl, Manchanda, and Argo (2001).

SCALE NAME: Purchase Frequency (Store Brands)

SCALE DESCRIPTION: Three, five-point statements are used to measure the frequency with which a person purchases brands owned and managed by the retailer, so-called "store brands."

SCALE ORIGIN: Ailawadi, Neslin, and Gedenk (2001) did not indicate any other source for the scale thus it is assumed that it was original to their study.

RELIABILITY: A composite reliability of .906 was reported for the scale (Ailawadi, Neslin, and Gedenk 2001).

VALIDITY: The items in this scale along with those belonging to two other scales were included in a confirmatory factor analysis. The fit of the measurement model was acceptable and general evidence was cited in support of the scale's discriminant validity.

REFERENCES:
Ailawadi, Kusum L., Scott A. Neslin, and Karen Gedenk (2001), "Pursuing the Value-Conscious Consumer: Store Brands Versus National Brand Promotions," *JM*, 65 (1), 71–89.

SCALE ITEMS: [1]

1. I buy store brands.

2. I look for store brands when I go shopping.

3. My shopping cart contains store brands for several products.

---

[1] The anchors Ailawadi, Neslin, and Gedenk (2001) used with this scale were *never* and *very often*.

SCALE NAME: Purchase Independence (Child from Parent)

SCALE DESCRIPTION: The scale is composed of several items using a four-point response scale to measure the degree to which a parent reports that a child exercises autonomy in the purchase of several products which the child will consume. Referred to by Carlson and Grossbart (1988) as *consumption independence* and *consumption dependence* by Rose (1999).

SCALE ORIGIN: The use of these items as a multi-item measure appears to be original to Carlson and Grossbart (1988). The items and response format used by Carlson and Grossbart (1988) was taken from the research of Ward et al. (1977) but the former appear to have been the first to treat the items as a summated measure. Rose (1999) added several items to the scale.

RELIABILITY: Carlson and Grossbart (1988) reported an alpha of .63 for their version of the scale. Rose (1999) reported alphas of .65 and .62 for the scale in the U.S. and the Japanese samples, respectively.

VALIDITY: No examination of scale validity was reported in either of the studies.

COMMENTS: The low alphas may indicate that a child's degree of autonomy is product-dependent and is not consistent across product categories.

REFERENCES:

Carlson, Les and Sanford Grossbart (1988), "Parental Style and Consumer Socialization of Children," *JCR*, 15 (June), 77–94.
Rose, Gregory M. and Les Carlson (1999), "Consumer Socialization, Parental Style, and Development Timetables in the United States and Japan," *JM*, 63 (July), 105–119.
Rose, Gregory M. (2002), Personal Correspondence.

SCALE ITEMS: [1]

Directions: Place a check to indicate how each of these products is usually purchased, either with your money or with your child's own money. Choose only one answer for each product.

1. candy (*sweet sweets* in Japanese questionnaire)

2. game or toy

3. snack food

4. sports equipment

5. magazines/comic books

6. child's clothing

7. cereal (*instant ramen* in Japanese questionnaire)

8. child's shoes

9. a restaurant

---

[1] The choices that respondents had to choose from were: *child chooses for self*, *child chooses but talks to parents first*, *parent chooses but talks to child first*, and *parent chooses and doesn't talk to child*. Carlson and Grossbart (1988) used the first five items (above) while Rose (1999, 2002) used #1-#3 and #6-#9.

SCALE NAME: Purchase Influence (Child's)

SCALE DESCRIPTION: The scale is composed of five-point Likert-type items measuring the degree to which a parent reports that a child's opinion should be included when purchase decisions are made for a variety of goods and services.

SCALE ORIGIN: The idea for the scale comes from a study reported by Jenkins (1979). However, he doesn't appear to have used the items in summated scale form so that aspect seems to be original to Carlson and Grossbart (1988; Grossbart, Carlson, and Walsh 1991).

RELIABILITY: Carlson and Grossbart (1988; Grossbart, Carlson, and Walsh 1991). reported an alpha of .84 for the scale. Rose (1999) reported alphas of .70 and .74 for the scale in the U.S. and the Japanese samples, respectively.

VALIDITY: No examination of scale validity was reported in any of the studies.

REFERENCES:

Carlson, Les and Sanford Grossbart (1988), "Parental Style and Consumer Socialization of Children," *JCR*, 15 (June), 77–94.

Grossbart, Sanford, Les Carlson, and Ann Walsh (1991), "Consumer Socialization and Frequency of Shopping with Children," *JAMS*, 19 (Summer), 155–163.

Jenkins, Roger L. (1979), "The Influence of Children in Family Decision Making: Parents' Perceptions," in *Advances in Consumer Research, V. 6*, William L. Wilkie, ed. Ann Arbor, Michigan: Association for Consumer Research 413–418.

Rose, Gregory M. and Roger L. Jenkins (1999), "Consumer Socialization, Parental Style, and Development Timetables in the United States and Japan," *JM*, 63 (July), 105–119.

SCALE ITEMS: [1]

My child's opinions should be included when we make purchase decisions for:

1. Major appliances

2. Automobiles

3. Furniture

4. Groceries (purchasing groceries)

5. Life Insurance

6. Vacations (selecting a vacation site)

7. General Purchases

8. Selecting a restaurant

9. Buying a house

---

[1] Each of the studies used verbal anchors on the response scale that ranged from *strongly disagree* (1) to *strongly agree* (5). Carlson and Grossbart (1988; Grossbart, Carlson, and Walsh 1991) used the first seven items (above). Rose (1999) used items 8 and 9 as well as the variations of 4 and 6 shown in parentheses.

SCALE NAME: Purchase Intention

SCALE DESCRIPTION: The scale is typically characterized by multiple Likert-like items used to measure the inclination of a consumer to buy a specified good or use a service. The various versions of the scale discussed here employed between two and four items. Most of the studies appear to have used seven-point response scales with the exception of Okechuku and Wang (1988) who used a nine-point format. Stafford (1998) modified the statements for use with services and called the scale *conative attitude toward the ad*.

SCALE ORIGIN: The source of this scale is a study of the physical attractiveness of models in advertisements (Baker and Churchill 1977). Consistent with the tripartite theory of attitudes, scales were developed to measure the cognitive, affective, and conative components of one's evaluation of an ad. Item-total correlations indicated that the three items expected to capture the conative component (#1, #2, and #3 below) were homogeneous. It should be noted that while the scale was developed to measure the conative dimension of one's attitude toward an ad, the statements actually measure the conative dimension of attitude toward the brand. Technically, therefore, this scale does not measure behavioral intention towards an ad although it could certainly be used with a product described in an ad.

RELIABILITY: Alphas of .73, .91, .81, .81, and .81 have been reported by Kilbourne (1986), Kilbourne, Painton and Ridley (1985), Neese and Taylor (1994), Perrien, Dussart, and Paul (1985), and Stafford (1998), respectively. Okechuku and Wang (1988) reported two alphas: .82 and .77 for clothing and shoe ads, respectively. The item-total correlations reported in their study also provide some evidence of scale item homogeneity.

VALIDITY: No examination of the scale's validity was reported by Neese and Taylor (1994) though the authors stated in general terms that they used item-total correlations and the results of a factor analysis to purify each of their scales.

The item-total correlations reported by Okechuku and Wang (1988) indicated that items composing this scale had much higher correlations with scores on this scale than with correlations with total scores on two other scales (cognitive and affective dimensions of attitude). This provides some evidence of convergent and discriminate validities although at the item level rather than the scale level.

As some evidence of content validity, Perrien, Dussart and Paul (1985) used items taken from the literature and tested with 15 marketing experts. All were unanimous in connecting the expected items with the proper dimensions of attitude (affective, cognitive, and conative).

COMMENTS: Several users of this scale referred to it as a semantic differential. However, it is described here as a Likert-type because it does not use a series of bi-polar adjectives but is instead composed of a series of statements responded to on a scale with the same verbal anchors.

REFERENCES:

Baker, Michael J. and Gilbert A. Churchill, Jr. (1977), "The Impact of Physically Attractive Models on Advertising Evaluations," *JMR*, 14 (November), 538–555.

Kilbourne, William E. (1986), "An Exploratory Study of Sex Role Stereotyping on Attitudes Toward Magazine Advertisements," *JAMS*, 14 (4), 43–46.

Kilbourne, William E., Scott Painton, and Danny Ridley (1985), "The Effect of Sexual Embedding on Responses to Magazine Advertisements," *JA*, 14 (2), 48–56.

Neese, William T. and Ronald D. Taylor (1994), "Verbal Strategies for Indirect Comparative Advertising," *JAR*, 34 (March/April), 56–69.

Okechuku, Chike and Gongrong Wang (1988), "The Effectiveness of Chinese Print Advertisements in North America," *JAR*, 28 (October/November), 25–34.

Perrien, Jean, Christian Dussart, and Francoise Paul (1985), "Advertisers and the Factual Content of Advertising," *JA*, 14 (1), 30–35, 53.

Stafford, Marla Royne (1998), "Advertising Sex-Typed Services: The Effects of Sex, Service Type, and Employee Type on Consumer Attitudes," *JA*, 27 (2), 65–82.

SCALE ITEMS: [1]

1. Would you like to try this _____?

2. Would you buy this _____ if you happened to see it in a store?

3. Would you actively seek out this _____ (in a store in order to purchase it)?

4. I would patronize this _____.

---

[1] This is the version of the scale reported by Baker and Churchill (1977) and the anchors on the seven-point response scale were *yes, definitely* and *no, definitely not*. Kilbourne, Painton, and Ridley (1985), Kilbourne (1986), and Neese and Taylor (1994) used phrases based upon these item. Okechuku and Wang (1988) appear to have used short phrases based upon these items. Perrien, Dussart, and Paul (1985) used items that referred to an ad the respondents had been exposed to and then asked questions similar to these items. Their scale also incorporated one bi-polar adjective (influential / not influential) that was included to measure the perceived power of the ad to affect purchase behavior. Stafford (1998) used items similar to #1, #3, #4 (above). Each statement began with the phrase "*If I needed a* _____ *service*" and was apparently responded to using a seven-point agree/disagree scale.

SCALE NAME: Purchase Intention

SCALE DESCRIPTION: The scale measures the likelihood that a consumer will buy a product he/she is knowledgeable of. The measure was referred to as *willingness to buy* by Dodds, Monroe, and Grewal (1991) as well as Grewal, Monroe, and Krishnan (1998). The version of the scale used by Dodds, Monroe, and Grewal (1991) had five items whereas the ones used by both Grewal, Monroe, and Krishnan (1998) and Grewal et al. (1998) had three.

SCALE ORIGIN: Dodds, Monroe, and Grewal (1991) stated that the items for this and two other scales were "developed from previous research" (p. 312) although the source of the items and the extent of the borrowing were not specified.

RELIABILITY: The scale was reported to have alphas of .97 and .96 for the two similar experiments in which they were used by Dodds, Monroe, and Grewal (1991). Average inter-item correlations were .97 and .96.

Grewal, Monroe, and Krishnan (1998) reported construct reliabilities of .92 and .95 for use of the scale in their first and second studies, respectively. Grewal et al. (1998) reported that their version of the scale had a construct reliability of .92.

VALIDITY: Dodds, Monroe, and Grewal (1991) stated that the results of an exploratory factor analysis indicated a three factor solution was found using items from this scale and two others. The suggestion was that the items in this scale loaded on one factor.

Grewal, Monroe, and Krishnan (1998) provided considerable evidence from both of their studies in support of the scale's unidimensionality, convergent validity, and discriminant validity.

A variety of tests conducted by Grewal et al. (1998) indicated the scale was unidimensional and showed evidence of discriminant validity. The variance extracted was .92.

REFERENCES:

Dodds, William B., Kent B. Monroe, and Dhruv Grewal (1991), "The Effects of Price, Brand, and Store Information on Buyers' Product Evaluations," *JMR*, 28 (August), 307–319.

Grewal, Dhruv, Kent B. Monroe, and R. Krishnan (1998), "The Effects of Price-Comparison Advertising on Buyer's Perceptions of Acquisition Value, Transaction Value, and Behavioral Intentions," *JM*, 62 (April), 46–59.

Grewal, Dhruv, R. Krishnan, Julie Baker, and Norm Borin (1998), "The Effect of Store Name, Brand Name and Price Discounts on Consumers' Evaluations and Purchase Intentions," *JR*, 74 (3), 331–352.

SCALE ITEMS: [1]

1. The likelihood of purchasing this product is . . .

2. If I were going to buy this product, I would consider buying the model at the price shown.

3. At the price shown, I would consider buying the product.

4. The probability that I would consider buying the product is . . .

5. My willingness to buy the product is . . .

6. If I were going to buy a _____, the probability of buying this model is:

7. I would purchase this _____.

[1] Dodds, Monroe, and Grewal (1991) used items 1 to 5; Grewal, Monroe, and Krishnan (1998) used item 4 and 6 as well as one similar to 1. Grewal et al. (1998) used items 4 and 7 plus one similar to 3. Items 2, 3, and 7 had *strongly disagree* (1) and *strongly agree* (7) as anchors while the rest used *very low* (1) and *very high* (7).

#337 *Purchase Intention*

SCALE NAME: Purchase Intention

SCALE DESCRIPTION: The scale is a Likert-type measure of the degree to which a consumer means to buy (or at least try) a specified brand in the future.

SCALE ORIGIN: Putrevu and Lord (1994) did not indicate the source of the scale. Although there is some conceptual similarity between this and other measures of the construct, the specific items appear to be distinct. Thus, it is likely that their scale is original.

The scale used by Coyle and Thorson (2001) is a combination of items borrowed from others. The first three items are from Putrevu and Lord (1994) whereas the last item is from Kim and Biocca (1997).

RELIABILITY: Putrevu and Lord (1994) reported an alpha of .91 (n = 100) for the scale. An alpha of .83 (n = 68) was reported for the version of the scale used by Coyle and Thorson (2001).

VALIDITY: No evidence of the scale's validity was presented in either of the studies.

REFERENCES:

Coyle, James R. and Esther Thorson (2001), "The Effects of Progressive Levels of Interactivity and Vividness in Web Marketing Sites," *JA*, 30 (Fall), 65–77.

Kim, Taeyong and Frank Biocca (1997), "Telepresence via Television: Two Dimensions of Telepresence May Have Different Connections to Memory and Persuasion," *Journal of Computer-Mediated Communication*, 3 (September), http://www.ascusc.org/jcmc/vol3/issue2/kim.html.

Putrevu, Sanjay and Kenneth R. Lord (1994), "Comparative and Noncomparative Advertising: Attitudinal Effects Under Cognitive and Affective Involvement Conditions," *JA*, 23 (June), 77–90.

SCALE ITEMS: [1]

1. It is very likely that I will buy *(brand)*.

2. I will purchase *(brand)* the next time I need a *(product)*.

3. I will definitely try *(brand)*.

4. Suppose that a friend called you last night to get your advice in his/her search for a *(product)*. Would you recommend him/her to buy a *(product)* from *(brand)*?

---

[1] The anchors for the first three items were *agree / disagree* whereas the anchors for the third item was *absolutely / absolutely not (*Coyle and Thorson 2001). Both studies used seven-point response formats for each item.

SCALE NAME: Purchase Intention

SCALE DESCRIPTION: It is a three-item, seven-point scale measuring the self-reported likelihood that a consumer will purchase a product based upon information he/she has read on the product's package.

SCALE ORIGIN: Although Burton, Garretson, and Velliquette (1999) have drawn inspiration from previous measures of intention, this scale appears to have been especially developed for use in their study.

RELIABILITY: An alpha of .89 was reported for the scale by Burton, Garretson, and Velliquette (1999).

VALIDITY: No explicit analysis was described bearing on the scale's validity.

REFERENCES:
Burton, Scot, Judith A. Garretson, and Anne M. Velliquette (1999), "Implications of Accurate Usage of Nutrition Facts Panel Information for Food Product Evaluations and Purchase Intentions," *JAMS*, 27 (4), 470–480.

SCALE ITEMS:

1. Would you be more likely or less likely to purchase the product, given the information shown on the package?
   more likely / less likely

2. Given the information on the front and back of the package, how probable is it that you would consider the purchase of the product?
   very probable / not probable

3. How likely would you be to purchase the product, given the information shown on the front and back of the package?
   very likely / very unlikely

SCALE NAME: Purchase Intention

SCALE DESCRIPTION: Likert-type statements are used to measure a person's stated interest in buying a product. Given the phrasing in the statements, the full six item scale is most suited for a product that has been presented in an ad which the consumer has been exposed to and is something that would affect the viewer's appearance (clothes, jewelry, cosmetics, exercise equipment). Bower (2001) only used three of the items and that subset is amenable for use in a wider variety of situations.

SCALE ORIGIN: Although some of the items are very similar to ones used in previous measures of the construct, in total the scale appears to be original to Bower (2001; Bower and Landreth (2001).

RELIABILITY: Alphas of .90 and .80 were reported for the scale by Bower and Landreth (2001) and Bower (2001), respectively.

VALIDITY: No explicit examination of the scale's validity was described by Bower and Landreth (2001). Bower (2001) used confirmatory factor analysis with items composing five scales, one of which was this scale. The evidence suggested a good fit. The scale's average variance extracted was .58. In addition, this was higher that the scale's squared correlation with the other scales. In total, this provides some evidence of the scale's convergent and discriminant validity.

REFERENCES:
Bower, Amanda B. (2003), Personal Correspondence.
Bower, Amanda B. (2001), "Highly Attractive Models in Advertising and the Women Who Loathe Them: The Implementations of Negative Affect for Spokesperson Effectiveness," *JA*, 30 (3), 51–63.
Bower, Amanda B. and Stacy Landreth (2001), "Is Beauty Best? Highly Versus Normally Attractive Models in Advertising" *JA*, 30 (1), 1–12.

SCALE ITEMS: [1]

1. I am eager to check out the product because of this advertisement.

2. I intend to try this product.

3. I am interested in seeing how the product looks on me.

4. I plan on buying this product.

5. It is likely that I will buy this product when it becomes available.

6. I would consider purchasing this product.

---

[1] Anchors for the response scale were *strong disagree* (1) and *strongly agree* (7). The items used by Bower (2001) were 1, 2, and 4. The items and anchors were provided by Bower (2003).

SCALE NAME: Purchase Intention (Product/Store)

SCALE DESCRIPTION: The scale is composed of three, seven-point Likert-type statements intended to capture a consumer's stated likelihood of purchasing a specified product at a particular store. The measure was referred to as *willingness to buy* by Sweeney, Soutar, and Johnson (1999).

SCALE ORIGIN: Sweeney, Soutar, and Johnson (1999) cited Dodds, Monroe, and Grewal (1991) as the source of the scale. However, examination of that scale (V. II, #302) indicates that it may be more accurate to say that the scale used by Sweeney, Soutar, and Johnson (1999) is an adaptation of the earlier scale.

RELIABILITY: An alpha of .95 was reported for the scale by Sweeney, Soutar, and Johnson (1999).

VALIDITY: Not much was said by the authors about this scale's validity but it was stated in general that all their scales exhibited discriminant validity by having their variance extracted being higher than the relevant squared structural path coefficients (Fornell and Larcker 1981).

REFERENCES:
Dodds, William B., Kent B. Monroe, and Dhruv Grewal (1991), "The Effects of Price, Brand, and Store Information on Buyers' Product Evaluations," *JMR*, 28 (August), 307–319.
Fornell, Claes and David F. Larcker (1981), "Evaluating Structural Equation Models with Unobservable Variables and Measurement Error," *JMR*, 18 (February), 39–50.
Sweeney, Jillian C., Geoffrey N. Soutar, and Lester W. Johnson (1999), "The Role of Perceived Risk in the Quality-Value Relationship: A Study in a Retail Environment," *JR*, 75 (1), 77–105.

SCALE ITEMS:

1. I would consider buying this product at this store.

2. I will purchase this product at this store.

3. There is a strong likelihood that I will buy this product at this store.

SCALE NAME: Purchase Involvement (Cognitive)

SCALE DESCRIPTION: The scale is composed of multiple seven-point semantic-differentials intended to measure the degree to which a consumer's involvement with a purchase is *thinking*-related (utilitarian motives) rather than *feeling* (affective motives).

SCALE ORIGIN: The items in this measure were first used by Ratchford (1987) in two separate scales: one measuring involvement with a purchase decision and another intended to capture the degree to which a decision is made on the basis of thinking rather than feeling. Putrevu and Lord (1994) indicate that they combined the items from these two scales based upon the work of Kim and Lord (1991). The latter demonstrated that there was greater validity and strategic value if the thinking scale was combined with the purchase involvement scale. Shamdasani, Stanaland, and Tan (2001) just used the purchase involvement part of the scale.

RELIABILITY: Alphas of .74 and .83 were reported for the versions of the scale used by Putrevu and Lord (1994) and Shamdasani, Stanaland, and Tan (2001), respectively.

VALIDITY: Evidence of the scale's unidimensionality comes from a factor analysis performed by Putrevu and Lord (1994). The analysis included the three items composing the Purchase Involvement (Affective) scale as well as the five items in this scale. The Varimax rotation produced good simple structure. Scale scores for the four products selected to represent the quadrants of the FCB Grid placed them in the correct cells, though not as well as hoped. This provides some limited evidence of the scales' predictive validity.

Shamdasani, Stanaland, and Tan (2001) did not address the validity of the scale.

REFERENCES:

Kim, Chung K. and Kenneth R. Lord (1991), "A New FCB Grid and Its Strategic Implications for Advertising," in *Proceedings of the Annual Conference of the Administrative Sciences Association of Canada (Marketing)*, Tony Schellinck, ed. Niagara Falls, Ontario: Administrative Sciences Association of Canada, 51–60.

Putrevu, Sanjay and Kenneth R. Lord (1994), "Comparative and Noncomparative Advertising: Attitudinal Effects Under Cognitive and Affective," *JA*, 23 (June), 77–90.

Ratchford, Brian T. (1987), "New Insights About the FCB Grid," *JAR*, 27 (4), 24–38.

Shamdasani, Prem N., Andrea J. S. Stanaland, and Juliana Tan (2001), "Location, Location, Location: Insights for Advertising Placement on the Web," *JAR*, 41 (July-August), 7–21.

SCALE ITEMS: [1]

1. unimportant decision / very important decision

2. decision requires little thought / decision requires a lot of thought

3. little to lose if you choose the wrong brand / a lot to lose if you choose the wrong brand

4. decision is not mainly logical or objective / decision is mainly logical or objective

5. decision is not based mainly on the functional facts / decision is based mainly on the functional facts

---

[1] Putrevu and Lord (1994) used all five items whereas Shamdasani, Stanaland, and Tan (2001) used just the first three. A seven-point response scale was used in both studies.

SCALE NAME: Purchase Likelihood (Sponsor's Products)

SCALE DESCRIPTION: The scale is composed of three, seven-point Likert type statements measuring the subjective likelihood that if a certain company supported a particular event then it would improve the chances that a consumer would buy the sponsor's products. The events examined by Speed and Thompson (2000) were related to sports.

SCALE ORIGIN: Although not explicitly stated by the authors, the scale appears to be original to the study by Speed and Thompson (2000). Some qualitative work by the authors led to generation of items for several scales used to create the independent variables in the model. This was followed by a pretest which aided in identifying items for deletion or modification. It was not clear whether or not the items used to create this scale and the other dependent measures were part of this process.

RELIABILITY: An alpha of .94 was reported for the scale by Speed and Thompson (2000).

VALIDITY: Based on data from the main study, a CFA was performed on items from this scale and two others (the dependent variables). The results provided evidence of this scale's convergent and discriminant validity.

REFERENCES:
Speed, Richard and Peter Thompson (2000), "Determinants of Sports Sponsorship Response," *JAMS*, 28 (2), 226–238.

SCALE ITEMS:

1. This sponsorship would make me more likely to use the sponsor's product.

2. This sponsorship would make me more likely to consider this company's products the next time I buy.

3. I would be more likely to buy from the sponsor as a result of this sponsorship.

SCALE NAME: Purchase Likelihood (Upon Child's Request)

SCALE DESCRIPTION: The scale is composed of three, five-point items measuring the probability that a parent would buy a product for a child when he/she asks for it. The scale was referred to as *yielding* by Rose (1999).

SCALE ORIGIN: The scale appears to be original to Rose (1999). Inspiration for the scale comes from Ward, Wackman, and Wartella (1977). A variation on the measure by Carlson and Grossbart (1988) can be found in V. I (#283) of this series.

RELIABILITY: Rose (1999) reported alphas of .66 and .56 for the scale in the U.S. and the Japanese samples, respectively.

VALIDITY: No examination of scale validity was reported by Rose (1999).

COMMENTS: The reliability of the scale is low enough that caution is urged in its use as currently configured.

REFERENCES:

Carlson, Les and Sanford Grossbart (1988), "Parental Style and Consumer Socialization of Children," *JCR*, 15 (June), 77–94.

Rose, Gregory M. and Scott Ward (1999), "Consumer Socialization, Parental Style, and Development Timetables in the United States and Japan," *JM*, 63 (July), 105–119.

Rose, Gregory M. (2002), Personal Correspondence.

Ward, Scott, Daniel B. Wackman, and Ellen Wartella (1977), *How Children Learn to Buy*, Beverly Hills, CA: Sage.

SCALE ITEMS: [1]

If your child asks for _____ how likely would you be to buy it?

1. candy

2. a game or toy

3. a specific type of clothing

[1] The verbal anchors used on the response scale ranged from *very unlikely* (1) to *very likely* (5) (Rose 2002).

SCALE NAME: Purchase Likelihood (With Child's Money)

SCALE DESCRIPTION: The scale is composed of three, five-point items measuring the probability that a parent would buy a product for a child on the condition that the child agrees to use his/her own money. The scale was referred to as *child's payment* by Rose (1999).

SCALE ORIGIN: The scale appears to be original to Rose (1999). Inspiration for the scale comes from Ward, Wackman, and Wartella (1977). A variation on the measure by Carlson and Grossbart (1988) can be found in V. I (#44) of this series.

RELIABILITY: Rose (1999) reported an alpha of .74 for the scale in both the U.S. and the Japanese samples.

VALIDITY: No examination of scale validity was reported by Rose (1999).

REFERENCES:

Carlson, Les and Sanford Grossbart (1988), "Parental Style and Consumer Socialization of Children," *JCR*, 15 (June), 77–94.

Rose, Gregory M. and Scott Ward (1999), "Consumer Socialization, Parental Style, and Development Time-tables in the United States and Japan," *JM*, 63 (July), 105–119.

Rose, Gregory M. (2002), Personal Correspondence.

Ward, Scott, Daniel B. Wackman, and Ellen Wartella (1977), *How Children Learn to Buy*, Beverly Hills, CA: Sage.

SCALE ITEMS: [1]

If your child asks for _____ how likely would you be to buy it only if your child agrees to use his/her own money?

1. candy

2. a game or toy

3. a specific type of clothing

[1] The verbal anchors used on the response scale ranged from *very unlikely* (1) to *very likely* (5) (Rose 2002).

#345 *Purchase Norms (Sports Fans)*

SCALE NAME: Purchase Norms (Sports Fans)

SCALE DESCRIPTION: The scale is composed of four, seven-point semantic differentials measuring the perception of a sports team fan of other respected fans regarding their approval of the purchase of a team sponsor's products.

SCALE ORIGIN: The scale stems were described as being similar to those used by Terry and Hogg (1996). However, the scale items themselves appear to be original to Madrigal (2000).

RELIABILITY: A composite reliability of .86 was reported for the scale by Madrigal (2000).

VALIDITY: Based on the CFA and other tests that were conducted on this and some other scales, Madrigal (2000) concluded that the scale was unidimensional and showed evidence of discriminant validity.

REFERENCES:

Madrigal, Robert (2000), "The Influence of Social Alliances with Sports Teams on Intentions to Purchase Corporate Sponsors' Products," *JA*, 29 (Winter), 13–24.

Terry, Deborah J. and Michael A Hogg (1996), "Group Norms and the Attitude-Behavior Relationship: A Role for Group Identification," *Personality and Social Psychological Bulletin*, 22 (August), 776–793.

SCALE ITEMS: [1]

Most other fans of this team whose opinion I value would probably think my decision to buy products or services from a company because it sponsors the _____ to be:

1. Admirable / silly

2. Smart / dumb

3. Makes sense / does not make sense

On the whole, would you say most other fans of this team who are important to you would approve or disapprove of your decision to buy a sponsor's products?

4. Approve / disapprove

---

[1] The name of the team should be placed in the blank of the initial scale stem.

SCALE NAME: Quality (Acting)

SCALE DESCRIPTION: The scale is composed of three items used to measure a theater attendee's perception of the quality of acting observed at a specified theater. The items utilized different anchors on their response scales. The scale was called *actor satisfaction* by Garbarino and Johnson (1999).

SCALE ORIGIN: Garbarino and Johnson (1999) indicated that they drew upon a variety of sources to develop the items.

RELIABILITY: Garbarino and Johnson (1999) reported the following alphas for the scales as used with three different subsets of theatergoers: .93 (individual ticket buyers), .85 (occasional subscribers), and .69 (consistent subscribers).

VALIDITY: Based on the variety of indicators they examined, Garbarino and Johnson (1999) made a general claim of good fit for their measurement model as well as evidence of good convergent validity. This scale performed adequately on a common test of discriminant validity, but not as well on a more conservative test.

REFERENCES:

Garbarino, Ellen and Mark S. Johnson (1999), "The Different Roles of Satisfaction, Trust, and Commitment in Customer Relationships," *JM*, 63 (April), 70–87.

SCALE ITEMS: [1]

1. How would you rate your overall satisfaction with the performances of the actors at this theater?

2. The actors at this theater are highly skilled.

3. How would you rate this theater compared to other off-Broadway companies on the quality of the acting?

---

[1] Response scale anchors were: *very dissatisfied / very satisfied* (#1), *strongly disagree / strongly agree* (#2), and *much worse / much better* (#3).

SCALE NAME: Quality (Environment)

SCALE DESCRIPTION: Seven, seven-point bi-polar adjectives are used to assess a person's evaluation of some environmental stimulus with an emphasis on affective descriptors. As used by Mattila and Wirtz (2001), the stimulus was a store's atmosphere and was called *store environment*.

SCALE ORIGIN: Mattila and Wirtz (2001) implied that they pretested a twelve-item measure of environmental quality by Fisher (1974). However, several of the items did not work well with their stimulus so the authors dropped them and added one of their own for the main study. Ultimately, of the seven items used by Mattila and Wirtz (2001), six were taken from the Fisher (1974) scale.

RELIABILITY: The alpha for the scale was .92 (Mattila and Wirtz 2001).

VALIDITY: No examination of the scale's validity was reported by Mattila and Wirtz (2001).

REFERENCES:
Fisher, Jeffrey David (1974), "Situation-Specific Variables as Determinants of Perceived Environmental Esthetic Quality and Perceived Crowdedness," *Journal of Research in Personality*, 8 (August), 177–188.
Mattila, Anna S. (2004), Personal Correspondence.
Mattila, Anna S. and Jochen Wirtz (2001), "Congruency of Scent and Music as a Driver of In-store Evaluations and Behaviour," *JR*, 77 (2), 273–289.

SCALE ITEMS: [1]

Directions: How did you find the store environment? Please rate the store environment on the following dimensions:

1. unattractive / attractive

2. uninteresting / interesting

3. bad / good

4. depressing / cheerful

5. dull / bright

6. uncomfortable / comfortable

7. pleasant / unpleasant

[1] The directions were provided by Mattila (2004).

SCALE NAME: Quality (Product)

SCALE DESCRIPTION: The scale is composed of several Likert-type items used to measure the perceived quality of a product with an emphasis on how it is thought it will last over time.

SCALE ORIGIN: Although similar to previous measures of product quality, the sets of items used by Grewal, Monroe, and Krishnan (1998) as well as Grewal et al. (1998) seem to be unique to their studies. The latter did have three items in common with the former as well as using three more items.

Both Sweeney, Soutar, and Johnson (1999) as well as Teas and Agarwal (2000) cited Dodds, Monroe, and Grewal (1991) as the source of their versions of the scale.

RELIABILITY: Grewal, Monroe, and Krishnan (1998) reported construct reliabilities of .79 (n = 361) and .77 (n = 328) for use of the scale in their first and second studies, respectively. The composite reliability for the version of the scale used by Grewal et al. (1998) was .91 (n = 309).

An alpha of .93 was reported for the scale by Sweeney, Soutar, and Johnson (1999). Alphas of .94 (wristwatch) and .96 (calculator) were reported for the version of the scale used by Teas and Agarwal (2000).

VALIDITY: A variety of evidence was provided by Grewal, Monroe, and Krishnan (1998) and Grewal et al. (1998) in support of the scale's unidimensionality, convergent validity, and discriminant validity. The variance extracted for the version of the scale used by Grewal et al. (1998) was .74.

Not much was said by Sweeney, Soutar, and Johnson (1999) about this scale's validity but it was stated in general that all their scales exhibited discriminant validity by having their variance extracted being higher than the relevant squared structural path coefficients (Fornell and Larcker 1981).

Teas and Agarwal (2000) showed for two sets of data that the items were unidimensional. Beyond this, no evidence bearing on the scale's validity was provided.

REFERENCES:

Dodds, William B., Kent B. Monroe, and Dhruv Grewal (1991), "The Effects of Price, Brand, and Store Information on Buyers' Product Evaluations," *JMR*, 28 (August), 307–319.

Fornell, Claes and David F. Larcker (1981), "Evaluating Structural Equation Models with Unobservable Variables and Measurement Error," *JMR*, 18 (February), 39–50.

Grewal, Dhruv, R. Krishnan, Julie Baker, and Norm Borin (1998), "The Effect of Store Name, Brand Name and Price Discounts on Consumers' Evaluations and Purchase Intentions," *JR*, 74 (3), 331–352.

Grewal, Dhruv, Kent B. Monroe, and R. Krishnan (1998), "The Effects of Price-Comparison Advertising on Buyer's Perceptions of Acquisition Value, Transaction Value, and Behavioral Intentions," *JM*, 62 (April), 46–59.

Sweeney, Jillian C., Geoffrey N. Soutar, and Lester W. Johnson (1999), "The Role of Perceived Risk in the Quality-Value Relationship: A Study in a Retail Environment," *JR*, 75 (1), 77–105.

Teas, R. Kenneth and Sanjeev Agarwal (2000), "The Effects of Extrinsic Product Cues on Consumers' Perceptions of Quality, Sacrifice, and Value," *JAMS*, 28 (2), 278–290.

#348 *Quality (Product)*

SCALE ITEMS: [1]

1. The _____ appears to be of good quality.

2. The _____ appears to be durable.

3. The _____ appears to be reliable.

4. The _____ appears to be dependable.

5. My image of the _____ is _____.

6. I view the _____ brand name positively.

7. The workmanship on this product would be good.

[1] The name of the product should be placed in the blanks. Grewal, Monroe, and Krishnan (1998) used items 1-3 and a seven-point response format. Grewal et al. (1998) used the first six items. The blank at the end of item 5 was not specified in the article but was likely to have been a positive descriptor such as *good*. The version of the scale used by Sweeney, Soutar, and Johnson (1999) used #7 and items similar to #2-#4 with a seven-point Likert-type response format. Teas and Agarwal (2000) used items the same or similar to #1-#4 and #7.

SCALE NAME: Quality (Product)

SCALE DESCRIPTION: The scale is composed of eight, seven-point semantic differentials used to measure a person's attitude regarding the quality of a particular product.

SCALE ORIGIN: The source of the scale used by Buchanan, Simmons, and Bickart (1999) was not specified. It appears to be original to their study though it draws on phrases and terms used in previous measures of product quality and brand attitude.

RELIABILITY: An alpha of .91 was reported for the scale by Buchanan, Simmons, and Bickart (1999).

VALIDITY: No examination of the scale's validity was reported by Buchanan, Simmons, and Bickart (1999).

REFERENCES:
Buchanan, Lauranne, Carolyn J. Simmons, and Barbara A. Bickart (1999), "Brand Equity Dilution: Retailer Display and Context Brand Effects," *JMR*, 36 (August), 345–355.

SCALE ITEMS:

1. good quality / poor quality

2. superior product / inferior product

3. better than average product / worse than average product

4. exceptional merchandise / ordinary merchandise

5. durable construction / flimsy construction

6. a lot of attention to details / very little attention to details

7. very good fabric / poor fabric

8. will last a long time / won't last a long time

#350 *Quality (Product)*

SCALE NAME: Quality (Product)

SCALE DESCRIPTION: Several brief descriptors are used to assess a person's attitude about the quality of manufactured products. Given the nature of the items the scale would be most appropriate for goods that are the result of factory production rather than services or agricultural products.

SCALE ORIGIN: The source of the scale used by Johar and Simmons (2000) was not stated, however, it appears to be original to them. They used the scale in several studies reported in their article, all of them composed of five items except the last one (Experiment 4) which had six.

RELIABILITY: The alphas Johar and Simmons (2000) reported for the scale were: .94 (pretest), .90 (Experiment 1), .87 (Experiment 3), and .92 (Experiment 4).

VALIDITY: No evidence relating to the scale's validity was provided (Johar and Simmons 2000).

REFERENCES:
Johar, Gita Venkataramani and Carolyn J. Simmons (2000), "The Use of Concurrent Disclosures to Correct Invalid Inferences," *JCR*, 26 (March), 307–322.

SCALE ITEMS: [1]

1. engineering and design

2. materials

3. manufacturing process

4. reliability

5. performance

6. quality

---

[1] Johar and Simmons (2000) used item 6 as part of the scale only in Experiment 4. It was used by itself as a single item measure in Experiment 2. The anchors for the response scale *very low* and *very high*.

SCALE NAME: Quality (Product)

SCALE DESCRIPTION : The scale is composed of six, five-point Likert-type statements attempting to capture a consumer's general sense of the quality of a specified brand.

SCALE ORIGIN: Although Yoo, Donthu, and Lee (2000) may have drawn inspiration from previous measures, especially Dodds, Monroe, and Grewal (1991), ultimately their scale appears to be original to them.

RELIABILITY: Yoo, Donthu, and Lee (2000) reported the scale to have a composite reliability of .93.

VALIDITY: Factor analyses (EFA and CFA) were used to check the dimensionality of this scale along with eight others used in the study. Based on the results, the authors concluded that all items loaded on their respective factors as expected providing some sense of the scales' convergent and discriminant validities. The average variance extracted for this scale was .68.

REFERENCES:
Dodds, William B., Kent B. Monroe, and Dhruv Grewal (1991), "The Effects of Price, Brand, and Store Information on Buyers' Product Evaluations," *JMR*, 28 (August), 307–319.
Yoo, Boonghee, Naveen Donthu, and Sungho Lee (2000), "An Examination of Selected Marketing Mix Elements and Brand Equity," *JAMS*, 28 (2), 195–211.

SCALE ITEMS: [1]

1. _____ is of high quality.

2. The likely quality of _____ is extremely high.

3. The likelihood that _____ would be functional is very high.

4. The likelihood that _____ is reliable is very high.

5. _____ must be of very good quality.

6. _____ appears to be of very poor quality. (r)

[1] The brand name of a product was placed in the blanks by Yoo, Donthu, and Lee (2000).

SCALE NAME: Quality (Supermarket Merchandise)

SCALE DESCRIPTION: The scale is composed of fifteen, five-point items tapping into a consumer's sense of the quality and breadth (variety) of items carried by a grocer.

SCALE ORIGIN: Sirohi, McLaughlin, and Wittink (1998) did not specify where their measure came from. It appears that it is original to their study.

RELIABILITY: Construct reliability was reported to be .97 (Sirohi, McLaughlin, and Wittink 1998).

VALIDITY: An average variance extracted of .72 was reported for the scale by Sirohi, McLaughlin, and Wittink (1998).

REFERENCES:
Sirohi, Niren, Edward W. McLaughlin, and Dick R. Wittink (1998), "A Model of Consumer Perceptions and Store Loyalty Intentions for a Supermarket Retailer," *JR*, 74 (2), 223–245.

SCALE ITEMS: [1]

1. Overall quality of merchandise purchased

2. Quality of produce department

3. Quality of meat department

4. Quality of deli

5. Quality of grocery items

6. Quality of in-store bakery

7. Quality of seafood department

8. Quality of frozen food section

9. Quality of dairy section

10. Quality of health and beauty aid department

11. Quality of private-label items

12. Rotation of perishables, so that they are always displayed fresh

13. Wide brand selection of grocery items

14. Variety of grocery items

15. Presence of items appropriate for a supermarket

---

[1] The response format for the items was a five-point scale ranging from *excellent* to *poor*.

SCALE NAME: Quality (TV Set)

SCALE DESCRIPTION: The purpose of the scale is to measure a person's perception of the quality of a particular television set. The scale is composed of five questions, each with a seven-point response format.

SCALE ORIGIN: The scale was apparently developed in one of several pretests conducted by Rao, Qu, and Ruekert (1999). The alpha at that point was .85.

RELIABILITY: Rao, Qu, and Ruekert (1999) reported alphas of .91 and .92 for the scale as used in Study 1 (n = 120) and 2 (n = 60), respectively.

VALIDITY: No examination of the scale's validity was reported by Rao, Qu, and Ruekert (1999). It was stated that in Study 1 only one factor emerged with an eigenvalue greater than 1. This is a very weak test of the scale's unidimensionality.

REFERENCES:
Rao, Akshay R., Lu Qu, and Robert W. Ruekert (1999), "Signaling Unobservable Product Quality Through a Brand Ally," *JMR*, 36 (May), 258–268.

SCALE ITEMS: [1]

1. What is your perception of the overall quality of this TV set?

2. What is your perception of the durability of this TV set?

3. What is your perception of the workmanship of this TV set?

4. What is your perception of the sound quality of this TV set?

5. What is your perception of the picture quality of this TV set?

[1] A seven-point response format was used by Rao, Qu, and Ruekert (1999) with anchors ranging from *very poor* (1) to *very good* (7).

SCALE NAME: Quality (Video Product)

SCALE DESCRIPTION: Six, seven-point items are used to measure the extent to which several attributes are characteristic of some video product or class of products. Although each item could be viewed as a belief, summarizing them implies that they are related to each other and are tapping into a common attribute (general product quality). Given the directions used by Gürhan-Canli and Maheswaran (2000), their scale measured one's attitude toward a class of products (electronics) manufactured in a specified country. They referred to the scale as *country-of-origin beliefs*.

SCALE ORIGIN: The scale is original to Gürhan-Canli and Maheswaran (2000).

RELIABILITY: The scale was reported to have an alpha of .88 (Gürhan-Canli and Maheswaran 2000).

VALIDITY: No evidence of the scale's validity was reported by Gürhan-Canli and Maheswaran (2000).

COMMENTS: The directions used by Gürhan-Canli and Maheswaran (2000) were: *Please rate the extent to which the following attributes are characteristic of Taiwanese electronic products.* When a country-of-origin effect is of no concern then different instructions could easily be used to simply measure a person's attitude about the quality of a specific electronic product such as a TV or video recorder.

REFERENCES:
Gurhan-Canli, Zeynep and Durairaj Maheswaran (2000), "Determinants of Country-of-Origin Evaluations," *JCR*, 27 (1), 96–108.

SCALE ITEMS: [1]

1. High picture quality

2. High sound quality

3. Easy to operate

4. Reliable

5. Nice design

6. Superior

7. Remote control

[1] The anchors used in the seven-point response scale by Gürhan-Canli and Maheswaran (2000) were *not at all characteristic* (1) and *very characteristic* (7).

SCALE NAME: Quality Consciousness

SCALE DESCRIPTION: The scale is composed of three, five-point Likert-type statements and attempts to assess the degree to which a consumer is intent on buying high quality products rather than compromising on quality to get a lower price.

SCALE ORIGIN: The source of the scale was not identified by Ailawadi, Neslin, and Gedenk (2001). Although the scale items bear some similarity to those developed by other authors (e.g., #284, V. III), it is probably safest to describe this scale as being original to the work of Ailawadi, Neslin, and Gedenk (2001).

RELIABILITY: A composite reliability of .85 was reported for the scale (Ailawadi, Neslin, and Gedenk 2001).

VALIDITY: The items in this scale along with those belonging to 14 other scales were included in a confirmatory factor analysis. The fit of the measurement model was acceptable and general evidence was cited in support of the scale's discriminant validity.

REFERENCES:
Ailawadi, Kusum L., Scott A. Neslin, and Karen Gedenk (2001), "Pursuing the Value-Conscious Consumer: Store Brands Versus National Brand Promotions," *JM*, 65 (1), 71–89.

SCALE ITEMS:

1. I will not give up high quality for a lower price.

2. I always buy the best.

3. It is important to me to buy high-quality products.

#356 *Racial Importance*

SCALE NAME: Racial Importance

SCALE DESCRIPTION: The three-item, seven-point scale attempts to measure the significance of one's racial status in his/her life.

SCALE ORIGIN: No information about the scale's origin was provided by Grier and Despandé (2001) but it would appear to have been developed by them for this study.

RELIABILITY: Grier and Despandé (2001) reported an alpha of .915 for the scale.

VALIDITY: No information regarding the scale's validity was reported.

REFERENCES:
Grier, Sonya A. and Rohit Despandé (2001), "Social Dimensions of Consumer Distinctiveness: The Influence of Social Status on Group Identity and Advertising Persuasion," *JMR*, 38 (May), 216–224.

SCALE ITEMS:

1. How much do you think about your race?
   Never / often

2. How important is your race to you?
   Unimportant / important

3. How relevant to your life is your race?
   Irrelevant / relevant

SCALE NAME: Reality of Television Portrayals

SCALE DESCRIPTION: The scale is composed of five, five-point Likert-type statements that measure the extent to which a person thinks that television provides an accurate portrayal of life the way it really is.

SCALE ORIGIN: Shrum, Wyer, and O'Guinn (1998) cited Rubin, Perse, and Taylor (1988) as the source of the scale but the origin appears to have been even earlier (Rubin 1981). A factor analysis in the study by Rubin, Perse, and Taylor (1988) indicated that out of 15 items measuring constructs related to TV viewing, the five items composing this scale loaded highest on the same dimension and loaded very low on the other dimensions. The alpha for the scale was .81 (n = 392).

RELIABILITY: The scale was used in the two studies reported by Shrum, Wyer, and O'Guinn (1998) but an alpha was only reported for the second study: .78 (n = 162).

VALIDITY: No information regarding the scale's validity was reported by Shrum, Wyer, and O'Guinn (1998).

REFERENCES:

Rubin, Alan M. (1981), "An Examination of Television Viewing Motivations," *Communication Research*, 8 (April), 141–165.

Rubin, Alan M., Elizabeth M. Perse, and Donald S. Taylor (1988), "A Methodological Examination of Cultivation," *Communication Research*, 15 (April), 107–134.

Shrum, L.J. (2000), Personal Correspondence.

Shrum, L.J., Robert S. Wyer, Jr., and Thomas C. O'Guinn (1998), "The Effects of Television Consumption on Social Perceptions: The Use of Priming Procedures to Investigate Psychological Processes," *JCR*, 24 (March), 447–458.

SCALE ITEMS: [1]

1. Television shows life as it really is.

2. Television presents things as they really are in life.

3. If I see something on television I can be sure it really is that way.

4. Television lets me see how other people live.

5. Television lets me see what happens in other places as if I'm really there.

[1] Although the exact items and response format were not stated by Shrum, Wyer, and O'Guinn (1998), according to Shrum (2000) they used the version shown above as described in Rubin, Perse, and Taylor (1988).

SCALE NAME: Refusal of Child's Purchase Requests (With Explanation)

SCALE DESCRIPTION: The scale is composed of three, five-point items measuring the likelihood that a parent would refuse to buy a product for a child when he/she asks for it but explain the reason for the decision to the child.

SCALE ORIGIN: The scale used by Rose (1999) is a variation on one used by Carlson and Grossbart (1988) that can be found in V. II, #211 of this series. That, in turn, was inspired by items used by Ward, Wackman, and Wartella (1977).

RELIABILITY: Rose (1999) reported alphas of .72 and .65 for the scale in the U.S. and the Japanese samples, respectively.

VALIDITY: No examination of scale validity was reported by Rose (1999).

REFERENCES:

Carlson, Les and Sanford Grossbart (1988), "Parental Style and Consumer Socialization of Children," *JCR*, 15 (June), 77–94.
Rose, Gregory M. and Scott Ward (1999), "Consumer Socialization, Parental Style, and Development Time-tables in the United States and Japan," *JM*, 63 (July), 105–119.
Rose, Gregory M. (2002), Personal Correspondence.
Ward, Scott, Daniel B. Wackman, and Ellen Wartella (1977), *How Children Learn to Buy*, Beverly Hills, CA: Sage.

SCALE ITEMS: [1]

If your child asks for _____ how likely would you be to refuse to buy it but give an explanation why?

1. candy

2. a game or toy

3. a specific type of clothing

---

[1] The verbal anchors used on the response scale ranged from *very unlikely* (1) to *very likely* (5) (Rose 2002).

SCALE NAME: Refusal of Child's Purchase Requests (Without Explanation)

SCALE DESCRIPTION: The scale is composed of three, five-point items measuring the likelihood that a parent would refuse to buy a product for a child when he/she asks for it and *not* explain the reason for the decision to the child.

SCALE ORIGIN: The scale used by Rose (1999) is a variation on one used by Carlson and Grossbart (1988) that can be found in V. I, #215 of this series. That, in turn, was inspired by items used by Ward, Wackman, and Wartella (1977).

RELIABILITY: Rose (2002) reported alphas of .83 and .87 for the scale in the U.S. and the Japanese samples, respectively.

VALIDITY: No examination of scale validity was reported by Rose (1999).

REFERENCES:

Carlson, Les and Sanford Grossbart (1988), "Parental Style and Consumer Socialization of Children," *JCR*, 15 (June), 77–94.
Rose, Gregory M. and Scott Ward (1999), "Consumer Socialization, Parental Style, and Development Timetables in the United States and Japan," *JM*, 63 (July), 105–119.
Rose, Gregory M. (2002), Personal Correspondence.
Ward, Scott, Daniel B. Wackman, and Ellen Wartella (1977), *How Children Learn to Buy*, Beverly Hills, CA: Sage.

SCALE ITEMS: [1]

If your child asks for _____ how likely would you be to just say "no" and that's that?

1. candy

2. a game or toy

3. a specific type of clothing

[1] The verbal anchors used on the response scale ranged from *very unlikely* (1) to *very likely* (5) (Rose 2002).

#360 *Regret*

SCALE NAME: Regret

SCALE DESCRIPTION: The scale is composed of three, seven-point Likert-type items measuring the displeasure a consumer experiences after a specific purchase decision when it appears possible that another brand should have been selected. Although it may be most natural for the scale to be completed by consumers with respect to their own regret, in the study by Tsiros and Mittal (2000) it had to do with the attribution of regret on others based on knowledge of what they had experienced. In other words, one party believes that another party who has made a "bad" purchase decision is feeling regretful about it.

SCALE ORIGIN: The scale is apparently original to Tsiros and Mittal (2000).

RELIABILITY: An alpha of .82 was reported for the scale (Tsiros and Mittal 2000).

VALIDITY: Little evidence relating to the scale's validity was reported by Tsiros and Mittal (2000). They did conduct confirmatory factor analysis of these three items along with three others intended to measure satisfaction. The results showed that the two sets of items loaded on their respective factors as expected. Further, a two-factor solution provided better fit than a one-factor solution.

REFERENCES:
Tsiros, Michael and Vikas Mittal (2000), "Regret: A Model of Its Antecedents and Consequences in Consumer Decision Making," *JCR*, 26 (March), 401–417.

SCALE ITEMS: [1]

1. _____ feel(s) sorry for choosing _____.

2. _____ regret(s) choosing _____.

3. _____ should have chosen _____.

---

[1] The name of the person experiencing the regret goes in the first blank. The name of the chosen product should be placed in the second blanks of items 1 and 2 whereas the name of another brand should go in the second blank of item 3.

SCALE NAME: Relational Benefits (Confidence)

SCALE DESCRIPTION: Six statements are used to measure the benefits above and beyond the core service performance that a consumer perceives receiving as a result of having a long-term relationship with a service provider. In particular, this scale is distinguished from two others also tapping into relational benefits (#363 and #366) by focusing on the comfort or security one feels by having a relationship with a specific service firm. This version of the scale used a six-point, Likert-type response format. Another version of the scale used the same items but with different directions (provided below) to measure the importance of this benefit. The anchors for this version were *very unimportant* and *very important*.

SCALE ORIGIN: The scale is original to Gwinner, Gremler, and Bitner (1998). The authors conducted depth interviews and then developed the items. The set of statements were pretested followed by improvements in item wording and directions before using them in the main study.

RELIABILITY: Alphas were .89 and .85 (n = 299) for the benefits received and importance versions of the scale, respectively (Gwinner 2000; Gwinner, Gremler, and Bitner 1998).

VALIDITY: No explicit examination of the scale's validity was reported by Gwinner, Gremler, and Bitner (1998). However, it is worthy of note that a factor analysis was conducted on sixteen items expected to tap into various dimensions of relational benefits. The six items in this scale clearly loaded on the same dimension. The factor structure fit well with what was expected based upon the authors' conceptual arguments as well as the results of their depth interview study.

REFERENCES:
Gwinner, Kevin P. (2000), Personal Correspondence.
Gwinner, Kevin P., Dwayne D. Gremler, and Mary Jo Bitner (1998), "Relational Benefits in Services Industries: The Customer's Perspective," *JAMS*, 26 (2), 101–114.

SCALE ITEMS:

Directions for Benefits Received version: The following questions ask about some benefits you may receive because of your relationship with the service provider you identified on the first page. Please write the name of the service provider you identified on the first page below. Indicate the degree to which you agree or disagree with each of the following statements.

Directions for Importance of Benefits version: We want to ask you some questions regarding how *important* certain relationship benefits are to you. Regardless of whether you receive these benefits in the relationship you rated on the previous page, please rate how important receiving these benefits are to you for this type of business.

1. I believe there is less risk that something will go wrong.

2. I feel I can trust the service provider.

3. I have more confidence the service will be performed correctly.

4. I have less anxiety when I buy the service.

5. I know what to expect when I go in.

6. I get the provider's highest level of service.

SCALE NAME: Relational Benefits (Functional)

SCALE DESCRIPTION: The four, seven-point Likert-type items are used to measure how much a person values the potential benefits received from interacting with a specific "sales associate" at a certain business. These benefits are above and beyond delivery of the core goods or services being purchased and have to do with more efficiently or effectively making the purchase decision.

SCALE ORIGIN: The scale is original to the study by Reynolds and Beatty (1999).

RELIABILITY: Reynolds and Beatty (1999) reported a composite reliability of .87 for the scale.

VALIDITY: A claim of convergent validity was made based upon the significance of the scale's loadings in the confirmatory factor analysis. Evidence of the discriminant validity of their two relational benefits measures (functional and social) came from noting that the variance extracted for each was much higher than the correlation between them.

REFERENCES:
Reynolds, Kristy E. and Sharon E. Beatty (1999), "Customer Benefits and Company Consequences of Customer-Salesperson Relationships in Retailing," *JR*, 75 (1), 11–32.

SCALE ITEMS:

1. I value the convenience benefits my sales associate provides me very highly.

2. I value the time saving benefits my sales associate provides me very highly.

3. I benefit from the advice my sales associate gives me.

4. I make better purchase decisions because of my sales associate.

SCALE NAME: Relational Benefits (Social)

SCALE DESCRIPTION: Five statements are used to measure the benefits above and beyond the core service performance that a consumer perceives receiving as a result of having a long-term relationship with a service provider. In particular, this scale is distinguished from two others also tapping into relational benefits (#361 and #366) by focusing on the familiarity or even friendship one feels by having a relationship with a specific service firm. This version of the scale used a six-point, Likert-type response format. Another version of the scale used the same items but with different directions (provided below) to measure the importance of this benefit. The anchors for this version were *very unimportant* and *very important*.

SCALE ORIGIN: The scale is original to Gwinner, Gremler, and Bitner (1998). The authors conducted depth interviews and then developed the items. The set of statements were pretested followed by improvements in item wording and directions before using them in the main study.

RELIABILITY: Alphas were .88 and .87 (n = 299) for the benefits received and importance versions of the scale, respectively (Gwinner 2000; Gwinner, Gremler, and Bitner 1998).

VALIDITY: No explicit examination of the scale's validity was reported by Gwinner, Gremler, and Bitner (1998). However, it is worthy of note that a factor analysis was conducted on sixteen items expected to tap into various dimensions of relational benefits. The five items in this scale clearly loaded on the same dimension. The factor structure fit well with what was expected based upon the authors' conceptual arguments as well as the results of their depth interview study.

REFERENCES:
Gwinner, Kevin P. (2000), Personal Correspondence.
Gwinner, Kevin P., Dwayne D. Gremler, and Mary Jo Bitner (1998), "Relational Benefits in Services Industries: The Customer's Perspective," *JAMS*, 26 (2), 101–114.

SCALE ITEMS:

Directions for Benefits Received version: The following questions ask about some benefits you may receive because of your relationship with the service provider you identified on the first page. Please write the name of the service provider you identified on the first page below. Indicate the degree to which you agree or disagree with each of the following statements.

Directions for Importance of Benefits version: We want to ask you some questions regarding how *important* certain relationship benefits are to you. Regardless of whether you receive these benefits in the relationship you rated on the previous page, please rate how important receiving these benefits are to you for this type of business.

1. I am recognized by certain employees.

2. I am familiar with the employee(s) who perform the service.

3. I have developed a friendship with the provider.

4. They know my name.

5. I enjoy certain social aspects of the relationship.

SCALE NAME: Relational Benefits (Social)

SCALE DESCRIPTION: The scale is composed of four, seven-point Likert-type items that are used to measure a consumer's sense of the potential benefits received from interacting with a specific "sales associate" at a certain business. These benefits are above and beyond delivery of the core goods or services being purchased and have to do with enjoying the salesperson as a individual.

SCALE ORIGIN: The scale is original to the study by Reynolds and Beatty (1999).

RELIABILITY: Reynolds and Beatty (1999) reported a composite reliability of .91 for the scale.

VALIDITY: A claim of convergent validity was made based upon the significance of the scale's loadings in a confirmatory factor analysis. Evidence of the discriminant validity of their two relational benefits measures (functional and social) came from noting that the variance extracted for each was much higher than the correlation between them.

REFERENCES:
Reynolds, Kristy E. and Sharon E. Beatty (1999), "Customer Benefits and Company Consequences of Customer-Salesperson Relationships in Retailing," *JR*, 75 (1), 11–32.

SCALE ITEMS:

1. The friendship aspect of my relationship with my sales associate is very important to me.

2. I enjoy spending time with my sales associate.

3. I value the close, personal relationship I have with my sales associate.

4. I enjoy my sales associate's company.

SCALE NAME: Relational Benefits (Social)

SCALE DESCRIPTION: Five-seven-point Likert-type statements are used to measure a customer's thoughts regarding the existence and degree of relationship with at least one employee of a service provider. Jones, Mothersbaugh, and Beatty (2000) referred to their scale as *interpersonal relationships*.

SCALE ORIGIN: Jones, Mothersbaugh, and Beatty (2000) stated that they adapted the scale from dissertation research by Gremler (1995). Indeed, the scale is conceptually similar to one reported by Gwinner, Gremler, and Bitner (1998) although the items themselves are different (See #363).

RELIABILITY: The reliability of the scale was .95 (both alpha and composite).

VALIDITY: Based on the CFA and other tests that were conducted on this and other scales, Jones, Mothersbaugh, and Beatty (2000) concluded that their version of the scale was unidimensional and showed evidence of discriminant validity. In addition, the scale was reported to have a variance extracted of .78.

REFERENCES:
Gremler, Dwayne D. (1995), "The Effect of Satisfaction, Switching Costs, and Interpersonal Bonds on Service Loyalty," unpublished doctoral dissertation, Arizona State University.
Gwinner, Kevin P., Dwayne D. Gremler, and Mary Jo Bitner (1998), "Relational Benefits in Services Industries: The Customer's Perspective," *JAMS*, 26 (2), 101–114.
Jones, Michael A., David L. Mothersbaugh, and Sharon E. Beatty (2000), "Switching Barriers and Repurchase Intentions in Services," *JR*, 79 (2), 259–274.

SCALE ITEMS: [1]

1. I feel like there is a "bond" between at least one employee at this _____ and myself.

2. I have developed a personal friendship with at least one employee at this _____.

3. I have somewhat of a personal relationship with at least one employee at this _____.

4. I am friends with at least one employee at this _____.

5. At least one employee at this _____ is familiar with me.

[1] A generic descriptor of the service provider should go in the blanks, e.g., bank.

SCALE NAME: Relational Benefits (Special Treatment)

SCALE DESCRIPTION: Five statements are used to measure the benefits above and beyond the core service performance that a consumer perceives receiving as a result of having a long-term relationship with a service provider. In particular, this scale is distinguished from two others also tapping into relational benefits (#361 and #363) by focusing on customization and economic benefits one receives by having a relationship with a specific service firm. This version of the scale used a six-point, Likert-type response format. Another version of the scale used the same items but with different directions (provided below) to measure the importance of this benefit. The anchors for this version were *very unimportant* and *very important*.

SCALE ORIGIN: The scale is original to Gwinner, Gremler, and Bitner (1998). The authors conducted depth interviews and then developed the items. The set of statements were pretested followed by improvements in item wording and directions before using them in the main study.

RELIABILITY: Alphas were .89 and .92 (n = 299) for the benefits received and importance versions of the scale, respectively (Gwinner 2000; Gwinner, Gremler, and Bitner 1998).

VALIDITY: No explicit examination of the scale's validity was reported by Gwinner, Gremler, and Bitner (1998). However, it is worthy of note that a factor analysis was conducted on sixteen items expected to tap into various dimensions of relational benefits. The five items in this scale clearly loaded on the same dimension. Based upon the authors' conceptual arguments as well as the results of their depth interview study it has been expected that these items would load on two different dimensions (economic and customization) rather than together on one.

REFERENCES:
Gwinner, Kevin P. (2000), Personal Correspondence.
Gwinner, Kevin P., Dwayne D. Gremler, and Mary Jo Bitner (1998), "Relational Benefits in Services Industries: The Customer's Perspective," *JAMS*, 26 (2), 101–114.

SCALE ITEMS:

Directions for Benefits Received version: The following questions ask about some benefits you may receive because of your relationship with the service provider you identified on the first page. Please write the name of the service provider you identified on the first page below. Indicate the degree to which you agree or disagree with each of the following statements.

Directions for Importance of Benefits version: We want to ask you some questions regarding how *important* certain relationship benefits are to you. Regardless of whether you receive these benefits in the relationship you rated on the previous page, please rate how important receiving these benefits are to you for this type of business.

1. I get discounts or special deals that most customers don't get.

2. I get better prices that most customers.

3. They do services for me that they don't do for most customers.

4. I am placed higher on the priority list when there is a line.

5. I get faster service than most customers.

SCALE NAME: Relationship Investment (Commercial Friendship)

SCALE DESCRIPTION: The scale has three, seven-point Likert-type statements and is intended to measure a customer's belief that a specific retailer has employees who get to know their regular customers over time and care about them. The scale was referred to as *interpersonal communication* by De Wulf, Odekerken-Schröder, and Iacobucci (2001).

SCALE ORIGIN: The scale seems to have been among those developed specifically for use in the studies by De Wulf, Odekerken-Schröder, and Iacobucci (2001) although its items bear some similarity to previous measures of commercial friendship (#118) and service quality (e.g., V. III. #338). Items were generated after conducting focus groups and depth interviews with consumers. Content validity was assessed using expert judges. The back-translation method was used to developed versions of the scales in American English and Dutch. Finally, the items were pretested in the U.S., Netherlands, and Belgium (Flemish-speaking area) and that led to only slight revisions.

RELIABILITY: Composite reliabilities were reported by De Wulf, Odekerken-Schröder, and Iacobucci (2001) for two types of stores for each of three countries. The reliabilities for food stores were .89, .87, and .89 for the U.S., Netherlands, and Belgium, respectively. For apparel stores, the reliabilities were .90, .87, and .83 for the U.S., Netherlands, and Belgium, respectively.

VALIDITY: A great deal of information regarding the scale's validity was provided by De Wulf, Odekerken-Schröder, and Iacobucci (2001). In brief, evidence was provided in support of the scale's unidimensionality as well as its convergent and discriminant validities. The average variance extracted for the six uses of the scale ranged from .61 to .74. Partial metric invariance across countries was supported too.

REFERENCES:
De Wulf, Kristof, Gaby Odekerken-Schröder, and Dawn Iacobucci (2001), "Investments in Consumer Relationships: A Cross-Country and Cross-Industry Exploration," *JM*, 65 (October), 33–50.

SCALE ITEMS:

1. This store takes the time to personally get to know regular customers.

2. This store often holds personal conversations with regular customers.

3. This store often inquires about the personal welfare of regular customers.

SCALE NAME: Relationship Investment (Overall)

SCALE DESCRIPTION: Three, seven-point Likert-type statements are intended to assess the degree to which a customer perceives that a specified store makes serious and significant efforts to strengthen and improve relationships with its regular customers.

SCALE ORIGIN: The scale seems to have been among those developed specifically for use in the studies by De Wulf, Odekerken-Schröder, and Iacobucci (2001). Items were generated after conducting focus groups and depth interviews with consumers. Content validity was assessed using expert judges. The back-translation method was used to developed versions of the scales in American English and Dutch. Finally, the items were pretested in the U.S., Netherlands, and Belgium (Flemish-speaking area) and that led to only slight revisions.

RELIABILITY: Composite reliabilities were reported by De Wulf, Odekerken-Schröder, and Iacobucci (2001) for two types of stores for each of three countries. The reliabilities for food stores were .92, .86, and .89 for the U.S., Netherlands, and Belgium, respectively. For apparel stores, the reliabilities were .93, .90, and .87 for the U.S., Netherlands, and Belgium, respectively.

VALIDITY: A great deal of information regarding the scale's validity was provided by De Wulf, Odekerken-Schröder, and Iacobucci (2001). In brief, evidence was provided in support of the scale's unidimensionality as well as its convergent and discriminant validities. The average variance extracted for the six uses of the scale ranged from .68 to .81. Full metric invariance across countries was supported too.

REFERENCES:
De Wulf, Kristof, Gaby Odekerken-Schröder, and Dawn Iacobucci (2001), "Investments in Consumer Relationships: A Cross-Country and Cross-Industry Exploration," *JM*, 65 (October), 33–50.

SCALE ITEMS:

1. This store makes efforts to increase regular customers' loyalty.

2. This store makes various efforts to improve its tie with regular customers.

3. This store really cares about keeping regular customers.

SCALE NAME: Relationship Investment (Preferential Treatment)

SCALE DESCRIPTION: The scale has three, seven-point Likert-type statements and is intended to measure a customer's belief that a specific retailer tends to treat its regular customers better than its nonregular ones.

SCALE ORIGIN: The scale seems to have been among those developed specifically for use in the studies by De Wulf, Odekerken-Schröder, and Iacobucci (2001). Items were generated after conducting focus groups and depth interviews with consumers. Content validity was assessed using expert judges. The back-translation method was used to developed versions of the scales in American English and Dutch. Finally, the items were pretested in the U.S., Netherlands, and Belgium (Flemish-speaking area) and that led to only slight revisions.

RELIABILITY: Composite reliabilities were reported by De Wulf, Odekerken-Schröder, and Iacobucci (2001) for two types of stores for each of three countries. The reliabilities for food stores were .90, .79, and .91 for the U.S., Netherlands, and Belgium, respectively. For apparel stores, the reliabilities were .89, .86, and .86 for the U.S., Netherlands, and Belgium, respectively.

VALIDITY: A great deal of information regarding the scale's validity was provided by De Wulf, Odekerken-Schröder, and Iacobucci (2001). In brief, evidence was provided in support of the scale's unidimensionality as well as its convergent and discriminant validities. The average variance extracted for the six uses of the scale ranged from .57 to .77. Full metric invariance across countries was supported too.

REFERENCES:
De Wulf, Kristof, Gaby Odekerken-Schröder, and Dawn Iacobucci (2001), "Investments in Consumer Relationships: A Cross-Country and Cross-Industry Exploration," *JM*, 65 (October), 33–50.

SCALE ITEMS:

1. This store makes greater efforts for regular customers than for nonregular customers.

2. This store offers better services to regular customers than to nonregular customers.

3. This store does more for regular customers than for nonregular customers.

SCALE NAME: Relationship Investment (Tangible Rewards)

SCALE DESCRIPTION: Three, seven-point Likert-type statements are used to measure an aspect of the investment made by a retailer in its relationships with customers, with the emphasis being on a customer's belief that the store provides something extra to its regular customers in exchange for their loyalty.

SCALE ORIGIN: The scale seems to have been among those developed specifically for use in the studies by De Wulf, Odekerken-Schröder, and Iacobucci (2001). Items were generated after conducting focus groups and depth interviews with consumers. Content validity was assessed using expert judges. The back-translation method was used to developed versions of the scales in American English and Dutch. Finally, the items were pretested in the U.S., Netherlands, and Belgium (Flemish-speaking area) and that led to only slight revisions.

RELIABILITY: Composite reliabilities were reported by De Wulf, Odekerken-Schröder, and Iacobucci (2001) for two types of stores for each of three countries. The reliabilities for food stores were .87, .80, and .80 for the U.S., Netherlands, and Belgium, respectively. For apparel stores, the reliabilities were .91, .87, and .86 for the U.S., Netherlands, and Belgium, respectively.

VALIDITY: A great deal of information regarding the scale's validity was provided by De Wulf, Odekerken-Schröder, and Iacobucci (2001). In brief, evidence was provided in support of the scale's unidimensionality as well as its convergent and discriminant validities. The average variance extracted for the six uses of the scale ranged from .57 to .77. Partial metric invariance across countries was supported too.

REFERENCES:
De Wulf, Kristof, Gaby Odekerken-Schröder, and Dawn Iacobucci (2001), "Investments in Consumer Relationships: A Cross-Country and Cross-Industry Exploration," *JM*, 65 (October), 33–50.

SCALE ITEMS:

1. This store rewards regular customers for their patronage.

2. This store offers regular customers something extra because they keep buying there.

3. This store offers discounts to regular customers for their patronage.

SCALE NAME: Relative Prices (Supermarket Merchandise)

SCALE DESCRIPTION: The scale is composed of five, five-point items measuring a consumer's sense of the general price level of a focal supermarket's products in comparison to those of other stores.

SCALE ORIGIN: The scale appears to be original to Sirohi, McLaughlin, and Wittink (1998) although they drew some inspiration from the studies by Conover (1986).

RELIABILITY: Construct reliability was reported to be .86 (Sirohi, McLaughlin, and Wittink 1998).

VALIDITY: An average variance extracted of .55 was reported for the scale by Sirohi, McLaughlin, and Wittink (1998).

REFERENCES:
Conover, Jerry N. (1986), "The Accuracy of Price Knowledge: Issues in Research Methodology," in *Advances in Consumer Research, V. 13*, Richard J. Lutz, ed. Provo, UT: Association for Consumer Research, 589–593.
Sirohi, Niren, Edward W. McLaughlin, and Dick R. Wittink (1998), "A Model of Consumer Perceptions and Store Loyalty Intentions for a Supermarket Retailer," *JR*, 74 (2), 223–245.

SCALE ITEMS: [1]

1. Comparison with charges made by alternative supermarkets for similar products.

2. Comparison with charges made by stores other than supermarkets for similar products.

3. Comparison of meat prices with other supermarkets.

4. Comparison of produce prices with other supermarkets.

5. Comparison of health and beauty aid prices with other supermarkets.

[1] The response format for the items was a five-point scale ranging from *much lower priced* to *much higher priced*.

SCALE NAME: Reliability of Theater Productions

SCALE DESCRIPTION: Four, five-point Likert-type items are used to measure a theater attendee's confidence in the quality and consistency of the shows produced by a specified theater. The scale was called *trust* by Garbarino and Johnson (1999).

SCALE ORIGIN: Garbarino and Johnson (1999) indicated that they drew upon a variety of sources to develop the items.

RELIABILITY: Garbarino and Johnson (1999) reported the following alphas for the scales as used with three different subsets of theatergoers: .93 (individual ticket buyers), .80 (occasional subscribers), and .73 (consistent subscribers).

VALIDITY: Based on the variety of indicators they examined, Garbarino and Johnson (1999) made a general claim of good fit for their measurement model as well as evidence of good convergent validity. There were several indications that the scale had adequate discriminant validity but with the individual ticket buyer sample the scale did not have discriminant validity with respect to a measure of satisfaction with the theater company.

REFERENCES:

Garbarino, Ellen and Mark S. Johnson (1999), "The Different Roles of Satisfaction, Trust, and Commitment in Customer Relationships," *JM*, 63 (April), 70–87.

SCALE ITEMS:

1. The performances at this theater always meet my expectations.

2. This theater can be counted on to produce a good show.

3. I cannot always trust performances at this theater to be good. (r)

4. This theater is a reliable off-Broadway theater company.

SCALE NAME: Reliance on Internal Reference Price

SCALE DESCRIPTION: The scale is composed of four, seven-point statements that measure the degree to which a consumer has other prices in mind when deciding if the price of a particular product is "good."

SCALE ORIGIN: The scale is original to the study of Burton et al. (1998). They said items were generated that were consistent with the construct's domain. The items were assessed in a pretest and less reliable ones were deleted from further use.

RELIABILITY: An alpha of .85 was reported for the scale by Burton et al. (1998).

VALIDITY: No information relating to the scale's validity was reported by Burton et al. (1998).

COMMENTS: Although the scale stem and first item mention a grocery store, the scale seems amenable for use in other contexts with some minor modification and retesting.

REFERENCES:
Burton, Scot (2000), Personal Correspondence.
Burton, Scot, Donald R. Lichtenstein, Richard G. Netemeyer, and Judith A. Garretson (1998), "A Scale for Measuring Attitude Toward Private Label Products and an Examination of Its Psychological and Behavioral Correlates," *JAMS*, 26 (4), 293–306.

SCALE ITEMS: [1]

To what extent do you think about the following in deciding if the price of a grocery item is a "good" price, or if a price is too high?

1. The price the brand normally sells for at the particular grocery store.

2. The price other stores are charging for the brand.

3. What a fair price for the brand would be.

4. The price you usually pay for the brand.

[1] One sample item was provided in the article by Burton et al. (1998). The other items were supplied personally by Burton (2000). The response scale used the following anchors: *do not think about at all* and *think about very much.*

SCALE NAME: Repatronage Intention

SCALE DESCRIPTION: The scale is composed of three, five-point items attempting to assess a person's likelihood of continuing to use an object. It is intended to tap into an aspect of loyalty. Given the phrasing of the items, the scale may not be widely usable for measuring the construct. They seem to best fit situations where a service or subscription is involved.

SCALE ORIGIN: The scale is apparently original to the study reported by Bolton, Kannan, and Bramlett (2000).

RELIABILITY: An alpha of .69 was reported for the scale (Bolton, Kannan, and Bramlett 2000).

VALIDITY: No examination of the scale's validity was reported by Bolton, Kannan, and Bramlett (2000).

REFERENCES:
Bolton, Ruth N., P.K. Kannan, and Matthew D. Bramlett (2000), "Implications of Loyalty Program Membership and Service Experiences for Customer Retention and Value," *JAMS*, 28 (1), 95–108.

SCALE ITEMS: [1]

1. How likely are you to recommend _____.

2. How likely are you to renew your _____.

3. How likely are you to increase your share of purchases with _____.

---

[1] The response scale used with these items ranged from *extremely likely* to *not at all likely*. The name of the product should be placed in the blanks. In the study by Bolton, Kannan, and Bramlett (2000), the product was a particular brand of credit card.

SCALE NAME: Response Difficulty

SCALE DESCRIPTION: The four-item, seven-point scale is intended to measure the perceived cognitive effort involved in answering a question. The scale was referred to as the *effort index* by Menon, Raghubir, and Schwarz (1995) and *accessibility manipulation* by Raghubir and Menon (1998).

SCALE ORIGIN: Although not explicitly stated, the scale appears to have been developed by Menon, Raghubir, and Schwarz (1995) for use in their study.

RELIABILITY: Alphas of .80 and .83 (n = 177) were reported by Menon, Raghubir, and Schwarz (1995) for the scale as used with regard to a question about regular behaviors and irregular behaviors, respectively. The scale was used in Studies 2 and 3 by Raghubir and Menon (1998) and alphas of .84 (n = 76) and .90 (n = 109), respectively, were reported.

VALIDITY: No examination of the scale's validity was discussed in either study.

REFERENCES:
Menon, Geeta, Priya Raghubir, and Norbert Schwarz (1995), "Behavioral Frequency Judgments: An Accessibility-Diagnosticity Framework," *JCR*, 22 (September), 212–228.
Raghubir, Priya (2000), Personal Correspondence.
Raghubir, Priya and Geeta Menon (1998), "AIDS and Me, Never the Twain Shall Meet: The Effects of Information Accessibility on Judgments of Risk and Advertising Effectiveness," *JCR*, 25 (June), 52–63.

SCALE ITEMS: [1]

Directions: The following questions pertain to how effortful you found the task. For each scale, please circle the number that best corresponds with your opinion.
 1. How would you rate the LEVEL OF DIFFICULTY of responding to this question?
    Not at all / Very difficult

 2. How would you rate the AMOUNT OF EFFORT it took you to respond to this question?
    No effort / A lot of effort

 3. How would you rate the AMOUNT OF TIME it took you to respond to this question?
    No time / A lot of time

 4. How would you rate the AMOUNT OF THOUGHT you had to put into responding to this question?
    No thought / A lot of thought

[1] The exact phrasing and structure of the scale was not described in the article by Menon, Raghubir, and Schwarz (1995) but is likely to have been the same as used by Raghubir and Menon (1998). The latter used the items as shown and a seven-point response format (Raghubir 2000).

SCALE NAME: Restriction of TV Viewing

SCALE DESCRIPTION: The scale is composed of three, five-point items measuring the degree to which a parent reports actively controlling when, what, and how much television a child is allowed to watch.

SCALE ORIGIN: The use of these items as a multi-item measure appears to be original to Carlson and Grossbart (1988). The items themselves, however, come from the research of Ward, Wackman, and Wartella (1977).

RELIABILITY: Carlson and Grossbart (1988) reported an alpha of .82 (n = 451) and a beta of .76 for the scale. Alphas of .89 (n = 389) and .85 (n = 237) were reported by Rose (Rose, Bush, and Kahle 1998; Rose 1999) for the scale in the U.S. and Japan, respectively.

VALIDITY: No examination of scale validity was reported by Carlson and Grossbart (1988) or Rose (Rose, Bush, and Kahle 1998; Rose 1999).

REFERENCES:

Carlson, Les and Sanford Grossbart (1988), "Parental Style and Consumer Socialization of Children," *JCR*, 15 (June), 77–94.

Rose, Gregory M. and Scott Ward (1999), "Consumer Socialization, Parental Style, and Development Time-tables in the United States and Japan," *JM*, 63 (July), 105–119.

Rose, Gregory M., Victoria D. Bush, and Lynn Kahle (1998), "The Influence of Family Communication Patterns on Parental Reactions toward Advertising: A Cross-National Examination," *JA*, 27 (4), 71–85.

Ward, Scott, Daniel B. Wackman, and Ellen Wartella (1977), *How Children Learn to Buy*, Beverly Hills, CA: Sage.

SCALE ITEMS: [1]

I place restrictions on:

1. . . . which programs my child can watch on TV.

2. . . . when my child can watch TV.

3. . . . how many hours each day my child can watch TV.

[1] Each of the studies appear to have used a five-point response scale with *very seldom* to *very often* as anchors.

SCALE NAME: Retailer's Institutional Action (Contribution to Community)

SCALE DESCRIPTION: The three-item, seven-point Likert-type scale is intended to measure a person's attitude about a retailer's adherence to unwritten rules of social conduct with the emphasis on how well it makes a positive contribution to the community in which it is located.

SCALE ORIGIN: One of the constructs studied by Handelman and Arnold (1999) was the "institutional actions" of an organization, that is, those things done by the organization that are considered to be "proper" within the norms of society. Three types of institutional actions were identified (family values, contribution to the community, support for the country) and three items were generated for each. The scales were then used as manipulation and confound checks.

RELIABILITY: An alpha of .9256 was calculated for the scale (Handelman 2002; Handelman and Arnold 1999). No information was provided about the reliability of the performative dimension overall (combining the items from the three subscales.)

VALIDITY: Handelman and Arnold (1999) reported on two rounds of examining the 18 items composing three performative scales and three institutional ones. While this provided some sense of the discriminant validities of these two sets of items, it also would appear to indicate that the sets of items measuring the three subdimensions within each factor did not exhibit discriminant validity.

REFERENCES:
Handelman, Jay M. (2002), Personal Correspondence.
Handelman, Jay M. and Stephen J. Arnold (1999), "The Role of Marketing Actions with a Social Dimension: Appeals to the Institutional Environment," *JM*, 63 (July), 33–48.

SCALE ITEMS: [1]

1. _____ is concerned about contributing positively to the community.

2. _____ contributes quite positively to their community.

3. People can rely on _____ to make a positive contribution to the community.

[1] The name of the retailer should be placed in the blanks.

SCALE NAME: Retailer's Institutional Action (Family Values)

SCALE DESCRIPTION: The scale is composed of three, seven-point Likert-type items intended to measure a person's attitude about a retailer's adherence to unwritten rules of social conduct with the emphasis on how well it supports families and their values.

SCALE ORIGIN: One of the constructs studied by Handelman and Arnold (1999) was the "institutional actions" of an organization, that is, those things done by the organization that are considered to be "proper" within the norms of society. Three types of institutional actions were identified (family values, contribution to the community, support for the country) and three items were generated for each. The scales were then used as manipulation and confound checks.

RELIABILITY: An alpha of .8066 was calculated for the scale (Handelman 2002; Handelman and Arnold 1999). No information was provided about the reliability of the institutional dimension overall (combining the items from the three subscales.)

VALIDITY: Handelman and Arnold (1999) reported on two rounds of examining the eighteen items composing three performative scales and three institutional ones. While this provided some sense of the discriminant validities of these two sets of items, it also would appear to indicate that the sets of items measuring the three subdimensions within each factor did not exhibit discriminant validity.

REFERENCES:
Handelman, Jay M. (2002), Personal Correspondence.
Handelman, Jay M. and Stephen J. Arnold (1999), "The Role of Marketing Actions with a Social Dimension: Appeals to the Institutional Environment," *JM*, 63 (July), 33–48.

SCALE ITEMS: [1]

1. _____ contributes positively to upholding family values.

2. _____ is concerned about supporting family values.

3. _____ has created an atmosphere that is welcoming to all family members.

---

[1] The name of the retailer should be placed in the blanks.

SCALE NAME: Retailer's Institutional Action (Support for Country)

SCALE DESCRIPTION: The three-item, seven-point Likert-type scale is intended to measure a person's attitude concerning a retailer's adherence to unwritten rules of social conduct with the emphasis on how well it supports the nation and identifies with it.

SCALE ORIGIN: One of the constructs studied by Handelman and Arnold (1999) was the "institutional actions" of an organization, that is, those things done by the organization that are considered to be "proper" within the norms of society. Three types of institutional actions were identified (family values, contribution to the community, support for the country) and three items were generated for each. The scales were then used as manipulation and confound checks.

RELIABILITY: An alpha of .8651 was calculated for the scale (Handelman 2002; Handelman and Arnold 1999). No information was provided about the reliability of the performative dimension overall (combining the items from the three subscales.)

VALIDITY: Handelman and Arnold (1999) reported on two rounds of examining the 18 items composing three performative scales and three institutional ones. While this provided some sense of the discriminant validities of these two sets of items, it also would appear to indicate that the sets of items measuring the three subdimensions within each factor did not exhibit discriminant validity.

REFERENCES:
Handelman, Jay M. (2002), Personal Correspondence.
Handelman, Jay M. and Stephen J. Arnold (1999), "The Role of Marketing Actions with a Social Dimension: Appeals to the Institutional Environment," *JM*, 63 (July), 33–48.

SCALE ITEMS: [1]

1. _____ will go out of its way to support _____ businesses.

2. _____ is proud to identify itself as a _____ company.

3. _____ has shown itself to have strong roots as a _____ company.

[1] The name of the retailer should be placed in the first blank of each sentence. The name of the country in which the retailer is operating should go in the second blank of each item (e.g., Canadian, American, German).

SCALE NAME: Retailer's Performative Action (Assortment)

SCALE DESCRIPTION: The three-item, seven-point Likert-type scale is intended to measure a person's attitude toward a retailer's performance with the emphasis on how wide an assortment of products are carried by the merchant in comparison to the competition.

SCALE ORIGIN: One of the constructs studied by Handelman and Arnold (1999) was the "performative actions" of an organization, that is, those things done by the organization that are consistent with the norms of competition. Based on a literature review, three key image attributes of retailers were identified (prices, assortment, location) and three items generated for each. These were then used as manipulation and confound checks.

RELIABILITY: An alpha of .8981 was calculated for the scale (Handelman 2002; Handelman and Arnold 1999). No information was provided about the reliability of the performative dimension overall (combining the items from the three subscales.)

VALIDITY: Handelman and Arnold (1999) reported on two rounds of examining the eighteen items composing three performative scales and three institutional ones. While this provided some sense of the discriminant validities of these two sets of items, it also would appear to indicate that the sets of items measuring the three subdimensions within each factor did not exhibit discriminant validity.

REFERENCES:
Handelman, Jay M. (2002), Personal Correspondence.
Handelman, Jay M. and Stephen J. Arnold (1999), "The Role of Marketing Actions with a Social Dimension: Appeals to the Institutional Environment," *JM*, 63 (July), 33–48.

SCALE ITEMS: [1]

1. _____ provides a wide assortment of products in its store.

2. A shopper at _____ can expect to find a wide assortment of products to choose from.

3. _____ offers a wider assortment of products than its competitors.

[1] The name of the retailer should be placed in the blanks.

SCALE NAME: Retailer's Performative Action (Location)

SCALE DESCRIPTION: The scale is composed of three, seven-point Likert-type items and is intended to measure a person's attitude about a retailer's performance with the emphasis on how easy it is viewed as being for shoppers to get to.

SCALE ORIGIN: One of the constructs studied by Handelman and Arnold (1999) was the "performative actions" of an organization, that is, those things done by the organization that are consistent with the norms of competition. Based on a literature review, three key image attributes of retailers were identified (prices, assortment, location) and three items generated for each. These were then used as manipulation and confound checks.

RELIABILITY: An alpha of .8685 was calculated for the scale (Handelman 2002; Handelman and Arnold 1999). No information was provided about the reliability of the performative dimension overall (combining the items from the three subscales.)

VALIDITY: Handelman and Arnold (1999) reported on two rounds of examining the eighteen items composing three performative scales and three institutional ones. While this provided some sense of the discriminant validities of these two sets of items, it also would appear to indicate that the sets of items measuring the three subdimensions within each factor did not exhibit discriminant validity.

REFERENCES:
Handelman, Jay M. (2002), Personal Correspondence.
Handelman, Jay M. and Stephen J. Arnold (1999), "The Role of Marketing Actions with a Social Dimension: Appeals to the Institutional Environment," *JM*, 63 (July), 33–48.

SCALE ITEMS: [1]

1. _____ is an easy store for shoppers to get to.

2. Most shoppers will find _____ easy to get to.

3. The average shopper will spend very little time getting to _____.

[1] The name of the retailer should be placed in the blanks.

SCALE NAME: Retailer's Performative Action (Prices)

SCALE DESCRIPTION: The three-item, seven-point Likert-type scale is intended to measure a person's attitude about a retailer's performance with the emphasis on how low and competitive its prices tend to be.

SCALE ORIGIN: One of the constructs studied by Handelman and Arnold (1999) was the "performative actions" of an organization, that is, those things done by the organization that are consistent with the norms of competition. Based on a literature review, three key image attributes of retailers were identified (prices, assortment, location) and three items generated for each. These were then used as manipulation and confound checks.

RELIABILITY: An alpha of .9201 was calculated for the scale (Handelman 2002; Handelman and Arnold 1999). No information was provided about the reliability of the performative dimension overall (combining the items from the three subscales.)

VALIDITY: Handelman and Arnold (1999) reported on two rounds of examining the 18 items composing three performative scales and three institutional ones. While this provided some sense of the discriminant validities of these two sets of items, it also would appear to indicate that the sets of items measuring the three subdimensions within each factor did not exhibit discriminant validity.

REFERENCES:
Handelman, Jay M. (2002), Personal Correspondence.
Handelman, Jay M. and Stephen J. Arnold (1999), "The Role of Marketing Actions with a Social Dimension: Appeals to the Institutional Environment," *JM*, 63 (July), 33–48.

SCALE ITEMS: [1]

1. A shopper will find _____ prices to be, on average, lower than the competition.

2. _____ offers its customers very low prices.

3. _____ prices are lower than their competitors' prices.

---

[1] The name of the retailer should be placed in the blanks.

SCALE NAME: Risk (General)

SCALE DESCRIPTION: Four, nine-point semantic differentials are used as an overall measure of a person's perceived risk with regard to some stimulus (product, event, etc.).

SCALE ORIGIN: Campbell and Goodstein (2001) did not indicate the source of the scale and it appears to be original to them.

RELIABILITY: The scale had alphas of .86 and .91 in the studies in which it was used by Campbell and Goodstein (2001).

VALIDITY: No examination of the scale's validity was reported by Campbell and Goodstein (2001).

COMMENTS: Although perceived risk has long been conceptualized as having a complex structure with two components (uncertainty and consequences) and different forms (financial, functional, etc.) (e.g., Bauer 1960; Cox 1967; Roselius 1971), this scale views it rather simply. It appears that the scenarios used with subjects by Campbell and Goodstein (2001) focused on social risk. However, the items are general enough that they seem to be amenable for use with the other types of risk as well.

REFERENCES:
Bauer, Raymond A. (1960), "Consumer Behavior as Risk Taking," in *Proceedings of the 43rd Conference of the American Marketing Association*, R. S. Hancock, ed. Chicago: American Marketing Association 389–398.
Campbell, Margaret C. and Ronald C. Goodstein (2001), "The Moderating Effect of Perceived Risk on Consumers' Evaluations of Product Incongruity: Preference for the Norm," *JCR*, 28 (December), 439–449.
Cox, Donald F. ed. (1967), *Risk Taking and Information Handling in Consumer Behavior*, Boston, MA: Harvard Univ. Press.
Roselius, Ted (1971), "Consumer Rankings of Risk Reduction Methods," *JM*, 35 (January), 56–61.

SCALE ITEMS:

1. not at all risky / extremely risky

2. not at all concerned / highly concerned

3. very unimportant / very important

4. not at all worried / very worried

SCALE NAME: Risk (General)

SCALE DESCRIPTION: The scale has five, five-point Likert-type statements that are used to measure the degree to which a person expresses doubts about the uncertainty of some service as well as its outcomes.

SCALE ORIGIN: Depending upon one's conceptualization of perceived risk, the construct can be notoriously difficult to measure. At one extreme it can be viewed as having two components (uncertainty and consequences) with one of those components (consequences) having several subdimensions (e.g., Bauer 1960; Cox 1967; Roselius 1971). At the other extreme, a general, unidimensional view is possible (e.g., Dowling and Staelin 1994). The latter was followed by Cox and Cox (2001) in developing this scale.

RELIABILITY: An alpha of .77 was reported for the scale (Cox and Cox 2001).

VALIDITY: No information regarding the scale's validity was provided by Cox and Cox (2001).

REFERENCES:

Bauer, Raymond A. (1960), "Consumer Behavior as Risk Taking," *Proceedings of the 43rd Conference of the American Marketing Association*, R. S. Hancock, ed. Chicago: American Marketing Association 389–398.

Cox, Dena and Anthony D. Cox (2001), "Communicating the Consequences of Early Detection: The Role of Evidence and Framing," *JM*, 65 (July), 91–103.

Cox, Donald F. ed. (1967), *Risk Taking and Information Handling in Consumer Behavior*, Boston, MA: Harvard University Press.

Dowling, Grahame R. and Richard Staelin (1994), "A Model of Perceived Risk and Intended Risk-handling Ability," *JCR*, 21 (June), 119–134.

Roselius, Ted (1971), "Consumer Rankings of Risk Reduction Methods," *JM*, 35 (January), 56–61.

SCALE ITEMS: [1]

1. Getting a _____ is risky.

2. _____ can lead to bad results.

3. _____ have uncertain outcomes.

4. Getting a _____ makes me feel anxious.

5. Getting a _____ would cause me to worry.

[1] A topic or product category name should be placed in the blank, e.g., mammogram examination.

SCALE NAME: Risk Averseness

SCALE DESCRIPTION: It is a three-item, five-point Likert-type summated ratings scale measuring the degree to which a person expresses a desire to avoid taking risks.

SCALE ORIGIN: The source of the scale was not stated by Donthu and Gilliland (1996) but it is likely to be original to their study.

RELIABILITY: Alphas of .78 (Donthu and Gilliland 1996) and .77 (Donthu and Garcia 1999) have been reported for the scale.

VALIDITY: No specific examination of the scale's validity was reported by Donthu and Gilliland (1996).

REFERENCES:
Donthu, Naveen and Adriana Garcia (1999), "The Internet Shopper," *JAR*, 39 (May/June), 52–58.
Donthu, Naveen and David Gilliland (1996), "The Infomercial Shopper," *JAR*, 36 (March/April), 69–76.

SCALE ITEMS:

1. I would rather be safe than sorry.

2. I want to be sure before I purchase anything.

3. I avoid risky things.

SCALE NAME: Risk Averseness

SCALE DESCRIPTION: The scale is composed of four, seven-point Likert-type statements that measure a consumer's thoughts about the degree to which he/she avoids taking risks in life.

SCALE ORIGIN: The scale is original to the study of Burton et al. (1998). They said items were generated that were consistent with the construct's domain. The items were assessed in a pretest and less reliable ones were deleted from further use.

RELIABILITY: An alpha of .78 was reported for the scale by Burton et al. (1998).

VALIDITY: No information relating to the scale's validity was reported by Burton et al. (1998).

REFERENCES:
Burton, Scot, (2000), Personal Correspondence.
Burton, Scot, Donald R. Lichtenstein, Richard G. Netemeyer, and Judith A. Garretson (1998), "A Scale for Measuring Attitude Toward Private Label Products and an Examination of Its Psychological and Behavioral Correlates," *JAMS*, 26 (4), 293–306.

SCALE ITEMS: [1]

1. I don't like to take risks.

2. Compared to most people I know, I like to "live life on the edge." (r)

3. I have no desire to take unnecessary chances on things.

4. Compared to most people I know, I like to gamble on things. (r)

---

[1] One sample item was provided in the article by Burton et al. (1998). The other items were supplied personally by Burton (2000).

SCALE NAME: Role Overload

SCALE DESCRIPTION: The Likert-type scale measures the degree to which a person expresses having time pressures due to the number of commitments and responsibilities one has in life. The abbreviated version of the scale used by Reynolds and Beatty (1999b) was referred to as *time poverty*.

SCALE ORIGIN: The scale was constructed and tested by Reilly (1982). After reviewing scales previously developed for organizational settings, the author and doctoral candidates wrote items more appropriate for female consumers. A number of items were tested on a convenience sample of 106 married women. Those items with weak item-total correlations were removed from the scale leaving thirteen items. Other properties of the scale are provided below.

Reynolds and Beatty (1999b) adapted the scale by using a subset of the items, two of those being slightly rephrased.

RELIABILITY: Reilly (1982) reported an alpha of .88 (n = 106) and item-total correlations from .544 to .797. An alpha of .86 (n = 310) was reported by Kaufman, Lane, and Lindquist (1991). Reynolds and Beatty (1999b) reported an alpha of .82 (n= 364) for the version of the scale they used.

VALIDITY: The validity of the scale has not specifically addressed in any of the studies. Reynolds and Beatty (1999b) did state, however, that the CFA they ran on several of their scales indicated the measurement model, including the items in this scale, had a good fit.

COMMENTS: Until validity is assessed there is some question whether the scale measures role overload, as purported, or rather time pressure. The two constructs may indeed be related but they are not the same thing. For example, there are likely to be some people who are quite busy just playing one role just as there may be others who handle multiple roles without expressing much conflict. Therefore, care must be exercised in assuming too much about what this scale can say in terms of the quantity of roles played but it does appear to indicate the degree of perceived stress despite the amount of role conflict.

The word "wives" in item 10 must be changed when using the scale with men and those women who are not married.

For another use of the scale see Bellizzi and Hite (1986).

REFERENCES:
Bellizzi, Joseph A. and Robert E. Hite (1986), "Convenience Consumption and Role Overload," *JAMS*, 14 (Winter), 1–9.
Kaufman, Carol Felker, Paul M. Lane, and Jay D. Lindquist (1991), "Exploring More than 24 Hours a Day: A Preliminary Investigation of Polychronic Time Use," *JCR*, 18 (December), 392–401.
Reilly, Michael D. (1982), "Working Wives and Convenience Consumption," *JCR*, 8 (March), 407–418.
Reynolds, Kristy E. and Sharon E. Beatty (1999b), "A Relationship Customer Typology," *JA*, 75 (4), 509–523.

#387 *Role Overload*

SCALE ITEMS: [1]

1. I have to do things I don't really have the time and energy for.

2. There are too many demands on my time.

3. I need more hours in the day to do all the things which are expected of me.

4. I can't ever seem to get caught up.

5. I don't ever seem to have any time for myself.

6. There are times when I can't meet everyone's expectations.

7. Sometimes I feel as if there are not enough hours in the day.

8. Many times I have to cancel commitments.

9. I seem to have to overextend myself in order to be able to finish everything I have to do.

10. I seem to have more commitments to overcome than some of the other wives I know.

11. I find myself having to prepare priority lists (lists which tell me which things I should do first) to get done all the things I have to do. Otherwise I forget because I have so much to do. *I forget things because I have so much to do.*

12. I feel I have to do things hastily and maybe less carefully in order to get everything done.

13. I just can't find the energy in me to do all the things expected of me. *I can't find the time to do all of the things expected of me.*

---

[1] Reilly (1982) as well as Kaufman, Lane, and Lindquist (1991) appear to have used a seven-point response format and all thirteen items. Reynolds and Beatty (1999b) used #4, #9, #12, and items similar to #11 and #13 (shown in italics) with a five-point response scale.

SCALE NAME: Sacrifice

SCALE DESCRIPTION: The three-item, nine-point scale measures the resources (money, time, effort) that are given up in order to obtain a specified service.

SCALE ORIGIN: Although Cronin, Brady, and Hult (2000) followed the definition of the construct used by previous researchers, the scale appears to be original to their study.

RELIABILITY: Cronin, Brady, and Hult (2000) reported a construct reliability of .69 for the scale.

VALIDITY: Confirmatory factor analysis was conducted by Cronin, Brady, and Hult (2000) on this scale and several others. Some evidence of the scale's discriminant validity came from noting that the average variance extracted was greater than the shared variances with the other constructs. However, the scale's average variance extracted was 43% which casts some doubt on its adequacy (Fornell and Larcker 1981).

COMMENTS: Based on the combined sample from six different service industries (n = 1944), the scale had a mean of 5.09 and a standard deviation of 1.50.

REFERENCES:

Cronin, Jr., J. Joseph, Michael K. Brady, and G. Tomas M. Hult (2000), "Assessing the Effects of Quality, Value, and Customer Satisfaction on Consumer Behavioral Intentions in Service Environments," *JR*, 79 (2), 193–218.

Fornell, Claes and David F. Larcker (1981), "Evaluating Structural Equation Models with Unobservable Variables and Measurement Error," *JMR*, 18 (February), 39–50.

SCALE ITEMS: [1]

1. The price charged to use this facility is:

2. The time required to use this facility is:

3. The effort that I must make to receive the services offered is:

[1] A nine-point response scale was used by Cronin, Brady, and Hult (2000) with anchors of *very low* and *very high*.

SCALE NAME: Satisfaction (Answering Questions)

SCALE DESCRIPTION: The three, seven-point Likert-type items are used to measure a respondent's attitude toward the process of responding to some questions they have just been asked. The context for the scale's usage was at the end of an experiment (Huffman and Kahn 1998).

SCALE ORIGIN: Huffman and Kahn (1998) stated that they adapted their scale from a measure of satisfaction with the shopping process developed by Fitzsimons (1996).

RELIABILITY: An alpha of .80 was reported for the scale (Huffman and Kahn 1998).

VALIDITY: No examination of the scale's validity was reported by Huffman and Kahn (1998).

REFERENCES:

Fitzsimons, Gavan (1996), "Out-of-Stocks and Consumer Satisfaction," doctoral dissertation, New York: Columbia University.

Huffman, Cynthia and Barbara E. Kahn (1998), "Variety for Sale: Mass Customization or Mass Confusion?" *JR*, 74 (4), 491–513.

SCALE ITEMS: [1]

1. I found the process of answering questions confusing. (r)

2. I found the process of answering questions tiring. (r)

3. I am dissatisfied with the experience of answering questions. (r)

---

[1] A seven-point *agree / disagree* response format was used by Huffman and Kahn (1998) in their first study and a nine-point format was used in the second study.

SCALE NAME: Satisfaction (Anticipated)

SCALE DESCRIPTION: The scale is composed of five, seven-point items attempting to assess a consumer's expected level of satisfaction *prior* to purchasing or using a product. The implication is that the respondents have been exposed to some information by the time they respond to the measure (e.g., promotion, word-of-mouth) but they have not committed themselves in the form of purchases yet.

SCALE ORIGIN: Although not explicitly stated, the scale appears to be original to the studies reported by Shiv and Huber (2000). The importance of the scale is that under some circumstances it may be a more appropriate measure of preference than the more typical choice, brand attitude, and purchase intention measures.

RELIABILITY: The scale was used with two stimuli in Experiment 1 and the alphas were .94 and .95 (Shiv and Huber 2000).

VALIDITY: No information regarding the scale's validity was reported by Shiv and Huber (2000).

REFERENCES:
Shiv, Baba and Joel Huber (2000), "The Impact of Anticipating Satisfaction on Consumer Choice," *JCR*, 27 (2), 202–216.

SCALE ITEMS:

1. I would be: dissatisfied / satisfied

2. I would be: unhappy / happy

3. I would feel: bad / good

4. I would think I did not do the right thing / I would think I did the right thing

5. I would think I was unwise / I would think I was wise

SCALE NAME: Satisfaction (Complaint Handling)

SCALE DESCRIPTION: Four, five-point Likert-type items compose the scale. The scale is used to measure the degree to which a customer who lodged a complaint is pleased with the way the problem was resolved. The context in which the respondents were given this scale was after being told to remember a recent service experience that led to their lodging a complaint.

SCALE ORIGIN: Although Tax, Brown, and Chandrashekaran (1998) may have drawn inspiration from previous measures, this scale appears to be original to their study. Apparently, the scale was refined in a pretest (n = 80).

RELIABILITY: An alpha of .96 (n = 257) was reported for the scale by Tax, Brown, and Chandrashekaran (1998).

VALIDITY: It is not clear what support if any was found for the validity of the scale in the study by Tax, Brown, and Chandrashekaran (1998).

REFERENCES:

Tax, Stephen S., Stephen W. Brown, and Murali Chandrashekaran (1998), "Customer Evaluations of Service Complaint Experiences: Implications for Relationship Marketing," *JM*, 62 (April), 60–76.

SCALE ITEMS:

1. I was not happy with how the organization handled my complaint. (r)

2. The organization did all that I expected to solve my problem.

3. The complaint was not handled as well as it should have been. (r)

4. I was pleased with the manner in which the complaint was dealt with.

SCALE NAME: Satisfaction (Consumption)

SCALE DESCRIPTION: The scale is used to measure a person's satisfaction with a product <u>after the selection/purchase has been made</u> and consumption/usage of the product has occurred. The context for the scale's usage was at the end of an experiment when subjects had made a selection between a variety of brands (Fitzsimons 2000; Huffman and Kahn 1998). The full version of the scale has six items whereas the abbreviated version has three.

SCALE ORIGIN: Huffman and Kahn (1998) stated that they adapted their scale from a measure of satisfaction by Fitzsimons (1996). Fitzsimons (2000) cited Fitzsimons, Greenleaf, and Lehmann (1997) as the source.

RELIABILITY: An alpha of .85 was reported for the scale (Huffman and Kahn 1998). Fitzsimons (2000) reported alphas for the scale ranging from .86 to .89.

VALIDITY: No examination of the scale's validity was reported by Huffman and Kahn (1998). The only information bearing on the scale's validity reported by Fitzsimons (2000) was that a factor analysis of the items in this scale and six items intended to measure another form of satisfaction (#393) showed that the items separately loaded on the expected dimensions. Further, the correlation of scores on the two scales was .36, suggesting that while they are related they are not measuring the same thing.

REFERENCES:

Fitzsimons, Gavan (1996), "Out-of-Stocks and Consumer Satisfaction," doctoral dissertation, New York: Columbia University.

Fitzsimons, Gavan (2000), "Consumer Response to Stockouts," *JCR*, 27 (2), 249–266.

Fitzsimons, Gavan, Eric A. Greenleaf, and Donald R. Lehmann (1997), "Decision and Consumption Satisfaction: Implications for Channel Relations," Marketing Studies Center Working Paper Series, No. 313, University of California, Los Angeles, 90095.

Huffman, Cynthia and Barbara E. Kahn (1998), "Variety for Sale: Mass Customization or Mass Confusion?," *JR*, 74 (4), 491–513.

SCALE ITEMS: [1]

1. How satisfied or dissatisfied are you with the _____ you choose?

2. I am very displeased with the _____ I purchased. (r)

3. I am very happy with the _____ I purchased.

4. My choice turned out better than I expected.

5. Given the identical set of alternatives to choose from, I would make the same choice again.

6. Thinking of an ideal example of the product I purchased, my choice was very close to the ideal example.

---

[1] Huffman and Kahn (1998) used the first three items and a seven-point *agree / disagree* response format was used with items 2 and 3 by in their first study and a nine-point format was used in their second study. The anchors for the response scale used with item 1 was *very dissatisfied / very satisfied*. Fitzsimons (2000) used all six items and a ten-point Likert-type response format (*strongly agree* to *strongly disagree*). The word *product* can be placed in the blanks or a generic term for the product category, e.g., *granola bar*.

SCALE NAME: Satisfaction (Decision)

SCALE DESCRIPTION: The ten-point scale is used to measure a person's satisfaction with the <u>process</u> of making a selection from among a set of alternative brands. The scale may be used prior to the consumer's consumption/usage of the product and is intended to be distinct from the form of satisfaction that can be measured after consumption has occurred. The full version of the scale has six items whereas the abbreviated version has three.

SCALE ORIGIN: Fitzsimons (2000) cited Fitzsimons, Greenleaf, and Lehmann (1997) as the source of the scale.

RELIABILITY: Alphas ranging from .78 to .83 were reported for the full version of the scale (Fitzsimons 2000.) Alphas of .82 and .83 were reported for the shorter version.

VALIDITY: The only information bearing on the scale's validity reported by Fitzsimons (2000) was that a factor analysis of the items in this scale and six intended to measure another form of satisfaction (#392) showed that the items separately loaded on the expected dimensions. Further, the correlation of scores on the two scales was .36, suggesting that while they are related they are not measuring the same thing.

REFERENCES:

Fitzsimons, Gavan (2000), "Consumer Response to Stockouts," *JCR*, 27 (2), 249–266.
Fitzsimons, Gavan, Eric A. Greenleaf, and Donald R. Lehmann, ed., (1997), "Decision and Consumption Satisfaction: Implications for Channel Relations," Marketing Studies Center Working Paper Series, No. 313, University of California, Los Angeles, 90095.

SCALE ITEMS: [1]

1. How satisfied or dissatisfied are you with your experience of deciding which product option to choose? (r)

2. I found the process of deciding which product to buy frustrating. (r)

3. Several good options were available for me to choose between.

4. I thought the choice selection was good.

5. I would be happy to choose from the same set of product options on my next purchase occasion.

6. I found the process of deciding which product to buy interesting. ·

---

[1] The anchors for the response scale used with item 1 was *extremely satisfied / extremely dissatisfied*. For the other items Fitzsimons (2000) used a ten-point Likert-type response format (*strongly agree* to *strongly disagree*). The short version of the scale used items 1, 2, and 6.

SCALE NAME: Satisfaction (Emotional)

SCALE DESCRIPTION: The five-item, nine-point scale is intended to measure the affective component of satisfaction one experiences after a purchase.

SCALE ORIGIN: Cronin, Brady, and Hult (2000) stated that they adapted a scale used by Westbrook and Oliver (1991). More accurately, the latter used ten subscales of DES-II (Izard 1977) to separately measure different consumption-related emotions. In contrast, Cronin, Brady, and Hult (2000) selected one item from five subscales and combined them into one measure.

RELIABILITY: Cronin, Brady, and Hult (2000) reported a construct reliability of .88 for the scale.

VALIDITY: Confirmatory factor analysis was conducted by Cronin, Brady, and Hult (2000) on this scale and several others. Some evidence of the scale's discriminant validity came from noting that the average variance extracted (60.7%) was greater than the shared variances with the other constructs.

Because the five items were taken from measures of different emotions the strong possibility exists that the scale is not unidimensional. Caution is urged in the scale's use until its dimensionality is confirmed. Even if the scale is shown to be unidimensional, two or more items will require reverse coding (see below).

COMMENTS: Based on the combined sample from six different service industries (n = 1944), the scale had a mean of 7.63 and a standard deviation of 1.75.

REFERENCES:
Brady, Michael (2003), Personal Correspondence.
Cronin, Jr., J. Joseph, Michael K. Brady, and G. Tomas M. Hult (2000), "Assessing the Effects of Quality, Value, and Customer Satisfaction on Consumer Behavioral Intentions in Service Environments," *JR*, 79 (2), 193–218.
Hult, G. Tomas M. (2003), Personal Correspondence.
Izard, Carroll E. (1977), *Human Emotions*, New York: Plenum Press.
Westbrook, Robert A. and Richard L. Oliver (1991), "The Dimensionality of Consumption Emotion Patterns and Consumer Satisfaction," *JCR*, 18 (June), 84–91.

SCALE ITEMS: [1]

Directions: Please choose the response (i.e., a number from 1-9) that best reflects the degree to which you feel the following emotions about this service facility. There are no right or wrong responses—we merely ask that you be as honest as possible.

1. interest—(defined as attentive, concentrating, alert)

2. enjoyment—(defined as delighted, happy, joyful)

3. surprise—(defined as surprised, amazed, astonished)

4. anger—(defined as enraged, angry, mad)

5. shame/shyness—(defined as sheepish, bashful, shy)

[1] A nine-point response scale was used by Cronin, Brady, and Hult (2000) with anchors of *not at all* and *very much*. Although not specified in the article, it would appear that at least two of the items (4 and 5) would need to be reverse coded when calculating scale scores. Details about the scale not given in the article were provided by Brady (2003) and Hult (2003).

SCALE NAME: Satisfaction (Evaluative)

SCALE DESCRIPTION: The scale is composed of three, nine-point Likert-type statements intended to measure the degree to which a consumer believes a decision he/she has made regarding a service-related purchase was the right one. Due to the third item in the scale, the facility used to provide the service is an integral aspect of what is being measured.

SCALE ORIGIN: Cronin, Brady, and Hult (2000) are the source of the scale although they cited Oliver (1997) as providing inspiration.

RELIABILITY: Cronin, Brady, and Hult (2000) reported a construct reliability of .85 for the scale.

VALIDITY: Confirmatory factor analysis was conducted by Cronin, Brady, and Hult (2000) on this scale and several others. Some evidence of the scale's discriminant validity came from noting that the average variance extracted (66.5%) was greater than the shared variances with the other constructs.

COMMENTS: Based on the combined sample from six different service industries (n = 1944), the scale had a mean of 6.37 and a standard deviation of 1.71.

REFERENCES:

Cronin, Jr., J. Joseph, Michael K. Brady, and G. Tomas M. Hult (2000), "Assessing the Effects of Quality, Value, and Customer Satisfaction on Consumer Behavioral Intentions in Service Environments," *JR*, 79 (2), 193–218.

Oliver, Richard L. (1997), *Satisfaction: A Behavioral Perspective on the Consumer*, New York: McGraw-Hill, Inc.

SCALE ITEMS: [1]

1. My choice to purchase this service was a wise one.

2. I think that I did the right thing when I purchased this service.

3. This facility is exactly what I needed for this service.

---

[1] A nine-point response scale was used by Cronin, Brady, and Hult (2000) with anchors of *strongly disagree* and *strongly agree*.

SCALE NAME: Satisfaction (General)

SCALE DESCRIPTION: In its fullest form, the scale is composed of twelve Likert-type items and measures a consumer's degree of satisfaction with a product he/she has recently purchased. Most of its uses have been in reference to the purchase of cars but Mano and Oliver (1993) appear to have adapted it so as to be general enough to apply to whatever product a respondent was thinking about. Mattila and Wirtz (2001) adapted a short version of the scale to measure customers' satisfaction with a shopping experience.

SCALE ORIGIN: The scale was originally generated and used by Westbrook and Oliver (1981) to measure consumer satisfaction with cars and with calculators. Four other satisfaction measures were used as well and their results compared in a multi-trait multi-method matrix. Convenience samples of students were used from two different universities (n = 68 + 107). In terms of internal consistency, the alphas were .93 and .96 as measured for cars in the two samples. For both samples, the scale showed strong evidence of construct validity by converging with like constructs and discriminating between unlike constructs. Compared to the other measures of satisfaction, this Likert version produced the greatest dispersion of individual scores while maintaining a symmetrical distribution.

RELIABILITY: Alphas of .95, .98, .94, and .94 were reported for the scale by Mano and Oliver (1993), Oliver (1993), Oliver and Swan (1989b), and Westbrook and Oliver (1991), respectively. Oliver, Rust, and Varki (1997) reported that the reliabilities were .89 and .87 in their first and second studies, respectively. The version of the scale used by Mattila and Wirtz (2001) had an alpha of .72.

VALIDITY: No specific examination of scale validity was reported in any of the studies. However, Mano and Oliver (1993) performed a factor analysis which provided evidence that the scale was unidimensional.

REFERENCES:
Mano, Haim and Richard L. Oliver (1993), "Assessing the Dimensionality and Structure of the Consumption Experience: Evaluation, Feeling, and Satisfaction," *JCR*, 20 (December), 451–466.
Mattila, Anna S. and Jochen Wirtz (2001), "Congruency of Scent and Music as a Driver of In-store Evaluations and Behaviour," *JR*, 77 (2), 273–289.
Oliver, Richard L. (1993), "Cognitive, Affective, and Attribute Bases of the Satisfaction Response," *JCR*, 20 (December), 418–430.
Oliver, Richard L., Roland T. Rust, and Sajeev Varki (1997), "Customer Delight: Foundations, Findings, and Managerial Insight," *JR*, 73 (3), 311–336.
Oliver, Richard L. and John E. Swan (1989b), "Equity and Disconfirmation Perceptions as Influences on Merchant and Product Satisfaction," *JCR*, 16 (December), 372–383.
Westbrook, Robert A. and Richard L. Oliver (1981), "Developing Better Measures of Consumer Satisfaction: Some Preliminary Results," in *Advances in Consumer Research, V. 8*, Kent B. Monroe, ed. Ann Arbor, MI: Association for Consumer Research 94–99.
Westbrook, Robert A. and Richard L. Oliver (1991), "The Dimensionality of Consumption Emotion Patterns and Consumer Satisfaction," *JCR*, 18 (June), 84–91.

SCALE ITEMS: [1]

1. This is one of the best _____ I could have bought.

2. This _____ is exactly what I need.

3. This _____ hasn't worked out as well as I thought it would. (r)

4. I am satisfied with my decision to buy this _____.

5. Sometimes I have mixed feelings about keeping it. (r)

6. My choice to buy this _____ was a wise one.

7. If I could do it over again, I'd buy a different make/model. (r)

8. I have truly enjoyed this _____.

9. I feel bad about my decision to buy this _____. (r)

10. I am <u>not</u> happy that I bought this _____. (r)

11. Owning this _____ has been a good experience.

12. I'm sure it was the right thing to buy this _____.

---

[1] Mano and Oliver (1993), Oliver (1993), and Westbrook and Oliver (1981) used five-point scales whereas Oliver and Swan (1989) used a seven-point format. Oliver, Rust, and Varki (1997) only used ten of these items (unspecified) and a five-point response scale. Mattila and Wirtz (2001) used seven-point items adapted from #4, #6, and #8.

SCALE NAME: Satisfaction (General)

SCALE DESCRIPTION: The seven-point semantic differential scale measures a consumer's degree of satisfaction with an object. The scale may be most suited for measuring a consumer's satisfaction with another party with whom a transaction has occurred or relationship has developed. The parties studied with this scale have been car salespeople (Oliver and Swan 1989a), hairstylists (Price and Arnould 1999), clothing/accessories salespeople (Reynolds and Beatty 1999a, 1999b), and banks (Jones, Mothersbaugh, and Beatty 2000).

SCALE ORIGIN: The scale used by Oliver and Swan (1989a and 1989b) was adapted from a seven item version of the scale discussed in Westbrook and Oliver (1981). There it was generated and used in measuring consumer satisfaction with cars and with calculators. Four other satisfaction measures were used as well and their results compared in a multi-trait multi-method matrix. Convenience samples of students were used from two different universities. In terms of internal consistency, the alphas were .91 or greater as measured for the two products and the two samples. For both products and samples, the scale showed strong evidence of construct validity by converging with like constructs and discriminating between unlike constructs.

The version of the scale used by Price and Arnould (1999) is similar to that used by Oliver and Swan (1989a and 1989b) but may have drawn upon phrasings from other satisfaction scales.

Reynolds and Beatty (1999a, 1999b) stated that they modified a scale developed by Ganesan (1994). Indeed, it is very similar (see V. III, #865) but it is also remarkably similar to those listed here which have been used with ultimate consumers rather than with channel partners.

RELIABILITY: The reliability of the version of the scale use by Jones, Mothersbaugh, and Beatty (2000) was .98 (both alpha and composite). The estimate of reliability provided by LISREL in Oliver and Swan (1989a) was .953 and had to do with a customer's expressed satisfaction with a car salesperson. LISREL estimates of .97 and .96 were reported for the scale when used to measure the consumer's satisfaction with the dealer and the salesperson, respectively (1989b).

Alphas of .97 (Study 3) and .95 (Study 4) were reported for the scale by Price and Arnould (1999) with regard to clients' satisfaction with their hairstylists. Reynolds and Beatty (1999a) reported composite reliabilities of .94 and .97 for satisfaction with a salesperson and a company, respectively. In Reynolds and Beatty (1999b), the alphas were .86 (sales associate) and .89 (store).

VALIDITY: Based on the CFA and other tests that were conducted on this and other scales, Jones, Mothersbaugh, and Beatty (2000) concluded that their version of the scale was unidimensional and showed evidence of discriminant validity. In addition, the scale was reported to have a variance extracted of .91.

A claim of convergent validity was made by Reynolds and Beatty (1999a) based upon the significance of the scales' λ loadings. Evidence of the discriminant validity of their two satisfaction measures (salesperson and company) came from noting that the variance extracted for each was much higher than the correlation between them.

REFERENCES:

Ganesan, Shankar (1994), "Determinants of Long-Term Orientation in Buyer-Seller Relationships," *JM*, 58 (April), 1–19.

Jones, Michael A., David L. Mothersbaugh, and Sharon E. Beatty (2000), "Switching Barriers and Repurchase Intentions in Services," *JR*, 79 (2), 259–274.

Oliver, Richard L. and John E. Swan (1989a), "Consumer Perceptions of Interpersonal Equity and Satisfaction in Transactions: A Field Survey Approach," *JM*, 53 (April), 21–35.

Oliver, Richard L. and John E. Swan (1989b), "Equity and Disconfirmation Perceptions as Influences on Merchant and Product Satisfaction," *JCR*, 16 (December), 372–383.

Price, Linda L. and Eric J. Arnould (1999), "Commercial Friendships: Service Provider-Client Relationships in Context," *JM*, 63 (October), 38–56.

Reynolds, Kristy E. and Sharon E. Beatty (1999a), "Customer Benefits and Company Consequences of Customer-Salesperson Relationships in Retailing," *JR*, 75 (1), 11–32.

Reynolds, Kristy E. and Sharon E. Beatty (1999b), "A Relationship Customer Typology," *JR*, 75 (4), 509–523.

Westbrook, Robert A. and Richard L. Oliver (1981), "Developing Better Measures of Consumer Satisfaction: Some Preliminary Results," in *Advances in Consumer Research, V. 8*, Kent B. Monroe, ed. Ann Arbor, MI: Association for Consumer Research 94–99.

SCALE ITEMS: [1]

Directions: Please indicate how satisfied you were with your _____ by checking the space that best gives your answer.

1. displeased me / pleased me

2. disgusted with / contented with

3. very dissatisfied with / very satisfied with

4. did a poor job for me / did a good job for me

5. poor choice in buying from that _____ / wise choice in buying from that _____

6. unhappy with / happy with

7. bad value / good value

8. frustrating / enjoyable

9. very unfavorable / very favorable

[1] The studies tended to use seven-point response formats except for Jones, Mothersbaugh, and Beatty (2000) who used ten. Oliver and Swan (1989a and 1989b) used items 1 to 6; Price and Arnould (1999) used item 7 and some phrases similar to 1, 3 to 6; Reynolds and Beatty (1999a, 1999b) used item 8 and others similar to 1, 2, and 6; and Jones, Mothersbaugh, and Beatty (2000) used items 1, 2, 3, 6, and 9.

SCALE NAME: Satisfaction (General)

SCALE DESCRIPTION: The scale is composed of three items intended to produce a overall evaluation of satisfaction. Given that the scale was created for use with a service encounter it may not be quite as suited for use as a satisfaction measure with respect to physical goods.

SCALE ORIGIN: Wirtz, Matilla and Tan (2000) drew upon several sources in developing this scale. They were apparently trying to make a short scale that would tap into three aspects of satisfaction (cognitive, affective, behavioral).

RELIABILITY: An alpha of .94 was reported for the scale (Wirtz, Matilla and Tan 2000).

VALIDITY: Wirtz, Matilla and Tan (2000) performed a confirmatory factor analysis on this scale and a couple of others with the results providing some evidence of each scale's convergent and discriminant validity. Further evidence of the satisfaction scale's discriminant validity came from noting that its average variance extracted (.99) was higher than it was for the squared correlation between it and any of the other two constructs (Fornell and Larcker 1981). Some evidence of nomological validity came from noting, as expected from previous research, satisfaction was not related to arousal but it was strongly related to pleasure.

REFERENCES:

Fornell, Claes and David F. Larcker (1981), "Evaluating Structural Equation Models with Unobservable Variables and Measurement Error," *JMR*, 18 (February), 39–50.

Wirtz, Jochen, Anna S. Matilla, and Rachel L.P. Tan (2000), "The Moderating Role of Target-Arousal on the Impact of Affect on Satisfaction-An Examination in the Context of Service Experience," *JR*, 76 (3), 347–365.

SCALE ITEMS: [1]

1. 0% / 100%

2. won't do it again / will do it again

3. terrible / delighted

---

[1] As used by Wirtz, Matilla and Tan (2000), items 1 and 2 had eleven-point response scales whereas the third item had a seven-point scale. Either the scores for each item should be standardized before calculating scale scores or they should each use the same number of response points.

SCALE NAME: Satisfaction (Life)

SCALE DESCRIPTION: The scale is composed of multiple statements with a six-point response format measuring a person's level of satisfaction with life including his/her accomplishments using a set of evoked standards (relatives, friends). The scale has also been referred to as *congruity life satisfaction* (Meadow et al. 1992).

SCALE ORIGIN: The scale used by Sirgy et al. (1998) was developed by Meadow et al. (1992). The latter provided evidence of the scale's internal consistency ($\alpha = .95$) and construct validity with two studies in which it was shown to be related to several demographic and psychograph variables as predicted.

RELIABILITY: Sirgy et al. (1998) used the scale with six different samples in five different countries. Alphas ranged from .744 for the Chinese sample (n = 191) to .934 for a sample of U.S. consumer panel (n = 233). The alpha for the pooled sample was .919 (n = 1226).

VALIDITY: Evidence of the scale's convergent validity was provided by Sirgy et al. (1998) based upon a pattern of correlations across samples between this scale and another measure of the same construct (Andrews and Withey 1976).

REFERENCES:

Andrews, Frank M. and S. B. Whitney (1976), *Social Indicators of Well-Being: America's Perception of Life Quality*, New York: Plenum Press.

Meadow, H. Lee, John T. Mentzer, Don R. Rahtz, and M. Joseph Sirgy (1992), "A Life Satisfaction Measure Based on Judgment Theory," *Social Indicators Research*, 26 (1), 23–59.

Sirgy M. Joseph, Dong-Jin Lee, Rustan Kosenko, H. Lee Meadow, Don Rahtz, Murris Cicic, Guang Xi-Jin, Duygun Yarsuvat, David L. Blenkhorn, and Newell Wright (1998), "Does Television Viewership Play a Role in the Perception of Quality of Life?" *Journal of Advertising*, 27 (Spring), 125–142.

SCALE ITEMS: [1]

1. Compared to your lifetime goals, ideals, and what you had ideally hoped to become, how satisfied are you?

2. Compared to what you feel you deserve to have happened to you considering all that you've worked for, how satisfied are you?

3. Compared to the accomplishments of your relatives (parents, brothers, sisters, etc.), how satisfied are you?

4. Compared to the accomplishments of your friends and associates, how satisfied are you?

5. Compared to the accomplishments of most people in your position, how satisfied are you?

6. Compared to where you've been and how far you have come along (the progress you made, the changes you have gone through, or the level of growth you have experienced), how satisfied are you?

7. Compared to what you have expected from yourself all along considering your resources, strengths, and weaknesses, how satisfied are you?

8. Compared to what you may have predicted about yourself becoming, how satisfied are you?

9. Compared to what you feel you should have accomplished so far, how satisfied are you?

10. Compared to what you feel is the minimum of what anyone in your position should have accomplished (and be able to accomplish), how satisfied are you?

[1] The response scale anchors were *very dissatisfied* (1) and *very satisfied* (6). Depending upon the country, some items were ultimately dropped when calculating scores. However, the scores for the pooled sample used all of the items.

SCALE NAME: Satisfaction (Performance)

SCALE DESCRIPTION: The scale is composed of three, seven-point Likert-type items measuring the level of satisfaction a consumer experiences with a product's performance. Although it may be most natural for the scale to be completed by consumers with respect to their own satisfaction, in the study by Tsiros and Mittal (2000) it had to do with the attribution of that reaction on others based on knowledge of what they had experienced. In other words, one party believes that another party who has made a certain purchase decision is feeling a certain way about it.

SCALE ORIGIN: Although some of the terms and phrases are similar to ones used in previous measures of satisfaction, this set of items as a whole appears to be original to Tsiros and Mittal (2000).

RELIABILITY: An alpha of .95 was reported for the scale (Tsiros and Mittal 2000).

VALIDITY: Little evidence relating to the scale's validity was reported by Tsiros and Mittal (2000). They did conduct confirmatory factor analysis of these three items along with three others intended to measure regret (#360). The results showed that the two sets of items loaded on their respective factors as expected. Further, a two-factor solution provided better fit than a one-factor solution.

REFERENCES:

Tsiros, Michael and Vikas Mittal (2000), "Regret: A Model of Its Antecedents and Consequences in Consumer Decision Making," *JCR*, 26 (March), 401–417.

SCALE ITEMS: [1]

1. _____ is happy with _____'s performance.

2. _____ is satisfied with _____'s performance.

3. _____ is disappointed with _____'s performance. (r)

[1] As used by Tsiros and Mittal (2000), the name of the person experiencing the regret goes in the first blank. If the scale is being filled out with respect to one's own satisfaction then some minor rephrasing will be necessary, e.g., *I am happy with . . ..* The name of the chosen product should be placed in the second blanks of the items.

SCALE NAME: Satisfaction (Relationship)

SCALE DESCRIPTION: Three Likert-type statements with a seven-point response format are used to assess the degree to which a customer feels he/she has a good relationship with a business.

SCALE ORIGIN: The source of the scale was not explicitly described by De Wulf, Odekerken-Schröder, and Iacobucci (2001) but it would appear to be original to their studies. The items appear to be among those that were developed using the back-translation method for versions in American English and Dutch and then pretested in the U.S., Netherlands, and Belgium (Flemish-speaking area).

RELIABILITY: Composite reliabilities were calculated for two types of stores for each of three countries (De Wulf, Odekerken-Schröder, and Iacobucci 2001). The reliabilities for food stores were .86, .76, and .82 for the U.S., Netherlands, and Belgium, respectively (Odekerken-Schröder 2004). For apparel stores, the reliabilities were .88, .84, and .78 for the U.S., Netherlands, and Belgium, respectively.

VALIDITY: Along with two other scales (relationship trustworthiness [#481] and commitment [#127]), De Wulf, Odekerken-Schröder, and Iacobucci (2001) used scale averages as indicators of a second-order factor (relationship quality). Evidence was provided in support of the scale's unidimensionality as well as its convergent validity.

REFERENCES:

De Wulf, Kristof, Gaby Odekerken-Schröder, and Dawn Iacobucci (2001), "Investments in Consumer Relationships: A Cross-Country and Cross-Industry Exploration," *JM*, 65 (October), 33–50.

Odekerken-Schröder, Gaby (2001), Personal Correspondence.

SCALE ITEMS: [1]

1. As a regular customer, I have a high quality relationship with this _____.

2. I am happy with the efforts this _____ is making towards regular customers like me.

3. I am satisfied with the relationship I have with this _____.

---

[1] An appropriate descriptor of the business entity should be placed in the blanks. De Wulf, Odekerken-Schröder, and Iacobucci (2001) used the term "store" but other general terms such as "retailer" and "service provider" are possible as are more specific terms such as "restaurant" and "wireless provider."

SCALE NAME: Satisfaction (Sales Process)

SCALE DESCRIPTION: The scale is composed of seven, seven-point Likert-type statements attempting to assess a customer's general level of satisfaction with several aspects of a particular sales event such as the terms of the agreement and the sales person involved. As written, the scale is most suited for a life insurance sale.

SCALE ORIGIN: Evans et al. (2000) indicated that they had tried to adapt items for their study from past research. No specific origin was cited for this scale and it appears to be unique enough that it may be safest to consider it to be original to their study. They said that all of their measures were modified based on pretesting.

RELIABILITY: An alpha of .90 was reported for the scale (Evans et al. 2000).

VALIDITY: No explicit evidence of the scale's validity was provided by Evans et al. (2000).

COMMENTS: Although the items could be adapted for use in other sales contexts, it is strongly urged that retesting of its psychometric properties be conducted. It is quite possible for a customer to have different levels of satisfaction associated with the various components of the sales process mentioned in the items. This, in turn, could lead to the scale not being unidimensional.

REFERENCES:
Evans, Kenneth R., Robert E. Kleine III, Timothy D. Landry, and Lawrence A. Crosby (2000), "How First Impressions of a Customer Impact Effectiveness in an Initial Sales Encounter," *JAMS*, 28 (4), 512–526.

SCALE ITEMS:

I am satisfied with the . . .

1. insurance and financial counseling I was given.

2. customer needs and insurance information that was communicated at the meeting.

3. agent as a life insurance agent.

4. quality and value of the policies that were offered.

5. social contact that took place.

6. agent as a financial service provider.

7. financial terms of the same discussed.

#403 *Satisfaction (Service Dimensions)*

SCALE NAME: Satisfaction (Service Dimensions)

SCALE DESCRIPTION: The scale is composed of six items measuring a customer's satisfaction with a recent retail experience with the emphasis being on various dimensions of the service received during the episode.

SCALE ORIGIN: Although not explicitly stated by Ofir and Simonson (2001), the scale seems to be original to their study. It is not clear why three different measures of the construct were used in their studies. The two most similar scales are presented together here and there was one not as similar (#408).

RELIABILITY: Alphas of .76 and .90 were reported for the versions of the scale used in Studies 3 and 5, respectively (Ofir and Simonson 2001).

VALIDITY: No information about the scale's validity was provided by Ofir and Simonson (2001).

REFERENCES:
Ofir, Chezy and Itmar Simonson (2001), "In Search of Negative Customer Feedback: The Effect of Expecting to Evaluate on Satisfaction Evaluations," *JMR*, 38 (May), 170–182.

SCALE ITEMS: [1]

Please indicate your level of satisfaction with each of the following:

1. Employee courtesy

2. Store cleanliness

3. Waiting time

4. Product selection

5. Professionalism of the cashier

6. Product display

7. Employee willingness to help

8. Convenience in shopping

9. Quality of the service

---

[1] The first six items were used by Ofir and Simonson (2001) in Study 3 and used response anchors that ranged from 1 (*not at all satisfied*) to 10 (*very satisfied*). The version of the scale used in Study 5 used items the same or similar to 1, 3, and 4 in addition to items 7-9.

SCALE NAME: Satisfaction (Service Provider's Location)

SCALE DESCRIPTION: The scale is composed of three, five-point statements used to measure the extent to which a customer expresses satisfaction with the aspects of a service provider that are related to the convenience of the provider's location relative to the customer's home, work, and route in-between.

SCALE ORIGIN: The three items in the scale by Ganesh, Arnold, and Reynolds (2000) were taken from research conducted by Rust and Zahorik (1993).

RELIABILITY: An alpha of .86 was reported for the scale (Ganesh, Arnold, and Reynolds 2000).

VALIDITY: While Ganesh, Arnold, and Reynolds (2000) did not examine the scale's validity they did include its items in an EFA along with items intended to measure other dimensions of satisfaction. All items shown below loaded strongly on the same factor with no significant cross-loadings.

REFERENCES:

Ganesh, Jaishanker, Mark J. Arnold, and Kristy E. Reynolds (2000), "Understanding the Customer Base of Service Providers: An Examination of the Differences Between Switchers and Stayers," *JM*, 64 (3), 65–87.

Rust, Roland T. and Anthony J. Zahorik (1993), "Customer Satisfaction, Customer Retention and Market Share," *JR*, 69 (Summer), 193–215.

SCALE ITEMS: [1]

1. How close the _____ is to my home.

2. How close the _____ is to my place of employment.

3. How convenient the _____ is to my route to work.

---

[1] The five-point response scale ranged from *very dissatisfied* to *very satisfied*. The generic term for the service provider should be placed in the blanks, e.g., bank.

SCALE NAME: Satisfaction (Service Provider's Personnel)

SCALE DESCRIPTION: Four, five-point statements are used to measure the extent to which a customer expresses satisfaction with the aspects of a service provider that are strongly related to the quality of employee/customer interaction.

SCALE ORIGIN: Three of the four items in the scale by Ganesh, Arnold, and Reynolds (2000) were taken from research conducted by Rust and Zahorik (1993).

RELIABILITY: An alpha of .92 was reported for the scale (Ganesh, Arnold, and Reynolds 2000).

VALIDITY: While Ganesh, Arnold, and Reynolds (2000) did not examine the scale's validity they did include its items in an EFA along with items intended to measure other dimensions of satisfaction. All items shown below loaded strongly on the same factor with no significant cross-loadings.

REFERENCES:

Ganesh, Jaishanker, Mark J. Arnold, and Kristy E. Reynolds (2000), "Understanding the Customer Base of Service Providers: An Examination of the Differences Between Switchers and Stayers," *JM*, 64 (3), 65–87.

Rust, Roland T. and Anthony J. Zahorik (1993), "Customer Satisfaction, Customer Retention and Market Share," *JR*, 69 (Summer), 193–215.

SCALE ITEMS: [1]

1. The friendliness of the _____ employees.

2. How well the _____ managers know me.

3. How well the _____ listens to my needs.

4. The quality of the service offered by the _____.

[1] The five-point response scale ranged from *very dissatisfied* to *very satisfied*. The generic term for the service provider should be placed in the blanks, e.g., bank.

SCALE NAME: Satisfaction (Service)

SCALE DESCRIPTION: Three, seven-point Likert-type statements compose the scale. The items are intended to measure the degree to which a customer of a service provider is satisfied with a service that has been experienced or received.

SCALE ORIGIN: Although drawing upon the many satisfaction measures developed previously, this scale is original to the study by Voss, Parasuraman, and Grewal (1998).

RELIABILITY: Average construct reliability was reported to be .83 (Voss, Parasuraman, and Grewal 1998).

VALIDITY: Voss, Parasuraman, and Grewal (1998) reported an average variance extracted of .63. Evidence was also supplied in support of the scale's convergent and discriminant validities.

REFERENCES:

Voss, Glenn B., A. Parasuraman, and Dhruv Grewal (1998), "The Roles of Price, Performance, and Expectations in Determining Satisfaction in Service Exchanges," *JM*, 62 (October), 46–61.

SCALE ITEMS: [1]

1. I was satisfied with the service provided.

2. I was delighted with the service provided.

3. I was unhappy with the service provided. (r)

---

[1] Responses to the items were made using a seven-point Likert-type scale using the following anchors: *disagree very strongly* (1) and *agree very strongly* (7).

SCALE NAME: Satisfaction (Service)

SCALE DESCRIPTION: The scale is composed of three, seven-point Likert-type items that gauge the general level of satisfaction a person expresses with regard to some specific service experience.

SCALE ORIGIN: The scale was developed by Keaveney and Parthasarathy (2001) after reviewing other measures.

RELIABILITY: An alpha of .75 was reported for the scale by Keaveney and Parthasarathy (2001).

VALIDITY: No examination of the scale's validity was reported by Keaveney and Parthasarathy (2001).

REFERENCES:
Keaveney, Susan M. and Madhavan Parthasarathy (2001), "Customer Switching Behavior in Online Services: An Exploratory Study of the Role of Selected Attitudinal, Behavioral, and Demographic Factors," *JAMS*, 29 (Fall), 374–390.

SCALE ITEMS:

1. On the whole, I am/was satisfied with my experience with this/that service.

2. Overall, my negative experience outweighs/outweighed my positive experience with this/that service. (r)

3. In general, I am/was happy with the service experience.

SCALE NAME: Satisfaction (Service)

SCALE DESCRIPTION: The five-item, five-point scale is intended to measure a customer's satisfaction with a service recently received with the emphasis on a problem solving or repair-type service.

SCALE ORIGIN: Although not explicitly stated by Ofir and Simonson (2001), the scale seems to be original to their study.

RELIABILITY: An alpha of .91 was reported for the scale as used in Study 1 by Ofir and Simonson (2001).

VALIDITY: No information about the scale's validity was provided by Ofir and Simonson (2001).

REFERENCES:
Ofir, Chezy and Itmar Simonson (2001), "In Search of Negative Customer Feedback: The Effect of Expecting to Evaluate on Satisfaction Evaluations," *JMR*, 38 (May), 170–182.

SCALE ITEMS: [1]

Please indicate your level of satisfaction with each of the following:

1. How well the problem was addressed.

2. The response time.

3. The time taken to solve the problem.

4. The technician's courtesy.

5. The level of assistance provided by the technician.

[1] The response scale used by Ofir and Simonson (2001) ranged from 1 (*not at all satisfied*) to 5 (*very satisfied*).

SCALE NAME: Satisfaction (Transaction Ease with Service Provider)

SCALE DESCRIPTION: The scale is composed of three, five-point statements that are used to measure the extent to which a customer expresses satisfaction with the aspects of a service provider that are related to the convenience of conducting business with it.

SCALE ORIGIN: Two of the items in the scale by Ganesh, Arnold, and Reynolds (2000) were taken from research conducted by Rust and Zahorik (1993).

RELIABILITY: An alpha of .75 was reported for the scale (Ganesh, Arnold, and Reynolds 2000).

VALIDITY: While Ganesh, Arnold, and Reynolds (2000) did not examine the scale's validity they did include its items in an EFA along with items intended to measure other dimensions of satisfaction. All items shown below loaded strongly on the same factor with no significant cross-loadings.

REFERENCES:
Ganesh, Jaishanker, Mark J. Arnold, and Kristy E. Reynolds (2000), "Understanding the Customer Base of Service Providers: An Examination of the Differences Between Switchers and Stayers," *JM*, 64 (3), 65–87.
Rust, Roland T. and Anthony J. Zahorik (1993), "Customer Satisfaction, Customer Retention and Market Share," *JR*, 69 (Summer), 193–215.

SCALE ITEMS: [1]

1. The number of *locations* the _____ has around town.

2. How many *employees* are available during busy times.

3. How convenient *their* hours are.

---

[1] The five-point response scale ranged from *very dissatisfied* to *very satisfied*. The generic term for the service provider should be placed in the blank of item 1, e.g., bank. The italized terms in the items are not those used by Ganesh, Arnold, and Reynolds (2000) but have been changed to make the statements more flexible for use with a variety of service providers rather than just banks.

SCALE NAME: Search Intention (External)

SCALE DESCRIPTION: Three, seven-point Likert-type items are used to measure the stated likelihood that a person will engage in external search behaviors before making a purchase decision with regard to some specified product in order to gather price information.

SCALE ORIGIN: The scale used by Grewal, Monroe, and Krishnan (1998) is based upon items used by Della Bitta, Monroe, and McGinnis (1981).

RELIABILITY: Grewal, Monroe, and Krishnan (1998) reported construct reliabilities of .88 (n = 361) and **.95** (n = 328) for use of the scale in their first and second studies, respectively.

VALIDITY: A variety of evidence was provided by the authors from both studies in support of the scale's unidimensionality, convergent validity, and discriminant validity (Grewal, Monroe, and Krishnan 1998).

REFERENCES:

Della Bitta, Albert J., Kent B. Monroe, and John M. McGinnis (1981), "Consumer Perceptions of Comparative Price Advertisements," *JMR*, 18 (November), 416–27.
Grewal, Dhruv, Kent B. Monroe, and R. Krishnan (1998), "The Effects of Price-Comparison Advertising on Buyer's Perceptions of Acquisition Value, Transaction Value, and Behavioral Intentions," *JM*, 62 (April), 46–59.

SCALE ITEMS: [1]

1. Before making a purchase decision, I would visit other stores that sell _____ to check their prices.

2. Before making a purchase decision, I would need to search for more information about prices of alternative _____.

3. Before making a purchase decision, I would visit other stores for a lower price.

---

[1] The name of the generic product should be placed in the blanks.

SCALE NAME: Self-Concept Clarity

SCALE DESCRIPTION: Twelve Likert-type statements are used to measure the degree which one's self beliefs "are clearly and confidently defined, internally consistent, and temporally stable" (Campbell et al. 1996, p. 141).

SCALE ORIGIN: The scale was created by Campbell et al. (1996). In an admiral series of studies, the authors provided support for various aspects of the scale's reliability and validity. For instance, the scale was found to be unidimensional, have high internal consistency (>.85) and high temporal stability (>.70) in both an eastern and a western culture. The scale was moderately correlated with a measure of social desirability bias (#462) but the authors did not take a position about what the implications were.

RELIABILITY: Tian, Bearden, and Hunter (2001) reported an alpha of .89 (n = 121) for the scale.

VALIDITY: No examination of the scales' validity was reported by Tian, Bearden, and Hunter (2001) although it was used in the process of validating other scales.

REFERENCES:

Campbell, Jennifer D., Paul D. Trapnell, Steven J. Heine, Ilana M. Katz, Loraine F. Lavallee, and Darrin R. Lehman (1996), "Self-Concept Clarity: Measurement, Personality Correlates, and Cultural Boundaries," *Journal of Personality and Social Psychology*, 70 (1), 141–156.

Tian, Kelly T., William O. Bearden, and Gary L. Hunter (2001), "Consumers' Need for Uniqueness: Scale Development and Validation," *JCR*, 28 (June), 50–66.

SCALE ITEMS: [1]

1. My beliefs about myself often conflict with one another. (r)

2. On one day I might have one opinion of myself and on another day I might have a different opinion. (r)

3. I spend a lot of time wondering about what kind of person I really am. (r)

4. Sometimes I feel that I am not really the person I appear to be. (r)

5. When I think about the kind of person I have been in the past, I'm not sure what I was really like. (r)

6. I seldom experience conflict between the different aspects of my personality.

7. Sometimes I think I know other people better than I know myself. (r)

8. My beliefs about myself seem to change very frequently. (r)

9. If I were asked to describe my personality, my description might end up being different from one day to another day. (r)

10. Even if I wanted to, I don't think I would tell someone what I'm really like. (r)

11. In general, I have a clear sense of who I am and what I am.

12. It is often hard for me to make up my mind about things because I don't really know what I want. (r)

[1] The response scale used by Campbell et al. (1996) ranged from 1 (*strongly disagree*) to 5 (*strongly agree*).

SCALE NAME: Self-Confidence (Clothes Shopping)

SCALE DESCRIPTION: The scale is composed of six, seven-point Likert-type statements measuring the degree of confidence a consumer has in his/her ability to shop for clothing and accessories.

SCALE ORIGIN: Although not explicitly stated by Reynolds and Beatty (1999b), the scale appears to be original to their study.

RELIABILITY: Reynolds and Beatty (1999b) reported an alpha of .90 (n= 364) for the scale.

VALIDITY: The validity of the scale was not addressed by Reynolds and Beatty (1999b). They did state, however, that the CFA they ran on several of their scales indicated the measurement model, including the items in this scale, had a good fit.

REFERENCES:
Reynolds, Kristy E. and Sharon E. Beatty (1999b), "A Relationship Customer Typology," *JR*, 75 (4), 509–523.

SCALE ITEMS:

1. I do not feel very confident in my ability to shop for clothing and accessories. (r)

2. I have the ability to choose the right clothes for myself.

3. I don't think I am a good clothing shopper. (r)

4. My self-confidence is high in selecting clothing.

5. I am not good at choosing clothing/accessories for most occasions. (r)

6. I feel very confident in putting together a good appearance.

SCALE NAME: Self-Confidence (Express Opinions)

SCALE DESCRIPTION: The scale is composed of five Likert-type statements that are used to measure one's tendency to "speak up" when dealing with marketers (e.g., salespersons) by expressing concerns and desires. Bearden, Hardesty, and Rose (2001) referred to this scale as the *marketplace interfaces* dimension of consumer self-confidence.

SCALE ORIGIN: Bearden, Hardesty, and Rose (2001) constructed the scale as part of a larger consumer self-confidence instrument. An admiral, multi-study process was used in which the instrument's psychometric quality was thoroughly tested and confirmed.

RELIABILITY: An alpha of .86 (n = 252 undergraduate students) was reported for the scale in Study 3 (Bearden, Hardesty, and Rose 2001). In addition, the stability of the scale (two-week test-retest) was checked along with the other dimensions of the instrument and found to be between .60 and .84.

VALIDITY: In the several studies conducted by Bearden, Hardesty, and Rose (2001) many types of validity were examined (content, convergent, discriminant, predictive, known-group). The evidence provides strong support for a claim of the scale being a valid measure of the construct.

REFERENCES:
Bearden, William O., David M. Hardesty, and Randall L. Rose, (2001), "Consumer Self-Confidence: Refinements in Conceptualization and Measurement," *JCR*, 28 (June), 121–134.

SCALE ITEMS:

1. I am afraid to "ask to speak to the manager."

2. I don't like to tell a salesperson something is wrong in the store.

3. I have a hard time saying "no" to a salesperson.

4. I am too timid when problems arise while shopping.

5. I am hesitant to complain when shopping.

SCALE NAME: Self-Confidence (Information Acquisition)

SCALE DESCRIPTION: Five Likert-type statements are used to measure a consumer's confidence in the ability he/she possesses to gather product information prior to a purchase by asking the right questions and finding the necessary answers.

SCALE ORIGIN: The scale is original to Bearden, Hardesty, and Rose (2001). It was developed as part of a larger consumer self-confidence instrument using an admiral, multi-study process in which the instrument's psychometric quality was thoroughly tested and confirmed.

RELIABILITY: An alpha of .82 (n = 252 undergraduate students) was reported for the scale in Study 3 (Bearden, Hardesty, and Rose 2001). In addition, the stability of the scale (two-week test-retest) was checked along with the other dimensions of the instrument and found to be between .60 and .84.

VALIDITY: In the several studies conducted by Bearden, Hardesty, and Rose (2001) many types of validity were examined (content, convergent, discriminant, predictive, known-group). The evidence provides strong support for a claim of the scale being a valid measure of the construct.

REFERENCES:
Bearden, William O., David M. Hardesty, and Randall L. Rose (2001), "Consumer Self-Confidence: Refinements in Conceptualization and Measurement," *JCR*, 28 (June), 121–134.

SCALE ITEMS:

1. I know where to find the information I need prior to making a purchase.

2. I know where to look to find the product information I need.

3. I am confident in my ability to research important purchases.

4. I know the right questions to ask when shopping.

5. I have the skills required to obtain needed information before making important purchases.

SCALE NAME: Self-Confidence (Information Processing)

SCALE DESCRIPTION: The scale is composed of ten Likert-like statements used to measure a person's confidence in his/her mental abilities. This measure attempts to focus on the *cognitive* dimension of general self-confidence rather than the social skills component.

SCALE ORIGIN: The scale is original to Wright (1975). He reported that the scale had a stability (two-week test-test correlation) of .69.

RELIABILITY: Alphas of .73 (Study 2) and .71 (Study 7) were reported for the scale by Bearden, Hardesty, and Rose (2001).

VALIDITY: No examination of the scale's validity was made by Bearden, Hardesty, and Rose (2001) although it was used in the process of validating a newer battery of consumer self-confidence scales, e.g., information acquisition self-confidence (#414).

REFERENCES:
Bearden, William O., David M. Hardesty, and Randall L. Rose, (2001), "Consumer Self-Confidence: Refinements in Conceptualization and Measurement," *JCR*, 28 (June), 121–134.
Wright, Peter (1975), "Factors Affecting Cognitive Resistance to Advertising," *JCR*, 2 (June), 1–9.

SCALE ITEMS: [1]

1. I have more trouble concentrating than most people. (r)

2. I am able to solve riddles and puzzles rapidly.

3. My mind seems to work slowly compared to those around me. (r)

4. I am totally confident about my ability to judge messages coming from the mass media.

5. I am certainly able to think quickly.

6. When I hear an argument being presented, I am quick to spot the weaknesses in it.

7. I usually have to stop and think for awhile before making up my mind even in unimportant matters.

8. My thoughts frequently race ahead faster than I can speak them.

9. I am never at a loss for words.

10. I don't seem to be very quick-witted. (r)

[1] Wright (1975) used a nine-point response scale with *definitely false* and *definitely true* as anchors. The nature of the response scale used by Bearden, Hardesty, and Rose (2001) is unknown.

SCALE NAME: Self-Confidence (Personal Outcomes)

SCALE DESCRIPTION: The scale is composed of five Likert-type statements that are used to measure one's confidence in his/her ability to buy the "right" brand that will lead to a satisfying outcome.

SCALE ORIGIN: The scale is original to Bearden, Hardesty, and Rose (2001). It was developed as part of a larger consumer self-confidence instrument using an admiral, multi-study process in which the instrument's psychometric quality was thoroughly tested and confirmed.

RELIABILITY: An alpha of .80 (n = 252 undergraduate students) was reported for the scale in Study 3 (Bearden, Hardesty, and Rose 2001). In addition, the stability of the scale (two-week test-retest) was checked along with the other dimensions of the instrument and found to be between .60 and .84.

VALIDITY: In the several studies conducted by Bearden, Hardesty, and Rose (2001) many types of validity were examined (content, convergent, discriminant, predictive, known-group). The evidence provides strong support for a claim of the scale being a valid measure of the construct.

REFERENCES:

Bearden, William O., David M. Hardesty, and Randall L. Rose (2001), "Consumer Self-Confidence: Refinements in Conceptualization and Measurement," *JCR*, 28 (June), 121–134.

SCALE ITEMS:

1. I often have doubts about the purchase decisions I make.

2. I frequently agonize over what to buy.

3. I often wonder if I've made the right purchase selection.

4. I never seem to buy the right thing for me.

5. Too often the things I buy are not satisfying.

SCALE NAME: Self-Confidence (Persuasion Knowledge)

SCALE DESCRIPTION: Six Likert-type statements are used to measure one's familiarity with the persuasion tactics used by marketers to sell products and having confidence in his/her ability to deal with those tactics.

SCALE ORIGIN: The scale is original to Bearden, Hardesty, and Rose (2001). It was developed as part of a larger consumer self-confidence instrument using an admiral, multi-study process in which the instrument's psychometric quality was thoroughly tested and confirmed.

RELIABILITY: An alpha of .83 (n = 252 undergraduate students) was reported for the scale in Study 3 (Bearden, Hardesty, and Rose 2001). In addition, the stability of the scale (two-week test-retest) was checked along with the other dimensions of the instrument and found to be between .60 and .84.

VALIDITY: In the several studies conducted by Bearden, Hardesty, and Rose (2001) many types of validity were examined (content, convergent, discriminant, predictive, known-group). The evidence provides strong support for a claim of the scale being a valid measure of the construct.

REFERENCES:
Bearden, William O., David M. Hardesty, and Randall L. Rose (2001), "Consumer Self-Confidence: Refinements in Conceptualization and Measurement," *JCR*, 28 (June), 121–134.

SCALE ITEMS:

1. I know when an offer is "too good to be true."

2. I can tell when an offer has strings attached.

3. I have no trouble understanding the bargaining tactics used by salespersons.

4. I know when a marketer is pressuring me to buy.

5. I can see through sales gimmicks used to get consumers to buy.

6. I can separate fact from fantasy in advertising.

SCALE NAME: Self-Confidence (Product Selection)

SCALE DESCRIPTION: The scale measures a consumer's opinion of the skill he/she possesses to choose the "best buy" from among alternatives in the same product category. The scale was referred to as *product-specific self-confidence* by Bearden, Hardesty, and Rose (2001).

SCALE ORIGIN: The scale is apparently original to Bearden, Hardesty, and Rose (2001).

RELIABILITY: An alpha of .69 was reported for the scale (Bearden, Hardesty, and Rose 2001).

VALIDITY: No examination of the scale's validity was reported by Bearden, Hardesty, and Rose (2001).

COMMENTS: The internal consistency of the scale is likely to suffer if the construct itself (confidence in selection ability) varies from category to category rather than being similar in degree across categories.

REFERENCES:
Bearden, William O., David M. Hardesty, and Randall L. Rose (2001), "Consumer Self-Confidence: Refinements in Conceptualization and Measurement," *JCR*, 28 (June), 121–134.

SCALE ITEMS: [1]

Directions: How confident would you be in your ability to choose the best buy from among alternatives available in the following good and service categories:

1. personal computers

2. legal services

3. exercise equipment

4. microwave ovens

5. cellular telephones

[1] The scale anchors were *not at all confident* (1) to *very confident* (7).

SCALE NAME: Self-Confidence (Social Outcomes)

SCALE DESCRIPTION: Five Likert-type statements are used to measure a consumer's confidence in his/her ability to buy the brand that will lead to satisfying reactions from friends and neighbors.

SCALE ORIGIN: Bearden, Hardesty, and Rose (2001) constructed the scale as part of a larger consumer self-confidence instrument. An admiral, multi-study process was used in which the instrument's psychometric quality was thoroughly tested and confirmed.

RELIABILITY: An alpha of .82 (n = 252 undergraduate students) was reported for the scale in Study 3 (Bearden, Hardesty, and Rose 2001). In addition, the stability of the scale (two-week test-retest) was checked along with the other dimensions of the instrument and found to be between .60 and .84.

VALIDITY: In the several studies conducted by Bearden, Hardesty, and Rose (2001) many types of validity were examined (content, convergent, discriminant, predictive, known-group). The evidence provides strong support for a claim of the scale being a valid measure of the construct.

REFERENCES:
Bearden, William O., David M. Hardesty, and Randall L. Rose (2001), "Consumer Self-Confidence: Refinements in Conceptualization and Measurement," *JCR*, 28 (June), 121–134.

SCALE ITEMS:

1. My friends are impressed with my ability to make satisfying purchases.

2. I impress people with the purchases I make.

3. My neighbors admire my decorating ability.

4. I have the ability to give good presents.

5. I get compliments from others on my purchase decisions.

SCALE NAME: Self-Confidence (Task)

SCALE DESCRIPTION: The scale is composed of three, seven-point semantic differentials measuring the degree to which a person feels certain about something. As used by Urbany et al. (1997), the confidence respondents had in their judgments of product quality was being measured. Similarly, Zhang and Budda (1999) examined the confidence respondents had in their perceptions of product performance.

SCALE ORIGIN: There is no information to indicate that the scale is anything other than original to the studies by Urbany et al. (1997). No source was cited by Zhang and Budda (1999).

RELIABILITY: Alphas of .93 (n = 200) and .94 (n = 393) were reported for the scale by Urbany et al. (1997). The scale had an alpha of .85 (n = 160) in the study by Zhang and Budda (1999).

VALIDITY: No examination of the scale's validity was reported by Urbany et al. (1997).

REFERENCES:
Urbany, Joel E., William O. Bearden, Ajit Kaicker, and Melinda Smith-de Borrero (1997), "Transaction Utility Effects When Quality is Uncertain," *JAMS*, 25 (Winter), 45–55.
Urbany, Joel E. and Richard Buda (1999), "Moderating Effects of Need for Cognition on Responses to Positively versus Negatively Framed Advertising Messages," *JA*, 28 (2), 1–15.

SCALE ITEMS: [1]

Please indicate the level of confidence you have in the ratings of quality you gave.

1. uncertain / certain

2. not sure / sure

3. not confident / confident

[1] The scale stem was not reported for either study but may have been somewhat similar to this one. The items shown are those used by Urbany et al. (1997); the version by Zhang and Budda (1999) was very similar but used *unsure* rather than *not sure* and *not certain* rather than *uncertain*.

SCALE NAME: Self-Efficacy (Health)

SCALE DESCRIPTION: The scale is composed of five, five-point Likert-type items intended to measure a person's beliefs that engaging in specific behaviors will mitigate health threats.

SCALE ORIGIN: Jayanti and Burns (1998) stated that they developed the scale for their study.

RELIABILITY: An alpha of .79 (n = 175) was reported for the scale by Jayanti and Burns (1998).

VALIDITY: Although rigorous examination of the scale's validity was not reported by Jayanti and Burns (1998), some general evidence related to the convergent and discriminant validities of all of their scales was mentioned.

REFERENCES:
Jayanti, Rama K. and Alvin C. Burns (1998), "The Antecedents of Preventive Health Care Behavior: An Empirical Study," *JAMS*, 26 (Winter), 6–15.

SCALE ITEMS:

1. I can avoid common health problems by reducing my sodium intake.

2. I can stay healthy longer by getting enough rest and sleep now.

3. Regular exercise helps me to avoid common health problems.

4. Taking care of my health now will reward me by not having problems later in life.

5. Having my physical done regularly has long-term advantages.

SCALE NAME: Self-Efficacy (Health)

SCALE DESCRIPTION: The scale is composed of five, five-point Likert-type items intended to measure a person's stated expectation to be able to successfully engage in behaviors that mitigate health threats.

SCALE ORIGIN: Jayanti and Burns (1998) stated that they developed the scale for their study.

RELIABILITY: An alpha of .72 (n = 175) was reported for the scale by Jayanti and Burns (1998).

VALIDITY: Although rigorous examination of the scale's validity was not reported by Jayanti and Burns (1998), some general evidence related to the convergent and discriminant validities of all of their scales was mentioned.

REFERENCES:

Jayanti, Rama K. and Alvin C. Burns (1998), "The Antecedents of Preventive Health Care Behavior: An Empirical Study," *JAMS*, 26 (Winter), 6–15.

SCALE ITEMS:

1. I usually make an attempt to eat a well-balanced diet.

2. I usually make an attempt to exercise regularly.

3. In the long-run, people who take care of themselves stay healthy.

4. People's ill health results from their own carelessness.

5. In general, I can do things that make me healthy.

SCALE NAME: Self-Esteem

SCALE DESCRIPTION: It is a ten-item Likert-type scale measuring the degree to which one approves of one's self. It does not necessarily imply that a person scoring high on the scale considers him/herself to be perfect or superior to others.

SCALE ORIGIN: The scale was constructed by Rosenberg (1965) for use in a study of high-school students. It was developed with at least four practical and theoretical considerations strongly in mind: that it be easy to administer, that it be completed quickly, that it be unidimensional, and that it have face validity. The Guttman scale of reproducibility was reported as .92 and its scalability was .72. The book provides considerable data that bears on the validity of the scale.

RELIABILITY: Alphas of .80, .86, and .81 were reported for the scale by Bearden and Rose (1990), Bearden, Hardesty, and Rose (2001), and Richins and Dawson (1992), respectively. Mick reported alphas of .87 and .80 for his Studies 1 and 2, respectively. Alphas of .86 and .87 were reported by Richins (1991) for the scale as used in Studies 2 and 3, respectively, with the alpha for the scale's use in Study 4 not being reported. Park, Mothersbaugh, and Feick (1994) reported an alpha of .86, with item-total correlations ranging from .48 to .66.

VALIDITY: The validity of the scale was not directly examined by Bearden and Rose (1990), Mick (1996), Park, Mothersbaugh, and Feick (1994), or Richins (1991; Richins and Dawson 1992).

REFERENCES:

Bearden, William O. and Randall L. Rose (1990), "Attention to Social Comparison Information: An Individual Difference Factor Affecting Consumer Conformity," *JCR*, 16 (March), 461–471.

Bearden, William O., David M. Hardesty, and Randall L. Rose (2001), "Consumer Self-Confidence: Refinements in Conceptualization and Measurement," *JCR*, 28 (June), 121–134.

Mick, David Glen (1996), "Are Studies of Dark Side Variables Confounded by Socially Desirable Responding? The Case of Materialism" *JCR*, 23 (September), 106–119.

Park, C. Whan, David L. Mothersbaugh, and Lawrence Feick (1994), "Consumer Knowledge Assessment," *JCR*, 21 (June), 71–82.

Richins, Marsha L. (1991), "Social Comparison and the Idealized Images of Advertising," *JCR*, 18 (June), 71–83.

Richins, Marsha L. and Scott Dawson (1992), "A Consumer Values Orientation for Materialism and Its Measurement: Scale Development and Validation," *JCR*, 19 (December), 303–316.

Richins, Marsha L., (1994), Personal Correspondence.

Rosenberg, Morris (1965), *Society and the Adolescent Self-Image*, Princeton, New Jersey: Princeton University Press.

#423 *Self-Esteem*

SCALE ITEMS: [1]

1. On the whole, I am satisfied with myself. (r)

2. At times I think I am no good at all.

3. I feel that I have a number of good qualities. (r)

4. I am able to do things as well as most other people. (r)

5. I feel I do not have much to be proud of.

6. I certainly feel useless at times.

7. I feel that I am a person of worth, at least on a equal plane with others. (r)

8. I wish I could have more respect for myself.

9. All in all, I am inclined to feel that I am a failure.

10. I take a positive attitude toward myself. (r)

[1] The four-point response scale was used by Rosenberg (1965), a five-point scale was used by Richins (1991) but it is not known how many points were on the scales as used by Bearden and Rose (1990), Bearden, Hardesty, and Rose (2001), Mick (1996) or Park, Mothersbaugh, and Feick (1994). The anchors used by Richins and Dawson (1992) were as follows: 0 = *not at all like me*, 1 = *a little like me*, 2 = *somewhat like me*, and 3 = *a lot like me* (Richins 1994).

SCALE NAME: Self-Esteem

SCALE DESCRIPTION: Twenty statements are used to measure the likelihood that a person expresses feelings of self-confidence, self-assurance, and self-esteem.

SCALE ORIGIN: The scale is a revision by Eagly (1967) of a measure presented earlier by Janis and Field (1959). The sample used by Eagly (1967) was composed of 144 college students. The split-half reliability for the scale was estimated to be .72 while the Spearman-Brown formula indicated internal consistency to be .84.

RELIABILITY: Alphas of .88 and .89 have been reported for the scale by Bearden et al. (1989) and Gulas and McKeage (2000), respectively.

VALIDITY: The validity of the scale was not examined in either study. However, it was used by Bearden et al. (1989) to help validate two other scales.

REFERENCES:

Bearden, William O., Richard G. Netemeyer, and Jesse E. Teel (1989), "Measurement of Consumer Susceptibility to Interpersonal Influence," *JCR*, 15 (March), 473–481.

Eagly, Alice H. (1967), "Involvement As a Determinant of Responses to Favorable and Unfavorable Information," *Journal of Personality and Social Psychology*, 7 (November), 1–15.

Gulas, Charles A. and Kim McKeage (2000), "Extending Social Comparison: An Examination of the Unintended Consequences of Idealized Advertising Imagery," *JA*, 29 (2), 17–28.

Janis, Irving L. and Peter B. Field (1959), "Sex Differences and Personality Factors Related to Persuasibility," in *Personality and Persuasibility*, Carl I. Hovland, Irving L. Janis, ed., New Haven, Conn.: Yale University Press 55–68.

SCALE ITEMS: [1]

1. How often do you have the feeling that there is *nothing* you can do well?

2. When you have to talk in front of a class or group of people your own age, how afraid or worried do you usually feel? (e.g., very afraid)

3. How often do you worry about whether other people like to be with you?

4. How often do you feel self-conscious?

5. How often are you troubled with shyness?

6. How often do you feel inferior to most of the people you know?

7. Do you ever think that you are a worthless individual?

8. How much do you worry about how well you get along with other people?

9. How often do you feel that you dislike yourself?

10. Do you ever feel so discouraged with yourself that you wonder whether anything is worthwhile?

11. How often do you feel that you have handled yourself well at a social gathering? (r)

12. How often do you have the feeling that you can do everything well? (r)

13. When you talk in front of a class or group of people of your own age, how pleased are you with your performance? (e.g., very pleased) (r)

14. How comfortable are you when starting a conversation with people whom you don't know? (e.g., very comfortable) (r)

15. How often do you feel that you are a successful person? (r)

16. How confident are you that your success in your future job or career is assured? (e.g., very confident) (r)

17. When you speak in a class discussion, how sure of yourself do you feel? (r)

18. How sure of yourself do you feel when among strangers? (r)

19. How confident do you feel that some day the people you know will look up to you and respect you? (r)

20. In general, how confident do you feel about your abilities? (r)

[1] Bearden et al. (1989) appear to have used a five-point response format ranging from *very often* to *practically never*. The response format used by Gulas and McKeage (2000) was not reported.

SCALE NAME: Self-Esteem (State)

SCALE DESCRIPTION: Twenty, five-point statements are used to measure a person's sense of self-esteem at a specific point in time. Thus, this is a *state* measure of a person's self-esteem rather than a more stable personality trait.

SCALE ORIGIN: The scale was developed by Heatherton and Polivy (1991). They drew upon items from Fleming and Courtney (1984), Pliner, Chaiken, and Flett (1990), as well as Janis and Field (1959). Initial testing indicated that scale had three subdimensions: performance, social, and appearance. Based on a study using 428 college students, the internal consistency was very high (alpha = .92).

RELIABILITY: An alpha of .89 was reported for the scale by Bearden, Hardesty, and Rose (2001).

VALIDITY: No examination of the scale's validity was provided by Bearden, Hardesty, and Rose (2001).

COMMENTS: Rigorous testing of the scale's psychometric structure was conducted by Bagozzi and Heatherton (1994) and provided evidence in support of representing the scale with either a partial aggregation model or a partial disaggregation model. How the scale is scored and its treatment in analyses should be determined by the way the construct is modeled.

REFERENCES:

Bagozzi, Richard P. and Todd F. Heatherton (1994), "A General Approach to Representing Multifaceted Personality Constructs: Application to State Self-Esteem," *Structural Equation Modeling*, 1 (1), 35–67.

Bearden, William O., David M. Hardesty, and Randall L. Rose (2001), "Consumer Self-Confidence: Refinements in Conceptualization and Measurement," *JCR*, 28 (June), 121–134.

Fleming, James S. and Barbara E. Courtney (1984), "The Dimensionality of Self-esteem: II. Hierarchical Facet Model for Revised Measurement Scales," *Journal of Personality and Social Psychology*, 46 (February), 404–421.

Heatherton, Todd F. and Janet Polivy (1991), "Development and Validation of a Scale for Measuring State Self-Esteem," *Journal of Personality and Social Psychology*, 60 (June), 895–910.

Janis, Irving L. and Peter B. Field (1959), "Sex Differences and Factors Related to Persuadibility," in *Personality and Persuadibility*, C. I. Hovland, and I. L. Janis, ed. New Haven, CT: Yale University Press, 55–68.

Pliner, Patricia, Shelly Chaiken, and Gordon L. Flett (1990), "Gender Differences in Concern with Body Weight and Physical Appearance Over the Lifespan," *Personality and Social Psychology Bulletin*, 16 (March), 263–273.

SCALE ITEMS:

Directions: This is a questionnaire designed to measure what you are thinking at this moment. There is, of course, no right answer for any statement. The best answer is what you feel is true of yourself at this moment. Be sure to answer all of the items, even if you are not certain of the best answer. Again, answer these questions as they are true for you RIGHT NOW.

#425 *Self-Esteem (State)*

Using the following scale, place a number in the box to the right of the statement that indicates what is true for you at this moment:

1 = not at all
2 = a little bit
3 = somewhat
4 = very much
5 = extremely

1. I feel confident about my abilities.

2. I am worried about whether I am regarded as a success or failure. (r)

3. I feel satisfied with the way my body looks right now.

4. I feel frustrated or rattled about my performance. (r)

5. I feel that I am having trouble understanding things that I read. (r)

6. I feel that others respect and admire me.

7. I am dissatisfied with my weight. (r)

8. I feel self-conscious. (r)

9. I feel as smart as others.

10. I feel displeased with myself. (r)

11. I feel good about myself.

12. I am pleased with my appearance right now.

13. I am worried about what other people think of me. (r)

14. I feel confident that I understand things.

15. I feel inferior to others at this moment. (r)

16. I feel unattractive. (r)

17. I feel concerned about the impression I am making. (r)

18. I feel that I have less scholastic ability right now than others. (r)

19. I feel like I'm not doing well. (r)

20. I am worried about looking foolish. (r)

SCALE NAME: Self-Monitoring

SCALE DESCRIPTION: The eighteen-item scale is intended to measure the extent to which a person observes and controls his/her expressive behavior for the purpose of managing a desired appearance to others.

SCALE ORIGIN: A twenty-five-item version was originally published by Snyder (1974) with the eighteen-item version being slightly abridged, having higher reliability, and being more "factorially pure" (Snyder and Gangestad 1986, p. 137). The shorter version was reported to have an internal consistency of over .70 but still may not be unidimensional. Criticism of the scale's validity as well as support for it are presented in Snyder and Gangestad (1986).

RELIABILITY: Alphas of .82 (Study 1) and .80 (Study 2) were reported for the scale by Aaker (1999).

VALIDITY: No examination of the scale's validity was reported by Aaker (1999).

REFERENCES:

Aaker, Jennifer L. (1999), "The Malleable Self: The Role of Self-Expression in Persuasion," *JMR*, 36 (February), 45–57.

Snyder, Mark (1974), "The Self-Monitoring of Expressive Behavior," *Journal of Personality and Social Psychology*, 30 (October), 526–537.

Snyder, Mark and Steve Gangestad (1986), "On the Nature of Self-Monitoring: Matters of Assessment, Matters of Validity," *Journal of Personality and Social Psychology*, 51 (1), 125–139.

SCALE ITEMS: [1]

1. I find it hard to imitate the behavior of other people. (F)

2. At parties and social gatherings, I do not attempt to do or say things that others will like. (F)

3. I can only argue for ideas which I already believe. (F)

4. I can make impromptu speeches even on topics about which I have almost no information. (T)

5. I guess I could put on a show to impress or entertain others. (T)

6. I would probably make a good actor. (T)

7. In a group of people I am rarely the center of attention. (F)

8. In different situations with different people, I often act like very different persons. (T)

9. I am not particularly good at making other people like me. (F)

10. I'm not always the person I appear to be. (T)

11. I would not change my opinions (or the way I do things) in order to please someone or win their favor. (F)

12. I have considered being an entertainer. (T)

13. I have never been good at games like charades or improvisational acting. (F)

14. I have trouble changing my behavior to suit different people and different situations. (F)

15. At a party I let others keep the jokes and stories going. (F)

16. I feel a bit awkward in public and do not show up quite as well as I should. (F)

17. I can look anyone in the eye and tell a lie with a straight face (if for a right end). (T)

18. I may deceive people by being friendly when I really dislike them. (T)

---

[1] High self-monitoring people are expected to answer True or False as indicated by the key at the end of each item whereas low self-monitoring people would likely answer in the other direction (Snyder and Gangestad 1986, p. 137).

SCALE NAME: Sensation Seeking

SCALE DESCRIPTION: The scale is composed of forty items intended to capture a person's need for varied and novel sensations as well as one's willingness to take the risks necessary to achieve those sensations. This is a measure of a personality *trait* rather than a situation-specific *state*. As used by Steenkamp and Baumgartner (1992), the measure was composed of forty items using a five-point Likert-type response scale. In contrast, Schoenbachler and Whittler (1996) used the original form of the scale that has forty *pairs* of items which the respondent is asked to choose between. Shoham, Rose, and Kahle (1998) used the ten items composing the thrill and adventure seeking subscale.

SCALE ORIGIN: The scale used by Steenkamp and Baumgartner (1992) was adapted from a scale constructed by Zuckerman (1979). The latter has been working on sensation seeking measures since the early 1960s and Form V is the name for the version adapted by Steenkamp and Baumgartner (1992). That version was composed of forty forced-choice pairs of items. Steenkamp and Baumgartner (1992) used nineteen of the negative statements and twenty-one of the positive statements in a Likert-type format. Form V has four subscales: thrill and adventure seeking, experience seeking, disinhibition, and boredom susceptibility.

Much information about the psychometric qualities of Form V can be found in Zuckerman (1979, Ch. 4). Briefly, the scale was found to be quite stable, with test-retest of .94. Analyzed separately for both sexes and for two cultures (English and Americans), internal consistency was above .80 for each of the four samples. Factor loadings and internal consistencies of the subscales were generally best for thrill and adventure seeking and worst for boredom susceptibility.

RELIABILITY: An alpha of .86 (n = 371) was reported for the total scale by Schoenbachler and Whittler (1996). A reliability (LISREL) of .806 (n = 223) was reported for the total scale by Steenkamp and Baumgartner (1992). Reliabilities of .79, .50, .72, and .50 were found for the thrill seeking, experience seeking, disinhibition, and boredom susceptibility subscales, respectively. Shoham, Rose, and Kahle (1998) reported an alpha of .83 (n = 155) for the thrill and adventure seeking subscale.

VALIDITY: Steenkamp and Baumgartner (1992) concluded that principal components factor analysis did not provide strong evidence of a unidimensional nor a four-dimensional structure. Scores on the scale had correlations of between .43 and .60 with three other measures of optimum stimulation level which provides some evidence of convergent validity. A confirmatory factor analysis of all four scales also provided some evidence of convergent validity since the sensation seeking scale loaded significantly on the underlying construct although not near as well as a couple of the other scales.

Although Shoham, Rose, and Kahle (1998) did not report examining the validity of the thrill and adventure seeking subscale they used, their results indicated the measure performed as expected in their model and, thus, provided some evidence of the subscale's nomological validity.

COMMENTS: Shoham, Rose, and Kahle (1998) translated the thrill and adventure seeking subscale into Hebrew before use with a sample of people in Israel.

REFERENCES:

Schoenbachler, Denise D. and Tommy E. Whittler (1996), "Adolescent Processing of Social and Physical Threat Communications," *JA*, 25 (Winter), 37–54.

Shoham, Aviv, Gregory M. Rose, and Lynn R. Kahle (1998), "Marketing of Risky Sports: From Intention to Action," *JAMS*, 26 (4), 307–321.

Steenkamp, Jan-Benedict E. M. and Hans Baumgartner (1992), "The Role of Optimum Stimulation Level in Exploratory Consumer Behavior," *JCR*, 19 (December), 434–448.

Zuckerman, Marvin (1979), *Sensation Seeking: Beyond the Optimum Level of Arousal*, Hillsdale, New Jersey: Lawrence Erlbaum Associates.

SCALE ITEMS:

1. A. I like "wild" uninhibited parties.[1]
   B. I prefer quiet parties with good conversation.[2]

2. A. There are some movies I enjoy seeing a second or even a third time.
   B. I can't stand watching a movie that I've seen before.[1,2]

3. A. I often wish I could be a mountain climber.[1,3]
   B. I can't understand people who risk their necks climbing mountains.[2]

4. A. I dislike all body odors.[2]
   B. I like some of the earthy body smells.[1]

5. A. I get bored seeing the same old faces.[1]
   B. I like the comfortable familiarity of everyday friends.[2]

6. A. I like to explore a strange city or section of town by myself, even if it means getting lost.[1,2]
   B. I prefer a guide when I am in a place I don't know well.

7. A. I dislike people who do or say things just to shock or upset others.[2]
   B. When you can predict almost everything a person will do and say he or she must be a bore.[1]

8. A. I usually don't enjoy a movie or play where I can predict what will happen in advance.[1,2]
   B. I don't mind watching a movie or play where I can predict what will happen in advance.

9. A. I have tried marijuana or would like to.[1,2]
   B. I would never smoke marijuana.

10. A. I would not like to try any drug which might product strange and dangerous effects on me.[2]
    B. I would like to try some of the new drugs that produce hallucinations.[1]

11. A. A sensible person avoids activities that are dangerous.[2]
    B. I sometimes like to do things that are a little frightening.[1,3]

12. A. I dislike "swingers."[2]
    B. I enjoy the company of real "swingers."[1]

13. A. I find that stimulants make me uncomfortable.
    B. I often like to get high (drinking liquor or smoking marijuana).[1,2]

14. A. I like to try new foods that I have never tasted before.[1,2]
    B. I order the dishes with which I am familiar, so as to avoid disappointment and unpleasantness.

15. A. I enjoy looking at home movies or travel slides.
    B. Looking at someone's home movies or travel slides bores me tremendously.[1,2]

16. A. I would like to take up the sport of water-skiing.[1,2,3]
    B. I would not like to take up water-skiing.

17. A. I would like to try surf-board riding.[1,2,3]
    B. I would not like to try surf-board riding.

18. A. I would like to take off on a trip with no pre-planned or definite routes, or timetable.[1]
    B. When I go on a trip I like to plan my route and timetable fairly carefully.[2]

19. A. I prefer the "down-to-earth" kinds of people as friends.[2]
    B. I would like to make friends in some of the "far-out" groups like artists or "hippies."[1]

20. A. I would not like to learn to fly an airplane.[3]
    B. I would like to learn to fly an airplane.[1,2]

21. A. I prefer the surface of the water to the depths.[2]
    B. I would like to go scuba diving.[13]

22. A. I would like to meet some persons who are homosexual (men or women).[1,2]
    B. I stay away from anyone I suspect of being "queer."

23. A. I would like to try parachute jumping.[1,2,3]
    B. I would never want to try jumping out of a plane with or without a parachute.

24. A. I prefer friends who are excitingly unpredictable.[1,2]
    B. I prefer friends who are reliable and predictable.

25. A. I am not interested in experience for its own sake.
    B. I like to have new and exciting experiences and sensations even if they are a little frightening, unconventional or illegal.[1,2]

26. A. The essence of good art is in its clarity, symmetry of form and harmony of colors.[2]
    B. I often find beauty in the "clashing" colors and irregular forms of modern painting.[1]

27. A. I enjoy spending time in the familiar surroundings of home.[2]
    B. I get very restless if I have to stay around home for any length of time.[1]

28. A. I like to dive off the high board.[1,2,3]
    B. I don't like the feeling I get standing on the high board (or I don't go near it at all).

29. A. I like to date members of the opposite sex who are physically exciting.[1]
    B. I like to date members of the opposite sex who share my values.[2]

30. A. Heavy drinking usually ruins a party because some people get loud and boisterous.
    B. Keeping the drinks full is the key to a good party.[12]

31. A. The worst social sin is to be rude.
    B. The worst social sin is to be a bore.[1,2]

32. A. A person should have considerable sexual experience before marriage.[1,2]
    B. It's better if two married persons begin their sexual experience with each other.

33. A. Even if I had the money I would not care to associate with flighty persons like those in the "jet set."[2]
    B. I could conceive of myself seeking pleasure around the world with the "jet set."[1]

34. A. I like people who are sharp and witty even if they do sometimes insult others.[1]
    B. I dislike people who have their fun at the expense of hurting the feelings of others.[2]

35. A. There is altogether too much portrayal of sex in movies.
    B. I enjoy watching many of the "sexy" scenes in movies.[1,2]

36. A. I feel best after taking a couple of drinks.[1,2]
    B. Something is wrong with people who need liquor to feel good.

37. A. People should dress according to some standards of taste, neatness, and style.
    B. People should dress in individual ways even if the effects are sometimes strange.[1,2]

38. A. Sailing long distances in small sailing crafts is foolhardy.[2]
    B. I would like to sail a long distance in a small but seaworthy sailing craft.[1,3]

39. A. I have no patience with dull or boring persons.[1,2]
    B. I find something interesting in almost every person I talk with.

40. A. Skiing fast down a high mountain slope is a good way to end up on crutches.
    B. I think I would enjoy the sensations of skiing very fast down a high mountain slope.[1,2,3]

[1] These are the items in each pair which indicate greater sensation-seeking.

[2] These are the items used by Steenkamp and Baumgartner (1992). When they are not the same as those marked by the endnote 1 then they must be reversed coded during the scoring process.

[3] Shoham, Rose, and Kahle (1998) used these ten items (the thrill and adventure seeking subdimension).

SCALE NAME: Service Quality (Ambience)

SCALE DESCRIPTION: The scale uses three, seven-point Likert-type statements to measure an aspect of service quality having to do with the extent to which a customer believes the physical environment of a provider's facilities are pleasant and important. Although not explicit in the statements, the scale was apparently intended to tap into non-visual aspects of a service provider's facilities (temperatures, smells, sounds) rather than visual aspects (#430).

SCALE ORIGIN: Although drawing some inspiration from previous studies of service quality, Brady and Cronin (2001) developed their own measures in order to ensure they had certain characteristics. The third-order factor model of service quality that they tested viewed overall service quality as having three primary dimensions: outcome, interaction, and environmental quality. In turn, each of those dimensions had three sub-dimensions. Ambience was confirmed as being most associated with the dimension of physical environment quality. A unique aspect of the scales constructed for each of the subdimensions is that they each have three items with one related to reliability, one related to responsiveness, and one related to empathy.

RELIABILITY: The construct reliability for the scale was .93.

VALIDITY: Based on a CFA, evidence of convergent and discriminant validity was provided. The AVE (average variance extracted) was 82%.

REFERENCES:
Brady, Michael K. and Joseph J. Cronin Jr. (2001), "Some New Thoughts on Conceptualizing Perceived Service Quality: A Hierarchical Approach," *JM*, 65 (July), 34–49.

SCALE ITEMS: [1]

1. At _____, you can rely on there being a good atmosphere.

2. _____'s ambience is what I'm looking for in a _____.

3. _____ understands that its atmosphere is important to me.

[1] The name of the service provider should be placed in the blanks except for the second blank of item 2 where a term or phrase for the appropriate generic category is used, e.g., amusement park.

SCALE NAME: Service Quality (Convenience Store)

SCALE DESCRIPTION: The sixteen-item, five-point scale attempts to measure a customer's attitude regarding the quality of a convenience store that offers gas as well as food. This scale is performance rather than expectations based. Further, it is not intended to be a measure of satisfaction although it is related to it.

SCALE ORIGIN: The scale is original to Hurley and Estelami (1998). Focus groups were conducted with store employees and consumers to determine what characteristics of the store were important. Checks were also made of prior research performed by the store as well as the industry association to make sure these attributes appeared to be important.

RELIABILITY: An alpha of .92 was reported for the scale by Hurley and Estelami (1998).

VALIDITY: To provide a sense of the scale's validity Hurley and Estelami (1998) examined the correlation between scale scores and two non-survey-related criterion variables that should theoretically be related with customer perceptions of store quality: sales revenue and store customer counts. Several service quality indexes based on the scale scores were calculated and correlated with the criterion variables. Scale mean correlated best. Despite this, a factor analysis conducted by the authors clearly showed that the scale was not uni-dimensional. Three dimensions were evident: items 1-8 loaded highest on a cleanliness factor; items 9-13 loaded highest on a food factor; and, the remaining three items loaded highest on an employee factor.

REFERENCES:
Hurley, Robert F. and Hooman Estelami (1998), "Alternative Indexes for Monitoring Customer Perceptions of Service Quality: A Comparative Evaluation in a Retail Context," *JAMS*, 26 (3), 209–221.

SCALE ITEMS: [1]

Directions: Please rate the store based on your typical experiences with it. Use the following five-point scale to rate each store attribute: 5 = *excellent*, 4 = *very good*, 3 = *good*, 2 = *fair*, 1 = *poor*.

1. cleanliness of gas station

2. cleanliness of sidewalk

3. cleanliness of parking

4. cleanliness of coffee area

5. cleanliness of fountain

6. cleanliness of food area

7. cleanliness of the register area

8. cleanliness of restrooms

9. food made the way you like

10. freshness of the food

11. food speed

12. cleanliness of food preparation employees

13. freshness of the coffee

14. employee friendliness

15. employee speed

16. employee appearance

[1] Only a portion of the directions were explicitly stated provided in the article. The phrasing here is a reconstruction based on the description provided.

SCALE NAME: Service Quality (Design)

SCALE DESCRIPTION: Three, seven-point Likert-type statements are used to assess an aspect of service quality having to do with the extent to which a customer believes the physical environment of a provider's facilities are notable and relevant. The scale was intended to tap into the visual aspects of a service provider's facilities (layout) rather than non-visual ones (#428).

SCALE ORIGIN: Although drawing some inspiration from previous studies of service quality, Brady and Cronin (2001) developed their own measures in order to ensure they had certain characteristics. The third-order factor model of service quality that they tested viewed overall service quality as having three primary dimensions: outcome, interaction, and environmental quality. In turn, each of those dimensions had three sub-dimensions. Ambience was confirmed as being most associated with the dimension of physical environment quality. A unique aspect of the scales constructed for each of the subdimensions is that they each have three items with one related to reliability, one related to responsiveness, and one related to empathy.

RELIABILITY: The construct reliability for the scale was .85.

VALIDITY: Based on a CFA, evidence of convergent and discriminant validity was provided. The AVE (average variance extracted) was 66%.

REFERENCES:

Brady, Michael K. and Joseph J. Cronin Jr. (2001), "Some New Thoughts on Conceptualizing Perceived Service Quality: A Hierarchical Approach," *JM*, 65 (July), 34–49.

SCALE ITEMS: [1]

1. This service provider's layout never fails to impress me.

2. _____'s layout serves my purposes.

3. _____ understands that the design of its facilities is important to me.

[1] The name of the service provider should be placed in the blanks.

SCALE NAME: Service Quality (Employees' Attitudes)

SCALE DESCRIPTION: Three, seven-point Likert-type statements are used to assess an aspect of service quality that has to do with the consumer's sense of the friendliness and positive demeanor expressed by the personnel with whom the customer has interacted.

SCALE ORIGIN: Although drawing considerable inspiration for the numerous measures of service quality that have been previously published (e.g., V. III #334-#359), Brady and Cronin (2001) developed their own measures in order to ensure they had certain characteristics. The third-order factor model of service quality that they tested viewed overall service quality as having three primary dimensions: outcome, interaction, and environmental quality. In turn, each of those dimensions had three subdimensions. Employee attitude was confirmed as being most associated with the dimension of interaction quality. A unique aspect of the scales constructed for each of the subdimensions is that they each have three items with one related to reliability, one related to responsiveness, and one related to empathy.

RELIABILITY: The construct reliability for the scale was .93.

VALIDITY: Based on a CFA, evidence of convergent and discriminant validity was provided. The AVE (average variance extracted) was 82%.

REFERENCES:
Brady, Michael K. and Joseph J. Cronin Jr. (2001), "Some New Thoughts on Conceptualizing Perceived Service Quality: A Hierarchical Approach," *JM*, 65 (July), 34–49.

SCALE ITEMS: [1]

1. You can count on the employees at _____ being friendly.

2. The attitude of _____'s employees demonstrates their willingness to help me.

3. The attitude of _____'s employees shows me that they understand my needs.

---

[1] The name of the service provider should be placed in the blanks.

SCALE NAME: Service Quality (Employees' Behaviors)

SCALE DESCRIPTION: The scale has three, seven-point Likert-type statements and measures an aspect of service quality that has to do with the degree to which a customer believes the personnel of a service provider act quickly and with an understanding of customer's needs.

SCALE ORIGIN: Although drawing considerable inspiration for the numerous measures of service quality that have been previously published (e.g., V. III #334-#359), Brady and Cronin (2001) developed their own measures in order to ensure they had certain characteristics. The third-order factor model of service quality that they tested viewed overall service quality as having three primary dimensions: outcome, interaction, and environmental quality. In turn, each of those dimensions had three subdimensions. Employee behavior was confirmed as being most associated with the dimension of interaction quality. A unique aspect of the scales constructed for each of the subdimensions is that they each have three items with one related to reliability, one related to responsiveness, and one related to empathy.

RELIABILITY: The construct reliability for the scale was .92.

VALIDITY: Based on a CFA, evidence of convergent and discriminant validity was provided. The AVE (average variance extracted) was 80%.

REFERENCES:
Brady, Michael K. and Joseph J. Cronin Jr. (2001), "Some New Thoughts on Conceptualizing Perceived Service Quality: A Hierarchical Approach," *JM*, 65 (July), 34–49.

SCALE ITEMS: [1]

1. I can count on _____'s employees taking actions to address my needs.

2. _____'s employees respond quickly to my needs.

3. The behavior of _____'s employees indicates to me that they understand my needs.

[1] The name of the service provider should be placed in the blanks.

SCALE NAME: Service Quality (Employees' Expertise)

SCALE DESCRIPTION: The scale has three, seven-point Likert-type statements that are intended to measure an aspect of service quality having to do with the extent to which a customer believes the personnel of a service provider have the requisite knowledge and skill to meet the customer's needs.

SCALE ORIGIN: Although drawing considerable inspiration for the numerous measures of service quality that have been previously published (e.g., V. III #334–#359), Brady and Cronin (2001) developed their own measures in order to ensure they had certain characteristics. The third-order factor model of service quality that they tested viewed overall service quality as having three primary dimensions: outcome, interaction, and environmental quality. In turn, each of those dimensions had three subdimensions. Employee expertise was confirmed as being most associated with the dimension of interaction quality. A unique aspect of the scales constructed for each of the subdimensions is that they each have three items with one related to reliability, one related to responsiveness, and one related to empathy.

RELIABILITY: The construct reliability for the scale was .91.

VALIDITY: Based on a CFA, evidence of convergent and discriminant validity was provided. The AVE (average variance extracted) was 77%.

REFERENCES:
Brady, Michael K. and Joseph J. Cronin Jr. (2001), "Some New Thoughts on Conceptualizing Perceived Service Quality: A Hierarchical Approach," *JM*, 65 (July), 34–49.

SCALE ITEMS: [1]

1. You can count on _____'s employees knowing their jobs.

2. _____ employees are able to answer my questions quickly.

3. The employees understand that I rely on their knowledge to meet my needs.

[1] The name of the service provider should be placed in the blanks.

SCALE NAME: Service Quality (Encounter Specific)

SCALE DESCRIPTION: The scale is composed of five, seven-point Likert-type statements intended to capture a consumer's sense of the helpfulness and attentiveness provided by employees at a store in which the customer has recently received service.

SCALE ORIGIN: Sweeney, Soutar, and Johnson (1999) were attempting to capture the perceived quality of the *process* of delivering a service rather than the quality of the *outcome*. Further, they were concerned about consumers' quality perceptions from a specific transaction experience rather than a more generalized attitude. Items for the scale were drawn from the assurance, responsiveness, and empathy dimensions of the SERVQUAL instrument (Parasuraman, Berry, and Zeithaml 1991).

RELIABILITY: An alpha of .93 was reported for the scale by Sweeney, Soutar, and Johnson (1999).

VALIDITY: Not much was said by the authors about this scale's validity but it was stated in general that all their scales exhibited discriminant validity by having their variance extracted being higher than the relevant squared structural path coefficients (Fornell and Larcker 1981). It was also stated that the items in the scale were unidimensional.

REFERENCES:

Fornell, Claes and David F. Larcker (1981), "Evaluating Structural Equation Models with Unobservable Variables and Measurement Error," *JMR*, 18 (February), Pages.

Parasuraman, A., Leonard L. Berry, and Valarie A. Zeithaml (1991), "Refinement and Reassessment of the SERVQUAL Scale," *JR*, 67 (Winter), 420–450.

Sweeney, Jillian C., Geoffrey N. Soutar, and Lester W. Johnson (1999), "The Role of Perceived Risk in the Quality-Value Relationship: A Study in a Retail Environment," *JR*, 75 (1), 77–105.

SCALE ITEMS:

1. The employees in this store were courteous.

2. The employees in this store were willing to help.

3. This store gave me personal attention.

4. The employees in this store gave me prompt service.

5. This store gave me individual attention.

SCALE NAME: Service Quality (Overall)

SCALE DESCRIPTION: The scale is composed of three, nine-point semantic differentials that are intended to measure a customer's global sense of the quality of service provided by a specified organization.

SCALE ORIGIN: The scale appears to have been developed by Cronin, Brady, and Hult (2000).

RELIABILITY: Cronin, Brady, and Hult (2000) reported a construct reliability of .88 for the scale.

VALIDITY: Confirmatory factor analysis was conducted by Cronin, Brady, and Hult (2000) on this scale and several others. Some evidence of the scale's discriminant validity came from noting that the average variance extracted (71.6%) was greater than the shared variances with the other constructs.

COMMENTS: Based on the combined sample from six different service industries (n = 1944), the scale had a mean of 6.41 and a standard deviation of 1.44.

REFERENCES:
Cronin, Jr., J. Joseph, Michael K. Brady, and G. Tomas M. Hult (2000), "Assessing the Effects of Quality, Value, and Customer Satisfaction on Consumer Behavioral Intentions in Service Environments," *JR*, 79 (2), 193–218.

SCALE ITEMS:

1. poor / excellent

2. inferior / superior

3. low standards / high standards

SCALE NAME: Service Quality (Past Experiences)

SCALE DESCRIPTION: Three, five-point semantic differential items compose the scale. The scale is used to allow customers to evaluate their past experiences with some specified organization. The context in which the respondents were given this scale was after being told to remember a recent service experience that led to their lodging a complaint. The scale stem directs the respondent to think of the state of the relationship prior to making the complaint. Unlike most other service quality measures this one does not focus on a particular facet but is a global-type measure.

SCALE ORIGIN: Although Tax, Brown, and Chandrashekaran (1998) may have drawn inspiration from previous measures, this scale appears to be original to their study.

RELIABILITY: An alpha of .93 (n = 257) was reported for the scale by Tax, Brown, and Chandrashekaran (1998).

VALIDITY: It is not clear what support if any was found for the validity of the scale in the study by Tax, Brown, and Chandrashekaran (1998).

REFERENCES:
Tax, Stephen S., Stephen W. Brown, and Murali Chandrashekaran (1998), "Customer Evaluations of Service Complaint Experiences: Implications for Relationship Marketing," *JM*, 62 (April), 60–76.

SCALE ITEMS:

How would you rate your experiences with this organization prior to the incident which led to the complaint:

1. Very poor / very good

2. Very negative / very positive

3. Terrible / excellent

SCALE NAME: Service Quality (Performance)

SCALE DESCRIPTION: The ten-item, nine-point scale attempts to measure a customer's perception of the performance-based quality of service provided by a specified organization. The items tap into several aspects of service quality but the emphasis is on the role played by employees.

SCALE ORIGIN: The items for the scale were developed by Cronin, Brady, and Hult (2000) based on detailed descriptions from Parasuraman, Zeithaml, and Berry (1985). Specifically, the latter proposed a ten dimensional model of service quality. Following that, Cronin, Brady, and Hult (2000) generated multi-item scales for each dimension. After several rounds of data collection and refinement 47 items were tested with 278 students. The ten items with the highest intercorrelations with the other items in their respective dimensions were selected for use in this scale.

RELIABILITY: Cronin, Brady, and Hult (2000) reported a construct reliability of .94 for the scale.

VALIDITY: Confirmatory factor analysis was conducted by Cronin, Brady, and Hult (2000) on this scale and several others. Some evidence of the scale's discriminant validity came from noting that the average variance extracted was greater than the shared variances with the other constructs. Despite this information, the origin of the scale items (deliberately drawn from ten dimensions) as well as an close examination of the items (provided below) indicate that the scale is multidimensional. Two dimensions are most obvious: employees (items 1-8) and facility (item 9 and 10). Caution is urged in the scale's use until it can be confirmed that it is unidimensional.

COMMENTS: Based on the combined sample from six different service industries (n = 1944), the scale had a mean of 6.61 and a standard deviation of 1.26.

REFERENCES:
Cronin, Jr., J. Joseph, Michael K. Brady, and G. Tomas M. Hult (2000), "Assessing the Effects of Quality, Value, and Customer Satisfaction on Consumer Behavioral Intentions in Service Environments," *JR*, 79 (2), 193–218.
Parasuraman, A., Valarie A. Zeithaml, and Leonard L. Berry (1985), "A Conceptual Model of Service Quality and Its Implications for Future Research," *JM*, 49 (Fall), 41–50.

SCALE ITEMS: [1]

1. Generally, the employees provide service reliably, consistently, and dependably.

2. Generally, the employees are willing and able to provide service in a timely manner.

3. Generally, the employees are competent (i.e., knowledgeable and skillful).

4. Generally, the employees are approachable and easy to contact.

5. Generally, the employees are courteous, polite, and respectful.

6. Generally, the employees listen to me and speak in a language that I can understand.

7. Generally, the employees are trustworthy, believable, and honest.

8. Generally, the employees make the effort to understand my needs.

9. Generally, this facility provides an environment that is free from danger, risk, or doubt.

10. Generally, the physical facilities and employees are neat and clean.

---

[1] A nine-point response scale was used by Cronin, Brady, and Hult (2000) with anchors of *very low* and *very high*.

SCALE NAME: Service Quality (Positive Experience)

SCALE DESCRIPTION: Three, seven-point Likert-type items are employed to assess the degree to which a customer believes a specified provider knows the type of experience desired by customers and, indeed, offers that quality of service. Given the instructions used with the scale items, the respondent should be focusing on the *outcome* of the service he/she has received in the past. The scale was called *valence* by Brady and Cronin (2001).

SCALE ORIGIN: Although drawing some inspiration from previous studies of service quality, Brady and Cronin (2001) developed their own measures in order to ensure they had certain characteristics. The third-order factor model of service quality that they tested viewed overall service quality as having three primary dimensions: outcome, interaction, and environmental quality. In turn, each of those dimensions had three sub-dimensions. Positive Experience was confirmed as being most associated with the dimension of outcome quality. A unique aspect of the scales constructed for each of the subdimensions is that they each have three items with one related to reliability, one related to responsiveness, and one related to empathy.

RELIABILITY: The construct reliability for the scale was .89.

VALIDITY: Based on a CFA, some evidence of convergent and discriminant validity was provided. The AVE (average variance extracted) was 73%.

REFERENCES:
Brady, Michael K. and Joseph J. Cronin Jr. (2001), "Some New Thoughts on Conceptualizing Perceived Service Quality: A Hierarchical Approach," *JM*, 65 (July), 34–49.

SCALE ITEMS: [1]

Directions: These questions refer to whether you think the outcome of your experience was good or bad.

1. When I leave _____, I usually feel that I had a good experience.

2. I believe _____ tries to give me a good experience.

3. I believe _____ knows the type of experience its customers want.

[1] The name of the service provider should be placed in the blanks.

SCALE NAME: Service Quality (Social Factors)

SCALE DESCRIPTION: Three, seven-point Likert-type statements are used to measure an aspect of service quality that involves the degree to which a customer thinks other patrons of a provider have an effect on the provider's ability to give satisfying service. Although not stated explicitly, the scale is intended to infer that the *presence* of other customers in the facilities when one is receiving service as well as the *quantity and quality* of those other customers has an influence on the service provided.

SCALE ORIGIN: Although drawing some inspiration from previous studies of service quality, Brady and Cronin (2001) developed their own measures in order to ensure they had certain characteristics. The third-order factor model of service quality that they tested viewed overall service quality as having three primary dimensions: outcome, interaction, and environmental quality. In turn, each of those dimensions had three sub-dimensions. Social Factors was confirmed as being most associated with the dimension of physical environment quality. A unique aspect of the scales constructed for each of the subdimensions is that they each have three items with one related to reliability, one related to responsiveness, and one related to empathy.

RELIABILITY: The construct reliability for the scale was .72.

VALIDITY: Based on a CFA, some evidence of convergent and discriminant validity was provided. However, the AVE (average variance extracted) was only 47%.

COMMENTS: The scale's quality could be improved by slight adjustments in the statements and/or instructions to specify that what is of interest is the *presence of other customers in the facility at the same time* as the respondent. Otherwise, the statements could be interpreted as referring to things the respondent has heard from other customers at some other place and time, e.g., word-of-mouth.

REFERENCES:
Brady, Michael K. and Joseph J. Cronin Jr. (2001), "Some New Thoughts on Conceptualizing Perceived Service Quality: A Hierarchical Approach," *JM*, 65 (July), 34–49.

SCALE ITEMS: [1]

1. I find that _____'s other customers consistently leave me with a good impression of its service.

2. _____'s other customers do not affect its ability to provide me with good service.

3. _____ understands that other patrons affect my perception of its service.

---

[1] The name of the service provider should be placed in the blanks.

SCALE NAME: Service Quality (Supermarket)

SCALE DESCRIPTION: The scale is composed of twenty-five, five-point items tapping into a person's sense of a supermarket's quality. The items focus on three dimensions of a store's quality: operations, appearance, and personnel.

SCALE ORIGIN: Sirohi, McLaughlin, and Wittink (1998) did not specify the source of the measure. It appears that it is original to their study.

RELIABILITY: Construct reliability was reported to be .97 (Sirohi, McLaughlin, and Wittink 1998).

VALIDITY: Sirohi, McLaughlin, and Wittink (1998) originally intended for the items in this scale to measure three different dimensions of store quality (as noted above in the scale description). However, their analysis showed that the average variance extracted for the three dimensions was low indicating that the constructs were not sufficiently distinct. The authors decided to pool the measures as formative indicators of a single construct. After a few of the original indicators were dropped (due to small loadings) the final version of the scale had an average variance extracted of .65.

REFERENCES:
Sirohi, Niren, Edward W. McLaughlin, and Dick R. Wittink (1998), "A Model of Consumer Perceptions and Store Loyalty Intentions for a Supermarket Retailer," *JR*, 74 (2), 223–245.

SCALE ITEMS: [1]

Store operations perception

1. Quality of operations (Hours, training, and staffing of employees)

2. Staffing enough employees to meet customer needs

3. Offering convenient hours of operation

4. Keeping deli, bakery open and providing services for extended hours

5. Providing adequate training of employees

6. Ability of manager to resolve questions and problems

Store Appearance perception

7. Rating of overall appearance of store

8. Providing a clean shopping environment

9. Having wide, open aisles

10. Having various departments in appropriate places in the store

11. Having well-marked aisle directories

12. Having a safe parking lot

13. Providing clean restrooms

14. Providing a pleasant shopping environment

Personnel Service Perception

15. Overall quality of services provided by personnel the customer interacts with

16. Quality of services provided by cashiers and baggers

17. Quality of services provided by customer service desk

18. Quality of services provided by employees at the deli counter

19. Quality of services provided by employees at the in-store bakery

20. Quality of services provided by employees in the meat department

21. Quality of services provided by employees at the seafood counter

22. Quality of services provided by employees in the produce department

23. Quality of services provided by store manager

24. Customer orientation of the supermarket

25. Provision of friendly and responsive service by the supermarket

[1] The response format for most of the items was a five point scale ranging from *excellent* to *poor*. One of the indicators for the Store Appearance facet as well as two items for the Personnel Service facet were responded to using a scale ranging from *strongly agree* to *strongly disagree*. However, the particular items were not identified.

SCALE NAME: Service Quality (Tangibles)

SCALE DESCRIPTION: The scale is composed of three, seven-point Likert-type statements measuring an aspect of service quality focused on the degree to which a customer says the provider knows that certain *physical aspects* of the service are important to patrons and, indeed, the respondent is pleased with them.

SCALE ORIGIN: Although drawing some inspiration from previous studies of tangible aspects of service quality (e.g., V. III #358 and #359), Brady and Cronin (2001) developed their own measures in order to ensure they had certain characteristics. The third-order factor model of service quality that they tested viewed overall service quality as having three primary dimensions: outcome, interaction, and environmental quality. In turn, each of those dimensions had three subdimensions. Tangibles was confirmed as being most associated with the dimension of outcome quality. A unique aspect of the scales constructed for each of the subdimensions is that they each have three items with one related to reliability, one related to responsiveness, and one related to empathy.

RELIABILITY: The construct reliability for the scale was .91.

VALIDITY: Based on a CFA, some evidence of convergent and discriminant validity was provided. The AVE (average variance extracted) was 76%.

REFERENCES:
Brady, Michael K. and Joseph J. Cronin Jr. (2001), "Some New Thoughts on Conceptualizing Perceived Service Quality: A Hierarchical Approach," *JM*, 65 (July), 34–49.

SCALE ITEMS: [1]

1. I am consistently pleased with the _____ at _____.

2. I like _____ because it has the _____ that I want.

3. _____ knows the kind of _____ its customers are looking for.

---

[1] The name of the service provider should be placed in the blanks (single). In the double-blanks some tangible aspect of the service should be specified. For example, for an amusement park it could be rides.

SCALE NAME: Service Quality (Waiting Time)

SCALE DESCRIPTION: The scale is composed of three, seven-point Likert-type statements and seems to measure an aspect of service quality involving the degree to which a customer thinks the time required for patrons to wait for service is important to the provider and, indeed, the wait time is acceptable.

SCALE ORIGIN: Although drawing some inspiration from previous studies of service quality, Brady and Cronin (2001) developed their own measures in order to ensure they had certain characteristics. The third-order factor model of service quality that they tested viewed overall service quality as having three primary dimensions: outcome, interaction, and environmental quality. In turn, each of those dimensions had three sub-dimensions. Wait Time was confirmed as being most associated with the dimension of outcome quality. A unique aspect of the scales constructed for each of the subdimensions is that they each have three items with one related to reliability, one related to responsiveness, and one related to empathy.

RELIABILITY: The construct reliability for the scale was .82.

VALIDITY: Based on a CFA, some evidence of convergent and discriminant validity was provided. The AVE (average variance extracted) was 61%.

REFERENCES:
Brady, Michael K. and Joseph J. Cronin Jr. (2001), "Some New Thoughts on Conceptualizing Perceived Service Quality: A Hierarchical Approach," *JM*, 65 (July), 34–49.

SCALE ITEMS: [1]

1. Waiting time at _____ is predictable.

2. _____ tries to keep my waiting time to a minimum.

3. This service provider understands that waiting time is important to me.

---

[1] The name of the service provider should be placed in the blanks.

SCALE NAME: Service Success Likelihood

SCALE DESCRIPTION: The scale is composed of four, seven-point semantic differentials intended to measure the perceived probability that a service will be successfully completed as intended.

SCALE ORIGIN: Hui, Thakor, and Gill (1998) did not specify the source of the scale. Although they appear to have drawn upon items used in previous scales, the measure as a whole may be original to their study.

RELIABILITY: An alpha of .90 (n = 90) was reported for the scale by Hui, Thakor, and Gill (1998).

VALIDITY: No examination of the scale's validity was reported by Hui, Thakor, and Gill (1998).

REFERENCES:
Hui, Michael K., Mrugank V. Thakor, and Ravi Gill (1998), "The Effect of Delay Type and Service Stage on Consumers' Reactions to Waiting," *JCR*, 24 (March), 469–479.

SCALE ITEMS: [1]

What is your sense that the service will be provided as you requested?

1. low / high

2. unlikely / likely

3. hopeless / hopeful

4. negative / positive

[1] Hui, Thakor, and Gill (1998) used a seven-point response scale with these items. The scale stem was not provided by the authors but may have been something like this.

SCALE NAME: Shop With Children

SCALE DESCRIPTION: The scale is composed of four, five-point items measuring the frequency with which a parent reports routinely taking a child along on shopping trips. This was referred to as *coshopping* by Carlson and Grossbart (1988; Grossbart, Carlson, and Walsh 1991) as well as Rose and Grossbart (1999).

SCALE ORIGIN: The use of items 1-3 as a multi-item measure appears to be original to Carlson and Grossbart (1988; Grossbart, Carlson, and Walsh 1991). They got ideas for some of the items, however, from the research of Ward, Wackman, and Wartella (1977). Item 4 may be original to Rose (1999).

RELIABILITY: Carlson and Grossbart (1988; Grossbart, Carlson, and Walsh 1991) reported an alpha of .79. Rose and Grossbart (1999) reported alphas of .80 and .82 for the scale in the U.S. and the Japanese samples, respectively.

VALIDITY: No examination of scale validity was reported in any of the studies. Carlson and Grossbart (1988; Grossbart, Carlson, and Walsh 1991) did report, however, that scores on this scale had a unspecified positive correlation with a measure of social desirability bias.

REFERENCES:

Carlson, Les and Sanford Grossbart (1988), "Parental Style and Consumer Socialization of Children," *JCR*, 15 (June), 77–94.

Grossbart, Sanford, Les Carlson, and Ann Walsh (1991), "Consumer Socialization and Frequency of Shopping with Children," *JAMS*, 19 (Summer), 155–163.

Rose, Gregory M. (2002), Personal Correspondence.

Rose, Gregory M. and Sanford Grossbart (1999), "Consumer Socialization, Parental Style, and Development Timetables in the United States and Japan," *JM*, 63 (July), 105–119.

Ward, Scott, Daniel B. Wackman, and Ellen Wartella (1977), *How Children Learn to Buy*, Beverly Hills, CA: Sage.

SCALE ITEMS: [1]

1. When I go grocery shopping, I take my child.

2. When I go general family shopping, I take my child.

3. When I shop for my child, I take him/her along.

4. Even if I could leave my children at home during shopping trips, I would rather taken them along because I believe children should participate in these activities.

---

[1] The anchors for the five-point response scale used in each of the studies were 1 = *very seldom*, 2 = *seldom*, 3 = *sometimes*, 4 = *often*, and 5 = *very often*. Carlson and Grossbart (1988; Grossbart, Carlson, and Walsh 1991) used the first three items (above) while Rose (2002; and Grossbart 1999) used all of them.

SCALE NAME: Shopping Convenience

SCALE DESCRIPTION: It is a three-item, five-point Likert-type summated ratings scale measuring the degree to which a person expresses a desire for convenience and simplicity particularly as it relates to gathering information about products and conducting shopping activity.

SCALE ORIGIN: The source of the scale was not stated by Donthu and Gilliland (1996) but it is likely to be original to their study.

RELIABILITY: Alphas of .71 (Donthu and Gilliland 1996) and .75 (Donthu and Garcia 1999) have been reported for the scale.

VALIDITY: No specific examination of the scale's validity was reported by Donthu and Gilliland (1996).

REFERENCES:
Donthu, Naveen and Adriana Garcia (1999), "The Internet Shopper," *JAR*, 39 (May/June), 52–58.
Donthu, Naveen and David Gilliland (1996), "The Infomercial Shopper," *JAR*, 36 (March/April), 69–76.

SCALE ITEMS:

1. I hate to spend time gathering information on products.

2. I do not like complicated things.

3. It is convenient to shop from home.

SCALE NAME: Shopping Enjoyment

SCALE DESCRIPTION: It is a three-item, five point Likert-type summated ratings scale measuring the enjoyment a consumer expresses receiving from the shopping experience. The scale was referred to as *emotional lift* by O'Guinn and Faber (1989; Faber and O'Guinn 1992). It was called *attitude toward shopping* by Donthu and Gilliland (1996).

SCALE ORIGIN: The scale was apparently original to O'Guinn and Faber (1989). The source of the variation used by Donthu and Gilliland (1996) was not stated.

RELIABILITY: Alphas of .89, .88, and .88 were reported for the scale by O'Guinn and Faber (1989; Faber and O'Guinn 1992), Donthu and Gilliland (1996), and Donthu and Garcia (1999), respectively.

VALIDITY: Beyond a factor analysis conducted by O'Guinn and Faber (1992) which indicated that the items loaded together, no specific examination of scale validity has been reported.

REFERENCES:
Donthu, Naveen and Adriana Garcia (1999), "The Internet Shopper," *JAR*, 39 (May/June), 52–58.
Donthu, Naveen and David Gilliland (1996), "The Infomercial Shopper," *JAR*, 36 (March/April), 69–76.
Faber, Ronald J. and Thomas C. O'Guinn (1992), "A Clinical Screener for Compulsive Buying," *JCR*, 19 (December), 459–469.
O'Guinn, Thomas C. and Ronald J. Faber (1989), "Compulsive Buying: A Phenomenological Exploration," *JCR*, 16 (September), 147–157.

SCALE ITEMS: [1]

1. I shop because buying things makes me happy.*

2. Shopping is fun.

3. I get a real "high" from shopping.

---

[1] Donthu and Gilliland (1996) as well as Donthu and Garcia (1999) used a shorter version of this item: *Buying things makes me happy.*

SCALE NAME: Shopping Enjoyment

SCALE DESCRIPTION: The scale is composed of several, seven-point Likert-type statements measuring the extent to which a consumer indicates that shopping is something he/she likes to do.

SCALE ORIGIN: The scale was developed in dissertation research conducted by Ellis (1995).

RELIABILITY: Beatty and Ferrell (1998) reported a composite reliability of .80 for the scale. An alpha of .95 was reported by Reynolds and Beatty (1999b) for the version of the scale they used.

VALIDITY: Although the details related to this scale were not provided, the implication was that it was unidimensional and showed sufficient evidence of convergent and discriminant validity (Beatty and Ferrell 1998). Reynolds and Beatty (1999b) stated that the CFA they ran on several of their scales indicated the measurement model, including the items in this scale, had a good fit.

REFERENCES:
Beatty, Sharon E. and M. Elizabeth Ferrell (1998), "Impulse Buying: Modeling Its Precursors," *JR*, 74 (2), 169–191.
Ellis, Kristy (1995), "The Determinants of the Nature and Types of Customer-Salesperson Relationships in a Retail Setting: An Empirical Study," doctoral dissertation, Tuscaloosa, AL: The University of Alabama.
Reynolds, Kristy E. and Sharon E. Beatty (1999b), "A Relationship Customer Typology," *JR*, 75 (4), 509–523.

SCALE ITEMS: [1]

1. Shopping is a waste of time. (r)

2. Shopping is not a way I like to spend any leisure time. (r)

3. Shopping is not entertaining to me. (r)

4. Shopping is not one of my favorite activities. (r)

5. I enjoy shopping more than most people do.

6. I love to go shopping when I can find the time.

7. Shopping is a good way for me to relax.

8. Shopping picks me up on a dull day.

---

[1] Beatty and Ferrell (1998) used the first four items (above). Reynolds and Beatty (1999b) used all of the items.

SCALE NAME: Shopping Enjoyment (Grocery)

SCALE DESCRIPTION: Five-point Likert-type statements are used to measure the degree to which a consumer believes shopping at a grocery store is a pleasant and likable activity to engage in.

SCALE ORIGIN: Although Urbany, Dickson, and Kalapurakal (1996) may have drawn inspiration from previous work, the scale appears to be original to their study. Ailawadi, Neslin, and Gedenk (2001) cited Urbany, Dickson, and Kalapurakal (1996) as the source of their scale but, as is shown below, some changes were made in the version they used.

RELIABILITY: An alpha of .93 was reported for the scale by Urbany, Dickson, and Kalapurakal (1996). The version used by Ailawadi, Neslin, and Gedenk (2001) had a composite reliability of .812.

VALIDITY: Ailawadi, Neslin, and Gedenk (2001) included the items in their version of the scale along with those belonging to 14 other scales in a confirmatory factor analysis. The fit of the measurement model was acceptable and general evidence was cited in support of the scale's discriminant validity.

Urbany, Dickson, and Kalapurakal (1996) tested the discriminant validity of their version of the scale using pairwise confirmatory factor analysis and six other measures. The evidence of three separate tests on each of the six pairs supported a claim of discriminant validity.

COMMENTS: Urbany, Dickson, and Kalapurakal (1996) reported a mean response of 3.34 on the scale. Although the scale has only been used with reference to grocery stores, the items appear to be amenable to minor adjustment so that they can be used with other types of stores or shopping.

REFERENCES:
Ailawadi, Kusum L., Scott A. Neslin, and Karen Gedenk (2001), "Pursuing the Value-Conscious Consumer: Store Brands Versus National Brand Promotions," *JM*, 65 (1), 71–89.
Urbany, Joel E., Peter R. Dickson, and Rosemary Kalapurakal (1996), "Price Search in the Retail Grocery Market," *JM*, 60 (April), 91–104.

SCALE ITEMS: [1]

1. I enjoy grocery shopping.

2. Grocery shopping is a chore. (r)

3. Grocery shopping is boring. (r)

4. Grocery shopping is a pain. (r)

5. I view grocery shopping in a positive way.

6. I like to finish my shopping as quickly as possible and get out of the store. (r)

---

[1] The items originally used by Urbany, Dickson, and Kalapurakal (1996) were #1-#5. The version used by Ailawadi, Neslin, and Gedenk (2001) had #6 and items similar to #1 and #2.

SCALE NAME: Shopping Enjoyment (With Technology Assistance)

SCALE DESCRIPTION: The scale is composed of seven-point Likert-type items used to measure the degree to which shopping that utilizes a technological device or system is viewed by a person as a pleasant and possibly even an exciting activity.

SCALE ORIGIN: Although bearing some similarity to more general measures of shopping enjoyment, this scale was apparently developed by Childers et al. (2001) for the specific context their studies were examining.

RELIABILITY: Using LISREL, the reliability of the scale was calculated to be .875 (hedonic motivations) and .928 (utilitarian motivations) in the studies reported by Childers et al. (2001).

VALIDITY: Discriminant validity was assessed using two different tests (the latent variable confidence interval tests and the χ^2 difference test). For both studies the evidence indicated that each scale, including shopping enjoyment, was measuring a distinctive construct.

COMMENTS: The phrase "technology assisted shopping" in each item (below) appears like it could be replaced with more specific names when wanting to adapt the scale for particular devices such as wireless PDAs.

REFERENCES:
Childers, Terry L., Christopher L. Carr, Joann Peck, and Stephen Carson (2001), "Hedonic and Utilitarian Motivations for Online retail Shopping Behavior," *JR*, 77 (Winter), 511–535.

SCALE ITEMS: [1]

1. Shopping with technology assisted shopping would make me feel good.

2. Shopping with technology assisted shopping would be boring. (r)

3. Shopping with technology assisted shopping would be exciting.

4. Shopping with technology assisted shopping would be enjoyable.

[1] Item 1 was eliminated from the scale during the purification stage of Study 2.

SCALE NAME: Shopping Intention

SCALE DESCRIPTION: The scale is a five-item, seven-point Likert-like measure of the self-reported likelihood that a consumer will shop at a specified store. The emphasis is on interaction with a particular clerk the consumer has some familiarity with.

SCALE ORIGIN: The origin of the scale was not described by Swinyard (1993) but it appears to be original.

RELIABILITY: An alpha of .94 was reported for the scale by both Mano (1999) and Swinyard (1993).

VALIDITY: The validity of the scale was not specifically addressed in either study.

REFERENCES:
Mano, Haim (1999), "The Influence of Pre-Existing Negative Affect on Store Purchase Intentions," *JR*, 75 (2), 149–172.
Swinyard, William R. (1993), "The Effects of Mood, Involvement, and Quality of Store Experience on Shopping Intentions," *JCR*, 20 (September), 271–280.

SCALE ITEMS: [1]

How likely or unlikely would you be to:

1. spend more time shopping in that department?

2. buy other items you need in the department?

3. spend more time shopping in the store?

4. let that clerk help with your other shopping?

5. make a purchase from that clerk?

[1] The anchors used by Swinyard (1993) were *unlikely* and *likely*.

SCALE NAME: Shopping Smart

SCALE DESCRIPTION: The scale is composed of four, seven-point Likert-type statements that measure a consumer's thoughts about the degree to which he/she is a smart shopper and considers that to be a positive behavior. Burton et al. (1998) referred to the scale as *smart shopper self-perception.*

SCALE ORIGIN: The scale is original to the study of Burton et al. (1998). The said items were generated that were consistent with the construct's domain. The items were assessed in a pretest and less reliable ones were deleted from further use.ccc

RELIABILITY: An alpha of .94 was reported for the scale by Burton et al. (1998).

VALIDITY: No information relating to the scale's validity was reported by Burton et al. (1998).

REFERENCES:
Burton, Scot (2000), Personal Correspondence.
Burton, Scot, Donald R. Lichtenstein, Richard G. Netemeyer, and Judith A. Garretson (1998), "A Scale for Measuring Attitude toward Private Label Products and an Examination of Its Psychological and Behavioral Correlates," *JAMS*, 26 (4), 293–306.

SCALE ITEMS: [1]

1. When I shop smartly, I feel like a winner.

2. When I go shopping, I take a lot of pride in making smart purchases.

3. Making smart purchases makes me feel good about myself.

4. I get a real sense of joy when I make wise purchases.

---

[1] One sample item was provided in the article by Burton et al. (1998). The other items were supplied personally by Burton (2000).

SCALE NAME: Shopping Value

SCALE DESCRIPTION: The four-item, seven-point Likert-type scale is intended to measure the perceived value of searching for the lowest product price by visiting several stores. Ideally, the scale assesses the consumer's sense of the benefits of shopping given the search costs involved.

SCALE ORIGIN: The source of the scale was not stated by Srivastava and Lurie (2001) but would appear to be original to their study.

RELIABILITY: An alpha of .78 was reported for the scale by Srivastava and Lurie (2001).

VALIDITY: No examination of the scale's validity was reported by Srivastava and Lurie (2001).

COMMENTS: The scale was developed for use in an experiment where subjects "visited" stores in a computer simulation. The task was to shop for a product at the stores with the goal of having the most money remaining after search costs and the product price were deducted from the amount they started with. If the scale is used in a different context then some adjustment in the phrasing of items 2 and 4 may be necessary, e.g., measuring consumers' general attitude toward the value of shopping.

REFERENCES:
Srivastava, Joydeep and Nicholas Lurie (2001), "A Consumer Perspective on Price-Matching Refund Policies: Effect on Price Perceptions and Search Behavior," *JCR*, 28 (September), 296–307.

SCALE ITEMS:

1. The benefit of finding the lowest price is worth the cost.

2. It is not worthwhile to shop most of the stores. (r)

3. The potential savings from finding a lower price is worth the cost.

4. It is worth the cost to visit most of the stores.

SCALE NAME: Shopping Value (Hedonic)

SCALE DESCRIPTION: The scale is a eleven-item, five-point Likert-type measure of the degree to which a consumer views a recent shopping trip as having been an entertaining and emotionally-driven activity. The shopping was enjoyed as an end in itself rather than as just a means to an end (obtaining goods and services). A seven-item, Russian version of the scale was developed by Griffin, Babin, and Modianos (2000).

SCALE ORIGIN: The scale is original to Babin, Darden, and Griffin (1994). The study approached the scale development process methodically with a concern about grounding the scales in theory as well as providing evidence of their psychometric quality.

A literature review, personal interviews, and focus group sessions were used to generate 71 items for this scale and a complimentary one (#454). Three experts were provided definitions of the constructs and asked to sort the items into one of three groups: hedonic, utilitarian, and other. Forty-eight items were agreed upon by all three judges. Five more were agreed upon by two judges and with further discussion they were retained for the next stage of analysis.

Data from a sample of 125 undergraduate students were used to purify the scales. The scales showed evidence of unidimensionality, reliability, as well as discriminant and convergent validity. Further testing was conducted to continue the validation process with a more diverse sample as discussed below.

RELIABILITY: An alpha of .91 (n = 118) was reported for the scale by Babin and Darden (1995). The construct reliability was .91 and variance extracted was .48. An alpha of .93 (n = 404) was reported for the scale as used by Babin, Darden, and Griffin (1994) and the item-total correlations ranged from .67 to .80. Griffin, Babin, and Modianos (2000) used the scale to compare U.S. (n = 386) and Russian (n = 128) shoppers. The alpha in both applications was .86 but a reduced, seven-item version was used with the Russian shoppers.

VALIDITY: The results of a confirmatory factor analysis supported the measurement model in both studies (Babin and Darden 1995; Babin, Darden, and Griffin 1994). This provides some limited evidence of the scale's unidimensionality as well as its convergent and discriminant validities. To investigate the scale's nomological validity, the Shopping Value (Hedonic) scale was correlated with other scales with which it was theorized to be related (Babin, Darden, and Griffin 1994). In general, the pattern of expectations was confirmed.

The Griffin, Babin, and Modianos (2000) study used a subset of the U.S. data reported previously in Babin, Darden, and Griffin (1994), thus, the validity was the same as described above. The Russian sample was somewhat different. The fit of the two-factor model was not good until four of the hedonic items were eliminated. With that modification, further examination of the scale was conducted to assess its cross-national validation. The authors' concluded that their data supported partial though not full measurement invariance.

COMMENTS: Note that this scale was constructed such that items are responded to after a shopping trip and refer specifically to that shopping trip. If there is interest in measuring a consumer's shopping orientation as a pattern followed over a longer period of time then another scale would have to be used (e.g., #446) or this one would have to be modified and retested.

See also Campo, Gijsbrechts, and Nisol (2000).

REFERENCES:
Babin, Barry J. and William R. Darden (1995), "Consumer Self-Regulation in a Retail Environment," *JR*, 71 (1), 47–70.

Babin, Barry J., William R. Darden, and Mitch Griffin (1994), "Work and /or Fun: Measuring Hedonic and Utilitarian Shopping Value," *JCR*, 20 (March), 644–656.

Campo, Katia, Els Gijsbrechts, and Patricia Nisol (2000), "Towards Understanding Consumer Response to Stock-Outs," *JR*, 79 (2), 219–242.

Griffin, Mitch, Barry J. Babin, and Doan Modianos (2000), "Shopping Values of Russian Consumers: The Impact of Habituation in a Developing Economy," *JR*, 76 (1), 33–52.

SCALE ITEMS: [1]

1. This shopping trip was truly a joy.

2. I continued to shop, not because I had to, but because I wanted to.

3. This shopping trip truly felt like an escape.

4. Compared to other things I could have done, the time spent shopping was truly enjoyable.

5. I enjoyed being immersed in exciting new products.

6. I enjoy this shopping trip for its own sake, not just for the items I may have purchased.

7. I had a good time because I was able to act on the "spur of the moment."

8. During the trip, I felt the excitement of the hunt.

9. While shopping, I was able to forget my problems.

10. While shopping, I felt a sense of adventure.

11. This shopping trip was not a very nice time out. (r)

---

[1] Each of the studies used the full scale with their American samples. The Russian version of the scale used by Griffin, Babin, and Modianos (2000) did <u>not</u> ultimately include items 3, 5, 7, and 9.

SCALE NAME: Shopping Value (Utilitarian)

SCALE DESCRIPTION: The scale is a four-item, five-point Likert-type measure of the degree to which a consumer agrees that a recent shopping trip allowed him/her to accomplish what was wanted (purchase of the items sought). The scale is supposed to tap into the view that shopping is primarily a means to an end (obtaining goods and services) rather than being enjoyed as an end in itself.

SCALE ORIGIN: The scale is original to Babin, Darden, and Griffin (1994). The study approached the scale development process methodically with a concern about grounding the scales in theory as well as providing evidence of their psychometric quality.

A literature review, personal interviews, and focus group sessions were used to generate 71 items for this scale and a complimentary one (#453). Three experts were provided definitions of the constructs and asked to sort the items into one of three groups: hedonic, utilitarian, and other. Forty-eight items were agreed upon by all three judges. Five more were agreed upon by two judges and with further discussion were retained for the next stage of analysis.

Data from a sample of 125 undergraduate students were used to purify the scales. The scales showed evidence of unidimensionality, reliability, as well as discriminant and convergent validity. Further testing was conducted to continue the validation process with a more diverse sample as discussed below.

A Russian version of the scale was developed by Griffin, Babin, and Modianos (2000). Translation equivalence was tested using the back-translation method.

RELIABILITY: An alpha of .76 (n = 118) was reported for the scale by Babin and Darden (1995). The construct reliability was .76 and variance extracted was .45. An alpha of .80 (n = 404) was reported for the scale as used by Babin, Darden, and Griffin (1994) and the item-total correlations ranged from .54 to .64. Griffin, Babin, and Modianos (2000) used the scale to compare U.S. (n = 386) and Russian (n = 128) shoppers. The alphas were reported to be .80 (U.S.) and .91 (Russian).

VALIDITY: The results of a confirmatory factor analysis supported the measurement model in both studies (Babin and Darden 1995; Babin, Darden, and Griffin 1994). This provides some limited evidence of the scale's unidimensionality as well as its convergent and discriminant validities. To investigate the scale's nomological validity, the Shopping Value (Utilitarian) scale was correlated with other scales with which it was theorized to be related. In general, the pattern of expectations was confirmed.

The Griffin, Babin, and Modianos (2000) study used a subset of the U.S. data reported previously in Babin, Darden, and Griffin (1994), thus, the validity was the same as described above. The Russian sample was somewhat different. The fit of the two-factor model was not good until four of the hedonic items were eliminated; the loadings of the utilitarian component were acceptable. Along with the modified version of the hedonic component, further examination of the scale was conducted to assess its cross-national validation. The authors' concluded that their data supported partial though not full measurement invariance.

COMMENTS: Note that this scale was constructed such that items are responded to after a shopping trip and refer specifically to that shopping trip. If there is interest in measuring a consumer's shopping orientation as a pattern followed over a longer period of time then another scale would have to be used (e.g., #446) or this one would have to be modified and retested.

REFERENCES:

Babin, Barry J. and William R. Darden (1995), "Consumer Self-Regulation in a Retail Environment," *JR*, 71 (1), 47–70.

#454 *Shopping Value (Utilitarian)*

Babin, Barry J., William R. Darden, and Mitch Griffin (1994), "Work and /or Fun: Measuring Hedonic and Utilitarian Shopping Value," *JCR*, 20 (March), 644–656.

Griffin, Mitch, Barry J. Babin, and Doan Modianos (2000), "Shopping Values of Russian Consumers: The Impact of Habituation in a Developing Economy," *JR*, 76 (1), 33–52.

SCALE ITEMS:

1. I accomplished just what I wanted to on this shopping trip.

2. I couldn't buy what I really needed. (r)

3. While shopping, I found just the item(s) I was looking for.

4. I was disappointed because I had to go to another store(s) to complete my shopping. (r)

SCALE NAME: Sincerity (Salesperson)

SCALE DESCRIPTION: Four, seven-point bipolar adjectives are used to measure a customer's attitude about a particular salesperson with the emphasis on the degree to which the salesperson was viewed as being honest rather than manipulative.

SCALE ORIGIN: Although the items and concepts have been used in previous scales that attempt to tap into the perceived credibility and honesty of message sources, this set of items appear to be original to Campbell and Kirmani (2000).

RELIABILITY: The scale was used by Campbell and Kirmani (2000) in a series of studies they described in the article, however, the reliability was reported only for the first study: alpha = .87 (n = 19).

VALIDITY: No information regarding the scale's validity was reported by Campbell and Kirmani (2000).

REFERENCES:
Campbell, Margaret C. and Amna Kirmani (2000), "Consumer's Use of Persuasion Knowledge: The Effects of Accessibility and Cognitive Capacity on Perceptions of an Influence Agent," *JCR*, 27 (1), 69–83.

SCALE ITEMS:

1. Sincere / insincere

2. Honest / dishonest

3. Not manipulative / manipulative

4. Not pushy / pushy

SCALE NAME: Sincerity (Sponsorship)

SCALE DESCRIPTION: The scale is composed of three, seven-point Likert type statements measuring a person's attitude about a company's reasons for sponsoring a sporting event, the emphasis being on the opinion that the sponsor genuinely has the "best interest" of the sport in mind.

SCALE ORIGIN: The scale is original to the study by Speed and Thompson (2000). Some qualitative work by the authors led to generation of items for this scale as well as several others. This was followed by a pretest which aided in identifying items for deletion or modification.

RELIABILITY: An alpha of .88 was reported for the scale by Speed and Thompson (2000).

VALIDITY: The initial qualitative work conducted by the authors provides some evidence of its content validity. Based on data from the main study, a CFA was performed on items from several scales. The results provided evidence of this scale's convergent and discriminant validity.

REFERENCES:
Speed, Richard and Peter Thompson (2000), "Determinants of Sports Sponsorship Response," *JAMS*, 28 (2), 226–238.

SCALE ITEMS:

1. The main reason the sponsor would be involved in the event is because the sponsor believes the event deserves support.

2. This sponsor would be likely to have the best interests of the sport at heart.

3. This sponsor would probably support the event even if it had a much lower profile.

SCALE NAME: Smoking-Related Beliefs (Poise)

SCALE DESCRIPTION: Six, nine-point semantic differentials are used to measure the self-confidence and independence-related characteristics a person associates with those who smoke. Two versions of the scale were used. One had to do with how a person thinks that smokers are perceived by others (reference group evaluations) and another focusing on how a person thinks that smokers perceive themselves (self evaluations).

SCALE ORIGIN: Pechmann and Shih (1999) reported that they drew 22 items from previous research (e.g., Burton at al. 1989). Factor analysis of responses to these items indicated that there were four dimensions, of which one was related to the perceived "poise" of a smoker.

RELIABILITY: The scale was found to have alphas of .93 (reference group evaluations) and .94 (self evaluations) (Pechmann 2002; Pechmann and Shih 1999).

VALIDITY: No examination of the scale's validity was reported by Pechmann and Shih (1999).

REFERENCES:

Burton, Dee, Steve Sussman, William B. Hansen, C. Anderson Johnson, and Brian R. Flay (1989), "Image Attributions and Smoking Intentions Among Seventh Grade Subjects," *Journal of Applied Social Psychology*, 19 (8), 656–664.

Pechmann, Cornelia (2002), Personal Correspondence.

Pechmann, Cornelia and Chuan-Fong Shih (1999), "Smoking Scenes in Movies and Antismoking Advertisements Before Movies: Effects on Youth," *JM*, 63 (July), 1–13.

SCALE ITEMS: [1]

1. insecure / confident

2. self-conscious / comfortable around others

3. controlled by others / his/her own person

4. not free to make own decisions / free to make own decisions

5. worried / contented

6. stressed out / relaxed

---

[1] For the "reference group" version, subjects were instructed to assume the role of a peer referent and answer the question: "How does a teenager who smokes look to you?" For the "self evaluation" version, they were asked to assume the role of a smoker and respond to the question: "If you were to smoke a cigarette, how do you think it would make you feel?" (Pechmann and Shih 1999, p. 5)

SCALE NAME: Smoking-Related Beliefs (Popularity)

SCALE DESCRIPTION: The scale is composed of six, nine-point semantic differentials measuring the desirability and coolness-related characteristics a person associates with those who smoke. Two versions of the scale were used. One had to do with how a person thinks that smokers are perceived by others (reference group evaluations) and another focusing on how a person thinks that smokers perceive themselves (self evaluations).

SCALE ORIGIN: Pechmann and Shih (1999) reported that they drew 22 items from previous research (e.g., Burton at al. 1989). Factor analysis of responses to these items indicated that there were four dimensions, of which one was related to the perceived "popularity" of a smoker.

RELIABILITY: The scale was found to have alphas of .94 (reference group evaluations) and .96 (self evaluations) (Pechmann 2002; Pechmann and Shih 1999).

VALIDITY: No examination of the scale's validity was reported by Pechmann and Shih (1999).

REFERENCES:

Burton, Dee, Steve Sussman, William B. Hansen, C. Anderson Johnson, and Brian R. Flay (1989), "Image Attributions and Smoking Intentions Among Seventh Grade Subjects," *Journal of Applied Social Psychology*, 19 (8), 656–664.

Pechmann, Cornelia (2002), Personal Correspondence.

Pechmann, Cornelia and Chuan-Fong Shih (1999), "Smoking Scenes in Movies and Antismoking Advertisements Before Movies: Effects on Youth," *JM*, 63 (July), 1–13.

SCALE ITEMS: [1]

1. disliked / well-liked

2. not fun to be with / fun to be with

3. not desirable to date / desirable to date

4. not sexy / sexy

5. not cute / cute

6. ugly looking / good looking

[1] For the "reference group" version, subjects were instructed to assume the role of a peer referent and answer the question: "How does a teenager who smokes look to you?" For the "self evaluation" version, they were asked to assume the role of a smoker and respond to the question: "If you were to smoke a cigarette, how do you think it would make you feel?" (Pechmann and Shih 1999, p. 5)

SCALE NAME: Smoking-Related Beliefs (Social Stature)

SCALE DESCRIPTION: The scale is composed of four, nine-point semantic differentials measuring the intelligence and success-related characteristics a person associates with those who smoke. Two versions of the scale were used. One had to do with how a person thinks that smokers are perceived by others (reference group evaluations) and another focusing on how a person thinks that smokers perceive themselves (self evaluations).

SCALE ORIGIN: Pechmann and Shih (1999) reported that they drew 22 items from previous research (e.g., Burton at al. 1989). Factor analysis of responses to these items indicated that there were four dimensions, of which one was related to the perceived social stature of a smoker.

RELIABILITY: The scale was found to have alphas of .91 (reference group evaluations) and .92 (self evaluations) (Pechmann 2002; Pechmann and Shih 1999).

VALIDITY: No examination of the scale's validity was reported by Pechmann and Shih (1999).

REFERENCES:

Burton, Dee, Steve Sussman, William B. Hansen, C. Anderson Johnson, and Brian R. Flay (1989), "Image Attributions and Smoking Intentions Among Seventh Grade Subjects," *Journal of Applied Social Psychology*, 19 (8), 656–664.

Pechmann, Cornelia (2002), Personal Correspondence.

Pechmann, Cornelia and Chuan-Fong Shih (1999), "Smoking Scenes in Movies and Antismoking Advertisements Before Movies: Effects on Youth," *JM*, 63 (July), 1–13.

SCALE ITEMS: [1]

1. Stupid / intelligent

2. Dumb / smart

3. Poor / rich

4. Unsuccessful / successful

[1] For the "reference group" version, subjects were instructed to assume the role of a peer referent and answer the question: "How does a teenager who smokes look to you?" For the "self evaluation" version, they were asked to assume the role of a smoker and respond to the question: "If you were to smoke a cigarette, how do you think it would make you feel?" (Pechmann and Shih 1999, p. 5)

SCALE NAME: Smoking-Related Beliefs (Vitality)

SCALE DESCRIPTION: Six, nine-point semantic differentials are used to measure the health and cleanliness-related characteristics a person associates with those who smoke. Two versions of the scale were used. One had to do with how a person thinks that smokers are perceived by others (reference group evaluations) and another focusing on how a person thinks that smokers perceive themselves (self evaluations).

SCALE ORIGIN: Pechmann and Shih (1999) reported that they drew 22 items from previous research (e.g., Burton at al. 1989). Factor analysis of responses to these items indicated that there were four dimensions, of which one was related to the perceived "vitality" of a smoker.

RELIABILITY: The scale was found to have alphas of .96 (reference group evaluations) and .96 (self evaluations) (Pechmann 2002; Pechmann and Shih 1999).

VALIDITY: No examination of the scale's validity was reported by Pechmann and Shih (1999).

REFERENCES:

Burton, Dee, Steve Sussman, William B. Hansen, C. Anderson Johnson, and Brian R. Flay (1989), "Image Attributions and Smoking Intentions Among Seventh Grade Subjects," *Journal of Applied Social Psychology*, 19 (8), 656–664.

Pechmann, Cornelia (2002), Personal Correspondence.

Pechmann, Cornelia and Chuan-Fong Shih (1999), "Smoking Scenes in Movies and Antismoking Advertisements Before Movies: Effects on Youth," *JM*, 63 (July), 1–13.

SCALE ITEMS: [1]

1. unhealthy / healthy

2. sick / well

3. unfit / fit

4. out of shape / athletic

5. unclean / clean

6. stinky / good smelling

---

[1] For the "reference group" version, subjects were instructed to assume the role of a peer referent and answer the question: "How does a teenager who smokes look to you?" For the "self evaluation" version, they were asked to assume the role of a smoker and respond to the question: "If you were to smoke a cigarette, how do you think it would make you feel?" (Pechmann and Shih 1999, p. 5)

SCALE NAME: Sociability

SCALE DESCRIPTION: The scale is composed of seven, seven-point Likert-type statements measuring the degree to which a person expresses interest and enjoyment in being around other people rather than being alone.

SCALE ORIGIN: The source of the scale was not explicitly stated by Reynolds and Beatty (1999b), although they indicated in general that their scales were drawn from previously developed measures.

RELIABILITY: Reynolds and Beatty (1999b) reported an alpha of .82 (n = 364) for the scale.

VALIDITY: The validity of the scale was not addressed by Reynolds and Beatty (1999b). They did state, however, that the CFA they ran on several of their scales indicated the measurement model, including the items in this scale, had a good fit.

REFERENCES:
Reynolds, Kristy E. and Sharon E. Beatty (1999b), "A Relationship Customer Typology," *JR*, 75 (4), 509–523.

SCALE ITEMS:

1. I like to be with people.

2. I prefer working with others than working alone.

3. I find spending time with people more enjoyable than solitary activities, such as reading a book.

4. I tend to be a loner. (r)

5. I prefer to do things alone. (r)

6. I am not very sociable. (r)

7. I do not like parties and social events. (r)

SCALE NAME: Social Desirability Bias

SCALE DESCRIPTION: It is a summated ratings scale purporting to measure the degree to which people describe themselves in socially acceptable terms in order to gain the approval of others. The original version of the scale has thirty-three items and uses a True/False response format. However, abbreviated versions have typically been used in marketing research and Likert-type response scales have been applied in a few cases.

SCALE ORIGIN: The scale was developed by Crowne and Marlowe (1960) by generating items related to behaviors that are culturally sanctioned but are unlikely to occur. Two sets of ten faculty and graduate student judges helped narrow an original inventory of 50 items down to the final set of thirty- three. An internal consistency of .88 (KR-20) was calculated for the scale using a sample of 10 male and 29 female undergraduates. Thirty-one of these same people completed the instrument a month later and a test-retest correlation of .89 was calculated. Scores of those 31 students plus 81 others in a course on exceptional children were found to have a correlation of .35 (p<.01) with scores on the Edward's Social Desirability Scale (1957). Considerable work was performed on correlating scale scores with MMPI variables. The authors interpreted the findings as being "more in accord with a definition of social desirability" than the Edwards scale.

Examinations of abbreviated versions of the scale can be found in Ballard, Crino, and Reubenfeld (1988), Fraboni and Cooper (1989), Reynolds (1982), as well as Strahan and Gerbasi (1972).

RELIABILITY: Most of the studies have not provided information regarding the reliability of the scale. The internal consistencies that have been reported have ranged from .70 (n = 144) by Richins and Dawson (1992; Richins 1994) to .83 (K-R 20, n = 198) by Moore et al. (1985).

VALIDITY: Grossbart, Carlson, and Walsh (1991) reported a beta of .50 for the modified version of the scale they used. Some evidence of the ten item version's convergent validity was provided by Goldsmith and Hofacker (1991) who reported a significant positive correlation between the social desirability scale and a lie scale (Eysenck 1958).

No specific examination of the scale's validity was conducted in the other studies. However, the scale has been typically used to provide evidence of other scales' discriminant validity.

COMMENTS: This scale is typically used when constructing scales for measuring particular constructs and not by itself. If the correlation between scores on the social desirability scale and another measure is high then that suggests the latter is measuring respondents' desire to answer in socially acceptable ways. If the correlation is low then it is evidence that the scale is relatively free of social desirability bias. However, caution is urged in the scale's use since it may not be unidimensional (e.g., Grossbart, Carlson, and Walsh 1991).

See other uses of the scale by: Bagozzi and Warshaw (1990); Carlson, Laczniak, and Walsh (2001); Childers, Houston, and Heckler (1985); Friedman and Churchill (1987); Lastovicka et al. (1999); Putrevu and Lord (1994); Raju (1980); Richins (1983); Saxe and Weitz (1982); Tian, Bearden, and Hunter (2001); Unger and Kernan (1983); Walsh, Laczniak, and Carlson (1998); and, Westbrook (1980, 1987). For further information on this scale and social desirability bias in general, refer to ***Psychology & Marketing*** (2000) where an entire issue was devoted to the topic.

REFERENCES:
Bagozzi, Richard P. (1994), Personal Correspondence.
Bagozzi, Richard P. and Paul R. Warshaw (1990), "Trying to Consume," *JCR*, 17 (September), 127–140.

Ballard, Rebecca, Michael D. Crino, and Stephen Rubenfeld (1988), "Social Desirability Response Bias and the Marlowe-Crowne Social Desirability Scale," *Psychological Reports*, 63 (August), 227–237.

Carlson, Les and Sanford Grossbart (1988), "Parental Style and Consumer Socialization of Children," *JCR*, 15 (June), 77–94.

Carlson, Les, Russell N. Laczniak, and Ann Walsh (2001), "Socializing Children about Television: An Intergenerational Study," *JAMS*, 29 (3), 276–288.

Childers, Terry L., Michael J. Houston, and Susan E. Heckler (1985), "Measurement of Individual Differences in Visual versus Verbal Information Processing," *JCR*, 12 (September), 125–134.

Crowne, Douglas P. and David Marlowe (1960), "A New Scale of Social Desirability Independent of Psychopathology," *Journal of Consulting Psychology*, 24 (August), 349–354.

Edwards, A. L. (1957), *The Social Desirability Variable in Personality Assessment and Research*, New York: Holt, Rinehart, and Winston.

Eyesnck, Hans J. (1958), "A Short Questionnaire for the Measurement of Two Dimensions of Personality," *Journal of Applied Psychology*, 42 (1), 14–17.

Fisher, Robert J. (1993), "Social Desirability Bias and the Validity of Indirect Questioning," *JCR*, 20 (September), 303–315.

Fraboni, Maryann and Douglas Cooper (1989), "Further Validation of Three Short Forms of the Marlowe-Crowne Scale of Social Desirability," *Psychological Reports*, 65 (2), 595–600.

Friedman, Margaret L. and Gilbert A. Churchill, Jr. (1987), "Using Consumer Perceptions and a Contingency Approach to Improve Health Care Delivery," *JCR*, 13 (March), 492–510.

Goldsmith, Ronald E. and Charles F. Hofacker (1991), "Measuring Consumer Innovativeness," *JAMS*, 19 (Summer), 209–221.

Grossbart, Sanford, Les Carlson, and Ann Walsh (1991), "Consumer Socialization and Frequency of Shopping with Children," *JAMS*, 19 (Summer), 155–163.

Lastovicka, John L., Lance A. Bettencourt, Renee Shaw Hughner, and Ronald J. Kuntze (1999), "Lifestyle of the Tight and Frugal: Theory and Measurement," *JCR*, 26 (June), 85–98.

Mick, David Glen (1996), "Are Studies of Dark Side Variables Confounded by Socially Desirable Responding? The Case of Materialism" *JCR*, 23 (September), 106–119.

Moore, Ellen M., William O. Bearden, and Jesse E. Teel (1985), "Use of Labeling and Assertions of Dependency in Appeals for Consumer Support," *JCR*, 12 (June), 90–96.

Psychology & Marketing (2000), 17 (February), 73-163.

Netemeyer, Richard G. (1997), Personal Correspondence.

Netemeyer, Richard G., Scot Burton, and Donald R. Lichtenstein (1995), "Trait Aspects of Vanity: Measurement and Relevance to Consumer Behavior," *JCR*, 21 (March), 612–626.

Putrevu, Sanjay and Kenneth R. Lord (1994), "Comparative and Noncomparative Advertising: Attitudinal Effects Under Cognitive and Affective Involvement Conditions," *JA*, 23 (June), 77–90.

Raju, P. S. (1980), "Optimum Stimulation Level: Its Relationship to Personality, Demographics, and Exploratory Behavior," *JCR*, 7 (December), 272–282.

Reynolds, William M. (1982), "Development of Reliable and Valid Short Forms of the Marlowe-Crowne Social Desirability Scale," *Journal of Clinical Psychology*, 38 (January), 119–125.

Richins, Marsha L. (1983), "An Analysis of Consumer Interaction Styles in the Marketplace," *JCR*, 10 (June), 73–82.

Richins, Marsha L. (1994), Personal Correspondence.

Richins, Marsha L. and Scott Dawson (1992), "A Consumer Values Orientation for Materialism and Its Measurement: Scale Development and Validation," *JCR*, 19 (December), 303–316.

Saxe, Robert and Barton A. Weitz (1982), "The SOCO Scale: A Measure of the Customer Orientation of Salespeople," *JMR*, 19 (August), 343–351.

Strahan, Robert and Kathleen Carrese Gerbasi (1972), "Short, Homogeneous Versions of the Marlowe-Crowne Social Desirability Scale," *Journal of Clinical Psychology*, 28 (April), 191–193.

Tian, Kelly T., William O. Bearden, and Gary L. Hunter (2001), "Consumers' Need for Uniqueness: Scale Development and Validation," *JCR*, 28 (June), 50–66.

Unger, Lynette S. and Jerome B. Kernan (1983), "On the Meaning of Leisure: An Investigation of Some Determinants of the Subjective Experience," *JCR*, 9 (March), 381–391.

Walsh, Ann D., Russell N. Laczniak, and Les Carlson (1998), "Mothers' Preferences for Regulating Children's Television," *JA*, 27 (3), 23–36.

Westbrook, Robert A. (1980), "Intrapersonal Affective Influences on Consumer Satisfaction with Products," *JCR*, 7 (June), 49–54.

Westbrook, Robert A. (1987), "Product/Consumption-Based Affective Responses and Postpurchase Processes," *JMR*, 24 (August), 258–270.

SCALE ITEMS: [1]

1. Before voting I thoroughly investigate the qualifications of all the candidates. (T)

2. I never hesitate to go out of my way to help someone in trouble. (T)

3. It is sometimes hard for me to go on with my work if I am not encouraged. (F)

4. I have never intensely disliked anyone. (T)

5. On occasion I have had doubts about my ability to succeed in life. (F)

6. I sometimes feel resentful when I don't get my way. (F)

7. I am always careful about my manner of dress. (T)

8. My table manners at home are as good as when I eat out in a restaurant. (T)

9. If I could get into a movie without paying and be sure I was not seen I would probably do it. (F)

10. On a few occasions, I have given up doing something because I thought too little of my ability. (F)

11. I like gossip at times. (F)

12. There have been times when I felt like rebelling against people in authority even though I knew they were right. (F)

13. No matter who I'm talking to, I'm always a good listener. (T)

14. I can remember "playing sick" to get out of something. (F)

15. There have been occasions when I took advantage of someone. (F)

16. I'm always willing to admit it when I've made a mistake. (T)

17. I always try to practice what I preach. (T)

18. I don't find it particularly difficult to get along with loud-mouthed, obnoxious people. (T)

19. I sometimes try to get even rather than forgive and forget. (F)

20. When I don't know something I don't at all mind admitting it. (T)

21. I am always courteous, even to people who are disagreeable. (T)

22. At times I have really insisted on having things my way. (F)

23. There have been occasions when I felt like smashing things. (F)

24. I would never think of letting someone else be punished for my wrongdoings. (T)

25. I never resent being asked to return a favor. (T)

26. I have never been irked when people expressed ideas very different from my own. (T)

27. I never make a long trip without checking the safety of my car. (T)

28. There have been times when I was quite jealous of the good fortune of others. (F)

29. I have almost never felt the urge to tell someone off. (T)

30. I am sometimes irritated by people who ask favors of me. (F)

31. I have never felt that I was punished without cause. (T)

32. I sometimes think when people have a misfortune they only got what they deserved. (F)

33. I have never deliberately said something that hurt someone's feelings. (T)

Carlson and Grossbart (1988; Grossbart, Carlson, and Walsh 1991): 1 to 19 T/F
Fisher (1993): 3, 6, 10, 12, 13, 15, 16, 19, 21, 26, 28, 30, and 33 T/F
Goldsmith and Hofacker (1991): 11, 15 to 17, 19, 22, 23, 25, 26, and 33 T/F
Mick (1996): 1 to 33 T/F
Netemeyer, Burton, and Lichtenstein (1995; Netemeyer 1997): 11, 15 to 17, 19, 22, 23, 25, 26, and 33 7-point
Richins and Dawson (1992): 6-8, 12, 16, 19, 21, 26, 30, and 33 5-point

[1] Respondents should receive a point each time they answer in a socially desirable manner. Social desirability is indicated if respondents answer as indicated at the end of each item above. For example, if a respondent answers "True" to #1 then that is considered to be answering in a socially desirable manner.

SCALE NAME: Source Influence

SCALE DESCRIPTION: The scale is composed of ten, seven-point statements intended to measure the extent to which a person thinks a specified person has provided information that was helpful in making a purchase decision. As used by Gilly et al. (1998), one version was used by an information seeker to rate the source while another version was used by the sources to rate themselves.

SCALE ORIGIN: Gilly et al. (1998) stated that the scale was developed in a separate (uncited) study apparently conducted by the same set of authors. In that earlier study the scale had seven items and an alpha of .74. At the suggestion of a reviewer, three additional items (#8–#10) were added to the scale for use in the second study reported by Gilly et al. (1998).

RELIABILITY: Alphas of .88 and .90 were reported by Gilly et al. (1998) when the scale was used with information seekers and their sources, respectively.

VALIDITY: Beyond some limited evidence of nomological validity, no information about the scale's validity was reported by Gilly et al. (1998).

REFERENCES:
Gilly, Mary C., John L. Graham, Mary Finley Wolfinbarger, and Laura J. Yale (1998), "A Dyadic Study of Interpersonal Information Search," *JAMS*, 26 (2), 83–100.

SCALE ITEMS: [1]

1. This person provided little new information. (r)

2. The opinion of this person will influence my choice about buying the product.

3. This person mentioned some things I had not considered.

4. This person provided some different ideas than other sources.

5. This person really didn't change my mind about buying the product. (r)

6. This person helped me make a decision about buying the product.

7. How much influence do you think this person will have on whether or not you purchase the product/service?

8. How much influence do you think this person will have on the product/service you actually buy?

9. How much influence do you think this person will have on the features you look for in this product/service?

10. How much influence do you think this person will have on the brand/provider of this product/service you buy?

[1] Items 1–6 used a seven-point *agree/disagree* format whereas the rest of the items used a seven-point response scale anchored by *very little influence/complete influence*.

SCALE NAME: Store Convenience Importance

SCALE DESCRIPTION: Three, five-point descriptors are used to measure the degree of importance a consumer places on some store attributes related to the convenience of shopping for a certain category of product.

SCALE ORIGIN: Although Kim and Kang (2001) did not indicate the origin of the scale they used, its contents are very similar to those used by Arora (1982) and those upon whose work he built. (See #146, V. I.)

RELIABILITY: Alphas of .70 (social clothes) and .74 (small electronics) were reported for the scale by Kim and Kang (2001).

VALIDITY: No examination of the scale's validity was reported by Kim and Kang (2001). They did state, however, that a factor analysis was conducted and showed a two-factor solution for the items shown below as well as the items composing a companion scale (#467). This pattern was the same for two product categories.

REFERENCES:
Arora, Raj (1982), "Consumer Involvement in Retail Store Positioning," *JAMS*, 10 (Spring), 109–124.
Kim, Youn-Kyung and Jikyeong Kang (2001), "The Effects of Ethnicity and Product on Purchase Decision Making," *JAR*, 41 (March-April), 39–48.

SCALE ITEMS:

Directions: When deciding where to shop for these two product categories, how important is each of the following store characteristics:[1]

1. Easy parking

2. Convenient location

3. Ease of return / exchange

[1] This scale stem was provided by Kang (2003). The product categories examined in their research were social clothes and small electronics.

SCALE NAME: Store Image

SCALE DESCRIPTION: Seven Likert-type statements are used to measure a consumer's perception of a retail store with an emphasis on the quality of the shopping atmosphere, the service, the merchandise, and the employees.

SCALE ORIGIN: Although inspiration was drawn from a previous scale (Baker, Grewal, and Parasuraman 1994), the scale used by Grewal et al. (1998) appears to have been developed for use in their study.

RELIABILITY: The composite reliability for the scale was reported to be .94 (Grewal et al. 1998).

VALIDITY: A variety of tests conducted by Grewal et al. (1998) indicated the scale was unidimensional and showed evidence of discriminant validity. The variance extracted was .80.

REFERENCES:
Baker, Julie, Dhruv Grewal, and A. Parasuraman (1994), "The Influence of Store Environment on Quality Inferences and Store Image," *JAMS*, 22 (4), 328–339.
Grewal, Dhruv, R. Krishnan, Julie Baker, and Norm Borin (1998), "The Effect of Store Name, Brand Name and Price Discounts on Consumers' Evaluations and Purchase Intentions," *JR*, 74 (3), 331–352.

SCALE ITEMS: [1]

The store:

1. is a pleasant place to shop.

2. offers an attractive shopping experience.

3. has a good store image.

4. has good overall service.

5. carries high quality merchandise.

6. has helpful salespeople.

7. has knowledgeable salespeople.

[1] Only abbreviated versions of the actual scale items were provided by Grewal et al. (1998). These are hypothetical reconstructions based on those brief phrases.

SCALE NAME: Store Image

SCALE DESCRIPTION: The scale is composed of three, five-point Likert-type statements attempting to capture a consumer's general image of a store or set of stores. The emphasis is on the quality of the brands that are carried and their popularity.

SCALE ORIGIN: Although Yoo, Donthu, and Lee (2000) drew inspiration from work by Dodds, Monroe, and Grewal (1991), ultimately their scale appears to be original to them.

RELIABILITY: Yoo, Donthu, and Lee (2000) reported the scale to have a composite reliability of .84.

VALIDITY: Factor analyses (EFA and CFA) were used to check the dimensionality of this scale along with eight others used in the study. Based on the results, the authors concluded that all items loaded on their respective factors as expected providing some sense of the scales' convergent and discriminant validities. The average variance extracted for this scale was .62.

REFERENCES:
Dodds, William B., Kent B. Monroe, and Dhruv Grewal (1991), "The Effects of Price, Brand, and Store Information on Buyers' Product Evaluations," *JMR*, 28 (August), 307–319.
Yoo, Boonghee, Naveen Donthu, and Sungho Lee (2000), "An Examination of Selected Marketing Mix Elements and Brand Equity," *JAMS*, 28 (2), 195–211.

SCALE ITEMS: [1]

1. The stores where I can buy _____ carry products of high quality.

2. The stores where I can buy _____ would be of high quality.

3. The stores where I can buy _____ have well-known brands.

[1] The name of a product category was placed in the blanks by Yoo, Donthu, and Lee (2000).

SCALE NAME: Store Image Importance

SCALE DESCRIPTION: The scale is composed of five, five-point descriptors towards which the respondent indicates the importance each has when deciding where to shop for a product in a specified category. In general, the items appear to be related to the status or quality image a store has.

SCALE ORIGIN: Although Kim and Kang (2001) did not indicate the origin of the scale they used, its contents are very similar to those used by Arora (1982) and those upon whose work he built. (See #146, V. I.)

RELIABILITY: An alphas of .82 was reported for the scale for both product categories by Kim and Kang (2001).

VALIDITY: No examination of the scale's validity was reported by Kim and Kang (2001). They did state, however, that a factor analysis was conducted and showed a two-factor solution for the items shown below as well as the items composing a companion scale (#464). This pattern was the same for two product categories.

REFERENCES:

Arora, Raj (1982), "Consumer Involvement in Retail Store Positioning," *JAMS*, 10 (Spring), 109–124.
Kim, Youn-Kyung and Jikyeong Kang (2001), "The Effects of Ethnicity and Product on Purchase Decision Making," *JAR*, 41 (March-April), 39–48.

SCALE ITEMS:

Directions: When deciding where to shop for these two product categories, how important is each of the following store characteristics:[1]

1. Up-to-date items

2. Well-known company

3. Well-known brand

4. Attractive display

5. Wide product selection

[1] This scale stem was provided by Kang (2003). The product categories examined in their research were social clothes and small electronics.

SCALE NAME: Substitutability of Information

SCALE DESCRIPTION: The scale is composed of four, seven-point Likert-type items used to measure the degree to which a person thinks that the product-related information provided by a technological device or system is similar to what could be gathered in-person.

SCALE ORIGIN: The scale appears to be original to the studies reported by Childers et al. (2001).

RELIABILITY: Using LISREL, the reliability of the scale was calculated to be .863 (hedonic motivations) and .783 (utilitarian motivations) in the studies reported by Childers et al. (2001).

VALIDITY: Discriminant validity was assessed using two different tests (the latent variable confidence interval tests and the χ^2 difference test). For both studies the evidence indicated that each scale, including substitutability, was measuring a distinctive construct.

COMMENTS: The phrase "technology assisted shopping" in each item (below) appears as if it could be replaced with more specific names when wanting to adapt the scale for particular devices such as wireless PDAs.

REFERENCES:
Childers, Terry L., Christopher L. Carr, Joann Peck, and Stephen Carson (2001), "Hedonic and Utilitarian Motivations for Online Retail Shopping Behavior," *JR*, 77 (Winter), 511–535.

SCALE ITEMS:

1. Use of technology assisted shopping will offer knowledge of a product similar to that available from an up-close personal examination.

2. Information available through using technology assisted shopping is a good substitute for that available from seeing and touching the product.

3. Use of technology assisted shopping would allow me to form an impression about a product similar to that from up-close examination.

4. Use of technology assisted shopping would allow me to judge a product's quality as accurately as an in-person appraisal of the product.

SCALE NAME: Support for the Retailer

SCALE DESCRIPTION: The four-item, seven-point Likert-type scale measures a person's political support (or lack thereof) for a retailer with emphasis on intentions to recommend the business to others, protesting against the business, and willingness to support zoning for the facility.

SCALE ORIGIN: Apparently the scale is original to Handelman and Arnold (1999) who generated eight items and then reduced the set down to four based upon results of the factor analyses.

RELIABILITY: An alpha of .8835 was calculated for the scale (Handelman 2002; Handelman and Arnold 1999).

VALIDITY: Handelman and Arnold (1999) used both EFA and CFA to purify and examine the structure of this scale and another one (#262). In the process of doing this, the authors' goal was to find the best fitting measurement model that discriminated between these two constructs while at the same time maintaining strong content validity in the resulting scales.

REFERENCES:
Handelman, Jay M. (2002), Personal Correspondence.
Handelman, Jay M. and Stephen J. Arnold (1999), "The Role of Marketing Actions with a Social Dimension: Appeals to the Institutional Environment," *JM*, 63 (July), 33–48.

SCALE ITEMS: [1]

1. If local politicians decided to grant a zoning permit to allow _____ to build a store in [our city], I would fully support this decision.

2. If asked to sign a list to join a boycott against _____, I would sign it. (r)

3. _____ is the last place that I would recommend to my friends. (r)

4. I would protest against the granting of a zoning permit for _____. (r)

[1] The name of the retailer should be placed in the blanks.

SCALE NAME: Susceptibility to Peer Influence

SCALE DESCRIPTION: The scale(s) measures the degree to which a person expresses the tendency to seek information about products by observing others' behavior and asking for their opinions. Bearden, Netemeyer, and Teel (1989) referred to the scale as *consumer susceptibility to interpersonal influence* (CSII) and defined it to be a consumer's "willingness to conform to the expectations of others regarding the purchase decision" (p. 473). They measured it using two scales with a total of twelve items in a seven-point response format. In contrast, the Boush, Friestad, and Rose (1994) version had just three items and a five-point response scale. The Day and Stafford (1997) version used all twelve items in one scale and apparently had a seven-point response format. The version used by Mangleburg and Bristol (1998) for the normative component had three items while four items were used to capture the informational component.

SCALE ORIGIN: This measure was constructed by Bearden, Netemeyer, and Teel (1989). A series of studies were conducted by the authors to determine the reliability and validity of the scale, only a portion of which are discussed here. Based upon a review of previous research, 166 items were generated that were suspected to measure one of the three hypothesized dimensions of interpersonal influence susceptibility: *informational, normative,* and *value expressiveness.* After ambiguous and essentially identical items were dropped, the content validity of the remaining items was evaluated by five judges. Then, the remaining items were rated again for their clarity in representing one of the dimensions of the construct by four more judges. Some other aspects of the analysis are described below.

Boush, Friestad, and Rose (1994) performed a pretest on items borrowed from the Bearden, Netemeyer, and Teel (1989). Two items were taken from the *informational* version of the CSII (V. I, #121) and one item was taken from the *normative* version (see V. I, #135). Some change is wording was also made.

Day and Stafford (1997) choose to combined the items from the two dimensions (*informational* and *normative*) of the original set of measures used by Bearden, Netemeyer, and Teel (1989). The former also modified the wording of items in some cases to make them more amenable to the retail context.

RELIABILITY: Bearden, Netemeyer, and Teel (1989) reported alphas for the eight-item normative dimension as being .87 (n = 220) and .88 (n = 141) in the first and second administrations, respectively. The alphas for the four-item informational dimension were .83 and .82 in the first and second administrations, respectively. Thirty-five students from the second administration participated in a test of the scales' three week stabilities (test-retest reliability). Correlations of .75 and .79 were reported between the scores for the informational and normative dimensions, respectively.

Alphas of .62 and .67 (n = 426 for both) were reported for the scale for its first and second administrations to middle school students, respectively by Boush, Friestad, and Rose (1994). The version of the scale used by Day and Stafford (1997) was reported to have an alpha of .87 (n = 126). Mangleburg and Bristol (1998) used the scales with high school students (n = 296) and reported composite reliabilities of .84 and .74 for the normative and informational components, respectively. Alphas of .93 and .88 were reported for the normative dimension of the scale as used by Bearden, Hardesty, and Rose (2001) and Sen, Gurhan-Canli, and Morwitz (2001), respectively.

VALIDITY: While there was initial effort by Bearden, Netemeyer, and Teel (1989) to develop separate scales to measure the three hypothesized dimensions of the construct (consumer susceptibility to interpersonal influence), there was strong evidence of discriminant and convergent validity for the informational dimension but not for the utilitarian and value expressive dimensions. Their items were combined to form one scale. Confirmatory factor analysis indicated a stable two-factor correlated structure (the normative and informational factors).

The validity of the scale was not specifically addressed in the study by Boush, Friestad, and Rose (1994). However, the authors did perform a principal components analysis of the combined items of this scale with those of another scale (V.III, #315). They reported that the results "yielded a simple structure solution" (p. 170).

COMMENTS: There is evidence that the full set of 12 items developed by Bearden, Netemeyer, and Teel (1989) is multidimensional. Yet, the studies by Boush, Friestad, and Rose (1994) as well as Day and Stafford (1997) combined items from both dimensions. Further testing appears to be called for to determine what is most appropriate.

As acknowledged by Boush, Friestad, and Rose (1994, p. 173), the internal consistency of their version of the scale is low enough to warrant caution in using it again, particularly with non-adolescents respondents.

See also Lastovicka et al. (1999).

REFERENCES:

Bearden, William O., Richard G. Netemeyer, and Jesse E. Teel (1989), "Measurement of Consumer Susceptibility to Interpersonal Influence," *JCR*, 15 (March), 473–481.

Bearden, William O., David M. Hardesty, and Randall L. Rose (2001), "Consumer Self-Confidence: Refinements in Conceptualization and Measurement," *JCR*, 28 (June), 121–134.

Boush, David M., Marian Friestad, and Gregory M. Rose (1994), "Adolescent Skepticism Toward TV Advertising and Knowledge of Advertiser Tactics," *JCR*, 21 (June), 165–175.

Day, Ellen and Marla Royne Stafford (1997), "Age-Related Cues in Retail Services Advertising: Their Effects on Younger Consumers," *JR*, 73 (2), 211–233.

Lastovicka, John L., Lance A. Bettencourt, Renee Shaw Hughner, and Ronald J. Kuntze (1999), "Lifestyle of the Tight and Frugal: Theory and Measurement," *JCR*, 26 (June), 85–98.

Mangleburg, Tamara F. and Terry Bristol (1998), "Socialization and Adolescents' Skepticism Toward Advertising," *JA*, 27 (3), 11–21.

Sen, Sankar, Zeynep Gurhan-Canli, and Vicki Morwitz (2001), "Withholding Consumption: A Social Dilemma Perspective on Consumer Boycotts," *JCR*, 28 (December), 399–417.

SCALE ITEMS: [1]

1. I rarely purchase the latest fashion styles until I am sure my friends approve of them.

2. It is important that others like the products and brands I buy.

3. When buying products, I generally purchase those brands that I think others will approve of.

4. If other people can see me using a product, I often purchase the brand they expect me to buy.

5. I like to know what brands and products make good impressions on others.

6. I achieve a sense of belonging by purchasing the same products and brands that others purchase.

7. If I want to be like someone, I often try to buy the same brands that they buy.

8. I often identify with other people by purchasing the same products and brands they purchase.

9. To make sure I buy the right product or brand, I often observe what others are buying and using.

10. If I have little experience with a product, I often ask my friends about the product.

11. I often consult other people to help choose the best alternative available from a product class.

12. I frequently gather information from friends or family about a product before I buy.

[1] Items 1–8 and 9–12 compose the normative and informational dimensions, respectively, as used by Bearden, Netemeyer, and Teel (1989). Boush, Friestad, and Rose (1994) used a five-point response format along with items similar to 3, 9, and 10. Day and Stafford (1997) used all twelve items but with slightly modified wording such that references to products and brands were changed to store or service firm. Mangleburg and Bristol (1998) used a seven-point Likert-type response format and items similar to 2, 3, and 5 to measure the normative component and items similar to #9–#12 to measure the informational component. Bearden, Hardesty, and Rose (2001) as well as Sen, Gurhan-Canli, and Morwitz (2001) just used the eight items measuring the normative dimension.

SCALE NAME: Switching Costs

SCALE DESCRIPTION: Three, seven-point Likert-type statements are used to measure a customer's thoughts regarding the degree of costs (time, money, and effort) that would be associated with changing service providers. Ganesh, Arnold, and Reynolds (2000) referred to their scale as a measure of *dependence*.

SCALE ORIGIN: Both Ganesh, Arnold, and Reynolds (2000) as well as Jones, Mothersbaugh, and Beatty (2000) stated that they adapted the scale from Ping (1993). There it was used in an industrial context (business-to-business). (See V. III, #897).

RELIABILITY: Alphas of .76 and .91 were reported for the scale as used by Ganesh, Arnold, and Reynolds (2000) and Jones, Mothersbaugh, and Beatty (2000), respectively.

VALIDITY: While Ganesh, Arnold, and Reynolds (2000) did not examine the scale's validity they did include its items in an EFA along with items intended to measure two other constructs. All items loaded strongly on the expected dimensions with no significant cross-loadings.

Based on the CFA and other tests that were conducted on this and other scales, Jones, Mothersbaugh, and Beatty (2000) concluded that their version of the scale was unidimensional and showed evidence of discriminant validity. In addition, the scale was reported to have a variance extracted of .76.

REFERENCES:

Ganesh, Jaishanker, Mark J. Arnold, and Kristy E. Reynolds (2000), "Understanding the Customer Base of Service Providers: An Examination of the Differences Between Switchers and Stayers," *JM*, 64 (3), 65–87.

Jones, Michael A., David L. Mothersbaugh, and Sharon E. Beatty (2000), "Switching Barriers and Repurchase Intentions in Services," *JR*, 79 (2), 259–274.

Ping, Robert A., Jr. (1993), "The Effects of Satisfaction and Structural Constraints on Retailer Exiting, Voice, Loyalty, Opportunism, and Neglect," *JR*, 69 (Fall), 320–352.

SCALE ITEMS: [1]

1. In general, it would be a hassle changing _____.

2. It would take a lot of time and effort changing _____.

3. For me, the costs in time, money, and effort to switch _____ are high.

---

[1] A generic descriptor of the service provider should go in the blanks, e.g., banks.

SCALE NAME: Telepresence (Website)

SCALE DESCRIPTION: The scale is composed of eight, seven-point Likert-type items that measure the degree to which a person has the sense of being at/in (*presence*) a remote/virtual environment (*tele*). Thus, afterwards the person is left with a feeling of having been psychologically transported to a "world" created at a website such that for a time it was as if they were there rather than the physical place where the viewing was done (home, office).

SCALE ORIGIN: The scale used by Coyle and Thorson (2001) was an adaptation of a scale developed by Kim and Biocca (1997). The latter proposed some antecedents and consequences of telepresence and then tested the model using the scale in the context of an infomercial on television. More specifically, their testing of the items indicated that there were two factors and they labeled them *arrival* and *departure*. They correspond to items #1–#5 and #6–#8, respectively. The results indicated that these two factors have differing effects on memory and attitude change.

RELIABILITY: An alpha of .93 (n = 68) was reported for the version of the scale used by Coyle and Thorson (2001).

VALIDITY: No evidence of the scale's validity was presented in the study by Coyle and Thorson (2001).

COMMENTS: Coyle and Thorson (2001) stated that their factor analysis indicated that there was just one factor and that is why they used all of the items as a single summated scale. This is in contrast to what Kim and Biocca (1997) did. As noted above, they viewed telepresence as a multidimensional construct and, in fact, their scale and model provided evidence of that. Given this, users should be aware that using these eight items as a unidimensional measure of telepresence may not be appropriate.

REFERENCES:

Coyle, James R. and Esther Thorson (2001), "The Effects of Progressive Levels of Interactivity and Vividness in Web Marketing Sites," *JA*, 30 (Fall), 65–77.

Kim, Taeyong and Frank Biocca (1997), "Telepresence via Television: Two Dimensions of Telepresence May Have Different Connections to Memory and Persuasion," *Journal of Computer-Mediated Communication*, 3 (September), http://www.ascusc.org/jcmc/vol3/issue2/kim.html.

SCALE ITEMS: [1]

1. When I left the _____ website, I felt like I came back to the "real world" after a journey.

2. The _____ website came to me and created a new world for me, and the world suddenly disappeared when I left the website.

3. While I was in the site, I felt I was in the world _____ created.

4. While I was in this site, my body was in the room, but my mind was inside the world created by _____.

5. While I was in this site, the world generated by _____ was more real or present for me compared to the "real world."

6. While I was in the _____ site, I sometimes forgot that I was in the middle of an experiment.

7. The world generated by _____ seemed to me only "something I saw" rather than "somewhere I visited." (r)

8. While I was in this site, my mind was in the room, not in the world created by _____. (r)

---

[1] The name of the website should be placed in the blanks.

SCALE NAME: Test Accuracy (Health)

SCALE DESCRIPTION: The four-item scale is intended to measure the subjective probability that a person assigns to the possibility that a medical test for a specific disease provides accurate results and can be believed as correctly indicating the presence of the disease (or lack thereof).

SCALE ORIGIN: The scale is original to Luce and Kahn (1999). They used a one-item version of the scale in their earlier studies (reported in the article) with the final study using the multi-item version.

RELIABILITY: An alpha of .80 was reported for the scale (Luce and Kahn 1999).

VALIDITY: Luce and Kahn (1999) did not examine the validity of the scale. However, they did state that the scale had a correlation of .67 with the one-item measure they had used.

REFERENCES:
Kahn, Barbara E. (2002), Personal Correspondence.
Luce, Mary Frances and Barbara E. Kahn (1999), "Avoidance or Vigilance? The Psychology of False-Positive Test Results," *JCR*, 26 (December), 242–259.

SCALE ITEMS: [1]

1. Some medical tests are very reliable and accurate so that you know the results they give you reflect your actual state of health or disease. Other medical tests are less reliable and accurate, so you worry that the results they give you do not reflect your actual condition. If you got tested for _____, how likely would it be for you to believe that the result was accurate?
   I would definitely BELIEVE my test result was accurate. / I would definitely NOT BELIEVE my test result was accurate.

2. A "Positive" test result means that something has shown up on the patient's test results that needs to be checked out. That something could be _____. How certain do you think it is that a person with a POSITIVE _____ test result HAS _____? (r)
   I believe that a person who has a POSITIVE _____ test result definitely DOES NOT HAVE _____. / I believe that a person who has a POSITIVE _____ test result definitely HAS _____.

3. How likely do you think it is that a person with a NEGATIVE _____ test result HAS _____?
   I believe that a person who has a NEGATIVE _____ test result definitely DOES NOT HAVE _____. / I believe that a person who has a NEGATIVE _____ test result definitely HAS _____.

4. Medical tests vary in terms of their accuracy, or whether they give correct results. How accurate do you think tests for _____ are, compared to other medical tests that you might get? (r)
   I think _____ tests are VERY BAD, compared to other tests. / I think _____ tests are VERY GOOD, compared to other tests.

[1] Items provided by Kahn (2002). The blanks should be used to describe the disease, illness, or problem of concern. In the case of Luce and Kahn (1999), the disease was Chlamydia.

SCALE NAME: Time Pressure

SCALE DESCRIPTION: Several statements with a Likert-type response format are used to measure a person's lack of free time for him/herself each day. This was referred to as "My Time Oriented" by Lumpkin (1985).

SCALE ORIGIN: It is not clear where the items originated nor where they were first used together as a multi-item scale. The earliest known usage of the items as a scale is Lumkpin and Darden (1982).

RELIABILITY: A composite reliability of .87 was reported for the scale used by Ailawadi, Neslin, and Gedenk (2001). Alphas of .59 and .6882 were calculated by Lumpkin and Darden (1982) and Lumpkin (1985), respectively.

VALIDITY: The items in the version of the scale used by Ailawadi, Neslin, and Gedenk (2001) were examined along with those belonging to 14 other scales in a confirmatory factor analysis. The fit of the measurement model was acceptable and general evidence was cited in support of the scale's discriminant validity.

In the studies by Lumpkin (1985; and Darden 1982), factor analysis indicated the items loaded together.

REFERENCES:

Ailawadi, Kusum L., Scott A. Neslin, and Karen Gedenk (2001), "Pursuing the Value-Conscious Consumer: Store Brands versus National Brand Promotions," *JM*, 65 (1), 71–89.
Lumpkin, James R. (1985), "Shopping Orientation Segmentation of the Elderly Consumer," *JAMS*, 13 (Spring), 271–289.
Lumpkin, James R. and William R. Darden (1982), "Relating Television Preference Viewing to Shopping Orientations, Lifestyles, and Demographics," *JA*, 11 (4), 56–67.

SCALE ITEMS: [1]

1. I take time off for leisure activities every day. (r)

2. I do things every day that are for "me." (r)

3. I set aside time each day for myself. (r)

4. I never seem to have enough time to do the things I want to.

5. I always seem to be in a hurry.

6. I have plenty of free time. (r)

7. Most days, I have no time to relax.

---

[1] Lumpkin (1985) used all six items whereas Lumpkin and Darden (1982) used just items 4, 5, and 6. Items 4, 5, and 7 were used by Ailawadi, Neslin, and Gedenk (2001).

SCALE NAME: Time Pressure (Specific Shopping Trip)

SCALE DESCRIPTION: Three, seven-point Likert-type statements are used to measure the degree to which a shopper expresses having a limited amount of time to use during a particular shopping episode. The scale was called *time available* by Beatty and Ferrell (1998).

SCALE ORIGIN: The scale was developed by Beatty and Ferrell (1998) after examining related measures used by Beatty and Smith (1987), Iyer (1989), and Jeon (1990).

RELIABILITY: Beatty and Ferrell (1998) reported a composite reliability of .66 for the scale.

VALIDITY: Although the details related to this scale were not provided, the implication was that it was unidimensional and showed sufficient evidence of convergent and discriminant validity (Beatty and Ferrell 1998).

REFERENCES:
Beatty, Sharon E. and M. Elizabeth Ferrell (1998), "Impulse Buying: Modeling Its Precursors," *JR*, 74 (2), 169–191.
Beatty, Sharon E. and Scott M. Smith (1987), "External Search Effort: An Investigation Across Several Product Categories," *JCR*, 14 (June), 83–95.
Iyer, Easwar S. (1989), "Unplanned Researching: Knowledge of Shopping Environment and Time Pressure," *JR*, 65 (Spring), 40–57.
Jeon, Jung-Ok (1990), "An Empirical Investigation of the Relationship Between Affective States, In-store Browsing, and Impulse Buying," doctoral dissertation, Tuscaloosa, AL: The University of Alabama.

SCALE ITEMS:

1. I have limited time available to me for this particular shopping trip. (r)

2. I am not rushed for time on this shopping trip.

3. The amount of time pressure I feel on this shopping trip could be described as:
   none / very high. (r)

SCALE NAME: Tolerance for Ambiguity

SCALE DESCRIPTION: It is a twelve-item, seven-point Likert-type scale measuring the degree of openness one has in general toward stimuli that are less than clear, puzzling, or indefinite.

SCALE ORIGIN: McQuarrie and Mick (1992) reported that they drew upon items that had been used in one or more of three previous studies (Budner 1962; MacDonald 1970; Norton 1975). A twenty-item scale was developed and tested. An alpha of .64 resulted which lead the authors to eliminate all items with item-total correlations less than .15. With another pretest sample, the twelve-item version of the scale yielded an alpha of .70.

RELIABILITY: As used by Phillips (2000, 2002), the scale had an alpha of .67. No information was provided by McQuarrie and Mick (1992) regarding the scale's reliability beyond what is noted above concerning its development.

VALIDITY: No specific testing of the scale's validity was reported by either McQuarrie and Mick (1992) or Phillips (2000).

COMMENTS: McQuarrie (1994) has indicated that this scale is barely adequate in its present form. Potential users are urged to review the larger list of tolerance-for-ambiguity items that can be found in Budner (1962), MacDonald (1970), and Norton (1975) and are encouraged to attempt revisions. Further, conceptually similar scales measuring exploratory tendencies (#167) and need-for-cognition (#283) could also be considered.

REFERENCES:

Budner, Stanley (1962), "Intolerance of Ambiguity as a Personality Variable," *Journal of Personality*, 30 (March), 29–50.

MacDonald, A. P. (1970), "Revised Scale for Ambiguity Tolerance: Reliability and Validity," *Psychological Reports*, 26 (June), 791–798.

McQuarrie, Edward F. and David Glen Mick (1992), "On Resonance: A Critical Pluralistic Inquiry into Advertising Rhetoric," *JCR*, 19 (Sept.), 180–197.

McQuarrie, Edward F. (1994), Personal Correspondence.

Norton, Robert W. (1975), "Measurement of Ambiguity Tolerance," *Journal of Personality Assessment*, 39 (6), 607–619.

Phillips, Barbara J. (2000), "The Impact of Verbal Anchoring on Consumer Response to Image Ads," *JA*, 29 (1), 15–24.

Phillips, Barbara J. (2002), Personal Correspondence.

SCALE ITEMS:

Directions: To help us understand you better we would like to know your opinions about some common objects, situations, and activities. There are no right or wrong answers and therefore your first response is important. Circle a number to indicate your agreement or disagreement.

1. I like movies or stories with definite endings. (r)

2. I always want to know what people are laughing at. (r)

3. I would like to live in a foreign country for a while.

4. A good job is one where what is to be done and how it is to be done are always clear. (r)

5. I tend to like obscure or hidden symbolism.

6. It really disturbs me when I am unable to follow another person's train of thought. (r)

7. I am tolerant of ambiguous situations.

8. A poem should never contain contradictions. (r)

9. Vague and impressionistic pictures appeal to me more than realistic pictures.

10. I don't like to work on a problem unless there is a possibility of coming out with a clear-cut and unambiguous answer. (r)

11. Generally, the more meanings a poem has, the better I like it.

12. I like parties where I know most of the people more than ones where all or most of the people are complete strangers. (r)

SCALE NAME: Travel Intentions

SCALE DESCRIPTION: The scale is composed of three, nine-point Likert-type statements that measure the extent of a person's plans to engage in activities related to traveling to a specific vacation destination.

SCALE ORIGIN: The scale appears to be original to the study by Krishnamurthy and Sujan (1999).

RELIABILITY: An alpha of .88 was reported for the scale (Krishnamurthy and Sujan 1999).

VALIDITY: No examination of the scale's validity was reported by Krishnamurthy and Sujan (1999).

REFERENCES:

Krishnamurthy, Parthasarathy and Mita Sujan (1999), "Retrospection versus Anticipation: The Role of the Ad under Retrospective and Anticipatory Self-Referencing," *JCR*, 26 (June), 55–69.

SCALE ITEMS: [1]

1. I am very likely to consider _____ as a vacation destination the next time I plan one.

2. I am very interested in getting a brochure on _____.

3. I am willing to call the 800 number to obtain a travel guide to _____.

[1] The name of the travel destination should be placed in the blanks.

SCALE NAME: Trust in Brand

SCALE DESCRIPTION: The scale is composed of four, seven-point Likert-type statements measuring the degree of confidence a consumer has in a brand and belief that it can be counted on to do what it is supposed to do.

SCALE ORIGIN: No information regarding the scale's origin was provided by Chaudhuri and Holbrook (2001). It seems to have been developed for use in their study.

RELIABILITY: An alpha of .81 was reported for the scale by Chaudhuri and Holbrook (2001).

VALIDITY: The only information bearing on the scale's validity reported by Chaudhuri and Holbrook (2001) was that there was evidence of its discriminant validity given that its average variance extracted was much higher than its squared correlation with the three other constructs with which it was compared.

REFERENCES:

Chaudhuri, Arjun and Morris B. Holbrook (2001), "The Chain of Effects from Brand Trust and Brand Affect to Brand Performance: The Role of Brand Loyalty," *JM*, 65 (April), 81–93.

SCALE ITEMS:

1. I trust this brand.

2. I rely on this brand.

3. This is an honest brand.

4. This brand is safe.

SCALE NAME: Trust in the Organization

SCALE DESCRIPTION: Four, five-point Likert-type items compose the scale. The scale is used to measure the degree to which a customer believes that an organization is honest and can be counted on. The context in which the respondents were given this scale was after being told to remember a recent service experience that led to their lodging a complaint.

SCALE ORIGIN: Tax, Brown, and Chandrashekaran (1998) borrowed and modified some items from a nine-item scale by Crosby, Evans, and Cowles (1990) that measured trust in a salesperson.

RELIABILITY: An alpha of .96 (n = 257) was reported for the scale by Tax, Brown, and Chandrashekaran (1998).

VALIDITY: It is not clear what support if any was found for the validity of the scale in the study by Tax, Brown, and Chandrashekaran (1998).

REFERENCES:

Crosby, Lawrence A., Kenneth R. Evans, and Deborah Cowles (1990), "Relationship Quality in Services Selling: An Interpersonal Influence Perspective," *JM*, 54 (July), 68–81.

Tax, Stephen S., Stephen W. Brown, and Murali Chandrashekaran (1998), "Customer Evaluations of Service Complaint Experiences: Implications for Relationship Marketing," *JM*, 62 (April), 60–76.

SCALE ITEMS:

1. I believed the organization could not be relied upon to keep its promises. (r)

2. I believed the organization was trustworthy.

3. I would find it necessary to be cautious in dealing with this organization. (r)

4. Overall, I believe this firm was honest.

SCALE NAME: Trust of Service Provider

SCALE DESCRIPTION: The three-item, five-point scale measures the extent to which one person believes that another person "knows best" in a certain situation. Due to the phrasing of the items and the context in which it was developed, the focus of the scale is on the perceived trust a client has in a specific service provider. The type of service provider studied by Price and Arnould (1999) was a hairstylist.

SCALE ORIGIN: The scale appears to be original to Price and Arnould (1999).

RELIABILITY: An alpha of .84 was reported for the scale by Price and Arnould (1999).

VALIDITY: No information about the scale's validity was provided by Price and Arnould (1999).

REFERENCES:
Price, Linda L. and Eric J. Arnould (1999), "Commercial Friendships: Service Provider-Client Relationships in Context," *JM*, 63 (October), 38–56.

SCALE ITEMS: [1]

1. I trust _____'s judgment.

2. _____ has a lot of experience and usually knows best.

3. _____ knows best in this situation.

[1] The name of the service provider should be placed in the blanks of the items.

SCALE NAME: Trustworthiness (Retailer)

SCALE DESCRIPTION: Three Likert-type statements with a seven-point response format are used to assess a customer's belief in a retailer's reliability and integrity.

SCALE ORIGIN: The source of the scale was not explicitly described by De Wulf, Odekerken-Schröder, and Iacobucci (2001) but it would appear to be original to their studies. The items appear to be among those that were developed using the back-translation method for versions in American English and Dutch and then pretested in the U.S., Netherlands, and Belgium (Flemish-speaking area).

RELIABILITY: Composite reliabilities were calculated for two types of stores for each of three countries (De Wulf, Odekerken-Schröder, and Iacobucci 2001). The reliabilities for food stores were .92, .83, and .85 for the U.S., Netherlands, and Belgium, respectively (Odekerken-Schröder 2004). For apparel stores, the reliabilities were .93, .88, and .86 for the U.S., Netherlands, and Belgium, respectively.

VALIDITY: Along with two other scales (relationship satisfaction [#401] and commitment [#127]), De Wulf, Odekerken-Schröder, and Iacobucci (2001) used scale averages as indicators of a second-order factor (relationship quality). Evidence was provided in support of the scale's unidimensionality as well as its convergent validity.

REFERENCES:

De Wulf, Kristof, Gaby Odekerken-Schröder, and Dawn Iacobucci (2001), "Investments in Consumer Relationships: A Cross-Country and Cross-Industry Exploration," *JM*, 65 (October), 33–50.
Odekerken-Schröder, Gaby (2004), Personal Correspondence.

SCALE ITEMS: [1]

1. This _____ gives me a feeling of trust.

2. I have trust in this _____ .

3. This _____ gives me a trustworthy impression.

___

[1] An appropriate descriptor of the business entity should be placed in the blanks. De Wulf, Odekerken-Schröder, and Iacobucci (2001) used the term "store" but other general terms such as "retailer" and "service provider" are possible as are more specific terms such as "restaurant" and "wireless provider."

SCALE NAME: TV Viewing (Escape Motivation)

SCALE DESCRIPTION: The five-item, five-point scale measures the frequency with which a person watches television as a way of mentally escaping discomforts of life such as boredom, loneliness, and other problems.

SCALE ORIGIN: The scale is original to Lin (1999) although she drew inspiration from previous studies.

RELIABILITY: The scale was reported to have an alpha of .76 (Lin 1999).

VALIDITY: Although no examination of the scale's validity was reported by Lin (1999) an exploratory factor analysis was conducted. This provided some evidence of the scale's unidimensionality.

REFERENCES:
Lin, Carolyn A. (1999), "Online-Service Adoption Likelihood," *JAR*, 39 (March/April), 79–89.
Lin, Carolyn A. (2001), Personal Correspondence.

SCALE ITEMS: [1]

Please tell me how often you watch TV for the following reasons:

1. To kill time.

2. To have company.

3. To not feel bored.

4. To forget about your problems.

5. To tune out what's going on around you.

---

[1] Responses to these statements were measured using the following scale: *never* (1), *rarely* (2), *sometimes* (3), *often* (4), and *very often* (5) (Lin 2001).

#483 *TV Viewing (Information Motivation)*

SCALE NAME: TV Viewing (Information Motivation)

SCALE DESCRIPTION: The scale is composed of four, five-point items that measure the frequency with which a person watches television in order to hear the local, national, and international news.

SCALE ORIGIN: The scale is original to Lin (1999) although she drew inspiration from previous studies.

RELIABILITY: The scale was reported to have an alpha of .86 (Lin 1999).

VALIDITY: Although no examination of the scale's validity was reported by Lin (1999) an exploratory factor analysis was conducted. This provided some evidence of the scale's unidimensionality.

REFERENCES:
Lin, Carolyn A. (1999), "Online-Service Adoption Likelihood," *JAR*, 39 (March/April), 79–89.
Lin, Carolyn A. (2001), Personal Correspondence.

SCALE ITEMS: [1]

Please tell me how often you watch TV for the following reasons:

1. To find out what's going on in your community.

2. To find out what's going on in your country.

3. To find out what's going on around the world.

4. To advance your intellectual growth.

[1] Responses to these statements were measured using the following scale: *never* (1), *rarely* (2), *sometimes* (3), *often* (4), and *very often* (5) (Lin 2001).

SCALE NAME: TV Viewing (Self-Concept Motivation)

SCALE DESCRIPTION: The five-item, five-point scale measures the frequency with which a person watches television as a way of determining his/her normalcy, i.e., that there are others who share the same thoughts and behaviors.

SCALE ORIGIN: The scale is original to Lin (1999) although she drew inspiration from previous studies.

RELIABILITY: The scale was reported to have an alpha of .88 (Lin 1999).

VALIDITY: Although no examination of the scale's validity was reported by Lin (1999) an exploratory factor analysis was conducted. This provided some evidence of the scale's unidimensionality.

REFERENCES:
Lin, Carolyn A. (1999), "Online-Service Adoption Likelihood," *JAR*, 39 (March/April), 79–89.
Lin, Carolyn A. (2001), Personal Correspondence.

SCALE ITEMS: [1]

Please tell me how often you watch TV for the following reasons:

1. To see whether there are people who think the way you do on TV.

2. To see whether there are people who feel the way you do on TV.

3. To see whether there are people who act the way you do on TV.

[1] Responses to these statements were measured using the following scale: *never* (1), *rarely* (2), *sometimes* (3), *often* (4), and *very often* (5) (Lin 2001).

#485 *Typicality (General)*

SCALE NAME: Typicality (General)

SCALE DESCRIPTION: Four, nine-point semantic differentials are used to measure the degree to which a person perceives some stimulus to have characteristics that make it fit into or belong to some category. In the study by Campbell and Goodstein (2001) respondents judged the extent to which a particular beverage was typical of "soft drinks."

SCALE ORIGIN: Campbell and Goodstein (2001) did not indicate the source of the scale but it appears to be original to them.

RELIABILITY: The scale had an alpha of .86 (Campbell and Goodstein 2001).

VALIDITY: No examination of the scale's validity was reported by Campbell and Goodstein (2001).

REFERENCES:
Campbell, Margaret C. and Ronald C. Goodstein (2001), "The Moderating Effect of Perceived Risk on Consumers' Evaluations of Product Incongruity: Preference for the Norm," *JCR*, 28 (December), 439–449.

SCALE ITEMS:

1. very typical / extremely atypical

2. not at all novel / extremely novel

3. not at all unusual / very unusual

4. matches very well / does not match at all well

SCALE NAME: Ubiquity (Sponsor)

SCALE DESCRIPTION: The scale is composed of three, seven-point Likert type statements measuring a person's sense of how likely a particular company is to be a sponsor of a variety of major sporting events. "Ubiquity" implies that the sponsor seems to be everywhere, visibly associated with lots of top sporting events.

SCALE ORIGIN: The scale is original to the study by Speed and Thompson (2000). Some qualitative work by the authors led to generation of items for this scale as well as several others. This was followed by a pretest which aided in identifying items for deletion or modification.

RELIABILITY: An alpha of .85 was reported for the scale by Speed and Thompson (2000).

VALIDITY: The initial qualitative work conducted by the authors provides some evidence of its content validity. Based on data from the main study, a CFA was performed on items from several scales. The results provided evidence of this scale's convergent and discriminant validity.

REFERENCES:
Speed, Richard and Peter Thompson (2000), "Determinants of Sports Sponsorship Response," *JAMS*, 28 (2), 226–238.

SCALE ITEMS:

1. This company sponsors many different sports.

2. It is very common to see this company sponsoring sporting events.

3. I expect this company to sponsor major events.

#487 *Uniqueness (Product)*

SCALE NAME: Uniqueness (Product)

SCALE DESCRIPTION: The scale is composed of three, seven-point Likert-type statements measuring the degree to which a consumer believes that, based on the advertising he/she has been exposed to, a specific brand of a product is distinct from the competition.

SCALE ORIGIN: The source of the scale was not stated by Dean (1999).

RELIABILITY: An alpha of .77 (n = 185) was reported for the scale (Dean 1999).

VALIDITY: No information regarding the scale's validity was reported (Dean 1999).

REFERENCES:
Dean, Dwane Hal (1999), "Brand Endorsement, Popularity, and Event Sponsorship as Advertising Cues Affecting Consumer Pre-Purchase Attitudes," *JA*, 28 (3), 1–12.

SCALE ITEMS: [1]

1. The advertised _____ "stands out" from other _____ brands.

2. The advertised _____ is very different from other _____ brands.

3. Compared to other _____ brands, the advertised _____ is "unique."

---

[1] The response scale had seven points and used anchors of *strongly disagree* and *strongly agree*. The name for the product category should be placed in the blanks.

SCALE NAME: Usage Intention

SCALE DESCRIPTION: The scale is composed of three, seven-point semantic differentials intended to measure the degree to which a person has tended to buy a certain brand of product. Unlike with the most popular measures of this sort (e.g., #92), the items in this scale are stated in the past tense but the assumption appears to be that by instructing respondents to describe their "anticipated actions" the measure should provide a sense of the consumers' intended future behavior.

SCALE ORIGIN: The origin of the scale used by Lane (2000) was not stated, however, it seems to have been developed for use in her study.

RELIABILITY: Lane (2000) used the scale with four brand extensions. The alphas were all very high (.91 to .94; Lane 2003).

VALIDITY: No examination of the scale's validity was reported by Lane (2000).

REFERENCES:
Lane, Vicki R. (2003), Personal Correspondence.
Lane, Vicki R. (2000), "The Impact of Ad Repetition and Ad Content on Consumer Perceptions of Incongruent Extensions," *JM*, 64 (2), 80–91.

SCALE ITEMS: [1]

Directions: Please circle the response that best describes your feelings, thoughts, and/or anticipated actions associated with _____.

1. Never chosen / always chosen

2. Unpreferred / preferred

3. Rarely used / always used

---

[1] Lane (2000) used these instructions above a section of the questionnaire that included these items as well as others. The name of the focal brand should be placed in the blank.

SCALE NAME: Usefulness of Technology to Assist Shopping

SCALE DESCRIPTION: Three, seven-point Likert-type items are used to measure the degree to which using a technological device or system is viewed by a person as improving his/her shopping ability.

SCALE ORIGIN: The construct and original scale were part of the Technology Acceptance Model (TAM) developed and tested by Davis (1986). The model became very popular and adjustments were made by other users over time and for varying contexts. Childers et al. (2001) drew upon Davis' (1989) usefulness scale and adapted it for their study, particularly so that it would better fit the shopping context.

RELIABILITY: Using LISREL, the reliability of the scale was calculated to be .920 (hedonic motivations) and .933 (utilitarian motivations) in the studies reported by Childers et al. (2001).

VALIDITY: Discriminant validity was assessed using two different tests (the latent variable confidence interval tests and the χ^2 difference test). For both studies the evidence indicated that each scale, including usefulness, was measuring a distinctive construct.

REFERENCES:

Childers, Terry L., Christopher L. Carr, Joann Peck, and Stephen Carson (2001), "Hedonic and Utilitarian Motivations for Online Retail Shopping Behavior," *JR*, 77 (Winter), 511–535.

Davis, Fred D (1986), "Technology Acceptance Model for Empirically Testing New End-User Information Systems: Theory and Results," doctoral dissertation, MIT Sloan School of Management, Cambridge, MA.

Davis, Fred D. (1989), "Perceived Usefulness, Perceived Ease of Use, and User Acceptance of Information Technology," *MIS Quarterly*, 19 (September), 319–340.

SCALE ITEMS:

1. Technology assisted shopping would improve my shopping productivity.

2. Technology assisted shopping would enhance my effectiveness in shopping.

3. Technology assisted shopping would improve my shopping ability.

SCALE NAME: Value (Economic)

SCALE DESCRIPTION: The scale is composed of four statements that attempt to assess the utility derived from the perceived economic value of a particular product. One way the scale is distinguished from that of a satisfaction scale is that it could be applied at various stages during the purchase decision process whereas satisfaction is usually measured *after* the decision.

SCALE ORIGIN: The scale is original to Sweeney and Soutar (2001) although they drew inspiration and items from the work of others as well as their previous work (Sweeney, Soutar, and Johnson 1999). The scale was part of a larger instrument developed to measure perceived value (PERVAL). The development occurred via a multistage process whereby focus groups were used to help generate items and judges were used to examine their content validity. Three quantitative studies were subsequently conducted to purify the instrument, test its dimensionality, and examine its reliability and validity. Ultimately, the nineteen-item PERVAL instrument with its four subscales was deemed by the authors to have "sound and stable psychometric properties" (p. 216).

RELIABILITY: For the first study (n = 273), Sweeney and Soutar (2001) did not identify the reliabilities for each subscale but they were said to be between .82 and .91. For Study 2 (n = 303), the composite reliability for the Price subscale was .80. The results for Study 3 were based on responses from customers of a furniture store (n = 323) and a car stereo center (n = 313) and the composite reliabilities for the Price subscale were .90 and .84, respectively.

VALIDITY: Beyond the validation described above, Sweeney and Soutar (2001) tested the psychometric quality of the instrument in the three studies using the typical procedures expected with confirmatory factor analysis. Each time the four-factor model was supported over competing ones. Repeatedly there was strong evidence of each scale's convergent and discriminant validities.

REFERENCES:
Soutar, Geoffrey N. (2004), Personal Correspondence.
Sweeney, Jillian C. and Geoffrey N. Soutar (2001), "Consumer Perceived Value: The Development of a Multiple Item Scale," *JR*, 77 (Summer), 203–220.
Sweeney, Jillian C., Geoffrey N. Soutar, and Lester W. Johnson (1999), "The Role of Perceived Risk in the Quality-Value Relationship: A Study in a Retail Environment," *JR*, 75 (1), 77–105.

SCALE ITEMS: [1]

1. _____ is reasonably priced.

2. _____ offers value for money.

3. _____ is a good product for the price.

4. _____ would be economical.

[1] The name of the product should be placed in the blanks. A seven-point Likert-type response format was used (Soutar 2004).

SCALE NAME: Value (Emotional)

SCALE DESCRIPTION: Five statements are used to measure the utility resulting from the affective reaction to a particular product. One way the scale is distinguished from that of a satisfaction scale is that it could be applied at various stages during the purchase decision process whereas satisfaction is usually measured *after* the decision.

SCALE ORIGIN: The scale is original to Sweeney and Soutar (2001) although they drew inspiration from the work of others. The scale was part of a larger instrument developed to measure perceived value (PER-VAL). The development occurred via a multi-stage process whereby focus groups were used to help generate items and judges were used to examine their content validity. Three quantitative studies were subsequently conducted to purify the instrument, test its dimensionality, and examine its reliability and validity. Ultimately, the nineteen-item PERVAL instrument with its four subscales was deemed by the authors to have "sound and stable psychometric properties" (p. 216).

RELIABILITY: For the first study (n = 273), Sweeney and Soutar (2001) did not identify the reliabilities for each subscale but they were said to be between .82 and .91. For Study 2 (n = 303), the composite reliability for the Emotional subscale was .94. The results for Study 3 were based on responses from customers of a furniture store (n = 323) and a car stereo center (n = 313) and the composite reliability for both was .86.

VALIDITY: Beyond the validation described above, Sweeney and Soutar (2001) tested the psychometric quality of the instrument in the three studies using the typical procedures expected with confirmatory factor analysis. Each time the four-factor model was supported over competing ones. Repeatedly there was strong evidence of each scale's convergent and discriminant validities.

REFERENCES:
Soutar, Geoffrey N. (2004), Personal Correspondence.
Sweeney, Jillian C. and Geoffrey N. Soutar (2001), "Consumer Perceived Value: The Development of a Multiple Item Scale," *JR*, 77 (Summer), 203–220.

SCALE ITEMS: [1]

1. _____ is one that I would enjoy.

2. _____ would make me want to use it.

3. _____ is one that I would feel relaxed about using.

4. _____ would make me feel good.

5. _____ would give me pleasure.

[1] The name of the product should be placed in the blanks. A seven-point Likert-type response format was used (Soutar 2004).

SCALE NAME: Value (Offer)

SCALE DESCRIPTION: Six Likert-type statements are used to measure a consumer's opinion of how good a deal is for a certain product at a certain price. The emphasis of several items is that the price is lower than could have been expected given one's knowledge of what is being charged elsewhere.

SCALE ORIGIN: Although Grewal et al. (1998) implied that Dodds, Monroe, and Grewal (1991) were the source of the scale, the items are different. Instead, it appears that Grewal et al. (1998) drew inspiration from that measure and others and then developed a new one for use in their study. (See V. III, #391 as well as #494 in this volume for similar measures.)

RELIABILITY: The composite reliability for the scale was reported to be .90 (Grewal et al. 1998).

VALIDITY: A variety of tests conducted by Grewal et al. (1998) indicated the scale was unidimensional and showed evidence of discriminant validity. The variance extracted was .74.

REFERENCES:

Dodds, William B., Kent B. Monroe, and Dhruv Grewal (1991), "The Effects of Price, Brand, and Store Information on Buyers' Product Evaluations," *JMR*, 28 (August), 307–319.

Grewal, Dhruv, R. Krishnan, Julie Baker, and Norm Borin (1998), "The Effect of Store Name, Brand Name and Price Discounts on Consumers' Evaluations and Purchase Intentions," *JR*, 74 (3), 331–352.

SCALE ITEMS:

1. This _____ appears to be a bargain.

2. The price is less than what I expect it to be.

3. The price is less than the average market price.

4. The price is less than what other retailers charge.

5. This _____ is a great deal.

6. At this price, I would save a lot of money.

#493 *Value (Offer)*

SCALE NAME: Value (Offer)

SCALE DESCRIPTION: The scale is composed of nine, seven-point Likert-type items that measure a consumer's attitude about a particular price-deal he/she has been exposed to.

SCALE ORIGIN: Although bearing some similarity to previous measures of value (e.g., V. III, #391), this set of items appears to be original to Grewal, Monroe, and Krishnan (1998).

RELIABILITY: Grewal, Monroe, and Krishnan (1998) reported construct reliabilities of .95 (n = 361) and .97 (n = 328) for use of the scale in their first and second studies, respectively.

VALIDITY: A variety of evidence was provided by the authors from both studies in support of the scale's unidimensionality, convergent validity, and discriminant validity (Grewal, Monroe, and Krishnan 1998). Especially abundant was the evidence indicating the discriminant validity between this scale and one measuring another type of value (#497).

COMMENTS: The product examined by Grewal, Monroe, and Krishnan (1998) was a bicycle. All of the scale items seem amenable for use with a variety of other products except for #9.

REFERENCES:

Grewal, Dhruv, Kent B. Monroe, and R. Krishnan (1998), "The Effects of Price-Comparison Advertising on Buyer's Perceptions of Acquisition Value, Transaction Value, and Behavioral Intentions," *JM*, 62 (April), 46–59.

SCALE ITEMS:

1. If I bought this _____ at _____, I feel I would be getting my money's worth.

2. I feel that I am getting a good quality _____ for a reasonable price.

3. After evaluating the advertised _____ features, I am confident that I am getting quality features for _____.

4. If I acquired this _____, I think I would be getting good value for the money I spend.

5. I think that given this _____'s features, it is good value for the money.

6. I feel that acquiring this _____ meets both my high quality and low price requirements.

7. Compared to the maximum price I would be willing to pay for this _____, the sale price conveys good value.

8. I would value this _____ as it would meet my needs for a reasonable price.

9. This _____ would be a worthwhile acquisition because it would help me exercise at a reasonable price.

SCALE NAME: Value (Product)

SCALE DESCRIPTION: The scale is used to measure the degree to which a consumer perceives that a product is a good value for the money given that one knows its price. The measure was referred to as *perceived value indicators* by Dodds, Monroe, and Grewal (1991).

SCALE ORIGIN: Dodds, Monroe, and Grewal (1991) stated that the items for this and two other scales were "developed from previous research" (p. 312) although the source of the items and the extent of the borrowing were not specified.

Sweeney, Soutar, and Johnson (1999) cited Dodds, Monroe, and Grewal (1991) as the source of their scale but adapted it so that complete statements were used instead of bi-polar phrases.

Buchanan, Simmons, and Bickart (1999) did not state the source of their scale but it appears to have been very similar to items in the Dodds, Monroe, and Grewal (1991) scale.

RELIABILITY: The scale was reported to have an alpha of .93 for both of the experiments in which it was used by Dodds, Monroe, and Grewal (1991). Average inter-item correlations were .73 and .72.

Alphas of .91 and .85 were reported for the versions of the scale used by Buchanan, Simmons, and Bickart (1999) and Sweeney, Soutar, and Johnson (1999), respectively. Teas and Agarwal (2000) reported alphas of .93 (wristwatch) and .94 (calculator) for their version of the scale.

VALIDITY: Quantitative results were not provided but Dodds, Monroe, and Grewal (1991) stated that the results of an exploratory factor analysis indicated a three factor solution was found using items from this scale and two others. The suggestion was that the items in this scale loaded on one factor.

Not much was said by Sweeney, Soutar, and Johnson (1999) about this scale's validity but it was stated in general that all their scales exhibited discriminant validity by having their variance extracted being higher than the relevant squared structural path coefficients (Fornell and Larcker 1981).

Teas and Agarwal (2000) showed for two sets of data that the items were unidimensional. They pointed out for one of the sets, one item (#1 below) had a moderate loading on a related scale (#348) although the item still loaded highest on the expected factor.

REFERENCES:

Buchanan, Lauranne, Carolyn J. Simmons, and Barbara A. Bickart (1999), "Brand Equity Dilution: Retailer Display and Context Brand Effects," *JMR*, 36 (August), 345–355.

Dodds, William B., Kent B. Monroe, and Dhruv Grewal (1991), "The Effects of Price, Brand, and Store Information on Buyers' Product Evaluations," *JMR*, 28 (August), 307–319.

Fornell, Claes and David F. Larcker (1981), "Evaluating Structural Equation Models with Unobservable Variables and Measurement Error," *JMR*, 18 (February), 39–50.

Sweeney, Jillian C., Geoffrey N. Soutar, and Lester W. Johnson (1999), "The Role of Perceived Risk in the Quality-Value Relationship: A Study in a Retail Environment," *JR*, 75 (1), 77–105.

Teas, R. Kenneth and Sanjeev Agarwal (2000), "The Effects of Extrinsic Product Cues on Consumers' Perceptions of Quality, Sacrifice, and Value," *JAMS*, 28 (2), 278–290.

#494 *Value (Product)*

SCALE ITEMS: [1]

1. The product is a:
   very poor value for the money / very good value for the money

2. The product is considered to be a good buy.
   strongly disagree / strongly agree

3. This product appears to be a bargain.
   strongly disagree / strongly agree

4. At the price shown the product is:
   very uneconomical / economical

5. The price shown for the product is:
   very unacceptable / acceptable

[1] Sweeney, Soutar, and Johnson (1999) used complete sentences similar to #1, #2, and #4. Likewise, the items used by Buchanan, Simmons, and Bickart (1999) seem to have been similar to #1, #3, and #5. The format of the version used by Teas and Agarwal (2000) was not described in detail but is likely to have been similar to what is shown above.

SCALE NAME: Value (Quality)

SCALE DESCRIPTION: The scale is composed of six statements measuring the utility resulting from the perceived quality and anticipated performance of a particular product. One way the scale is distinguished from that of a satisfaction scale is that it could be applied at various stages during the purchase decision process whereas satisfaction is usually measured *after* the decision.

SCALE ORIGIN: The scale is original to Sweeney and Soutar (2001) although they drew inspiration and items from the work of others as well as their previous work (Sweeney, Soutar, and Johnson 1999). The scale was part of a larger instrument developed to measure perceived value (PERVAL). The development occurred via a multi-stage process whereby focus groups were used to help generate items and judges were used to examine their content validity. Three quantitative studies were subsequently conducted to purify the instrument, test its dimensionality, and examine its reliability and validity. Ultimately, the nineteen-item PERVAL instrument with its four subscales was deemed by the authors to have "sound and stable psychometric properties" (p. 216).

RELIABILITY: For the first study (n = 273), Sweeney and Soutar (2001) did not identify the reliabilities for each subscale but they were said to be between .82 and .91. For Study 2 (n = 303), the composite reliability for the Quality subscale was .91. The results for Study 3 were based on responses from customers of a furniture store (n = 323) and a car stereo center (n = 313) and the composite reliabilities for the Quality subscale were .95 and .94, respectively.

VALIDITY: Beyond the validation described above, Sweeney and Soutar (2001) tested the psychometric quality of the instrument in the three studies using the typical procedures expected with confirmatory factor analysis. Each time the four-factor model was supported over competing ones. Repeatedly there was strong evidence of each scale's convergent and discriminant validities.

REFERENCES:
Soutar, Geoffrey N. (2004), Personal Correspondence.
Sweeney, Jillian C. and Geoffrey N. Soutar (2001), "Consumer Perceived Value: The Development of a Multiple Item Scale," *JR*, 77 (Summer), 203–220.
Sweeney, Jillian C., Geoffrey N. Soutar, and Lester W. Johnson (1999), "The Role of Perceived Risk in the Quality-Value Relationship: A Study in a Retail Environment," *JR*, 75 (1), 77–105.

SCALE ITEMS: [1]

1. _____ has consistent quality.

2. _____ is well made.

3. _____ has an acceptable standard of quality.

4. _____ has poor workmanship. (r)

5. _____ would *not* last a long time. (r)

6. _____ would perform consistently.

[1] The name of the product should be placed in the blanks. A seven-point Likert-type response format was used (Soutar 2004).

SCALE NAME: Value (Social)

SCALE DESCRIPTION: Four statements are used to assess the utility derived from the perceived ability of a particular product to enhance its user's self-concept and social approval.

SCALE ORIGIN: The scale is original to Sweeney and Soutar (2001) although they drew inspiration from the work of others. The scale was part of a larger instrument developed to measure perceived value (PERVAL). The development occurred via a multi-stage process whereby focus groups were used to help generate items and judges were used to examine their content validity. Three quantitative studies were subsequently conducted to purify the instrument, test its dimensionality, and examine its reliability and validity. Ultimately, the nineteen-item PERVAL instrument with its four subscales was deemed by the authors to have "sound and stable psychometric properties" (p. 216).

RELIABILITY: For the first study (n = 273), Sweeney and Soutar (2001) did not identify the reliabilities for each subscale but they were said to be between .82 and .91. For Study 2 (n = 303), the composite reliability for the Social subscale was .82. The results for Study 3 were based on responses from customers of a furniture store (n = 323) and a car stereo center (n = 313) and the composite reliabilities for the Social subscale were .92 and .91, respectively.

VALIDITY: Beyond the validation described above, Sweeney and Soutar (2001) tested the psychometric quality of the instrument in the three studies using the typical procedures expected with confirmatory factor analysis. Each time the four-factor model was supported over competing ones. Repeatedly there was strong evidence of each scale's convergent and discriminant validities.

REFERENCES:
Soutar, Geoffrey N. (2004), Personal Correspondence.
Sweeney, Jillian C. and Geoffrey N. Soutar (2001), "Consumer Perceived Value: The Development of a Multiple Item Scale," *JR*, 77 (Summer), 203–220.

SCALE ITEMS: [1]

1. _____ would help me to feel acceptable.

2. _____ would improve the way I am perceived.

3. _____ would make a good impression on other people.

4. _____ would give its owner social approval.

---

[1] The name of the product should be placed in the blanks. A seven-point Likert-type response format was used (Soutar 2004).

SCALE NAME: Value (Transaction Enjoyment)

SCALE DESCRIPTION: Three, seven-point Likert-type items are used to measure the pleasure one feels in getting a good deal. The items suggest that not only is the person glad to be saving money but that a positive emotional reaction is felt. Further, the items assume the respondent has been exposed to some particular deal and is reacting to it as well as giving a sense of his/her enjoyment in getting similar deals.

SCALE ORIGIN: Although similar in some ways to previous measures (e.g., #237), this set of items appears to be original to Grewal, Monroe, and Krishnan (1998).

RELIABILITY: Grewal, Monroe, and Krishnan (1998) reported construct reliabilities of .85 (n = 361) and .85 (n = 328) for use of the scale in their first and second studies, respectively.

VALIDITY: A variety of evidence was provided by the authors from both studies in support of the scale's unidimensionality, convergent validity, and discriminant validity (Grewal, Monroe, and Krishnan 1998). Especially abundant was the evidence indicating the discriminant validity between this scale and one measuring another type of value (#493).

REFERENCES:

Grewal, Dhruv, Kent B. Monroe, and R. Krishnan (1998), "The Effects of Price-Comparison Advertising on Buyer's Perceptions of Acquisition Value, Transaction Value, and Behavioral Intentions," *JM*, 62 (April), 46–59.

SCALE ITEMS:

1. Taking advantage of a price-deal like this makes me feel good.

2. I would get a lot of pleasure knowing that I would save money at this reduced sale price.

3. Beyond the money I save, taking advantage of this price will give me a sense of joy.

SCALE NAME: Value (Travel Effort)

SCALE DESCRIPTION: The scale is composed of three, seven-point semantic differentials attempting to capture a consumer's sense of the value of the drive required to get to some specified retail store. The aspect being focused on appears to be whether the unpleasantness of the drive and the effort involved are viewed as worthwhile in order to be able to shop at the store. The measure was referred to by Soman (1998) as *perceived aversiveness of the effort*.

SCALE ORIGIN: The scale appears to be original to Soman (1998).

RELIABILITY: An alpha of .9384 was reported for the scale (Soman 1998).

VALIDITY: No evidence of the scale's validity was reported by Soman (1998).

REFERENCES:
Soman, Dilip (1998), "The Illusion of Delayed Incentives: Evaluating Future Effort-Money Transactions," *JMR*, 35 (November), 427–437.

SCALE ITEMS: [1]

The drive to the retail location is:

1. pleasant / aversive

2. not a waste of time / a waste of time

3. not at all effortful / extremely effortful

---

[1] Soman (1998) used a seven-point response scale with these semantic differentials such that the one on the left (above) received a 1 while the one on the right received a 7.

SCALE NAME: Value Consciousness

SCALE DESCRIPTION: A seven-item, seven-point Likert-type scale measuring the concern a consumer has for paying low prices contingent on some product quality expectations.

SCALE ORIGIN: The scale is original to Lichtenstein, Netemeyer, and Burton (1990). Five marketing academicians judged the appropriateness of 33 items generated to represent the construct. Eighteen items remained after this procedure. Based upon a second round of five additional judges assessing the face validity of the items, fifteen items were retained. The items were then interspersed throughout a questionnaire given to 263 undergraduate and graduate business students. The seven items composing the final version of the scale were those that had corrected item-total correlations equal to or greater than .40. Confirmatory factor analysis provided evidence that the items were unidimensional and had discriminant validity. The construct reliability was calculated to be .80.

RELIABILITY: As in the pretest, the internal consistency of the scale was calculated by Lichtenstein, Netemeyer, and Burton (1990) to be .80 and item-total correlations were above .40. The main study by Lichtenstein, Ridgway, and Netemeyer (1993) also showed an alpha for the scale of .82. Burton et al. (1998) reported an alpha of .86. In Study 1 by Burton, Lichtenstein, and Netemeyer (1999) an alpha of .86 was reported; in Study 2 it was merely reported to be greater than .85. Lastovicka et al. (1999) reported an alpha of .91.

VALIDITY: In the process of validating another scale (#26), Burton et al. (1998) conducted multiple tests of the scale's discriminant validity. The evidence provided support for a claim of discriminant validity for the Value Consciousness scale as well.

Lastovicka et al. (1999) used this scale in the process of validating another scale (#177). Based upon that, their data indicated that scores on the value consciousness scale were significantly related to frugality but not to a measure of response bias (#91).

Confirmatory factor analysis was used by Lichtenstein et al (1990, 1993) in both studies to conclude that the scale was unidimensional and showed evidence of discriminant validity.

REFERENCES:
Burton, Scot, Donald R. Lichtenstein, and Richard G. Netemeyer (1999), "Exposure to Sales Flyers and Increased Purchases in Retail Supermarkets," *JAR*, 39 (September/October), 7–14.

Burton, Scot, Donald R. Lichtenstein, Richard G. Netemeyer, and Judith A. Garretson (1998), "A Scale for Measuring Attitude Toward Private Label Products and an Examination of Its Psychological and Behavioral Correlates," *JAMS*, 26 (4), 293–306.

Lastovicka, John L., Lance A. Bettencourt, Renee Shaw Hughner, and Ronald J. Kuntze (1999), "Lifestyle of the Tight and Frugal: Theory and Measurement," *JCR*, 26 (June), 85–98.

Lichtenstein, Donald R., Richard D. Netemeyer, and Scot Burton (1990), "Distinguishing Coupon Proneness From Value Consciousness: An Acquisition-Transaction Utility Theory Perspective," *JM*, 54 (July), 54–67.

Lichtenstein, Donald R., Nancy M. Ridgway, and Richard G. Netemeyer (1993), "Price Perceptions and Consumer Shopping Behavior: A Field Study," *JMR*, 30 (May), 234–245.

SCALE ITEMS:

1. I am very concerned about low prices, but I am equally concerned about product quality.

2. When grocery shopping, I compare the prices of different brands to be sure I get the best value for the money.

3. When purchasing a product, I always try to maximize the quality I get for the money I spend.

4. When I buy products, I like to be sure that I am getting my money's worth.

5. I generally shop around for lower prices on products, but they still must meet certain quality requirements before I buy them.

6. When I shop, I usually compare the "price per ounce" information for brands I normally buy.

7. I always check the prices at the grocery store to be sure I get the best value for the money I spend.

SCALE NAME: Values (Self)

SCALE DESCRIPTION: The scale is composed of several phrases that appear to capture the degree to which a person places importance on values related directly to self such as self-respect, self-fulfillment, and a sense of accomplishment. Shim and Eastlick (1998) referred to this scale as *self-actualizing*.

SCALE ORIGIN: The scale used by Corfman, Lehmann, and Narayanan (1991) seems to be original to their study but the items themselves come from the List of Values (LOV) developed by Kahle (1983). Nine values composed LOV but the analysis conducted by Corfman, Lehmann, and Narayanan (1991) indicated that the three values specified below were tapping into the same factor.

Likewise, Shim and Eastlick (1998) factor analyzed the nine LOV items and found two factors. Five items had loadings on this factor (>.61), three loaded on the other factor (#501), and one was excluded because of its high loadings on both factors.

RELIABILITY: An alpha of .74 (n = 735) was reported for the version of the scale used by Corfman, Lehmann, and Narayanan (1991). Shim and Eastlick (1998) reported an alpha of .86 for their version of the scale.

VALIDITY: Corfman, Lehmann, and Narayanan (1991) factor analyzed the items composing LOV and settled on a three factor solution that accounted for 64% of the variance. The items composing this scale all had high loadings on the second factor providing some evidence of the scale's unidimensionality.

In addition to conducting an exploratory factor analysis, Shim and Eastlick (1998) used LISREL to examine the measurement model. They arrived at a two factor solution. The standardized loadings on this factor were reasonably high and significant. The variance extracted was .564.

COMMENTS: In analyzing the nine LOV items, a two factor solution was used by Shim and Eastlick (1998) whereas a three factor solution was used by both Corfman, Lehmann, and Narayanan (1991) as well as Homer and Kahle (1988). For this reason, the Shim and Eastlick (1998) version of the scale combines items that were part of two factors in the other studies. All three studies should be examined closely in addition to the original work by Kahle (1983) before deciding which items to use in future studies for measuring this construct.

REFERENCES:

Corfman, Kim P., Donald R. Lehmann, and Sunder Narayanan (1991), "Values, Utility, and Ownership: Modeling the Relationships for Consumer Durables," *JR*, 67 (Summer), 184–204.

Homer, Pamela M. and Lynn R. Kahle (1988), "A Structural Equation Test of the Value-Attitude-Behavior Hierarchy," *Journal of Personality and Social Psychology*, 54 (4), 638–646.

Kahle, Lynn R., ed. (1983), *Social Values and Social Change*, New York: Praeger Publishers.

Shim, Soyeon and Mary Ann Eastlick (1998), "The Hierarchical Influence of Personal Values on Mall Shopping Attitude and Behavior," *JR*, 74 (1), 139–160.

#500 *Values (Self)*

SCALE ITEMS: [1]

1. self-respect

2. sense of accomplishment

3. self-fulfillment

4. security

5. being well-respected

---

[1] Shim and Eastlick (1998) used all of the items whereas Corfman, Lehmann, and Narayanan (1991) used just the first three. The anchors used by Shim and Eastlick (1998) were *not important at all* (1) and *extremely important* (7). A six-point response format was used by Corfman, Lehmann, and Narayanan (1991) but the anchors were not specified.

SCALE NAME: Values (Social)

SCALE DESCRIPTION: The scale is composed of three, seven-point Likert-type phrases that appear to capture the degree to which a person places importance on socially-related values such as belongingness and friendly relationships. Shim and Eastlick (1998) referred to this scale as *social affiliation*.

SCALE ORIGIN: The scale used by Shim and Eastlick (1998) seems to be original to their study but the items themselves come from the List of Values (LOV) developed by Kahle (1983). Shim and Eastlick (1998) factor analyzed the nine LOV items and found two factors. Three items had loadings on this factor ($\geq$ .60), five loaded on the other factor (#500) and one was excluded because of its high loadings on both factors.

RELIABILITY: Shim and Eastlick (1998) reported an alpha of .76 for their version of the scale.

VALIDITY: In addition to conducting an exploratory factor analysis, Shim and Eastlick (1998) used LISREL to examine the measurement model. The standardized loadings on this factor were reasonably high and significant. The variance extracted was .536.

COMMENTS: The face validity of this set of items is suspect since item #1 does not "fit" with the other two in terms of its meaning. Further, factor analyses by others do not show these items being unidimensional (e.g., Corfman, Lehmann, and Narayanan 1991; Homer and Kahle 1988; and, Kahle 1983.) Further analysis of this set of items appears to be called for before it is used in future research.

REFERENCES:

Corfman, Kim P., Donald R. Lehmann, and Sunder Narayanan (1991), "Values, Utility, and Ownership: Modeling the Relationships for Consumer Durables," *JR*, 67 (Summer), 184–204.

Homer, Pamela M. and Lynn R. Kahle (1988), "A Structural Equation Test of the Value-Attitude-Behavior Hierarchy," *Journal of Personality and Social Psychology*, 54 (4), 638–646.

Kahle, Lynn R., ed. (1983), *Social Values and Social Change*, New York: Praeger Publishers.

Shim, Soyeon and Mary Ann Eastlick (1998), "The Hierarchical Influence of Personal Values on Mall Shopping Attitude and Behavior," *JR*, 74 (1), 139–160.

SCALE ITEMS: [1]

1. Excitement

2. Sense of belonging

3. Friendly relationships with others

[1] The anchors used by Shim and Eastlick (1998) were *not important at all* (1) and *extremely important* (7).

SCALE NAME: Variety-Seeking Tendency

SCALE DESCRIPTION: It is a three-item, five-point Likert-type summated ratings scale measuring the degree to which a person expresses a desire to try new and different things.

SCALE ORIGIN: The source of the scale was not stated by Donthu and Gilliland (1996) but it is likely to be original to their study.

RELIABILITY: Alphas of .87 (Donthu and Gilliland 1996) and .84 (Donthu and Garcia 1999) have been reported for the scale.

VALIDITY: No specific examination of the scale's validity was reported by Donthu and Gilliland (1996).

REFERENCES:
Donthu, Naveen and Adriana Garcia (1999), "The Internet Shopper," *JAR*, 39 (May/June), 52–58.
Donthu, Naveen and David Gilliland (1996), "The Infomercial Shopper," *JAR*, 36 (March/April), 69–76.

SCALE ITEMS:

1. I like to try different things.

2. I like a great deal of variety.

3. I like new and different styles.

SCALE NAME: Verbal-Visual Processing Style

SCALE DESCRIPTION: The full version of the scale has twenty-two statements measuring a person's preference for processing information in either a verbal or a visual modality. The measure was referred to as the *Style of Processing (SOP)* scale by Childers, Houston, and Heckler (1985).

SCALE ORIGIN: The scale is original to Childers, Houston, and Heckler (1985). The measure was developed after work with another measure, the Verbal-Visualizer Questionnaire (VVQ, Richardson 1977) failed to have satisfactory reliability or dimensionality. Thirty-six new items were generated in addition to using six from the VVQ. After administering the 42-item scale to 35 undergraduate students, item-total correlations were used to construct the final 22-item scale. Half of the items tapped the visual component and the other half tapped the verbal component. This final version of the scale included the six items from the VVQ.

The version of the scale used by Bezjian-Avery, Calder, and Iacobucci (1998) had only eight items. They did not indicate the reasoning for use of those particular items.

RELIABILITY: Bezjian-Avery, Calder, and Iacobucci (1998) reported an alpha of .88 (n = 96) for the overall scale.

An alpha of .88 (n = 54) was reported by Childers, Houston, and Heckler (1985) for the overall scale. The eleven items measuring the verbal component had an alpha of .81 and the eleven items measuring the visual component had an alpha of .86.

The overall scale had an alpha of .73 (n = 124) and alphas of .72 and .73 were calculated for the verbal and visual subscales, respectively, by Miller and Marks (1992; Marks 1994). Likewise, Burns, Biwas, and Babin (1993) reported alphas of .75 and .74 for the verbal and visual subscales (n = 377), respectively.

An alpha of .70 was reported for the visual subscale by McQuarrie and Mick (1999).

VALIDITY: Evidence of the scale's discriminant validity came from the insignificant correlations with two measures of processing ability (not style) by Childers, Houston, and Heckler (1985). It also had no correlation with a measure of social desirability. Criterion validity was evident due to the scale's significant correlations with measures of recall and recognition. None of the other studies reported any examination of the scale's validity.

McQuarrie and Mick (1999) intended to use the scale to distinguish between those who process verbally and those who process visually. Scores for the two subscales were expected to be somewhat opposite. Based on a pilot test, however, no linear association was found between them. Given this, they only used the visual subscale. This finding suggests that further testing of the scale is necessary.

COMMENTS: Although Childers, Houston, and Heckler (1985) preferred to compute a single score for the items in this scale, they did point out that some researchers might desire to treat the visual and verbal components as separate dimensions.

See also a revised version of the scale for which several forms of validity were provided (Heckler, Childers, and Houston 1993).

REFERENCES:
Bezjian-Avery, Alexa, Bobby Calder, and Dawn Iacobucci (1998), "New Media Interactive Advertising vs. Traditional Advertising," *JAR*, 38 (July/August), 23–32.
Burns, Alvin C., Abhijit Biwas, and Laurie A. Babin (1993), "The Operation of Visual Imagery as a Mediator of Advertising Effects," *JA*, 22 (June), 71–85.

Childers, Terry L., Michael J. Houston, and Susan E. Heckler (1985), "Measurement of Individual Differences in Visual Versus Verbal Information Processing," *JCR*, 12 (September), 125–134.

Heckler, Susan E., Terry L. Childers, and Michael J. Houston (1993), "On the Construct Validity of the SOP Scale," *Journal of Mental Imagery*, 17 (3 & 4), 119–132.

Marks, Lawrence J., (1994), Personal Correspondence.

McQuarrie, Edward F. and David Glen Mick (1999), "Visual Rhetoric in Advertising: Text-Interpretive, Experimental, and Reader-Response Analyses," *JCR*, 26 (June), 37–54.

Miller, Darryl W. and Lawrence J. Marks (1992), "Mental Imagery and Sound Effects in Radio Commercials," *JA*, 21 (4), 83–93.

Richardson, Alan (1977), "Verbalizer-Visualizer: A Cognitive Style Dimension," *Journal of Mental Imagery*, 1 (1), 109–125.

SCALE ITEMS: [1]

Directions: The aim of this exercise is to determine the style or manner you use when carrying out different mental tasks. Your answers to the questions should reflect the manner in which you typically engage in each of the tasks mentioned. There are no right or wrong answers, we only ask that you provide honest and accurate answers. Please answer each question by circling one of the four possible responses. For example, if I provided the statement, "I seldom read books," and this was your typical behavior, even though you might read say one book a year, you would circle the "ALWAYS TRUE" response.

1. I enjoy dong work that requires the use of words. (W)

2. There are some special times in my life that I like to relive by mentally "picturing" just how everything looked. (P) (r)

3. I can never seem to find the right word when I need it. (W) (r)

4. I do a lot of reading. (W)

5. When I'm trying to learn something new, I'd rather watch a demonstration than read how to do it. (P) (r)

6. I think I often use words in the wrong way. (W) (r)

7. I enjoy learning new words. (W)

8. I like to picture how I could fix up my apartment or a room if I could buy anything I wanted. (P) (r)

9. I often make written notes to myself. (W)

10. I like to daydream. (P) (r)

11. I generally prefer to use a diagram than a written set of instructions. (P) (r)

12. I like to "doodle". (P) (r)

13. I find it helps to think in terms of mental pictures when doing many things. (P) (r)

14. After I meet someone for the first time, I can usually remember what they look like, but not much about them. (P) (r)

15. I like to think of synonyms for words. (W)

16. When I have forgotten something, I frequently try to form a mental picture to remember it. (P) (r)

17. I like learning new words. (W)

18. I prefer to read instructions about how to do something rather than have someone show me. (W)

19. I prefer activities that don't require a lot of reading. (W) (r)

20. I seldom daydream. (P)

21. I spend very little time attempting to increase my vocabulary. (W) (r)

22. My thinking often consists of mental "pictures" or images. (P) (r)

[1] (W) = Verbal Items, (P) = Visual Items. Childers, Houston, and Heckler (1985) used a four-point response scale ranging from *always true* (1) to *always false* (4). Burns, Biwas, and Babin (1993) apparently used a seven-point response scale with the items. Bezjian-Avery, Calder, and Iacobucci (1998) used items 1, 3, 5, 10, 11, 18, 19, and 22. Only the visual items were ultimately used by McQuarrie and Mick (1999).

SCALE NAME: Visualizing Ease

SCALE DESCRIPTION: The three-item, seven-point semantic-differential is intended to assess the ease with which a stimulus has evoked visual images. The scale was used as a manipulation check in an experiment by Shiv and Fedorikhin (1999) with two snacks, chocolate cake and fruit salad, to see if the presentation mode of the snacks (real versus photographs) made a difference in the ease with which subjects could see themselves eating the snack. The scale was referred to as *vividness* by Shiv and Fedorikhin (1999).

SCALE ORIGIN: Shiv and Fedorikhin (1999) developed the scale by drawing upon the one-item measures used previously (Keller and Block 1997; McGill and Anand 1989).

RELIABILITY: Alphas of .81 and .79 were reported for the scale as used with cake and fruit salad, respectively (Shiv and Fedorikhin 1999).

VALIDITY: No examination of the scale's validity was reported by Shiv and Fedorikhin (1999). However, some evidence of the scale's validity is implied in the finding that visualizing was significantly more likely with real snacks compared to photographs.

REFERENCES:

Keller, Punam Anand and Lauren G. Block (1997), "Vividness Effects: A Resource-Matching Perspective," *JCR*, 24 (December), 295–304.

McGill, Ann and Punam Anand Keller (1989), "The Effect of Vivid Attributes on the Evaluation of Alternatives: The Role of Differential Attention and Cognitive Elaboration," *JCR*, 16 (September), 188–196.

Shiv, Baba and Alexander Fedorikhin (1999), "Heart and Mind in Conflict: The Interplay of Affect and Cognition in Consumer Decision Making," *JCR*, 26 (December), 278–292.

SCALE ITEMS: [1]

1. not easy to visualize myself consuming the _____ / easy to visualize myself consuming the _____

2. not easy to imagine myself consuming the _____ / easy to imagine myself consuming the _____

3. not easy to picture myself consuming the _____ / easy to picture myself consuming the _____

[1] The name of the food item should be placed in the blanks.

SCALE NAME: Volunteerism (Perceived Group Need)

SCALE DESCRIPTION: The scale is composed of four, seven-point Likert-type statements measuring the degree to which a person thinks that a nonprofit organization needs his/her help.

SCALE ORIGIN: Although not explicitly stated in the article, the scale appears to be original to Fisher and Ackerman (1998).

RELIABILITY: An alpha of .86 was reported for the scale by Fisher and Ackerman (1998).

VALIDITY: The scale's validity was not explicitly tested by Fisher and Ackerman (1998).

REFERENCES:
Fisher, Robert J. (2000), Personal Correspondence.
Fisher, Robert J. and David Ackerman (1998), "The Effects of Recognition and Group Need on Volunteerism: A Social Norm Perspective," *JCR*, 25 (December), 262–275.

SCALE ITEMS: [1]

Based on the poster, I think that:

1. the _____ really needs my help.

2. every person who volunteers will make a difference.

3. I would make a difference by volunteering my time.

4. my contribution to the _____ is important.

---

[1] The items and scale stem were provided by Fisher (2000). The name of the nonprofit entity should go in the blanks. The scale stem appears to be amenable for change for other situations, e.g., "based on my experience..."

SCALE NAME: Volunteerism (Recognition)

SCALE DESCRIPTION: The scale is composed of four, seven-point Likert-type statements measuring the degree to which a person thinks that those people who volunteer to help raise funds for a nonprofit organization are properly rewarded for their effort.

SCALE ORIGIN: Although not explicitly stated in the article, the scale appears to be original to Fisher and Ackerman (1998).

RELIABILITY: An alpha of .90 was reported for the scale by Fisher and Ackerman (1998).

VALIDITY: The scale's validity was not explicitly tested by Fisher and Ackerman (1998). However, given that the scale was used to show that recognition of volunteerism was successfully manipulated in the experiment some evidence of its predictive validity was provided.

REFERENCES:
Fisher, Robert J. (2000), Personal Correspondence.
Fisher, Robert J. and David Ackerman (1998), "The Effects of Recognition and Group Need on Volunteerism: A Social Norm Perspective," *JCR*, 25 (December), 262–275.

SCALE ITEMS: [1]

Based on the poster, I think that:

1. the _____ shows its appreciation to those who volunteer.

2. fundraising volunteers receive special recognition for their help.

3. the _____ rewards fundraising volunteers.

4. volunteers are properly thanked by the _____.

---

[1] The items and scale stem were provided by Fisher (2000). The name of the nonprofit entity should go in the blanks. The scale stem appears to be amenable for changing to something more broadly applicable such as "based on my experience..."

SCALE NAME: Volunteerism (Social Approval Expectations)

SCALE DESCRIPTION: The scale is composed of four, ten-point items measuring the degree of approval or disapproval a person thinks would be received from various parties if he/she volunteered to help a particular nonprofit organization.

SCALE ORIGIN: Although not explicitly stated in the article, the scale appears to be original to Fisher and Ackerman (1998).

RELIABILITY: An alpha of .81 was reported for the scale by Fisher and Ackerman (1998).

VALIDITY: The scale's validity was not explicitly tested by Fisher and Ackerman (1998).

COMMENTS: The organization studied by Fisher and Ackerman (1998) was a business college at a major university. Some modification in the items will be necessary if the scale is to be used for a non-academic entity.

REFERENCES:
Fisher, Robert J. (2000), Personal Correspondence.
Fisher, Robert J. and David Ackerman (1998), "The Effects of Recognition and Group Need on Volunteerism: A Social Norm Perspective," *JCR*, 25 (December), 262–275.

SCALE ITEMS: [1]

If you volunteered for the _____, would people in each of the following groups disapprove or approve of your decision?

1. your friends at _____?

2. other volunteers?

3. other _____ students?

4. _____ faculty?

[1] The items and scale stem were provided by Fisher (2000). The response scale ranged from *strongly disapprove* (0) to *strongly approve* (9). The university name was used in the blanks of the items whereas the name for the fundraising organization involved with the business college was used in the blank of the scale stem.

#508 *Vulnerability (Health)*

SCALE NAME: Vulnerability (Health)

SCALE DESCRIPTION: The three-item scale is intended to measure a person's sense of the probability that he/she will contract a certain illness or disease.

SCALE ORIGIN: The scale is original to Luce and Kahn (1999). They used a one-item version of the scale in their earlier studies (reported in the article) with the final study using the multi-item version.

RELIABILITY: An alpha of .87 was reported for the scale (Luce and Kahn 1999).

VALIDITY: Luce and Kahn (1999) did not examine the validity of the scale. However, they did state that the scale had a correlation of .82 with the one item measure they had used.

REFERENCES:
Kahn, Barbara E. (2002), Personal Correspondence.
Luce, Mary Frances and Barbara E. Kahn (1999), "Avoidance or Vigilance? The Psychology of False-Positive Test Results," *JCR*, 26 (December), 242–259.

SCALE ITEMS: [1]

1. How likely do you think it would be that you will be diagnosed with _____. More likely that I WILL NOT BE DIAGNOSED with _____. / More likely that I WILL BE DIAGNOSED with _____.

2. Are you more or LESS likely to get _____. I am MORE likely to get _____. / I am LESS likely to get _____.

3. Think about your behavior and lifestyle one more time. How vulnerable are you, personally, to _____. I am NOT vulnerable AT ALL. / I am VERY vulnerable.

---

[1] Items provided by Kahn (2002). The blanks should be used to explicate the disease, illness, or problem of concern as well as the target audience. In the case of Luce and Kahn (1999), the disease was Chlamydia and the audience was students at a particular university.

SCALE NAME: Website Visit Intention

SCALE DESCRIPTION: The three, seven-point Likert-type statements are used to measure a person's inclination to return to a website. The implication is that the person is already familiar with the website based upon one or more exposures to it. Due to one of its items, the scale also taps into the degree to which one would recommend a website to others.

SCALE ORIGIN: Coyle and Thorson (2001) did not cite any previous study as the source of the first two items (shown below) but borrowed the last item from Kim and Biocca (1997) who used it as a single-item measure. Thus, as a summated measure, this scale appears to be original to Coyle and Thorson (2001).

RELIABILITY: An alpha of .75 (n = 68) was reported for the scale (Coyle and Thorson 2001).

VALIDITY: No examination of the scale's validity was reported by Coyle and Thorson (2001).

REFERENCES:
Coyle, James R. and Esther Thorson (2001), "The Effects of Progressive Levels of Interactivity and Vividness in Web Marketing Sites," *JA*, 30 (Fall), 65–77.
Kim, Taeyong and Frank Biocca (1997), "Telepresence via Television: Two Dimensions of Telepresence May Have Different Connections to Memory and Persuasion," *Journal of Computer-Mediated Communication*, 3 (September), http://www.ascusc.org/jcmc/vol3/issue2/kim.html.

SCALE ITEMS: [1]

1. It is very likely that I will return to this site.

2. I will return to this site the next time I need a _____.

3. Suppose that a friend called you last night to get your advice in his/her search for a _____. Would you recommend him/her to visit _____'s website?

---

[1] The anchors for the first two items were *agree/disagree* whereas the anchors for the third item was *absolutely / absolutely not* (Coyle and Thorson 2001). Also, the blank at the end of item #2 as well as the first blank in item #3 should contain the name of the product category while the second blank in item #3 should have the name of the brand.

SCALE NAME: Willingness To Be Tested (Health)

SCALE DESCRIPTION: The scale is composed of three statements intended to measure a person's sense of the likelihood that he/she would get a specified medical test. Although similar to a measure of behavioral intention, this scale is assessing something more hypothetical. The phrasing of the items indicate the respondent is to imagine what he/she *might do* under certain conditions with respect to the focal behavior whereas intention scales usually attempt to measure what the person actually *plans to do*.

SCALE ORIGIN: The scale is original to Luce and Kahn (1999). They used a one-item version of the scale in their earlier studies (reported in the article) with the final study using the multi-item version.

RELIABILITY: An alpha of .87 was reported for the scale (Luce and Kahn 1999).

VALIDITY: Luce and Kahn (1999) did not examine the validity of the scale. However, they did state that the scale had a correlation of .70 with the one item measure they had used.

REFERENCES:
Kahn, Barbara E. (2002), Personal Correspondence.
Luce, Mary Frances and Barbara E. Kahn (1999), "Avoidance or Vigilance? The Psychology of False-Positive Test Results" *JCR*, 26 (December), 242–259.

SCALE ITEMS: [1]

1. If it was possible for you to get a confidential and low cost appointment to see a doctor and get a _____ test, please indicate how likely you would be to do so.
   I would definitely NOT GET tested for _____. / I would definitely GET tested for _____.

2. Again, imagine you could get a confidential, low cost _____. Please indicate whether you are MORE or LESS likely than other _____ to get the test.
   I am MORE likely to get tested. / I am LESS likely to get tested.

3. If you could get a confidential, low cost _____ test, would you think it was an important thing for you to go ahead and do? That is, would you make getting the test a priority?
   It would NOT be important to me to get tested. / It would be VERY important to me to get tested.

[1] Items provided by Kahn (2002). The blanks should be used to explicate the disease, illness, or problem of concern. In the case of Luce and Kahn (1999), the disease was Chlamydia. The second blank in item #2 named a reference group for respondents to compare themselves to (e.g., other students at a specified university).

SCALE NAME: Word-of-Mouth Intentions (Positive)

SCALE DESCRIPTION: Three, seven-point statements are used to measure the extent to which a person (a client) expresses willingness to recommend a certain service provider to others. The type of service provider studied by Price and Arnould (1999) was a hairstylist.

SCALE ORIGIN: The scale appears to be original to Price and Arnould (1999).

RELIABILITY: An alpha of .95 was reported for the scale by Price and Arnould (1999).

VALIDITY: No information about the scale's validity was provided by Price and Arnould (1999).

REFERENCES:
Price, Linda L. and Eric J. Arnould (1999), "Commercial Friendships: Service Provider-Client Relationships in Context," *JM*, 63 (October), 38–56.

SCALE ITEMS: [1]

1. I would recommend this _____ to someone who seeks my advice.

2. I say positive things about this _____ to other people.

3. I would recommend this _____ to others.

[1] The term for the <u>category</u> of service provider should be placed in the blanks, e.g., hairstylist.

Part II

Advertising-Related Scales

SCALE NAME: Absurdity of the Ad

SCALE DESCRIPTION: The scale is composed of seven, seven-point uni-polar items used to measure a person's belief that a certain ad is bizarre and irrational. This attitude is likely to have been evoked because of the incongruous juxtaposition of stimuli in the ad (images, sounds, text) such that little or no logical interpretation is possible.

SCALE ORIGIN: The scale is original to Arias-Bolzmann, Chakraborty, and Mowen (2000). Using the items from a previous version of the scale (Arias-Bolzmann and Mowen 1992), several more items were added and then evaluated in a pretest to the main study. The fourteen-item set was reduced to the seven listed here.

RELIABILITY: An alpha of .86 was reported for the scale by Arias-Bolzmann, Chakraborty, and Mowen (2000).

VALIDITY: No explicit examination of the scale's validity was made by Arias-Bolzmann, Chakraborty, and Mowen (2000). However, the scale was used as a manipulation check and, indeed, there was a significant difference between the groups that were exposed to ads supposed to be absurd and those exposed to ads not expected to be absurd. Since the former group rated their ads as more absurd than the latter group this provides some limited evidence of the scale's predictive validity.

REFERENCES:

Arias-Bolzmann, Leopoldo (2002), Personal Correspondence.

Arias-Bolzmann, Leopoldo and John C. Mowen (1992), "Absurd Images in Cigarette Advertising: An Empirical Investigation," in *Marketing: Perspectives for the 1990s*, Robert L. King, ed., Southern Marketing Association 295–299.

Arias-Bolzmann, Leopoldo, Goutam Chakraborty, and John C. Mowen (2000), "Effects of Absurdity in Advertising: The Moderating Role of Product Category Attitude and the Mediating Role of Cognitive Responses," *JA*, 29 (1), 35–48.

SCALE ITEMS: [1]

1. bizarre

2. unique

3. unusual

4. illogical

5. absurd

6. comical

7. unreal

---

[1] A seven-point Likert-type response format was used with these items (Arias-Bolzmann 2002).

SCALE NAME: Ad Preference Index

SCALE DESCRIPTION: The scale is composed of seven forced-choice statements assessing the preference a person has for one of two advertisements to which he/she has been exposed, both promoting the same product.

SCALE ORIGIN: Brunel and Nelson (2001) modified a measure used previously by Snyder and DeBono (1985). The latter called their scale an *index of favorability toward advertisements*. It had twelve items but only three were identified in the article. The estimates of internal consistency on the forced-choice index (KR-20) ranged from .91 to .95.

RELIABILITY: The alpha for the scale was reported to be greater than .85 (Brunel and Nelson 2001).

VALIDITY: No examination of the scale's validity was reported by Brunel and Nelson (2001). The items were said, however, to have loaded on the same factor.

COMMENTS: As used by Brunel and Nelson (2001), responses to the items were coded as 1 or 0 depending upon which advertisement a person chose. A summated score was then calculated with the possible range being 0 to 7.

Item 6 (below) and possibly 7 will have to be modified or eliminated if this scale is used with ads for something other than a charitable organization.

REFERENCES:
Brunel, Frederic F. and Michelle R. Nelson (2001), "Explaining Gendered Responses to 'Help-Self' and 'Help-Others' Charity Ad Appeals: The Mediating Role of World-Views," *JA*, 29 (3), 15–28.
Snyder, Mark and Kenneth G. DeBono (1985), "Appeals to Image and Claims About Quality: Understanding the Psychology of Advertising," *Journal of Personality and Social Psychology*, 49 (3), 586–597.

SCALE ITEMS:

1. Overall, which ad do you think is better?

2. Which one appeals to you more?

3. Which ad do you think would be more successful?

4. Which ad do you think will stick in people's minds more?

5. For products of this type, which ad do you think is more typical of the way this product is sold?

6. If you were considering donating to this organization, which ad would be more likely to convince you to donate?

7. Which ad do you think would create a more favorable image of the organization?

SCALE NAME: Ad Usage

SCALE DESCRIPTION: The scale is composed of four, five-point Likert-type statements measuring the extent to which a consumer reports consulting advertisements before making purchase decisions in order to make "better" decisions.

SCALE ORIGIN: The scale used by Bush, Smith, and Martin (1999) was directly adapted from a scale by Bearden, Netemeyer, and Teel (1989). (See #191 in V. III.) Whereas the latter's scale had to do with one's tendency to seek information about products by observing others' behavior, the former's involves seeking information from advertising.

RELIABILITY: An alpha of .80 was reported for the scale by Bush, Smith, and Martin (1999).

VALIDITY: No examination of the scale's validity was reported by Bush, Smith, and Martin (1999).

REFERENCES:

Bearden, William O., Richard G. Netemeyer, and Jesse E. Teel (1989), "Measurement of Consumer Susceptibility to Interpersonal Influence," *JCR*, 15 (March), 473–481.

Bush, Alan J., Rachel Smith, and Craig Martin (1999), "The Influence of Consumer Socialization Variables on Attitude Toward Advertising: A Comparison of African-Americans and Caucasians," *JA*, 28 (3), 13–24.

Martin, Craig A. (2001), Personal Correspondence.

SCALE ITEMS: [1]

1. To make sure I buy the right product or brand, I often look at advertisements to see what others are buying and using.

2. If I have little experience with a product, I often check with advertisements.

3. I often consult advertisements to help choose the best alternative available from a product class.

4. I often gather information from advertisements about products before I buy.

[1] The statements were provided by Martin (2001).

SCALE NAME: Ad-Evoked Image (Spirited)

SCALE DESCRIPTION: The scale is composed of three, seven-point unipolar descriptors and measures the extent to which an advertisement triggers a visual image with a sense of vigor and youthfulness.

SCALE ORIGIN: Hung (2001) cited a working paper by Batra (1997) as the source of 36 items for measuring image responses. All 36 items were used in the study but in the final analysis only the 11 items which were found to compose viable factors were used to make scales.

RELIABILITY: An alpha of .93 was reported for the scale (Hung 2001).

VALIDITY: Hung (2001) did not report an explicit examination of the scale's validity but some limited evidence was provided. A factor analysis of 36 image items produced four factors, one of which was the one shown here. In addition, it had an average variance extracted of .81.

REFERENCES:

Batra, Rajeev (1997), "Building Brand Equity through Advertising," working paper, University of Michigan Business School.

Hung, Kineta (2001), "Framing Meaning Perceptions with Music: The Case of Teaser Ads," *Journal of Advertising*, 30 (3), 39–49.

SCALE ITEMS: [1]

Directions: The images and personalities projected in the commercial are . . .

1. pioneering

2. youthful

3. spirited

---

[1] A seven-point response format was used by Hung (2001) but the anchors were not described. They could have been of the *agree / disagree* type.

SCALE NAME: Ad-Evoked Image (Successful)

SCALE DESCRIPTION: Four, uni-polar descriptors are used to measure the degree to which an advertisement triggers a visual image with aspects of status and achievement.

SCALE ORIGIN: Hung (2001) cited a working paper by Batra (1997) as the source of 36 items for measuring image responses. All 36 items were used in the study but in the final analysis only the 11 items which were found to compose viable factors were used to make scales.

RELIABILITY: An alpha of .97 was reported for the scale (Hung 2001).

VALIDITY: Hung (2001) did not report an explicit examination of the scale's validity but some limited evidence was provided. A factor analysis of 36 image items produced four factors, one of which was the one shown here. In addition, it had an average variance extracted of .89.

REFERENCES:

Batra, Rajeev (1997), "Building Brand Equity through Advertising," working paper, University of Michigan Business School.

Hung, Kineta (2001), "Framing Meaning Perceptions with Music: The Case of Teaser Ads," *Journal of Advertising*, 30 (3), 39–49.

SCALE ITEMS: [1]

The images and personalities projected in the commercial are . . .

1. upper- class

2. shrewd

3. successful

4. clever

[1] A seven-point response format was used by Hung (2001) but the anchors were not described. They could have been of an *agree / disagree* style.

SCALE NAME: Advertising Avoidance (Direct Mail)

SCALE DESCRIPTION: The scale is composed of three, seven-point items intended to measure the extent to which a person reports engaging in behaviors that indicate he/she tries to avoid direct mail advertising.

SCALE ORIGIN: The scale appears to be original to Elliot and Speck (1998). In their earlier article based upon the same data they presented similar scales for other media (Speck and Elliot 1997).

RELIABILITY: An alpha of .62 (n = 946) was reported for the scale by Elliot and Speck (1998).

VALIDITY: No examination of the scale's validity was reported by Elliot and Speck (1998).

COMMENTS: The internal consistency of the scale is low. Further work is called for to improve its psychometric qualities.

REFERENCES:

Elliott, Michael T. and Paul Surgi Speck (1998), "Consumer Perceptions of Advertising Clutter and Its Impact Across Various Media," *JAR*, 38 (January/February), 29–41.
Speck, Paul Surgi and Michael T. Elliot (1997), "Predictors of Advertising Avoidance in Print and Broadcast Media," *JA*, 26 (Fall), 61–76.

SCALE ITEMS: [1]

How often do you . . .

1. ask companies to take you off their mailing lists?

2. discard "bulk rate" mail without opening it?

3. discard the promotional material in your monthly statement without reading it?

[1] The response format used by Elliot and Speck (1998) was a seven-point scale anchored by *never* (1) and *always* (7).

SCALE NAME: Advertising Avoidance (Magazines)

SCALE DESCRIPTION: The scale is composed of three, seven-point items measuring the extent to which a person reports engaging in behaviors that indicate he/she tries to avoid ads appearing in magazines.

SCALE ORIGIN: The scale appears to be original to Speck and Elliot (1997). They imply that the measures used in their main study had undergone a great deal of refinement since they were "based on previous research, input from academic and industry reviewers, and two pretests" (p. 67).

RELIABILITY: An alpha of .66 (n = 946) was reported for the scale by Speck and Elliot (1997; Elliot and Speck 1998).

VALIDITY: No examination of the scale's validity was reported by Speck and Elliot (1997; Elliot and Speck 1998).

COMMENTS: The article by Elliot and Speck (1998) appears to be based upon the same data as used by Speck and Elliot (1997). The internal consistency of the scale is low enough to justify caution in its use until its psychometric quality can be improved.

REFERENCES:
Elliott, Michael T. and Paul Surgi Speck (1998), "Consumer Perceptions of Advertising Clutter and Its Impact Across Various Media," *JAR*, 38 (January/February), 29–41.
Speck, Paul Surgi and Michael T. Elliot (1997), "Predictors of Advertising Avoidance in Print and Broadcast Media," *JA*, 26 (Fall), 61–76.

SCALE ITEMS: [1]

How often do you . . .

1. rip out or discard advertising inserts before reading a magazine?

2. flip past large advertising sections in a magazine?

3. ignore magazine ads?

---

[1] The response format used by Speck and Elliot (1997; Elliot and Speck 1998) was a seven-point scale anchored by *never* (1) and *always* (7).

SCALE NAME: Advertising Avoidance (Newspapers)

SCALE DESCRIPTION: The scale is composed of three, seven-point items measuring the extent to which a person reports engaging in behaviors that indicate he/she tries to avoid or ignore ads appearing in newspapers.

SCALE ORIGIN: The scale appears to be original to Speck and Elliot (1997). They imply that the measures used in their main study had undergone a great deal of refinement since they were "based on previous research, input from academic and industry reviewers, and two pretests" (p. 67).

RELIABILITY: An alpha of .89 (n = 946) was reported for the scale by Speck and Elliot (1997; Elliot and Speck 1998).

VALIDITY: No examination of the scale's validity was reported by Speck and Elliot (1997; Elliot and Speck 1998).

COMMENTS: The article by Elliot and Speck (1998) appears to be based upon the same data as used by Speck and Elliot (1997).

REFERENCES:

Elliott, Michael T. and Paul Surgi Speck (1998), "Consumer Perceptions of Advertising Clutter and Its Impact Across Various Media," *JAR*, 38 (January/February), 29–41.

Speck, Paul Surgi and Michael T. Elliot (1997), "Predictors of Advertising Avoidance in Print and Broadcast Media," *JA*, 26 (Fall), 61–76.

SCALE ITEMS: [1]

How often do you . . .

1. discard advertising inserts before you read a newspaper?

2. skip over newspaper pages that are mainly advertising?

3. ignore newspaper ads?

---

[1] The response format used by Speck and Elliot (1997; Elliot and Speck 1998) was a seven-point scale anchored by *never* (1) and *always* (7).

SCALE NAME: Advertising Avoidance (Radio)

SCALE DESCRIPTION: The scale is composed of three, seven-point items measuring the extent to which a person reports engaging in behaviors that indicate he/she tries to avoid listening to radio commercials.

SCALE ORIGIN: The scale appears to be original to Speck and Elliot (1997). They imply that the measures used in their main study had undergone a great deal of refinement since they were "based on previous research, input from academic and industry reviewers, and two pretests" (p. 67).

RELIABILITY: An alpha of .83 (n = 946) was reported for the scale by Speck and Elliot (1997; Elliot and Speck 1998).

VALIDITY: No examination of the scale's validity was reported by Speck and Elliot (1997; Elliot and Speck 1998).

COMMENTS: The article by Elliot and Speck (1998) appears to be based upon the same data as used by Speck and Elliot (1997).

REFERENCES:
Elliott, Michael T. and Paul Surgi Speck (1998), "Consumer Perceptions of Advertising Clutter and Its Impact Across Various Media," *JAR*, 38 (January/February), 29–41.
Speck, Paul Surgi and Michael T. Elliot (1997), "Predictors of Advertising Avoidance in Print and Broadcast Media," *JA*, 26 (Fall), 61–76.

SCALE ITEMS: [1]

How often do you . . .

1. switch radio stations during commercials?

2. skip past radio stations that are in commercial?

3. tune out radio commercials?

[1] The response format used by Speck and Elliot (1997; Elliot and Speck 1998) was a seven-point scale anchored by *never* (1) and *always* (7).

SCALE NAME: Advertising Avoidance (Television)

SCALE DESCRIPTION: The scale is composed of three, five-point Likert-type statements used to measure a person's dislike of TV commercials and the tendency to engage in behaviors to avoid exposure to them.

SCALE ORIGIN: The scale was developed by Gupta and Gould (1997) as part of a larger instrument examining a variety of issues related to the use of branded products in movies. The authors generated 30 items, had them reviewed by colleagues, and then pretested them with a small sample of college students. Based on that, some revision occurred and the final instrument was developed for use in their main study. Those results were factor analyzed and indicated the presence of seven factors. Reliabilities were checked for scales based on items with high loadings on those factors. Only the first four factors had alphas greater than .60 and were used further in their analyses. The alpha for the scale measuring TV ad avoidance was .66.

The sample in the Gupta and Gould (1997) study were Americans. That same set of data was incorporated into the study by Gould, Gupta, and Grabner-Kräuter (2000) where it was compared to findings with samples of French and Austrians. With the French sample, an English version of the instrument was used since the respondents were expected to understand the language. With the Austrian sample, the instrument was translated into German.

RELIABILITY: An alpha of .67 was reported for the scale by Gould, Gupta, and Grabner-Kräuter (2000).

VALIDITY: The validity of the scale was not explicitly addressed by Gould, Gupta, and Grabner-Kräuter (2000). However, they did indicate that separate factor analyses were run for the data from the three different countries. The same four factor structure was found in each case although the items composing each factor were not completely the same. Given that the purpose of their study was to make cross-cultural comparisons the authors decided to stick with the same scales as reported in Gupta and Gould (1997).

REFERENCES:

Gould, Stephen J., Pola B. Gupta, and Sonja Grabner-Kräuter (2000), "Product Placement in Movies: A Cross-Cultural Analysis of Austrian, French and American Consumers' Attitudes Toward This Emerging, International Promotional Medium," *JA*, 29 (Winter), 41–58.

Gupta, Pola B. and Stephen J. Gould (1997), "Consumers' Perceptions of the Ethics and Acceptability of Product Placements in Movies: Product Category and Individual Differences," *Journal of Current Issues & Research in Advertising*, 19 (Spring), 37–50.

SCALE ITEMS:

1. I hate watching ads on television.

2. While watching a TV program, I frequently flip channels to escape watching ads.

3. When an ad appears on my TV, I stop looking at the screen until the program starts again.

SCALE NAME: Advertising Avoidance (Television)

SCALE DESCRIPTION: The scale is composed of seven-point items measuring the extent to which a television viewer reports engaging in behaviors that indicate he/she is trying to avoid commercials when they come on.

SCALE ORIGIN: The scale appears to be original to Speck and Elliot (1997). They imply that the measures used in their main study had undergone a great deal of refinement since they were "based on previous research, input from academic and industry reviewers, and two pretests" (p. 67)

RELIABILITY: Alphas of .80 and .76 have been reported for the scale by Elliot and Speck (1998) and Speck and Elliot (1997), respectively.

VALIDITY: No examination of the scale's validity was reported by either Elliot and Speck (1998) or Speck and Elliot (1997).

COMMENTS: The article by Elliot and Speck (1998) appears to be based upon the same data as used by Speck and Elliot (1997).

REFERENCES:
Elliott, Michael T. and Paul Surgi Speck (1998), "Consumer Perceptions of Advertising Clutter and Its Impact across Various Media," *JAR*, 38 (January/February), 29–41.
Speck, Paul Surgi and Michael T. Elliot (1997), "Predictors of Advertising Avoidance in Print and Broadcast Media," *JA*, 26 (Fall), 61–76.

SCALE ITEMS: [1]

How often do you . . .

1. leave the room during TV commercials?

2. skip past TV channels that are in commercial?

3. tune out TV commercials?

4. switch TV channels during commercials?

5. lower the TV's volume during commercials?

---

[1] The response format used by both Elliot and Speck (1998) and Speck and Elliot (1997) was a seven-point scale anchored by *never* (1) and *always* (7). The latter used just three items in their version of the scale: #2–#4.

SCALE NAME: Affective Response to Ad (Approval)

SCALE DESCRIPTION: The scale is composed of nine, semantic differential phrases measuring a person's reaction to an ad he/she has been exposed to with the emphasis on the positive and/or pleasurable types of feelings that were experienced.

SCALE ORIGIN: Bhat, Leigh, and Wardlow (1998) conducted a pretest that exposed students to the ads used in the main study and asked them to write down thoughts and emotions they experienced while viewing the ads. These comments were independently coded by two people as falling into twelve emotion categories. Two items were selected for representing each of the twelve emotions and were employed in the main study.

RELIABILITY: An alpha of .893 was reported for the scale by Bhat, Leigh, and Wardlow (1998).

VALIDITY: No explicit examination of the scale's validity was reported by Bhat, Leigh, and Wardlow (1998). However, the 24 feeling items (referred to under Origin above) were subjected to exploratory factor analysis. The nine items of this scale loaded high on the same factor and provides a sense of their unidimensionality.

REFERENCES:
Bhat, Subodh, Thomas W. Leigh, and Daniel L. Wardlow (1998), "The Effect of Consumer Prejudices on Ad Processing: Heterosexual Consumers' Responses to Homosexual Imagery in Ads," *JA*, 27 (4), 9–28.

SCALE ITEMS:

1. not at all stimulated / very stimulated

2. not at all interested / very interested

3. not at all involved / very involved

4. not at all happy / very happy

5. not at all envious / very envious

6. not at all curious / very curious

7. not at all loving / very loving

8. not at all excited / very excited

9. not at all wishful / very wishful

SCALE NAME: Affective Response to Ad (Disapproval)

SCALE DESCRIPTION: The scale is composed of ten, semantic differential phrases measuring a person's reaction to an ad he/she has been exposed to with the emphasis on the negative types of feelings that were experienced.

SCALE ORIGIN: Bhat, Leigh, and Wardlow (1998) conducted a pretest that exposed students to the ads used in the main study and asked them to write down thoughts and emotions they experienced while viewing the ads. These comments were independently coded by two people as falling into twelve emotion categories. Two items were selected for representing each of the twelve emotions and were employed in the main study.

RELIABILITY: An alpha of .933 was reported for the scale by Bhat, Leigh, and Wardlow (1998).

VALIDITY: No explicit examination of the scale's validity was reported by Bhat, Leigh, and Wardlow (1998). However, the 24 feeling items (referred to under Origin above) were subjected to exploratory factor analysis. The ten items of this scale loaded high on the same factor and provides a sense of their unidimensionality.

REFERENCES:
Bhat, Subodh, Thomas W. Leigh, and Daniel L. Wardlow (1998), "The Effect of Consumer Prejudices on Ad Processing: Heterosexual Consumers' Responses to Homosexual Imagery in Ads," *JA*, 27 (4), 9–28.

SCALE ITEMS:

1. not at all skeptical / very skeptical

2. not at all disgusted / very disgusted

3. not at all contemptuous / very contemptuous

4. not at all angry / very angry

5. not at all distrustful / very distrustful

6. not at all irritated / very irritated

7. not at all uneasy / very uneasy

8. not at all scornful / very scornful

9. not at all revolted / very revolted

10. not at all worried / very worried

SCALE NAME: Affective Response to Ad (Negative Feelings)

SCALE DESCRIPTION: This measure is composed of several uni-polar items and is purported to measure the degree of negative feelings a consumer reports experiencing when exposed to a specific advertisement. The scale has been used over time with varying numbers of items.

There is an important distinction between this measure and one such as #562. As Mooradian stated in the directions used with his scale, subjects were to describe "reactions to the ad, not to how you would describe the ad" (1996, p. 101). Admittedly, there should be a high correspondence between the two but they are still theoretically distinct constructs.

SCALE ORIGIN: Madden, Allen, and Twible (1988) cited Abelson et al. (1982), Madden (1982), and Nowlis (1970) as sources of their items. Mooradian's (1996) version of the scale is very similar to one used by Goodstein, Edell, and Moore (1990). Ultimately, most of the items composing the various versions of the scale can be found in the Reaction Profile for TV Commercials developed by Wells, Leavitt and McConville (1971). Aylesworth, Goodstein, and Kalra (1999) cited Edell and Burke (1987) as the source of their items. Coulter (1998) cited Edell and Burke (1987) as well as Plutchik (1980).

RELIABILITY: An alpha of .58 (n = 56) was reported for the version of the scale used by Aylesworth, Goodstein, and Kalra (1999). Burke and Edell (1989) reported an alpha of .88 (n = 191). The version used by Coulter (1998) had an alpha of .89. Alphas of .96 (n = 29) and .89 (n = 32) were reported by Edell and Burke (1987). Madden, Allen, and Twible (1988) reported a composite reliability of .75 (n = 143) for their version of the measure. Alphas of .81 (n = 78) and .80 (n = 73) were reported by Mooradian for the versions of the scale used in his Studies 1 and 2, respectively. It should be noted that while Study 2 used a simple summated scale, Study 1 was based on the factor scores of 59 items.

VALIDITY: All of the studies used factor analyses to some degree for purifying the measures but the validity of the scale has not been thoroughly examined. Madden, Allen, and Twible (1988) did find some support for the discriminant validity of their abbreviated version of the measure. Specifically, while discriminant validity was found between negative affective response and positive affective response (#527), the claim could not be made for negative affective response and overall attitude-toward-the-ad (#562).

COMMENTS: Several different constructs appear to be represented by the full set of items presented below. Some of them appear to represent a disinterested type of feeling (e.g., # 1, #6, #8) while others reflect a sense of skepticism (e.g., #2, #7, #13). An even more intensely negative feeling is shown in several of the other terms (e.g., #3, #5, #10). Users should select items based upon their face validity for the facet of interest and then use factor analysis to evaluate and refine the scale's unidimensionality.

REFERENCES:

Abelson, Robert P., Donald R. Kinder, Mark D. Peters, and Susan T. Fisk (1982), "Affective and Semantic Components in Political Person Perceptions," *Journal of Personality and Social Psychology*, 42 (April), 619–630.

Aylesworth, Andrew B., Ronald C. Goodstein, and Ajay Kalra (1999), "Effect of Archetypal Embeds on Feelings: An Indirect Route to Affecting Attitudes?" *JA*, 28 (3), 73–81.

Burke, Marian Chapman and Julie A. Edell (1989), "The Impact of Feelings on Ad-Based Affect and Cognitions," *JMR*, 26 (February), 69–83.

Coulter, Keith S. (1998), "The Effects of Affective Responses to Media Context on Advertising Evaluations," *JA*, 27 (4), 41–51.

Edell, Julie E. and Marian C. Burke (1987), "The Power of Feelings in Understanding Advertising Effects," *JCR*, 14 (December), 421–33.

Goodstein, Ronald C., Julie A. Edell, and Mairian Chapman Moore (1990), "When are Feelings Generated? Assessing the Presence and Reliability of Feelings Based on Storyboards and Animatics" in *Emotion in Advertising*, Stuart J. Agres, Julie A. Edell, Tony M. Dubitsky, ed. New York: Quorum Books 175–193.

Madden, Thomas J. (1982), "Humor in Advertising: Application of a Hierarchy of Effects Paradigm," doctoral dissertation, University of Massachusetts.

Madden, Thomas J., Chris T. Allen, and Jacquelyn L. Twible (1988), "Attitude Toward the Ad: An Assessment of Diverse Measurement Indices Under Different Processing Sets," *JMR*, 25 (August), 242–252.

Mooradian, Todd A. (1996), "Personality and Ad-Evoked Feelings: The Case for Extraversion and Neuroticism," *JAMS*, 24 (Spring), 99–109.

Nowlis, Vincent (1970), "Mood, Behavior and Experience," in *Feelings and Emotions*, Magda B. Arnold, ed. New York: Academic Press Inc. 261–277.

Plutchik, Robert (1980), *Emotion: A Psychoevolutionary Synthesis*, New York: Harper and Row Publishers, Inc.

Wells, William D., Clark Leavitt, and Maureen McConville (1971), "A Reaction Profile for TV Commercials," *JAR*, 11 (December), 11–17.

SCALE ITEMS: [1]

Directions: We would like you to tell us how the ad you just saw made you feel. We are interested in your reactions to the ad, not how you would describe it. Please tell us how much you felt each of these feelings while you were watching this commercial. If you felt the feeling *very strongly,* put a 5; *strongly,* put a 4; *somewhat strongly,* put a 3; *not very strongly,* put a 2; *not at all,* put a 1.

1. Bored

2. Critical

3. Defiant

4. Depressed

5. Disgusted

6. Disintegrated

7. Dubious

8. Dull

9. Lonely

10. Offended

11. Regretful

12. Sad

13. Skeptical

14. Suspicious

15. Angry

16. Annoyed

17. Bad

18. Fed-up

19. Insulted

20. Irritated

21. Repulsed

22. Upset/Disturbed

23. Fearful

Aylesworth, Goodstein, and Kalra (1999): 1, 3, 1, 12, 14, 23 5-point
Burke and Edell (1989): 1–14 5-point
Coulter (1998): 11, 12, 15, 22 5-point
Edell and Burke (1987): 1–20 (Study 1); 1–14 (Study 2) both 5-point
Madden, Allen, and Twible (1988): 19–21 6-point
Mooradian (1996): 2, 6, 10, 13, 14 (Study 2) both 5-point

[1] These directions and scale anchors were used by Edell and Burke (1987) as well as Burke and Edell (1989). In contrast, Aylesworth, Goodstein, and Kalra (1999) used the following to anchor their response scale: *did not experience the feeling at all* (1) and *experienced the feeling very strongly* (5).

SCALE NAME: Affective Response to Ad (Overall)

SCALE DESCRIPTION: Twelve descriptors are used to measure a person's affective reaction to a particular advertisement he/she has been exposed to. A seven-point response scale was used with the items. The authors (Singh et al. 2000) referred to the scale as *attitude-toward-the-ad-affective* but, more precisely, the scale appears to measure the feelings evoked by an ad rather than one's assessment of the ad itself such as other scales do, e.g., #562.

SCALE ORIGIN: Singh et al. (2000) stated that they adopted the scale from Madden, Allen, and Twible (1988). It is more accurate to say that the items were among those tested by Madden, Allen, and Twible. Factor analysis indicated that the set represented at least three dimensions. They did not use these twelve items as a set and, in fact, developed two scales with eight of the items (one positive and one negative) and the other items were dropped for lack of fit.

RELIABILITY: An alpha of .80 was reported for the scale by Singh et al. (2000).

VALIDITY: No examination of the scale's validity was reported by Singh et al. (2000).

COMMENTS: Given the results of the rigorous analysis conducted by Madden, Allen, and Twible (1988), it is rather clear that this set of items is unlikely to be tapping into one and the same dimension. Further testing is called for before these items are used together as a summated scale.

REFERENCES:
Madden, Thomas J., Chris T. Allen, and Jacquelyn L. Twible (1988), "Attitude Toward the Ad: An Assessment of Diverse Measurement Indices Under Different Processing Sets," *JMR*, 25 (August), 242–252.
Singh, Surendra N., V. Parker Lessig, Dongwook Kim, Reetika Gupta, and Mary Ann Hocutt (2000), "Does Your Ad Have Too Many Pictures?" *JAR*, 40 (Jan-Apr), 11–27.

SCALE ITEMS: [1]

1. Insulted

2. Good

3. Cheerful

4. Irritated

5. Impatient

6. Pleased

7. Repulsed

8. Amused

9. Confused

10. Stimulated

11. Shocked

12. Soothed

<hr>

[1] The anchors for the response scale were *very much so* (7) and *not at all* (1).

SCALE NAME: Affective Response to Ad (Upbeat Feelings)

SCALE DESCRIPTION: This measure is composed of several uni-polar items and is purported to measure the degree of "upbeat" feelings a consumer reports experiencing when exposed to a specific advertisement. The scale has been used with varying numbers of items.

There is an important distinction between this measure and one such as #562. As Mooradian stated in the directions used with his scale, subjects were to describe "reactions to the ad, not to how you would describe the ad" (1996, p. 101). Admittedly, there should be a high correspondence between the two but they are still theoretically different constructs.

SCALE ORIGIN: All or most of the items composing the various versions of the scale can be found in the Reaction Profile for TV Commercials developed by Wells, Leavitt and McConville (1971). Madden, Allen, and Twible (1988) cited Abelson et al. (1982), Madden (1982), and Nowlis (1970) as sources of their items. Aylesworth, Goodstein, and Kalra (1999) cited Edell and Burke (1987) as the source of their items. Coulter (1998) cited Edell and Burke (1987) as well as Plutchik (1980).

RELIABILITY: An alpha of .87 (n = 56) was reported for the version of the scale used by Aylesworth, Goodstein, and Kalra (1999). Burke and Edell (1989) reported an alpha of .95 (n = 191). The version used by Coulter (1998) had an alpha of .93. Alphas of .98 (n = 29) and .95 (n = 32) were reported by Edell and Burke (1987). Madden, Allen, and Twible (1988) reported a composite reliability of .89 (n = 143) for their version of the measure. Alphas of .94 (n = 78) and .91 (n = 73) were reported by Mooradian for the versions of the scale used in his Studies 1 and 2, respectively. It should be noted that while Study 2 used a simple summated scale, Study 1 was based on the factor scores of 59 items.

VALIDITY: The validity of the scale has not been adequately addressed in any of the studies though Madden, Allen, and Twible (1988) did find some support for the discriminant validity of their measure. All of the studies used factor analyses to some degree for purifying the measures.

REFERENCES:
Abelson, Robert P., Donald R. Kinder, Mark D. Peters, and Susan T. Fisk (1982), "Affective and Semantic Components in Political Person Perceptions," *Journal of Personality and Social Psychology*, 42 (April), 619–630.
Aylesworth, Andrew B., Ronald C. Goodstein, and Ajay Kalra (1999), "Effect of Archetypal Embeds on Feelings: An Indirect Route to Affecting Attitudes?" *JA*, 28 (3), 73–81.
Burke, Marian Chapman and Julie A. Edell (1989), "The Impact of Feelings on Ad-Based Affect and Cognitions," *JMR*, 26 (February), 69–83.
Coulter, Keith S. (1998), "The Effects of Affective Responses to Media Context on Advertising Evaluations," *JA*, 27 (4), 41–51.
Edell, Julie E. and Marian C. Burke (1987), "The Power of Feelings in Understanding Advertising Effects," *JCR*, 14 (December), 421–33.
Madden, Thomas J. (1982), "Humor in Advertising: Application of a Hierarchy of Effects Paradigm," doctoral dissertation, University of Massachusetts.
Madden, Thomas J., Chris T. Allen, and Jacquelyn L. Twible (1988), "Attitude Toward the Ad: An Assessment of Diverse Measurement Indices Under Different Processing Sets," *JMR*, 25 (August), 242–252.
Mooradian, Todd A. (1996), "Personality and Ad-Evoked Feelings: The Case for Extraversion and Neuroticism," *JAMS*, 24 (Spring), 99–109.

Nowlis, Vincent (1970), "Mood, Behavior and Experience," in *Feelings and Emotions*, Magda B. Arnold, ed. New York: Academic Press Inc. 261–277.

Plutchik, Robert (1980), *Emotion: A Psychoevolutionary Synthesis*, New York: Harper and Row Publishers, Inc.

Wells, William D., Clark Leavitt, and Maureen McConville (1971), "A Reaction Profile for TV Commercials," *JAR*, 11 (December), 11–17.

SCALE ITEMS: [1]

Directions: We would like you to tell us how the ad you just saw made you feel. We are interested in your reactions to the ad, not how you would describe it. Please tell us how much you felt each of these feelings while you were watching this commercial. If you felt the feeling *very strongly,* put a 5; *strongly,* put a 4; *somewhat strongly,* put a 3; *not very strongly,* put a 2; *not at all,* put a 1.

1. Active

2. Alive

3. Amused

4. Attentive

5. Attractive

6. Carefree

7. Cheerful

8. Confident

9. Creative

10. Delighted

11. Elated

12. Energetic

13. Happy

14. Humorous

15. Independent

16. Industrious

17. Inspired

18. Interested

19. Joyous

20. Lighthearted

21. Playful

22. Pleased

23. Proud

24. Satisfied

25. Silly

26. Stimulated

27. Strong

28. Adventurous

29. Enthusiastic

30. Excited

31. Exhilarated

32. Good

33. Lively

34. Soothed

35. Aroused

36. Caring

Aylesworth, Goodstein, and Kalra (1999): 3, 4, 7, 8, 13, 17, 18, 23, 24, 26, 35, 36 5-point
Burke and Edell (1989): 1–27 5-point
Coulter (1998): 3, 13, 18, 22 5-point
Edell and Burke (1987): 1–24, 26–33 (Study 1); 1–24, 26, 27 (Study 2) both 5-point
Madden , Allen, and Twible (1988): 7, 22, 26, 32, 34 6-point
Mooradian (1996): 3, 6, 7, 13, 21, 25 (Study 2) both 5-point

[1] These directions and scale anchors were used by Edell and Burke (1987) as well as Burke and Edell (1989). In contrast, Aylesworth, Goodstein, and Kalra (1999) used the following to anchor their response scale: *did not experience the feeling at all* (1) and *experienced the feeling very strongly* (5).

SCALE NAME: Affective Response to Ad (Warm Feelings)

SCALE DESCRIPTION: This measure is composed of several uni-polar items and is purported to measure the degree of "warm" feelings a consumer reports experiencing when exposed to a specific advertisement. The scale has been used with varying numbers of items.

There is an important distinction between this measure and one such as #562. As Mooradian stated in the directions used with his scale, subjects were to describe "reactions to the ad, not to how you would describe the ad" (1996, p. 101). Admittedly, there should be a high correspondence between the two but they are still theoretically distinct constructs.

SCALE ORIGIN: The scale was developed by Edell and Burke in a pilot test described in an appendix to their 1987 article. Sixty people recruited on a college campus viewed sixteen TV commercials. Afterwards, they were asked to write down any feelings the ads evoked. They also were given a checklist of 169 terms to use to describe their affective responses to the ads. Sixty of the checklist items and nine more from the open-ended task were used as the initial feelings inventory which was subsequently factor analyzed in study one. Three feelings factors were produced: upbeat (#527), negative (#525), and warm.

RELIABILITY: An alpha of .87 (n = 56) was reported for the version of the scale used by Aylesworth, Goodstein, and Kalra (1999). Burke and Edell (1989) reported an alpha of .89 (n = 191). Alphas of .93 (n = 29) and .90 (n = 32) were reported by Edell and Burke (1987). Alphas of .71 (n = 78) and .91 (n = 73) were reported by Mooradian for the versions of the scale used in his Studies 1 and 2, respectively. It should be noted that while Study 2 used a simple summated scale, Study 1 was based on the factor scores of 59 items.

VALIDITY: The validity of the scale has not been adequately addressed in any of the studies though all of them used factor analyses to some degree for purifying the measures.

REFERENCES:

Aylesworth, Andrew B., Ronald C. Goodstein, and Ajay Kalra (1999), "Effect of Archetypal Embeds on Feelings: An Indirect Route to Affecting Attitudes?" *JA*, 28 (3), 73–81.

Burke, Marian Chapman and Julie A. Edell (1989), "The Impact of Feelings on Ad-Based Affect and Cognitions," *JMR*, 26 (February), 69–83.

Edell, Julie E. and Marian C. Burke (1987), "The Power of Feelings in Understanding Advertising Effects," *JCR*, 14 (December), 421–33.

Mooradian, Todd A. (1996), "Personality and Ad-Evoked Feelings: The Case for Extraversion and Neuroticism," *JAMS*, 24 (Spring), 99–109.

SCALE ITEMS: [1]

Directions: We would like you to tell us how the ad you just saw made you feel. We are interested in your reactions to the ad, not how you would describe it. Please tell us how much you felt each of these feelings while you were watching this commercial. If you felt the feeling *very strongly,* put a 5; *strongly,* put a 4; *somewhat strongly,* put a 3; *not very strongly,* put a 2; *not at all,* put a 1.

1. Affectionate

2. Calm

3. Concerned

4. Contemplative

5. Emotional

6. Hopeful

7. Kind

8. Moved

9. Peaceful

10. Pensive

11. Sentimental

12. Warmhearted

13. Touched

Aylesworth, Goodstein, and Kalra (1999): 1, 6–9, 11, 12 5-point
Burke and Edell (1989): 1–12 5-point
Edell and Burke (1987): 1–13 (Study 1); 1–12 (Study 2) both 5-point
Mooradian (1996): 1, 6, 7, 9, 12 (Study 2) both 5-point

[1] These directions and scale anchors were used by Edell and Burke (1987) as well as Burke and Edell (1989). In contrast, Aylesworth, Goodstein, and Kalra (1999) used the following to anchor their response scale: *did not experience the feeling at all* (1) and *experienced the feeling very strongly* (5).

SCALE NAME: Agency Selection Criteria (Account Team)

SCALE DESCRIPTION: Four, seven-point phrases are used to measure the extent to which a person believes the quality of key account-related personnel are important when choosing an advertising agency. As written, the scale does not measure a person's attitude toward a specific agency but rather the role this criterion should play in general when making a selection among agencies.

SCALE ORIGIN: The scale appears to have been developed by Fam and Waller (1999) although they drew upon items and concepts used in previous studies (e.g., Cagley 1986; Wackman, Salmon, and Salman 1986).

RELIABILITY: An alpha of .68 was reported for the scale (Fam and Waller 1999).

VALIDITY: The validity of the scale was not specifically addressed by Fam and Waller (1999). An exploratory factor analysis with Varimax rotation was conducted on the 33 selection items included in the study. The results led the authors to a eight factor solution with the items shown below loading highest on the same factor. Despite this, the loading of one item (#4 below) was very low (.413) probably because it does not tap very well into the same content as the other items. This may also account for the low internal consistency of the scale. Elimination of this item and retesting of the scale should be strongly considered.

COMMENTS: In the study by Fam and Waller (1999) the respondents were account directors at ad agencies. The items seem amenable for use with others such as potential clients although some pretesting is advised.

REFERENCES:
Cagley, James W. (1986), "A Comparison of Advertising Agency Selection Factors: Advertiser and Agency Perceptions," *JAR*, 26 (June), 39–44.
Fam, Kim Shyan and David S. Waller (1999), "Factors in Winning Accounts: The Views of Agency Account Directors in New Zealand," *JAR*, 39 (May/June), 21–32.
Wackman, Daniel B., Charles T. Salmon, and Caryn C. Salman (1986), "Developing an Advertising Agency-Client Relationship," *JAR*, 26 (December), 21–28.

SCALE ITEMS: [1]

1. The extent of top management participation in client service.

2. The agency people pitching for the account are those who will be working on the account.

3. The quality of agency people assigned to the account.

4. The cost consciousness of the agency.

[1] Responses to these items were captured by Fam and Waller (1999) using a seven-point scale with 1 indicating *no importance* and 7 indicating *high importance*.

SCALE NAME: Agency Selection Criteria (Creative)

SCALE DESCRIPTION: The five, seven-point items are used to measure the degree of importance a person believes should be placed on an advertising agency's creative ability. As written, the scale does not measure a person's attitude toward a specific agency's ability but rather the role this criterion should play in general when making a selection among agencies.

SCALE ORIGIN: The scale appears to have been developed by Fam and Waller (1999) although they drew upon items and concepts used in previous studies (e.g., Cagley 1986; Wackman, Salmon, and Salman 1986).

RELIABILITY: An alpha of .70 was reported for the scale (Fam and Waller 1999).

VALIDITY: The validity of the scale was not specifically addressed by Fam and Waller (1999). An exploratory factor analysis with Varimax rotation was conducted on the 33 selection items included in the study. The results led the authors to a eight factor solution with the items shown below loading highest on the same factor. Despite this, the loading of one item (#5 below) was very low (.402) probably because it does not tap into the same content as the other items. Elimination of this item and retesting of the scale should be strongly considered.

COMMENTS: In the study by Fam and Waller (1999) the respondents were account directors at ad agencies. The items seem amenable for use with others such as potential clients though some pretesting is advised.

REFERENCES:
Cagley, James W. (1986), "A Comparison of Advertising Agency Selection Factors: Advertiser and Agency Perceptions," *JAR*, 26 (June), 39–44.
Fam, Kim Shyan and David S. Waller (1999), "Factors in Winning Accounts: The Views of Agency Account Directors in New Zealand," *JAR*, 39 (May/June), 21–32.
Wackman, Daniel B., Charles T. Salmon, and Caryn C. Salman (1986), "Developing an Advertising Agency-Client Relationship," *JAR*, 26 (December), 21–28.

SCALE ITEMS: [1]

1. The overall strength of creative product.

2. The willingness of the agency to interact with the client in developing creative strategy.

3. The need for the agency to thoroughly understand characteristics of the client's business.

4. The agency's creative philosophy.

5. The agency's strategic planning ability.

---

[1] Responses to these items were captured by Fam and Waller (1999) using a seven-point scale with 1 indicating *no importance* and 7 indicating *high importance*.

SCALE NAME: Agency Selection Criteria (Reputation)

SCALE DESCRIPTION: The scale is composed of five, seven-point items that are intended to measure the extent to which a person believes the reputation of an advertising agency is a very important criterion that should be used by a client when making the selection decision.

SCALE ORIGIN: The scale appears to have been developed by Fam and Waller (1999) although they drew upon items and concepts used in previous studies (e.g., Cagley 1986; Wackman, Salmon, and Salman 1986).

RELIABILITY: An alpha of .74 was reported for the scale (Fam and Waller 1999).

VALIDITY: The validity of the scale was not specifically addressed by Fam and Waller (1999). However, an exploratory factor analysis with Varimax rotation was conducted on the 33 selection items included in the study. The results led the authors to an eight-factor solution with the items shown below loading highest on the same factor.

COMMENTS: In the study by Fam and Waller (1999) the respondents were account directors at ad agencies. The items seem amenable for use with others such as potential clients though some pretesting is advised.

REFERENCES:

Cagley, James W. (1986), "A Comparison of Advertising Agency Selection Factors: Advertiser and Agency Perceptions," *JAR*, 26 (June), 39–44.

Fam, Kim Shyan and David S. Waller (1999), "Factors in Winning Accounts: The Views of Agency Account Directors in New Zealand," *JAR*, 39 (May/June), 21–32.

Wackman, Daniel B., Charles T. Salmon, and Caryn C. Salman (1986), "Developing an Advertising Agency-Client Relationship," *JAR*, 26 (December), 21–28.

SCALE ITEMS: [1]

1. Awards received by the agency.

2. Previous accounts lost and reasons for the breakups.

3. Response of past or existing clients as referees.

4. Degree of business growth and record of agency performance.

5. Agency has international affiliations.

[1] Responses to these items were captured by Fam and Waller (1999) using a seven-point scale with 1 indicating *no importance* and 7 indicating *high importance*.

SCALE NAME: Agency Selection Criteria (Resources)

SCALE DESCRIPTION: The scale is composed of six, seven-point items that are intended to measure the extent to which a person believes the breadth of services available from an advertising agency is a very important criterion that should be used by a client when making the selection decision.

SCALE ORIGIN: The scale appears to have been developed by Fam and Waller (1999) although they drew upon items and concepts used in previous studies (e.g., Cagley 1986; Wackman, Salmon, and Salman 1986).

RELIABILITY: An alpha of .81 was reported for the scale (Fam and Waller 1999).

VALIDITY: The validity of the scale was not specifically addressed by Fam and Waller (1999). However, an exploratory factor analysis with Varimax rotation was conducted on the 33 selection items included in the study. The results led the authors to an eight-factor solution with the items shown below loading highest on the same factor.

COMMENTS: In the study by Fam and Waller (1999) the respondents were account directors at ad agencies. The items seem amenable for use with others such as potential clients though some pretesting is advised.

REFERENCES:

Cagley, James W. (1986), "A Comparison of Advertising Agency Selection Factors: Advertiser and Agency Perceptions," *JAR*, 26 (June), 39–44.

Fam, Kim Shyan and David S. Waller (1999), "Factors in Winning Accounts: The Views of Agency Account Directors in New Zealand," *JAR*, 39 (May/June), 21–32.

Wackman, Daniel B., Charles T. Salmon, and Caryn C. Salman (1986), "Developing an Advertising Agency-Client Relationship," *JAR*, 26 (December), 21–28.

SCALE ITEMS: [1]

1. The general structure and handling of accounts.

2. The agency resources in all areas including account services, creative, and media.

3. Integration of the media function into the agency's planning process.

4. The agency can provide a full range of services.

5. The ability to buy media at favorable rates.

6. The employee stability of the agency.

---

[1] Responses to these items were captured by Fam and Waller (1999) using a seven-point scale with 1 indicating *no importance* and 7 indicating *high importance*.

SCALE NAME: Agency Selection Criteria (Shared Purpose)

SCALE DESCRIPTION: The scale is composed of three, seven-point items that are intended to measure the degree of importance a person places on the integrity of an advertising agency and agreement on goals. As written, the scale does not measure a person's attitude toward a specific agency but rather the role this criterion should play in general when making a selection among agencies.

SCALE ORIGIN: The scale appears to have been developed by Fam and Waller (1999) although they drew upon items and concepts used in previous studies (e.g., Cagley 1986; Wackman, Salmon, and Salman 1986).

RELIABILITY: An alpha of .70 was reported for the scale (Fam and Waller 1999).

VALIDITY: The validity of the scale was not specifically addressed by Fam and Waller (1999). However, an exploratory factor analysis with Varimax rotation was conducted on the 33 selection items included in the study. The results led the authors to an eight-factor solution with the items shown below loading highest on the same factor.

COMMENTS: In the study by Fam and Waller (1999) the respondents were account directors at ad agencies. The items seem amenable for use with others such as potential clients though some pretesting is advised.

REFERENCES:

Cagley, James W. (1986), "A Comparison of Advertising Agency Selection Factors: Advertiser and Agency Perceptions," *JAR*, 26 (June), 39–44.

Fam, Kim Shyan and David S. Waller (1999), "Factors in Winning Accounts: The Views of Agency Account Directors in New Zealand," *JAR*, 39 (May/June), 21–32.

Wackman, Daniel B., Charles T. Salmon, and Caryn C. Salman (1986), "Developing an Advertising Agency-Client Relationship," *JAR*, 26 (December), 21–28.

SCALE ITEMS: [1]

1. Complete agreement on goals and objectives.

2. Evidence of agency-initiated projects that have come to fruition.

3. The willingness of the agency to make recommendations and object to advertiser decisions.

[1] Responses to these items were captured by Fam and Waller (1999) using a seven-point scale with 1 indicating *no importance* and 7 indicating *high importance*.

SCALE NAME: Agency Selection Criteria (Strategic)

SCALE DESCRIPTION: The three, seven-point items are used to measure the degree of importance a person believes should be placed on an advertising agency's ability to provide assistance in developing business strategy when making a choice among agencies. As written, the scale does not measure a person's attitude toward a specific agency's ability but rather the role this criterion should play in general when making a selection among agencies.

SCALE ORIGIN: The scale appears to have been developed by Fam and Waller (1999) although they drew upon items and concepts used in previous studies (e.g., Cagley 1986; Wackman, Salmon, and Salman 1986).

RELIABILITY: An alpha of .79 was reported for the scale (Fam and Waller 1999).

VALIDITY: The validity of the scale was not specifically addressed by Fam and Waller (1999). However, an exploratory factor analysis with Varimax rotation was conducted on the 33 selection items included in the study. The results led the authors to an eight-factor solution with the items shown below loading highest on the same factor.

COMMENTS: In the study by Fam and Waller (1999) the respondents were account directors at ad agencies. The items seem amenable for use with others such as potential clients though some pretesting is advised.

REFERENCES:
Cagley, James W. (1986), "A Comparison of Advertising Agency Selection Factors: Advertiser and Agency Perceptions," *JAR*, 26 (June), 39–44.
Fam, Kim Shyan and David S. Waller (1999), "Factors in Winning Accounts: The Views of Agency Account Directors in New Zealand," *JAR*, 39 (May/June), 21–32.
Wackman, Daniel B., Charles T. Salmon, and Caryn C. Salman (1986), "Developing an Advertising Agency-Client Relationship," *JAR*, 26 (December), 21–28.

SCALE ITEMS: [1]

1. The agency can provide assistance in long-term business development/strategic direction.

2. The agency can provide commentary and information on global market trends.

3. The agency can provide assistance in development of marketing plans.

[1] Responses to these items were captured by Fam and Waller (1999) using a seven-point scale with 1 indicating *no importance* and 7 indicating *high importance*.

SCALE NAME: Attention to Sponsor's Promotion

SCALE DESCRIPTION: The scale is composed of three, seven-point Likert type statements measuring the subjective likelihood that if a certain company supported a particular event then it would improve the chances that a consumer would attend to and remember the sponsor's promotion. The events examined by Speed and Thompson (2000) were related to sports.

SCALE ORIGIN: Although not explicitly stated by the authors, the scale appears to be original to the study by Speed and Thompson (2000). Some qualitative work by the authors led to generation of items for several scales used to create the independent variables in the model. This was followed by a pretest which aided in identifying items for deletion or modification. It was not clear whether or not the items used to create this scale and the other dependent measures were part of this process.

RELIABILITY: An alpha of .91 was reported for the scale by Speed and Thompson (2000).

VALIDITY: Based on data from the main study, a CFA was performed on items from this scale and two others (the dependent variables). The results provided evidence of this scale's convergent and discriminant validity.

REFERENCES:
Speed, Richard and Peter Thompson (2000), "Determinants of Sports Sponsorship Response," *JAMS*, 28 (2), 226–238.

SCALE ITEMS:

This sponsorship would make me more likely to:

1. notice the sponsor's name on other occasions.

2. pay attention to the sponsor's advertising.

3. remember the sponsor's promotion.

SCALE NAME: Attention to the Advertisement

SCALE DESCRIPTION: The scale is composed of multiple statements using a seven-point response format to indicate the extent of cognitive resources a person indicates having devoted to an advertisement, the product in an ad, or a portion of an ad.

SCALE ORIGIN: The scales were originally developed by Laczniak, Muehling, and Grossbart (1989). Muehling, Stoltman, and Grossbart (1990) indicated that the scale had previously been used by Cohen (1983) and Mitchell (1979). They used two versions of the scale, the first version measuring the amount of attention paid to the written message in an ad while the second version measured the visual aspects of the ad. A slightly modified version of the scale was used with broadcast ads by Bucholz and Smith (1991) to measure the amount of attention paid to a computer. Laczniak and Muehling (1993) used the scale to measure the attention paid to the written message in an ad. Stevenson, Bruner, and Kumar (2000) adapted the scale slightly for use with a commercial run at a website.

RELIABILITY: Alphas of .91, .95, .94, .76 were reported for the versions of the scale used by Bruner and Kumar (2000), Bucholz and Smith (1991), Laczniak and Muehling (1993), and Stevenson, Bruner, and Kumar (2000), respectively. Muehling, Stoltman, and Grossbart (1990) reported alphas of .94 (written message) and .86 (visual aspects).

VALIDITY: No examination of scale validity was reported in any of the studies.

REFERENCES:

Bruner II, Gordon C. and Anand Kumar (2000), "Web Commercials and Advertising Hierarchy-of-Effects," *JAR*, 40 (Jan-Apr), 35–42.

Bucholz, Laura M. and Robert E. Smith (1991), "The Role of Consumer Involvement in Determining Cognitive Response to Broadcast Advertising," *JA*, 1 (20), 4–17.

Laczniak, Russell N., Darrel D. Muehling, and Sanford Grossbart (1989), "Manipulating Message Involvement in Advertising Research," *JA*, 3 (16), 3–12.

Laczniak, Russell N. and Darrel D. Muehling (1993), "The Relationship Between Experimental Manipulations and Tests of Theory in an Advertising Message Involvement Context," *JA*, 3 (22), 59–74.

Muehling, Darrel D., Jeffrey J. Stoltman, and Sanford Grossbart (1990), "The Impact of Comparative Advertising on Levels of Message Involvement," *JA*, 4 (19), 41–50.

Stevenson, Julie, Gordon C. Bruner II, and Anand Kumar (2000), "Webpage Background and Viewer Attitudes," *JAR*, 40 (January/April), 29–34.

SCALE ITEMS: [1]

1. How much attention did you pay to _____.

2. How much did you concentrate on _____.

3. How involved were you with _____.

4. How much thought did you put into evaluating _____.

5. How much did you notice _____.

Bruner and Kumar (2000): 1, 2, 5
Bucholz and Smith (1991): 1–5
Laczniak and Muehling (1993): 1–5
Muehling, Stoltman, and Grossbart (1990): 1, 2, 5
Muehling, Stoltman, and Grossbart (1990): 1, 2, 5
Stevenson, Bruner, and Kumar (2000): 1, 2, 5

---

[1] Most if not all of the studies used verbal anchors on their response scales ranging from *none / not at all* to *very much*.

SCALE NAME: Attitude Toward Advertising

SCALE DESCRIPTION: The scale is composed of ten, five-point Likert-type statements measuring a person's attitude toward advertising across a variety of media and whether or not it is enjoyable or interesting.

SCALE ORIGIN: The measure originates from a dissertation published by Moschis (1978).

RELIABILITY: Alphas of .54 (Moschis 1981) and .76 (Bush, Smith, and Martin 1999) have been reported for the scale.

VALIDITY: No examination of the scale's validity has been reported.

COMMENTS: The low internal consistencies indicate that the scale may not be very reliable. This could be due to the items lacking unidimensionality. Caution is urged in use of the scale until validation occurs.

REFERENCES:
Bush, Alan J., Rachel Smith, and Craig Martin (1999), "The Influence of Consumer Socialization Variables on Attitude Toward Advertising: A Comparison of African-Americans and Caucasians," *JA*, 28 (3), 13–24.
Moschis, George P. (1978), *Acquisition of the Consumer Role by Adolescents,* Research Monograph, 82, Georgia State University: Publishing Services Division.
Moschis, George P. (1981), "Patterns of Consumer Learning," *JAMS*, 9 (Spring), 110–126.

SCALE ITEMS:

1. Most television commercials are fun to watch.

2. When I see or hear something new advertised, I often want to buy it.

3. Advertisements help people buy things that are best for them.

4. Most radio commercials are annoying. (r)

5. I think there should be less advertising than there is now. (r)

6. Most advertising that comes through the mail is junk and not worth looking at. (r)

7. Most magazine advertisements are enjoyable to look at.

8. Most advertisements tell the truth.

9. I don't pay much attention to advertising. (r)

10. Most newspaper advertisements are enjoyable to look at.

SCALE NAME: Attitude Toward Advertising

SCALE DESCRIPTION: Five, five-point Likert-type statements are used to measure consumer attitudes about advertising in general. A seven-item version of the scale with similar psychometric properties is also available.

SCALE ORIGIN: The scale was developed by Gaski and Etgar (1986). Using a formula described in the article, the scale can be combined with data from several other measures to form an index of consumer attitudes toward marketing-related activities. The authors request that the index be referred to as the University of Notre Dame/Market Facts Index of Consumer Sentiment toward Marketing. Some items were taken or adapted from the literature but the majority were written especially for the index. Pretesting involved 50 members of the Market Facts mail panel completing the index.

RELIABILITY: A seven-item version of the scale used by Gaski and Etgar (1986) had an alpha of .761 and the item-total correlations were .31 or higher. Two items with the lowest item-total correlations were eliminated leaving a scale with an alpha of .760.

   The five item version used by Baumgartner and Steenkamp (2001) in their pan-European survey was .74 with alphas for individual countries ranging from .62 to .78.

VALIDITY: Gaski and Etgar (1986) conducted a factor analysis of the twenty items composing their entire index. The five items composing each of four scales loaded most heavily on their respective factors and had extremely low loadings on the other three factors.

   The purpose of the study by Baumgartner and Steenkamp (2001) was to examine response styles as a source of contamination in questionnaire measures and the effect that might have on validity of conclusions drawn from such data. Although most of the results were reported at an overall level one finding pertinent to this scale was that the mean level of contamination in scale scores was estimated to be 4% (ranging from 1%–13% for 11 European countries), lower than the average amount of contamination found for the 14 scales examined.

COMMENTS: Baumgartner and Steenkamp (2001) described the version they used as having five items, four being reverse scored. Given that, it would appear they used items 2–5 and 7 and that all of those except 5 were reversed scored so that higher scores could be interpreted as better attitudes.

REFERENCES:

Baumgartner, Hans and Jan-Benedict E.M. Steenkamp (2001), "Response Styles in Marketing Research: A Cross-National Investigation," *JMR*, 38 (May), 143–156.

Gaski, John F. and Michael J. Etzel (1986), "The Index of Consumer Sentiment toward Marketing," *JM*, 50 (July), 71–81.

SCALE ITEMS: [1]

1. Most advertising provides consumers with essential information. (r)

2. Most advertising is very annoying.

3. Most advertising makes false claims.

4. If most advertising was eliminated, consumers would be better off.

5. I enjoy most ads. (r)

6. Advertising should be more closely regulated.

7. Most advertising is intended to deceive rather than to inform consumers.

[1] The five-item version of the scale did not include #1 and #6.

SCALE NAME: Attitude Toward Advertising

SCALE DESCRIPTION: It is a three-item, five-point Likert-type summated ratings scale measuring the degree to which a person expresses a positive attitude toward advertising in general, particularly in the sense of it being credible and useful.

SCALE ORIGIN: The source of the scale was not stated by Donthu and Gilliland (1996) but it is likely to be original to their study.

RELIABILITY: Alphas of .75 (Donthu and Gilliland 1996) and .78 (Donthu and Garcia 1999) have been reported for the scale.

VALIDITY: No specific examination of the scale's validity has been reported.

REFERENCES:
Donthu, Naveen and Adriana Garcia (1999), "The Internet Shopper," *JAR*, 39 (May/June), 52–58.
Donthu, Naveen and David Gilliland (1996), "The Infomercial Shopper," *JAR*, 36 (March/April), 69–76.

SCALE ITEMS:

1. Advertisements provide useful information.

2. I think that advertisements are often deceptive. (r)

3. I usually do not pay attention to advertisements. (r)

SCALE NAME: Attitude Toward Advertising

SCALE DESCRIPTION: The scale is composed of four, seven-point semantic differentials measuring a consumer's general attitude toward the advertising within a specified medium. The media studied by Elliot and Speck (1998) were television, radio, magazines, newspapers, Yellow Pages, and direct mail.

SCALE ORIGIN: Although this construct has been measured before, use of this particular set of items appears to be original to Elliot and Speck (1998).

RELIABILITY: Elliot and Speck (1998) used the scale with the six media they studied. The alphas ranged from .82 (Yellow Pages) to .92 (direct mail).

VALIDITY: No examination of the scale's validity was reported by Elliot and Speck (1998).

COMMENTS: According to the premise underlying the semantic differential, items should be constructed so that the poles are adjective pairs describing opposites of the semantic continuum (Dawes and Smith 1985, p. 534; Osgood, Suci, and Tannenbaum 1957, pp. 29, 83). It is arguable whether this requirement is being met for the items composing this scale since they have the form $X / not X$. The possibility exists that items of this form compromise the assumption that the midpoint of the scale is meant to be used when respondents associate the object with *neither* pole of the adjective pair. The practical significance of this compromise is unknown but one implication is that the full variance of the construct is not being captured well by the scale.

REFERENCES:

Dawes, Robyn M. and Tom L. Smith (1985), "Attitude and Opinion Measurement," in *Handbook of Social Psychology*, 3rd ed., Gardner Lindzey, Elliot Aronson, ed., 1,New York: Random House 509–566.
Elliott, Michael T. and Paul Surgi Speck (1998), "Consumer Perceptions of Advertising Clutter and Its Impact Across Various Media," *JAR*, 38 (January/February), 29–41.
Osgood, Charles E., George J. Suci, and Percy H. Tannenbaum (1957), *The Measurement of Meaning*, Urbana: University of Illinois Press.

SCALE ITEMS:

1. interesting / not interesting

2. enjoyable / not enjoyable

3. informative / not informative

4. believable / not believable

SCALE NAME: Attitude Toward Advertising (Credibility)

SCALE DESCRIPTION: Three, five-point Likert-type statements are used to measure the degree which a person believes that advertising in general is plausible and convincing. The items are general enough so that they can refer to advertising in general or to advertising on a specific medium. The scale was not, however, developed for use with a specific ad.

SCALE ORIGIN: The key terms in the items have been used in advertising attitude scales previously although no known scale has used this set of items. In that sense then, the scale may be original to Brackett and Carr (2001).

RELIABILITY: An alpha of .773 was estimated by Brackett and Carr (2001; Carr 2003).

VALIDITY: No examination of the scale's validity was reported by Brackett and Carr (2001).

REFERENCES:
Brackett, Lana K. and Benjamin N. Carr, Jr. (2001), "Cyberspace Advertising vs. Other Media: Consumer vs. Mature Student Attitudes," *JAR*, 41 (5), 23–32.
Carr, Benjamin N. Jr. (2003), Personal Correspondence.

SCALE ITEMS: [1]

Directions: When you respond to each statement, think in general about advertising in all of its various forms that you have been exposed to, not a single advertisement or advertising for a particular type of product or service.

Advertising on _____:

1. is credible.

2. is trustworthy.

3. is believable.

[1] Directions such as this appear to have been used in the study. If the items are used with respect to a particular medium then the name of that medium should be placed in the blank of the scale stem.

SCALE NAME: Attitude Toward Advertising (Disbelief)

SCALE DESCRIPTION: The scale is composed of three, six-point Likert-type statements used to assess a person's opinion of advertising in general with an emphasis on the extent of its unbelievability.

SCALE ORIGIN: Without being specific, Burnett (2000) stated that some of the items composing this scale and two others were original while others had been used for years by Market Facts. Response data were split in half and the item-total correlations in each were compared. The strongest items common to both halves were then factor analyzed. Ultimately, ten items remained which represented three factors.

RELIABILITY: An alpha of .73 was reported for the scale (Burnett 2000).

VALIDITY: No examination of validity was reported by Burnett (2000) beyond the purification procedures referred to above.

REFERENCES:
Burnett, John J. (2000), "Gays: Feelings about Advertising and Media Used," *JAR*, 40 (Jan-Apr), 75–84.

SCALE ITEMS:

1. Ads insult my intelligence.

2. I don't believe ads.

3. Ads are never objective.

SCALE NAME: Attitude Toward Advertising (Entertaining)

SCALE DESCRIPTION: The scale is composed of three Likert-type statements measuring the degree to which a person believes that advertising in general is entertaining. The items are general enough so that they can refer to advertising in general or to advertising in a specific medium. The scale was not, however, developed for use with a specific ad.

SCALE ORIGIN: Brackett and Carr (2001) employed the same scales as used by Ducoffe (1996) who, in turn, built upon a scale he had developed in previous research (Ducoffe 1995).

RELIABILITY: Alphas of .85 and .729 were estimated by Ducoffe (1996) and Brackett and Carr (2001; Carr 2003), respectively.

VALIDITY: No examination of the scale's validity was reported by Ducoffe (1996) or Brackett and Carr (2001).

REFERENCES:
Ducoffe H. Robert (1995), "How Consumers Assess the Value of Advertising," *Journal of Current Issues and Research in Advertising*, 17 (1), 1–18.
Ducoffe H. Robert (1996), "Advertising Value and Advertising on the Web," *JAR*, 36 (September/October), 21–35.
Brackett, Lana K. and Benjamin N. Carr, Jr. (2001), "Cyberspace Advertising vs. Other Media: Consumer vs. Mature Student Attitudes," *JAR*, 41 (5), 23–32.
Carr, Benjamin N., Jr. (2003), Personal Correspondence.

SCALE ITEMS: [1]

Directions: When you respond to each statement, think in general about advertising in all of its various forms that you have been exposed to, not a single advertisement or advertising for a particular type of product or service.

Advertising on _____:

1. is entertaining.

2. is enjoyable.

3. is pleasing.

---

[1] Directions such as this appear to have been used in the studies. If the items are used with respect to a particular medium then the name of that medium should be placed in the blank of the scale stem. The response scale used by Ducoffe (1996) had seven points whereas Brackett and Carr (2001) used a five-point scale. See the latter for details about this issue.

SCALE NAME: Attitude Toward Advertising (Informative)

SCALE DESCRIPTION: The scale is composed of three Likert-type statements measuring the degree to which a person believes that advertising in general provides useful product-related information. The items are general enough so that they can refer to advertising in general or to advertising in a specific medium. The scale was not, however, developed for use with a specific ad.

SCALE ORIGIN: Brackett and Carr (2001) employed the same scales as used by Ducoffe (1996) who, in turn, built upon a scale he had developed in previous research (Ducoffe 1995).

RELIABILITY: Alphas of .82 and .657 were estimated by Ducoffe (1996) and Brackett and Carr (2001; Carr 2003), respectively.

VALIDITY: No examination of the scale's validity was reported by Ducoffe (1996) or Brackett and Carr (2001).

REFERENCES:

Ducoffe H. Robert (1995), "How Consumers Assess the Value of Advertising," *Journal of Current Issues and Research in Advertising*, 17 (1), 1–18.
Ducoffe H. Robert (1996), "Advertising Value and Advertising on the Web," *JAR*, 36 (September/October), 21–35.
Brackett, Lana K. and Benjamin N. Carr, Jr. (2001), "Cyberspace Advertising vs. Other Media: Consumer vs. Mature Student Attitudes," *JAR*, 41 (5), 23–32.
Carr, Benjamin N., Jr. (2003), Personal Correspondence.

SCALE ITEMS: [1]

Directions: When you respond to each statement, think in general about advertising in all of its various forms that you have been exposed to, not a single advertisement or advertising for a particular type of product or service.

Advertising on _____:

1. Is a good source of product information.

2. Supplies relevant product information.

3. Provides timely information.

---

[1] Directions such as this appear to have been used in the studies. If the items are used with respect to a particular medium then the name of that medium should be placed in the blank of the scale stem. The response scale used by Ducoffe (1996) had seven points whereas Brackett and Carr (2001) used a five-point scale. See the latter for details about this issue.

SCALE NAME: Attitude Toward Advertising (Informative)

SCALE DESCRIPTION: The scale is composed of three five-point Likert-type statements measuring the extent to which a person expresses several beliefs that have to do with the ability of advertising (in general) to provide useful information.

SCALE ORIGIN: Although the concepts behind the items can be found in several previous measures these items as a set appear to be original to the study by Smit and Neijens (2000). Using the items in this scale and two others the authors were attempting to assess what they called *affinity for advertising*. They viewed this scale as measuring the *information* dimension.

RELIABILITY: Referring to the reliabilities for this scale and two others across the four media, the authors said that most had alphas above .65 (Smit and Neijens 2000). An exception was for newspapers where the alpha for this scale was .61. (The other individual alphas were not reported.)

VALIDITY: No examination of the scale's validity was reported by Smit and Neijens (2000). They did, however, run a factor analysis for each of the four media and concluded that there were three factors among the statements they used.

COMMENTS: Without knowing more about this scale's quality, potential users should be cautious about depending upon it.

REFERENCES:
Smit, Edith and Peter C. Neijens (2000), "Segmentation Based on Affinity for Advertising," *JAR*, 40 (4), 35–43.

SCALE ITEMS: [1]

1. Advertising on/in _____ provides me with useful information about bargains.

2. Advertising on/in _____ provides me with meaningful information about the product use of other consumers.

3. Advertising on/in _____ provides me with useful information about new products.

[1] The name of the medium should be placed in the blanks. Smit and Neijens (2000) used a five-point response scale with *strongly disagree* (1) and *strongly agree* (5) as the anchors.

SCALE NAME: Attitude Toward Advertising (Irritating)

SCALE DESCRIPTION: Three Likert-type statements are used to measure the extent to which a person believes that advertising is annoying. The items are general enough so that they can refer to advertising in general or to advertising in a specific medium. The scale was not, however, developed for use with a specific ad.

SCALE ORIGIN: Brackett and Carr (2001) employed the same scales as used by Ducoffe (1996) who, in turn, built upon a scale he had developed in previous research (Ducoffe 1995).

RELIABILITY: Alphas of .78 and .581 were estimated by Ducoffe (1996) and Brackett and Carr (2001; Carr 2003), respectively.

VALIDITY: No examination of the scale's validity was reported by Ducoffe (1996) or Brackett and Carr (2001).

REFERENCES:
Ducoffe H. Robert (1995), "How Consumers Assess the Value of Advertising," *Journal of Current Issues and Research in Advertising*, 17 (1), 1–18.
Ducoffe H. Robert (1996), "Advertising Value and Advertising on the Web," *JAR*, 36 (September/October), 21–35.
Brackett, Lana K. and Benjamin N. Carr, Jr. (2001), "Cyberspace Advertising vs. Other Media: Consumer vs. Mature Student Attitudes," *JAR*, 41 (5), 23–32.
Carr, Benjamin N., Jr. (2003), Personal Correspondence.

SCALE ITEMS: [1]

Directions: When you respond to each statement, think in general about advertising in all of its various forms that you have been exposed to, not a single advertisement or advertising for a particular type of product or service.

Advertising on _____:

1. insults people's intelligence.

2. is annoying.

3. is irritating.

[1] Directions such as this appear to have been used in the studies. If the items are used with respect to a particular medium then the name of that medium should be placed in the blank of the scale stem. The response scale used by Ducoffe (1996) had seven points whereas Brackett and Carr (2001) used a five-point scale. See the latter for details about this issue.

SCALE NAME: Attitude Toward Advertising (Negative)

SCALE DESCRIPTION: The scale is composed of five, five-point Likert-type statements measuring the extent to which a person expresses a variety of negative beliefs about advertising in general.

SCALE ORIGIN: Although the concepts behind the items can be found in several previous measures these items as a set appear to be original to the study by Smit and Neijens (2000). Using the items in this scale and two others the authors were attempting to assess what they called *affinity for advertising*. They viewed this scale as measuring the *irritation* dimension.

RELIABILITY: Referring to the reliabilities for this scale and two others across the four media, the authors said that most had alphas above .65 (Smit and Neijens 2000). (The individual alphas were not reported.)

VALIDITY: No examination of the scale's validity was reported by Smit and Neijens (2000). They did, however, run a factor analysis for each of the four media and concluded that there were three factors among the statements they used.

COMMENTS: Without knowing more about this scale's quality, potential users should be cautious about depending upon it.

REFERENCES:
Smit, Edith and Peter C. Neijens (2000), "Segmentation Based on Affinity for Advertising," *JAR*, 40 (4), 35–43.

SCALE ITEMS: [1]

1. For me, advertising on / in _____ appears at inconvenient moments.

2. For me, advertising on / in _____ is too loud.

3. For me, advertising on / in _____ has no credibility.

4. For me, advertising on / in _____ is repeated too often.

5. For me, all ads are alike.

[1] The name of the medium should be placed in the blanks. Smit and Neijens (2000) used a five-point response scale with *strongly disagree* (1) and *strongly agree* (5) as the anchors.

SCALE NAME: Attitude Toward Advertising (Portrayal of Homosexuals)

SCALE DESCRIPTION: Three, six-point Likert-type items are used to assess a person's opinion of advertising in general as it relates to its portrayal of homosexuals.

SCALE ORIGIN: Without being specific, Burnett (2000) stated that some of the items composing this scale and two others were original while others had been used for years by Market Facts. It seems likely, however, that the items in this scale were among the ones that were original to this study. Response data were split in half and the item-total correlations in each were compared. The strongest items common to both halves were then factor analyzed. Ultimately, ten items remained which represented three factors.

RELIABILITY: An alpha of .64 was reported for the scale (Burnett 2000).

VALIDITY: No examination of validity was reported by Burnett (2000) beyond the purification procedures referred to above.

COMMENTS: The internal consistency of the scale is low enough that caution should be exercised in its use. Further, some effort should be made to improving its reliability and evaluating its validity.

REFERENCES:
Burnett, John J. (2000), "Gays: Feelings about Advertising and Media Used," *JAR*, 40 (Jan-Apr), 75–84.

SCALE ITEMS:

1. Ads are condescending to homosexuals.

2. Ads are only useful if they portray homosexuals accurately.

3. Ads tend to portray stereotypes of homosexuals.

SCALE NAME: Attitude Toward Advertising (Usefulness)

SCALE DESCRIPTION: Three Likert-type statements are used to measure the extent to which a person believes that advertising has value and is important. The items are general enough so that they can refer to advertising in general or to advertising in a specific medium. The scale was not, however, developed for use with a specific ad.

SCALE ORIGIN: Brackett and Carr (2001) employed the same scales as used by Ducoffe (1996) who, in turn, built upon a scale he had developed in previous research (Ducoffe 1995).

RELIABILITY: Alphas of .84 and .71 were estimated by Ducoffe (1996) and Brackett and Carr (2001; Carr 2003), respectively.

VALIDITY: No examination of the scale's validity was reported by Ducoffe (1996) or Brackett and Carr (2001).

REFERENCES:
Ducoffe H. Robert (1995), "How Consumers Assess the Value of Advertising," *Journal of Current Issues and Research in Advertising*, 17 (1), 1–18.
Ducoffe H. Robert (1996), "Advertising Value and Advertising on the Web," *JAR*, 36 (September/October), 21–35.
Brackett, Lana K. and Benjamin N. Carr, Jr. (2001), "Cyberspace Advertising vs. Other Media: Consumer vs. Mature Student Attitudes," *JAR*, 41 (5), 23–32.
Carr, Benjamin N., Jr. (2003), Personal Correspondence.

SCALE ITEMS: [1]

Directions: When you respond to each statement, think in general about advertising in all of its various forms that you have been exposed to, not a single advertisement or advertising for a particular type of product or service.

Advertising on _____ :

1. is useful.

2. is valuable.

3. is important.

[1] Directions such as this appear to have been used in the studies. If the items are used with respect to a particular medium then the name of that medium should be placed in the blank of the scale stem. The response scale used by Ducoffe (1996) had seven points whereas Brackett and Carr (2001) used a five-point scale. See the latter for details about this issue.

SCALE NAME: Attitude Toward Advertising (Usefulness)

SCALE DESCRIPTION: The scale is composed of four, six-point Likert-type statements used to assess a person's opinion of advertising in general with an emphasis on the helpfulness of the information in making consumer decisions.

SCALE ORIGIN: Without being specific, Burnett (2000) stated that some of the items composing this scale and two others were original while others had been used for years by Market Facts. Response data were split in half and the item-total correlations in each were compared. The strongest items common to both halves were then factor analyzed. Ultimately, ten items remained which represented three factors.

RELIABILITY: An alpha of .91 was reported for the scale (Burnett 2000).

VALIDITY: No examination of validity was reported by Burnett (2000) beyond the purification procedures referred to above.

REFERENCES:
Burnett, John J. (2000), "Gays: Feelings about Advertising and Media Used," *JAR*, 40 (Jan-Apr), 75–84.

SCALE ITEMS:

1. Ad information helps decisions.

2. I use ads to make decisions.

3. Media provides useful information.

4. Family and friends provide better information than ads. (r)

SCALE NAME: Attitude Toward Direct Marketing

SCALE DESCRIPTION: It is a three-item, five-point Likert-type summated ratings scale measuring one's attitude about direct marketing activities being aimed at him/her.

SCALE ORIGIN: The source of the scale was not stated by Donthu and Gilliland (1996) but it is likely to be original to their study.

RELIABILITY: Alphas of .70 (Donthu and Gilliland 1996) and .72 (Donthu and Garcia 1999) have been reported for the scale.

VALIDITY: No specific examination of the scale's validity has been reported.

COMMENTS: A close reading of the items suggests that the scale is probably tapping into more than one dimension.

REFERENCES:
Donthu, Naveen and Adriana Garcia (1999), "The Internet Shopper," *JAR*, 39 (May/June), 52–58.
Donthu, Naveen and David Gilliland (1996), "The Infomercial Shopper," *JAR*, 3 (March/April), 69–76.

SCALE ITEMS:

1. Phone solicitations are an invasion of my privacy. (r)

2. I enjoy receiving junk mail.

3. I often use catalogues to shop for products.

SCALE NAME: Attitude Toward the Ad (Activity Judgments)

SCALE DESCRIPTION: The scale is composed of uni-polar items used to capture a dimension of one's attitude toward a certain advertisement with the emphasis on how exciting and playful it is. This is in contrast to measures of one's *affective reaction* to an ad. In other words, the object of the description is an ad, not merely one's emotional response to it. See scales such as #523–#528 for examples of the latter type.

SCALE ORIGIN: In one sense, the source of the scale is Burke and Edell (1986). However, they in turn drew all of the items from the pool of words used in construction of the Reaction Profile Scales by Wells, Leavitt and McConville (1971).

RELIABILITY: Alphas of .82 (n = 56), .93 (n = 184), and .91 (n = 191) were reported for the versions of the scale used by Aylesworth, Goodstein, and Kalra (1999), Burke and Edell (1986), and Burke and Edell (1989), respectively. Edell and Burke (1987) reported alphas of .95 (n = 29) and .90 (n = 32) for the versions they used for Studies 1 and 2, respectively.

VALIDITY: In several studies, Burke and Edell (1986, 1989; Edell and Burke 1987) factor analyzed a large number of descriptors. Virtually identical factors were found in each case. Three factors emerged and were labeled evaluation, activity and gentleness. This three factor structure was also found by Aylesworth, Goodstein, and Kalra (1999, p. 76).

REFERENCES:

Aylesworth, Andrew B., Ronald C. Goodstein, and Ajay Kalra (1999), "Effect of Archetypal Embeds on Feelings: An Indirect Route to Affecting Attitudes?" *JA*, 28 (3), 73–81.

Burke, Marian C. and Julie A. Edell (1986), "Ad Reactions Over Time: Capturing Changes in the Real World," *JCR*, 13 (June), 114–118.

Burke, Marian C. and Julie A. Edell (1989), "The Impact of Feelings on Ad Based Affect and Cognitions," *JMR*, 26 (February), 69–83.

Edell, Julie E. and Marian C. Burke (1987), "The Power of Feelings in Understanding Advertising Effects," *JCR*, 14 (December), 421–433.

Wells, William D., Clark Leavitt, and Maureen McConville (1971), "A Reaction Profile for TV Commercials," *JAR*, 11 (December), 11–17.

SCALE ITEMS: [1]

Directions: Please tell us how well you think each of the words listed below describes the ad you have just seen by putting a number to the right of the word. Here, we are interested in your thoughts about the ad, not the brand or product class. If you think the word describes the ad extremely well, put a 5; very well, put a 4; fairly well, put a 3; not very well, put a 2; not at all well, put a 1.

1. Energetic

2. Exciting

3. Humorous

4. Imaginative

5. Ingenious

6. Merry

7. Novel

8. Playful

9. Unique

10. Vigorous

11. Amusing

12. Enthusiastic

13. Exhilarating

14. Jolly

15. Original

16. Likable

17. Worth remembering

Aylesworth, Goodstein, and Kalra (1999): 1, 3, 4, 5, 8–10, 16, 17 5-point
Burke and Edell (1986): 1–15 5-point
Burke and Edell (1989): 1–10 5-point
Edell and Burke (1987, Study 1): 1–15 5-point
Edell and Burke (1987, Study 2): 1–10 5-point

[1] These directions and scale anchors were used by Edell and Burke (1987) as well as Burke and Edell (1989). In contrast, Aylesworth, Goodstein, and Kalra (1999) used the following to anchor their response scale: *does not describe the ad well at all* (1) and *describes the ad extremely well* (5).

SCALE NAME: Attitude Toward The Ad (Affective)

SCALE DESCRIPTION: The scales consist of various bi-polar adjectives presumed to measure more of the *affective* component of a person's attitude about a particular advertisement as opposed to the cognitive component. Most of these scales were used as part of a pair to measure the cognitive and affective components of a person's attitude. Some of the scales were developed with the apparent notion that they were general evaluative measures. However, the work done by Bruner (1995, 1998) suggests that they have more in common with measures of the *affective* component than they do with general evaluative measures. Work conducted by Petty (Crites, Fabrigar, and Petty 1994; Petty, Wegener, and Fabrigar 1997) supports the notion of separately measuring the affective, cognitive, and general evaluative aspects of attitudes.

SCALE ORIGIN: The source of most of the scales is unclear because most authors did not specify their origin. However, using methods described by Bruner (1995, 1998), a large portion, maybe as much as half, appear to be original with the remaining being either borrowed or modified from previous research. In a general sense, the basis for these scales can be traced to the work with semantic differentials pioneered by Osgood, Suci, and Tannenbaum (1957). Another source used by several authors, especially those who have wanted to measure both the affective and cognitive components of an attitude, is Baker and Churchill (1977).

RELIABILITY: The internal consistencies reported for the various versions of the scale have ranged from .75 (Petroshius and Crocker 1989) to .95 (Olney, Holbrook, and Batra 1991). Reliabilities for individual studies are listed at the end of the SCALE ITEMS section along with the specific scale items used in a study.

VALIDITY: Little validity information was provided, per se, in most of the studies. Petroshius and Crocker (1989) used factor analysis as a reliability check, noting that the affective and cognitive components in attitude toward the ad comprised 56% of the variance. Janiszewski (1988) reported unidimensionality (ML Confirmatory analysis) and support for an assumption of independence of errors in measure. Zinkhan and Zinkhan (1985) used factor analysis to reduce the items in the Response Profile (Schlinger 1979) to four semantic differential scales applicable to print ads for financial services.

COMMENTS: See also Leong, Ang, and Tham (1996) and Zinkhan and Zinkhan (1985).

REFERENCES:

Baker, Michael J. and Gilbert A. Churchill (1977), "The Impact of Physically Attractive Models on Advertising Evaluations," *JMR*, 14 (November), 538–555.

Bruner II, Gordon C. (1995), "The Psychometric Quality of Aad Scales," *Office of Scale Research Technical Report #9501*, Dept. of Marketing, Southern Illinois University.

Bruner II, Gordon C. (1998), "Standardization & Justification: Do Aad Scales Measure Up?" *Journal of Current Issues & Research in Advertising*, 20 (Spring), 1–18.

Burton Scot and Donald R. Lichtenstein (1988), "The Effect of Ad Claims and Ad Context on Attitude Toward the Advertisement," *JA*, 17 (1), 3–11.

Crites, Stephen L. Jr., Leandre R. Fabrigar, and Richard E. Petty (1994), "Measuring the Affective and Cognitive Properties of Attitudes: Conceptual and Methodological Issues," *Personality and Social Psychology Bulletin*, 20 (December), 619–634.

Janiszewski, Chris (1988), "Preconscious Processing Effects: The Independence of Attitude Formation and Conscious Thought," *JCR*, 15 (September), 199–209.

Kilbourne, William E., Scott Painton, and Danny Ridley (1985), "The Effect of Sexual Embedding on Responses to Magazine Advertisements," *JA*, 14 (2), 48–56.

Kilbourne, William E. (1986), "An Exploratory Study of the Effect of Sex Role Stereotyping on Attitudes Toward Magazine Advertisements," *JAMS*, 14 (Winter), 43–46.

Laczniak, Russell N. and Darrel D. Muehling (1993), "The Relationship Between Experimental Manipulations and Tests of Theory in an Advertising Message Involvement Context," *JA*, 3 (22), 59–74.

Leong, Siew Meng, Swee Hoon Ang, and Lai Leng Tham (1996), "Increasing Brand Name Recall in Print Advertising Among Asian Consumers," *JA*, 25 (Summer), 65–81.

Okechuku, Chike and Gongrong Wang (1988), "The Effectiveness of Chinese Print Advertisements in North America," *JAR*, 28 (October/November), 25–34.

Olney, Thomas J., Morris B. Holbrook, and Rajeev Batra (1991), "Consumer Responses to Advertising: The Effects of Ad Content, Emotions, and Attitude toward the Ad on Viewing Time," *JCR*, 17 (March), 440–453.

Osgood, Charles E., George J. Suci, and Percy H. Tannenbaum (1957), *The Measurement of Meaning*, Urbana: University of Illinois Press.

Perrien, Jean, Christian Dussart, and Francoise Paul (1985), "Advertisers and the Factual Content of Advertising," *JA*, 14 (1), 30–35, 53.

Petroshius, Susan M. and Kenneth E. Crocker (1989), "An Empirical Analysis of Spokesperson Characteristics on Advertisement and Product Evaluations," *JAMS*, 17 (Summer), 217–225.

Petty, Richard E., Duane T. Wegener, and Leandre R. Fabrigar (1997), "Attitudes and Attitude Change," *Annual Review of Psychology*, 481, 609–647.

Rosenberg, Edward, Rik Pieters, and Michel Wedel (1997), "Visual Attention to Advertising: A Segment-Level Analysis," *JCR*, 24 (December), 305–314.

Schlinger, Mary Jane (1979), "A Profile of Responses to Commercials," *JAR*, 19 (2), 37–46.

Sorescu, Alina B. and Betsy D. Gelb (2000), "Negative Competitive Advertising: Evidence Favoring Fine-Tuning," *JA*, 29 (Winter), 25–40.

Stafford, Marla Royne (1998), "Advertising Sex-Typed Services: The Effects of Sex, Service Type, and Employee Type on Consumer Attitudes," *JA*, 27 (2), 65–82.

Zhang, Yong (1996), "Responses to Humorous Advertising: The Moderating Effect of Need for Cognition," *JA*, 25 (Spring), 15–32.

Zhang, Yong and Betsy D. Gelb (1996), "Matching Advertising Appeals to Culture: The Influence of Products' Use Conditions," *JA*, 25 (Fall), 29–46.

Zinkhan, George M. and Christian F. Zinkhan (1985), "Response Profiles and Choice Behavior: An Application to Financial Services," *JA*, 14 (3), 39–51, 66.

SCALE ITEMS:

Scale items used in specific studies are listed below with an indication of the number of response points used if known. Although two studies may be shown below to have used one or more of the same items it should not automatically be concluded that the items were exactly the same. Judgment was used to determine when a bi-polar adjective was similar to one used before or when it was unique. Slight differences in the bi-polar adjectives used such as *extremely good* versus *good* and *uninteresting* versus *not interesting* were counted the same for purposes of the list here. Note that Stafford (1998) used a modified version of this approach by using very simple statements and a Likert-type response format.

1. good / bad

2. not irritating / irritating

3. interesting / boring

4. appealing / unappealing

5. impressive / unimpressive

6. attractive / unattractive

7. eye-catching / not eye-catching

8. pleasant / unpleasant

9. likable / unlikable

10. soothing / not soothing

11. warm hearted / cold hearted

12. uplifting / depressing

13. affectionate / not affectionate

14. dynamic / dull

15. refreshing / depressing

16. enjoyable / not enjoyable

17. worth watching / not worth watching

18. beautiful / ugly

19. entertaining / not entertaining

20. agreeable / disagreeable

Burton and Lichtenstein (1988): 6, 8, 10, 11, 12, 13 9-point [.86]
Janiszewski (1988): 1, 4, 6, 8, 9 9-point [.91, .93]
Kilbourne (1986): 4, 5, 6 7-point [.88]
Kilbourne, Painton and Ridley (1985): 4, 5, 6 [.77]
Laczniak and Muehling (1993): 1, 3, 4, 6, 8, 9, 14, 15, 16 7-point [.93]
Okechuku and Wang (1988): 3, 4, 5, 6, 7 [.88, .86]
Olney, Holbrook, and Batra (1991): 8, 16, 17, 19 [.95]
Perrien, Dussart and Paul (1985): 3, 6, 8, 20 7-point [.80]
Petroshius and Crocker (1989): 3, 4, 5, 6, 7 7-point [.75-.87]
Rosenberg, Pieters, and Wedel (1997): 1, 6, 17 5-point [.77]
Sorescu and Gelb (2000): 1, 9*, 16, 18 7-point [.88, .92]
Stafford (1998): 4, 5, 6, 7 7-point Likert-type [.87]
Zhang (1996): 2, 3, 8, 9 9-point [.92]
Zhang and Gelb (1996): 2, 3, 8, 9 9-point [.92]

SCALE NAME: Attitude Toward the Ad (Cognitive)

SCALE DESCRIPTION: The scales consist of various bipolar adjectives presumed to measure more of the *cognitive* content (rather than the affective content) of a subject's evaluation of an advertisement. Most of these scales were part of a pair used together to measure the cognitive and affective components of a person's attitude. Some of the scales were developed with the apparent notion that they were general evaluative measures. However, the work done by Bruner (1995, 1998) indicated that they had more in common with measures of the cognitive component than they did with general evaluative measures. In addition, work conducted by Petty (Crites, Fabrigar, and Petty 1994; Petty, Wegener, and Fabrigar 1997) supports the notion of separately measuring the affective, cognitive, and general evaluative aspects of attitudes.

SCALE ORIGIN: The source of most of the scales is unclear because most authors did not specify their origin. However, using methods described by Bruner (1995, 1998), it is estimated that about a third were borrowed intact from previously published studies with the remaining being either original or modified from previous research. In a general sense, the basis for these scales can be traced to the work with semantic differentials pioneered by Osgood, Suci, and Tannenbaum (1957). Another source used by several authors, especially those who have wanted to measure both the affective and cognitive components of an attitude, is Baker and Churchill (1977).

RELIABILITY: The reported internal consistencies have ranged from .52 (Petroshius and Crocker 1989) to .91 (Peterson, Wilson, and Brown 1992). Reliabilities for individual studies are listed at the end of the SCALE ITEMS section along with the specific scale items used in a study.

VALIDITY: Little validity information was provided, per se, in most of the studies. Several used exploratory factor analysis to provide evidence of unidimensionality. Only Burton and Lichtenstein (1988) were more rigorous in their examination of the scale's validity. They subjected their original fifteen items to a confirmatory factor analysis to arrive at six affective and five cognitive items. They also used a separate sample to see if subjects perceived the affective items as more emotional or "feeling state" descriptive than the cognitive items. The results were highly significant in the expected direction.

COMMENTS: A close examination the list of items indicates that not all of them are particularly cognitive. Some of them would appear to tap more into the affective component of an attitude (e.g., #7-#10, #13). This probably reflects an author's view of what an attitude is and some of the authors appear to have thought they were measuring attitudes in general. It was the judgment here, however, that each of these scales skewed more towards being measures of the cognitive component than they did to being measures of the affective component or more general evaluative scales. Researchers interested in measuring just the cognitive component are advised to use a set of items that has been tested in a previous study and appears to be more purely tapping into the cognitive component.

See also Zinkhan and Zinkhan (1985).

REFERENCES:
Baker, Michael J. and Gilbert A. Churchill (1977), "The Impact of Physically Attractive Models on Advertising Evaluations," *JMR*, 14 (November), 538–555.

Bruner II, Gordon C. (1995), "The Psychometric Quality of Aad Scales," *Office of Scale Research Technical Report* #9501, Dept. of Marketing, Southern Illinois University.

Bruner II, Gordon C. (1998), "Standardization & Justification: Do Aad Scales Measure Up?" *Journal of Current Issues & Research in Advertising*, 20 (Spring), 1–18.

Burton Scot and Donald R. Lichtenstein (1988), "The Effect of Ad Claims and Ad Context on Attitude Toward the Advertisement," *JA*, 17 (1), 3–11.

Crites, Stephen L. Jr., Leandre R. Fabrigar, and Richard E. Petty (1994), "Measuring the Affective and Cognitive Properties of Attitudes: Conceptual and Methodological Issues," *Personality and Social Psychology Bulletin*, 20 (December), 619–634.

Donthu, Naveen (199), (2), "Comparative Advertising Intensity," *JAR*, 32 (6), 53–58.

Donthu, Naveen (1998), "A Cross-Country Investigation of Recall of and Attitude toward Comparative Advertising," *JA*, 27 (2), 111–122.

Kilbourne, William E., Scott Painton, and Danny Ridley (1985), "The Effect of Sexual Embedding on Responses to Magazine Advertisements," *JA*, 14 (2), 48–56.

Kilbourne, William E. (1986), "An Exploratory Study of the Effect of Sex Role Stereotyping on Attitudes Toward Magazine Advertisements," *JAMS*, 14 (Winter), 43–46.

Lord, Kenneth R., Myung-Soo Lee, and Paul L. Sauer (1994), "Program Context Antecedents of Attitude toward Radio Commercials," *JAMS*, 22 (1), 3–15.

Miniard, Paul W., Sunil Bhatla, and Randall L. Rose (1990), "On the Formation and Relationship of Ad and Brand Attitudes: An Experimental and Causal Analysis," *JMR*, 27 (August), 290–303.

Okechuku, Chike and Gongrong Wang (1988), "The Effectiveness of Chinese Print Advertisements in North America," *JAR*, 28 (October/November), 25–34.

Olney, Thomas J., Morris B. Holbrook, and Rajeev Batra (1991), "Consumer Responses to Advertising: The Effects of Ad Content, Emotions, and Attitude toward the Ad on Viewing Time," *JCR*, 17 (March), 440–453.

Osgood, Charles E., George J. Suci, and Percy H. Tannenbaum (1957), *The Measurement of Meaning*, Urbana: University of Illinois Press.

Perrien, Jean, Christian Dussart, and Francoise Paul (1985), "Advertisers and the Factual Content of Advertising," *JA*, 14 (1), 30–35, 53.

Peterson, Robert A., William R. Wilson, and Steven P. Brown (1992), "Effects of Advertised Customer Satisfaction Claims on Consumer Attitudes and Purchase Intention," *JAR*, 2 (32), 34–40.

Petroshius, Susan M. and Kenneth E. Crocker (1989), "An Empirical Analysis of Spokesperson Characteristics on Advertisement and Product Evaluations," *JAMS*, 17 (Summer), 217–225.

Petty, Richard E., Duane T. Wegener, and Leandre R. Fabrigar (1997), "Attitudes and Attitude Change," *Annual Review of Psychology*, 48 (1), 609–647.

Zinkhan, George M. and Christian F. Zinkhan (1985), "Response Profiles and Choice Behavior: An Application to Financial Services," *JA*, 14 (3), 39–51, 66.

SCALE ITEMS:

Scale items used in specific studies are listed below with indication of the number of response points used for a scale, if known. Although two studies may be shown below to have used one or more of the same items it should not automatically be concluded that the items were exactly the same. Judgement was used to determine when a bi-polar adjective was similar to one used before or when it was unique. Slight differences in the bi-polar adjectives used were counted the same for purposes of the list here. If every truly different set of bi-polar adjectives were listed separately here the list of items would have been much longer.

1. interesting / boring

2. trustworthy / untrustworthy

#554 *Attitude Toward the Ad (Cognitive)*

3. persuasive / not at all persuasive

4. informative / uninformative

5. believable / unbelievable

6. effective / not at all effective

7. appealing / unappealing

8. impressive / unimpressive

9. attractive / unattractive

10. eye-catching / not eye-catching

11. clear / not clear

12. convincing / unconvincing

13. overall liking / disliking

14. clear / imprecise

15. complete / incomplete

16. well structured / badly structured

17. likely / unlikely

18. meaningful / meaningless

19. valuable / not valuable

20. important to me / not important to me

21. strong / weak

22. helpful / not helpful

23. useful / not useful

Burton and Lichtenstein (1988) (cognitive): 3, 4, 5, 6, 12 9-point [.73]
Donthu (1992): 4, 5, 7, 8, 9, 10, 11, 12, 13, 17 7-point [.88]
Donthu (1998): 4, 5, 7, 8, 9, 10, 11, 12, 13, 17 7-point [.82]

Kilbourne (1986) (cognitive): 2, 4, 5 7-point [.65]
Kilbourne, Painton and Ridley (1985) (cognitive): 2, 4, 5 [.57]
Lord, Lee, and Sauer (1994) (claim): 3, 5, 21 [.72]
Miniard, Bhatla, and Rose (1990) (claim): 3, 4, 5, 21 [.82]
Okechuku and Wang (1988) (cognitive): 4, 5, 11 9-point [.61, .72]
Olney, Holbrook, and Batra (1991) (utilitarianism): 4, 20, 22, 23 [.90]
Perrien, Dussart and Paul (1985) (cognitive): 4, 14, 15, 16 7-point [.78]
Peterson, Wilson, and Brown (1992): 1, 3, 4, 6, 7 5-point [.91]
Petroshius and Crocker (1989) (cognitive): 4, 5, 11 7-point [.52]

SCALE NAME: Attitude Toward the Ad (Cognitive)

SCALE DESCRIPTION: Multiple semantic differentials are used to assess the degree to which an ad (or the message portion of it) is viewed as being rational and useful.

SCALE ORIGIN: The version of the scale used by Hirschman (1986) appears to have been developed by Hirschman and Solomon (1984). In that study, the authors explored consumers' perceptions of visual versus verbal ads on three dimensions: functional utility, aesthetic value, and familiarity. Respondents were exposed to two ads in their questionnaires and the two alphas reported were .80 and .82.

   The source of the scale used by Cox and Cox (2001) was not given and might be original except that most of its items come from various attitude-toward-the-ad measures that have been used over time. Due to its conceptual similarity to the scale used by Hirschman (1986) and the overlap in items, it is included here rather than by itself.

RELIABILITY: An alpha of .74 was reported for the version of the scale used by Cox and Cox (2001). The alpha for the version used by Hirschman (1986) was not specifically reported.

VALIDITY: No examination of the scale's validity was reported by Hirschman (1986) or Cox and Cox (2001) but the study by Hirschman and Solomon (1984) showed that, as hypothesized, verbal ads were consistently scored higher on this dimension than visual ads. This gives a limited sense of the scale's nomological validity.

REFERENCES:

Cox, Dena and Anthony D. Cox (2001), "Communicating the Consequences of Early Detection: The Role of Evidence and Framing," *JM*, 65 (July), 91–103.

Hirschman, Elizabeth C. (1986), "The Effect of Verbal and Pictorial Advertising Stimuli on Aesthetic, Utilitarian and Familiarity Perceptions," *JA*, 15 (2), 27–34.

Hirschman, Elizabeth C. and Michael R. Solomon (1984), "Utilitarian, Aesthetic, and Familiarity Response to Verbal versus Visual Advertisements," in *Advances in Consumer Research*, T. C. Kinnear, ed. Ann Arbor, MI: Association for Consumer Research, 426–431.

SCALE ITEMS: [1]

1. logical / not logical

2. educational / not educational

3. informative / not informative

4. factual / not factual

5. useful / not useful

6. believable / not believable

7. realistic / not realistic

8. good / bad

9. appropriate / not inappropriate

10. helpful / not helpful

---

[1] Hirschman (1986) used items #1–#5 as the anchors on a seven-point response scale. Cox and Cox (2001) used items #2, #4–#10 and, although not clear, it also appeared to be a seven-point response format.

SCALE NAME: Attitude Toward the Ad (Cognitive)

SCALE DESCRIPTION: The scale appears to measure one's attitude toward some specific advertisement with an emphasis on the beliefs one holds about particular attributes the ad may or may not have. These characteristics would be generally considered as positive and desirable. The scale used by Homer (1995) was called the design factor.

SCALE ORIGIN: Although the specific versions used by Homer (1995) and Stafford (1998) appear to be original to their studies they both draw on key descriptors used many times previously in semantic differential versions of the scale to capture the cognitive component of an attitude (#554).

RELIABILITY: Alphas of .89 and .78 were reported for the versions of the scale used by Homer (1995) and Stafford (1998), respectively.

VALIDITY: No examination of the scale's validity was reported by Homer (1995) or Stafford (1998). The former did state, however, that a factor analysis was conducted and the items in this scale loaded on the same dimension.

REFERENCES:
Homer, Pamela M. (1995), "Ad Size as an Indicator of Perceived Advertising Costs and Effort: The Effects on Memory and Perceptions," *JA*, 24 (Winter), 1–12.
Stafford, Marla Royne (1998), "Advertising Sex-Typed Services: The Effects of Sex, Service Type, and Employee Type on Consumer Attitudes," *JA*, 27 (2), 65–82.

SCALE ITEMS: [1]

The ad . . .

1. was believable

2. was interesting

3. was informative

4. was well-designed

5. was easy-to-follow

6. was attention-getting

7. was clear

---

[1] Homer (1995) used the first six items (above) with the following scale anchors: *not at all descriptive of the ad / described the ad very well.* In contrast, Stafford (1998) used items 1, 3, and 7 with a Likert-type response format. Both authors used seven-point scales.

SCALE NAME: Attitude Toward the Ad (Comprehension)

SCALE DESCRIPTION: The scale is composed of semantic differential items intended to measure the difficulty a person has understanding the meaning of an advertisement.

SCALE ORIGIN: Although some of these words and phrases have been used in various ad-related studies in the past, it appears that the use of this set of items to measure this construct is original to McQuarrie and Mick (1999).

RELIABILITY: Alphas of .87 and .89 were reported for the versions of the scale used by McQuarrie and Mick (1999) and Phillips (2000), respectively.

VALIDITY: No explicit examination of the scale's validity was reported by McQuarrie and Mick (1999) or Phillips (2000).

COMMENTS: See also Hung (2001).

REFERENCES:
Hung, Kineta (2001), "Framing Meaning Perceptions with Music: The Case of Teaser Ads," *JA*, 30 (3), 39–49.
McQuarrie, Edward F. and David Glen Mick (1999), "Visual Rhetoric in Advertising: Text-Interpretive, Experimental, and Reader-Response Analyses," *JCR*, 26 (June), 37–54.
Phillips, Barbara J. (2000), "The Impact of Verbal Anchoring on Consumer Response to Image Ads," *JA*, 29 (1), 15–24.

SCALE ITEMS: [1]

1. easy to understand / difficult to understand

2. straightforward / confusing

3. the meaning is certain / the meaning is ambiguous

---

[1] McQuarrie and Mick (1999) used all three items but Phillips (2000) only used the first two.

SCALE NAME: Attitude Toward the Ad (Evaluative Judgments)

SCALE DESCRIPTION: The scale is composed of unipolar items used to capture a general evaluative dimension of one's attitude about a certain advertisement. This is in contrast to measures of one's *affective reaction* to an ad. In other words, the object of the description is an ad, not merely one's emotional response to it. See scales such as #523–#528 for examples of the latter type.

SCALE ORIGIN: In one sense, the source of the scale is Burke and Edell (1986). However, they in turn drew all of the items from the pool of words used in construction of the Reaction Profile Scales by Wells, Leavitt and McConville (1971).

RELIABILITY: Alphas of .77 (n = 56), .93 (n = 184), and .89 (n = 191) were reported for the versions of the scale used by Aylesworth, Goodstein, and Kalra (1999), Burke and Edell (1986), and Burke and Edell (1989), respectively. Edell and Burke (1987) reported alphas of .93 (n = 29) and .90 (n = 32) for the versions they used for Study 1 and Study 2, respectively.

VALIDITY: In several studies, Burke and Edell (1986, 1989; Edell and Burke 1987) factor analyzed a large number of descriptors. Virtually identical factors were found in each case. Three factors emerged and were labeled evaluation, activity and gentleness. This three-factor structure was also found by Aylesworth, Goodstein, and Kalra (1999, p. 76).

REFERENCES:
Aylesworth, Andrew B., Ronald C. Goodstein, and Ajay Kalra (1999), "Effect of Archetypal Embeds on Feelings: An Indirect Route to Affecting Attitudes?" *JA*, 28 (3), 73–81.
Burke, Marian C. and Julie A. Edell (1986), "Ad Reactions Over Time: Capturing Changes in the Real World," *JCR*, 13 (June), 114–118.
Burke, Marian C. and Julie A. Edell (1989), "The Impact of Feelings on Ad Based Affect and Cognitions," *JMR*, 26 (February), 69–83.
Edell, Julie E. and Marian C. Burke (1987), "The Power of Feelings in Understanding Advertising Effects," *JCR*, 14 (December), 421–433.
Wells, William D., Clark Leavitt, and Maureen McConville (1971), "A Reaction Profile for TV Commercials," *JAR*, 11 (December), 11–17.

SCALE ITEMS: [1]

Instructions: Please tell us how well you think each of the words listed below describes the ad you have just seen by putting a number to the right of the word. Here, we are interested in your thoughts about the ad, not the brand or product class. If you think the word describes the ad extremely well, put a 5; very well, put a 4; fairly well, put a 3; not very well, put a 2; not at all well, put a 1.

1. Believable

2. For me

3. Informative

4. Interesting

5. Irritating (r)

6. Meaningful to me

7. Phony (r)

8. Ridiculous (r)

9. Terrible (r)

10. Valuable

11. Worth remembering

12. Convincing

13. Important to me

14. Stupid (r)

15. Bad (r)

Aylesworth, Goodstein, and Kalra (1999): 1, 3, 5, 7, 8, 15 5-point
Burke and Edell (1986): 1–14 5-point
Burke and Edell (1989): 1–11 5-point
Edell and Burke (1987, Study 1): 1–14 5-point
Edell and Burke (1987, Study 2): 1–11 5-point

[1] These directions and scale anchors were used by Edell and Burke (1987) as well as Burke and Edell (1989). In contrast, Aylesworth, Goodstein, and Kalra (1999) used the following to anchor their response scale: *does not describe the ad well at all* (1) and *describes the ad extremely well* (5).

SCALE NAME: Attitude Toward the Ad (Gentleness)

SCALE DESCRIPTION: The scale is composed of uni-polar items used to capture a dimension of one's attitude toward a certain advertisement with the emphasis on how soothing and tender it is. This is in contrast to measures of one's *affective reaction* to an ad. In other words, the object of the description is an ad, not merely one's emotional response to it. See scales such as #523–#528 for examples of the latter type.

SCALE ORIGIN: In one sense, the source of the scale is Burke and Edell (1986). However, they in turn drew all of the items from the pool of words used in construction of the Reaction Profile Scales by Wells, Leavitt and McConville (1971).

RELIABILITY: Alphas of .78 (n = 56), .86 (n = 184), and .89 (n = 191) were reported for the versions of the scale used by Aylesworth, Goodstein, and Kalra (1999), Burke and Edell (1986), and Burke and Edell (1989), respectively. Edell and Burke (1987) reported alphas of .88 (n = 29) and .87 (n = 32) for the versions they used for Studies 1 and 2, respectively.

VALIDITY: In several studies, Burke and Edell (1986, 1989; Edell and Burke 1987) factor analyzed a large number of descriptors. Virtually identical factors were found in each case. Three factors emerged and were labeled evaluation, activity and gentleness. This three factor structure was also found by Aylesworth, Goodstein, and Kalra (1999, p. 76).

REFERENCES:

Aylesworth, Andrew B., Ronald C. Goodstein, and Ajay Kalra (1999), "Effect of Archetypal Embeds on Feelings: An Indirect Route to Affecting Attitudes?" *JA*, 28 (3), 73–81.

Burke, Marian C. and Julie A. Edell (1986), "Ad Reactions Over Time: Capturing Changes in the Real World," *JCR*, 13 (June), 114–118.

Burke, Marian C. and Julie A. Edell (1989), "The Impact of Feelings on Ad Based Affect and Cognitions," *JMR*, 26 (February), 69–83.

Edell, Julie E. and Marian C. Burke (1987), "The Power of Feelings in Understanding Advertising Effects," *JCR*, 14 (December), 421–433.

Wells, William D., Clark Leavitt, and Maureen McConville (1971), "A Reaction Profile for TV Commercials," *JAR*, 11 (December), 11–17.

SCALE ITEMS: [1]

Instructions: Please tell us how well you think each of the words listed below describes the ad you have just seen by putting a number to the right of the word. Here, we are interested in your thoughts about the ad, not the brand or product class. If you think the word describes the ad extremely well, put a 5; very well, put a 4; fairly well, put a 3; not very well, put a 2; not at all well, put a 1.

1. Gentle

2. Serene

3. Soothing

4. Tender

5. Lovely

Aylesworth, Goodstein, and Kalra (1999): 1–3 5-point
Burke and Edell (1986): 1–5 5-point
Burke and Edell (1989): 1–4 5-point
Edell and Burke (1987, Study 1): 1–5 5-point
Edell and Burke (1987, Study 2): 1–4 5-point

[1] These directions and scale anchors were used by Edell and Burke (1987) as well as Burke and Edell (1989). In contrast, Aylesworth, Goodstein, and Kalra (1999) used the following to anchor their response scale: *does not describe the ad well at all* (1) and *describes the ad extremely well* (5).

SCALE NAME: Attitude Toward the Ad (Happiness)

SCALE DESCRIPTION: The scale is a three-item, seven-point measure of one's attitude toward a specific advertisement with an emphasis on the extent to which it expresses some emotion-like qualities related to happiness. Note that the way in which the scale stem is phrased the scale measures what one thinks the ad expresses rather than the emotion one has experienced in reaction to the ad.

SCALE ORIGIN: The scale is original to the study by Aaker and Williams (1998). They cited Frijda (1986) as well as Edell and Burke (1987) as the source of the items. In a pretest with 12 American and 13 Chinese students, the scale was found to have an alpha of .89.

RELIABILITY: Aaker and Williams (1998) reported that the scale had an alpha of .86 (n = 151).

VALIDITY: No evidence of the scale's validity was presented in the article by Aaker and Williams (1998).

REFERENCES:

Aaker, Jennifer L. and Patti Williams (1998), "Empathy versus Pride: The Influence of Emotional Appeals Across Cultures," *JCR*, 25 (December), 241–261.

Edell, Julia A. and Marian Chapman Burke (1987), "The Power of Feelings in Understanding Advertising Effects," *JCR*, 14 (December), 421–433.

Frijda, Nico (1986), *The Emotions*, New York: Cambridge University Press.

SCALE ITEMS: [1]

Directions: Please indicate how much the following emotions describe the advertisement for _____ by circling one number for each word below.

1. happy

2. cheerful

3. delighted

[1] The response scale used for these items was anchored by *not at all* (1) and *very strongly* (7). The brand name should be placed in the blank.

SCALE NAME: Attitude Toward the Ad (Message)

SCALE DESCRIPTION: The scale is composed of seven, seven-point bi-polar adjectives used to measure a person's attitude toward the message portion of an advertisement or some other form of commercial communication (e.g., infomercial).

SCALE ORIGIN: Although the source of the scale is a dissertation by Singh (1994), the scale is similar to previous measures of attitude-toward-the-ad and attitude-toward-the-offer.

RELIABILITY: Alphas of .88 (initial) and .82 (replication) were reported for the scale by Singh, Balasubramanian, and Chakraborty (2000).

VALIDITY: No examination of the scale's validity was reported by Singh, Balasubramanian, and Chakraborty (2000).

REFERENCES:

Singh, Mandeep (1994), "A Theoretical and Empirical Examination of Infomercials," doctoral dissertation, Southern Illinois University, Carbondale, Illinois.

Singh, Mandeep, Siva K. Balasubramanian, and Goutam Chakraborty (2000), "A Comparative Analysis of Three Communication Formats: Advertising, Infomercial, and Direct Experience," *JA*, 29 (Winter), 59–75.

SCALE ITEMS:

Directions: Please indicate your attitude toward the marketing message on the following scales:

1. Good / Bad

2. Like / Dislike

3. Irritating / Not Irritating

4. Interesting / Uninteresting

5. Fair / Deceptive

6. Favorable / Unfavorable

7. Harmless / Harmful

SCALE NAME: Attitude Toward the Ad (Overall)

SCALE DESCRIPTION: The scales consist of various bipolar adjectives presumed to measure the subject's general evaluation of an advertisement. The scales are similar in that their items are not specific to the advertisements under investigation although certain adjectives may or may not be appropriate for every advertisement one may wish to assess.

Seven-point scales seem to be the most popular response format but five- and nine-point scales have been used as well. These scales are commonly symbolized by Aad and appear to be considered overall evaluations of an ad as opposed to measuring just the affective (#553) or cognitive (#554) components of an attitude.

Work conducted in recent years both in general psychology (Crites, Fabrigar, and Petty 1994; Petty, Wegener, and Fabrigar 1997) as well as with advertising (Bruner 1995, 1998) support the notion of separately measuring the affective, cognitive, and general evaluative aspects of attitudes.

With the potential exception of attitude-toward-the-brand (#59), this scale and its variations have been used more than any other in scholarly marketing research.

SCALE ORIGIN: The source of most of the scales is unclear because authors did not specify their origin. However, related investigation suggests that about a third are original with the remaining being either borrowed or modified from previous research (Bruner 1995, 1998). In a general sense, the basis for these scales can be traced to the work with semantic differentials pioneered by Osgood, Suci, and Tannenbaum (1957). With specific reference to work in marketing, the most common source is Mitchell and Olson (1981). Theirs is a common form of the scale to use when one wants to measure an overall evaluative response to an ad.

Taylor, Miracle, and Wilson (1997) developed a Korean version of the scale using the back-translation method.

RELIABILITY: Reported internal consistencies have ranged from below .69 (Kamins, Marks, and Skinner 1991) to as high as .98 (Sujan, Bettman, and Baumgartner 1993; Goodstein 1993). See last section for specific reliabilities.

VALIDITY: Little validity information, per se, was provided in most of the studies. Mitchell and Olson (1981) developed the background for using evaluative belief statements as measures of attitude from Fishbein and Ajzen (1975) and Ahtola (1975) and utilized only those four items loading together out of seven original ones in there study. Stout and Burda (1989) used a manipulation check to assess the manipulation of brand dominance, but not for Aad.

A factor analysis was performed by Bezjian-Avery, Calder, and Iacobucci (1998) on items composing their attitude toward the brand (#59) and attitude toward the ad scales. Each set of items appeared to be unidimensional with no cross-loadings greater than .34.

Madden, Allen, and Twibble (1988) reported substantive discriminant validity between ad evaluation and a measure of positive affect. Marginal discriminant validity between ad evaluation and a measure of negative affect is claimed. Both principle components and confirmatory factor analysis support the unidimensionality of the scale measure of the ad evaluation construct.

Machleit and Wilson (1988) tested their eight-item scale for dimensionality since they acknowledged the possibility that it might tap into both affective and cognitive factors. Their results indicated that there "was not evidence to support discriminant validity between the affective and cognitive dimensions" and they decided to treat the items as an overall measure of Aad.

COMMENTS: While these scales represent a generally recognized method for measuring attitude toward an ad they have relied heavily on researcher judgement with respect to which specific adjective pairs are appropriate for a given situation. In addition, there has been little rigorous testing of validity. Given this and all of the alternatives that are available, future users are urged to <u>not</u> generate more items or unique sets of items. Instead, it is suggested that they examine the previously published alternatives and select the one that is most appropriate for their study and has shown the most evidence of validity.

An additional concern is that there seems to be a lack of concern regarding the premise underlying use of the semantic differential. The semantic differential should be constructed so that the items are anchored by adjectives describing opposites on the semantic continuum. It is arguable whether this requirement is being met in those many cases where researchers have used bi-polar adjectives of the form X/not X. Scale items of this form violate the assumption that the midpoint of the scale is meant to be used when the respondent associates the object with neither pole of the adjective pair (Dawes and Smith 1985, p. 534; Osgood, Suci, and Tannenbaum 1957, pp. 29, 83). For example, the mid-point between *interesting* and *boring* would be *neither boring nor interesting*. That is different from the mid-point of a uni-polar set such as *interesting/not interesting*. There the mid-point would be something like *slightly interesting*. The degree to which this violation affects scale scores and interpretation is unknown.

See also Fennis and Bakker (2001), Mooradian (1996), Moore and Harris (1996), as well as Rubin, Mager, and Friedman (1982). The latter two studies appear to have used many of the same items as listed below but not as summated rating scales.

REFERENCES:

Aaker, Jennifer L. (2000b), "Accessibility or Diagnosticity? Disentangling the Influence of Culture on Persuasion Processes and Attitudes," *JCR*, 26 (March), 340–357.

Aaker, Jennifer L. and Patti Williams (1998), "Empathy versus Pride: The Influence of Emotional Appeals Across Cultures," *JCR*, 25 (December), 241–261.

Ahtola, Olli T. (1975), "The Vector Model of PREFERENCES: An Alternative to the Fishbein Model," *JMR*, 12 (February), 52–59.

Andrews, J. Craig (2001), Personal Correspondence.

Andrews, J. Craig, Scot Burton, and Richard G. Netemeyer (2001), "Are Some Comparative Nutrition Claims Misleading? The Role of Nutrition Knowledge, Ad Claim Type and Disclosure Conditions," *JA*, 29 (3), 29–42.

Andrews, J. Craig, Richard G. Netemeyer, and Scot Burton (1998), "Consumer Generalization of Nutrient Content Claims in Advertising," *JM*, 62 (October), 62–75.

Appiah, Osei (2001), "Ethnic Identification on Adolescents' Evaluations of Advertisements," *JAR*, 41 (5), 7–22.

Arias-Bolzmann, Leopoldo, Goutam Chakraborty, and John C. Mowen (2000), "Effects of Absurdity in Advertising: The Moderating Role of Product Category Attitude and the Mediating Role of Cognitive Responses," *JA*, 29 (1), 35–48.

Aylesworth, Andrew B., Ronald C. Goodstein, and Ajay Kalra (1999), "Effect of Archetypal Embeds on Feelings: An Indirect Route to Affecting Attitudes?" *JA*, 28 (3), 73–81.

Aylesworth, Andrew B. and Scott B. MacKenzie (1998), "Context Is Key: The Effect of Program-Induced Mood on Thoughts about the Ad," *JA*, 27 (Summer), 17–31.

Babin, Laurie and Alvin C. Burns (1997), "Effects of Print Ad Pictures and Copy Containing Instructions to Imagine on Mental Imagery That Mediates Attitudes," *JA*, 26 (Fall), 33–44.

Baumgartner, Sujan, and Padgett Baumgartner (1997), "Patterns of Affective Reactions to Advertisements: The Integration of Moment-to-Moment Responses into Overall Judgments," *JMR*, 34 (May), 219–232.

Bezjian-Avery, Alexa, Bobby Calder, and Dawn Iacobucci (1998), "New Media Interactive Advertising vs. Traditional Advertising," *JAR*, 38 (July/August), 23–32.

Bhat, Subodh, Thomas W. Leigh, and Daniel L. Wardlow (1998), "The Effect of Consumer Prejudices on Ad Processing: Heterosexual Consumers' Responses to Homosexual Imagery in Ads," *JA*, 27 (4), 9–28.

Boles, James and Scot Burton (1992), "An Examination of Free Elicitation and Response Scale Measures of Feelings and Judgments Evoked by Television Advertisements," *JAMS*, 20 (Summer), 225–233.

Brunel, Frederic F. and Michelle R. Nelson (2001), "Explaining Gendered Responses to "Help-Self" and "Help-Others" Charity Ad Appeals: The Mediating Role of World-Views," *JA*, 29 (3), 15–28.

Bruner II, Gordon C. (1995), "The Psychometric Quality of Aad Scales," *Office of Scale Research Technical Report #9501*, Dept. of Marketing, Southern Illinois University.

Bruner II, Gordon C. (1998), "Standardization and Justification: Do Aad Scales Measure Up?" *Journal of Current Issues and Research in Advertising*, 20 (Spring), 1–18.

Bruner II, Gordon C. and Anand Kumar (2000), "Web Commercials and Advertising Hierarchy-of-Effects," *JAR*, 40 (Jan-Apr), 35–42.

Bucholz, Laura M. and Robert E. Smith (1991), "The Role of Consumer Involvement in Determining Cognitive Response to Broadcast Advertising," *JA*, 1 (20), 4–17.

Burnkrant, Robert E. and H. Rao Unnava (1995), "Effects of Self-Referencing on Persuasion," *JCR*, 22 (June), 17–26.

Burns, Alvin C., Abhijit Biswas, and Laurie A. Babin (1993), "The Operation of Visual Imagery as a Mediator of Advertising Effects," *JA*, 2 (22), 71–85.

Coulter, Keith S. (1998), "The Effects of Affective Responses to Media Context on Advertising Evaluations," *JA*, 27 (4), 41–51.

Cox, Dena Saliagas and William B. Locander (1987), "Product Novelty: Does It Moderate the Relationship Between Ad Attitudes and Brand Attitudes?" *JA*, 16 (3), 39–44.

Cox, Dena S. and Anthony D. Cox (1988), "What Does Familiarity Breed? Complexity as a Moderator of Repetition Effects in Advertisement Evaluation," *JCR*, 15 (June), 111–116.

Chattopadhyay, Amitava and Kumal Basu (1990), "Humor in Advertising: The Moderating Role of Prior Brand Evaluation," *JMR*, 27 (November), 466–476.

Chattopadhyay, Amitava and Prakash Nedungadi (1992), "Does Attitude toward the Ad Endure? The Moderating Effects of Attention and Delay," *JCR*, 19 (June), 26–33.

Crites, Stephen L. Jr., Leandre R. Fabrigar, and Richard E. Petty (1994), "Measuring the Affective and Cognitive Properties of Attitudes: Conceptual and Methodological Issues," *Personality and Social Psychology Bulletin*, 20 (December), 619–634.

Darley, William K. and Robert E. Smith (1993), "Advertising Claim Objectivity: Antecedents and Effects," *JM*, 57 (October), 100–113.

Darley, William K. and Robert E. Smith (1995), "Gender Differences in Information Processing Strategies: An Empirical Test of the Selectivity Model in Advertising Response," *JA*, 24 (Spring), 41–56.

Dawes, Robyn M. and Tom L. Smith (1985), "Attitude and Opinion Measurement," in *Handbook of Social Psychology, 3rd ed., Vol. 1*, Gardner Lindzey and Elliot Aronson, ed. New York: Random House, 509–566.

Day, Ellen and Marla Royne Stafford (1997), "Age-Related Cues in Retail Services Advertising: Their Effects on Younger Consumers," *JR*, 73 (2), 211–233.

Droge, Cornelia (1989), "Shaping the Route to Attitude Change: Central Versus Peripheral Processing Through Comparative Versus Noncomparative Advertising," *JMR*, 26 (May), 193–204.

Ellen, Pam Scholder and Paula Fitzgerald Bone (1998), "Does It Matter If It Smells? Olfactory Stimuli As Advertising Executional Cues," *JA*, 27 (4), 29–39.

Fennis, Bob M. and Arnold B. Bakker (2001), "Stay Tuned-We Will Be Back Right After These Messages: Need to Evaluate Moderates the Transfer of Irritation in Advertising," *JA*, 30 (3), 15–25.

Fishbein, Martin and Icek Ajzen (1975), *Belief, Attitude, Intention and Behavior: An Introduction to Theory and Research*, Reading, MA: Addison-Wesley.

Forehand, Mark R., and Rohit Deshpande (2001), "What We see Makes Us Who We Are: Priming Ethnic Self-Awareness and Advertising Response," *JMR*, 38 (August), 336–348.

Gardner, Meryl Paula (1985), "Does Attitude Toward the Ad Affect Brand Attitude Under a Brand Evaluation Set?" *JMR*, 22 (May), 192–198.

Goldsmith, Ronald E., Barbara A. Lafferty, and Stephen J. Newell (2001), "The Impact of Corporate Credibility and Celebrity Credibility on Consumer Reaction to Advertisements and Brands," *JA*, 29 (3), 30–54.

Goodstein, Ronald C. (1993), "Category-based Applications and Extensions in Advertising: Motivating More Extensive Ad Processing," *JCR*, 20 (June), 87–99.

Ha, Louisa (1997), Personal Correspondence.

Ha, Louisa (1996), "Advertising Clutter in Consumer Magazines: Dimensions and Effects," *JAR*, 36 (July/August), 76–84.

Hastak, Manoj and Jerry C. Olson (1989), "Assessing the Role of Brand Related Cognitive Responses as Mediators of Communications Effects on Cognitive Structure," *JCR*, 15 (March), 444–456.

Hill, Ronald Paul (1988), "An Exploration of the Relationship Between AIDS-Related Anxiety and the Evaluation of Condom Advertisements," *JA*, 17 (Winter), 35–42.

Hill, Ronald Paul (1989), "An Exploration of Voter Responses to Political Advertisements," *JA*, 18 (Winter), 14–22.

Homer, Pamela M. (1995), "Ad Size as an Indicator of Perceived Advertising Costs and Effort: The Effects on Memory and Perceptions," *JA*, 24 (Winter), 1–12.

Homer, Pamela M. and Lynn Kahle (1990), "Source Expertise, Time of Source Identification, and Involvement in Persuasion: An Elaborative Processing Perspective," *JA*, 1 (19), 30–39.

Kalra, Ajay and Ronald C. Goodstein (1998), "The Impact of Advertising Positioning Strategies on Consumer Price Sensitivity," *JMR*, 35 (May), 210–224.

Kamins, Michael A. (1990), "An Investigation into the 'Match-Up' Hypothesis in Celebrity Advertising: When Beauty May be Only Skin Deep," *JA*, 19 (Spring), 4–13.

Kamins, Michael A., Lawrence J. Marks, and Deborah Skinner (1991), "Television Commercial Evaluation in the Context of Program Induced Mood: Congruency Versus Consistency Effects," *JA*, 20 (Summer), 1–14.

Kellaris, James J., Anthony D. Cox, and Dena Cox (1993), "The Effect of Background Music on Ad Processing: A Contingency Explanation," *JM*, 57 (October), 114–124.

Keller, Kevin Lane (1987), "Memory Factors in Advertising: The Effect of Advertising Retrieval Cues on Brand Evaluations," *JCR*, 14 (December), 316–333.

Keller, Kevin Lane (1991a), "Cue Compatibility and Framing in Advertising," *JMR*, 28 (February), 42–57.

Keller, Kevin Lane (1991b), "Memory and Evaluation Effects in Competitive Advertising Environments," *JCR*, 17 (March), 463–476.

Kempf, Deanna S. and Robert E. Smith (1998), "Consumer Processing of Product Trial and the Influence of Prior Advertising: A Structural Modeling Approach," *JMR*, 35 (August), 325–338.

Kirmani, Amna (1997), "Advertising Repetition as a Signal of Quality: If It's Advertised So Much, Something Must Be Wrong," *JA*, 26 (Fall), 77–86.

Krishnamurthy, Parthasarathy and Mita Sujan (1999), "Retrospection versus Anticipation: The Role of the Ad under Retrospective and Anticipatory Self-Referencing," *JCR*, 26 (June), 55–69.

Lohse, Gerald L. and Dennis L. Rosen (2001), "Signaling Quality and Credibility in Yellow Pages Adverting: The Influence of Color and Graphics on Choice," *JA*, 30 (2), 73–85.

Lord, Kenneth R., Myung-Soo Lee, and Paul L. Sauer (1994), "Program Context Antecedents of Attitude toward Radio Commercials," *JAMS*, 22 (1), 3–15.

Lord, Kenneth R., Myung-Soo Lee, and Paul L. Sauer (1995), "The Combined Influence Hypothesis: Central and Peripheral Antecedents of Attitude toward the Ad," *JA*, 24 (Spring), 73–85.

Machleit, Karen A. and R. Dale Wilson (1988), "Emotional Feelings and Attitude toward the Advertisement: The Roles of Brand Familiarity and Repetition," *JA*, 17 (3), 27–35.

Machleit, Karen A., Chris T. Allen, and Thomas J. Madden (1993), "The Mature Brand and Brand Interest: An Alternative Consequence of Ad-Evoked Affect," *JM*, 57 (October), 72–82.

MacInnis, Deborah J. and C. Whan Park (1991), "The Differential Role of Characteristics of Music on High- and Low-Involvement Consumers' Processing of Ads," *JCR*, 18 (September), 161–173.

MacInnis, Deborah J. and Douglas M. Stayman (1993), "Focal and Emotional Integration: Constructs, Measures, and Preliminary Evidence," *JA*, 22 (Winter), 51–65.

MacKenzie, Scott B. and Richard J. Lutz (1989), "An Empirical Examination of the Structural Antecedents of Attitude toward the Ad in an Advertising Pretesting Context," *JM*, 53 (April), 48–65.

MacKenzie, Scott B. and Richard A. Spreng (1992), "How Does Motivation Moderate the Impact of Central and Peripheral Processing on Brand Attitudes and Intentions?" *JCR*, 18 (March), 519–529.

Macklin, M. Carole, Norman T. Bruvold, and Carol Lynn Shea (1985), "Is it Always as Simple as 'Keep It Simple!'?" *JA*, 14 (4), 28–35.

Madden, Thomas J., Chris T. Allen, and Jacquelyn L. Twibble (1988), "Attitude toward the Ad: An Assessment of Diverse Measurement Indices under Different Processing Sets," *JMR*, 25 (August), 242–252.

McQuarrie, Edward F. and David G. Mick (1992), "On Resonance: A Critical Pluralistic Inquiry into Advertising Rhetoric," *JCR*, 19 (September), 180–197.

McQuarrie, Edward F. and David G. Mick (1999), "Visual Rhetoric in Advertising: Text-Interpretive, Experimental, and Reader-Response Analyses," *JCR*, 26 (June), 37–54.

Miller, Darryl W. and Lawrence J. Marks (1992), "Mental Imagery and Sound Effects in Radio Commercials," *JA*, 4 (21), 83–93.

Miniard, Paul W., Sunil Bhatla, and Randall L. Rose (1990), "On the Formation and Relationship of Ad and Brand Attitudes: An Experimental and Causal Analysis," *JMR*, 27 (August), 290–303.

Mitchell, Andrew A. (1986), "The Effect of Verbal and Visual Components of Advertisements on Brand Attitudes and Attitude toward the Advertisement," *JCR*, 13 (June), 12–24.

Mitchell, Andrew A. and Jerry C. Olson (1981), "Are Product Attribute Beliefs the Only Mediator of Advertising Effects on Brand Attitude?" *JMR*, 18 (August), 318–332.

Mooradian, Todd A. (1996), "Personality and Ad-Evoked Feelings: The Case for Extraversion and Neuroticism," *JAMS*, 24 (Spring), 99–109.

Moore, David J. and William D. Harris (1996), "Affect Intensity and the Consumer's Attitude toward High Impact Emotional Advertising Appeals," *JA*, 25 (Summer), 37–50.

Muelhing, Darrel D. (1987), "Comparative Advertising: The Influence Attitude-toward-the-Ad on Brand Evaluation," *JA*, 16 (4), 43–49.

Murry, John P. Jr., John L. Lastovicka, and Surendra N. Singh (1992), "Feeling and Liking Responses to Television Programs: An Examination of Two Explanations for Media-Context Effects," *JCR*, 18 (March), 441–451.

Osgood, Charles E., George J. Suci, and Percy H. Tannenbaum (1957), *The Measurement of Meaning*, Urbana: University of Illinois Press.

Petty, Richard E., Duane T. Wegener, and Leandre R. Fabrigar (1997), "Attitudes and Attitude Change," *Annual Review of Psychology*, 48 (1), 609–647.

Pham, Michel Tuan (1996), "Cue Representation and Selection Effects of Arousal on Persuasion," *JCR*, 22 (March), 373–387.

Phillips, Barbara J. (2000), "The Impact of Verbal Anchoring on Consumer Response to Image Ads," *JA*, 29 (1), 15–24.

Prakash, Ved (1992), "Sex Roles and Advertising Preferences," *JAR*, 3 (32), 43–52.

Rubin, Vicky, Carol Mager, and Hershey H. Friedman (1982), "Company President Versus Spokesperson in Television Commercials," *JAR*, 22 (August/September), 31–33.

Schuhwerk, Melody E. and Roxanne Lefkoff-Hagius (1995), "Green or Non-Green? Does Type of Appeal Matter When Advertising a Green Product?" *JA*, 24 (Summer), 45–54.

Severn, Jessica, George E. Belch, and Michael A. Belch (1990), "The Effects of Sexual and Non-Sexual Advertising Appeals and Information Level on Cognitive Processing and Communication Effectiveness," *JA*, 19 (Spring), 14–22.

Shiv, Baba, Julie A. Edell, and John W. Payne (1997), "Factors Affecting the Impact of Negatively and Positively Framed Ad Messages," *JCR*, 24 (December), 285–294.

Simpson, Penny M., Steve Horton, and Gene Brown (1996), "Male Nudity in Advertisements: A Modified Replication and Extension of Gender and Product Effects," *JAMS*, 24 (Summer), 257–262.

Singh, Surendra N. and Catherine A. Cole (1993), "The Effects of Length, Content, and Repetition on Television Commercial Effectiveness," *JMR*, 30 (February), 91–104.

Singh, Surendra N., V. Parker Lessig, Dongwook Kim, Reetika Gupta, and Mary Ann Hocutt (2000), "Does Your Ad Have Too Many Pictures?" *JAR*, 40 (Jan-Apr), 11–27.

Smith, Robert E. (1993), "Integrating Information From Advertising and Trial: Processes and Effects on Consumer Response to Product Information," *JMR*, 30 (May), 204–219.

Stafford, Marla Royne (1996), "Tangibility in Services Advertising: An Investigation of Verbal Versus Visual Cues," *JA*, 25 (Fall), 13–28.

Stafford, Marla Royne (1998), "Advertising Sex-Typed Services: The Effects of Sex, Service Type, and Employee Type on Consumer Attitudes," *JA*, 27 (2), 65–82.

Stafford, Marla Royne (1999), Personal Correspondence.

Stafford, Marla Royne and Ellen Day (1995), "Retail Services Advertising: The Effects of Appeal, Medium, and Service," *JA*, 24 (Spring), 57–71.

Steenkamp, Jan-Benedict E. M. and Hans Baumgartner (1992), "The Role of Optimum Stimulation Level in Exploratory Consumer Behavior," *JCR*, 19 (December), 434–448.

Stevenson, Julie, Gordon C. Bruner II, and Anand Kumar (2000), "Webpage Background and Viewer Attitudes," *JAR*, 40 (January/April), 29–34.

Stout, Patricia A. and Benedicta L. Burda (1989), "Zipped Commercials: Are They Effective?" *JA*, 18 (4), 23–32.

Sujan, Mita, James R. Bettman, and Hans Baumgartner (1993), "Influencing Consumer Judgments Using Autobiographical Memories: A Self-Referencing Perspective," *JMR*, 30 (November), 422–436.

Taylor, Charles R., Gordon E. Miracle, and R. Dale Wilson (1997), "The Impact of Information Level on the Effectiveness of U.S. and Korean Television Commercials," *JA*, 26 (Spring), 1–18.

Toncar, Mark and James Munch (2001), "Consumer Responses to Tropes in Print Advertising," *JA*, 30 (1), 55–65.

Tripp, Carolyn, Thomas D. Jensen, and Les Carlson (1994), "The Effects of Multiple Product Endorsements by Celebrities on Consumers' Attitudes and Intentions," *JCR*, 20 (March), 535–547.

Whittler, Tommy E. and Joan DiMeo (1991), "Viewer's Reaction to Racial Cues in Advertising Stimuli," *JAR*, 6 (31), 37–46.

Yi, Youjae (1990), "Cognitive and Affective Priming Effects of the Context for Print Advertisements," *JA*, 19 (Summer), 40–48.

Yi, Youjae (1993), "Contextual Priming Effects in Print Advertisements: The Moderating Role of Prior Knowledge," *JA*, 1 (22), 1–10.

SCALE ITEMS: [1]

Rate your beliefs about the ad on these dimensions:

1. good / bad

2. like / dislike

3. not irritating / irritating

4. interesting / boring

5. inoffensive / offensive

6. persuasive / not at all persuasive

7. informative / uninformative

8. believable / unbelievable

9. effective / not at all effective

10. appealing / unappealing

11. attractive / unattractive

12. favorable / unfavorable

13. fair / unfair

14. pleasant / unpleasant

15. fresh / stale

16. nice / awful

17. honest / dishonest

18. convincing / unconvincing

19. likable / unlikable

20. agreeable / disagreeable

21. tasteful / tasteless

22. artful / artless

23. valuable / not valuable

24. familiar / unfamiliar

25. positive / negative

26. dynamic / dull

27. refreshing / depressing

28. enjoyable / not enjoyable

29. useful / useless

30. entertaining / not entertaining

31. satisfactory / unsatisfactory

32. well made / poorly made

33. fond of / not fond of

34. not insulting / insulting

35. original / unoriginal

36. refined / vulgar

37. sensitive / insensitive

38. appropriate / inappropriate

39. clear / not clear

40. simple / complex

41. overall liking / overall disliking

42. not annoying / annoying

43. outstanding / poor

44. for me / not for me

45. strong / weak

Aaker (2000b): 1, 12, 19* 7-point [.87]
Aaker and Williams (1998): 1, 12, 19* 7-point [.95]
Appiah (2001): 1, 4, 10*, 11*, 19*, 23*, 25, 29, 43, 44, 45 7-point [.94-.96]
Arias-Bolzmann, Chakraborty, and Mowen (2000): 1, 2, 12, 25 7-point [.95]
Andrews, Burton and Netemeyer (2001): 1, 12, 25 7-point [.93]
Andrews, Netemeyer, and Burton (1998; Andrews 2001): 1, 12, 25 7-point [.93]
Aylesworth and MacKenzie (1998): 1, 12, 14 7-point
Aylesworth, Goodstein, and Kalra (1999): 1, 12, 19* 7-point [.95]
Babin and Burns (1997): 1, 4, 12, 14, 16 7-point [.89]
Baumgartner, Sujan, and Padgett (1997): 1, 12, 14, 25 9-point [.92]
Bezjian-Avery, Calder, and Iacobucci (1998): 1, 6, 10, 11, 18, 39, 40, 41 7-point
Bhat, Leigh, and Wardlow (1998): 1, 2, 12 7-point [.94]
Boles and Burton (1992): 1, 2, 12 7-point* [.91]
Brunel and Nelson (2001): 1, 2*, 3, 14 7-point
Bruner and Kumar (2000): 1, 2, 3, 4* 7-point [.87]
Bucholz and Smith (1991): 1, 3, 4 7-point [.92]
Burnkrant and Unnava (1995): 1, 12, 25 7-point [.95]
Burns, Biswas, and Babin (1993): 1, 4, and three unidentified items [.88]
Chattopadhyay and Basu (1990): 3, 4, 14, 19 9-point [.91]
Chattopadhyay and Nedungadi (1992): 1, 4, 14, 19 9-point [.86]
Coulter (1998): 1, 2*, 12, 25 7-point [.90]
Cox and Cox (1988): 1, 14, 19 9-point [.90]
Cox and Locander (1987): 1, 14, 19 9-point [.90]
Darley and Smith (1993): 1, 3, 4* 7-point [.75]
Darley and Smith (1995): 1, 3, 4*, 14 7-point [.81]
Day and Stafford (1997): 1, 2, 12, 25 7-point [.92]
Droge (1989): 1, 3, 4, 5 7-point [.806, .893]
Ellen and Bone (1998): 1, 3, 4*, 14, 19, 28 7-point [.93]
Forehand and Deshpande (2001): 1, 2, 7, 14, 29 7-point [91]
Gardner (1985): 1, 2, 3, 4 7-point [.78 and .86]
Goldsmith, Lafferty and Newell (2001): 1, 12, 14 7-point [.93]
Goodstein (1993): 1, 12, 19 7-point [.98]
Ha (1996): 2, 4*, 14, 29, 30 7-point [.95]
Hastak and Olson (1989): 1, 2, 14, 16 7-point [.90]
Hill (1988): 1, 2, 3, 4, 12 5-point [.89-.92]
Hill (1988): 14, 16, 21, 37 5-point [.82-.94]
Hill (1989): 1, 2, 3, 4, 12 5-point [.86]
Hill (1989): 14, 16, 21, 37 5-point [.83]
Homer (1995): 1, 2, 12, 14, 20, 23, 25, 29, 38 9-point [.95]

Homer and Kahle (1990): 4, 12, 25 9-point [.82]

Kalra and Goodstein (1998): 1*, 2*, 12* 7-point [.97, .91]

Kamins (1990): 1, 14, 20, 31 7-point [.85]

Kamins, Marks, and Skinner (1991): 1, 14, 31 5-point [.69]

Kellaris, Cox, and Cox (1993): 1, 4, 14, 19, 21 7-point [.88]

Keller (1987): 1, 4, 10, 19 7-point [.92]

Keller (1991a): 1, 4, 10, 19 7-point [.89]

Keller (1991b): 1, 2, 4, 10 7-point [.89]

Kempf and Smith (1998): 1, 2, 14 [.90]

Kirmani (1997): 1, 3, 4, 14 7-point [.84]

Krishnamurthy and Sujan (1999): 1, 14, 19*, 28 9-point [.89]

Lohse and Rosen (2001): 1, 12, 14 7-point [.92]

Lord, Lee, and Sauer (1994, 1995): 1, 12, 14 7-point [.86]

Machleit and Wilson (1988): 1, 2*, 3, 12, 28*, 32, 33, 34 7-point [.95, .96]

Machleit, Allen, and Madden (1993): 1, 4, 14, 19, 21, 22 [.91, .93]

MacInnis, and Park (1991): 1, 10, 12, 19 7-point [.95]

MacInnis and Stayman (1993): 1, 2, 10, 25 7-point [.93]

MacKenzie and Lutz (1989): 1, 12, 14 7-point [.88]

MacKenzie and Spreng (1992): 1, 12, 14 7-point [.88]

Macklin, Bruvold and Shea (1985): 1, 13, 14, 15, 16, 17 7-point [.85]

Madden, Allen and Twibble (1988): 1, 4, 14, 19, 21, 22 [.88]

McQuarrie and Mick (1992): 2, 14, 28 7-point [.92]

McQuarrie and Mick (1999): 2, 14, 28* [.90]

Miller and Marks (1992): 1, 2, 3, 4 5-point [.86]

Miniard, Bhatla, and Rose (1990): 1, 2, 3, 4, 9 7-point [.92]

Mitchell (1986): 1, 2, 3, 4 5-point [.90]

Mitchell and Olsen (1981): 1, 2, 3, 4 5-point [.87]

Muehling (1987): 1, 10, 11, 14, 26, 27, 28 7-point

Murry, Lastovicka, Singh (1992): 1, 2, 3, 4, 12 [.88]

Pham (1996): 1, 2, 12, 31 5-point [.95, .93]

Phillips (2000): 1, 2, 28 7-point [.89]

Prakash (1992): 1, 2, 3, 4 7-point [.82]

Schuhwerk and Lefkoff-Hagius (1995): 1, 4, 8, 12, 14, 18 7-point [.87]

Severn, Belch, and Belch (1990): 4, 5, 12, 30, 35 7-point

Shiv, Edell, and Payne (1997): 1, 10, 19* 7-point [.85]

Simpson, Horton, and Brown (1996): 1, 2, 12, 25 9-point [.965]

Singh and Cole (1993): 1, 4, 7, 8, 14, 18, 19, 21, 22, 24, 30, 34, 36 7-point [.93]

Singh et al. (2000): 1, 4, 7, 8, 14, 18, 19*, 21, 22, 24*, 30* 7-point [.91]

Smith (1993): 1, 12, 14 7-point [.92]

Stafford (1996): 1, 2, 12, 25 [.96]

Stafford (1998): 1, 2, 12, 25 7-point [.95]

Stafford and Day (1995): 1, 2, 3, 4* 7-point [.90]

Steenkamp and Baumgartner (1992): 1, 12, 14, 25 7-point [.93, .89]

Stout and Burda (1989): 2, 12 7-point [.89]

Stevenson, Bruner, and Kumar (2000): 1, 2, 3, 4* 7-point [.91]

Sujan, Bettman, and Baumgartner (1993): 1, 12, 14, 25 9-point [.98]

#562 *Attitude Toward the Ad (Overall)*

Taylor, Miracle, and Wilson (1997): 1, 2, 25, 32 7-point [.95, .96]
Toncar, Mark and James Munch (2001): 1, 14, 25 7-point [.89]
Tripp, Jensen, and Carlson (1994): 1, 3*, 4*, 19 7-point [.84]
Whittler and DiMeo (1991): 6, 11, 12 15-point [.87]
Yi (1990): 1, 2, 3, 4 7-point [.85]
Yi, (1993): 1, 2, 3, 4 7-point [.80]

[1] Directions could be something like this. For ease of reporting, the positive anchors (when clear) are listed on the left. Below that, scale items used in specific studies are listed with an indication of the points on the response scale, if known. Although two studies may be shown to have used one or more of the same items it should not automatically be concluded that the items were exactly the same. Judgment was used to determine the similarity of adjectives. Slight differences in the bi-polar adjectives used such as *extremely bad* versus *bad* and *uninteresting* versus *not interesting* or *boring* were counted the same for purposes of the list here but are noted with an asterisk (*). If every truly different set of bi-polar adjectives were listed separately here the list of items would have been much longer. Finally, for each study in which it is known, the reliability of the particular set of items that was used is shown in brackets.

SCALE NAME: Attitude Toward the Ad (Overall)

SCALE DESCRIPTION: A four-item, seven-point scale is used to assess a person's attitude toward some specific advertisement. Unlike the more popular approach that depends primarily on simple bi-polar adjectives, this scale is composed of sets of brief, opposing, complete sentences.

SCALE ORIGIN: Although the first known use of this scale was by Holbrook and Batra (1987), the core bi-polar adjectives began to be common in the measurement of the construct during the 1980s.

RELIABILITY: Alphas of .99 and .81 have been reported for the scale by Holbrook and Batra (1987) and Shamdasani, Stanaland, and Tan (2001), respectively.

VALIDITY: The validity of the scale has not been specifically addressed in the studies.

REFERENCES:
Holbrook, Morris B. and Rajeev Batra (1987), "Assessing the Role of Emotions as Mediators of Consumer Responses to Advertising," *JCR*, 14 (December), 404–420.
Shamdasani, Prem N., Andrea J. S. Stanaland, and Juliana Tan (2001), "Location, Location, Location: Insights for Advertising Placement on the Web," *JAR*, 41 (July/August), 7–21.

SCALE ITEMS:

1. I dislike the ad / I like the ad.

2. I react unfavorably to the ad / I react favorably to the ad.

3. I feel negative toward the ad / I feel positive toward the ad.

4. The ad is bad / The ad is good.

SCALE NAME: Attitude Toward The Ad (Overall)

SCALE DESCRIPTION: The scale is composed of five statements and uses a seven-point, Likert-type response format. The items are intended to measure a person's attitude toward a particular advertisement.

SCALE ORIGIN: Although the key descriptors in the statements have been commonly used in semantic differential measures of attitude-toward-the-ad in the past, the set of statements used by Lee and Mason (1999) appears to be original to their study.

RELIABILITY: An alpha of .91 was reported for the scale (Lee and Mason 1999). Lee (2000) reported an alpha of .93 for use of the scale with two different ads.

VALIDITY: No evidence of the scale's validity was reported in either study. (1999).

REFERENCES:
Lee, Yih Hwai (2000), "Manipulating Ad Message Involvement through Information Expectancy: Effects on Attitude Evaluation and Confidence," *JA*, 29 (2), 29–43.
Lee, Yih Hwai and Charlotte Mason (1999), "Responses to Information Incongruency in Advertising: The Role of Expectancy, Relevancy, and Humor," *JCR*, 26 (September), 156–169.

SCALE ITEMS:

1. I dislike the ad. (r)

2. The ad is appealing to me.

3. The ad is attractive to me.

4. The ad is interesting to me.

5. I think the ad is bad. (r)

SCALE NAME: Attitude Toward the Ad (Peacefulness)

SCALE DESCRIPTION: The scale is a three item, seven-point measure of one's attitude toward a specific advertisement with an emphasis on the extent to which it expresses some emotion-like qualities related to peacefulness. Note that the way in which the scale stem is phrased the scale measures what one thinks the ad expresses rather than the emotion one has experienced in reaction to the ad.

SCALE ORIGIN: The scale is original to the study by Aaker and Williams (1998). They cited Frijda (1986) as well as Edell and Burke (1987) as the source of the items. In a pretest with 12 American and 13 Chinese students, the scale was found to have an alpha of .93.

RELIABILITY: Aaker and Williams (1998) reported that the scale had an alpha of .93 (n = 151).

VALIDITY: No evidence of the scale's validity was presented in the article by Aaker and Williams (1998).

REFERENCES:

Aaker, Jennifer L. and Patti Williams (1998), "Empathy versus Pride: The Influence of Emotional Appeals Across Cultures," *JCR*, 25 (December), 241–261.

Edell, Julia A. and Marian Chapman Burke (1987), "The Power of Feelings in Understanding Advertising Effects," *JCR*, 14 (December), 421–433.

Frijda, Nico (1986), *The Emotions*, New York: Cambridge University Press.

SCALE ITEMS: [1]

Directions: Please indicate how much the following emotions describe the advertisement for _____ by circling one number for each word below.

1. calm

2. peaceful

3. serene

[1] The response scale used for these items was anchored by *not at all* (1) and *very strongly* (7). The brand name should be placed in the blank.

SCALE NAME: Attitude Toward the Ad (Pride)

SCALE DESCRIPTION: The scale is a three-item, seven-point measure of one's attitude toward a specific advertisement with an emphasis on the extent to which it expresses some emotion-like qualities related to pride. Note that the way in which the scale stem is phrased the scale measures what one thinks the ad expresses rather than the emotion one has experienced in reaction to the ad.

SCALE ORIGIN: The scale is original to the study by Aaker and Williams (1998). They cited Frijda (1986) as well as Edell and Burke (1987) as the source of the items. In a pretest with 10 American and 10 Chinese students, the scale was found to have an alpha of .90.

RELIABILITY: The scale was used in both Study 1 and 2 by Aaker and Williams (1998) with alphas of .93 (n = 150) and .90 (n = 151) being reported, respectively.

VALIDITY: No evidence of the scale's validity was presented in the article by Aaker and Williams (1998).

REFERENCES:
Aaker, Jennifer L. and Patti Williams (1998), "Empathy versus Pride: The Influence of Emotional Appeals Across Cultures," *JCR*, 25 (December), 241–261.
Edell, Julia A. and Marian Chapman Burke (1987), "The Power of Feelings in Understanding Advertising Effects," *JCR*, 14 (December), 421–433.
Frijda, Nico (1986), *The Emotions*, New York: Cambridge University Press.

SCALE ITEMS: [1]

Directions: Please indicate how much the following emotions describe the advertisement for _____ by circling one number for each word below.

1. proud

2. confident

3. excited

---

[1] The response scale used for these items was anchored by *not at all* (1) and *very strongly* (7). The brand name should be placed in the blank.

SCALE NAME: Attitude Toward the Ad (Warmth)

SCALE DESCRIPTION: The scale is a three-item, seven-point measure of one's attitude toward a specific advertisement with an emphasis on the extent to which it expresses some emotion-like qualities related to warmth. Note that the way in which the scale stem is phrased the scale measures what one thinks the ad expresses rather than the emotion one has experienced in reaction to the ad. The scale was loosely referred to as *empathy* by Aaker and Williams (1998).

SCALE ORIGIN: The scale is original to the study by Aaker and Williams (1998). They cited Frijda (1986) as well as Edell and Burke (1987) as the source of the items. In a pretest with 10 American and 10 Chinese students, the scale was found to have an alpha of .93.

RELIABILITY: The scale was used in both Study 1 and 2 by Aaker and Williams (1998) with an alpha of .87 (n1 = 150, n2 = 151) being reported in both cases.

VALIDITY: No evidence of the scale's validity was presented in the article by Aaker and Williams (1998).

REFERENCES:

Aaker, Jennifer L. and Patti Williams (1998), "Empathy versus Pride: The Influence of Emotional Appeals Across Cultures," *JCR*, 25 (December), 241–261.

Edell, Julia A. and Marian Chapman Burke (1987), "The Power of Feelings in Understanding Advertising Effects," *JCR*, 14 (December), 421–433.

Frijda, Nico (1986), *The Emotions*, New York: Cambridge University Press.

SCALE ITEMS: [1]

Directions: Please indicate how much the following emotions describe the advertisement for _____ by circling one number for each word below.

1. warmhearted

2. emotional

3. moving

[1] The response scale used for these items was anchored by *not at all* (1) and *very strongly* (7). The brand name should be placed in the blank.

SCALE NAME: Attitude Toward The Advertiser

SCALE DESCRIPTION: The scales consist of various bi-polar adjectives designed to capture a consumer's overall evaluation of a specified advertiser.

SCALE ORIGIN: Each of the studies described here uses a slightly different version of the scale and it is not clear what the origin is. Only Simpson, Horton, and Brown (1996) indicated a source; they cited MacKenzie and Lutz (1989) and modified their scale by adding one more item.

RELIABILITY: Cronbach's alphas of .93 (Lohse and Rosen 2001), .96 (Muehling 1987), .90 (Mackenzie and Lutz 1989), .96 (Simpson, Horton, and Brown 1996), and .97 (Speed and Thompson 2000) were reported for the various versions of the scale.

VALIDITY: No examination of the scale's validity was reported in any of the studies.

REFERENCES:

Lohse, Gerald L. and Dennis L. Rosen (2001), "Signaling Quality and Credibility in Yellow Pages Adverting: The Influence of Color and Graphics on Choice," *JA*, 30 (2), 73–85.

Mackenzie, Scott B. and Richard J. Lutz (1989), "An Empirical Examination of the Structural Antecedants of Attitude Toward the Ad in an Advertising Pretesting Context," *JM*, 53 (April), 48–65.

Muehling, Darrel D. (1987), "Comparative Advertising: The Influence of Attitude-Toward-the-Brand on Brand Evaluation," *JA*, 16 (4), 43–49.

Simpson, Penny M., Steve Horton, and Gene Brown (1996), "Male Nudity in Advertisements: A Modified Replication and Extension of Gender and Product Effects," *JAMS*, 24 (Summer), 257–262.

Speed, Richard and Peter Thompson (2000), "Determinants of Sports Sponsorship Response," *JAMS*, 28 (2), 226–238.

SCALE ITEMS: [1]

Please rate the advertiser of this ad using the following scales.

1. good / bad

2. pleasant / unpleasant

3. favorable / unfavorable

4. positive / negative

5. reputable / not reputable

Lohse and Rosen (2001): 1, 2, 3 7-point
Mackenzie and Lutz (1989): 1, 2, 3, 7-point
Muehling (1987): 1, 3, 4 7-point
Simpson, Horton, and Brown (1996): 1, 2, 3, 5 9-point
Speed and Thompson (2000): 1, 2, 3, 6 7-point

---

[1] The scale stem could be stated something like what is shown here. The "advertiser" might also be referred to as "the sponsor" or "the company."

SCALE NAME: Attitude Toward the Banner Ad

SCALE DESCRIPTION: The scale is composed of eight, five-point Likert-type statements meant to assess a person's general, overall attitude about a particular banner ad he/she has seen.

SCALE ORIGIN: Cho, Lee, and Tharp (2001) did not specify the source of the scale. Although it could be assumed that the scale as a whole is original to these authors, the key descriptors in each item have been routinely used to measure this construct in more typical contexts, e.g., #562.

RELIABILITY: The alpha for the scale was calculated to be .87 (Cho 2001).

VALIDITY: No examination of the scale's validity was reported by Cho, Lee, and Tharp (2001).

REFERENCES:
Cho, Chang-Hoan (2001), Personal Correspondence.
Cho, Chang-Hoan, Jung-Gyo Lee, and Marye Tharp (2001), "Different Forced-Exposure Levels to Banner Advertisements," *JAR*, 41 (July-August), 45–56.

SCALE ITEMS:

1. I like this banner ad.

2. This banner ad is entertaining.

3. This banner ad is useful.

4. This banner ad is important.

5. This banner ad is interesting.

6. This banner ad is informative.

7. I would enjoy seeing this banner ad again.

8. This banner ad is good.

SCALE NAME: Attitude Toward the Brand in the Ad

SCALE DESCRIPTION: The scale is composed of four statements and uses a seven-point, Likert-type response format. The items are intended to measure a person's attitude toward a particular brand featured in an ad that the person has been exposed to.

SCALE ORIGIN: Although most of the key descriptors in the statements have been commonly used in semantic differential measures of attitude-toward-the-brand in the past, the set of statements used by Lee and Mason (1999) appears to be original to their study.

RELIABILITY: An alpha of .92 was reported for the scale (Lee and Mason 1999). Lee (2000) reported alphas of .93 (computer) and .89 (monitor) for use of the scale with two different ads.

VALIDITY: No evidence of the scale's validity was reported by Lee and Mason (1999).

REFERENCES:
Lee, Yih Hwai (2000), "Manipulating Ad Message Involvement through Information Expectancy: Effects on Attitude Evaluation and Confidence," *JA*, 29 (2), 29–43.
Lee, Yih Hwai and Charlotte Mason (1999), "Responses to Information Incongruency in Advertising: The Role of Expectancy, Relevancy, and Humor," *JCR*, 26 (September), 156–169.

SCALE ITEMS:

1. The brand in the ad is likely to possess the stated ad claims.

2. I react favorably to the brand.

3. I feel positively towards the brand.

4. I dislike the brand. (r)

SCALE NAME: Attitude Toward the Commercial

SCALE DESCRIPTION: Three, five-point Likert-type statements are used to assess a person's general attitude toward a specific advertisement. As currently phrased, the scale is most suited for use with TV and radio commercials but the term "advertisement" could be substituted for "commercial" to make the scale amenable for use in print ads.

SCALE ORIGIN: No information about the source of the scale was provided by Fennis and Bakker (2001) but it appears to be original to their study.

RELIABILITY: An alpha of .80 was reported for the scale (Fennis and Bakker 2001).

VALIDITY: No examination of the scale's validity was reported by Fennis and Bakker (2001).

REFERENCES:
Fennis, Bob M. (2003), Personal Correspondence.
Fennis, Bob M. and Arnold B. Bakker (2001), "Stay Tuned-We Will Be Back Right After These Messages: Need to Evaluate Moderates the Transfer of Irritation in Advertising," *JA*, 30 (3), 15–25.

SCALE ITEMS: [1]

1. I found the _____ commercial good.

2. I found the _____ commercial enjoyable.

3. I considered the _____ commercial to be positive.

[1] The statements were provided by Fennis (2003). The response scale ranged from *totally disagree* (1) to *totally agree* (5). The brand name of the product should be placed in the blanks.

SCALE NAME: Attitude Toward the Endorser

SCALE DESCRIPTION: The scale is composed of three, nine-point semantic differentials intended to measure a person's attitude about another person whose statement or likeness is used in ads as a form of support and endorsement for a specified product.

SCALE ORIGIN: The source of the scale was not identified by Till and Shimp (1998). However, it is merely an adaptation of a variety of scales used previously to measure a similar construct: attitude toward the advertiser (#568).

RELIABILITY: An alpha of .98 was reported for the scale (Till and Shimp 1998).

VALIDITY: No examination of the scale's validity was reported by Till and Shimp (1998).

REFERENCES:
Till, Brian D. and Terence A. Shimp (1998), "Endorsers In Advertising: The Case of Negative Celebrity Information," *JA*, 27 (Spring), 67–82.

SCALE ITEMS:

1. good / bad

2. favorable / unfavorable

3. positive / negative

SCALE NAME: Attitude Toward the Infomercial

SCALE DESCRIPTION: Six, five-point Likert-type statements are used to measure the degree to which a viewer has a positive attitude about a particular infomercial. The scale was called *advertising effectiveness* by Agee and Martin (2001).

SCALE ORIGIN: Although not explicitly stated by the authors (Agee and Martin 2001), the scale appears to be original to their study.

RELIABILITY: An alpha of .79 was reported for the scale (Agee and Martin 2001).

VALIDITY: No examination of the scale's validity was reported by Agee and Martin (2001). They did, however, state that factor analysis was used to determine the dimensions underlying the full set of items used in their survey instrument. The six items composing this scale loaded highest on the same factor.

REFERENCES:
Agee, Tom and Brett A. S. Martin (2001), "Planned or Impulse Purchases? How to Create Effective Infomercials" *JAR*, 41 (November/December), 35–42.

SCALE ITEMS: [1]

1. I found the infomercial interesting and informative.

2. I found the infomercial entertaining and fun to watch.

3. The demonstrations of how the product worked were very helpful in making my decision to buy.

4. I could relate to the people in the ad who tried the product.

5. The host or celebrity in the ad made me feel the product was a good one.

6. I often check TV listings to see when infomercials are on.

[1] The response scale used by Agee and Martin (2001) for these items had the following anchors: *agree strongly* (1) and *disagree strongly* (5).

SCALE NAME: Attitude Toward the Manufacturer (Responsible)

SCALE DESCRIPTION: The scale is composed of three, seven-point Likert-type statements measuring the degree to which a consumer has a positive attitude toward the company that makes a product featured in an ad the consumer has been exposed to. The emphasis is on the company's status with regard to societal obligations, thus, the scale was called *corporate citizenship* by Dean (1999).

SCALE ORIGIN: The source of the scale was not stated by Dean (1999).

RELIABILITY: An alpha of .90 (n = 185) was reported for the scale (Dean 1999).

VALIDITY: No information regarding the scale's validity was reported (Dean 1999).

COMMENTS: Depending upon the nature of the sample, there may be many respondents who do not have a clear understanding of item #1 (below).

REFERENCES:
Dean, Dwane Hal (1999), "Brand Endorsement, Popularity, and Event Sponsorship as Advertising Cues Affecting Consumer Pre-Purchase Attitudes," *JA*, 28 (3), 1–12.

SCALE ITEMS: [1]

1. The company that makes the advertised _____ is a good "corporate citizen."

2. The company that makes the advertised _____ cares about its customers.

3. The company that makes the advertised _____ is socially responsible.

---

[1] The response scale had seven points and used anchors of *strongly disagree* and *strongly agree*. The name for the product category should be placed in the blanks.

SCALE NAME: Attitude Toward the Manufacturer (Trust)

SCALE DESCRIPTION: The scale is composed of seven-point Likert-type statements measuring the degree to which a consumer has a positive attitude toward the company that makes a product featured in an ad the consumer has been exposed to. The emphasis is on the high regard and respect felt by the consumer toward the manufacturer, thus, the scale was called *manufacturer esteem* by Dean (1999). It was referred to more generally by Dean and Biswas (2001) as *attitude toward the manufacturer*.

SCALE ORIGIN: The source of the scale was not stated by Dean (1999; Dean and Biswas 2001) but it would appear to be original to him.

RELIABILITY: An alpha of .83 (n = 185) was reported for the scale used in Dean (1999); alphas of .92 (n = 229) and .90 (n = 237) were reported for the version of the scale used in Dean and Biswas (2001).

VALIDITY: No information regarding the scale's validity was reported by Dean (1999). However, Dean and Biswas (2001) described the results of an EFA as well as a CFA of the items composing the four multi-item scales used in their two studies. All items loaded as expected. The AVE of the scale was above .70 in both studies and met a strict criterion of discriminant validity (Fornell and Larcker 1981).

REFERENCES:

Dean, Dwane Hal (1999), "Brand Endorsement, Popularity, and Event Sponsorship as Advertising Cues Affecting Consumer Pre-Purchase Attitudes," *JA*, 28 (3), 1–12.

Dean, Dwane Hal (2003), Personal Correspondence.

Dean, Dwane Hal and Abhijit Biswas (2001), "Third-Party Organization Endorsement of Products: An Advertising Cue Affecting Consumer Prepurchase Evaluation of Goods and Services," *JA*, 30 (4), 41–57.

Fornell, Claes and David F. Larcker (1981), "Evaluating Structural Equation Models with Unobservable Variables and Measurement Error," *JMR*, 18 (February), 39–50.

SCALE ITEMS: [1]

1. Compared to other _____ brands, I hold the manufacturer of the advertised _____ in high regard.

2. The company that makes the advertised _____ deserves my respect.

3. I can trust the company that makes the advertised _____.

4. I admire the advertised _____ company.

---

[1] The response scale had seven points and used anchors of *strongly disagree* and *strongly agree*. The name for the product category should be placed in the blanks. Dean (1999) reported using the first three items (above) while items 1 and 4 as well as items similar to 2 and 3 were used by Dean and Biswas (2001; Dean 2003).

SCALE NAME: Attitude Toward the Spokesperson (Likeability)

SCALE DESCRIPTION: Four sets of bi-polar adjectives are used to assess a person's opinion of the actor or spokesperson featured in an advertisement with an emphasis on the person's favorability.

SCALE ORIGIN: The scale appears to have been developed by Whittler and Dimeo (1991).

RELIABILITY: Alphas of .94 and .87 were reported by Forehand and Deshpande (2001) and Whittler and Dimeo (1991), respectively.

VALIDITY: No examination of the scale's validity was reported in the studies.

REFERENCES:
Forehand, Mark R. and Rohit Deshpande (2001), "What We see Makes Us Who We Are: Priming Ethnic Self-Awareness and Advertising Response," *JMR*, 38 (August), 336–348.
Whittler, Tommy E. and Joan DiMeo (1991), "Viewer's Reaction to Racial Cues in Advertising Stimuli," *JAR*, 6 (31), 37–46.

SCALE ITEMS: [1]

1. warm / cold

2. likeable / unlikable

3. sincere / insincere

4. friendly / unfriendly

---

[1] Forehand and Deshpande (2001) used a typical seven-point response format contrasted with Whittler and Dimeo (1991) who used a fifteen-point scale.

SCALE NAME: Attitude Toward the Spokesperson (Similarity)

SCALE DESCRIPTION: The scale has been used to measure a consumer's perceived homogeneity with an actor or model in an advertisement. Visual similarity is just part of the comparison. Whittler (1991; and Dimeo 1991) used a four-item, fifteen-point version of the scale whereas Appiah (2001) used a five-item, seven-point version.

SCALE ORIGIN: Appiah (2001) cited Whittler (1989) as the source of the scale who in turn, along with Whittler and DiMeo (1991), cited McKirnan, Smith, and Hamayan (1983) as the source.

RELIABILITY: Whittler and DiMeo (1991) reported a Cronbach's alpha of .86. Whittler (1991) reported Cronbach's alphas of .72 in Study 1 and .86 in Study 2. The version of the scale used by Appiah (2001) has alphas ranging from .86 to .91 for the three ads it was used with.

VALIDITY: No examination of the scale's validity was reported in any of the studies.

REFERENCES:

Appiah, Osei (2001), "Ethnic Identification on Adolescents' Evaluations of Advertisements," *JAR*, 41 (5), 7–22.

Appiah, Osei (2003), Personal Correspondence.

McKirnan, D. J., C. Smith, and E. V. Hamayan (1983), "A Sociolinguistic Approach to the Belief Similarity Model of Racial Attitudes," *Journal of Experimental Social Psychology*, 19 (5), 434–447.

Whittler, Tommy E. (1989), "Viewers' Processing of Actor's Race and Message Claims in Advertising Stimuli," *Psychology and Marketing*, 6 (Winter), 287–309.

Whittler, Tommy E. and Joan DiMeo (1991), "Viewer's Reaction to Racial Cues in Advertising Stimuli," *JAR*, 6 (31), 37–46.

Whittler, Tommy E. (1991), "The Effects of Actors' Race in Commercial Advertising: Review and Extension," *JA*, 1 (20), 54–60.

SCALE ITEMS: [1]

Directions: Please tell us how similar or dissimilar you are to the character(s) pictured in the ad on the following traits. Please circle only one number from 1 (*Not at all Similar*) to 7 (*Very Similar*).

1. How similar are you to the character(s) pictured in the ad on overall lifestyle?

2. How similar are you to the character(s) pictured in the ad on cultural background?

3. How similar are you to the character(s) pictured in the ad on dress?

4. How similar are you to the character(s) pictured in the ad on appearance?

5. How similar are you to the character(s) pictured in the ad on basic values ?

[1] This is the form of the scale used by Appiah (2001; 2003). Whittler (1991; and Dimeo 1991) just used the key words (underlined) from items 1, 2, 4, and 5.

SCALE NAME: Attitude Toward TV Advertising

SCALE DESCRIPTION: It is a seven-item, Likert-type summated ratings scale measuring a person's opinion about television commercials in general.

SCALE ORIGIN: The scale was originally constructed and tested by Rossiter (1977). His purpose was to develop a measure of attitude toward television commercials which could be reliably used with children. Twelve initial items were tested on a group of 20 third graders. Based upon this, some items were either eliminated or reworded. A seven-item version was then tested on a sample of 208 suburban Philadelphia kids. The sample was mostly middle class, in grades four through six, and had similar proportions of each gender for each grade level. Item-total correlations ranged from .49 to .67 and the internal consistency (KR-20) was computed to be .69. The scale was administered to the children a month later and the test-retest correlation was .67.

RELIABILITY: Carlson and Grossbart (1988) reported an alpha of .73 and a beta of .62 for the scale. Riecken and Samli (1981) reported an alpha of .60, a one week test-rest correlation of .59, and item-total correlations for each item greater than .50. Alphas of .73 and .71 were reported by Rose, Bush, and Kahle (1998) for the scale in the U.S. and Japan, respectively.

VALIDITY: No examination of scale validity was reported in any of the studies. However, Riecken and Samli (1981) indicated that one factor accounting for 82.7% of the total item variance emerged in a factor analysis they conducted.

COMMENTS: See also a use of this scale by Wiman (1983).

REFERENCES:

Carlson, Les and Sanford Grossbart (1988), "Parental Style and Consumer Socialization of Children," *JCR*, 15 (June), 77–94.

Riecken, Glen and A. Coskun Samli (1981), "Measuring Children's Attitudes Toward Television Commercials: Extension and Replication," *JCR*, 8 (June), 57–61.

Rose, Gregory M., Victoria D. Bush, and Lynn Kahle (1998), "The Influence of Family Communication Patterns on Parental Reactions toward Advertising: A Cross-National Examination," *JA*, 27 (4), 71–85.

Rossiter, John R. (1977), "Reliability of a Short Test Measuring Children's Attitudes Toward TV Commercials," *JCR*, 3 (March), 179–184.

Wiman, Alan R. (1983), "Parental Influence and Children's Responses to Television Advertising," *JA*, 12 (1), 12–18.

SCALE ITEMS: [1]

1. Television commercials tell the truth. (r)

2. Most television commercials are in poor taste and very annoying.

3. Television commercials tell only the good things about a product; they don't tell you the bad things.

4. I like most television commercials. (r)

5. Television commercials try to make people buy things they don't really need.

6. You can always believe what the people in commercials say or do. (r)

7. The products advertised the most on TV are always the best to buy. (r)

---

[1] Rossiter (1977) as well as Riecken and Samli (1981) used four-point response scales to eliminate the tendency of children to select a midpoint answer so as to avoid attention to the question. Carlson and Grossbart (1988) used five-point scales; Rose, Bush, and Kahle (1998) used seven.

SCALE NAME: Attitude Toward TV Advertising (Skepticism)

SCALE DESCRIPTION: The scale is composed of four, seven-point Likert-type statements that measure a person's attitude toward television commercials with an emphasis on the negative such as the extent to which ads are annoying and exaggerated.

SCALE ORIGIN: The scale appears to be original to Mangleburg and Bristol (1998) although they received inspiration for some of their items from previous measures. While they only cite Gaski and Etzell (1986, V. I, # 292), there is some resemblance to measures by Rossiter (1977, #578) and Alwitt and Prabhaker (1992, V. II, #339) as well.

RELIABILITY: A composite reliability of .64 (n = 296 high school students) was reported for the scale by Mangleburg and Bristol (1998).

VALIDITY: Although confirmatory factor analysis was conducted by Mangleburg and Bristol (1998), the exact details bearing on the validity of this scale were not reported.

REFERENCES:
Alwitt, Linda F. and Paul R. Prabhaker (1992), "Functional and Belief Dimensions of Attitudes to Television Advertising," *JAR*, 32 (5), 30–42. (3205).
Gaski, John F. and Michael J. Etzell (1986), "The Index of Consumer Sentiment Toward Marketing," *JM*, 50 (July), 71–81.
Mangleburg, Tamara F. and Terry Bristol (1998), "Socialization and Adolescents' Skepticism Toward Advertising," *JA*, 27 (3), 11–21.
Rossiter, John R. (1977), "Reliability of a Short Test Measuring Children's Attitudes Toward TV Commercials," *JCR*, 3 (March), 179–184. (478).

SCALE ITEMS:

1. Advertisers often exaggerate claims made about their products.

2. Televisions ads tell only the good things about products.

3. Most television advertising is very annoying.

4. Television advertising does not tell much useful information about products.

SCALE NAME: Attitude Toward TV Advertising Aimed at Children

SCALE DESCRIPTION: The scale measures the degree to which a person expresses reservations about advertising, particularly food ads, being aimed at children. In all of the studies the scale was filled out by parents but it appears to be amenable for use with any adult sample.

SCALE ORIGIN: Carlson and Grossbart (1988) indicated that they adapted a scale from earlier work by Crosby and Grossbart (1984). In the latter's study, the scale had an alpha of .813 (n = 563). Rose, Bush, and Kahle (1998) also cited Crosby and Grossbart (1984) as the source of their scale, however, they dropped one of the original items and added two as noted below.

RELIABILITY: Carlson and Grossbart (1988) reported an alpha of .81 (n = 451) and a beta of .72 for the scale. Alphas of .78 (n = 389) and .71 (n = 237) were reported by Rose, Bush, and Kahle (1998) for the scale in the U. S. and Japan, respectively.

VALIDITY: No examination of scale validity was reported by Carlson and Grossbart (1988) or Rose, Bush, and Kahle (1998).

REFERENCES:

Carlson, Les and Sanford Grossbart (1988), "Parental Style and Consumer Socialization of Children," *JCR*, 15 (June), 77–94.

Crosby, Lawrence A. and Sanford L. Grossbart (1984), "Parental Style Tendencies and Concern about Children's Advertising," in *Current Issues in Research in Advertising*, James H. Leigh and Claude R. Martin, Jr. eds. Ann Arbor, MI: Division of Research, Graduate School of Business Administration, 43–63.

Rose, Gregory M., Victoria D. Bush, and Lynn Kahle (1998), "The Influence of Family Communication Patterns on Parental Reactions toward Advertising: A Cross-National Examination," *JA*, 27 (4), 71–85.

SCALE ITEMS: [1]

1. There is too much food advertising directed at children.

2. Advertisers use tricks and gimmicks to get children to buy their products.

3. Advertising to children makes false claims about the nutrition content of food products.

4. There is too much sugar in the foods advertised to children.

5. Advertising teaches children bad eating habits.

6. Advertising directed at children leads to family conflict.

7. All advertising should be banned on shows that are watched by children 5 or under.

8. It's the parent's responsibility to explain advertisements to their children.

---

[1] Crosby and Grossbart (1984) as well as Carlson and Grossbart (1988) used items #1–#6 with five-point Likert-type response formats. Rose, Bush, and Kahle (1998) used items #1, #2, #4–#8 in a five-point Likert-type format.

SCALE NAME: Attitude Toward TV Advertising Aimed at Children

SCALE DESCRIPTION: The scale is composed of five, five-point Likert-type items intended to measure a person's (adult) attitude toward television advertising directed at kids. The tone of most of the items is negative. The scale does not measure one's attitude toward a specific commercial but instead attempts to gauge a person's attitude about allowing TV advertising in general that has children as the intended audience.

SCALE ORIGIN: The scale appears to be original to Walsh, Laczniak, and Carlson (1998).

RELIABILITY: An alpha of .82 (n = 151) was reported by Walsh, Laczniak, and Carlson (1998).

VALIDITY: No examination of the scale's validity was reported by Walsh, Laczniak, and Carlson (1998).

REFERENCES:
Walsh, Ann D., Russell N. Laczniak, and Les Carlson (1998), "Mothers' Preferences for Regulating Children's Television," *JA*, 27 (3), 23–36.

SCALE ITEMS:

1. Children's television is nothing but commercials.

2. TV commercials directed toward children are unethical.

3. TV advertising takes advantage of children's inability to understand selling techniques.

4. Television commercials directed toward children use fair selling techniques to promote products. (r)

5. TV commercials with the same characters as in television programs should NOT be allowed during the program (e.g., *Power Ranger* toys during a *Power Ranger* episode.)

SCALE NAME: Attitude Toward Use of English in a Commercial

SCALE DESCRIPTION: The scale is composed of eight descriptors and a five-point Likert-type response scale to measure a person's opinion about the use of English in a commercial. The scale makes most sense when used in a non-English-speaking country where ads are being run or considered which will use English. It is also likely that the scale itself will not be administered in English but will be translated to the appropriate language.

As used by Gerritsen et al. (2000), the measure was used in Holland with respect to a specific commercial after Dutch subjects had been exposed to it. However, it appears to be amenable for use with ads in general.

SCALE ORIGIN: The scale is original to the study reported by Gerritsen et al. (2000). These authors said that these particular descriptors were selected for use in the scale because "they are often used in discussion on the use of English . . . ." (p. 23).

RELIABILITY: The scale was used with six commercials and it was reported that in each case the alpha was over .80 (Gerritsen et al. 2000).

VALIDITY: No examination of the scale's validity was reported by Gerritsen et al. (2000).

COMMENTS: The four negative items and the four positive ones began as two separate scales but the authors decided to combine them because the scores "showed a high correlation" (Gerritsen et al. 2000, p. 23). If this set of items is to be used again then a factor analysis is urged since it is quite possible that the items are not unidimensional. This becomes doubly important if and when these items are translated for use in other languages.

REFERENCES:
Gerritson, Marinel, Hubert Korzilius, Frank Van Meurs, and Inge Gijsbers (2000), "English in Dutch Commercials: Not Understood and Not Appreciated," *JAR*, 40 (4), 17–31.

SCALE ITEMS:

1. poetic
2. easygoing
3. functional
4. sympathetic
5. irritating
6. superfluous
7. affected
8. arrogant

SCALE NAME: Attitude Toward Web Advertising

SCALE DESCRIPTION: The scale is composed of five, seven-point Likert-type statements that are intended to measure a person's general attitude about advertising on the web, not what they think about any particular ad or website.

SCALE ORIGIN: The items used by Shamdasani, Stanaland, and Tan (2001) were used previously by Cho 1999) although the latter does not appear to have used them as a summated ratings scale.

RELIABILITY: An alpha of .82 was reported for the scale (Shamdasani, Stanaland, and Tan 2001).

VALIDITY: No examination of the scale's validity was reported by Shamdasani, Stanaland, and Tan (2001).

REFERENCES:
Cho, Chang-Hoan (1999), "How Advertising Works on the WWW: Modified Elaboration Likelihood Model," *Journal of Current Issues & Research in Advertising*, 21 (Spring), 33–50.
Shamdasani, Prem N., Andrea J. S. Stanaland, and Juliana Tan (2001), "Location, Location, Location: Insights for Advertising Placement on the Web," *JAR*, 41 (July-August), 7–21.

SCALE ITEMS:

1. Web advertising supplies valuable information in general.

2. Web advertising is irritating in general.

3. Web advertising is entertaining in general.

4. Web advertising is valuable in general.

5. Web advertising is necessary on the web.

SCALE NAME: Beauty (Advertising Model)

SCALE DESCRIPTION: Three, seven-point statements are used to measure a person's opinion of the relative physical attractiveness of a model (female) featured in an ad as compared to other models that one normally sees.

SCALE ORIGIN: The scale is apparently original to Bower (2001).

RELIABILITY: An alpha of .80 was reported for the scale (Bower 2001).

VALIDITY: No explicit examination of the scale's validity was described by Bower (2001).

COMMENTS: To make the scale appropriate for assessing the beauty of male models some simple word changes will be necessary. However, it should be kept in mind that in the two studies by Bower (2001), the scale was only applied to female models and only completed by female respondents. Thus, further testing is necessary before it can be safely assumed the scale can be reliably used by males with regard to male models.

REFERENCES:
Bower, Amanda B. (2003), Personal Correspondence.
Bower, Amanda B. (2001), "Highly Attractive Models in Advertising and the Women Who Loathe Them: The Implementations of Negative Affect for Spokesperson Effectiveness," *JA*, 30 (3), 51–63.

SCALE ITEMS: [1]

1. Relative to other female models seen in advertising, this model's beauty makes her:
   Much less noticeable / much more noticeable

2. Compared to other female models I normally see in advertisements, this model's beauty is: *far below average / far above average*

3. This model's superior beauty would stand out among other models in a magazine.
   Strongly disagree / strongly agree

---

[1] Items and anchors were provided by Bower (2003).

SCALE NAME: Believability of the Information

SCALE DESCRIPTION: Seven-point semantic differentials are used to measure the extent to which some specific information to which a consumer has been exposed is viewed as being true and acceptable. If using instructions similar to Gürhan-Canli and Maheswaran (2000), the respondent's attention can be focused on something specific in the information, e.g., a claim made about the product.

SCALE ORIGIN: The scale is original to Gürhan-Canli and Maheswaran (2000). A slight variation in the scale was used later by Sen, Gürhan-Canli, and Morwitz (2001).

RELIABILITY: The scale by Gürhan-Canli and Maheswaran (2000) was reported to have alphas of .87 (Study 1) and .77 (Study 2). Alphas of .87 (Study 1) and .86 (Study 2) were reported for the version of the scale used by Sen, Gürhan-Canli, and Morwitz (2001).

VALIDITY: No evidence of the scale's validity was reported in either study.

REFERENCES:

Gürhan-Canli, Zeynep and Durairaj Maheswaran (2000), "Determinants of Country-of-Origin Evaluations," *JCR*, 27 (1), 96–108.

Sen, Sankar, Zeynep Gürhan-Canli, and Vicki Morwitz (2001), "Withholding Consumption: A Social Dilemma Perspective on Consumer Boycotts," *JCR*, 28 (December), 399–417.

SCALE ITEMS: [1]

Directions: Please describe your perceptions of the information provided to you by answering each of the following questions. For each question please circle one number on each scale that best describes your perceptions. *In your opinion the claim made was*:

1. Not at all believable / highly believable

2. Not at all true / absolutely true

3. Not at all acceptable / totally acceptable

4. Not at all credible / very credible

---

[1] These are the directions used by Gürhan-Canli and Maheswaran (2000). By changing the final phrase in the scale directions (shown in italics) the scale can be made to focus on some other aspect of the information. By deleting it altogether the scale would evaluate the information in general. In the study by Sen, Gürhan-Canli, and Morwitz (2001) the scale was used with regard to a mock newspaper article that subjects were asked to read. Items 1–3 are those by Gürhan-Canli and Maheswaran (2000) whereas Sen, Gürhan-Canli, and Morwitz (2001) used 1, 2, and 4.

SCALE NAME: Brand Advertising Intensity

SCALE DESCRIPTION: The scale is composed of three, five-point Likert-type statements attempting to capture a consumer's relative sense of the amount of advertising that is conducted for a specified brand compared to its competing brands.

SCALE ORIGIN: In developing their scale, Yoo, Donthu, and Lee (2000) built upon items originally used by Kirmani and Wright (1989).

RELIABILITY: Yoo, Donthu, and Lee (2000) reported the scale to have a composite reliability of .87.

VALIDITY: Factor analyses (EFA and CFA) were used to check the dimensionality of this scale along with eight others used in the study. Based on the results, the authors concluded that all items loaded on their respective factors as expected providing some sense of the scales' convergent and discriminant validities. The average variance extracted for this scale was .70.

REFERENCES:

Kirmani, Amna and Peter Wright (1989), "Money Talks: Perceived Advertising Expense and Expected Product Quality," *JCR*, 16 (December), 344–353.
Yoo, Boonghee, Naveen Donthu, and Sungho Lee (2000), "An Examination of Selected Marketing Mix Elements and Brand Equity," *JAMS*, 28 (2), 195–211.

SCALE ITEMS: [1]

1. _____ is intensively advertised.

2. The ad campaigns for _____ seem very expensive compared to campaigns for competing brands.

3. The ad campaigns for _____ are seen frequently.

---

[1] The brand name of a product was placed in the blanks by Yoo, Donthu, and Lee (2000).

SCALE NAME: Celebrity Endorser (Credibility)

SCALE DESCRIPTION: The scale is composed of three, five-point items measuring the importance of certain attributes of a celebrity if that person is to be hired as an endorser in advertising. The attributes in this scale have to do with the celebrity's risk of being controversial and his/her trustworthiness.

SCALE ORIGIN: No information about the scale's source was provided by Erdogan, Baker, and Tagg (2001). It appears the scale is original but that they drew upon measures used in previous studies.

RELIABILITY: An alpha of .72 was reported for the scale (Erdogan, Baker, and Tagg 2001).

VALIDITY: Although no examination of the scale's validity was reported by Erdogan, Baker, and Tagg (2001) they did provide evidence from an EFA that showed the scale to be unidimensional.

REFERENCES:
Erdogan, Zafer B., Michael J. Baker, and Stephen Tagg (2001), "Selecting Celebrity Endorsers: The Practitioner's Perspective," *JAR*, 41 (3), 39–48.

SCALE ITEMS: [1]

1. Celebrity controversy risk

2. Celebrity prior endorsements

3. Celebrity trustworthiness

---

[1] These are the items as shown in the article by Erdogan, Baker, and Tagg (2001); longer phrases may have actually been used but were not reported. The anchors used with the response scale were *very unimportant* (1) and *very important* (5).

SCALE NAME: Celebrity Endorser (Expertise)

SCALE DESCRIPTION: Five, five-point items are used to measure the importance of certain celebrity attributes if that person is to be hired as an endorser in advertising. The attributes in this scale have to do with the celebrity's profession and whether or not he/she is a user of the brand. The scale was called *profession* by Erdogan, Baker, and Tagg (2001).

SCALE ORIGIN: No information about the scale's source was provided by Erdogan, Baker, and Tagg (2001). It appears the scale is original but that they drew upon measures used in previous studies.

RELIABILITY: An alpha of .68 was reported for the scale (Erdogan, Baker, and Tagg 2001).

VALIDITY: Although no examination of the scale's validity was reported by Erdogan, Baker, and Tagg (2001) they did provide evidence from an EFA that showed the scale to be unidimensional.

COMMENTS: The low alpha indicates that the scale should be improved before used further.

REFERENCES:
Erdogan, Zafer B., Michael J. Baker, and Stephen Tagg (2001), "Selecting Celebrity Endorsers: The Practitioner's Perspective," *JAR*, 41 (3), 39–48.

SCALE ITEMS: [1]

1. Whether celebrity is a brand user

2. Celebrity profession

3. Celebrity EQUITY membership status

4. Celebrity expertise

5. Risk of celebrity overshadowing brands

[1] These are the items as shown in the article by Erdogan, Baker, and Tagg (2001); longer phrases may have actually been used but were not reported. The anchors used with the response scale were *very unimportant* (1) and *very important* (5).

#589 *Celebrity Endorser (Match-Up)*

SCALE NAME: Celebrity Endorser (Match-Up)

SCALE DESCRIPTION: The scale is composed of four, five-point items measuring the degree to which a person believes certain attributes of a celebrity are important if that person is to be an endorser in advertising. The attributes in this scale have to do with the physical attractiveness of the celebrity as well as the fit between the endorser, the product, and the target audience. The scale was called *congruence* by Erdogan, Baker, and Tagg (2001).

SCALE ORIGIN: No information about the scale's source was provided by Erdogan, Baker, and Tagg (2001). It appears the scale is original but that they drew upon measures used in previous studies.

RELIABILITY: An alpha of .71 was reported for the scale (Erdogan, Baker, and Tagg 2001).

VALIDITY: Although no examination of the scale's validity was reported by Erdogan, Baker, and Tagg (2001) they did provide evidence from an EFA that showed the scale to be unidimensional.

REFERENCES:
Erdogan, Zafer B., Michael J. Baker, and Stephen Tagg (2001), "Selecting Celebrity Endorsers: The Practitioner's Perspective," *JAR*, 41 (3), 39–48.

SCALE ITEMS: [1]

1. Celebrity physical attractiveness

2. Celebrity-target audience match

3. Celebrity-product/brand match

4. The stage of the celebrity life cycle

---

[1] These are the items as shown in the article by Erdogan, Baker, and Tagg (2001); longer phrases may have actually been used but were not reported. The anchors used with the response scale were *very unimportant* (1) and *very important* (5).

SCALE NAME: Child's Understanding of Advertising Practices

SCALE DESCRIPTION: The scale is composed of five, eleven-point statements measuring at what age a parent believes that a normal child is aware of the advertising-related activities that are used to influence them.

SCALE ORIGIN: The items are original to Rose (1999). This scale and a companion one were envisioned as capturing a "developmental timetable" dimension. This has to do with a parent's beliefs about typical ages when certain emotional and cognitive developments occur in children.

RELIABILITY: Alphas of .77 (U.S.) and .82 (Japan) were reported for the scale by Rose (1999).

VALIDITY: The validity of the scale was not addressed by Rose (1999). However, results of a factor analysis of the items in this scale and those of another related scale (#140) were presented. It showed that the items proposed for the two scales loaded appropriately for both the U.S. and the Japanese samples.

REFERENCES:
Rose, Gregory M. (2002), Personal Correspondence.
Rose, Gregory M. (1999), "Consumer Socialization, Parental Style, and Development Timetables in the United States and Japan," *JM*, 63 (July), 105–119.

SCALE ITEMS: [1]

Directions: Now we would like to find out at what age you believe a typical child can do each of the following things:

1. understand that not all advertisements are true.

2. tell when an advertiser is exaggerating.

3. understand the difference between a television program and a television advertisement.

4. understand that actors that endorse a product may not really use that product.

5. understand that television characters are just pretending or playing a role.

---

[1] The response format for these items was anchored by 2 to 12+ with the numbers referring to a child's age (Rose 2002).

SCALE NAME: Client Conflict With Agency

SCALE DESCRIPTION: The scale is composed of three, seven-point Likert-type statements that are used to measure the degree of disagreement and frustration that a client states having with his/her representative(s) at the company's advertising agency.

SCALE ORIGIN: Although Beard (1996, 1999) drew inspiration from similar work by others (e.g., Michell, Cataquet, and Hague 1992), the scale he used appears to be original.

RELIABILITY: Alphas of .90 and .84 were reported for the scale by Beard in his 1996 and 1999 studies, respectively.

VALIDITY: No examination of the scale's validity was reported by Beard in either study (1996, 1999).

REFERENCES:
Beard, Fred (1996), "Marketing Client Role Ambiguity as a Source of Dissatisfaction in Client AD Agency Relationships," *JAR*, 36 (September/October), 9–20.
Beard, Fred (1999), "Client Role Ambiguity and Satisfaction in Client-Ad Agency Relationships," *JAR*, 39 (March/April), 69–78.
Michell, Paul, Harold Cataquet, and Stephen Hague (1992), "Establishing the Causes of Dissatisfaction in Agency-Client Relations," *JAR*, 32 (2), 41–48.

SCALE ITEMS:

1. Agency representatives and I often have trouble agreeing on objectives and strategies for our advertising.

2. I often think it would be easier to work with a different ad agency representative, or even with another agency altogether.

3. I often become frustrated when trying to reach a decision with my ad agency representatives.

SCALE NAME: Client Role Ambiguity (Goal Clarity)

SCALE DESCRIPTION: Five, seven-point statements are used to measure the degree of certainty an advertising client has about the outcome goals of his/her part of the client/agency relationship.

SCALE ORIGIN: The source of the scale used by Beard (1996, 1999) is Sawyer (1992). The latter presented a reconceptualization of role ambiguity such that it had two dimensions: role clarity and process clarity. The composite reliability for the goal clarity scale was .919 and the variance extracted was .695. See Sawyer (1992) for details of the scale's validity as well as support for the two dimensional model.

RELIABILITY: Alphas of .90 and .86 were reported for the scale by Beard in his 1996 and 1999 studies, respectively.

VALIDITY: No examination of the scale's validity was reported by Beard in either study (1996, 1999). However, a factor analysis of this scale and a companion scale (#593) indicated that the items loaded on their respective factors.

REFERENCES:
Beard, Fred (1996), "Marketing Client Role Ambiguity as a Source of Dissatisfaction in Client AD Agency Relationships," *JAR*, 36 (September/October), 9–20.
Beard, Fred (1999), "Client Role Ambiguity and Satisfaction in Client-Ad Agency Relationships," *JAR*, 39 (March/April), 69–78.
Sawyer, John E. (1992), "Goal and Process Clarity: Specification of Multiple Constructs of Role Ambiguity and a Structural Model of Their Antecedents and Consequences," *Journal of Applied Psychology*, 77 (2), 130–142.

SCALE ITEMS: [1]

1. What my duties and responsibilities are in my work with the ad agency.

2. What the goals and objectives are for my work with the ad agency.

3. How my efforts related to the overall objectives of my work with the agency.

4. The expected results of my work with the agency.

5. The aspects of my work that will lead to positive evaluations from agency representatives.

[1] A seven-point response format anchored by *very certain / very uncertain* was used by Beard (1996, 1999).

SCALE NAME: Client Role Ambiguity (Process Clarity)

SCALE DESCRIPTION: The scale is composed of four, seven-point statements that are used to measure the degree of certainty an advertising client has about performing his/her part of the client/agency relationship.

SCALE ORIGIN: The source of the scale used by Beard (1996, 1999) is Sawyer (1992). The latter presented a reconceptualization of role ambiguity such that it had two dimensions: role clarity and process clarity. The composite reliability for the process clarity scale was .904 and the variance extracted was .656. See Sawyer (1992) for details of the scale's validity as well as support for the two dimensional model.

RELIABILITY: Alphas of .86 and .83 were reported for the scale by Beard in his 1996 and 1999 studies, respectively.

VALIDITY: No examination of the scale's validity was reported by Beard in either study (1996, 1999). However, a factor analysis of this scale and a companion scale (#592) indicated that the items loaded on their respective factors.

REFERENCES:

Beard, Fred (1996), "Marketing Client Role Ambiguity as a Source of Dissatisfaction in Client AD Agency Relationships," *JAR*, 36 (September/October), 9–20.

Beard, Fred (1999), "Client Role Ambiguity and Satisfaction in Client-Ad Agency Relationships," *JAR*, 39 (March/April), 69–78.

Sawyer, John E. (1992), "Goal and Process Clarity: Specification of Multiple Constructs of Role Ambiguity and a Structural Model of Their Antecedents and Consequences," *Journal of Applied Psychology*, 77 (2), 130–142.

SCALE ITEMS: [1]

1. How to divide my time among the tasks required of my job.

2. How to schedule my activities when working with the agency.

3. How to determine the appropriate procedures for each task I need to perform in my work with the agency.

4. The job procedures I use to do my work with the agency are correct and proper.

[1] A seven-point response format anchored by *very certain / very uncertain* was used by Beard (1996, 1999).

SCALE NAME: Client Satisfaction (Agency Performance)

SCALE DESCRIPTION: The scale is composed of four, seven-point Likert-type statements that are used to measure the degree of satisfaction a client has with its advertising agency based upon its work process and performance.

SCALE ORIGIN: Although inspiration for the items came from previous research (e.g., Wackman, Salmon, and Salmon 1986/1987), the scale as a whole appears to be original to Beard (1996).

RELIABILITY: Alphas of .85 and .79 were reported for the scale by Beard in his 1996 and 1999 studies, respectively.

VALIDITY: No examination of the scale's validity was reported by Beard in either study (1996, 1999).

REFERENCES:
Beard, Fred (1996), "Marketing Client Role Ambiguity as a Source of Dissatisfaction in Client AD Agency Relationships," *JAR*, 36 (September/October), 9–20.

Beard, Fred (1999), "Client Role Ambiguity and Satisfaction in Client-Ad Agency Relationships," *JAR*, 39 (March/April), 69–78.

Wackman, Daniel B., Charles T. Salmon, and Caryn C. Salmon (1986/1987), "Developing an Advertising Agency-Client Relationship," *JAR*, 26 (6), 21–28.

SCALE ITEMS:

1. The ad agency I work with does good creative work.

2. The ad agency I work with gives good marketing advice.

3. The ad agency I work with has good account management.

4. The ad agency I work with has a good understanding of our business.

SCALE NAME: Client Satisfaction (Personal Relationships)

SCALE DESCRIPTION: The scale is composed of three, seven-point Likert-type statements that are used to measure the degree of satisfaction a client has with its advertising agency based upon the personal relationships with agency personnel.

SCALE ORIGIN: Although the items were drawn from the work of Wackman, Salmon, and Salmon 1986/1987), their usage as a summated scale appears to be original to Beard (1996).

RELIABILITY: Alphas of .79 and .69 were reported for the scale by Beard in his 1996 and 1999 studies, respectively.

VALIDITY: No examination of the scale's validity was reported by Beard in either study (1996, 1999).

COMMENTS: The scale may not be unidimensional given that the last item (#3) appears to tap into a different construct. Testing of the scale's dimensionality is called for.

REFERENCES:

Beard, Fred (1996), "Marketing Client Role Ambiguity as a Source of Dissatisfaction in Client AD Agency Relationships," *JAR*, 36 (September/October), 9–20.

Beard, Fred (1999), "Client Role Ambiguity and Satisfaction in Client-Ad Agency Relationships," *JAR*, 39 (March/April), 69–78.

Wackman, Daniel B., Charles T. Salmon, and Caryn C. Salmon (1986/1987), "Developing an Advertising Agency-Client Relationship," *JA*, 26 (6), 21–28.

SCALE ITEMS:

1. I have a good personal relationship with the ad agency's account service people.

2. I have a good personal relationship with the ad agency's creative people.

3. My ad agency representatives show strong leadership.

SCALE NAME: Client Tension With Agency

SCALE DESCRIPTION: Three, seven-point Likert-type statements are used to measure the level of anxiety and loss of control felt by the client regarding its working relationship with its advertising agency.

SCALE ORIGIN: Beard (1996, 1999) stated that he had adapted items used by Singh (1993). However, an examination of the two sets of items shows the resemblance to be small enough that it is probably best to think of Beard's scale as original.

RELIABILITY: Alphas of .88 and .87 were reported for the scale by Beard in his 1996 and 1999 studies, respectively.

VALIDITY: No examination of the scale's validity was reported by Beard in either study (1996, 1999).

REFERENCES:
Beard, Fred (1996), "Marketing Client Role Ambiguity as a Source of Dissatisfaction in Client AD Agency Relationships," *JAR*, 36 (September/October), 9–20.
Beard, Fred (1999), "Client Role Ambiguity and Satisfaction in Client-Ad Agency Relationships," *JAR*, 39 (March/April), 69–78.
Singh, Jagdip (1993), "Boundary Role Ambiguity: Facets, Determinants, and Impacts," *JM*, 57 (April), 11–31.

SCALE ITEMS:

1. I often feel a lot of anxiety associated with my work with the ad agency.

2. I often feel nervous or jumpy when I have to work with my ad agency representatives.

3. I often feel a loss of control over the outcomes resulting from my work with the ad agency.

SCALE NAME: Community Image Importance

SCALE DESCRIPTION: The scale is composed of three, seven-point statements intended to assess the importance a person places on maintaining a positive image in the community when it comes to deciding whether or not to air an advertisement. As studied by Wicks and Abernethy (2001), the respondent was a TV sales manager or other station employee who was familiar with the station's clearance policy. Further, the type of advertisement they examined was infomercials.

SCALE ORIGIN: Apparently, the scale items had been used in previous studies by the lead author (e.g., Wicks 1997) but this was the first time they had been used as part of a summated scale.

RELIABILITY: An alpha of .72 was reported for the scale (Wicks and Abernethy 2001).

VALIDITY: No examination of the scale's validity was reported by Wicks and Abernethy (2001). They did state, however, that the items loaded on a single factor.

REFERENCES:
Wicks, Jan LeBlanc (1997), "Which Factors Primarily Influence the Number of Infomercial Hours a Commercial Television Station Airs," *Journal of Media Economics*, 10 (1), 29–38.
Wicks, Jan LeBlanc and Abernethy (2001), "Effective Consumer Protection or Benign Neglect? A Model of Television Infomercial Clearance" *JA*, 30 (1), 41–54.

SCALE ITEMS: [1]

Directions: Please indicate how important each of the following statements is considered when deciding whether to refuse to air an ad.

1. Serve the public interest, convenience and necessity.

2. Maintain a positive image in the community.

3. The ad's content is in poor taste, e.g., ad content would offend most viewers in your community.

[1] A seven-point response scale anchored by *very important* and *not important* was used with these items.

SCALE NAME: Comparison with Advertising Model

SCALE DESCRIPTION: Three seven-point statements are used to measure the extent to which a person thinks a model featured in an ad is likely for viewers to compare themselves with. Bower (2001) viewed this as a form of social comparison in that one compares him- or herself to another person on one or more personally relevant attributes to see if there is cause for concern (envy, jealousy, lower self-worth).

SCALE ORIGIN: The scale is apparently original to Bower (2001).

RELIABILITY: An alpha of .71 was reported for the scale (Bower 2001).

VALIDITY: No explicit examination of the scale's validity was described by Bower (2001).

COMMENTS: To make the scale appropriate for use with males some simple word changes will be necessary. However, it should be kept in mind that in the two studies by Bower (2001), the scale was only applied to female models and only completed by female respondents. Thus, further testing is necessary before it can be safely assumed the scale can be reliably used by males and/or with regard to male models.

REFERENCES:
Bower, Amanda B. (2003), Personal Correspondence.
Bower, Amanda B. (2001), "Highly Attractive Models in Advertising and the Women Who Loathe Them: The Implementations of Negative Affect for Spokesperson Effectiveness," *JA*, 30 (3), 51–63.

SCALE ITEMS: [1]

1. I think most of my friends would compare themselves to the model in this advertisement.
   strong disagree / strongly agree

2. If the average woman interested in using this type of product noticed this advertisement, how likely is it that she would compare herself to the model?
   very unlikely / very likely

3. If you were to notice this advertisement in a magazine, how likely is it that you would compare yourself to the model?
   very unlikely / very likely

[1] Items and anchors were provided by Bower (2003).

SCALE NAME: Consistency of Thoughts and Ad

SCALE DESCRIPTION: The scale is composed of three, nine-point Likert-type statements that measure the degree to which a person agrees that the information communicated in an ad he/she has been exposed to corresponds with an experience the person has in mind.

SCALE ORIGIN: The scale appears to be original to the study by Krishnamurthy and Sujan (1999). Subjects in the experiment were instructed to think of a vacation experience for two minutes and then relate the ad to the experience they thought about.

RELIABILITY: An alpha of .72 was reported for the scale (Krishnamurthy and Sujan 1999).

VALIDITY: No examination of the scale's validity was reported by Krishnamurthy and Sujan (1999).

COMMENTS: The scale was developed for use by Krishnamurthy and Sujan (1999) with respect to ads for a vacation destination. With some slight modification to item #3 the scale appears to be amenable for use with other contexts.

REFERENCES:

Krishnamurthy, Parthasarathy and Mita Sujan (1999), "Retrospection versus Anticipation: The Role of the Ad under Retrospective and Anticipatory Self-Referencing," *JCR*, 26 (June), 55–69.

SCALE ITEMS: [1]

1. The ad was inconsistent with my thoughts. (r)

2. I thought about a _____ dissimilar to what was shown in the ad. (r)

3. I found it easy to integrate my thoughts with the surroundings and activities shown in the ad.

[1] The name of the context should be placed in the blanks. The context examined in the study by Krishnamurthy and Sujan (1999) was a vacation experience.

SCALE NAME: Contextual Detail in Ads (Visual)

SCALE DESCRIPTION: The scale is composed of four, nine-point Likert-type statements that measure the degree to which a person agrees that the visual elements of an advertisement contain informative details relevant to the context surrounding consumption of the product.

SCALE ORIGIN: The scale appears to be original to the study by Krishnamurthy and Sujan (1999).

RELIABILITY: An alpha of .86 was reported for the scale (Krishnamurthy and Sujan 1999).

VALIDITY: Although examination of the scale's validity was not explicitly reported by Krishnamurthy and Sujan (1999) some information can be gleaned from its use as a manipulation check. The scale was used to determine if the two versions of the ad successfully manipulated contextual detail perceived by subjects in the experiment. Indeed, it did, thus, providing some evidence of the scale's concurrent validity.

COMMENTS: The scale was developed for use by Krishnamurthy and Sujan (1999) with respect to ads for a vacation destination. With some slight modification the items appear to be amenable for use with other contexts.

REFERENCES:
Krishnamurthy, Parthasarathy and Mita Sujan (1999), "Retrospection Versus Anticipation: The Role of the Ad Under Retrospective and Anticipatory Self-Referencing," *JCR*, 26 (June), 55–69.

SCALE ITEMS: [1]

1. The ad was visually detailed in terms of what people do on a _____.

2. The ad clearly showed activities that could be part of a _____.

3. The ad clearly showed pictures of the various objects and surroundings one would expect to see on a _____.

4. The ad provided a visual summary of a _____.

[1] The name of the focal context should be placed in the blanks. The context examined in the study by Krishnamurthy and Sujan (1999) was a particular vacation destination, thus, each item contained the phrase "tropical vacation."

SCALE NAME: Creativity (Advertisement)

SCALE DESCRIPTION: Fifteen, seven-point semantic differentials are used to measure the degree to which an advertisement is viewed as being original, well-made, and logical.

SCALE ORIGIN: The scale used by White and Smith (2001) was taken from a larger instrument developed by O'Quin and Besemer (1989). That instrument was made to judge the creativity of products and used fifty-five items to measure eleven dimensions of the construct. Due to the potential fatigue in completing the full instrument and the low marginal utility compared to an abridged version, White and Smith (2001) only used items for the three dimensions most relevant to advertisements.

RELIABILITY: The scale used by White and Smith (2001; White 2003) had an alpha of .91.

VALIDITY: No examination of the scale's validity was reported by White and Smith (2001). Given the three different dimensions intentionally being tapped into by the fifteen items, the scale as a whole is probably not unidimensional. Future users are urged to carefully examine the dimensionality of the items before treating the scale as if it is unidimensional.

COMMENTS: Although the application made by White and Smith (2001) was to advertisements, the scale appears amenable for use with other creative aspects of marketing such as sales presentations, sales promotion, event marketing, etc.

REFERENCES:
O'Quin, Karen and Susan Besemer (1989), "The Development, Reliability, and Validity of the Revised Creative Product Semantic Scale," *Creativity Research Journal*, 2 (4), 267–278.
White, Alisa (2003), Personal Correspondence.
White, Alisa and Bruce L. Smith (2001), "Assessing Advertising Creativity Using the Creative Product Semantic Scale," *JAR*, 41 (November/December), 27–34.

SCALE ITEMS:

Originality subscale

1. Overused / fresh

2. Predictable / novel

3. Usual / unusual

4. Ordinary / unique

5. Conventional / original

Logical subscale

1. Illogical / logical

2. Senseless / makes sense

3. Irrelevant / relevant

4. Inappropriate / appropriate

5. Inadequate / adequate

Well-Crafted subscale

1. Bungling / skillful

2. Botched / well-made

3. Crude / well-crafted

4. Sloppy / meticulous

5. Careless / careful

SCALE NAME: Credibility

SCALE DESCRIPTION: The scale is composed of various semantic differentials measuring one or more dimensions of a source's credibility. Most of the uses reported here focused on the trustworthiness dimension and just a few measured the other two dimensions: expertise and attractiveness. The following applications of the scale (or parts of it) have been made: credibility of a nutrition claim in an ad (Andrews, Netemeyer, and Burton 1998; Andrews 2001; Andrews, Burton and Netemeyer 2001); credibility of merchant supplied price information (Lichtenstein and Bearden 1989); credibility of a store's ad (Bobinski, Cox, and Cox 1996); the trustworthiness and expertise of a company (Goldsmith, Lafferty and Newell 2001); a website's reputation (Shamdasani, Stanaland, and Tan 2001); trustworthiness, expertise, and attractiveness of print ad models (Bower and Landreth 2001); trustworthiness of noncelebrity product endorsers (Moore, Mowen, and Reardon 1994); and, credibility of celebrity endorsers (Ohanian 1990, 1991; Till and Busler 2000; Tripp, Jensen, and Carlson 1994). While the focus in Ohanian (1990) was on the development of a semantic differential version of the scale, Likert and Staple versions were developed as well though the exact phrasing of the items was not given in the article.

SCALE ORIGIN: Lichtenstein and Bearden (1989) as well as Moore, Mowen, and Reardon (1994) did not give any information about the origin of their scales. Lohse and Rosen (2001) cited Mackenzie and Lutz (1989) as the source of the items they used. While Tripp, Jensen, and Carlson (1994) cited McCroskey (1966) as the source of their measure, they actually used only one of his six items. Shamdasani, Stanaland, and Tan (2001) cited both Ohanian (1990) as well as Lichtenstein and Bearden (1989) as the sources of their scale. Ohanian was the only source cited by Bower and Landreth (2001) as well as Till and Busler (2000).

Ohanian (1990, 1991) engaged in considerable developmental work in construction of her three dimensional scale. While she conducted several exploratory and confirmatory analyses to refine the scales, she cites Bowers and Phillips (1967) and Whitehead (1968) as sources for the items she began with.

RELIABILITY: Alphas of .89 (Andrews, Netemeyer, and Burton 1998; Andrews 2001), .89 (Andrews, Burton and Netemeyer 2001), .91 (Bobinski, Cox, and Cox 1996), .78 (Lichtenstein and Bearden 1989), .71 (Lohse and Rosen 2001), .80 (Moore, Mowen, and Reardon 1994), .94 (Shamdasani, Stanaland, and Tan 2001), and .88 (Tripp, Jensen, and Carlson 1994) have been reported for the various versions of the scale. The trustworthiness and expertise subscales were reported to have alphas of .85 and .88, respectively, by Goldsmith, Lafferty and Newell (2001).

Bower and Landreth (2001) conducted two studies of models in advertisements in which each of the three subscales were used and had the following alphas: .85 and .86 (attractiveness), .92 and .93 (trustworthiness), and .91 and .94 (expertise). An alpha of .89 was reported for the expertise dimension by Bower (2001).

Ohanian (1990) reported construct reliabilities for each subscale for each of two celebrity endorsers. The reliabilities were .893 and .904 for attractiveness, .885 and .892 for expertise, and .895 and .896 for trustworthiness. Specific alpha coefficients were not reported by Ohanian (1991) but she did calculate them for both males and females and for four different celebrity endorser test ads. The alphas were described as being .82 or higher in each case.

Likewise, Till and Busler (2000) provided alphas for each of the subscales: .94 (attractiveness), .95 (trustworthiness), and .94 (expertise).

VALIDITY: Most of the studies have not reported any assessment of the scale's validity. Tripp, Jensen, and Carlson (1994) did indicate that the scale had a beta coefficient of .51 suggesting the scale might not be unidimensional. However, further testing using confirmatory factor analysis is necessary to better determine the scale's dimensionality.

Although no rigorous evaluation of the scale's validity was discussed in the article by Goldsmith, Lafferty and Newell (2001) it was stated that all of the scale items in their study were examined via principle axis factor analysis with oblique rotation. All of the items were described as loading as expected and those intended to measure "corporate credibility" loaded on two factors (trustworthiness and expertise). This provides some rudimentary evidence of the scales' convergent and discriminant validity.

Ohanian (1990) tested nomological validity by relating scores on the subscales to several self-reported behaviors. The hypothesized pattern was basically confirmed. Convergent and discriminant validity were examined using the multitrait-multimethod matrix and the analyses supported a claim of acceptable convergent and discriminant validity for the subscales. Average variance extracted was between .61 and .65 for each subscale.

COMMENTS: The evidence indicates that credibility is a multidimensional construct, thus, users should not expect to accurately capture the full construct in just one, unidimensional scale. They should either use one subscale to measure the focal dimension of interest, such as trustworthiness, or use multiple scales to measure multiple dimensions.

REFERENCES:

Andrews, J. Craig (2001), Personal Correspondence.

Andrews, J. Craig, Scot Burton, and Richard G. Netemeyer (2001), "Are Some Comparative Nutrition Claims Misleading? The Role of Nutrition Knowledge, Ad Claim Type and Disclosure Conditions," *JA*, 29 (3), 29–42.

Andrews, J. Craig, Richard G. Netemeyer, and Scot Burton (1998), "Consumer Generalization of Nutrient Content Claims in Advertising," *JM*, 62 (October), 62–75.

Bobinski, George S. Jr., Dena Cox, and Anthony Cox (1996), "Retail 'Sale' Advertising, Perceived Retailer Credibility, and Price Rationale," *JR*, 72 (3), 291–306.

Bower, Amanda B. (2001), "Highly Attractive Models in Advertising and the Women Who Loathe Them: The Implementations of Negative Affect for Spokesperson Effectiveness," *JA*, 30 (3), 51–63.

Bower, Amanda B. and Stacy Landreth (2001), "Is Beauty Best? Highly versus Normally Attractive Models in Advertising," *JA*, 30 (1), 1–12.

Bowers, John W. and William A. Phillips (1967), "A Note on the Generality of Source Credibility Scales," *Speech Monographs*, 34 (August), 185–186.

Goldsmith, Ronald E., Barbara A. Lafferty, and Stephen J. Newell (2001), "The Impact of Corporate Credibility and Celebrity Credibility on Consumer Reaction to Advertisements and Brands," *JA*, 29 (3), 30–54.

Lichtenstein, Donald R. and William O. Bearden (1989), "Contextual Influences on Perceptions of Merchant-Supplied Reference Prices," *JCR*, 16 (June), 55–66.

Lohse, Gerald L. and Dennis L. Rosen (2001), "Signaling Quality and Credibility in Yellow Pages Adverting: The Influence of Color and Graphics on Choice," *JA*, 30 (2), 73–85.

Mackenzie, Scott B. and Richard J. Lutz (1989), "An Empirical Examination of the Structural Antecedants of Attitude toward the Ad in an Advertising Pretesting Context," *JM*, 53 (April), 48–65.

McCroskey, James C. (1966), "Scales for the Measurement of Ethos," *Speech Monographs*, 33 (March), 65–72.

Moore, David J., John C. Mowen, and Richard Reardon (1994), "Multiple Sources in Advertising Appeals: When Product Endorsers Are Paid by the Advertising Sponsor," *JAMS*, 22 (Summer), 234–243.

Ohanian, Roobina (1990), "Construction and Validation of a Scale to Measure Celebrity Endorsers' Perceived Expertise, Trustworthiness, and Attractiveness," *JA*, 19 (3), 39–52.

#602 *Credibility*

Ohanian, Roobina (1991), "The Impact of Celebrity Spokes Persons' Perceived Image on Consumer's Intention to Purchase," *JAR*, 31 (1), 46–54.

Shamdasani, Prem N., Andrea J. S. Stanaland, and Juliana Tan (2001), "Location, Location, Location: Insights for Advertising Placement on the Web," *JAR*, 41 (July-August), 7–21.

Till, Brian D. and Michael Busler (2001), "The Match-Up Hypothesis: Physical Attractiveness, Expertise, and the Role of Fit on Brand Attitude, Purchase Intent and Brand Beliefs," *JA*, 29 (3), 1–14.

Tripp, Carolyn, Thomas D. Jensen, and Les Carlson (1994), "The Effects of Multiple Product Endorsements by Celebrities on Consumers' Attitudes and Intentions," *JCR*, 20 (March)), 535–547.

Whitehead, Jack L. (1968), "Factors of Source Credibility," *Quarterly Journal of Speech*, 54 (1), 59–63.

SCALE ITEMS: [1]

1. insincere / sincere

2. dishonest / honest

3. not dependable / dependable

4. not trustworthy / trustworthy

5. not credible / credible

6. biased / not biased

7. not believable / believable

8. disreputable / reputable

9. unreliable / reliable

10. untruthful / truthful

11. not an expert / expert

12. inexperienced / experienced

13. unknowledgeable / knowledgeable

14. unqualified / qualified

15. unskilled / skilled

16. unattractive / attractive

17. not classy / classy

18. ugly / beautiful

19. plain / elegant

20. not sexy / sexy

21. unconvincing / convincing

Andrews, Burton and Netemeyer (2001): 4*, 5, 7* 7-point
Andrews, Netemeyer, and Burton (1998; Andrews 2001): 4*, 5, 7* 7-point
Bobinski, Cox, and Cox (1996): 1*, 2*, 3*, 4*, 5* 7-point
Bower (2001): 11, 12, 13
Bower and Landreth (2001): 1–4, 9, 11–20 7-point
Goldsmith, Lafferty and Newell (2001): 2, 4*, 10*, 11, 12, 15 7-point
Lichtenstein and Bearden (1989): 1–5 9-point
Lohse and Rosen (2001): 6, 7, 21 7-point
Moore, Mowen, and Reardon (1994): 1, 6, 7, 10 7-point
Ohanian (1990, 1991): 1–4, 9, 11–20
Shamdasani, Stanaland, and Tan (2001): 1–4, 9, 11–15 7-point
Till and Busler (2000): 1–4, 9, 11–20 9-point
Tripp, Jensen, and Carlson (1994): 1, 2, 4, 5–8 7-point

[1] As used by Ohanian (1990, 1991), items for measuring each of the three dimensions were: #1-#4, #9 (trustworthiness), #11-#15 (expertise), and #16-#20 (attractiveness). The items shown with an asterisk were slight variations on those shown.

SCALE NAME: Direct Mail Usage (Retailer)

SCALE DESCRIPTION: The scale has three, seven-point Likert-type statements and is intended to measure a customer's belief that a specific retailer frequently uses direct mail to provide information to its regular customers.

SCALE ORIGIN: The scale seems to have been among those developed specifically for use in the studies by De Wulf, Odekerken-Schröder, and Iacobucci (2001). Items were generated after conducting focus groups and depth interviews with consumers. Content validity was assessed using expert judges. The back-translation method was used to developed versions of the scales in American English and Dutch. Finally, the items were pretested in the U.S., Netherlands, and Belgium (Flemish-speaking area) and that led to only slight revisions.

RELIABILITY: Composite reliabilities were reported by De Wulf, Odekerken-Schröder, and Iacobucci (2001) for two types of stores for each of three countries. The reliabilities for food stores were .89, .76, and .83 for the U.S., Netherlands, and Belgium, respectively. For apparel stores, the reliabilities were .93, .94, and .93 for the U.S., Netherlands, and Belgium, respectively.

VALIDITY: A great deal of information regarding the scale's validity was provided by De Wulf, Odekerken-Schröder, and Iacobucci (2001). In brief, evidence was provided in support of the scale's unidimensionality as well as its convergent and discriminant validities. The average variance extracted for the six uses of the scale ranged from .51 to .84. Partial metric invariance across countries was supported too.

REFERENCES:
De Wulf, Kristof, Gaby Odekerken-Schröder, and Dawn Iacobucci (2001), "Investments in Consumer Relationships: A Cross-Country and Cross-Industry Exploration," *JM*, 65 (October), 33–50.

SCALE ITEMS:

1. This store often sends mailings to regular customers.

2. This store keeps regular customers informed through mailings.

3. This store often informs regular customers through brochures.

SCALE NAME: Ease of Measurement

SCALE DESCRIPTION: The Likert-type scale is composed of four, seven-point statements measuring the respondent's attitude about the ease with which the effect of advertising for a product can be measured.

SCALE ORIGIN: Although not explicitly stated as such, the source of the scale appears to be Spake et al. (1999).

RELIABILITY: An alpha of .88 was reported by Spake et al. (1999). The composite reliability was .825.

VALIDITY: The authors provided some evidence of the scale's convergent and discriminant validity (Spake et al. 1999). Variance extracted was reported to be .586.

COMMENTS: The scale was developed for use with client advertising managers. However, the items appear to be amenable for use with other types of respondents, e.g., market researchers, accountants.

REFERENCES:
Spake, Deborah F. (2001), Personal Correspondence.
Spake, Deborah F., Giles D'Souza, Tammy Neal Crutchfield, and Robert M. Morgan (1999), "Advertising Agency Compensation: An Agency Theory Explanation," *JA*, 28 (3), 53–72.

SCALE ITEMS: [1]

For my product or service:

1. It is easy to measure the sales effect of advertising.

2. It is easy to measure the communications effect of advertising.

3. It is easy to measure the success of the ad campaign.

4. It is hard to know if we accomplished our advertising objectives. (r)

[1] The scale stem and items were provided by Spake (2001).

SCALE NAME: Effectiveness (Product's Impact on Model's Beauty)

SCALE DESCRIPTION: The scale is composed of three, seven-point statements used to measure a person's opinion of the role played by an advertised product with the advertising model's physical beauty, i.e., to what extent was the product responsible for the model's beauty. The scale was referred to as *product arguments* by Bower (2001).

SCALE ORIGIN: No information about the scale's source was provided by Bower (2001) but it appears to be original to her.

RELIABILITY: An alpha of .67 was reported for the scale (Bower 2001).

VALIDITY: Confirmatory factor analysis was used on this scale along with four other scales. The fit indices provided support for the measurement model (Bower 2001). A cause for concern for this scale comes, however, from its low AVE (average variance extracted) of .42. A minimum of .50 is desired (Fornell and Larcker 1981) with lower numbers indicating that the variance explained by the construct is less than the variance due to measurement error and bringing the validity of the scale into question.

REFERENCES:

Bower, Amanda B. (2003), Personal Correspondence.

Bower, Amanda B. (2001), "Highly Attractive Models in Advertising and the Women Who Loathe Them: The Implementations of Negative Affect for Spokesperson Effectiveness," *JA*, 30 (3), 51–63.

Fornell, Claes and David F. Larcker (1981), "Evaluating Structural Equation Models with Unobservable Variables and Measurement Error," *JMR*, 18 (February), 39–50.

SCALE ITEMS: [1]

1. How influential do you believe the advertised product was in improving the model's appearance?
   not at all influential / very influential

2. I believe that the advertised product positively affected the model's beauty.
   strongly disagree / strongly agree

3. The model is more beautiful as a result of her use of the advertised product
   strongly disagree / strongly agree

[1] The items were provided by Bower (2003).

SCALE NAME: Effectiveness of the Ad

SCALE DESCRIPTION: The seven-item scale is intended to measure a person's evaluation of an advertisement he/she has been exposed to with an emphasis on how informative it is and how influential it could be.

SCALE ORIGIN: Although not stated explicitly, the scale seems to be original to the study by Moreau, Markman, and Lehmann (2001).

RELIABILITY: The alpha reported for the scale by Moreau, Markman, and Lehmann (2001) was .80.

VALIDITY: No information regarding the scale's validity was reported by Moreau, Markman, and Lehmann (2001).

REFERENCES:
Moreau, Page C. (2004), Personal Correspondence.
Moreau, Page C., Arthur B. Markman, and Donald R. Lehmann (2001), "What Is It? Categorization Flexibility and Consumers' Responses to Really New Products," *JCR*, 27 (4), 489–498.

SCALE ITEMS: [1]

1. Please rate the overall effectiveness of the ad on the scale below:
   Not at All Effective / Very Effective

2. Please provide your overall evaluation of the ad on the scale below:
   Bad / Good

3. The ad helped me to learn more about the product.
   Agree / Disagree

4. After viewing this ad, I have a better understanding of the product.
   Agree / Disagree

5. After reading the ad, I have a lot of unanswered questions about the product's features and the way that it works. (r)
   Agree / Disagree

6. How realistic is the ad?
   Very Realistic / Not at All Realistic

7. How effective do you think the ad would be in influencing consumers' purchase intentions?
   Very Effective / Not at All Effective

[1] These items were provided by Moreau (2004).

SCALE NAME: Elaboration

SCALE DESCRIPTION: The scale is composed of six semantic differential items intended to measure the amount, complexity, and range of cognitive complexity evoked by an advertisement. Half of the items are meant to tap into imagistic responses while the other half tap into discursive responses.

SCALE ORIGIN: Three of the scale's items (#1–#3, below) came from a study by Unnava and Burnkrant (1991) who used them to measure the imagery-provoking ability of ad copy (a = .81). The origin of the other three items was not stated and would appear to be original to McQuarrie and Mick (1999).

RELIABILITY: An alpha of .87 was reported for the scale by McQuarrie and Mick (1999).

VALIDITY: No explicit examination of the scale's validity was reported by McQuarrie and Mick (1999) although they did state that the set of items was unidimensional based upon factor analysis.

REFERENCES:
McQuarrie, Edward F. and David Glen Mick (1999), "Visual Rhetoric in Advertising: Text-Interpretive, Experimental, and Reader-Response Analyses," *JCR*, 26 (June), 37–54.
Unnava, H. Rao and Robert E. Burnkrant (1991), "An Imagery-Processing View of the Role of Pictures in Print Advertisements," *JMR*, 28 (May), 226–231.

SCALE ITEMS:

1. Provokes / does not provoke imagery

2. Vivid / dull

3. Interesting / boring

4. I had many thoughts in response / I had few thoughts in response

5. The ad has multiple meanings / the ad has one meaning

6. The ad has rich, complex meaning(s) / the ad has simple meaning(s)

SCALE NAME: Fit (Ad/Object)

SCALE DESCRIPTION: The five-item Likert-type scale measures the degree to which a person believes an advertisement is consistent with something else. In the study by Ellen and Bone (1998) the focus was on the scent of a scratch-and-sniff panel attached to an ad and whether the ad was consistent with it. Two of the items used nine-point response formats while the other three had five-point scales. Item scores were standardized then summed.

SCALE ORIGIN: Ellen and Bone (1998) cited MacInnis and Park (1991) as having a similar scale but it appears to be similar in concept only. The items used in the two studies are sufficiently unique to conclude they produced different scales.

RELIABILITY: An alpha of .89 was reported of the scale by Ellen and Bone (1998).

VALIDITY: No examination of the scale's validity was reported by Ellen and Bone (1998).

COMMENTS: Although the items were developed for use with scent, it appears they can be easily adapted for use with other constructs that researchers might examine for their fit with an ad, e.g., product taste, brand image, company image, self-concept.

REFERENCES:
Ellen, Pam Scholder (2004), Personal Correspondence.
Ellen, Pam Scholder and Paula Fitzgerald Bone (1998), "Does It Matter If It Smells? Olfactory Stimuli As Advertising Executional Cues," *JA*, 27 (4), 29–39.
MacInnis, Deborah J. and C. Whan Park (1991), "The Differential Role of Characteristics of Music on High- and Low-Involvement Consumers' Processing of Ads," *JCR*, 18 (September), 161–173.

SCALE ITEMS: [1]

1. The _____ for the advertisement was consistent with what was in the ad.

2. It is clear to me that the _____ was related to what was in the ad.

3. The _____ fit the picture used in the ad.

4. The _____ was appropriate for the information advertised about [object/scene].

5. The picture of the [object/scene] matched the _____ used.

---

[1] The first two items used nine-point response formats while the other three items used five-point scales (Ellen 2004). The word "scent" was used in the blanks by Ellen and Bone (1998).

SCALE NAME: Fit (Brand/Endorser)

SCALE DESCRIPTION: Three, nine-point semantic differentials are used to measure the extent of perceived compatibility between the endorser of a product in an advertisement and the brand being featured.

SCALE ORIGIN: Till and Busler (2000) did not state the source of the scale but it would appear to be original to their study.

RELIABILITY: An alpha of .99 was reported for the scale (Till and Busler 2000).

VALIDITY: No examination of the scale's validity was reported by Till and Busler (2000).

REFERENCES:
Till, Brian D. and Michael Busler (2001), "The Match-Up Hypothesis: Physical Attractiveness, Expertise, and the Role of Fit on Brand Attitude, Purchase Intent and Brand Beliefs," *JA*, 29 (3), 1–14.

SCALE ITEMS: [1]

I think the combination of _____ and _____:

1. Does not belong with / belongs with

2. Does not go together / goes together

3. Does not fit together / fits together

[1] The names of the brand and the endorser should be provided in the blanks.

SCALE NAME: Fit (Model/Consumer)

SCALE DESCRIPTION: Three Likert-type statements are used to assess a person's opinion of the extent to which a model in an advertisement is physically similar to him/herself.

SCALE ORIGIN: The scale is apparently original to Bower and Landreth (2001).

RELIABILITY: An alpha of .74 was reported for the scale (Bower and Landreth 2001).

VALIDITY: No explicit examination of the scale's validity was described by Bower and Landreth (2001).

REFERENCES:
Bower, Amanda B. (2003), Personal Correspondence.
Bower, Amanda B. and Stacy Landreth (2001), "Is Beauty Best? Highly Versus Normally Attractive Models in Advertising," *JA*, 30 (1), 1–12.

SCALE ITEMS: [1]

1. I feel that the model in the advertisement and I are very much alike.

2. I can identify physically with the model in the advertisement.

3. I find that the model in the advertisement is like me.

[1] Anchors for the response scale were *strongly disagree* (1) and *strongly agree* (7). The items and anchors were provided by Bower (2003).

SCALE NAME: Goal Congruence (Agency/Firm)

SCALE DESCRIPTION: The Likert-type scale is composed of three, seven-point statements measuring the respondent's attitude about similarity of values and beliefs held in common by a company and its advertising agency with an emphasis on how they treat their customers and their employees. The scale was called *goal conflict* by Spake et al. (1999).

SCALE ORIGIN: Although Spake et al. (1999) were inspired by a *shared values* scale by Morgan and Hunt (1994), their items are different enough to be considered a distinct, original scale.

RELIABILITY: An alpha of .81 was reported by Spake et al. (1999). The composite reliability was .833.

VALIDITY: The authors provided some evidence of the scale's convergent and discriminant validity (Spake et al. 1999). Variance extracted was reported to be .63.

COMMENTS: The scale was developed for use with client advertising managers. However, with some slight rephrasing of the scale stem the items appear to be amenable for use with other types of respondents either within the client firm or working for the advertising agency.

REFERENCES:
Morgan, Robert M. and Shelby D. Hunt (1994), "The Commitment-Trust Theory of Relationship Marketing," *JM*, 58 (July), 20–38.
Spake, Deborah F. (2001), Personal Correspondence.
Spake, Deborah F., Giles D'Souza, Tammy Neal Crutchfield, and Robert M. Morgan (1999), "Advertising Agency Compensation: An Agency Theory Explanation," *JA*, 28 (3), 53–72.

SCALE ITEMS: [1]

My advertising agency and my firm:

1. Share similar values.

2. Share similar beliefs about how a business should treat its customers.

3. Share similar beliefs about how a business should treat its employees.

[1] The scale stem and items were provided by Spake (2001).

SCALE NAME: Helpfulness of the Ad

SCALE DESCRIPTION: The scale is composed of four, seven-point Likert-type statements measuring the degree to which a consumer believes that the information provided in an advertisement facilitates an understanding of the product's quality.

SCALE ORIGIN: The source of the scale was not explicitly stated by Dean and Biswas (2001) but it would appear to be original to them. They explained that the purpose of the scale was to determine the *value* of an ad to a consumer in terms of its information helping to complete the search process for the consumer.

RELIABILITY: Alphas of .80 (n = 229) and .87 (n = 237) were reported for the versions of the scale used in Dean and Biswas (2001).

VALIDITY: Dean and Biswas (2001) described the results of an EFA as well as a CFA of the items composing the four multi-item scales used in their two studies. All items loaded as expected. The AVE of the scale was above .50 in both studies and met a strict criterion of discriminant validity (Fornell and Larcker 1981).

REFERENCES:

Dean, Dwane Hal (2003), Personal Correspondence.

Dean, Dwane Hal and Abhijit Biswas (2001), "Third-Party Organization Endorsement of Products: An Advertising Cue Affecting Consumer Prepurchase Evaluation of Goods and Services," *JA*, 30 (4), 41–57.

Fornell, Claes and David F. Larcker (1981), "Evaluating Structural Equation Models with Unobservable Variables and Measurement Error," *JMR*, 18 (February), 39–50.

SCALE ITEMS: [1]

Based on information in the ad . . .

1. I can predict the performance of the advertised _____.

2. I can evaluate the quality of the advertised _____.

3. I can estimate how satisfied I would be with the advertised _____.

4. I can compare the advertised _____ to other brands of _____.

---

[1] Items provided by Dean (2003). The response scale had seven points and used anchors of *strongly disagree* and *strongly agree*. The name for the product category should be placed in the blanks.

SCALE NAME: Importance of Advertising

SCALE DESCRIPTION: The Likert-type scale is composed of four, seven-point statements measuring the respondent's attitude about the role that advertising plays in the market success of a product.

SCALE ORIGIN: Although not explicitly stated as such, the source of the scale appears to be Spake et al. (1999).

RELIABILITY: An alpha of .79 was reported by Spake et al. (1999). The composite reliability was .713.

VALIDITY: Variance extracted was reported to be a rather low .385 (Spake et al. 1999). Despite this, the authors provided some evidence of the scale's convergent and discriminant validity.

COMMENTS: The scale was developed for use with client advertising managers. However, the items appear to be amenable for use with other types of respondents, e.g., consumers, non-advertising professionals. Given the very low average variance extracted, however, further purification is called for.

REFERENCES:
Spake, Deborah F., Giles D'Souza, Tammy Neal Crutchfield, and Robert M. Morgan (1999), "Advertising Agency Compensation: An Agency Theory Explanation," *JA*, 28 (3), 53–72.

SCALE ITEMS:

1. Advertising is one of the most important determinants of market success.

2. The firms that devote the most resources to advertising are most profitable.

3. Firms that do not advertise are not successful.

4. In order to remain competitive, a firm must advertise.

SCALE NAME: Importance of Payment Information

SCALE DESCRIPTION: The scale is composed of four statements used to measure the importance placed by a viewer on information provided in an infomercial regarding the means of paying for the product being offered.

SCALE ORIGIN: Although not explicitly stated by the authors (Agee and Martin 2001), the scale appears to be original to their study.

RELIABILITY: An alpha of .64 was reported for the scale (Agee and Martin 2001).

VALIDITY: No examination of the scale's validity was reported by Agee and Martin (2001). They did, however, state that factor analysis was used to determine the dimensions underlying the full set of items used in their survey instrument. The four items composing this scale loaded highest on the same factor.

COMMENTS: The scale seems to be amenable for use with typical length advertisements although its reliability is rather low and indicates a need for improvement in the scale's psychometric quality.

REFERENCES:
Agee, Tom and Brett A. S. Martin (2001), "Planned or Impulse Purchases? How to Create Effective Infomercials," *JAR*, 41 (November/December), 35–42.

SCALE ITEMS: [1]

1. Easy payment plan with credit card

2. Money back guarantee

3. The amount of information provided

4. Buying at home, free number

---

[1] The instructions used with these items were not described by Agee and Martin (2001). They were probably something like the following: *please indicate how important each of the following were as you decided whether or not to buy the advertised product.* The response scale had the following anchors: *very important* (1) and *not important at all* (5).

SCALE NAME: Importance of Testimonials

SCALE DESCRIPTION: Three statements are used to measure the importance placed by a viewer on positive comments and endorsements made by people in an infomercial. The scale was called *comments and demonstrations* by Agee and Martin (2001).

SCALE ORIGIN: Although not explicitly stated by the authors (Agee and Martin 2001), the scale appears to be original to their study.

RELIABILITY: An alpha of .74 was reported for the scale (Agee and Martin 2001).

VALIDITY: No examination of the scale's validity was reported by Agee and Martin (2001). They did, however, state that factor analysis was used to determine the dimensions underlying the full set of items used in their survey instrument. The three items composing this scale loaded highest on the same factor.

COMMENTS: The scale seems to be amenable for use with typical length advertisements simply by replacing the word *infomercial* in item 3 (below) with *ad* or *commercial*.

REFERENCES:
Agee, Tom and Brett A. S. Martin (2001), "Planned or Impulse Purchases? How to Create Effective Infomercials," *JAR*, 41 (November/December), 35–42.

SCALE ITEMS: [1]

1. Testimonials from satisfied users.

2. Comments by an expert.

3. People like me in the infomercial who seemed to benefit from using the product.

[1] The instructions used with these items were not described by Agee and Martin (2001). They were probably something like the following: *please indicate how important each of the following were as you decided whether or not to buy the advertised product.* The response scale had the following anchors: *very important* (1) and *not important at all* (5).

SCALE NAME: Interest in Product (Prior to Ad Exposure)

SCALE DESCRIPTION: The scale is composed of three, five-point Likert-type statements used to measure the extent to which a consumer indicates awareness and interest in a product similar to the advertised one *before* seeing it promoted on TV or in stores.

SCALE ORIGIN: Although not explicitly stated by the authors (Agee and Martin 2001), the scale appears to be original to their study.

RELIABILITY: An alpha of .63 was reported for the scale (Agee and Martin 2001).

VALIDITY: No examination of the scale's validity was reported by Agee and Martin (2001). They did, however, state that factor analysis was used to determine the dimensions underlying the full set of items used in their survey instrument. The three items composing this scale loaded highest on the same factor.

COMMENTS: The scale's reliability is rather low and indicates a need for improvement in its psychometric quality.

REFERENCES:
Agee, Tom and Brett A. S. Martin (2001), "Planned or Impulse Purchases? How to Create Effective Infomercials," *JAR*, 41 (November/December), 35–42.

SCALE ITEMS: [1]

1. I had seen TV ads for other products like this before.

2. I thought a lot about similar products that I had seen in shops or on TV.

3. I had been looking around for a product like this, even before I saw the TV ad.

---

[1] The response scale used by Agee and Martin (2001) for these items had the following anchors: *strongly agree* (1) and *strongly disagree* (5).

SCALE NAME: Intergenerational Communication (Promotion-Related)

SCALE DESCRIPTION: The scale is composed of four, seven-point statements measuring beliefs about promotion and product quality issues that have been communicated in some way from a parent to a child. Two versions of the scale are presented (below). One has to do with the *frequency* with which these beliefs have been communicated by the parents. The other focuses on the *degree of influence* the parent's opinions have had on the child.

SCALE ORIGIN: The scale is original to Viswanathan, Childers, and Moore (2000). It is part of a larger instrument they developed called IGEN, referring to intergenerational communication and influence. The instrument as a whole covers three dimensions (skills, preferences, and attitudes) and two versions of scales for those three dimensions (*frequency* and *degree of influence*). Initially, 37 items were generated. After a thorough pretest which involved examination of dimensionality, reliability, and validity the set was reduced to 12 items with each dimension represented by four items.

RELIABILITY: Viswanathan, Childers, and Moore (2000) reported the following alphas for the *frequency* version of the scale: .65 (U.S.), .74 (Thailand), .64 (young adults), .72 (parents). For the *degree of influence* version the alphas were .66 (U.S.), .77 (Thailand), .64 (college students), .79 (students' parents).

VALIDITY: The pretest and three follow-up studies thoroughly examined the scales' psychometric quality (Viswanathan, Childers, and Moore 2000). The evidence appeared to favor a three factor model and a variety of evidence was found in support of each scales' convergent, discriminant, and nomological validities.

COMMENTS: Data for Studies 1 and 2 were collected along with the data referred to in Childers and Rao (1992).

REFERENCES:

Childers, Terry L. and Akshay R. Rao (1992), "The Influence of Familial and Peer-Based Reference Groups on Consumer Decisions," *JCR*, 19 (Sept), 198–211.

Viswanathan, Madhubalan, Terry L. Childers, and Elizabeth S. Moore (2000), "The Measurement of Intergenerational Communication and Influence on Consumption: Development, Validation, and Cross-Cultural Comparison of the IGEN Scale," *JAMS*, 28 (3), 406–424.

SCALE ITEMS: [1]

Directions: The following set of questions deals with the communication and influence that your family may have on your purchasing behavior. Two questions follow each statement. The first pertains to whether your parents/family have communicated in some way the basic idea behind the statement to you. The second question deals with how much you were influenced by your parents/family and their opinions.

1. Their views about product information provided by different types of advertising.

2. The role that advertising plays in purchase decisions (i.e., whether it helps or hinders purchase decisions).

3. Their views on whether price should be used as an indicator of product quality.

4. Whether to rely upon salespeople to educate you when making a purchase decision.

---

[1] The frequency version of the scale would have the following question after each item: "have your parents communicated this to you? *Very often / never.*" The degree of influence version would have the following question after each item: "how much were you influenced by their opinions on this issue? *A large extent / not at all.*"

SCALE NAME: Involvement (Ad Message)

SCALE DESCRIPTION: The scale appears to measure how much a person reports actively processing some information stimuli s/he has been exposed to. In Lord, Lee, and Sauer (1994, 1995) the stimuli were mock radio commercials embedded in a recorded radio program. They referred to this measure as *commercial processing motivation* (CPM, 1994) and later as *response involvement* (1995). The stimulus toward which respondents were exposed in the study by Ahluwalia, Unnava, and Burnkrant (2001) was not clearly described but apparently was a folder containing a variety of information about the focal product including a *Consumer Reports*-type article and draft copies of advertisements.

SCALE ORIGIN: No information was provided by Lord, Lee, and Sauer (1994, 1995) as to the source of the scale but it would appear to be original to their study.

RELIABILITY: Alphas of .93 and .89 were reported for the scale by Lord, Lee, and Sauer (1994) and (1995), respectively. Ahluwalia, Unnava, and Burnkrant (2001) reported an alpha of .85 for their version of the scale.

VALIDITY: The validity of the scale was not specifically addressed in the studies by Lord, Lee, and Sauer (1994, 1995). However, some support for the scale's validity comes from the finding that those who scored higher in the involvement scale also scored higher on a "recognition memory index" created to determine the degree to which respondents could accurately respond to statements made about the ads they heard.

REFERENCES:

Ahluwalia, Rohini, H. Rao Unnava, and Robert E. Burnkrant (2001), "The Moderating Role of Commitment on the Spillover Effect of Marketing Communications," *JMR*, 38 (Nov), 458–470.

Lord, Kenneth R., Myung-Soo Lee, and Paul L. Sauer (1994), "Program Context Antecedents of Attitude toward Radio Commercials," *JAMS*, 22 (1), 3–15.

Lord, Kenneth R., Myung-Soo Lee, and Paul L. Sauer (1995), "The Combined Influence Hypothesis: Central and Peripheral Antecedents of Attitude Toward the Ad," *JA*, 24 (Spring), 73–85.

SCALE ITEMS: [1]

1. very uninvolved / very involved

2. concentrating very little / concentrating very hard

3. paying very little attention / paying a lot of attention

4. I carefully considered the advertising claims about the *(product name)*.
   strongly disagree / strongly agree

---

[1] Lord, Lee, and Sauer (1994) used each of the above items, a seven-point response format, and a scale stem that read *"While listening to the radio commercials I was. . ."* The first three items were used by Ahluwalia, Unnava, and Burnkrant (2001) with a seven-point response scale but the type of scale stem and/or directions they used is unknown.

SCALE NAME: Involvement (Ad Message)

SCALE DESCRIPTION: A four-item, nine-point scale measuring the cognitive effort a person reports having expended with regard to processing an advertisement. The scale was called *motivation to process* by Ellen and Bone (1998).

SCALE ORIGIN: Although Petty and Cacioppo (1986) were cited for contributing the concept, the scale itself appears to have been developed by Ellen and Bone (1998) for their study.

RELIABILITY: An alpha of .93 was reported of the scale by Ellen and Bone (1998).

VALIDITY: No examination of the scale's validity was reported by Ellen and Bone (1998).

REFERENCES:

Ellen, Pam Scholder and Paula Fitzgerald Bone (1998), "Does It Matter If It Smells? Olfactory Stimuli as Advertising Executional Cues" *JA*, 27 (4), 29–39.

Petty, Richard E. and John T. Cacioppo (1986), *Communication and Persuasion: Central and Peripheral Routes to Attitude Change*, New York: Springer-Verlag.

SCALE ITEMS:

1. To what extent did you try to evaluate the information in the ad?
   (not at all / very much)

2. How much effort did you put into evaluating the information in the ad?
   (no effort at all / a great deal of effort)

3. I paid close attention to the advertisement.
   (disagree / agree)

4. I carefully read the copy in the advertisement.
   (disagree / agree)

SCALE NAME: Involvement (Ad Message)

SCALE DESCRIPTION: The scale is composed of seven items meant to measure a person's motivation to process the information content of an advertisement.

SCALE ORIGIN: This scale is apparently original to Baker and Lutz (2000). The construct itself has been studied previously and has been referred to as AMI (advertising message involvement), e.g., Muehling, Stoltman, and Grossbart (1990).

RELIABILITY: An alpha of .90 was reported for the scale by Baker and Lutz (2000).

VALIDITY: Although the article did not explicitly discuss tests of the scale's validity, some limited evidence comes from the use of the scale as a manipulation check. Specifically, there were three conditions in the experiment that were manipulated in terms of AMI. The scale showed that, indeed, subjects in the three conditions significantly differed in AMI in the expected direction.

REFERENCES:
Baker, William E., and Richard J. Lutz (2000), "An Empirical Test of an Updated Relevance-Accessibility Model of Advertising Effectiveness," *JA*, 29 (1), 1–14.
Muehling, Darrel D., Jeffrey J. Stoltman, and Sanford Grossbart (1990), "The Impact of Comparative Advertising on Levels of Message Involvement," *JA*, 19 (4), 41–50.

SCALE ITEMS: [1]

1. Very low / very high

2. Very motivated / very unmotivated (r)

3. Very intense / not at all intense (r)

4. Mattered a lot / didn't matter (r)

5. I tried to memorize the content of the advertisements.

6. I explicitly compared the content of the three advertisements as I listened to them.

7. Basically, I disregarded the advertisements. (r)

---

[1] A seven-point response format was used with these items, the last three items utilizing *agree / disagree* anchors. The scale stem and/or directions used are unknown.

SCALE NAME: Involvement (Ad Message)

SCALE DESCRIPTION: Six, seven-point phrases are used to measure a person's motivation to process information in the message portion of an advertisement.

SCALE ORIGIN: This scale is original to Lee (2000) though inspiration for the items was attributed to Andrew (1988).

RELIABILITY: Alphas of .96 (computer ad) and .95 (monitor ad) were reported for the scale by Lee (2000).

VALIDITY: Although the article did not explicitly discuss tests of the scale's validity, some limited evidence comes from the use of the scale as a manipulation check. Specifically, there were two conditions in the experiment that were manipulated in terms of advertising information expectancy, a factor thought to have a negative relationship with AMI. The scale showed that, indeed, subjects in the two conditions significantly differed in AMI in the expected direction.

REFERENCES:

Andrew, J. Craig (1988), "Motivation, Ability, and Opportunity to Process Information: Conceptual and Experimental Manipulation Issues," in *Advances in Consumer Research, V. XV*, Michael J. Houston ed. Provo, UT: Association for Consumer Research, 219–225.

Lee, Yih Hwai (2000), "Manipulating Ad Message Involvement through Information Expectancy: Effects on Attitude Evaluation and Confidence," *JA*, 29 (2), 29–43.

SCALE ITEMS: [1]

Directions: Using the following statements to fill in the blank, indicate the extent to which you agree with the statement: *I was _____ the content of the advertisement.*

1. paying attention to

2. concentrating on

3. thinking about

4. focusing on

5. spending effort looking at

6. carefully reading

[1] The exact phrases and scale stem were not provided in the article and were recreated here based upon the information that was provided. Agreement appears to have been measured via a seven-point Likert-type scale.

SCALE NAME: Involvement (Ad Message)

SCALE DESCRIPTION: Six statements are used to measure the degree to which a person says he/she was interested in and paid attention to an advertisement he/she is familiar with (and had probably just been exposed to).

SCALE ORIGIN: Although some of the items are similar to ones used previously to measure ad involvement, the scale as a whole appears to be original to this study by Cox and Cox (2001).

RELIABILITY: An alpha of .96 was reported for the scale (Cox and Cox 2001).

VALIDITY: No information regarding the scale's validity was provided by Cox and Cox (2001). However, some sense of its nomological validity comes from the fact that it showed, as a manipulation check, that an anecdotal message was significantly more involving than a statistical one.

REFERENCES:
Cox, Dena and Anthony D. Cox (2001), "Communicating the Consequences of Early Detection: The Role of Evidence and Framing," *JM*, 65 (July), 91–103.

SCALE ITEMS: [1]

1. I got involved in what the ad had to say.

2. The message seemed relevant to me.

3. This ad really made me think.

4. This ad was thought-provoking.

5. The _____ was very interesting.

6. I felt strong emotions while reading this ad.

[1] A topic or product category name should be placed in the blank, e.g., breast cancer awareness. Although Cox and Cox (2001) did not describe the response format used with these items, it appears to have been a seven-point, agree/disagree scale.

SCALE NAME: Involvement (Brand Response)

SCALE DESCRIPTION: The scale is composed of six items meant to measure a person's motivation to process information from an advertisement at the time of brand choice.

SCALE ORIGIN: This scale is apparently original to Baker and Lutz (2000). The construct itself was referred to as BRI (brand response involvement).

RELIABILITY: An alpha of .90 was reported for the scale by Baker and Lutz (2000).

VALIDITY: Although the article did not explicitly discuss tests of the scale's validity, some limited evidence comes from the use of the scale as a manipulation check. Specifically, there were three conditions in the experiment that were manipulated in terms of BRI. The scale showed that, indeed, subjects in the three conditions significantly differed in BRI in the expected direction.

REFERENCES:
Baker, William E., and Richard J. Lutz (2000), "An Empirical Test of an Updated Relevance-Accessibility Model of Advertising Effectiveness," *JA*, 29 (1), 1–14.

SCALE ITEMS: [1]

1. Very motivated / very unmotivated (r)

2. Mattered a lot / didn't matter (r)

3. Of strong concern / of no concern

4. Meant nothing / meant a lot

5. I tried very hard to recall all of the advertising information I could about each brand before I made my brand choice.

6. I tried very hard to compare all of the pluses and minuses of each advertised brand before I made my choice.

[1] A seven-point response format was used with these items, the last two items utilizing *agree / disagree* anchors. The scale stem and/or directions used are unknown.

SCALE NAME: Irritation With Commercials

SCALE DESCRIPTION: The scale measures the degree to which a set of commercials a person has been exposed to is viewed as unpleasant and annoying using seven, five-point Likert-type statements.

SCALE ORIGIN: No information about the source of the scale was provided by Fennis and Bakker (2001) but it appears to be original to their study.

RELIABILITY: An alpha of .87 was reported for the scale (Fennis and Bakker 2001).

VALIDITY: No examination of the scale's validity was reported by Fennis and Bakker (2001) although they did state a confirmatory factor analysis of the items showed the items were unidimensional.

COMMENTS: Although the items are stated such that they refer to a set of commercials the respondent has been exposed to, they might be amenable for use with a single commercial or, at the other extreme, commercials in general. However, some rephrasing and retesting would be advisable.

REFERENCES:
Fennis, Bob M. (2003), Personal Correspondence.
Fennis, Bob M. and Arnold B. Bakker (2001), "Stay Tuned-We Will Be Back Right After These Messages: Need to Evaluate Moderates the Transfer of Irritation in Advertising," *JA*, 30 (3), 15–25.

SCALE ITEMS: [1]

1. I found the commercials quite annoying.

2. I found the commercials quite irritating.

3. I was bored by the commercials.

4. The commercials were bothersome to me.

5. The commercials constituted a pleasant break from the program. (r)

6. The commercials distracted unpleasantly from the program.

7. The commercials formed a troublesome, irritating interference with the program.

[1] The statements were provided by Fennis (2003). The response scale ranged from *totally disagree* (1) to *totally agree* (5).

SCALE NAME: Mood Evoked by Ad

SCALE DESCRIPTION: A six-item, nine-point semantic differential scale measuring the emotion evoked by an ad that a person has been exposed to. The scale was called *mood* by Ellen and Bone (1998).

SCALE ORIGIN: Ellen and Bone (1998) cited Mehrabian and Russell (1974, p. 216) as the source of the items. Indeed, the items are part of an eighteen-item instrument those authors developed to measure either an emotional trait or state. Four of the items used by Ellen and Bone (1998) came from the *pleasure* dimension of the instrument and two items came from the *arousal* dimension.

RELIABILITY: An alpha of .89 was reported of the scale by Ellen and Bone (1998).

VALIDITY: No examination of the scale's validity was reported by Ellen and Bone (1998). There is some doubt about the scale's unidimensionality given that it was clear from the studies by Mehrabian and Russell (1974) that the items were tapping into different emotional dimensions.

REFERENCES:

Ellen, Pam Scholder and Paula Fitzgerald Bone (1998), "Does It Matter If It Smells? Olfactory Stimuli As Advertising Executional Cues," *JA*, 27 (4), 29–39.

Mehrabian, Albert and James A. Russell (1974), *An Approach to Environmental Psychology*, Cambridge, MA: The MIT Press.

SCALE ITEMS:

1. satisfied / unsatisfied

2. happy / unhappy

3. hopeful / despairing

4. wide-awake / sleepy

5. aroused / unaroused

6. pleased / annoyed

SCALE NAME: New Product Attributes (Learning Costs)

SCALE DESCRIPTION: The scale is composed of three, nine-point Likert-type items measuring the degree to which a consumer views there to be "learning costs" associated with the advertised new features of a product, that is, the cognitive effort required to become familiar and experienced with the features in order to use them effectively.

SCALE ORIGIN: Mukherjee and Hoyer (2001) did not specify the source of the scale but it would appear to be original to their work.

RELIABILITY: The scale had an alpha of .84 (Mukherjee 2003).

VALIDITY: No examination of the scale's validity was reported by Mukherjee and Hoyer (2001).

REFERENCES:
Mukherjee, Ashesh (2003), Personal Correspondence.
Mukherjee, Ashesh and Wayne D. Hoyer (2001), "The Effect of Novel Attributes on Product Evaluation," *JCR*, 28 (December), 462–472.

SCALE ITEMS: [1]

Directions: The following questions relate to the new features offered by the advertised product (e.g., _____).

Learning to effectively use the new features is likely to take a lot of:

1. time.

2. effort.

3. energy.

[1] A nine-point Likert-type response format (*strongly disagree / strongly agree*) was used with these items (Mukherjee 2003). The new features can be listed in the blank at the end of the scale instructions.

SCALE NAME: New Product Attributes (Value Added)

SCALE DESCRIPTION: Three, nine-point statements are used to measure the extent to which a consumer believes that the advertised new features of a product provide additional benefits and value to the product.

SCALE ORIGIN: Mukherjee and Hoyer (2001) did not specify the source of the scale but it would appear to be original to their work.

RELIABILITY: The scale had an alpha of .91 (Mukherjee 2003).

VALIDITY: No examination of the scale's validity was reported by Mukherjee and Hoyer (2001).

REFERENCES:
Mukherjee, Ashesh (2003), Personal Correspondence.
Mukherjee, Ashesh and Wayne D. Hoyer (2001), "The Effect of Novel Attributes on Product Evaluation," *JCR*, 28 (December), 462–472.

SCALE ITEMS: [1]

Directions: The following questions relate to the new features offered by the advertised product (e.g., _____).

1. It is likely that the new features will offer advantages to the consumer.
   strongly disagree / strongly agree

2. How likely is it that the new features will add value to the advertised product?
   not at all likely / very likely

3. The new features are likely to perform well.
   strongly disagree / strongly agree

[1] This phrasing of the items was provided by Mukherjee (2003). The new features can be listed in the blank at the end of the scale instructions.

#628 *Normalcy*

SCALE NAME: Normalcy

SCALE DESCRIPTION: Four Likert-type statements are used to measure a person's opinion of the degree to which a model in a specific advertisement looks like a normal person rather than being unusual in some way (e.g., very attractive).

SCALE ORIGIN: The scale is apparently original to Bower and Landreth (2001).

RELIABILITY: Alphas of .83 (Study 1) and .79 (Study 2) were reported for the scale (Bower and Landreth 2001).

VALIDITY: No explicit examination of the scale's validity was described by Bower and Landreth (2001). However, since the scale was used a manipulation check showed that a model who was considered to be highly attractive scored lower (less normal) than a model considered to be "normal" then that provides some limited evidence of the scale's validity.

COMMENTS: To make the scale appropriate for assessing the normalcy of male models a simple word change will be necessary in item 1 (below). However, it should be kept in mind that in the two studies by Bower and Landreth (2001) the scale was <u>only</u> applied to female models and <u>only</u> completed by female respondents. Thus, further testing is necessary before it can be assumed the scale can be reliably used by males with regard to male models.

REFERENCES:

Bower, Amanda B. (2003), Personal Correspondence.
Bower, Amanda B. and Stacy Landreth (2001), "Is Beauty Best? Highly Versus Normally Attractive Models in Advertising," *JA*, 30 (1), 1–12.

SCALE ITEMS: [1]

1. This model is an example of an ordinary woman.

2. I would consider this model to be "normal looking."

3. A good word to describe this model is "unrealistic." (r)

4. This model looks like a regular person.

---

[1] Anchors for the response scale were *strongly disagree* (1) and *strongly agree* (7). The items and anchors were provided by Bower (2003).

SCALE NAME: Persuasiveness of the Ad (Cognitive Change)

SCALE DESCRIPTION: The scale is composed of four, seven-point statements intended to measure the degree to which a person believes that an advertisement has influenced him/her to be more knowledgeable or to think differently about a topic. Given this, the scale appears to be a measure of the extent to which an ad is effective in making changes in one's cognitions about some topic.

SCALE ORIGIN: Although no source of the scale was specified by Reichert, Heckler, and Jackson (2001) it appears to be original to their study.

RELIABILITY: An alpha of .79 was reported for the scale (Reichert, Heckler, and Jackson 2001).

VALIDITY: No information regarding the scale's validity was reported by Reichert, Heckler, and Jackson (2001).

REFERENCES:
Reichert, Tom (2003), Personal Correspondence.
Reichert, Tom, Susan E. Heckler, and Sally Jackson (2001), "The Effects of Sexual Marketing Appeals on Cognitive Processing and Persuasion," *JA*, 30 (1), 13–27.

SCALE ITEMS: [1]

1. Did the ad cause you to think differently about _____?

2. How much did the ad cause you to want to make any changes in how you behave regarding _____?

3. How much did the ad increase your awareness of _____?

4. Was the ad a good way to explain the importance of _____?

[1] The response scale was anchored by *very much* (1) and *not at all* (7). The items shown here were provided by Reichert (2003).

SCALE NAME: Persuasiveness of the Information

SCALE DESCRIPTION: Three, seven-point semantic differentials are used to measure the extent to which some specific product information to which a consumer has been exposed is viewed as being convincing and powerful. If using instructions similar to Gürhan-Canli and Maheswaran (2000), the respondent's attention can be focused on something specific in the information, e.g., message arguments related to the product.

SCALE ORIGIN: The scale is original to Gürhan-Canli and Maheswaran (2000). A slight variation in the scale was used later by Sen, Gürhan-Canli, and Morwitz (2001).

RELIABILITY: The scale by Gürhan-Canli and Maheswaran (2000) was reported to have alphas of .85 (Study 1) and .83 (Study 2). Alphas of .92 (Study 1) and .93 (Study 2) were reported for the version of the scale used by Sen, Gürhan-Canli, and Morwitz (2001).

VALIDITY: No evidence of the scale's validity was reported by Gürhan-Canli and Maheswaran (2000).

REFERENCES:
Gürhan-Canli, Zeynep and Durairaj Maheswaran (2000), "Determinants of Country-of-Origin Evaluations," *JCR*, 27 (1), 96–108.
Sen, Sankar, Zeynep Gürhan-Canli, and Vicki Morwitz (2001), "Withholding Consumption: A Social Dilemma Perspective on Consumer Boycotts," *JCR*, 28 (December), 399–417.

SCALE ITEMS: [1]

Directions: Please describe your perceptions about the strength of the arguments presented in the message. In your opinion, the message arguments were:

1. very weak / very strong

2. not very convincing / very convincing

3. not very powerful / very powerful

4. not very persuasive / very persuasive

---

[1] These are the directions used by Gürhan-Canli and Maheswaran (2000). By changing the directions, the scale can be made to focus on some other aspect of the information or on the information stimulus as a whole. In the study by Sen, Gürhan-Canli, and Morwitz (2001) the scale was used with regard to a mock boycott announcement that subjects were asked to read. Items 1–3 are those by Gürhan-Canli and Maheswaran (2000) whereas Sen, Gürhan-Canli, and Morwitz (2001) used 1, 2, and 4.

SCALE NAME: Post-Exposure Elaboration

SCALE DESCRIPTION: The scale is composed of four, five-point Likert-type statements used to measure the degree that a viewer of an infomercial thought a lot about the product and the information provided about it before making the decision to purchase the product.

SCALE ORIGIN: Although not explicitly stated by the authors (Agee and Martin 2001), the scale appears to be original to their study.

RELIABILITY: An alpha of .83 was reported for the scale (Agee and Martin 2001).

VALIDITY: No examination of the scale's validity was reported by Agee and Martin (2001). They did, however, state that factor analysis was used to determine the dimensions underlying the full set of items used in their survey instrument. The four items composing this scale loaded highest on the same factor.

COMMENTS: Although the scale was used with reference to infomercials in the study by Agee and Martin (2001) it appears to be amenable for use with typical length advertisements simply by replacing the word *infomercial* in items 1 and 2 (below) with *ad* or *commercial*.

REFERENCES:
Agee, Tom and Brett A. S. Martin (2001), "Planned or Impulse Purchases? How to Create Effective Infomercials" *JAR*, 41 (November/December), 35–42.

SCALE ITEMS: [1]

1. I thought a lot about the infomercial before I decided to buy.

2. The infomercial made me think a lot about the product before I decided to buy.

3. I thought a lot about the reasons given for buying it.

4. Before I decided, I thought a lot about whether I might benefit from the product.

---

[1] The response scale used by Agee and Martin (2001) for these items had the following anchors: *strongly agree* (1) and *strongly disagree* (5).

SCALE NAME: Product Information Content

SCALE DESCRIPTION: The scale is composed of four, seven-point statements used to measure a person's sense of the amount of relevant product information that is provided in a commercial communication to which he/she has been exposed.

SCALE ORIGIN: The source of the scale is apparently Meyers-Levy and Perrachio (1992). Their version of the scale focused on the amount of information viewer's received from one of three different mock ads that differed in the camera angles used to take product photographs. In contrast, Singh, Balasubramanian, and Chakraborty (2000) used the scale to gauge how much information viewer's thought was contained in the message portion of three infomercials.

RELIABILITY: Alphas of .85 (Experiment 1) and .83 (Experiment 2) were reported by Meyers-Levy and Perrachio (1992). The scale was used by Singh, Balasubramanian, and Chakraborty (2000) in the pretest phase of their studies and had an alpha of .73 (Singh 1994).

VALIDITY: No examination of the scale's validity was reported in these studies.

REFERENCES:
Meyers-Levy, Joan and Laura A. Peracchio (1992), "Getting an Angle in Advertising: The Effect of Camera Angle on Product Evaluations," *JMR*, 29 (November), 454–461.
Singh, Mandeep (1994), "A Theoretical and Empirical Examination of Infomercials," doctoral dissertation, Southern Illinois University, Carbondale, IL.
Singh, Mandeep, Siva K. Balasubramanian, and Goutam Chakraborty (2000), "A Comparative Analysis of Three Communication Formats: Advertising, Infomercial, and Direct Experience," *JA*, 29 (Winter), 59–75.

SCALE ITEMS: [1]

Directions: Please evaluate the TV commercial on each of the following scales.

1. The amount of relevant product information provided by the video segment is _____.

2. The amount of product knowledge communicated is _____.

3. The aid the video segment offered in making valid judgments is _____.

4. The aid the video segment provided in portraying the details of the product is _____.

[1] This is the version of the scale used by Singh (1994; Singh, Balasubramanian, and Chakraborty 2000). The response scale varied from *low* (1) to *high* (7).

SCALE NAME: Product Placement (General)

SCALE DESCRIPTION: Four, five-point Likert-type statements are used to measure a person's attitude about the practice of putting branded products in movies as props for commercial purposes.

SCALE ORIGIN: The scale was developed by Gupta and Gould (1997) as part of a larger instrument examining a variety of issues related to the use of branded products in movies. The authors generated 30 items, had them reviewed by colleagues, and then pretested them with a small sample of college students. Based on that, some revision occurred and the final instrument was developed for use in their main study. Those results were factor analyzed and indicated the presence of seven factors. Reliabilities were checked for scales based on items with high loadings on those factors. Only the first four factors had alphas greater than .60 and were used further in their analyses. The alpha for the general product placement scale was .66.

The sample in the Gupta and Gould (1997) study were Americans. That same set of data was incorporated into the study by Gould, Gupta, and Grabner-Kräuter (2000) where it was compared to findings with samples of French and Austrians. With the French sample, an English version of the instrument was used since the respondents were expected to understand the language. With the Austrian sample, the instrument was translated into German.

RELIABILITY: An alpha of .71 was reported for the scale by Gould, Gupta, and Grabner-Kräuter (2000).

VALIDITY: The validity of the scale was not explicitly addressed by Gould, Gupta, and Grabner-Kräuter (2000). However, they did indicate that separate factor analyses were run for the data from the three different countries. The same four-factor structure was found in each case although the items composing each factor were not completely the same. Given that the purpose of their study was to make cross-cultural comparisons the authors decided to stick with the same scales as reported in Gupta and Gould (1997).

REFERENCES:

Gupta, Pola B. and Stephen J. Gould (1997), "Consumers' Perceptions of the Ethics and Acceptability of Product Placements in Movies: Product Category and Individual Differences," *Journal of Current Issues & Research in Advertising*, 19 (Spring), 37–50.

Gould, Stephen J., Pola B. Gupta, and Sonja Grabner-Kräuter (2000), "Product Placement in Movies: A Cross-Cultural Analysis of Austrian, French and American Consumers' Attitudes Toward This Emerging, International Promotional Medium," *JA*, 29 (Winter), 41–58.

SCALE ITEMS:

1. I will not go to a movie if I know beforehand that brands are placed prominently in the movie for commercial purposes.

2. I hate seeing brand name products in movies if they are placed for commercial purposes.

3. I don't mind if movie producers receive money or other compensation from manufacturers for placing their brands in the movies. (r)

4. It is highly unethical to influence the captive audience by using brand name products in movies.

SCALE NAME: Product Placement (Preference)

SCALE DESCRIPTION: Five, five-point Likert-type statements are used to measure a person's attitude about branded products being used in movies as props with the emphasis appearing to be on their preference of whether or not they should be used. The scale was referred to as *perceived realism* by Gupta and Gould (1997) and Gould, Gupta, and Grabner-Kräuter (2000).

SCALE ORIGIN: The scale was developed by Gupta and Gould (1997) as part of a larger instrument examining a variety of issues related to the use of branded products in movies. The authors generated 30 items, had them reviewed by colleagues, and then pretested them with a small sample of college students. Based on that, some revision occurred and the final instrument was developed for use in their main study. Those results were factor analyzed and indicated the presence of seven factors. Reliabilities were checked for scales based on items with high loadings on those factors. Only the first four factors had alphas greater than .60 and were used further in their analyses. The alpha for the scale measuring the appropriateness of product placement was .79.

The sample in the Gupta and Gould (1997) study were Americans. That same set of data was incorporated into the study by Gould, Gupta, and Grabner-Kräuter (2000) where it was compared to findings with samples of French and Austrians. With the French sample, an English version of the instrument was used since the respondents were expected to understand the language. With the Austrian sample, the instrument was translated into German.

RELIABILITY: An alpha of .71 was reported for the scale by Gould, Gupta, and Grabner-Kräuter (2000).

VALIDITY: The validity of the scale was not explicitly addressed by Gould, Gupta, and Grabner-Kräuter (2000). However, they did indicate that separate factor analyses were run for the data from the three different countries. The same four-factor structure was found in each case although the items composing each factor were not completely the same. Given that the purpose of their study was to make cross-cultural comparisons the authors decided to stick with the same scales as reported in Gupta and Gould (1997).

REFERENCES:
Gupta, Pola B. and Stephen J. Gould (1997), "Consumers' Perceptions of the Ethics and Acceptability of Product Placements in Movies: Product Category and Individual Differences," *Journal of Current Issues & Research in Advertising*, 19 (Spring), 37–50.
Gould, Stephen J., Pola B. Gupta, and Sonja Grabner-Kräuter (2000), "Product Placement in Movies: A Cross-Cultural Analysis of Austrian, French and American Consumers' Attitudes Toward This Emerging, International Promotional Medium," *JA*, 29 (Winter), 41–58.

SCALE ITEMS:

1. I prefer to see real brands in movies rather than fake/fictitious brands. (r)

2. Movies should use fictitious brands rather than existing brands.

3. The presence of brand name products in a movie makes it more realistic. (r)

4. I don't mind if brand name products appear in movies. (r)

5. The placement of brands in movies should be completely banned.

SCALE NAME: Product Placement (Restriction)

SCALE DESCRIPTION: The scale is composed of three, five-point Likert-type statements used to measure a person's attitude about banning the use of branded tobacco and liquor products in movies primarily due to the potential influence it could have on children.

SCALE ORIGIN: The scale was developed by Gupta and Gould (1997) as part of a larger instrument examining a variety of issues related to the use of branded products in movies. The authors generated 30 items, had them reviewed by colleagues, and then pretested them with a small sample of college students. Based on that, some revision occurred and the final instrument was developed for use in their main study. Those results were factor analyzed and indicated the presence of seven factors. Reliabilities were checked for scales based on items with high loadings on those factors. Only the first four factors had alphas greater than .60 and were used further in their analyses. The alpha for the scale measuring restriction of product placement was .71.

The sample in the Gupta and Gould (1997) study were Americans. That same set of data was incorporated into the study by Gould, Gupta, and Grabner-Kräuter (2000) where it was compared to findings with samples of French and Austrians. With the French sample, an English version of the instrument was used since the respondents were expected to understand the language. With the Austrian sample, the instrument was translated into German.

RELIABILITY: An alpha of .72 was reported for the scale by Gould, Gupta, and Grabner-Kräuter (2000).

VALIDITY: The validity of the scale was not explicitly addressed by Gould, Gupta, and Grabner-Kräuter (2000). However, they did indicate that separate factor analyses were run for the data from the three different countries. The same four-factor structure was found in each case although the items composing each factor were not completely the same. Given that the purpose of their study was to make cross-cultural comparisons the authors decided to stick with the same scales as reported in Gupta and Gould (1997).

REFERENCES:

Gupta, Pola B. and Stephen J. Gould (1997), "Consumers' Perceptions of the Ethics and Acceptability of Product Placements in Movies: Product Category and Individual Differences," *Journal of Current Issues & Research in Advertising*, 19 (Spring), 37–50.

Gould, Stephen J., Pola B. Gupta, and Sonja Grabner-Kräuter (2000), "Product Placement in Movies: A Cross-Cultural Analysis of Austrian, French and American Consumers' Attitudes Toward This Emerging, International Promotional Medium," *JA*, 29 (Winter), 41–58.

SCALE ITEMS:

1. Use of brand name tobacco, beer and liquor products should be banned from PG and PG-13 rated movies because kids watch such movies.

2. Brand name tobacco, beer and liquor products should only be used in R-rated movies as kids don't watch such movies.

3. Cigarette product placements in movies should be banned completely since cigarette ads are banned on TV.

SCALE NAME: Quality (Ad Stimulus Production)

SCALE DESCRIPTION: The scale is composed of three, seven-point Likert-type statements used to measure a person's attitude toward a commercial communication (e.g., ad, infomercial) he/she has been exposed to with an emphasis on how professionally the stimulus has been produced, i.e., the *form* of the message rather than its information content.

SCALE ORIGIN: The source of the scale is unclear but may have been dissertation research by Singh (1994). The scale was used by Singh, Balasubramanian, and Chakraborty (2000) in the pretest phase of their studies.

RELIABILITY: The scale had an alpha of .78 (Singh 1994; Singh, Balasubramanian, and Chakraborty 2000).

VALIDITY: No examination of the scale's validity was reported by Singh, Balasubramanian, and Chakraborty (2000).

REFERENCES:
Singh, Mandeep (1994), "A Theoretical and Empirical Examination of Infomercials," doctoral dissertation, Southern Illinois University, Carbondale, IL.
Singh, Mandeep, Siva K. Balasubramanian, and Goutam Chakraborty (2000), "A Comparative Analysis of Three Communication Formats: Advertising, Infomercial, and Direct Experience," *JA*, 29 (Winter), 59–75.

SCALE ITEMS:
Directions: Please evaluate the TV commercial on each of the following scales:

1. The execution quality of the video segment is very good.

2. The video segment appeared professionally produced.

3. The overall quality of the video segment is excellent.

SCALE NAME: Quality (Advertised Product)

SCALE DESCRIPTION: The scale is composed of seven-point Likert-type statements measuring the degree to which a consumer believes that a specific brand of a product is better than the competition based upon the advertising he/she has been exposed to.

SCALE ORIGIN: The source of the scale was not stated by Dean (1999; Dean and Biswas 2001) but it would appear to be original to him.

RELIABILITY: An alpha of .86 (n = 185) was reported for the scale used in Dean (1999); alphas of .87 (n = 229) and .88 (n = 237) were reported for the version of the scale used in Dean and Biswas (2001).

VALIDITY: No information regarding the scale's validity was reported by Dean (1999). However, Dean and Biswas (2001) described the results of an EFA as well as a CFA of the items composing the four multi-item scales used in their two studies. All items loaded as expected. The AVE of the scale was above .60 in both studies and met a strict criterion of discriminant validity (Fornell and Larcker 1981).

REFERENCES:

Dean, Dwane Hal (1999), "Brand Endorsement, Popularity, and Event Sponsorship as Advertising Cues Affecting Consumer Pre-Purchase Attitudes," *JA*, 28 (3), 1–12.

Dean, Dwane Hal (2003), Personal Correspondence.

Dean, Dwane Hal and Abhijit Biswas (2001), "Third-Party Organization Endorsement of Products: An Advertising Cue Affecting Consumer Prepurchase Evaluation of Goods and Services," *JA*, 30 (4), 41–57.

Fornell, Claes and David F. Larcker (1981), "Evaluating Structural Equation Models with Unobservable Variables and Measurement Error," *JMR*, 18 (February), 39–50.

SCALE ITEMS: [1]

1. Compared to other _____ brands, the advertised _____ is a superior product.

2. The advertised _____ is the best in its product class.

3. The advertised _____ will perform better than other _____ brands.

4. The advertised _____ is the best brand of _____ I will find.

5. Among _____, the advertised company is definitely a quality brand.

---

[1] The response scale had seven points and used anchors of *strongly disagree* and *strongly agree*. The name for the product category should be placed in the blanks. Dean (1999) reported using the first three items (above) while items 4 and 5 as well as items similar to 1 and 3 were used by Dean and Biswas (2001; Dean 2003).

SCALE NAME: Quality (Advertised Product)

SCALE DESCRIPTION: Five, seven-point semantic differentials are used to assess the degree of quality a consumer believes that a specific good or service has based upon some advertising for the product he/she has been exposed to.

SCALE ORIGIN: Although Lohse and Rosen (2001) cited a couple of articles they received some inspiration from, the scale itself appears to be original to their study.

RELIABILITY: An alpha of .87 was reported for the scale (Lohse and Rosen 2001).

VALIDITY: No information regarding the scale's validity was provided in the article by Lohse and Rosen (2001).

REFERENCES:
Lohse, Gerald L. and Dennis L. Rosen (2001), "Signaling Quality and Credibility in Yellow Pages Adverting: The Influence of Color and Graphics on Choice," *JA*, 30 (2), 73–85.

SCALE ITEMS:

1. low quality / high quality

2. inexperienced / experienced

3. unreliable / reliable

4. inexpensive / expensive

5. unsuccessful / successful

SCALE NAME: Relevance of the Information

SCALE DESCRIPTION: Three, seven-point semantic differentials are used to measure the extent to which some product information to which a consumer has been exposed is viewed as being helpful in making a product evaluation. The emphasis appears to be on the content of the information versus the form/style in which it is presented. The scale was referred to as *diagnosticity* by Ahluwalia, Unnava, and Burnkrant (2001).

SCALE ORIGIN: The source of the scale is not clear. Based on the information provided by Gürhan-Canli and Maheswaran (2000), the measure would appear to be original to their study. However, Ahluwalia, Unnava, and Burnkrant (2001) cited Klar (1990) as the source of the scale. While there are some differences between their two versions, the similarities between the items are so striking that it seems unlikely that they come from totally different sources.

RELIABILITY: Alphas of .70 and .80 were reported for the versions of the scale used by Ahluwalia, Unnava, and Burnkrant (2001) and Gürhan-Canli and Maheswaran (2000), respectively.

VALIDITY: No evidence of the scale's validity was reported by Ahluwalia, Unnava, and Burnkrant (2001) or Gürhan-Canli and Maheswaran (2000).

REFERENCES:

Ahluwalia, Rohini, H. Rao Unnava, and Robert E. Burnkrant (2001), "The Moderating Role of Commitment on the Spillover Effect of Marketing Communications," *JMR*, 38 (Nov), 458–470.

Gurhan-Canli, Zeynep and Durairaj Maheswaran (2000), "Determinants of Country-of-Origin Evaluations," *JCR*, 27 (1), 96–108.

Klar, Yechiel (1990), "Linking Structures and Sensitivity to Judgment-Relevant Information in Statistical and Logical Reasoning Tasks," *Journal of Personality and Social Psychology*, 59 (5), 841–858.

SCALE ITEMS: [1]

1. Please indicate the degree to which the information provided was relevant or irrelevant for your evaluation of _____ products.
   Irrelevant / relevant

2. Please indicate the degree to which the information was useful in your evaluation of _____ products.
   The information was of no use / the information was of great use

3. Please indicate the degree to which the information provided was indicative of how good or bad _____ products are.
   Not at all indicative / very indicative

[1] The blanks were filled by Gürhan-Canli and Maheswaran (2000) with a phrase indicating a country-of-origin and a class of products, e.g., Taiwanese electronic products. By leaving that part of the statements out the scale can be used in a wider variety of situations where the interest is just in the relevance of some product information rather than anything related to where the product was made. The semantic differentials used by Ahluwalia, Unnava, and Burnkrant (2001) were very similar to those shown above but it is not known if the stems shown above with each item were used or if, instead, a general set of directions was provided.

SCALE NAME: Risk of Purchase

SCALE DESCRIPTION: The scale is composed of four, seven-point Likert-type statements measuring the degree to which a consumer believes that purchase of a product featured in an ad he/she has been exposed to would be risky.

SCALE ORIGIN: The source of the scale was not explicitly stated by Dean and Biswas (2001) but it would appear to be original to them.

RELIABILITY: Alphas of .88 (n = 229) and .87 (n = 237) were reported for the versions of the scale used in Dean and Biswas (2001).

VALIDITY: Dean and Biswas (2001) described the results of an EFA as well as a CFA of the items composing the four multi-item scales used in their two studies. All items loaded as expected. The AVE of the scale was above .60 in both studies and met a strict criterion of discriminant validity (Fornell and Larcker 1981).

REFERENCES:
Dean, Dwane Hal (2003), Personal Correspondence.
Dean, Dwane Hal and Abhijit Biswas (2001), "Third-Party Organization Endorsement of Products: An Advertising Cue Affecting Consumer Prepurchase Evaluation of Goods and Services," *JA*, 30 (4), 41–57.
Fornell, Claes and David F. Larcker (1981), "Evaluating Structural Equation Models with Unobservable Variables and Measurement Error," *JMR*, 18 (February), 39–50.

SCALE ITEMS: [1]

1. Purchase of the advertised _____ would probably be a wrong choice.

2. Purchase of the advertised _____ would be a very risky choice.

3. It is likely that the consumer would be unsatisfied with the advertised _____.

4. It is likely that the advertised _____ would not meet the expectations of the consumer.

[1] Items provided by Dean (2003). The response scale had seven points and used anchors of *strongly disagree* and *strongly agree*. The name for the product category should be placed in the blanks.

SCALE NAME: Romance Between Couple in Ad

SCALE DESCRIPTION: The scale is composed of three, seven-point Likert-type statements measuring the extent to which a viewer agrees that there is a romantic attraction between two people in an advertisement. To clarify, the scale does not measure whether the viewer *feels* romantic while watching the ad nor whether the ad as a whole is romantic but just that it appears the two people in the ad are behaving romantically.

SCALE ORIGIN: The scale was used as a manipulation check in the experiment conducted by Bhat, Leigh, and Wardlow (1998). The source of the measure was not identified but would appear to have been developed by the authors for use in their study.

RELIABILITY: An alpha of .768 was reported for the scale by Bhat, Leigh, and Wardlow (1998).

VALIDITY: No examination of the scale's validity was reported by Bhat, Leigh, and Wardlow (1998).

REFERENCES:
Bhat, Subodh, Thomas W. Leigh, and Daniel L. Wardlow (1998), "The Effect of Consumer Prejudices on Ad Processing: Heterosexual Consumers' Responses to Homosexual Imagery in Ads," *JA*, 27 (4), 9–28.

SCALE ITEMS:

1. There seems to be romantic interest between the couple in the ad.

2. The couple in the ad seem to be physically attracted to each other.

3. The two people in the ad seem to be having a dating relationship.

SCALE NAME: Standard of Living (Comparison with Typical TV Family)

SCALE DESCRIPTION: The scale is composed of seven, five-point Likert-type statements measuring how a person compares his/her family's standard of living (financial well-being, status, happiness) compared to the typical people shown on television, with the emphasis being on families shown in commercials.

SCALE ORIGIN: The scale is apparently original to Sirgy et al. (1998).

RELIABILITY: Sirgy et al. (1998) used the scale with six different samples in five different countries. Alphas ranged from .591 for the Chinese sample (n = 191) to .824 for the Canadian sample (n = 180). The alpha for the pooled sample was .735 (n = 1226).

VALIDITY: Examination of the scale's validity was not reported by Sirgy et al. (1998) except to the extent that use of CFA provided evidence that the items were unidimensional.

REFERENCES:

Sirgy M. Joseph, Dong-Jin Lee, Rustan Kosenko, H. Lee Meadow, Don Rahtz, Murris Cicic, Guang Xi-Jin, Duygun Yarsuvat, David L. Blenkhorn, and Newell Wright (1998), "Does Television Viewership Play a Role in the Perception of Quality of Life?" *Journal of Advertising*, 27 (Spring), 125–142.

SCALE ITEMS: [1]

1. I am more well off financially than most people shown on television commercials.

2. The average family we see in most ads has a higher standard of living than my own family. (r)

3. Advertisers seem to show that people are upper middle class and happy. (r)

4. I usually find that I am materially better off than the typical family shown on television.

5. I believe that my family's standard of living is below that of the typical family shown on television. (r)

6. Most television commercials show upscale families using advertised products and services. (r)

7. I consider my family to be lower class compared to the typical family they show on television. (r)

---

[1] Depending upon the country, some items were ultimately dropped when calculating scores. The scores for the pooled sample used the first five items.

SCALE NAME: TV Programming (Broadcasters' Responsibilities)

SCALE DESCRIPTION: The scale is composed of nine, five-point Likert-type items intended to measure the extent to which a person believes that television broadcasters should be proactive in controlling the programming, including commercials, that are aimed at children.

SCALE ORIGIN: The scale appears to be original to Walsh, Laczniak, and Carlson (1998).

RELIABILITY: An alpha of .81 (n = 151) was reported by Walsh, Laczniak, and Carlson (1998).

VALIDITY: No examination of the scale's validity was reported by Walsh, Laczniak, and Carlson (1998).

REFERENCES:
Walsh, Ann D., Russell N. Laczniak, and Les Carlson (1998), "Mothers' Preferences for Regulating Children's Television," *JA*, 27 (3), 23–36.

SCALE ITEMS:

1. Broadcasters should make clear distinctions between children's TV programs and commercials.

2. Broadcasters should increase viewing options for children.

3. Television networks should control Saturday morning programs for children.

4. Television networks should prohibit "host selling" (i.e., using the same characters in ads that are shown during a TV program about the character).

5. Television broadcasters need to have standards so that program needs of children are fulfilled.

6. Networks should offer more hours of educational programming for children.

7. Broadcasters should set standards which regulate children's television program content.

8. Broadcasters should be responsible for improving the content of children's television programming.

9. Television executives should develop guides for developers of children's television programs.

SCALE NAME: TV Programming (Need For Government Regulation)

SCALE DESCRIPTION: The scale is composed of nine, five-point Likert-type items intended to measure the extent to which a person believes that there is a need for government regulation of programming (including commercials) aimed at children.

SCALE ORIGIN: The scale appears to be original to Walsh, Laczniak, and Carlson (1998).

RELIABILITY: An alpha of .89 (n = 151) was reported by Walsh, Laczniak, and Carlson (1998).

VALIDITY: No examination of the scale's validity was reported by Walsh, Laczniak, and Carlson (1998).

REFERENCES:
Walsh, Ann D., Russell N. Laczniak, and Les Carlson (1998), "Mothers' Preferences for Regulating Children's Television," *JA*, 27 (3), 23–36.

SCALE ITEMS:

1. New laws should be enacted to create a better television environment for children.

2. Further government regulation is needed to improve television programs directed toward children.

3. Laws should be passed to provide more hours of educational viewing for children.

4. Television commercials directed at children should be banned.

5. Lack of adequate government control of television allows advertisers to take advantage of kids.

6. Commercials that use popular program characters to sell products to kids should be banned.

7. Government's regulation of television programming for children is in the best interest of kids.

8. Legal regulations need to be imposed upon broadcasters to improve children's television.

9. The government should pose limits on the time devoted to commercials during children's viewing times.

SCALE NAME: TV Programming (Need For Independent Regulation)

SCALE DESCRIPTION: The scale is composed of five, five-point Likert-type items intended to measure the extent to which a person believes that there is a need for an organization, independent of parties involved in marketing products, to control television programming aimed at children. As one of the items indicates, the independent organization is envisioned as being composed of parents, educators, and broadcasters; government is not specifically mentioned.

SCALE ORIGIN: The scale appears to be original to Walsh, Laczniak, and Carlson (1998).

RELIABILITY: An alpha of .84 (n = 151) was reported by Walsh, Laczniak, and Carlson (1998).

VALIDITY: No examination of the scale's validity was reported by Walsh, Laczniak, and Carlson (1998).

REFERENCES:
Walsh, Ann D., Russell N. Laczniak, and Les Carlson (1998), "Mothers' Preferences for Regulating Children's Television," *JA*, 27 (3), 23–36.

SCALE ITEMS:

1. An independent organization is needed to rate the educational level of children's TV programs.

2. An independent organization of parents, educators, and broadcasters should be formed to control children's TV.

3. Parent groups should be formed to improve children's television programs.

4. Monitoring of children's TV by an independent organization is needed.

5. Television advertising directed at children needs to be regulated by people who are *NOT* directly involved with the selling of products to children.

SCALE NAME: TV Viewing (Child's Verbal Interaction with Mother)

SCALE DESCRIPTION: Five, four-point statements are used to measure how frequently a child says it talks with its mother about things shown on TV.

SCALE ORIGIN: The scale appears to be original to Carlson, Laczniak, and Walsh (2001).

RELIABILITY: An alpha of .81 was reported for the scale by Carlson, Laczniak, and Walsh (2001).

VALIDITY: No examination of the scale's validity was reported by Carlson, Laczniak, and Walsh (2001).

REFERENCES:

Carlson, Les, Russell N. Laczniak, and Ann Walsh (2001), "Socializing Children about Television: An Intergenerational Study," *JAMS*, 29 (3), 276–288.

SCALE ITEMS: [1]

1. I ask my mom what things mean on TV.

2. I talk to my mom about TV programs.

3. My mom tells me about things on TV that I am not sure about.

4. I tell my mom about things I have seen on TV.

5. If I don't know what something means on a TV show, I ask my mom.

---

[1] The anchors on the response scale were *never, sometimes, most of the time,* and *all of the time.*

SCALE NAME: TV Viewing (Child's View of Mother's Control)

SCALE DESCRIPTION: Nine, four-point statements are used to measure how frequently a child believes his/her mother does things to control his/her TV viewing.

SCALE ORIGIN: The scale appears to be original to Carlson, Laczniak, and Walsh (2001).

RELIABILITY: An alpha of .73 was reported for the scale by Carlson, Laczniak, and Walsh (2001).

VALIDITY: No examination of the scale's validity was reported by Carlson, Laczniak, and Walsh (2001).

REFERENCES:

Carlson, Les, Russell N. Laczniak, and Ann Walsh (2001), "Socializing Children about Television: An Intergenerational Study," *JAMS*, 29 (3), 276–288.

SCALE ITEMS: [1]

1. I have to do my homework before I can watch TV.

2. When I am bad, my mom won't let me watch TV.

3. When my mom is going to be gone, she tells me not to watch some shows.

4. I have to ask my mom before I watch TV.

5. My mom knows what I watch on TV.

6. My mom picks out the videos I watch.

7. Before we rent a video, my mom has to say it is okay.

8. My mom asks me about what I watch on TV.

9. My friends get to watch TV shows that my mom will not let me watch.

[1] The anchors on the response scale were *never, sometimes, most of the time,* and *all of the time.*

SCALE NAME: TV Viewing (Child's View of Mother's Opinion)

SCALE DESCRIPTION: The scale is composed of five, four-point statements measuring the frequency which a child believes that his/her mother makes statements that would indicate she has a negative attitude toward TV, with an emphasis on the inappropriateness of things kids are exposed to.

SCALE ORIGIN: The scale appears to be original to Carlson, Laczniak, and Walsh (2001).

RELIABILITY: An alpha of .72 was reported for the scale by Carlson, Laczniak, and Walsh (2001).

VALIDITY: No examination of the scale's validity was reported by Carlson, Laczniak, and Walsh (2001).

REFERENCES:
Carlson, Les, Russell N. Laczniak, and Ann Walsh (2001), "Socializing Children about Television: An Intergenerational Study," *JAMS*, 29 (3), 276–288.

SCALE ITEMS: [1]

1. My mom thinks that toys advertised on TV are junk.

2. My mom tells me that TV shows have too much killing.

3. My mom says there is too much fighting on TV shows.

4. My mom thinks that food advertised on TV is junk food.

5. My mom says the evening shows on TV are bad for kids.

[1] The anchors on the response scale were *never, sometimes, most of the time,* and *all of the time.*

SCALE NAME: TV Viewing (Frequency)

SCALE DESCRIPTION: The scale is composed of thirteen, five-point items measuring the frequency with which a person reports watching specific types of programs on television.

SCALE ORIGIN: Bush, Smith, and Martin (1999) stated that they built upon a scale originally used by Moschis and Churchill (1978). The latter's scale had seven items and an alpha of .67.

RELIABILITY: An alpha of .77 was reported for the scale by Bush, Smith, and Martin (1999).

VALIDITY: No examination of the scale's validity was reported by Bush, Smith, and Martin (1999).

REFERENCES:

Bush, Alan J., Rachel Smith, and Craig Martin (1999), "The Influence of Consumer Socialization Variables on Attitude Toward Advertising: A Comparison of African-Americans and Caucasians," *JA*, 28 (3), 13–24.
Martin, Craig A. (2001), Personal Correspondence.
Moschis, George P. and Gilbert A. Churchill, Jr. (1978), "Consumer Socialization: A Theoretical and Empirical Analysis," *JMR*, 15 (November), 599–609.

SCALE ITEMS: [1]

I watch:

1. Cartoons

2. Situation comedies

3. Drama/adventure

4. Sports

5. Music television

6. Crime/detective

7. Soap operas

8. Daytime television

9. Variety/comedy

10. Movies

11. Public television

12. News

13. News documentaries

[1] Responses to these items were captured on a five-point scale with the following anchors: *everyday*, *once a week*, *once a month*, *several times a year*, and *never* (Martin 2001). Also, examples were provided for each category listed.

SCALE NAME: TV Viewing (Parents' Responsibilities)

SCALE DESCRIPTION: The scale is composed of seven, five-point Likert-type items intended to measure the extent to which a person believes that parents should control what their children watch on television. In the studies by Walsh, Laczniak, and Carlson (1998; Carlson, Laczniak, and Walsh 2001) the scale was responded to by mothers but it appears to be amenable for use with other groups as well.

SCALE ORIGIN: The scale appears to be original to Walsh, Laczniak, and Carlson (1998).

RELIABILITY: An alpha of .76 was reported for the scale by both Carlson, Laczniak, and Walsh (2001) and Walsh, Laczniak, and Carlson (1998).

VALIDITY: No examination of the scale's validity was reported by Carlson, Laczniak, and Walsh (2001) or Walsh, Laczniak, and Carlson (1998).

REFERENCES:

Carlson, Les, Russell N. Laczniak, and Ann Walsh (2001), "Socializing Children About Television: An Intergenerational Study," *JAMS*, 29 (3), 276–288.

Walsh, Ann D., Russell N. Laczniak, and Les Carlson (1998), "Mothers' Preferences for Regulating Children's Television," *JA*, 27 (3), 23–36.

SCALE ITEMS:

1. Parents should play a large role in determining what kids watch on TV.

2. Children should be taught by parents about the difference between TV ads and programs.

3. Parents should watch television with their children.

4. Parents need to discuss TV programs and commercials with their children.

5. Parents should carefully monitor children's viewing of TV programs intended for adult audiences.

6. Family rules are absolutely necessary to control what kids watch on television.

7. Parents should be aware of the television programs their children watch.

SCALE NAME: TV Viewing (Time Spent)

SCALE DESCRIPTION: The scale is composed of three, open-ended statements intended to measure the extent to which one watches television, the emphasis being on the number of hours spent watching TV per day.

SCALE ORIGIN: The scale used by Sirgy et al. (1998) appears to be original to their study although they built upon simpler measures used by Morgan (1984) and Richins (1987).

RELIABILITY: Sirgy et al. (1998) used the scale with six different samples in five different countries. Alphas ranged from .426 for the Chinese sample (n = 191) to .796 for a sample of U.S. college students (n = 234). The alpha for the pooled sample was .699 (n = 1226).

VALIDITY: Examination of the scale's validity was not reported by Sirgy et al. (1998) except to the extent that use of CFA provided evidence that the three items were unidimensional.

REFERENCES:

Morgan, Michael (1984), "Heavy Television Viewing and Perceived Quality of Life," *Journalism Quarterly*, 61 (Autumn), 499–504, 740.

Richins, Marsha L. (1987), "Media, Materialism, and Human Happiness," in *Advances in Consumer Research*, *V. 14*, Melanie Wallendorf and Paul Anderson, eds. Ann Arbor, MI: Association for Consumer Research, 352–356.

Sirgy M. Joseph, Dong-Jin Lee, Rustan Kosenko, H. Lee Meadow, Don Rahtz, Murris Cicic, Guang Xi-Jin, Duygun Yarsuvat, David L. Blenkhorn, and Newell Wright (1998), "Does Television Viewership Play a Role in the Perception of Quality of Life?" *Journal of Advertising*, 27 (Spring), 125–142.

SCALE ITEMS:

1. How much time did you spend watching television yesterday? ___ hours

2. How much time do you usually spend watching television every day? ___ hours

3. On an average day, about how much time, if any, do you personally spend watching television? ___ hours

#652 *Typicality (Commercial)*

SCALE NAME: Typicality (Commercial)

SCALE DESCRIPTION: The scale is composed of four, seven-point statements used to measure the extent to which a viewer considers a commercial message to which he/she has been exposed to be like other commercial messages.

SCALE ORIGIN: The source of the scale is apparently Meyers-Levy and Perrachio (1992). Their version of the scale focused on the typicality of three different mock ads that differed in the camera angles used to take product photographs. In contrast, Singh, Balasubramanian, and Chakraborty (2000) used the scale to gauge the typicality of the message portion of three infomercials.

RELIABILITY: Alphas of .65 (Experiment 1) and .85 (Experiment 2) were reported by Meyers-Levy and Perrachio (1992). The scale was used by Singh, Balasubramanian, and Chakraborty (2000) in the pretest phase of their studies and had an alpha of .26 (Singh 1994). It is unclear why this alpha is so low; a double-check with the author (Singh 2002) indicated that is indeed what was calculated.

VALIDITY: No examination of the scale's validity was reported in these studies.

REFERENCES:

Meyers-Levy, Joan and Laura A. Peracchio (1992), "Getting an Angle in Advertising: The Effect of Camera Angle on Product Evaluations," *JMR*, 29 (November), 454–461.

Singh, Mandeep (1994), "A Theoretical and Empirical Examination of Infomercials," doctoral dissertation, Southern Illinois University, Carbondale, IL.

Singh, Mandeep (2002), Personal Correspondence.

Singh, Mandeep, Siva K. Balasubramanian, and Goutam Chakraborty (2000), "A Comparative Analysis of Three Communication Formats: Advertising, Infomercial, and Direct Experience," *JA*, 29 (Winter), 59–75.

SCALE ITEMS: [1]

Directions: Please evaluate the TV commercial on each of the following scales.

1. The degree to which the video segment was unusual. (r)

2. The degree to which the video segment was typical of TV advertisements.

3. The degree to which the video segment was different from advertisements seen on television. (r)

4. The degree to which the video segment was as might be expected in ads for this product.

---

[1] This is the version of the scale used by Singh (1994; Singh, Balasubramanian, and Chakraborty 2000). The response scale varied from *low* (1) to *high* (7).

SCALE NAME: Visual Imaging

SCALE DESCRIPTION: The scale is composed of four statements that are intended to measure the extent to which an ad has stimulated a person to form mental images of what was being described verbally in the ad copy. It is not clear whether the scale taps more into a person's propensity for visualization or an ad's propensity for stimulating visualization; it appears to lean more toward the latter.

SCALE ORIGIN: The scale used by Unnava, Agarwal, and Haugtvedt (1996) was developed by Unnava and Burnkrant (1991). The earlier study reported an alpha of .89 based on a sample of 107 undergraduate students.

RELIABILITY: An alpha of .94 (n = 100) was reported for the scale by Unnava, Agarwal, and Haugtvedt (1996). Singh et al. (2000) reported an alpha of .91 (n = 404) in their usage of the scale.

VALIDITY: No evidence of the scale's validity has been reported.

REFERENCES:

Singh, Surendra N., V. Parker Lessig, Dongwook Kim, Reetika Gupta, and Mary Ann Hocutt (2000), "Does Your Ad Have Too Many Pictures?" *JAR*, 40 (Jan-Apr), 11–27.

Unnava, H. Rao and Robert E. Burnkrant (1991), "An Imagery-Processing View of the Role of Pictures in Print Advertisements," *JMR*, 28 (May), 226–231.

Unnava, H. Rao, Sanjeev Agarwal, and Curtis P. Haugtvedt (1996), "Interactive Effects of Presentation Modality and Message-Generated Imagery on Recall of Advertising Information," *JCR*, 23 (June), 81–88.

SCALE ITEMS: [1]

1. The ad brought pictures or images to my mind that helped clarify what was said in the ad.

2. As I read the ad, I formed pictures or images about much of what was being discussed in the ad.

3. I found myself thinking of images when I read the ad.

4. It was easy to form images or pictures of what was being said in the ad.

[1] As used by Unnava, Agarwal, and Haugtvedt (1996), the scale used a seven-point Likert-type response format. The response scale use by Singh et al. (2000) was not described.

SCALE NAME: Vividness of the Ad

SCALE DESCRIPTION: The scale is composed of four, nine-point bi-polar adjectives that measure the strength with which an advertisement has evoked imagery.

SCALE ORIGIN: The scale appears to be original to the study by Krishnamurthy and Sujan (1999) though it bears similarity to some previous scales, e.g., #484 and #485 in V. III.

RELIABILITY: An alpha of .87 was reported for the scale (Krishnamurthy and Sujan 1999).

VALIDITY: No examination of the scale's validity was reported by Krishnamurthy and Sujan (1999).

REFERENCES:
Krishnamurthy, Parthasarathy and Mita Sujan (1999), "Retrospection Versus Anticipation: The Role of the Ad Under Retrospective and Anticipatory Self-Referencing," *JCR*, 26 (June), 55–69.

SCALE ITEMS: My thoughts while viewing the ad were:

1. abstract / concrete

2. dull / vivid

3. vague / clear

4. not imageful / imageful

READING LIST FOR
SCALE DEVELOPMENT AND USE
··

Below is a list of articles and books one could peruse when trying to better understand psychometrics and related issues. In this limited list the emphasis is on literature focusing on the field of marketing written in recent years but some oft cited pieces from earlier years and important publications from other fields are mentioned as well. A longer list is available at *http://www.siu.edu/departments/coba/osr/read.html*.

American Educational Research Association (AERA), American Psychological Association (APA), & National Council on Measurement in Education (NCME) (1999), *Standards for Educational and Psychological Testing*, Washington, D.C.: American Educational Research Association.

Bagozzi, Richard P. and Youjae Yi (1991), "Multitrait-Multimethod Matrices in Consumer Research," *JCR*, 17 (March), 426−439.

Baumgartner, Hans and Jan-Benedict E. M. Steenkamp (2001), "Response Styles in Marketing Research: A Cross-National Investigation," *JMR*, 38 (May), 143−156.

Boyle, Gregory J. (1991), "Does Item Homogeneity Indicate Internal Consistency or Item Redundancy in Psychometric Scales?" *Personality & Individual Differences*, 12 (3), 291−294.

Bradlow, Eric T. and Gavan J. Fitzsimons (2001), "Subscale Distance and Item Clustering Effects in Self-Administered Surveys: A New Metric," *JMR*, 38 (May), 254−261.

Bruner II, Gordon C. (1998), "Standardization & Justification: Do Aad Scales Measure Up?," *Journal of Current Issues & Research in Advertising*, 20 (Spring), 1−18.

Bruner II, Gordon C. (2003), "Combating Scale Proliferation," *Journal of Targeting, Measurement & Analysis*, 11 (4), 362−372.

Bruner II, Gordon C. and Paul J. Hensel (1993), "Multi-Item Scale Usage in Marketing Journals: 1980 to 1989," *JAMS*, 21 (Fall), 339−344.

Campbell, Donald T. and Donald W. Fiske (1959), "Convergent Validity and Discriminant Validity by the Multitrait-Multimethod Matrix," *Psychological Bulletin*, 56 (March), 81−105.

Churchill, Gilbert A., Jr. (1979), "A Paradigm for Developing Better Measures of Marketing Constructs," *JMR*, 16 (February), 64−73.

Clark, Lee Anna and David Watson (1995), "Constructing Validity: Basic Issues in Objective Scale Development," *Psychological Assessment*, 7 (3), 309−319.

Cortina, Jose M. (1993), "What is Coefficient Alpha? An Examination of Theory and Applications," *Journal of Applied Psychology*, 78 (1), 98−104.

Cronbach, Lee J. (1951), "Coefficient Alpha and the Internal Structure of Tests," *Psychometrika*, 16 (September), 297−334.

Crowne, Douglas P. and David Marlowe (1960), "A New Scale of Social Desirability Independent of Psychopathology," *Journal of Consulting Psychology*, 24 (August), 349−354.

DeVellis, Robert F. (2003), *Scale Development: Theory and Applications*, Newbury Park, CA: Sage Publications, Inc.

Diamantopoulous, Adamantios and Heidi M. Winklhofer (2001), "Index Construction with Formative Indicators: An Alternative to Scale Development," *JMR*, 38 (May), 269–277.

Embretson, Susan E., Steve Reise, Steven Paul Reise (2000), *Item Response Theory for Psychologists*, Mahwah, NJ: Lawrence Erlbaum Associates, Inc.

Finn, Adam and Ujwal Kawande (1997), "Reliability Assessment and Optimization of Marketing Measurement," *JMR*, 34 (May), 262–275.

Finn, Adam and Ujwal Kawande (2004), "Scale Modification: Alternative Approaches and Their Consequences," *JR*, 80 (1), 37–52.

Flynn, Leisa Reinecke and Dawn Pearcy (2001), "Four Subtle Sins in Scale Development: Some Suggestions for Strengthening the Current Paradigm," *International Journal of Marketing Research*, 43 (4), 409–423.

Gerbing, David W. and James C. Anderson (1988), "An Updated Paradigm for Scale Development Incorporating Uni-dimensionality and Its Assessment," *JMR*, 25 (May), 186–192.

Herche, Joel and Brian Engelland (1996), "Reversed-Polarity Items and Scale Unidimensionality," *JAMS*, 24 (4), 366–374.

Jarvis, Cheryl Burke, Scott B. MacKenzie, and Philip M. Podsakoff (2003), "A Critical Review of Construct Indicators and Measurement Model Misspecification in Marketing and Consumer Research," *JCR*, 30 (September), 199–218.

Journal of Business Research (2004), "Special Issue: Measurement Validation in Market Research," 57 (2).

Little, Todd D., Ulman Lindenberger, and John R. Nesselroade (1999), "On Selecting Indicators for Multivariate Measurement and Modeling With Latent Variables: When 'Good' Indicators Are Bad and 'Bad' Indicators Are Good," *Psychological Methods*, 4 (2), 192–211.

Netemeyer, Richard G., William O. Bearden, and Subhash Sharma (2003), *Scaling Procedures: Issues and Applications*, Newbury Park, CA: Sage Publications, Inc.

Nunnally, Jum C. and Ira H. Bernstein (1994), *Psychometric Theory*, New York: McGraw-Hill.

Peterson, Robert A. (1994), "A Meta-Analysis of Cronbach's Coefficient Alpha," *JCR*, 21 (September), 381–391.

Reise, Steven P., Keith F. Widaman, and Robin H. Pugh (1993), "Confirmatory Factor Analysis and Item Response Theory: Two Approaches for Exploring Measurement Invariance," *Psychological Bulletin*, 114 (3), 552–566.

Rossiter, John R. (2002), "The C-OAR-SE Procedure for Scale Development in Marketing," *International Journal of Research in Marketing*, 19 (4), 305–335.

Santor, Darcy A. and J. O. Ramsay (1998), "Progress in the Technology of Measurement: Applications of Item Response Models," *Psychological Assessment*, 10 (4), 345–359.

Schuman, Howard and Stanley Presser (1996), *Questions and Answers in Attitude Surveys: Experiments on Question Form, Wording, and Context*, Thousand Oaks, CA: Sage Publications.

Singh, Jagdip, Roy D. Howell, and Gary K. Rhoads (1990), "Adaptive Designs for Likert-Type Data: An Approach for Implementing Marketing Surveys," *JMR*, 27 (August), 304–321.

Steenbergen, Mario R. (2000), "Item Similarity in Scale Analysis," *Political Analysis*, 8 (March), 261–283.

Steenkamp, Jan-Benedict E.M. and Hans C.M. van Trijp (1991), "The Use of LISREL in Validating Marketing Constructs," *International Journal of Research in Marketing*, 8, 283–299.

Wong, Nancy, Aric Rindfleisch, and James E. Burroughs (2003), "Do Reverse-Worded Items Confound Measures in Cross-Cultural Consumer Research? The Case of the Material Values Scale," *JCR*, 30 (June), 72–91.

Author Index

The numbers following authors' names refer to the *scale number* located at the top of each page.

Subject Index

The numbers following keywords refer to the *scale number* located at the top of each page.